marketing management

a strategic, value-based approach

marketing management

a strategic, value-based approach

Gregory Whitwell
University of Melbourne

Bryan A. Lukas
University of Melbourne

Peter Doyle
University of Warwick

John Wiley & Sons Australia, Ltd

First published 2003 by
John Wiley & Sons Australia, Ltd
33 Park Road, Milton, Qld 4064

Offices also in Sydney and Melbourne

Typeset in 10/13 Berkeley

Australian edition © 2003 John Wiley & Sons Australia, Ltd

Authorised adaptation of the original, *Value-Based Marketing:
Marketing Strategies for Corporate Growth and Shareholder Value*
(ISBN 0-471-87727-1), published by John Wiley & Sons Ltd,
Chichester, United Kingdom.

National Library of Australia
ISBN 0 470 80096 8

Whitwell, Greg.
Marketing management: A value-based approach.

Includes index.
ISBN 0 470 80096 8.

1. Marketing — Management. I. Doyle, Peter, 1943– .
II. Lukas, Bryan A. III. Doyle, Peter, 1943– Value-based
marketing. IV. Title.

658.802

Edited by Robi van Nooten, On-Track Editorial Services, and
Daniel Logovik.

Cover image: © Copyright 2000 PhotoDisc, Inc

Printed in Singapore by
Markono Print Media Pte Ltd

10 9 8 7 6 5 4 3 2 1

contents

Part 2
Deciding where to
compete   127

about the authors

Gregory Whitwell

is Associate Professor of Marketing and Director of the Master of Applied Commerce (Marketing) in the Faculty of Economics and Commerce at the University of Melbourne, and was previously Associate Dean (International) and Associate Dean (Graduate Studies). He was trained in economics and economic history before moving into marketing. He holds several academic awards, including the Academy of the Social Sciences in Australia medal for excellence in scholarship, a Best Paper award from the American Marketing Association and a Good Teaching and Teaching Innovation Award at the University of Melbourne. Gregory has published three academic texts, written chapters in 12 books and has published numerous journal articles. He is an active consultant to both public and private institutions.

Bryan A. Lukas

is Associate Professor of Marketing and Director of the Master of Applied Commerce program in the Faculty of Economics and Commerce at the University of Melbourne. He has received several academic awards, including two Best Paper awards from the American Marketing Association. At the University of Melbourne he has been awarded the Faculty's Individual Award for Good Teaching. Bryan has published two academic texts in the areas of marketing research and marketing management. His research has appeared in numerous journals, including the *Journal of Management*, *Journal of the Academy of Marketing Science* and *Journal of Business Research*. He has run executive programs for managers in the United States and Australia and has acted as a consultant to many firms. He is a member of the Australian and New Zealand Marketing Association, American Marketing Association and Academy of Marketing Science.

Peter Doyle

is Professor of Marketing and Strategic Management at the Warwick Business School, University of Warwick. His research has twice led him to be awarded the President's Medal of the Operational Research Society and the Best Paper Award of the American Marketing Association. He also has been voted 'Outstanding Teacher' on numerous university and corporate courses. Peter is the author of many papers that have appeared in journals such as the *Journal of Marketing*, *Journal of Marketing Research*, *Management Science* and the *Economic Journal*. His other recent academic texts are in the areas of marketing management, strategy and innovation. He has run executive programs for senior managers throughout Europe, the United States, South America, Australia and the Far East. Peter has acted as a consultant to many international companies in Europe and the United States and advised professional bodies, including Britain's Cabinet Office, the Institute of Chartered Accountants, the Institute of Directors, the CBI, the Pacific–Asian Management Institute and the Singapore Department of Trade.

acknowledgements

Many people have influenced this book. We have benefited from the ideas of many colleagues including John McGee, Andrew Pettigrew, John Saunders, Howard Thomas and Robin Wensley, Andrew Ehrenberg, Ken Simmonds, Jean-Claude Larréché, Marcel Corstjens, David Montgomery, V. Srinivasan, Dave Cook, Ian Fenwick, Graham Hooley, Davis Jobber, Jim Lynch, Paul Michelle, Richard Cyert, Herbert Simon and Robert Lucas.

The book is influenced by the cooperation of managers from the following organisations: 3M, Arthur Andersen, Andersen Consulting, AstraZeneca, British Airways, BMP DDB Omnicom, BP-Amoco, British Telecom, Cabinet Office, Cadbury-Schweppes, Coca-Cola, Dixons, FedEx, Hewlett Packard, IBM, ICI, Johnson & Johnson, J. Walter Thompson, KPMG, Marks & Spencer, Mars, Nestlé, Novartis, Ogilvy, Philips, PriceWaterhouseCoopers, Saatchi & Saatchi, Safeway, Shell, Tesco, Unilever, Wal-Mart, WH Smith and Woolworths.

Finally, we would like to thank Mark John Roberts for helping us select and prepare the pedagogical material embedded in the chapters and the Teaching Manual; his assistance was invaluable. We are also pleased to be associated with Janine Burford, Catherine Spedding and Robi van Nooten, who have guided us through this project.

D. P. Norton, *Harvard Business Review*, Sept.–Oct. 1993, pp. 138–9, Copyright © 1993 by the Harvard Business School Publishing Corporation; all rights reserved; pp. 165–6: John Lyons is an independent non-executive company director specialising in strategy research and marketing. john.lyons@bigpond.com. Reproduced with permission; pp. 174–5: Stephen Dabkowski, *The Age*, 27 December 2001. Reproduced with permission; pp. 193–4: David Blake, *Shares*, May 2001. Reproduced with permission; pp. 196–7: Tim Treadgold, *BRW*, 13–19 September 2001, by permission of Journalists Copyright; p. 209: Rochelle Burbury, *AFR*, 8–9 December 2001. Reproduced with permission; p. 218: Cathy Bolt, *Australian Financial Review*, 20 November 2001; p. 232: Reproduced with permission from ANZ Bank; pp. 236–7: Michael Cave, *Australian Financial Review BOSS*, May 2001. Reproduced with permission; p. 239: *Interbrand, The World's Greatest Brands*, Macmillan, 1996. Reproduced with permission of Palgrave Macmillan; pp. 242–3: Rochelle Burbury, *AFR*, 22–23 July 2000. Reproduced with permission; p. 246: From *Creating Powerful Brands* by Leslie de Chernatony and Malcolm H. B. McDonald. Reprinted by permission of Elsevier Science Limited; p. 247: Rochelle Burbury, *AFR*, 30 November 2001. Reproduced with permission; p. 251: Rochelle Burbury, *AFR*, 13 November 2001. Reproduced with permission; p. 260: Tim Treadgold, *BRW*, 5 May 2000, by permission of Journalists Copyright; pp. 278–9: First published 2000. Reproduced with permission from Knowledge@Wharton (http://knowledge.wharton.upenn.edu). © 2000 the Trustees of the University of Pennsylvania. All rights reserved *and* First published 2001. Reproduced with permission from Knowledge@Wharton (http://knowledge.wharton.upenn.edu). © 2001 The Trustees of the University of Pennsylvania. All rights reserved; p. 282: James Thomson, *BRW*, 29 June 2001, by permission of Journalists Copyright; pp. 282–3: Neil Shoebridge, *BRW*, 18 January 1999, by permission of Journalists Copyright; p. 289: Alan Kallir, *The Australian Financial Review*, Friday 4 May 2001. Reproduced with permission. © Alan J. Kallir, Insight Partners; p. 318: Reproduced with permission from Gordon Mills Consulting; pp. 326–7: Paul McIntyre, *BRW*, 7–13 February 2002. Reproduced with permission; pp. 336–7: Simon Lloyd, *BRW*, 27 September–3 October 2001, by permission of Journalists Copyright; pp. 340–1: Peter Crayford, *The Australian Financial Review Weekend*, 28 March–1 April 2002. Reproduced with permission; p. 346: Jan McCallum, *BRW*, 23–29 August 2002, by permission of Journalists Copyright; p. 354: Simon Lloyd, *BRW*, 23–29 August 2001, by permission of Journalists Copyright; p. 356: Michelle Hannen, *BRW*, 27 September–3 October 2001, by permission of Journalists Copyright; pp. 363–4: Reproduced with permission from Bill Bennett; pp. 366–7: Simon Lloyd, *BRW*, 11–17 October 2001, by permission of Journalists Copyright; pp. 370–1: Simon Lloyd, *BRW* online, 12 April 2001, by permission of Journalists Copyright; p. 372: Reproduced with permission from Nielsen Media Research; p. 397: Adapted from *B&T Weekly*, 'Australia's ten most effective marketers', www.bandt.com.au. Reproduced with permission of Reed Business Information; pp. 400–1: © Fred Pawle, *AFR BOSS*, 2002; pp. 405–6: Simon Lloyd, *BRW* online, 30 March 2001, by permission of Journalists Copyright; p. 429: From *Principles of Internet Marketing* 1st edn by W. Hanson © 2000 Reprinted with permission of South-Western — a division of Thomson Learning www.thomsonrights.com, Fax 800 730–2215; pp. 438–9: Michelle Hannen, *BRW*, 31 January–6 February 2002, by permission of Journalists Copyright.

preface

The objectives of this book are ambitious: to redefine the purpose of marketing and how its contribution should be measured. The result of this redefinition is a concept of marketing that is more practical and more relevant to the objectives of today's top management. Specifically, we argue that the purpose of marketing is to contribute to maximising shareholder value and that marketing strategies must be evaluated in terms of how much value they create for investors. This new approach, which we call *value-based marketing*, does not overthrow the existing body of marketing knowledge. On the contrary, value-based marketing makes the existing knowledge more relevant and practical by giving it greater clarity and focus.

Many senior managers notice a paradox in how firms perceive marketing. On the one hand, every chief executive and mission statement puts marketing at the very top of the agenda. Getting closer to customers and meeting their needs is seen as the cornerstone of building a world-class company. A market orientation is regarded as the essential coordinating focus for all the disciplines and processes of the business. At the same time, marketing professionals, marketing departments and marketing education are not highly regarded. Few chief executives are from a marketing background, most companies do not have a marketing director on the board and marketing qualifications often are not treated seriously. One leading consulting firm called marketing departments 'a millstone around an organisation's neck'.

What accounts for this paradox of marketing being paramount but market professionals being disregarded? The main problem is that the marketing discipline has not been clear about what its objectives are. Most strategy proposals emanating from marketing staff justify investments in advertising or marketing, in terms of increasing consumer awareness, sales volume or market share. But most boards of directors are sceptical about such measures having any clear relation to the firm's long-run profitability. Marketing managers rarely see the necessity of linking marketing spending to the financial value of the business. Given today's enormous pressures on top managers to generate higher returns to shareholders, the fact that the voice of marketing gets disregarded at senior management levels is hardly surprising. The situation cannot be resolved until marketing professionals learn to justify marketing strategies in relevant financial terms.

When managers can show that marketing does increase returns to the owners of the firm, marketing can obtain a much more pre-eminent role in the boardrooms of industry. The discipline itself can also obtain more respect for its greater rigour and direction. The purpose of this book is to demonstrate how marketing creates value for shareholders and to provide managers with the practical tools for developing and evaluating marketing strategies using modern shareholder value analysis.

The premise of the book

Increasingly, the rhetoric used by top managers and boards is that the primary task of management is to maximise returns to shareholders. There is growing acceptance by today's executives that unless they demonstrate their ability to enhance shareholder value, they are likely to be replaced, new capital becomes difficult to obtain and their business is put at risk. Shareholder returns grow when a company increases its dividends or when its share price rises. Outside top management, the idea of running a business to maximise shareholder value remains controversial. But today's managers know that unless they do maximise shareholder value, their jobs become vulnerable, the business is put at risk and new capital is difficult to obtain. In competitive capital markets, earning returns that shareholders regard as acceptable is a necessity for survival.

Much of the controversy surrounding maximising shareholder returns occurs because the concept is misunderstood. Most misunderstanding occurs among managers. Managers confuse maximising shareholder value with maximising profits. The two concepts are completely different. Maximising profits is about short-term management: cutting costs, reducing investment and downsizing. The approach is totally antithetical to developing long-term marketing strategies and building world-class businesses. By contrast, maximising shareholder value is a long-term concept — about building businesses that last. Despite what managers believe, investors see through short-term tactics that temporarily boost profits. Often share prices actually fall when companies announce cuts in spending on marketing and less ambitious long-term goals.

Value-based marketing is founded on shareholder value analysis — a well-accepted body of financial theory and set of techniques. Shareholder value analysis states that the value of a business is increased when managers make decisions that increase the discounted value of all future cash flows. We show in this book that shareholder value analysis offers enormous opportunities to marketing. First, the adoption of shareholder value analysis enables the purpose of marketing in commercial firms to be clearly defined as one of building intangible assets that increase shareholder returns. Second, the technique explains how marketing strategies need to be evaluated: they are worth pursuing if they increase the net present value of the firm's long-term cash flow. Third, rigorously exploring the effects on shareholder value makes it harder for boards to make arbitrary cuts in marketing budgets and similar measures to boost short-term earnings.

The most important contribution of value-based marketing is to make the shareholder value concept more useful. While more and more chief executives are espousing that their job is to maximise shareholder value, all too often it has become associated with cutting costs and downsizing. In many companies shareholder value is an accounting tool rather than a general management concept. What many executives understand is that shareholder value is more about growth and grasping new market opportunities than reducing expenses. All the companies that have created the greatest value for shareholders in the past decade — Dell, Flight Centre, GE, Harvey Norman and Qantas — are market-led, high-growth companies. As we show in the book, creating shareholder value is really about identifying emerging opportunities, putting together marketing strategies that can enable firms to rapidly obtain critical mass and building lasting relationships with customers. Shareholder value is not built in accounting departments.

The structure of the book

The book is in three parts. Part 1, 'A New Basis for Marketing Management', presents the principles of value-based marketing and comprises three chapters. The first chapter, on marketing and shareholder value, is divided into three distinct sections. The chapter discusses the major challenges of managing in the 21st Century, provides an overview of the principles of shareholder value analysis, and explains the synergies between marketing and shareholder value. Chapter 2 presents a step-by-step guide to shareholder value analysis and discusses alternative approaches to measuring shareholder value. Chapter 3 discusses the three principal drivers of shareholder value. The nature, importance and interrelatedness of the financial, marketing and organisational value drivers are discussed.

Part 1 is organised to provide flexibility for both instructors and students. Not everyone has the time or the inclination to study shareholder value analysis in depth. Accordingly, in designing their course, instructors may consider skipping chapter 2, 'The Shareholder Value Approach'. They can do so, knowing that section 2 of chapter 1 is designed to present the basics of shareholder value analysis and to introduce all the terms that are needed to understand the discussion in Parts 2 and 3 of the text. We certainly encourage readers to explore chapter 2, even though they may not do so as part of the formal curriculum.

Part 2, 'Deciding Where to Compete', focuses on how to develop strategies that lead to value-creating growth and comprises three chapters. Chapter 4 discusses the development of value-based marketing strategies for current and new businesses. Chapter 5 explains how to assess the current position of the business and its prospects. Chapter 6 explores the strategic focus that a firm may choose to adopt, and explains why growth is so important to creating shareholder value and how managers can organise to accelerate growth.

After deciding where to compete, the next critical requirement for a business is the implementation of high-value strategies. Accordingly, Part 3 is titled 'Deciding How to Compete' and comprises six chapters. Chapter 7 considers intangible assets and the role of the brand in building shareholder value. Chapter 8 re-examines pricing from a value perspective and shows how the current theory of pricing often leads to decisions that are too short-term in their orientation. Chapter 9 discusses products, which we define as anything that delivers a benefit needed by a customer. Chapter 10 is concerned with the distribution channels that the business employs to reach its target market. Chapter 11 explores the role of promotion and communication investments in creating long-term value and how to decide on how much should be spent. The final chapter considers the far-reaching implications of the information revolution on business strategies and marketing.

Many marketing texts of the past few years added on an obligatory chapter on e-commerce. This book is different. Digital technology, the Internet and the new opportunities for customisation affect every aspect of marketing and, indeed, business generally. Accordingly, we seek to recognise these impacts from the beginning and weave the theme of the revolution in information technology throughout the work.

A note for instructors and students

This book is written for managers and aspiring managers seeking responsibility for the economic performance of their businesses. The book is especially suitable for use in advanced undergratuate, MBA and EMBA classes, and may also be used in strategy and management classes that are based on shareholder value principles, as well as specialised business programs. Although written with an Australian and New Zealand audience in mind, we also recognise that businesses compete in a global environment and, therefore, make liberal use of examples of European and North American companies.

Readers will become aware quickly that this book is not a 'one-minute manager' type of read. We provide a rigorous presentation of some of the most challenging ideas in modern marketing. The book asks the reader to grapple and integrate current work not just from marketing but, also, from finance, economics, strategy and information systems. The text is fully referenced with the latest research and most influential papers. The ideas in this book are so important that we hope that the reader feels the challenge is worth taking up. Managers of tomorrow are going to need to be technically accomplished if they are to contribute effectively to the development of their businesses in our rapidly changing world.

This book is written in a readable style and includes many examples that keep it highly practical and close to the issues in the real world. Each chapter begins with a *scene setter*. This material may be an extract from an interview, a discussion piece or a study of a particular company that relates to the topics pursued in the chapter. Relevant material, usually based on articles from the business and financial press, are offered as boxed inserts within the chapter. These are provided either as a *marketing insight* or a *marketing management in practice*. Each chapter concludes with a *case study* of a particular company, complete with questions.

To assist readers, we preface each chapter with a list of *chapter objectives*. At the end of the chapter, we include a *summary* of the key points. To encourage class discussion, we provide, in addition to the end-of-chapter case study questions, a set of *review questions*, *discussion questions* and *debate questions*. Unless otherwise stated, all references to dollars are to Australian dollars.

The accompanying instructor's resource guide includes a guide to some of the ways in which these questions can be answered. We also provide for instructors a set of PowerPoint slides for each chapter. A test bank of multiple-choice questions is also available.

Gregory Whitwell
Bryan A. Lukas
Peter Doyle
October 2002

Part 1

A new basis for marketing management

Marketing and shareholder value

By the time you have completed this chapter, you will be able to:

- describe the new marketing challenges faced by today's managers
- understand the central role of shareholder value
- comprehend the nature of shareholder value analysis and the key concepts it employs
- assess why marketing managers have lost influence in the boardroom
- recognise why marketing is the bedrock of shareholder value analysis
- identify how the profession and discipline of marketing needs to change to make it more relevant to top management.

scene setter

ANZ and the challenges of being customer-centric: An interview with John McFarlane

John McFarlane [managing director of ANZ Banking Group] is proving a skilful player as he tries to move the ANZ up the banking charts — one eye on the analysts, the other on customers and staff.

Q: Why did you decide on a business model that effectively breaks the ANZ into [16 different businesses]?

A: It is really the big forces that are at work that have driven our strategy. The main driver of our strategy in Australia — and probably it is true in the rest of the world — is the need to reach the customer. It is fundamental. In Australia, particularly in the consumer side of the business, there has been quite a degree of inertia in the system and stickiness that has allowed the institutions to get away with less than perfect service. That can't last. We have to respond to customer behaviour and social forces. It is very hard to do but it is essential.

Q: Your view of the branch network is also different.

A: The focus has been on rationalising the traditional branch network that was positioned in earlier times and not configured for how people want to bank today. There is this need to shift and retain access to customers and obtain new customers.

*'The ratings agencies want to see
sticky funding and sticky funding
comes from consumers.'*
John McFarlane,
Managing Director,
ANZ Banking Group

Q: Can you keep shareholders happy with such a strategy?

A: Sometimes the analysts grimace about these things but you cannot meet the needs of the market all the time, even if you try. You can do that but you would gyrate from side to side as they get one strategy or another into their heads. You have to listen to the analysts but you can't keep changing your strategy ... Banking is more about execution of strategy than strategy itself.

Q: Is globalisation a big force on the bank?

A: It is an atomising force, an unbundling force. Specialists are likely to break into your market, big investment banks, big fund managers ... Global players will win in markets open to global competition — they are specialists. The easiest to penetrate will be cards, investment banking, capital markets, foreign exchange.

Q: And technology. Is that the hottest topic in banking at the moment?

A: There's a lot of elements there, like the Internet. You can rationalise platforms, disaggregate. Becoming a series of specialist businesses is the way to go. That doesn't mean the share-of-customer model still is not valuable. It is not discredited in that

your best prospect is your existing customer. But customers are unbundling. That really means you have got to find the best of two worlds. Find growth businesses and then link them together — that is a great paradigm.

Q: So where to for ANZ? Will you grow by making more acquisitions? (ANZ [in April 2002] entered a $38 billion joint venture with ING.)

A: The problem with ANZ was that we had a solid return on investment but we got it by having the highest financial leverage, and so the highest cost of capital and the riskiest proposition. We had 80 per cent corporate customers. Our cost of capital was too high so we were probably producing marginal EVA (economic value added). ANZ had to radically transform its business.

Source: Extracts from Andrew Cornell, 'The fixer', *AFR Boss*, May 2002, pp. 37–8.

Introduction

What do Qantas, General Electric, Flight Centre, Coca-Cola Amatil, Harvey Norman, BP-Amoco, Cadbury and BRL Hardy have in common? All have been very successful for the past decade or longer in both sales and financial performance. All are market leaders. In fact, most are bywords for successful marketing and brand building. Finally, all are explicitly led and managed with the objective of maximising shareholder value.

Many managers have confused maximising shareholder value and maximising profitability. The two are completely different. Maximising profitability is short term and invariably erodes a company's long-term market competitiveness. It is about cutting costs and shedding assets to produce quick improvements in earnings. By neglecting new market opportunities and failing to invest, such strategies destroy rather than create economic value. Strategies aimed at maximising shareholder value are different. They focus on identifying growth opportunities and building competitive advantage. They punish short-term strategies that destroy assets and fail to capitalise on the company's core capabilities.

Marketing and shareholder value need each other to reach their full potential. A major problem for marketing is that it has not been integrated with the modern concept of financial value creation. This has handicapped the ability of marketing managers to contribute to top management decision making. Yet marketing-led growth is at the heart of value creation. Without effective marketing, the shareholder value concept becomes little more than another destructive technique gearing management to rationalisation and short-term profits.

This chapter is one of three that make up part 1 of this book. Together the three chapters address the principles of value-based marketing. They provide an introduction to the challenges facing marketing, assess the importance of marketing within the organisation, outline the nature and significance of shareholder value, and analyse the key drivers of shareholder value.

value-based marketing: the process that seeks to maximise returns to shareholders by developing relationships with valued customers and creating a differential advantage

In this chapter, **value-based marketing** is presented as a new approach, which integrates marketing directly into the process of creating value for shareholders. Value-based marketing, we argue, makes the shareholder concept more valuable and marketing more effective. We define value-based marketing as the process that seeks to maximise returns to shareholders by developing relationships with valued customers and creating a competitive advantage.

Before we can explain in more detail the nature and basis of value-based marketing, two things need to be clearly understood. The first is the major changes affecting the business environment in recent decades. These changes are described in 'Managing in the twenty-first century', the next section of this chapter. The aim is to provide a better understanding of the pressures that contemporary managers face and the reasons why a new approach to marketing is warranted.

The second prerequisite is to be clear on just what is meant by the term 'shareholder value'. Thus, the second section of this chapter, 'Shareholder value: An introduction', provides an overview of the shareholder value approach by introducing the key concepts and assumptions that inform it.

The aim is to provide readers with a basic understanding that is sufficient to appreciate the material covered in parts 2 and 3 of this book. For those readers who would like a more detailed discussion of the shareholder approach, chapter 2 provides a fuller account of shareholder value analysis and of the key steps that it entails.

The shareholder approach is not without controversy. Hence, another purpose of the second section is to outline and analyse some of the main challenges and criticisms encountered by proponents of the notion of shareholder value. Here, attention is directed to the debate that organisations should seek to maximise the interests of all stakeholders, rather than just shareholders. The more technical criticisms of shareholder value analysis are considered in chapter 2.

Having discussed the market challenges that contemporary managers face, and having outlined the nature of the shareholder approach, we are in a position, in the section 'Marketing and shareholder value: A synergistic relationship', to introduce value-based marketing. The major theme in this section is the synergies between marketing and shareholder value. Marketing, it is argued, needs to embrace the shareholder value approach if it is to have a greater impact on business strategy. Just as importantly, shareholder value itself is greatly improved by the input provided by marketing.

A much more detailed discussion of these synergies — and of the concept of value-based marketing — is provided in chapter 3. That chapter is organised around the concept of value drivers. We argue there that the financial value drivers that generate shareholder value are themselves directly and critically influenced by marketing activities. A key theme of this book is that shareholder value analysis is essentially a method for analysing strategies; marketing's principal contribution is to provide those strategies. Part 2 of this book provides a guide to how such strategies can be developed and managed. Part 3 analyses the constituent parts of the process.

Section 1 | Managing in the 21st Century

The enormous changes in the global market environment explain today's pressures for greater management effectiveness. Competitive capitalism is Darwinian in nature. Businesses succeed when they meet the needs of customers more effectively than their competitors. Corporate profitability depends primarily on the company's ability to offer products that customers choose to pay for. But what products customers regard as attractive is a function of the market environment. What is an appealing computer, retail store or banking service today will not be tomorrow. Technological change, new competition and changing needs make yesterday's solutions obsolete and create the opportunity for new answers.

The result is that most companies do not usually last very long. De Geus calculated that the average life expectancy of a Western company is well below 20 years.[1] The period over which a successful firm can maintain a profitable competitive advantage is usually even shorter. Normally, any innovation in products or processes is quickly copied and the surplus profit is competed away. Even where a company endures and grows, its true profitability normally erodes. Studies show that the average company does not maintain a return above its cost of capital for more than seven or eight years.[2]

While the period over which the average business is successful is short, there are companies that do better. There are a few examples of companies that have survived and maintained successful economic performance over a much longer period. Currently, examples would include General Electric, Qantas, News Corporation, Coca-Cola, Merck, BP-Amoco and Shell. However, quoting examples of excellent companies is a hazardous venture. Great companies have a tendency to go belly-up when the environment changes fundamentally. A recent and powerful example of this is the Australian airline, Ansett. Another is the Tasmanian manufacturer of high-speed aluminium catamarans, Incat. Few leaders have the perspicacity, courage or capabilities to overturn the strategies, systems and organisation which created their past achievement.

Environmental change

macroenvironment: the broad outside forces affecting all markets, including the major economic, demographic, political, technological and cultural developments

microenvironment: the specific developments affecting the firm's individual industry or market: its customers, competitors and suppliers

Environmental changes affecting the performance of the business can be categorised as macro or micro. **Macroenvironmental** changes are the broad outside forces affecting all markets. These include the major economic, demographic, political, technological and cultural developments taking place today. The **microenvironment** refers to the specific developments affecting the firm's individual industry: its customers, competitors and suppliers. These developments reflect the impacts of the macroenvironmental changes on the specific industry (see figure 1.1).

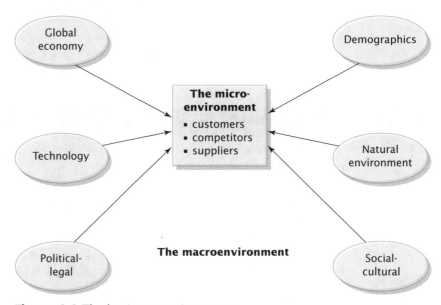

Figure 1.1 The business environment

Today, this macroenvironment is experiencing unique historical changes which are fundamentally redrawing the business and social landscape. These changes have been given various names including the 'post-industrial society', the 'global village', the 'third wave' and, perhaps most accurately, the 'information age'.

Social scientists describe three periods of economic evolution in the Western world: the *agricultural era*, which lasted from around 8000 BC to the mid-eighteenth century; the *industrial era*, which lasted until the late twentieth century; and finally what we will call the *information age*, which began in the 1960s and will last for decades to come.[3] These dates are, of course, approximate and overlapping. The first era was based on agriculture, with physical labour being the driver of any wealth that was achieved. This eventually gave way to the second era sparked by the industrial revolution, when machinery replaced muscle power, and factories replaced agriculture as the dominant employer, leading to an enormous growth in both agricultural and industrial productivity.

While the agricultural era lasted for thousands of years, the industrial age lasted only two hundred. The 1960s began to see the end of the industrial era and the beginning of the new information age. Employment in manufacturing began to drop in all the advanced countries and the service sector became the new focus for growth. Blue-collar workers who operated equipment in crowded factories were increasingly replaced by white-collar workers working individually or in small teams using computers and scientific knowledge in office environments. Today, information technology is rapidly replacing factories and machine power as the source of productivity growth and competitiveness.

The transitional periods between the three great waves of change have not been smooth. In figure 1.2 each wave is represented by an 'S' curve that shows an early period of turbulence, followed by a long spell of maturity, and then its eventual demise as new technologies take over. The last decades of the twentieth century witnessed the period of turbulence marking the birth of the information age and the death of the industrial era. The turbulence included record levels of mergers and acquisitions, the collapse of communism in the former USSR and its satellites, and economic crises in South-East Asia. All these reflect old second-wave industries and social organisations being pushed aside in the competitive environment of the new information age.

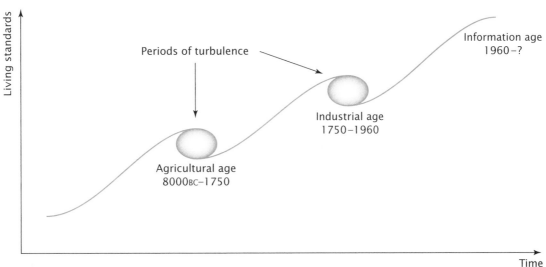

Figure 1.2 The three waves of economic change

Four aspects in particular of the new information age require fundamental strategic and organisational responses from management:
1. the globalisation of markets
2. changing industrial structures
3. the information revolution
4. rising customer expectations.

The globalisation of markets

The new information age has seen a dramatic shift to global markets and competition. Across more and more industries, firms that are not building global operations and marketing capabilities are losing out. Recent decades have seen an enormous growth of international trade in goods, services and capital. The General Agreement on Tariffs and Trade (GATT) and its successor organisation, the World Trade Organisation (WTO), have been the means of negotiating a general lowering of barriers to trade between countries and an opening up of markets. The stimulus to this liberalisation of trade has been experience. Governments have seen, often painfully, that protecting home industries and markets from competition does not work. It only leads to higher inflation, lower economic growth and domestic companies lacking the levels of efficiency and entrepreneurial skills ever to be internationally competitive. Other stimuli to the globalisation of markets and competition have been faster and cheaper transportation and a continuing telecommunications revolution that has made global communications cheap, simple and effective. Finally, the barriers to participation in world trade have often come down dramatically. Today, any business can open an Internet web site and market to customers from the other side of the world, just as easily as to its customers around the corner.

The result has been the emergence of new transnational companies organised to maximise the opportunities to be gained from the new global marketplace and to minimise the costs of serving it. Companies like Microsoft, General Electric, Intel, Merck, IBM, Dell and McDonald's are selling in all the key markets. Their supply chains are equally global, with materials and components sourced from the cheapest locations, assembly and logistics organised from the most effective regional bases, and research and development located where relevant knowledge is most accessible.

In most sectors, small domestically oriented companies lack the economies of scale to remain competitive over the longer run. The scale economies of the transnational companies lie not so much in manufacturing costs but in information and knowledge. The new focused transnationals like Intel, AOL and Cisco win out because they can afford to spend more on research and development, on building brands, on information technology and on marketing. Once new opportunities are identified they can also marshal the resources that are necessary to capitalise and develop the market.

Changing industrial structures

The information age is changing the nature of the profit opportunities available to businesses. Many markets that were once at the very heart of the economy have ceased to offer profit opportunities for Western firms. Other new markets are rapidly emerging that offer enormous profit opportunities to companies that can move fast and decisively to capitalise on them.

Manufacturing industries can be divided into two types. One type comprises traditional industries such as textiles, coal mining, heavy chemicals, steel and auto manufacturing, which are relatively labour intensive and make heavy use of raw materials. These industries are relocating rapidly to the developing countries, which have a comparative cost advantage. Such industries also generally suffer the problem of substantial excess manufacturing capacity because these new countries have invested too aggressively in seeking to gain market shares. The result has been falling prices and very poor returns on investment.

The second type of industries are the information- and knowledge-based ones such as pharmaceuticals, communications equipment, electronics and computers, aerospace and biotechnology. Here, labour costs are typically less than 5 per cent of total costs. Most of the costs are information related: research, design, development, testing, marketing, customer service and support. These are where the profit and growth opportunities occur for information-age companies. Contrary to the popular view, in most Western countries, manufacturing output has not declined in recent decades. What has changed is the switch away from traditional labour-intensive industries to those that are information based. Second, there has been a sharp decline in manufacturing employment — notably blue-collar work, as these jobs have been automated or moved to the developing countries.

Overall employment has been maintained in information-age countries by the rapid growth of the service sector. Service-sector output has been growing at least twice as fast as manufacturing output in recent decades. In advanced countries, services now account for two-thirds of economic output. As living standards continue to rise, consumers spend relatively more on services rather than on goods. Health, education, travel, financial services, entertainment and restaurants are all growth markets. Information technology has also become a massive service industry. Another reason why this will continue is that the output of the new information-based manufacturing industries is increasingly distributed in service form. For example, pharmaceutical companies or book publishers, rather than exporting drugs or books, will license the rights to produce them. In the future, many items such as music and news will be increasingly downloaded from the Internet rather than bought in the form of a physical product such as a CD.

The information revolution

Rapid scientific and technological changes continue to radically reshape many industries. But the most dramatic and far-reaching changes of the current era result from the revolution in information technology. Initiated by the development of the mainframe and the personal computer in the 1960s and 1970s, its full implications only really became apparent in the 1990s with the explosion in use of the Internet. By 2001, less than a decade after the emergence of the World Wide Web, a fundamental change in business and society had occurred — a critical mass of people, over 400 million, at home and at work, are able to communicate electronically with one another at essentially zero cost, using universal, open standards.

The Internet, together with the emergence of broadband cellular radio networks, is creating an explosion in connectivity that is revolutionising almost every aspect of business. First, it changes the firm's internal value chain — the way people inside the business organise to design, produce, market, deliver and support its products. In the past, businesses had to organise through hierarchies and bureaucracy because information was expensive, and difficult and slow to obtain. Today, **intranets**, which instantly and costlessly connect individuals within companies for the exchange of information, make obsolete the need for hierarchical functions. Instead, cross-functional teams and informal networking are encouraged, which in turn facilitate flatter, lower-cost organisational structures, faster responses and better customer service.

Second, the information revolution changes the way the business works with its suppliers. Where partnerships are important, information technology can make them much closer. **Extranets**, which connect companies to each other, can seamlessly integrate buyer and seller into a **virtual business**. A typical example is the jeans maker, Levi. Over the Internet it continuously obtains information about the sizes and styles of its jeans being sold by its major retailers. Levi then electronically orders more fabric for immediate delivery from the Milliken Company, its fabric supplier. Milliken, in turn, relays an order for more fibre to Du Pont, its fibre supplier. In this way the partners take out cost throughout the supply chain, minimise inventory holding and have up-to date information to enable them to respond quickly to changes in consumer demand.

On the other hand, where buyers see price as more important than partnerships, the new availability of information will undermine the suppliers' relationships with customers. For example, many component buyers are now posting their purchasing requirements on Internet bulletin boards and inviting bids from anybody inclined to respond. The information revolution increases the information available to buyers and reduces the cost of switching suppliers. In general, the bargaining power of buyers is radically increased.

Finally, the information revolution significantly changes the nature of marketing and the **marketing mix**. Traditionally, buyers chose suppliers for both the qualities of the products and the information they supplied. For example, retailers like Toys 'R' Us or PC World prospered by offering shoppers a wider selection of merchandise. But such formats are now undermined by search engines on the Internet, which can offer consumers much more choice than any store. This has created many new huge business opportunities for companies able to exploit the informational advantage of the Internet. These include specialist facilitators like Microsoft, Yahoo! and AOL, which assist consumers in their search for information. Others have reconfigured the traditional industry chain to capitalise on electronic communications. Among the most successful has been Amazon.com, which in only four years created the world's biggest book retailing operation, selling its wares globally over the Internet. In more recent years it has greatly expanded the product categories sold online.

In many markets, information technology is leading to **disintermediation** — the elimination of agents between the supplier and the consumer. Buyers are finding that they no longer need retailers, agents or brokers; they can buy at lower cost, and more conveniently, directly from the manufacturer over the telephone or the Internet. Companies like Dell in computers and Direct Line in insurance rapidly grew to market leadership by exploiting this strategic window. When the seller deals directly with end consumers the opportunity is

intranet: web sites internal to the company and available only to its employees

extranet: web sites that connect the intranet of an organisation with its trading partners, suppliers and distributors

virtual business: an online business; one conducted on the Internet

marketing mix: a set of operating decisions, sometimes referred to as the four Ps — product, price, promotion and place

disintermediation: the elimination of intermediaries or agents between the supplier and the consumer

then created to build databases which record *learning* about individual consumer wants and buying behaviour. The seller can then create added value by tailoring messages and even products for individual consumers. The information revolution then begins to change marketing from mass communications and standardised brands to one-to-one customised marketing. For the innovators this offers the opportunity for higher profit margins, greater loyalty and a bigger share of the customer's spending.[4]

These changes are converting the marketing assets of many of the traditional market leaders into liabilities. Bank branch networks, many shops and boutiques, and experienced sales forces are all at risk as customers communicate electronically.

Rising customer expectations

The information age has brought a marked rise in customer expectations. Buyers have grown to expect higher quality, competitive prices, and better and faster service. The most important causes have been the globalisation of competition and the deregulation of markets. Once markets were opened up to today's aggressive international competitors, companies that lacked a customer orientation or that had inefficient cost structures were soon in trouble. The new wave of Japanese exporters such as Sony, Toyota and Matsushita in the 1960s showed Western companies the new standards of quality required to stay competitive. Concepts like *kaisen* (continuous incremental improvement), Total Quality Management (TQM), and such schemes as the US Baldridge Awards and the European ISO 9000 certification had real effects in raising quality standards. During the 1970s and 1980s major excess capacity became a characteristic of more and more industries — for example, cars, steel, chemicals, electrical goods, agricultural products and banking. This further shifted the priority to gaining customer preference in **hypercompetitive markets**. Finally, the explosion of information technology gave management new tools for serving customers better: tools to continuously monitor customer needs and to improve the internal processes and supply chains that would enable them to meet, and indeed exceed, customer expectations.

hypercompetitive markets: markets subject to intense competition and high levels of environmental turbulence

market segmentation: dividing a market into discrete categories of consumers who share particular characteristics and who have a similar need

Initially, the response to meeting customer needs better was **market segmentation**. Companies brought out an increasing number of product variants to meet the diverse needs of their customers. Nike had 347 types of running shoes, Procter & Gamble had 207 brands and sizes of detergent, United Distillers introduced nine line extensions of its Johnnie Walker brand of scotch whisky, credit card companies offered green, blue, gold and platinum versions, each with minor differences in the service offering, and so on. Media too became more segmented: mass-circulation newspapers and magazines were replaced by a proliferating array of specialists. Digital technology also facilitated an explosive growth of the number of radio and television channels.

mass customisation: offering products tailored to the individual customer and made to order

The problem with market segmentation was that it was expensive and limited in effectiveness. More variants meant higher manufacturing costs and spiralling inventory levels leading to lower profits and asset turnover. By 2000, the information revolution was beginning to offer a better alternative — **mass customisation**. Media and products could be tailored to the individual customer and made to order, using modern high technology communications and manufacturing systems. Information technology now allows companies to record all the information they obtain from consumers through their personal, written, telephone or Internet communications with the company. Creating a database allows companies to learn about the buying behaviour and preferences of customers and to communicate individually and directly with them. Direct marketing creates the opportunity for a dialogue, allowing a precise specification of the customer's wants.

one-to-one marketing: a form of marketing involving mass customisation and two-way direct communication between the producer and the consumer

Companies like Dell Computer Corporation have shown how direct marketing can be allied to a fast response supply chain to produce customised products delivered to the customer's door 48 hours after the order.[5] For the customer, **one-to-one marketing** offers a precise fit to his or her individual requirements. For the supplier, it means higher margins and lower investment requirements.

Strategic and organisational implications

Companies survive only if they can adapt to this rapidly changing environment (see figure 1.3). This changing environment determines what products customers will find attractive. It also determines the technologies that will be available for companies to produce and market these products. **Strategy** refers to the business's overall plan for deploying resources to create a differential advantage in its markets. **Organisation** refers to the capabilities the firm possesses and how its staff are led, coordinated and motivated to implement the strategy.

strategy: the business's overall plan for deploying resources to create a differential advantage in its markets

organisation: the capabilities the firm possesses and how its staff are led, coordinated and motivated to implement strategy

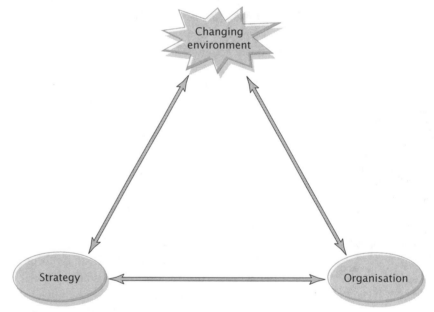

Figure 1.3 Adapting to a changing environment

Today, the changes in the marketing environment are so momentous that they require radical strategic and organisational change from virtually all companies. Gone are the days when managers could stick to tried and tested formulas to provide continuous growth and profitability. Globalisation, new industrial structures, rapidly changing technologies and new customer expectations are quickly eroding yesterday's markets, while creating phenomenal new opportunities for those that can move fast and decisively to capitalise on the changing environment.

Today, five main issues stand out for management:

1. participation strategy
2. marketing strategy
3. operations strategy
4. global strategy
5. organisational imperatives.

Participation strategy

As the environment changes, the opportunities to achieve profitable growth change too. Some markets cease to have potential and should be exited; others offer great opportunities and require high investment, innovative strategies and new organisations. Managers have to decide which markets to participate in. To do this they have to objectively assess, first, the future attractiveness of the markets in which they operate. Because they differ in intensity of competition and price pressures from customers, some markets will become much more profitable than others. In general, the greatest opportunities will occur in services — such as, entertainment, education, the Internet, software and mobile telecommunications. Other markets are extremely unlikely to generate returns for shareholders. Many of the old labour- and raw-material intensive industries such as textiles, steel and heavy chemicals fall into this category. Second, managers need to assess their **competitive potential**. With today's fierce global competition, unless a business can create a differential advantage, in terms of either low total cost or a superior product that can command a price premium from customers, it will not earn an adequate return.

competitive potential:
an organisation's assessment of the extent to which it is able, now or in the future, to compete in a market

Marketing strategy

The information revolution is making obsolete the marketing strategies of many traditional industry leaders. It destroys barriers to entry and transforms the structure of many industries. Who needs a branch network when customers can bank more conveniently on the Web? Who needs retailers and distributors when you can sell direct to consumers? Every aspect of marketing comes up for renewal.

The customer and product mix needs to be strategically reappraised. The information revolution will increase the need for firms to focus. Many firms have too many low-value customers who do not want long-term relationships. They also often have too many products bundled together by the classic informational logic of one-stop shopping. However, one-stop shopping loses its premium for customers once information is readily available. Specialists can then generally offer lower prices or superior service by focusing their operations around a single product or customer group.

Pricing strategies also need reviewing. The globalisation of markets, the new euro currency and information technology all make prices more transparent and comparable. Businesses not offering value to customers will see their market shares eroding at accelerating rates. The information revolution is having its most dramatic impacts on promotion and distribution strategies. The company's web site is increasingly becoming both the first port of call for customers looking for information and a crucial source of knowledge about customers for the company. More fundamentally, the Internet is offering more and more companies the opportunity to eliminate intermediaries and deal with consumers directly.

Operations strategy

To implement a new marketing strategy requires the firm to create an operations strategy capable of delivering it. Companies need to construct a supply chain that can produce the right goods and services, at the right price, in the right place, at the right time. With today's global competition and rising customer expectations, this right strategy usually means low prices, rapid delivery, reliable quality and up-to-date technology.

To meet these demanding expectations, a new business model is emerging among today's leading-edge companies built around coordination and focus. We will call this the **direct business model** (see figure 1.4). Perhaps the most famous exponent of this model is Dell Computer Corporation, a market leader in desktop computer sales. The new model fundamentally reshapes the firm's downstream and upstream activities. **Downstream**, the new business model is built around bypassing the dealer, selling direct to the customer and making to order. Generally the communications take place over the telephone or the Internet. Selling direct has the crucial advantage of enabling the firm rather than the intermediary to control the relationship with the customer. Information from customers enables the firm to add value and develop loyalty by customising the offer and the communications to the customer's exact requirements. Information also gives the firm leverage over its suppliers because it owns the brand and the customer relationships. The new direct business model also cuts distribution costs, eliminates inventories and reduces risks by enabling better forecasting of consumer demand.

direct business model: a business model involving direct sales to the end user and, usually, close cooperation with suppliers

downstream: that part of the supply chain in which the product moves from the producer to the buyer

Traditional model: value chain with transactions between independent parties

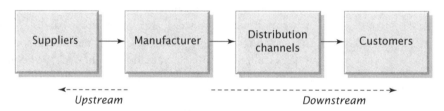

Direct business model: eliminates distributors

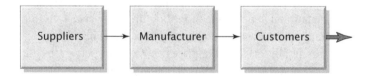

Virtual integration: develops direct model further by using IT to integrate supply chain partners and customers

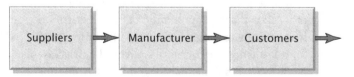

Figure 1.4 The evolution of a new business model

upstream: that part of the supply chain in which the producer obtains the parts, components and/or raw materials with which to make the product

vertical integration: achieving control and coordination of the procurement of supplies and/or of distribution by owning those who provide the supplies or distribute the product

virtual integration: achieving control and coordination through information rather than through ownership

Upstream, the model is built around close cooperation with suppliers. Manufacturing and logistics is outsourced to a carefully selected set of partners. These suppliers are linked electronically to the firm and treated like an internal department. Instead of **vertical integration** (control and coordination through ownership) we have **virtual integration** (control and coordination through information). This reduces the assets required to support rapid growth, minimises financial risk and maximises flexibility. It frees management to focus on what adds most value today — delivering solutions and systems to customers. The direct business model creates genuine value through customer focus, supplier partnerships, mass customisation and just-in-time manufacturing.

Global strategy

In today's connected world, every company now needs a global strategy. Industries are globalising at a rush and companies that are not leading, or at least participating, in the new alliances, are becoming non-viable. Manufacturing tended to globalise first but now services are following rapidly. For example, a series of mega-mergers in the 1990s globalised accounting, financial services and most of the advertising industry into a small number of huge global groups. Regional and global groupings are also beginning to emerge in telecommunications, banking, contract services and many other areas.

In business-to-business markets — to which most companies belong — the pressure to globalise comes from their customers, which operate across the world. Procter & Gamble and IBM want suppliers and business partners that can interface with their own far-flung geographical operations. The opportunity to spread the costs and lever the investments in research, development and technology also favours global players. Finally, being dependent on a single country market leaves today's local player highly vulnerable. Strategically it is in a weak position to counter-attack against a strong global player moving into its market and being willing to cross-subsidise its entry from profits earned in other markets.

As in most areas of business today, there are big advantages in speed and decisiveness when it comes to global strategy. The longer management prevaricates, the fewer the options are available and the higher the price that has to be paid.

Organisational imperatives

To implement new strategies requires new organisations. What is different about organisations in the information age? First, employees are different. Blue-collar workers have given way to knowledge professionals. Part-timers and women make up an increasing proportion of the staff. The skills of the new knowledge workers make them less dependent on the company and more mobile. Motivating them requires different work environments and incentives from the past. Second, information and communications technology now permits new and more effective ways for people within the firm to relate to one another and to relate to others in the supply chain.

Finally, the new strategies ushered in by the information age require different responses from staff. A customer orientation becomes more important since more of the staff are now directly involved in providing customer service and customising products and solutions. The priority consumers now give to convenience and speed of response demands much greater empowerment and commitment from staff. The pressure on prices and the need to provide greater shareholder value also drive management to seek higher productivity and better utilisation of assets.

The direction of organisational changes is clear. **Delayering** has been one major move. Information technology has enabled companies to reduce the number of levels of middle management, providing for greater customer orientation, lower costs and faster response. Second, enhanced connectivity is breaking down functional barriers within firms, permitting a much greater use of cross-functional teams, which again makes for faster response and greater customer focus. The same forces have increased the flow of information between firms, facilitating more effective networks to lever the firm's capabilities with those of its business partners. The final change has been a greater focus on shareholder value. Investors are putting much more pressure on managers either to deliver superior returns or return the cash to shareholders.

The implications of the changing environment for strategy and organisation, and hence for the firm's ability to achieve longer term growth and profitability, can be summarised in five principles:

1. **Strategy must fit the environment**. Companies can remain competitive only when they have products which today's customers regard as offering superior value. Perceived value is shaped by the changing macro- and microenvironments within which the firm and its customers operate.

2. **Successful strategies erode**. Winning formulas eventually lose out because the environment changes. Competitors copy successful products and processes. Changing tastes and new technologies make yesterday's successes obsolete.

3. **Effectiveness is more important than efficiency**. Old formulas cannot be preserved by downsizing and cost reduction. Innovative solutions have a way of coming down in cost to offer superior value across all dimensions of value. Success in the information age is about renewal rather than retrenchment.

4. **Speed and decisiveness**. Being first mover when new opportunities occur can carry great advantages. With no direct competition it is much easier to demonstrate a competitive advantage. However, being first is not sufficient; the innovator has to create a critical mass in terms of market share. This requires managers decisively shifting resources out of yesterday's businesses into the new opportunities.

5. **Organisational adaptation**. Creating these dynamic, customer-oriented businesses that are needed for the new millennium requires leadership and organisational transformation of a high order.

delayering:
removing or reducing the number of managerial layers within an organisation

Section 2 | Shareholder value: An introduction

The onset of environmental turbulence has raised questions about the very purpose of organisations, their primary responsibilities and their objectives. The argument presented in this book is that value must be judged in terms of the value provided to the firm's owners. In publicly listed companies, the owners are the shareholders. From the shareholders' perspective, managers are their agents, acting on their behalf. The primary managerial objective should be to take actions that enhance shareholder value: indeed, that maximise the returns for the firm's owners. As this suggests, proponents of the notion of shareholder value take it as given that management need to think in terms of how investors are evaluating their business. Management need to have a capital market focus and to understand investor behaviour.

The environmental changes discussed in the previous section help to explain why, in recent years, the notions of value-based management and shareholder value analysis have spread rapidly. The increased interest in shareholder value has been triggered, in particular, by the enormous growth of equity markets around the world caused by economic expansion and the declining role of government investment in industry. Capital controls have been substantially eased, if not entirely eliminated. At the same time, institutional investors have grown in importance.

While government investment is motivated by complex political concerns, the objectives of private equity investors are much simpler and clearer. Private investors expect the pension, insurance and mutual funds that invest their money to maximise their performance. This in turn causes the fund managers to increasingly demand value from the companies in which they invest.

Companies are now competing internationally not only for customers but also for capital. The most important criterion for attracting equity capital is its expected economic return. The information revolution is also making markets more efficient. Computers and modelling software now make it much quicker to run shareholder value analyses and test the implications of a company's strategic thinking. The quantity and quality of information available to investors have also increased exponentially in recent years. Finally, the sophistication of modern tele-communications means that money can now travel around the world in seconds. All these trends mean that managers are under increasing scrutiny from the people whose money they are using. As Young and O'Byrne put it, 'capital isn't "sticky" anymore; capital can move. And move it will, whenever investors believe their capital will be more productively employed somewhere else.'[6]

Basic principles

At the heart of the shareholder value approach is the notion that an attempt must be made to measure the impact of a proposed strategy, and that measurement should focus on the contribution that the strategy makes to generating cash flow for the organisation. Furthermore, the focus should not be on short-term effects but on what happens to cash flow over the longer term.

To pursue these points in more detail, the appropriate starting point is to note that **shareholder value analysis (SVA)** recognises that the implementation of strategic decisions generates a stream of cash flows over a number of years. SVA emphasises the importance of cash flow because this determines how much is available to pay shareholders and debtors. Particular attention, as noted, is paid to long-term cash flows. One of the tenets of SVA is that, contrary to what many managers believe, investors have a long-term perspective. Investors appreciate, for example, that a strategy that yields considerable long-term gains may have a negative impact on both short-term earnings and cash flow, and factor this into their evaluation.

In determining whether a proposed strategy is one that will add value, it is necessary first to assess as accurately as possible the anticipated future cash flows that it will generate. Second, the present value of these future cash flows needs to be calculated. To do this, we discount them by multiplying them by the **discount factor**. Discounting reflects that money has a time value. Because cash can earn

shareholder value analysis (SVA): a formal process in which strategies are analysed to determine whether and to what extent their implementation would increase shareholder value

discount factor: the present value of $1 received at a stated future date; calculated as $1/(1 + r)^t$ where r is the discount rate and t is the year

18

interest, cash received today is worth more than the same amount received a year or more in the future. The idea of using **discounted cash flow (DCF)** techniques for evaluating individual projects, particularly capital budget proposals, is not new. Indeed, it has been the standard for evaluating capital projects for 40 years. But it was not until the 1980s that firms began seriously using DCF for broader strategic planning purposes. It is only now that it is being considered for evaluating marketing strategies. One of the givens in SVA is that the principles of DCF can be used to determine the value of the organisation as a whole. Properly done, this can be used to determine whether the organisation, and not just an individual project, is one that increases the wealth of the shareholders and thereby provides shareholder value. The argument is that shareholder value, and not the traditional accounting-based measures of corporate performance, should be the primary metric for assessing the firm's ongoing operations.

In SVA, the estimated future cash flows are discounted using something called the **cost of capital**. A key consideration in understanding the cost of capital is that those who provide funds to an organisation — be it in the form of debt or equity — have a variety of choices as to where and to whom they will provide capital. That which is provided to one organisation is now no longer available to be provided to another. In choosing one alternative over another, investors incur an **opportunity cost**. The cost of capital measures this opportunity cost. It is the percentage return that investors expect to receive as the minimum reward for providing capital.

Consider an investor who has invested in a (fictitious) pharmaceutical company called Alpha Drugs. In making this decision, she was aware that she had several alternatives. One was to spend the money, perhaps on buying furniture. Another was to invest not in the stock market but in long-term Australian Government bonds. This, essentially, would have been a risk-free strategy in that the chances of default are close to zero. Our investor would have received a guaranteed annual interest rate and full payment of the principal at the expiry of the bond. Instead, however, she chose to invest in the stock market, but only because she expected to receive a sufficiently high rate of return to compensate her for the risks involved. Having decided to invest her available funds in the stock market, her next task was to choose a particular company. In deciding upon Alpha Drugs, our investor is now expecting to receive, in the way of dividends and share price appreciation, a rate of return that compensates her for parting with her money and which is superior to what she could have got by investing in long-term government bonds. Our investor also considered Beta Drugs, another pharmaceutical company and one subject to similar sorts of market risks to those faced by Alpha. Her opportunity cost, therefore, was that, by investing in Alpha, she forsook the opportunity to invest in Beta. Our investor will not be satisfied unless Alpha is able to provide her with a rate of return that is at least as good as that which Beta provides its investors.

The cost of capital has two components — the cost of debt and the cost of equity — reflecting the two sources of capital funding on which firms rely. The two are combined as a weighted average, reflecting the firm's financing structure. For example, in pursuing a particular strategy a firm may plan to raise, say, 70 per cent of its future capital by equity finance and 30 per cent by debt. If the firm has calculated its cost of equity to be 11.7 per cent, then the weighted cost for equity finance is 8.2 per cent (70 per cent of 11.7). Likewise, if it has

weighted average cost of capital (WACC): the cost of equity and the cost of debt combined and weighted according to their relative contribution to the organisation's financing or capital structure

total shareholder returns: the combined returns to shareholders in the form of dividend payments and share price appreciation

calculated its cost of debt to be 6 per cent, then the weighted cost for debt finance is 1.8 per cent (30 per cent of 6). The overall cost of capital (known as the **weighted average cost of capital**) is 8.2 + 1.8 = 10 per cent.

In choosing to tie up their capital with a particular company, the suppliers of equity capital are interested in overall returns, or what are known as **total shareholder returns** (see marketing insight 'The shareholders' friends'). They have expectations with respect not only to the stream of future dividend payments but also the extent to which there will be an appreciation in the share price. The overall returns that they seek are influenced partly by their perceptions of the riskiness of the investment. Investors want returns that compensate them appropriately for the level of risk that they bear. As a rule, the higher the risk, the greater is the desired return. The cost of capital is a risk-weighted measure, since it incorporates the risk that investors perceive to be associated with the investment.

Marketing insight: **The shareholders' friends**

In 2001, consulting firm, A.T. Kearney, was commissioned to rank Australia's 100 largest listed companies (by market capitalisation) in terms of their total shareholder return (TSR). This was calculated as an average over five years.

TSR, a measure of share price growth plus dividend growth, is the most direct measure of the return that shareholders receive from their investment in a company. It is also the most commonly used tool for boards wanting to set performance standards. All companies in A.T. Kearney's top 10 have maintained an average TSR of 40% or more during the past five years. The top performer was Cochlear, a manufacturer of bionic ears, with a 54% increase in revenue for the year ending June 30, 2001, and a 54% increase in TSR. Cochlear's five-year TSR averaged 56%. Closely following was Toll Holdings, the transport and logistics company, with a five-year average TSR of 54%. The top ten performers were:

1. Cochlear
2. Toll Holdings
3. Challenger International
4. Aristocrat Leisure
5. Corporate Express
6. Flight Centre
7. Lang Corporation
8. Sonic Healthcare
9. CSL
10. Perpetual Trustees

The survey showed that only 48 companies had been able to maintain an average TSR above the cost of equity (a result A. T. Kearney calls superior shareholder return (SSR)) over the past five years. The cost of equity for the 100 companies in the survey averaged 10%. 32 companies made it into the very good category with a TSR of 5% or more above the cost of equity over 5 years.

'A company that is producing a positive SSR is adding value for its shareholders,' says Peter Munro, a principal at A. T. Kearney.

'That is what all companies aspire to, but this survey demonstrates that it is a high hurdle. It is very difficult to create value consistently for any length of time. This is what makes the performance of the chief executives in the top quartile so remarkable.'

The survey shows a strong correlation between revenue growth and TSR. Munro notes that revenue growth is the prerequisite for the creation of long-term shareholder value. 'You can't cost-cut your way to greatness. Cost-cutting can improve shareholder value but it tends to work as a one-off. Once you have cut your costs, investors expect that you will keep costs low or cut them even more, so any additional improvement in cost management tends to produce little extra shareholder value.'

Leading companies in the survey, Munro observed, were innovators that drive consolidation in their industries so that they can achieve economies of scale and greater efficiency. They are also active in managing their portfolio of assets. Munro says that creating strong shareholder value is not limited to companies in growth industries: there is no sectoral advantage when it comes to creating value for shareholders.

Source: Adapted from John Kavanagh, 'Superstar performers', *BRW*, 1–7 November 2001, pp. 62–6.

A company has failed to provide value unless the cash return on its investments is in excess of the company's cost of capital. In terms of the example noted earlier, the cash return has to be greater than 10 per cent (the weighted average cost of capital). The practical requirement of this principle is that the company needs to ensure that the returns that it provides to its investors are at least as high as what they could have expected to earn elsewhere if they had invested their funds in businesses with a similar degree of risk. The cost of capital is a threshold — a hurdle rate — that must be bettered. If the company fails to do this, investors will withdraw their funds and capital will migrate in search of better returns elsewhere. We can summarise this by saying that it is only when shareholder returns exceed equity cost that shareholder value is created.

It needs to be stressed that SVA does not itself generate strategies. Rather, it seeks to identify those strategies that create shareholder value. The cost of capital, as noted earlier, is used for discounting the estimated future cash flows to give them a present value. The challenge for the analyst — a considerable one — is to obtain an accurate estimate of future cash flows. The estimates are made for two periods. One is the **explicit forecast period**. This is the time during which the proposed strategy has run its course and provided for the organisation a competitive advantage. Another determinant of the length of the explicit forecast period is the assessment by managers of the length of time for which they can sensibly make estimates of sales, costs and investments. Generally this would be for a period of no more than about seven or eight years. The other is the post-forecast period. The value of cash flow during the post-forecast period is known by a variety of names: **continuing value**, terminal value and residual value.

While it is difficult to obtain reliable estimates of cash flows, an even greater challenge is deciding upon the discount rate, the cost of capital. Since the object of the DCF procedure is to determine whether to proceed with a particular strategy or to choose between a variety of alternative strategies, a mistake in calculating the cost of capital could have a prejudicial effect on decision making. Unfortunately, as will be discussed in chapter 2, the cost of capital is not easily calculated.

Sometimes, investors, analysts and management themselves use proxy measures of shareholder value. One of these is based on the **market-to-book (M/B) ratio**. This reflects the stock market's judgment on the expected financial performance of a company (see figure 1.5). This ratio is a useful insight for measuring how successful management have been in maximising shareholder value. The main determinant of **market value** is the ability of management to seize profitable investment opportunities. Company size can be measured by its book value or **book equity**: the accounting value of its equity. The market capitalisation is simply the product of these two components. For example, a market-to-book ratio of 3 and a book value of $10 billion equates to a market capitalisation of $30 billion. A useful proxy for determining whether shareholder value has been created is to see whether the market value of the shares exceeds its book value.

To evaluate a new strategy proposed by the management team, the future effects of this strategy must be separated from the results of past strategies and investments. The current share price reflects both the values derived from

explicit forecast period: the period during which a proposed strategy can be expected to provide for the organisation a competitive advantage and for which managers feel that they can sensibly make estimates of sales, costs and investments

continuing value: the value of the cash flow generated during the post-forecast period

market-to-book (M/B) ratio: the market value of the business divided by the book equity ratio

market value: the actual value of equity as reflected in the market price of shares multiplied by the number of shares

book equity: the value of shareholders' funds as recorded in the published accounts of the business

these past decisions as well as shareholders' expectations about what the current management team will do. To judge the current strategy, we need to focus on the incremental effect on shareholder value.

Shareholder value as a measure of success and of strategic vulnerability

The value of a company measures the views of professional investors about the ability of management to master the changing market environment outlined earlier. When a company is seen to be in an attractive market, pursuing a strategy that has a good chance of building a sustainable differential advantage, then the value of the company rises. An attractive market and a winning formula should mean that the company will be able to earn a return on its investment above the cost of capital. In this situation management find it easy to attract outside funds, to make acquisitions and to grow.

When investors perceive a company to be stuck in unattractive markets and to be lacking a differential advantage, they naturally do not want to invest. The value of the company then declines, making the company difficult to attract resources and making it vulnerable to acquisition.

The value of a company is increased by making the business better. But even if the company performs well, it could still be too small to remain independent. It may be worth more to a larger company with global ambitions than it is as a stand-alone business. Good companies as well as bad companies get bought. The difference is that in the former case, shareholders are well rewarded in the higher price that the acquirer has to pay. If managers want to be able to control their own destiny in today's global economy — to remain independent — the company has to get bigger as well as get better.

Companies that do not manage for value find capital more difficult and costly to obtain, handicapping their growth potential. They also become vulnerable more quickly. Non-executive shareholders and fund managers are becoming notably more proactive in removing top management when they fail to create value for shareholders. Chief executives recently removed in this way include those at General Motors, IBM, American Express and Kodak in the United States, and Marks & Spencer, Mirror Group, Sears and BP in the United Kingdom. Finally, acquisition is a potent threat. When a weak market-to-book ratio indicates a **value gap** — that is, a difference between the value of the company if it were operated to maximise shareholder value and its current value — an invitation appears for an acquirer to bid for it and replace the existing management.

value gap: the difference between the value of a company if it were operated to maximise shareholder value and its current value

The implications of this can be seen in figure 1.5. The management consultants, McKinsey, suggest that companies can be mapped into four groups:[7]

1. **Vulnerable.** Companies like A and B, using relatively small amounts of financial capital and generating relatively low returns, are vulnerable to acquisition. These are often businesses that have been left in mature, unattractive industries and are still focused on the domestic market. They are commonly taken over by larger competitors that can generate higher returns from the same asset base. To have a future, these vulnerable companies need either to radically improve the performance of their existing businesses or divest them and reinvest the capital in more attractive industries. The Australian biscuits manufacturer, Arnott's, was an example of such a company. It is now owned by the US multinational, Campbells.

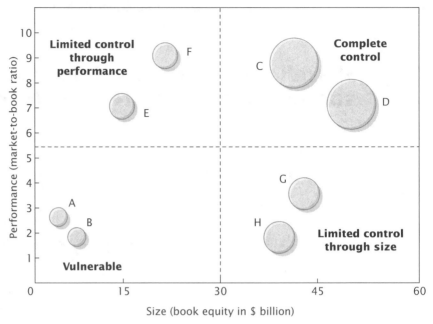

Figure 1.5 Strategic control as a function of performance and size

2. **Complete control**. At the opposite extreme are companies like C and D, which are generating high returns from a large capital base. Examples might be Intel, General Electric and Alcoa World Alumina Australia. Typically these companies are in attractive markets, competing globally and with competitive advantages that give them high market shares. Their high multiples enable them to acquire competitors, and protect them from being acquisition targets themselves. The challenge facing these companies is protecting their positions against the onslaught of new competitors while simultaneously identifying new opportunities to grow sales and profits.

3. **Limited control through performance**. Companies like E and F in the upper left quadrant obtain high returns from relatively small amounts of invested capital. Examples are 3Com, Cable and Wireless and Reuters. They are often specialist niche players in attractive high-tech segments. Their good performance makes them an expensive acquisition. But, in the longer run, they are vulnerable to bigger companies that believe they can lever their specialist skills by taking them into global or broader markets. The information technology and service sectors are full of young, successful businesses that fall into this category. To maintain control, these companies need to grow aggressively by adding new products and new markets. Computershare provides a good example of how this might be done (see marketing management case in practice 'Computershare's move into value-added services').

4. **Limited control through size**. H and G are large companies producing low returns on capital. Today they include such companies as General Motors, Coles Myer and Credit Lyonnais. Despite their poor performance they are difficult to acquire because of their sheer size. They are generally older companies, in mature, asset-intensive industries. Their challenge is to improve performance by divesting assets that produce low returns and

using the proceeds to capture more attractive opportunities. Should they fail, they are likely eventually to be acquired or merged as part of the cost consolidation process in the industry.

Shareholder value analysis allows management to compare the value of alternative marketing strategies. They can objectively examine which strategy is most likely to increase the market value of the company. They can explore where a particular plan is likely to take them on the strategic vulnerability map (see figure 1.5). Will it move the company towards the area of 'complete control' or towards increased 'vulnerability'?

Marketing management in practice: Computershare's move into value-added services

Topping the list of [Australian companies with] the fastest-growing overseas revenues [in the five-year period to end-2001], Computershare (CPU) is a company that has used the technology, knowledge and cashflow generated in Australia to expand rapidly into foreign markets. Today, a review of CPU's operating divisions looks like a who's who of desirable English-speaking markets, with revenues sourced from Australia, Britain, the United States, South Africa, New Zealand, Hong Kong and Canada.

In order to find out how this once small Australian company managed to expand into the only company in the world able to offer registry services on a global scale, one need only look at what it does.

CPU is a share registrar. It maintains a list of a client's shareholders, for a fee, based on the number of shareholders on the register. Around the world, registry systems are managed in roughly the same way as in Australia, so CPU was able to use technology and processes developed in Australia to drive efficiencies across the world.

During the expansion, CPU has widened the product offering from straight vanilla registry services to value-added services. Operations of divisions such as Document Services (printing and mail-out of shareholder documents such as dividend cheques and annual reports) and Computershare Analytics (analysis of shareholding patterns for take-overs and strategic shareholder management) complement registry operations. Movement into employee share plans is a key area for future growth and will be serviced off an adjusted SCRIP platform.

In 1997, CPU began its foreign expansion in earnest by acquiring Registry Managers of New Zealand. Consolidation of the Australian, NZ and British registry market became available, and the Ernst & Young and KPMG Registry businesses were added to the fold. Acquisitions followed in 1998 in Scotland, Ireland and South Africa, with a half share of Central Registration Hong Kong acquired in 1999. The registry business of Harris Bank (US) and the Bank of Montreal were included in 2000, along with the Merrill Lynch ESPP business. In early 2001, the remaining interests in Hong Kong were bought, along with non-registry operations in the United States and Australia.

Despite dominant market share in many countries, there are still some growth opportunities. Registry operations in Britain and the US have the potential to increase its market share substantially over time, while industry expectations for employee share plans, equivalent to only 3 per cent of revenue last year, are for significant medium-term growth.

As the only registrar with a multinational presence, CPU has a distinct advantage in selling the global aspect of its service, and more contracts should be added to the worldwide employee share plan contract for BP over time.

On a less global scale, a strategic relationship between competitors Lloyds TSB (UK) and ASX/Perpetual Registrars has the potential to attract multinational clients in the future. Current registry clients present an accessible market for selling employee share plan business, as well as Document Services and Analytics, as cross-selling penetration rates remain low ...

Source: Extract from Ian Huntley and Jack Russell, 'Local paper chase goes global', *Shares*, December 2001, p. 63.

The key to economic value creation is the company's ability to achieve or maintain a differential advantage in a changing market environment. Accurately assessing alternative strategies is critical in determining whether a company becomes more or less vulnerable. For an example of how shareholder value can be used to make the appropriate strategic choices, see marketing insight 'A European airline analyses marketing strategies'.

| Marketing insight: | **A European airline analyses marketing strategies** |

A major European airline believed that deregulation would inevitably lead to greater price competition as new 'no-frills' airlines entered the market. Companies such as Virgin, Ryanair, EasyJet and others had already announced big expansion plans. The airline's review of the industry led it to conclude that its recent market share losses would accelerate unless a new strategy was developed.

Management eventually identified three alternative marketing strategies. The parity strategy involved seeking to hold market share by reducing prices towards the level of the new competitors. A major cost reduction exercise would run alongside this plan. The premium strategy would refocus the airline around business and first-class passengers. It would include a switch to smaller aeroplanes, with fewer seats for economy passengers. The dual-brand strategy envisaged the launch of an entirely new airline codenamed 'Merit'. Merit would be positioned as a no-frills discount airline that would match or even undercut the prices of the new competitors. Here, the aim would be to achieve market leadership in both the regular and the discount sectors.

Management made detailed projections of sales, profit margins and investment requirements under the three strategies. On the basis of this analysis they calculated the shareholder value added with each alternative:

Alternative strategy   Shareholder value added
1. Parity strategy   − $120 million
2. Premium strategy   + $210 million
3. Dual-brand strategy   + $555 million

Faced with the analysis, the board of directors had no hesitation in accepting management's radical strategy of dual branding and the new airline was launched ten months later. The parity strategy was demonstrated to be disastrous because, while it stopped the erosion of market share, it led to a huge decline in profitability per passenger. The premium strategy did create value but it was inferior to dual branding because of the effect of the decline in passengers carried.

The board believed that shareholder value analysis had proved its worth. The SVA challenged management to identify and develop new strategies. It encouraged them to think radically, which was necessary with rapid environmental changes increasingly making the status quo a non-viable strategic option. Finally, it provided a criterion for rationally and objectively evaluating strategic choices. All too often in the past, key decisions had been made on the basis of subjective judgments, marketing 'hype' or political wrangling, which had subsequently proved to be wrong.

Challenges to shareholder value

The modern shareholder value movement started in the United States and the United Kingdom but, with the globalisation of trade and capital flows, it is sweeping into other major countries. Although a growing number of Australian companies have espoused their commitment to shareholder value — in rhetoric if not necessarily in practice — the 'arrival' of the shareholder value movement is perhaps best indicated by the annual survey by BRW of Australia's most admired business leaders. In response to the question,

'What are the key attributes of business success?', long-term shareholder value was not ranked in the 2000 survey but came in at fourth in the 2001 survey (see table 1.1). Furthermore, the most common reason for nominating a most admired business leader in the 2002 BRW survey was 'focusing on shareholder value', which was cited by 27% of respondents.

Table 1.1 What are the key attributes of business success?

| | % OF RESPONDENTS | |
ATTRIBUTE	2002	2001
Ability to recruit, develop and retain talented people	86	78
Long-term shareholder value	54	40
Customer relationship management	48	47
High quality product/services	42	43
Capacity to deliver growth	38	38
Commitment to the community, environment	29	27
Innovation	28	32
Effective use of corporate assets	22	26
Strong corporate brand image	20	25
Effective use of new technology	16	20
Successful deployment of intellectual capital	10	15

Source: Stuart Washington, 'Mr Consistency', *BRW*, 29 August–4 September 2002, p. 61.

A chorus of complaint, however, has paralleled the increased interest in SVA. The more technical complaints are discussed in chapter 2. Here, the focus is on the objections that have been raised to the philosophical assertion, central to shareholder value, that the primary objective of managers is to maximise the returns for shareholders.

Shareholders versus other stakeholders

Many writers have pointed out that a company has social responsibilities and that shareholders are not the only stakeholders in the business. It is argued that in seeking to maximise shareholder value, managers ignore these social responsibilities and fail to balance the different stakeholder interests. That these stakeholders may have interests which conflict with those of shareholders is clear. It is also true that they often have longer-term relationships with the company than its shareholders. Today's shareholders are normally financial investors rather than individuals with emotional and long-term personal ties to the business. These other stakeholders fall into the following groups:

- **Employees.** The legitimacy of the claims of employees lies in the long-term commitment many of them make to the firm. In today's information age companies, the special skills of employees also represent **intangible assets** that are generally more important in creating value than the traditional balance-sheet items. The objectives of employees are normally a combination of

intangible assets: non-material assets such as technical expertise, brands or patents

employment security, compensation and job satisfaction. Each of these, but particularly security, can conflict sharply with a strategy based on maximising shareholder value. In rapidly changing markets, value-based management will unfortunately often dictate closure or disposals of businesses.

• **Managers.** The separation of ownership and control in the twentieth century increased the ability of top managers to pursue interests that were not aligned to those of shareholders. Managers have often seen growth and short-term profits as more closely linked to personal rewards in terms of salaries and prestige than shareholder value. Managers, too, are typically more risk averse in searching for opportunities than shareholders would wish. If the company invests in a risky project, shareholders can always balance the risk by portfolio diversification. Managers, however, have their jobs on the line, and so are hurt more by failure.

• **Customers.** Without customer value there can be no shareholder value. Even the most focused financial manager understands that the source of a company's long-term cash flow is its satisfied customers. Many managers, especially those with a marketing background, have therefore gone on to argue that maximising customer satisfaction should be the primary goal. The problem is that providing customer satisfaction does not automatically lead to shareholder value. Delighting customers with lower prices than competitors or superior quality and features cannot provide a sustainable advantage if the cost of delivering all this (including the cost of capital) exceeds the price they are paying. The unconstrained maximisation of customer satisfaction certainly conflicts with a shareholder value orientation.

• **Suppliers.** Today's virtually integrated companies are clearly dependent upon the cooperation and commitment of their network of suppliers. Competition has moved on from competition between individual companies to competition between networks. Suppliers in these networks want long-term security, predictability and satisfactory margins. Again, value management in today's volatile markets will mean that the firm cannot guarantee these relationships. Changing technologies, evolving consumer needs and new sources of supply will bring conflicts between the aspirations of traditional suppliers for stability and the ambitions of shareholders for value.

• **Community.** The local and national communities where the firm is located will also have interests in the firm's behaviour. Social responsibilities can be divided into those arising from what the firm does *to* the society, and what it can do *for* it. The former are the negative impacts — pollution and environmental damage — which arise as by-products of the firm's activities, and which communities increasingly want stopped. The latter are tasks which communities often want businesses to take on — such as preserving employment, helping minorities or improving schooling. Social impacts are caused by, and are the responsibility of, the firm. Social problems, on the other hand, are dysfunctions of society. Accepting responsibility for these social problems can bring sharp conflicts with the goal of maximising shareholder value.

Clearly, then, conflicts can and do arise between shareholders and other stakeholders — but these conflicts are essentially short-term. The long-term situation is different, for there are strong market incentives for value-maximising firms to take into account other stakeholder interests. Crucial is the need to attract, retain and motivate the new 'knowledge workers' whose specialist skills and efforts determine the firm's ultimate competitiveness.[8] Shareholder interest dictates that the firm offers competitive salaries and safe and attractive working conditions. Similarly, it would be suicidal in today's competitive markets not to be dedicated to satisfying customers. Investing in market research, new product development, quality and customer service are central to value management.

This is to put the case negatively. Stern and Shiely express it more positively:

> [A] company will enhance shareholder value if it undertakes creative initiatives to foster the well-being of its employees, if it works in close harness with its suppliers and cultivates their loyalty, if it knows its customers intimately and takes pains to meet their specific needs, and if it wins a reputation in the community as a good corporate citizen. In the long run, there is a harmony of interest between the shareholders and the other stakeholders.[9]

Ultimately the claims of all stakeholders depend on the firm's ability to generate sufficient cash to meet them. This in turn depends on the firm's competitiveness. The share price reflects the firm's competitiveness. The market value of a company is based on the most informed estimates of its ability to create a competitive advantage and to achieve profitable growth in its markets. Goals which undermine this focus increase costs, misallocate investment and reduce the ability of the firm to compete. While in the short run, employees or managers might be better off, in today's global markets, the non-optimal use of resources is not sustainable, as will become evident in the firm's declining profits and growth performance. All stakeholders are vulnerable when managements fail to create shareholder value.

For this reason, it is indeed true that, from a long-term perspective, there is a mutuality of interest between shareholders and other stakeholders. This is not to suggest, however, that top management should eschew shareholder value as the primary goal in favour of 'balancing the interests of stakeholders'. Do anything other than this and the company's strategy loses clarity and focus. Management can be lured into making investments for reasons of prestige or public relations. They hold on to business units that have no chance of generating economic returns or go on to make ill-considered diversifications. When this occurs a value gap begins to emerge, eventually precipitating a takeover, with all the unpleasant consequences for employees, managers and the community.

Many critics of value management forget who shareholders are. Often they are demonised as a small group of wealthy, self-serving individuals set apart from ordinary people. For countries like Australia, New Zealand, the United States and the United Kingdom, nothing could be further from the truth. Half of all adult Australians own shares: in November 2000 some 52 per cent of Australian adults were involved in the share market, either through direct shareholdings or indirectly through a managed fund. Australia has the highest level of direct share ownership in the world, with about 41 per cent of adults, as of August 2000, holding equity in listed companies. The corresponding proportion in the United Kingdom was 39 per cent, the United States 32 per cent and New Zealand 31 per cent. In Australia, direct share ownership rose quickly (from 20.4 per cent in 1997 and 31.9 per cent in 1998), largely because of the privatisation of a number of former government-owned and mutual organisations.[10] In countries like the United Kingdom and the United States, virtually every household owns shares indirectly through pension funds and other institutional savings. These institutions own 50 per cent of all shares in the United States and 80 per cent in the United Kingdom and Japan. Almost everyone now is affected by the market value of shares. Losses, whether due to poor management or incurred in the pursuit of other stakeholder interests, come out of the pockets of employees, pensioners and other individuals with savings. As governments around the world shift pension and social security provision from the public sector to individuals, shareholders become even more 'us' rather than 'them'. Self-interest will increasingly pressure business executives and fund managers to maximise shareholder value.

Motivational and operational complaints about shareholder value

There are two other fundamental and related criticisms of the shareholder value objective. The first is that it does not motivate staff to achieve high performance. The second criticism is that it is not operational: it does not tell employees and managers what to do at a practical level.

There are several reasons why maximising shareholder value may not be aspirational. One is that few of the staff will normally be significant shareholders themselves. Another is that they cannot see a direct link between their own specific jobs and the share prices of the company as a whole, so there is little point in simply instructing an employee that they should be aiming to increase stock value. Third, share prices often move as a result of macroeconomic factors and market forces unrelated to the performance of management.

It is also true that the very term 'shareholder value' is often misrepresented — and too often used by managers who should know better — as an excuse for mindless cost cutting in the name of achieving ever-higher stock prices. It is also sometimes interpreted, incorrectly, to mean that organisations can and should have no other goal than making shareholders wealthier. As Hamel and Prahalad point out, an organisation's strategic intent — its animating dream, its source of emotional and intellectual energy — requires a sense of direction, a sense of discovery and a sense of destiny.[11] To express the firm's vision as nothing other than shareholder value maximisation will not provide this. Ehrhardt puts the point well:

> People are more creative and productive when they feel they are part of an organization that is doing something important and worthwhile. They often get this feeling as a result of a well-articulated and fully enacted corporate vision. Still, achieving superior 'return on equity does not, as a goal, mobilize the most noble forces of our soul'. In other words, the maximization of shareholder value isn't a particularly effective element in a corporate vision.[12]

What is needed, therefore, is the development of broader statements of purpose that inspire the organisation in a way that will generate improvements in shareholder value. This point is considered further in chapter 4, which focuses on value-based marketing strategy.

Operationally, the problem with shareholder value as an objective is that, as noted earlier, while value-based management provides a criterion for strategies to be selected and evaluated, it does not say how these strategies can be constructed. Before a strategy can be put forward for SVA, a method for identifying the need for strategic change must exist. Then, there must be a process of constructing strategic options that have prospects of creating differential advantages and enabling the business to generate cash flows that exceed costs, including the cost of capital. If these two prior processes are not well understood, SVA can easily become over-focused on downsizing — getting rid of non-performing business units — rather than on exploiting growth opportunities.

How then can these problems be overcome and the two criticisms met? In order both to motivate staff and operationalise SVA, management need a deep understanding of what the value drivers of the business will be in the future. This is why value-based management should not be thought of as a financial technique: it depends on all the knowledge and skills within the firm. A well-grounded understanding of the fundamental value generators allows managers to overcome the motivational and operational limitations of SVA. It can assign objectives, tasks and resources to measures of marketing, operations and financial performance that automatically lead to increases in shareholder value. The nature of these value drivers is considered in detail in chapter 3.

Section 3 | Marketing and shareholder value: A synergistic relationship

Marketing's lost influence

In today's information age, marketing professionals should have become more important in the top councils of business. First, the central issue facing all firms now is understanding and adapting to rapidly changing markets — globalisation, new competition, rising customer expectations and the implications of the information revolution on how companies market. Second, marketing, rather than production, skills have become the key to creating differential advantage. More and more leading branded goods companies follow the lead of the likes of Coca-Cola, Dell, Nike, Bodyshop and Armani in outsourcing all their manufacturing to outside suppliers, often in the developing countries. Others, like General Electric and IBM, are seeing their future not in selling products, but in providing services that offer tailored solutions to the needs of individual customers. Third, marketing performance is the root source of shareholder value. The firm's opportunity to create cash is based first and foremost on its ability to create a differential advantage that will enable it to attract and retain customers paying satisfactory prices.

But rather than gaining in influence, marketing professionals, whose expertise is in identifying these market opportunities and building customer relationships, appear to have lost influence in the boardrooms of industry. A recent survey, for example, found that only 12 of the chief executives of Britain's top 100 companies had experience in a marketing job. Only 57 per cent of larger companies had marketing represented on the board. The survey found that while all companies considered profit at each board meeting, only one in three regularly reviewed customer attitudes to the company and its brands.[13] Several of the major consulting companies have also observed the waning influence of marketing departments in many companies.[14] The situation in Australia is no different, as is made clear in marketing insight 'Unease in the marketing department: Troubles down under'. (The scene setter 'The emerging importance of value-based marketing strategy' in chapter 4 provides additional information.)

Unease in the marketing department: Troubles down under

There's a sense of unease creeping into the marketing departments of Australian companies. The unrelenting drive to build shareholder value and the likelihood of changes to accounting standards so that brands can be valued has put more pressure than ever before on marketers to prove their worth.

Whether boom or bust, the marketing budget is usually the first to be slashed if costs need to be reined in or profits need to be plumped. Many marketers have been unable to justify their existence to chief executives who more often than not are unfamiliar with the value of marketing or who view it as a cost rather than an investment.

A recent study into marketing measurement and value by Dr Chris Styles, from the University of New South Wales's School of Marketing, along with the Australian Marketing Institute (AMI) found that, although 44 per cent of marketers believed marketing contributed to shareholder value, only 10 per cent of chief financial officers, 11 per cent of board directors and 22 per cent of CEOs agreed. Yet the challenge of measuring effectiveness was considered important by only 12 per cent of marketers.

'The influence of marketing at board level should be substantial but it is not. Marketers seem to be their own worst enemy when it comes to marketing themselves,' Styles says. 'If marketers don't start taking the initiative and make themselves heard, we are in for another round of unimaginative downsizing, mergers and share buybacks. This would not only be bad news for marketers but also for shareholders and customers.'

Marketing experts agree that marketers need to be able to measure the performance of not only their campaigns but also themselves ...

'There is a revolution occurring across the marketing landscape, rather belatedly, about the roles of accountability and optimising strategic performance,' says Gary Neat from the Adshan Group. 'There is scrutiny of marketing performance and return on investment from CEOs, who in turn are under pressure from boards increasingly uneasy about marketing performance. They can't measure marketing strength, they can't value brands and there's very little marketing experience on boards.'

Neat says it was a huge increase in demand from companies to measure marketing that led him to establish Marketing Audits as a new division of his company.

'[Marketing directors] were very secure in their own ability, but they've been quite blatant that they need an independent view of their capabilities to take to the chief financial officer in justifying marketing expenditure,' he says.

Tony Hart, the president of the Australian Marketing Institute, agrees. 'Performance per se is the big talking point [among marketers]. If the department and the brand are not performing, you're not performing,' he says. 'For a marketer as an individual it is a major concern. A lot of things make an impact on performance that are outside the marketer's control, and it causes a lot of stress among marketers.'

Marketing consultant Dianne Davis, of Davis & Associates, says the financial community has started to see the value of brands and marketing, necessitating a different measurement system from marketers. 'You're seeing fund managers and analysts starting to factor brands, customer satisfaction and retention into their analysis,' she says. 'They are realising that to get a good health check of a company they have to go beyond financials.'

The University of New South Wales study found that margins were considered important by 81 per cent of marketers but they only reached the board in 46 per cent of cases. The 'softer' measures of customer satisfaction were considered important by 62 per cent of marketers but reached the board in 14 per cent of cases; and for brand health, the figures were 48 per cent and 21 per cent respectively. Marketing measures were used in total shareholder return in only 8 per cent of cases, in cash flow return on investment in 4 per cent of cases and in economic value-added measure in 14 per cent of cases.

According to marketing practitioner Mike Slater, a director of Slater Marketing Group, measuring brand value in particular should be embraced by marketers because it propels their role back into the boardroom. 'As it starts to become a hot topic, it's something which focuses more on the financials of how you measure [brands] versus what the marketing director does, which is how you grow [brands],' he says.

Marketers, according to Styles, need to both speak the language of the boardroom to be heard and agitate for board representation to help their cause. 'If you talk about asset building, for example, brands and customer relationships, and shareholder value and present metrics that relate to them,' he says, 'you will command more attention than if you just show copy reels of your latest expensive television commercials.'

... Colin Wilson-Brown, the chief executive of Foote Cone & Belding who also chairs the Advertising Federation of Australia's Advertising Effectiveness Awards, says: 'Too many advertisers lack a realistic understanding of what advertising can or cannot achieve. There is frequently a lack of rigour in setting clear objectives, matched only by a lack of commitment to determining the outcome of advertising campaigns.'

But Davis believes Australia is at a watershed between traditional methods of measuring marketing performance based on mass marketing, such as market share, to measurement based around a one-to-one model of customer share ...

'There are two key drivers of this change. Technology [such as] data warehousing and mining tools, the Internet, wireless applications and CRM [customer relationship management] systems are enabling companies to implement a customer-centric view of measurement. And the investment community and shareholders are increasingly looking at non-financial elements in their assessment of shareholder value and company performance; for example, customer retention/customer loyalty, brand equity, environmental policy, corporate ethics and so on.'

The propensity of companies to turn first to the marketing budget when costs need to be cut will not diminish until marketers prove their worth. 'The real issue is the ability of marketing directors to demonstrate that the things they do have an impact. If they're not able to do that, they are faced with the likelihood of having funds removed,' says Rod Slater, another director from Slater Marketing Group.

Source: Extracts from Rochelle Burbury, 'The new measuring schtick', *AFR Boss*, May 2001, pp. 15–17.

Why does the lack of marketing professionalism in the boardroom matter? It matters because top managers will lack expert guidance on how their customers and competitors' strategies are changing. New market opportunities and threats are unlikely to be recognised speedily and, once recognised, acted upon decisively. If senior management are not focusing on customers and markets, it will mean that other issues fill the agenda. Evidence suggests that managers become preoccupied with short-term budgets, operating rather than strategic issues and, when difficulties arise, retrenchment rather than renewal. Such myopia is, in the long run, antithetical to genuine value-creating strategies.

Several factors account for this paradox of the growing importance of marketing with the lack of influence of marketing professionals in top management. Of fundamental importance has been the failure of the marketing discipline to incorporate the concept of shareholder value. As a result, there is no criteria for judging the success of a marketing strategy or comparing alternatives. This in turn means it is difficult to accept marketing recommendations on product policy, pricing, promotions or, indeed, any element of the marketing mix. All too often marketing managers think a strategy is sensible if it increases sales or market share.[15] But astute top managers know that strategies to maximise market share will very rarely make economic sense.

More sophisticated marketing managers will be tempted to use projected profits or return on investment to rationalise their marketing proposals. Unfortunately, this approach has the opposite bias and leads to an under-investment in marketing and a failure to capitalise on opportunities. Modern marketing has not incorporated current strategic valuation techniques and has consequently become marginalised in many boardrooms. The marketing discipline lacks the framework for engaging in the strategic debate.

Because the link between marketing strategy and shareholder value has not been made, boards have tended to look at two other more transparent strategies. One has been cost reduction — sometimes disguised by more appealing names such as reengineering, downsizing or right sizing. Unfortunately, in a time of rapid market change, such actions are invariably only palliatives at best. The other common remedy has been acquisition. Acquisitions have broken all records in recent years. They have been seen as a way of generating value by adding top-line growth and by permitting a reduction in average costs. But, again, the evidence is that three out of four acquisitions fail to add value for the acquiring company.[16] Excessive bid premiums, cultural differences between the businesses and a failure to rejuvenate the company's marketing orientation appear to be the major weaknesses.

The failure to place marketing strategy at the centre of the corporate agenda cannot be laid solely at the door of the marketing profession. Financial management has also failed to bridge the marketing–finance interface. Top management still focus on company accounts that measure only the historical cost of assets and omit internally developed brands and other intangible assets. Yet these marketing assets are now by far the most important sources of shareholder value. The market-to-book ratios for the *Fortune 500* average over 4, implying that over 75 per cent of the value of these companies lies in their brands and other marketing-based intangibles. Companies whose goal is maximising shareholder value need a framework for placing the development and management of marketing assets at the centre of their planning processes. It is these marketing assets — brands, market knowledge and customer and partner relationships — that have become the key generators of long-term profits in the information age.

Marketing's new opportunity

Shareholder value analysis is becoming the new standard because of the increasing realisation of the defects of conventional accounting. We argue in chapter 2 that accounting profits encourage an excessively short-term view of business. They also encourage an under-investment in information-based assets — staff, brands, and customer and supplier relationships. In the information age, the accounting focus on tangible assets makes little sense now that these intangible assets are the overwhelming source of value creation. Shareholder value analysis (SVA) can avoid both these biases. But to achieve its potential, SVA needs marketing. Similarly, marketing needs SVA if it is to make a real contribution to strategy.

Shareholder value needs marketing

SVA is tautological without a marketing strategy. The shareholder value principle is that a business should be run to maximise the return on the shareholders' investment. SVA provides a tool for calculating the shareholder value added from any given growth, profit and investment projection. But what drives these growth, profit and investment requirements is outside the financial model. SVA does not address how managers can develop strategies that can accelerate growth, increase profit margins and lever investments. These are the objectives of marketing strategy. For example, returning to the earlier airline problem (see marketing insight 'A European airline analyses marketing strategies'), SVA was able to identify which of the three strategies presented was best, but developing the innovative dual-branding plan came solely from an understanding of the market dynamics and a creative approach to serving different customer segments.

The heart of SVA, as explained earlier, is that economic value is created only when the business earns a return on investment that exceeds its cost of capital. Economic theory suggests that, in competitive markets, this will only occur when it has a differential advantage in cost or product superiority. Without a unique advantage, competition will drive profits down to the cost of capital. Creating shareholder value is then essentially about building a sustainable competitive advantage — a reason why customers should consistently prefer to buy from one company rather than others. Marketing provides the tools for creating this differential advantage. These are frameworks for researching and analysing customer needs, techniques for competitive analysis, and systems for measuring and enhancing consumer preference. Effective marketing input allows SVA to be dynamic and growth oriented. Without it, SVA is static, merely focusing on ways of reducing costs and assets to produce a temporary fillip to cash flow.

The inputs to the SVA model are largely estimates about marketing variables. Key inputs are future sales volumes and prices. The other inputs are costs, investment and the cost of capital. Each of these variables depends on careful analysis and projections of the market. As with all models, the lesson is 'garbage in, garbage out'. Poor judgments about the future behaviour of customers and competitors will make worthless any conclusions from SVA.

SVA only deals with the latter stages of strategic planning. Any decision problem has four steps:

1. perceiving a need to change
2. identifying alternative courses of action
3. evaluating the options
4. making the choice.

SVA only provides answers for the last two steps. It does not provide for the continuing analysis of the firm's markets and technologies that is needed to alert management to emerging problems and opportunities. Nor does it suggest alternative strategies — these have to be discovered elsewhere. For example, SVA is not going to alert management to the opportunities of the Internet or identify great new product or distribution ideas. These are most likely to be generated by staff who are close to customers. Just as marketing needs to be augmented to include developments in finance, so finance needs to be extended and broadened to include developments in marketing.

Marketing needs shareholder value

SVA is a great opportunity for marketing professionals. It can bring to the fore the real value drivers in today's globally competitive markets. The shareholder value approach provides a language for integrating marketing more effectively with other functions within the business. The language of the modern board is finance. Actions have to be justified to the board in terms of their ability to increase the financial value of the business. Integrating SVA provides marketing with the means to communicate to other disciplines more effectively than in the past how marketing activities increase the value of the firm. It provides the framework and language for integrating marketing more effectively with the other functions in the business.

The shareholder value approach also helps marketing properly define its objective and thereby gives marketing the opportunity to play a pivotal role in the strategy formulation process. Traditionally, marketing has tended to see increasing customer loyalty and market share as ends in themselves. But today, top management requires that marketing view its ultimate purpose as contributing to increasing shareholder value. No longer can marketers afford to rely on the untested assumption that increases in customer satisfaction and market share will translate automatically into higher financial performance. This dilemma now suggests a reformulation of the marketing discipline as about developing and managing intangible assets — customer and channel relationships and brands — to maximise economic value.[17]

Another benefit of value-based analysis is that it can be used to demonstrate that marketing investments contribute to value creation. For example, investments in brand building that, under conventional accounting procedures, would be discouraged because they reduce current profits can be shown as having a clear positive impact on the share price using shareholder value analysis.

Finally, value-based analysis makes it harder for boards to make arbitrary cuts in marketing budgets to boost short-term earnings. Indeed, management has found cutting marketing investment an easy target when it needs fast profit increases. SVA gives marketing a powerful tool to demonstrate that these short-term cuts are more likely to destroy rather than build value.

The changing role of marketing

The centrality of marketing in creating growth and shareholder value suggests a new role for marketing both as a discipline and a function (see table 1.2). Traditionally, marketing has been seen as about satisfying the needs of customers more effectively than competitors. The assumption has been that if the company satisfied its customers and won market share, positive financial results would automatically follow. Unfortunately, top management knows that this is not necessarily true. Marketing expenditures, like any other resources, can be wasted, and satisfied customers are not necessarily profitable ones. The concept of marketing that will make it more effective in tomorrow's boardroom is one of contributing to the creation of shareholder value. This concept suggests the following description:

> Marketing is the process that seeks to maximise returns to shareholders by developing relationships with valued customers and creating a differential advantage.

Table 1.2 The changing role of marketing

	PAST	FUTURE
Objective of marketing	Create customer value	Create shareholder value
Marketing strategy	Increase market share	Develop and manage marketing assets
Assumptions	Positive market performance leads to positive financial performance	Marketing strategies need to be tested in value terms
Contribution	Knowledge of customers, competitors and channels	Knowledge of how to lever marketing to increase shareholder value
Focus of marketing	Marketing orientation	General management
Skills of marketing	Specialist	Specialist + general
Advocacy	Importance of understanding customers	Marketing's role in creating shareholder value
Concept of assets	Tangible	Intangible
Rationale	Improves profits	Increases shareholder value
Performance measures	Market share, customer satisfaction, and return on sales and investment	Shareholder value: discounted cash flows

This new concept of marketing shifts it from being a specialist activity to an integral part of the general management process. Where in the past marketing management were seen as experts on customers, channels and competitors, in the future they should be seen as experts on how marketing and growth can increase shareholder value. To do this, marketers need to extend their skill base to add expertise in modern financial planning techniques. In the past, marketers have often allowed themselves to be trapped by accounting-oriented management into seeking to justify their marketing strategies in terms of improving immediate earnings. Such a short-term approach is invariably destructive because marketing is primarily about creating and managing assets. Investments in brands and customer relationships — like research and development — rarely pay off in the period in which they occur. They are made to generate and defend cash flows, often for many years ahead. Familiarity with shareholder value analysis has become an essential tool for demonstrating that marketing produces an economic return.

Summary

1. Companies grow and prosper when they efficiently meet the needs of customers. However, efficient products are soon made obsolete by rapid environmental changes that create new customer needs, introduce new competition and offer new technologies that provide better answers. Maintaining success requires continual change.
2. As the world moves into the new millennium, four particular changes are reshaping the environment of business: the globalisation of markets, changing industrial structures, the information revolution, and rising consumer expectations.
3. Increasing shareholder returns are the best measure of business performance. The market value of a business reflects investors' views of the ability of managers to create long-term profits that exceed its cost of capital.

4. Marketing has lost influence in business because marketing strategies are not effectively linked to shareholder value creation. Growth of sales or market share are not reliable measures of operating performance. The real role of marketing is to create and utilise marketing assets to create future cash flows with a positive net present value.

5. In most companies, shareholder value has mistakenly come to be associated with downsizing and rationalisation. Such strategies do not create sustainable increases in cash flow or shareholder value. In today's rapidly changing markets, the greatest increases in value accrue to companies that identify new market opportunities and put in place market-led strategies that promise high future earnings growth.

6. Without effective marketing, shareholder value is a trivial concept. Shareholder value analysis allows management to evaluate alternative strategies, but only marketing insight and investment can create worthwhile strategies in the first place.

 key terms

book equity, p. 20
competitive potential, p. 13
continuing value, p. 20
cost of capital, p. 18
delayering, p. 16
direct business model, p. 14
discount factor, p. 17
discounted cash flow (DCF), p. 18
disintermediation, p. 10
downstream, p. 14
explicit forecast period, p. 20
extranet, p. 10
hypercompetitive markets, p. 11
intangible assets, p. 25
intranet, p. 10
macroenvironment, p. 6
market segmentation, p. 11
market-to-book (M/B) ratio, p. 20
market value, p. 20

marketing mix, p. 10
mass customisation, p. 11
microenvironment, p. 6
one-to-one marketing, p. 12
opportunity cost, p. 18
organisation, p. 12
shareholder value analysis (SVA), p. 17
strategy, p. 12
total shareholder returns, p. 19
upstream, p. 15
value-based marketing, p. 4
value gap, p. 21
vertical integration, p. 15
virtual business, p. 10
virtual integration, p. 15
weighted average cost of capital, p. 19

  **review** questions

1. How have the major environmental changes that constitute the information age affected the task of managing?

2. What is the essence of the shareholder value approach?

3. How can shareholder value analysis be used as a measure of strategic vulnerability?

4. What are the main complaints raised against the notion that businesses should concentrate on maximising shareholder value?

5. Why has the marketing function become marginalised in today's boardroom and how can it redeem its status?

6. Critically analyse the SVA approach to evaluation of strategies and its contribution to strategic planning.

discussion questions

1. Which of the following do you think poses the most profound challenge for managers: the globalisation of markets, changing industrial structures, the information revolution, or rising customer expectations?
2. Explain the notion that shareholder value analysis does not itself generate strategies.
3. Why do companies that do not manage for value become vulnerable?
4. Why might the goal of maximising customer value conflict with the goal of maximising shareholder value?
5. Explain why shareholder value needs marketing, and why marketing needs shareholder value.

debate questions

1. Are customer expectations different now to what they were 50 years ago?
2. Rather than strategy fitting the environment, should an attempt be made by organisations to mould the environment to their advantage?
3. Should the interests of shareholders prevail over other stakeholders?
4. In the long run, is there a mutuality of interest between shareholders and other stakeholders?
5. Has marketing only itself to blame for its demise in the corporate boardroom?

case study | Coles Myer — The challenges ahead

Appointed in August 2001 to his new position as chief executive at Coles Myer, John Fletcher faces a tough challenge. The ailing retailer faces an angry investment community, demanding major changes from the new CEO and his management team. Just as Fletcher's managers have to persuade him to retain the businesses they run, he has to persuade Australian and international fund managers — who hold 78 per cent of Coles Myer stock — to change their collective mind about the retailer.

In the 12 months to 31 July 2001, the food and liquor business had an EBIT of $514.7 million on sales of $14.4 billion, a margin of 3.5 per cent. The general merchandise and apparel business (excluding Katies) produced an EBIT of $103.3 million, on sales of $8.9 billion, a margin of 1.1 per cent.

The changes that Fletcher is seeking at Coles Myer will focus on the following:

- Sale of non-core businesses (e.g. Red Rooster)
- Asset write-downs
- Closure of poor performers (e.g. Myer Direct)
- Margin improvement in the ailing general merchandise and apparel business (including Myer-Grace Bros, Kmart and Target)
- Cost cutting
- Entrance into the financial services sector
- Restructuring of loyalty programs
- Corporate culture transformations
- People management
- Supply chain management.

Corporate culture

One challenge that faces Fletcher is breaking down the myriad of cultures that have developed in Coles Myer with the aim being to build a unified customer-focused culture. After the merger of G. J. Coles and Myer Emporium in 1985, several 'silos' were allowed to develop in the company. Changing the culture will be particularly difficult, especially in a company with 162 000 employees. A retail analyst at Deutsche Bank, Nikki Thomas, says the cultural problems at Coles Myer are perhaps the biggest obstacle that lies ahead. Cultural change is risk laden: morale can slump; productivity can fall; the clash between old and new staff can cause valuable staff to quit.

(continued)

People management

Incompetent senior managers and a board with limited retail experience also fuelled the company's downfall. According to Fletcher, 'the highest priority is people. Priority one is getting the team right. That then allows you to establish the feel of the place or culture, and values going forward, which then leads you to be able to do sensible work with the team that is going to deliver on the strategy.'

Fletcher plans to build the right management team by hiring new people, introducing new performance measures for more accountable management, and cross-fertilisation between divisions. 'If we have the right people, we have the market positioning to win.'

Significant appraisal and restructuring of the senior management team is urgently required and may be a problematic process. The people running the general merchandise and apparel division, Kmart and Target, joined the company from North American retailers. They lack local retailing experience. In an industry where the consumer holds the power in the relationship, a thorough understanding of the market and its vagaries is essential.

Cost reductions

Operation Right Now is the title that has been accorded to Fletcher's strategy. He is confident that the program will 'reduce operating expenses, improve margins and enhance competitiveness'.

This strategy will be achieved across all areas of the business, from operational concerns to staff reduction. Since September 2001, staff cuts were introduced in general merchandise and apparel with the aim of producing annual savings of $90 million from 2003–04 onwards. The next phase commenced in January 2002 and centred on rationalisation of Head Office operations. Following this, the online division and food and drink division will be tackled.

Stock levels running exorbitantly high have only served to undermine Coles Myer's value. The future concern will be with stock turns, the number of times a retailer turns over its entire stock in a year. Faster turnaround increases net profit through a reduction in inventory costs.

Supply chain management

Fletcher also has, as a central aim, efficiency improvement and cost reduction with a fully integrated supply chain system. 'There would appear to be a better way of doing what we are doing now. If we are going to run a fully integrated supply chain, you need a lot of computers, talking to each other, through the steps from buying inventory to merchandising and stores.' The cost of this, according to industry sources, will be more than $150 million. JB Were analyst, George Batsakis, says that Coles Myer's current net investment in stock is about $1 billion or 85 cents a share. He argues that a better supply chain system will free up funds which can then be re-invested in growth initiatives or returned to shareholders.

Loyalty programs

Another key area for review and overhauling will be Coles Myer's loyalty programs. $176 million a year is spent on running the shareholder discount card. The 500 000 retail investors want the shareholder discount card kept, but institutional investors want it ditched to boost earnings. The head of Australian equities at ING Investment Management, John Morgan, says ING has not held shares in Coles Myer for at least five years and will not do so until the company gets rid of the shareholder discount card and shows evidence that things are changing. The challenge, according to Roger Corbett, managing director of Woolworths, will be to attract domestic and international institutional support, while retaining those shareholders who are there for the discount card.

Fletcher's strategy is now in the 'fix it or sell it' stage, with a focus on improving the value of the existing business. Fixing the current situation is paramount; however, Fletcher must not be myopic and ignore growth opportunities. In Britain, Tesco now has a thriving financial services sector offering a spectrum of financial products, differentiating the traditional retail offer and meeting customer demands for one-stop shopping.

Most consumers will be oblivious to the radical internal restructuring that is taking place. They can expect, however, to be confronted with marketing campaigns designed to reposition Coles Myer's various businesses. The aim is to communicate clearly to shoppers the differences between the chains. Kmart will be positioned as a deep discount family store, Target as a trend-based retail store, and Myer-Grace as serving the middle to upper class with a full department store range.

Fletcher knows that it will take many years and radical restructuring will be required to achieve the turnaround. The investment community is not known for its patience, but is willing to allow him 12 months to reveal tangible progress. The investment community regards Fletcher as one of Australia's best chief executives. Will he be able to meet the challenges that lie ahead?

Source: Adapted from Adele Ferguson, Coles Myer: The big fix, *BRW*, 22–28 November 2001, pp. 46–53.

Questions

1. Discuss the impact that the information age has had on Coles Myer. How has the company adapted to the changed retailing landscape?
2. What issues should John Fletcher address regarding the existing business units?
3. What appears to be the biggest challenge that Fletcher faces in restructuring the company?
4. What immediate strategies for cost reduction are open to Fletcher and what are the long-term implications of these strategies in terms of increased shareholder value?
5. What do you consider to be the best option for Fletcher in addressing the issue of the existing loyalty program?

end notes

1. Arie de Geus, *The Living Company*, Boston, MA: Harvard Business School Press, 1997.
2. Andrew Black, Philip Wright with John Davies, *In Search of Shareholder Value*, 2nd edn, London: Prentice Hall, 2001.
3. See, for example, Jeremy Hope and Tony Hope, *Competing in the Third Wave*, Boston: Harvard Business School Press, 1997; Peter Drucker, *Managing in a Time of Great Change*, Harmondsworth: Penguin Books, 1995.
4. Tom Peppers and Martha Rogers, *Enterprise One-to-One*, New York: Doubleday, 1997.
5. Joan Magretta, 'The power of virtual integration: An interview with Dell Computer's Michael Dell', *Harvard Business Review*, March/April 1998, pp. 72–85.
6. S. David Young and Stephen F. O'Byrne, *EVA and Value-based Management: A Practical Guide to Implementation*, New York: McGraw-Hill, p. 8.
7. Lowell L. Bryan, Timothy G. Lyons and James Rosenthal, 'Corporate strategy in a globalizing world: The market capitalization imperative', *McKinsey Quarterly*, no. 3, 1998, pp. 6–19.
8. Peter F. Drucker, *Management Challenges for the 21st Century*, Oxford: Butterworth Heinemann, 1999, pp. 133–60.
9. Joel M. Stern and John S. Shiely with Irwin Ross, *The EVA Challenge: Implementing Value-added Change in an Organization*, New York: John Wiley & Sons, 2001, p. 53.
10. Australian Stock Exchange, 'Shareownership Update', November 2000, www.asx.com.au.
11. Gary Hamel and C. K. Prahalad, *Competing for the Future*, Boston: Harvard Business School Press, 1994, pp. 141–9.
12. Michael C. Erhardt, *The Search for Value: Measuring the Company's Cost of Capital*, Boston: Harvard Business School Press, 1994, p. 4.
13. Stephen Callender, 'The industry's profile', *Marketing*, 14 January, 1999, p. 7.
14. Peter Doyle, 'Marketing in the new millennium', *European Journal of Marketing*, **29**(13), 1995, pp. 23–41.
15. These are the main objectives sought by marketers; see Leslie Butterfield (ed.), *Excellence in Advertising*, Oxford: Butterworth Heinemann, 1999, pp. 268–71.
16. 'Why too many mergers miss the mark', *The Economist*, 4 January 1997.
17. Rajendra K. Srivastava, Tasadduq A. Shervani and Liam Fahey, 'Market-based assets and shareholder value: A framework for analysis', *Journal of Marketing*, **62**, 1998, pp. 2–18.

2

The shareholder value approach

chapter objectives

By the time you have completed this chapter, you will be able to:

- describe the principles of shareholder value
- understand the basic steps in conducting shareholder value analysis
- describe the differences between the free cash flow approach to shareholder valuation and the economic value-added approach
- assess the problems and limitations in operationalising shareholder value analysis
- explain why shareholder value is superior to accounting-based performance measures.

scene setter

A brew tipped to improve with age

The big difference between Foster's and its chief rivals, Southcorp and BRL Hardy, is the obvious one — Foster's is a brewer as well as a wine maker. But there are other differences that set Foster's apart, including the business it owns in the US, Beringer Wine Estates.

While all Australian wine companies will be hit by the rising Australian dollar, a big part of Foster's wine operations are overseas based, and relatively immune from currency fluctuations. If there is any effect, a fall in the US dollar helps Beringer, the biggest part of Foster's wine business, which trades as Beringer Blass Wine Estates.

Failure of the market to understand the difference is frustrating Foster's chief executive, Ted Kunkel. He wants Foster's to be known as an 'international multi-beverage' company with beer providing the engine room of steady earnings, and wine the double-digit growth.

'Basically, we took the cash flow of the whole business and spent it in putting together what is arguably the best premium wine business in the world today,' Kunkel says. 'In terms of our business, we believe the mix is exactly right. No other wine company can support its accelerated growth without having the support of a beer company. There are needs in terms of working capital, and capital to buy businesses.'

> *'Of the five business deadly sins, the first and easily the most common is the worship of high profit margins.'*
>
> Peter F. Drucker

There is also another force at work — a spread of risk, and the capacity to grow businesses at different times. For the past few years, the investment world has watched breathlessly as wine shares have boomed. Nothing rises forever, and few industries fall forever ...

But the rush to market Foster's to the new tune of 'the world's third most profitable wine company' has confused the outside world. Investors can see the change, but they can also see that buying Beringer has meant a dramatic increase in debt, which stands at $3.6 billion, and a complete change in the business profile where agricultural risk (grape glut, drought, floods and insect plagues) have assumed a greater importance than when Foster's was more of an industrial stock producing beer.

What Kunkel found annoying was the treatment of Foster's after the release of its half-year results on 12 February [2002] ... [t]he doomsayers pointed to what looked like poor cash flow numbers caused by a build-up of stocks at Beringer and a timing difference in the payment of excise duty to the Australian Government ...

How the wine division evolved is a business lesson. When Foster's acquired Mildara Blass in 1996, it paid a premium which reduced the return to Foster's to about 7.5 per cent on the funds employed, less than Foster's' weighted average cost of capital (WACC) of around 10 per cent. Time, capital and management saw Mildara Blass grow to a 14 per cent return.

'We own the process, if you like, of doing exactly the same thing with Beringer,' Kunkel says. 'We paid a premium for Beringer; clearly the return of our whole wine business went down. If you believe analysts' consensus then you would be saying that Beringer would be getting back close to the WACC. After that [reaching the WACC] we would like to see a business of that size develop up to a mid-teens return on capital employed. That's our aim over the next four to five years.'

Source: Adapted from Tim Treadgold, 'A brew tipped to improve with age', *Shares*, June 2002, pp. 24–8.

Introduction

This chapter provides a guide to the principles of valuation that underpin value-based marketing. It contains some challenging technical material. The ideas will be unfamiliar to most marketing managers. But there is nothing here that cannot be mastered by anyone willing to spend time on the material. The techniques described here position marketing managers to become much more involved and proactive in developing business strategy. They are the same techniques that boards, consultants, analysts and sophisticated investors use to evaluate business strategies. Without these tools, marketing managers risk being left behind in influencing the big strategic issues facing their businesses. These techniques provide the best framework for evaluating marketing strategy and demonstrating the effectiveness of marketing. In addition, as will be shown in the following chapters, they lead to a fundamentally different approach to thinking about marketing issues and developing the marketing mix.

The chapter begins with a reminder that shareholder value analysis (SVA) is primarily an evaluative tool for analysing the present value of the anticipated cash flow from a strategy proposal. It then outlines the major steps that should be pursued in conducting SVA. In doing this, an attempt is made to minimise the technical complexities involved, and to concentrate instead on fundamental principles. The two commonly accepted approaches to SVA are then discussed: the cash flow method and the economic profit (or EVA®) approach. Both lead to the same results, but it is argued here that the cash flow method provides more insights for marketing. Accordingly, this is the main focus of the chapter and of the book. Some of the main concerns expressed about the technical aspects of SVA are then discussed, and consideration is given to the issue of whether the concept of shareholder value is relevant to non-publicly listed companies. Finally, the case is made that shareholder value, even with its limitations, is markedly superior to accounting-based measures of business performance. In essence, the shareholder value approach sees a business's value in terms of its anticipated future cash flows, appropriately discounted. By contrast, the conventional, or accounting, approach is concerned with 'book value': the initial cost of (tangible) investments, reduced by a predetermined depreciation schedule (with possible adjustments made for the effects of inflation on replacement costs).

How shareholder value analysis acts as an evaluative tool

For all its insistence on the pre-eminence of shareholders, shareholder value analysis (SVA) recognises that other stakeholders have claims that need to be met. Customers insist on products that meet their quality and price expectations. Employees demand satisfactory pay and working conditions. Suppliers want to be reimbursed according to agreed terms. Payments to shareholders are *residual* payments: dividends are received only after other stakeholders have been paid. To meet the requirements of all claimants, proponents of SVA point out, long-term cash flow is of critical importance. The funding of the investment needed for future growth and for meeting customer needs, of wage payments that will help to attract and retain employees, and of the financial obligations to suppliers and bondholders — all depend heavily on cash flow.

SVA, then, takes as its starting point the importance of generating cash flow over the long run. It is in essence a technique for trying to determine what the present value of anticipated future cash flow will be. It thereby facilitates strategic choices, for it provides a guide to how much value will be created.

A company committed to the achievement of shareholder value is one that is committed to measuring performance, and doing this in a transparent and consistent manner. This may seem trite but it needs to be said that a characteristic of companies implementing SVA is the desire to do something more than simply issue periodic accounting results to meet legal requirements, and to use something other than just gut feelings in deciding which strategy to pursue. Instead, there is a commitment to careful measurement of the performance of product lines, business units, the entire company, the strategies contemplated for each of these levels of the organisation and the amount to be paid to senior executives. A company committed to shareholder value is also one that is committed to a particular *way* of measuring performance. It is a commitment to the use of a particular set of tools, those derived principally from the techniques of discounted cash flow analysis. It is also a philosophical insistence that performance should not be assessed by dwelling on short-term results but should instead employ a long-term approach. Finally, it is a view that recognises that an external perspective — that of investors — should be used for internal analysis.

The point will be made repeatedly in this book that, while we can readily acknowledge the technical difficulties of conducting SVA, the really challenging task for managers is not SVA as such but that of generating and implementing strategies that yield differential advantage. SVA does not itself produce such strategies. Rather, as noted, it is a technique for evaluating strategies and for monitoring the organisation's achievements in implementing them. It can also act as an incentive mechanism (see marketing insight 'Linking chief executives' pay to long-run performance'). It is, to repeat, a measurement tool underpinned by a particular view of what should be measured and how it should be measured.

Shareholder value analysis: A step-by-step guide

It is helpful to think of SVA as consisting of five steps:[1]

1. The first is to establish a benchmark for decisions about the future by analysing the business's historical performance.
2. Next, management must determine the appropriate discount rate to be applied to estimates of future cash flows. To do this, they need to estimate something called the cost of capital.
3. Management must then forecast future performance. The aim here is to determine the nature, strength and durability of the company's differential advantage. This in turn provides the background against which estimates of future cash flows can be made. The focus in this step is on the 'forecast period' — the finite period during which the strategy under analysis is to be implemented.
4. The next task is to determine what cash flows will be in the period beyond the forecast period. To use the terminology of SVA, the task is to estimate 'continuing' or 'residual' value, the value of the business in the post-forecast period.
5. Finally, management need to calculate and interpret the results.

Each of these five steps is discussed in more detail below.

Marketing insight: **Linking chief executives' pay to long-run performance**

David Crawford, the national chairman of KPMG and a director of BHP, says that the time horizon of companies is an important issue for boards and chief executives. 'Are you there to maximise short-term profitability? Are you there to maximise long-tem profitability? Or are you there to get a balance?' The smart answer, he says, has to be balance. 'But if you are rewarding executives based on today's performance, then there is a tendency for them to seek shorter-term rewards.' ...

Paul Kerin, managing director of the management consulting firm, A. T. Kearney, says the total value of chief executive packages has increased threefold compared with the income of the general Australian population in the past 10 years. Their base salaries, however, have not moved as much because a greater proportion of the salary package is being tied to performance.

'Ten years ago, most chief executives got measured on an earnings-per-share or profit target,' Kerin says. 'It was fairly simplistic, and 90 per cent got rewarded whether they met the target or not. They are evaluated in a different way now, much more weighted towards the creation of shareholder value.'

Kerin says that because chief executives are being judged more by the shareholder value they create, they are more focused on long-term results. This is because share prices usually reflect expectations of the company's performance.

He says the chief executives of Australia's 100 biggest companies (based on market capitalisation) receive about half of their total potential remuneration as base salary and the other half is 'at risk'. Of the half that is at risk, Kerin says about 15–20 per cent is linked to the company's profit performance (a short-term measure) and the rest is linked to creating shareholder value (a long-term measure).

However, Kerin says that about 25 per cent of the chief executives in the top 100 companies are measured only on share-price growth. He says share-price growth takes no account of dividends, and dividend policies can be changed to boost share price. 'If my compensation was tied to simple growth in share price I would have a strong incentive to recommend to the board that we should cut dividend payout ratio and retain more cash in the company so the value of the shares would go up.'

Source: Extracts from Jan McCallum, 'Tough at the top', *BRW*, 22 June 2001, pp. 54–9.

Step 1: Analyse historical performance

The starting point for a company wishing to develop and analyse forecasts of future performance is to have a thorough appreciation of its past performance. In conducting such an analysis, Copeland, Koller and Murrin recommend that it is necessary not simply to assess cash flows but to analyse also the company's return on invested capital (ROIC), a metric most commonly associated with the approach to shareholder valuation called economic value added (and discussed in a later section of this chapter).[2] It is important also to analyse the determinants or drivers of both historic cash flow and ROIC.

Calculating ROIC requires two things: a measure of the income the company is generating, and a measure of the total amount invested by the company's investors. The income measure involves two main steps. First, operating expenses are deducted from sales revenue to get operating earnings. Taxes are then deducted. This gives us something called **NOPAT** (net operating profits after tax). It should be noted here that the data for calculating measures such as ROIC are to be found in the traditional accounting statements and that these have to be reorganised to give them less of an accounting, and more of an economic, perspective on the company. The nature of these adjustments, however, need not detain us here.[3] To measure

NOPAT: net operating profits after tax

invested capital, we sum working capital and property, plant and equipment. Management can then calculate ROIC as follows:

$$\text{ROIC} = \frac{\text{NOPAT}}{\text{Invested capital}}$$

Copeland, Koller and Murrin explain that:

ROIC is a better analytical tool for understanding the company's performance than other return measures such as return on equity or return on assets because it focuses on the true operating performance of the company. Return on equity mixes operating performance with financial structure, making peer group analysis or trend analysis less meaningful because you can't understand the underlying operating performance of the company. The return on total assets (ROA) is inadequate because it includes a number of inconsistencies between the numerator and the denominator. Non-interest bearing liabilities are not deducted from the denominator, total assets. Yet, the implicit financing cost of these liabilities is included in the expenses of the company and, therefore, deducted from the numerator.[4]

A comparison of ROIC and the cost of capital (the latter will be explained shortly) reveals whether the company has created value: when ROIC exceeds the cost of capital, value has been created; when it is below the cost of capital, value has been destroyed. ROIC is important too because it, together with the proportion of profits invested for growth, drives cash flow. And it is cash flow that drives value.

Step 2: Estimate the cost of capital

SVA is fundamentally about estimating future cash flows and then expressing their present value by using a suitable discount rate. The **cost of capital** is the discount rate used for valuation purposes. Underpinning the cost of capital is the idea that those who *supply* capital are looking for a minimum rate of return as a reward for providing their money, and that those who *consume* capital have an obligation to provide suppliers with a return that at the very least equals what they could have earned if their funds had been invested in companies of similar risk. Companies that provide a rate of return in excess of the cost of capital are, in effect, justifying the decision of investors to tie up their capital in the business.

cost of capital: the opportunity cost, or expected return, that investors forgo by investing in the company rather than in other comparable shares

In coming to grips with the nature and purpose of the cost of capital, it is necessary to understand what is entailed in the act of investing. In effect, investors choose not to spend their funds immediately and decide instead to purchase the right to a stream of future cash flows. Before making this decision, they need to ask themselves how much this future cash flow is worth to them today. In answering this, they have to estimate the magnitude of the future cash flow that will be generated by the investment (the size of the cash flow and how long it will continue), the time they will have to wait before they begin to receive the anticipated cash flow, and the uncertainty or risk that the cash flow will not in fact occur in the way they anticipate. Implicit in the act of investing, therefore, is the expectation by investors that future cash flows will provide them with adequate compensation for choosing not to spend now or, to put it differently, that it will provide sufficient reward for having to wait for the receipt of cash. Furthermore, the rate of return sought by investors will vary according to their perceptions of the degree of risk that the investment entails: the higher the risk, the greater the desired rate of return.

discounted cash flow (DCF): future cash flows multiplied by the discount factor to obtain the present value of the cash flows

The **discounted cash flow (DCF)** approach to valuation captures these ideas. Most commonly it is used to determine the *present value* of an asset. It may be, for example, that an asset is expected to generate a cash flow of $2 million in each of the next four years. To convert this stream of cash flows to its present value, it is necessary to 'discount' them at an interest rate, or rate of return, that incorporates the risk that is thought to be attached to the cash flows. Using the DCF model, and employing a discount rate of 10 per cent, the present value of the four years of cash flow of $2 million is $6.4 million. The model is also used to determine the **net present value (NPV)** of an asset. This is simply the present value plus the initial investment to acquire the asset. If, for example, management invested $5 million initially to obtain the above four years of cash flows, then the NPV would be $1.4 million.

net present value (NPV): the net contribution of a strategy to the wealth of shareholders: present value of cash flows minus initial investment

The cash flows are discounted for two simple reasons. Both of them were alluded to above. First, cash today is worth more than cash tomorrow, since money today can be invested to start earning immediately. This is the principle of the time value of money: the use of a discount rate incorporates the idea that investors must be paid to wait because they would rather have cash today than tomorrow. Second, because risky returns are worth less than safe ones, they are penalised by a higher discount rate. The current rates of return available in the capital market are used to determine how much to discount for time and risk. By calculating the present value of an asset, management are in effect estimating the maximum amount people will pay for it, if they have the alternative of investing elsewhere in ventures of comparable risk.

The basic conclusion is that investors should only invest in assets with positive net present values — otherwise they would have done better to invest elsewhere. SVA simply takes these same ideas and uses them to value businesses and marketing strategies. The discount rate, as noted, is referred to as the cost of capital. This, in essence, is the return — the minimum reward for providing capital — which investors expect to receive if they were to invest their capital elsewhere in assets of comparable risk. As such, it is an opportunity cost. Deciding to invest in company A rather than company B, when both have similar levels of risk, is to forgo the potential benefit provided by B, and it is this benefit that is captured by the cost of capital. The decision to invest in A indicates that the investor has decided that the return provided by company A will be higher than B, the next best alternative.

How, then, is the cost of capital estimated? The answer, in essence, is that three things need to be done:

1. develop a target capital structure for the company so that market value weights can be assigned
2. estimate the cost of debt finance
3. estimate the cost of equity finance.

» 1. Develop the target capital structure to determine value weights

While the basic principles of discounting future cash flows can be readily understood and appreciated by non-financial managers, such as marketing managers, it is frequently the case that such managers have difficulty coming to grips with the notion of a 'cost of capital' and with why it is the appropriate choice for discounting purposes. They assume that the cost of capital simply refers to the interest paid on loans. They thereby make two errors: they ignore other forms of financing, and they think of actual costs rather than opportunity costs.

capital structure: the relative dependence of a business on equity versus debt as sources of funding

weighted average cost of capital (WACC): the cost of equity and the cost of debt combined and weighted according to their relative contribution to the organisation's financing or capital structure

Companies use both debt and equity as a means of financing. The **capital structure** of an organisation indicates the relative dependence of the organisation on these two methods of financing. The cost of capital is a weighted average. It incorporates the degree of reliance on debt vis-à-vis equity as well as the different levels of risk attached to each of these forms of financing. Because the **weighted average cost of capital (WACC)** is used to discount future cash flows, it should theoretically reflect a different capital structure for each of the years in which it is to be applied. The standard practice, however, is to apply a single WACC to the entire forecast period, and to use a target capital structure rather than the structure currently in place. That said, an estimate of the current capital structure will provide critical input in developing the target capital structure. So too will an examination of the capital structure of similar companies.

» 2. Estimate the cost of debt finance

Calculating the first component of the cost of capital, the cost of debt, is relatively straightforward. It is based on the cost of new debt, not historic debt. It is also the after-tax cost that is calculated since interest on debt is tax deductible. If a company has some publicly quoted debt — for example, a corporate bond — the current cost of debt can be obtained directly by looking at market prices and yield quotes. When this information is not directly available, it has to be estimated. One way is to observe the yield on debt of companies in a related sector and to use a rating agency such as Moody's or Standard and Poor's to estimate a premium or discount to the published yield figure.

» 3. Estimate the cost of equity finance

The second component of the cost of capital, the cost of equity, is more difficult to estimate. The cost of equity is the expected return which will attract investors to purchase or hold the company's shares instead of those of other companies. This expected return will vary with the specific risk attached to the company's shares.

The method of estimating the cost of equity financing is based on the capital asset pricing model (CAPM), a framework at the core of the corporate finance discipline. The model certainly has its critics but it remains remarkably resilient. It suggests that the cost of equity can be divided into two components: a risk-free rate and an equity risk premium. The latter has two elements: the general or market risk premium (the amount by which the average return on shares exceeds the risk-free rate) and the specific risk attached to the shares of a particular company (known as the systematic risk).

The risk-free rate of return

Bonds differ from equity in that the former entails a promise that there will be regular interest payments and that the principal will be paid on maturity. Even with bonds, however, there is the risk of the debt issuer defaulting or missing an interest payment. The only bonds that could be considered risk-free are government bonds (and even here, as the recent example of Argentina shows, there are occasional, if infrequent, exceptions). As a rule, however, there is a zero default risk associated with the debt obligations of sovereign governments. The yield on government bonds acts, therefore, as a baseline return for any investor. What this means is that rational investors will not be tempted to invest in anything other than government bonds unless they expect superior rates of return to this baseline. The rate of return has to compensate them for moving outside the risk-free zone. Conventionally, since the cost of capital is used to discount cash flows over the forecast period, the risk-free rate will be the yield on longer-term government bonds, those that prevail over the length of the planning cycle. The yield on ten-year government bonds is commonly favoured. In mid-2002, this was approximately 6 per cent in Australia and 5 per cent in the United States.

The market-risk premium

This is the extra amount (the premium) to be made on average by investing in equities as compared to risk-free government bonds. As such, it is a measure of the opportunity cost of investing in the overall equity market. There has been much debate about what the market-risk premium is (a figure of 5–6 per cent is commonly suggested for the United States) and how it is best calculated. The premium can be assessed ex post by using historical data to analyse how equities have performed relative to bonds (such analyses show that the market-risk premium varies considerably over time and from one country to another, and that it is not always positive). Alternatively, it can be done ex ante by trying to determine what realistically will be demanded by institutional investors to move from the apparent certainties of the bond market and into the uncertain world of the equity market.[5]

The systematic risk

This refers to the specific riskiness attached to a particular company's shares. It is commonly referred to as the **beta coefficient** (a term used in the CAPM formula). This is the aspect of the model that has attracted the most debate. Beta is a measure of the association between changes in the share price of an individual company and the change in the main market index in which the share is quoted. It captures the extent to which a company's share price moves in line with the market as a whole. If the share price moves more than the market average, the beta coefficient exceeds 1.0; if it moves less than the market average, the coefficient will be less than 1.0. Financial service companies regularly calculate these coefficients from data on past share movements and publish them for interested parties. As of early 2002, to provide some Australian examples, the retail company, Woolworths, had a beta of 0.50; the chemical company, Orica, had a beta of 0.98; Tabcorp's was 1.07; Paperlinx's was 1.33; while Looksmart had a beta of 2.00.[6]

The higher the beta, the greater the volatility of the share, and the greater the risk associated with it. This in turn implies that the higher the beta, the higher will be the return demanded by investors. Empirical research has confirmed the conventional notion that investors seeking superior returns have to be willing to take greater risk: as a rule, there is a positive relationship between betas (and hence risk) and stock returns. There is also research, however, which questions the relationship, suggesting in some cases that it is not as strong as the model indicates, or that there is a point beyond which an increase in risk is not associated with a commensurate increase in return. There has also been debate about whether the relationship holds at all.[7] There are alternatives to CAPM-based betas, notably arbitrage pricing theory, but for all the debate associated with it, the former continues to receive widespread support.

beta coefficient: a measure of the association between changes in the share price of an individual company and the change in the main market index in which the share is quoted

Once each of the elements of the CAPM formula have been analysed, it is a simple matter of calculating the cost of equity by multiplying the market risk premium by the systematic risk factor (beta), and then adding this to the risk-free rate of return. And once the cost of equity has been determined, the WACC can be calculated.

» Calculating the WACC

Suppose a company's after-tax cost of debt is 8 per cent and its estimated cost of equity is 12 per cent. It plans to raise future capital, and has determined that its target capital structure will be 35 per cent by way of debt and 65 per cent by new equity. The cost of capital is:

	WEIGHT (%)	COST (%)	WEIGHTED COST (%)
Debt (after tax)	35	8	2.8
Equity	65	12	7.8
Cost of capital			10.6

The WACC of 10.6 per cent is what the company should use for discounting anticipated future cash flows.

Black and Wright summarise the critical role that the WACC plays as a hurdle rate in measuring success:

> The WACC is an expression of what return a company must earn if it is to justify the financial assets it uses … It is entirely market-driven: if the assets cannot earn that return, then investors will eventually withdraw their funds from the business … From the manager's point of view, the WACC establishes the *market relevant hurdle rate against which success has to be measured* … It is not just a question of ensuring that the business earns returns that are equivalent to its WACC. If the business is to prosper in the longer term, it has to earn more than that WACC. It is only when this condition is met that we can talk about the creation of shareholder value.[8]

This also underlines the importance of carefully calculating the WACC. Interpretations of whether value has been created or destroyed are heavily dependent on an accurate assessment of the discount rate, a point considered in more detail later.

Step 3: Estimate value in the forecast period

Step 3 involves an assessment of future cash flow. This may be for a period as short as three years, or as much as 10 years after the introduction of the strategy under consideration. Step 4, discussed in detail in the next section, also involves a forecast of cash flow, but this time for the period after the strategy has run its course. Before describing step 3, it is necessary to explain the problems faced in both it and step 4. The rationale for dividing the future into two discrete periods needs also to be explained.

» Dealing with an uncertain future: The challenges of steps 3 and 4

The challenge in both steps 3 and 4 is to deal with the fact that the future is inherently unknowable. Nevertheless, forecasts of future performance, and the cash flows associated with them, must be made. They will only be as good as the analytical skills and efforts of those undertaking the forecasts. Funda-mental to the task of forecasting is to ensure that it is based on a strategic perspective, one that incorporates a careful analysis of market opportunities and trends, and of the company's competitive situation. As Copeland, Koller and Murrin describe it, 'developing a strategic perspective essentially means crafting a plausible story about the company's future performance', one that provides the context for the financial forecast.[9] Part 2 of this book has much to say about how this strategic perspective can be developed.

The problem of trying to forecast future performance is identified later in this chapter as one of the major limitations of SVA. Day and Fahey are perfectly correct when they note that 'The hard numbers in the projections of cash flow … obscure numerous judgment calls and give a deceptive precision to the estimated value'.[10] The point will be made in the discussion of Step 5 that, because of these judgment calls, it is necessary to develop a variety of scenarios and to subject all forecasts to sensitivity analyses. Day and Fahey note in addition that there are a variety of problems that may compromise and bias the translation of strategic moves into cash flow forecasts. There may be, for example, a natural bias that arises from concentrating on the information that is easiest to retrieve and/or from a tendency to focus on the particular outcome that management believe will occur. When there is selective perception, conflicting evidence may be ignored. Another example is the possibility that management may use, as their baseline measure, a figure that assumes a continuation of the status quo, but it is unlikely that the status quo will prevail because of market dynamics and actions taken by competitors.

It would be wrong, however, to conclude that these problems constitute reasons for not making forecasts. They should be seen, instead, as a warning of the need to be conscious of such biases and to try to guard against them. It is all too easy to use the existence of such problems as an excuse for sticking with gut feelings as a basis for strategic decisions, rather than attempting any sort of forecasting.

Courtney points out that managers tend to accept a binary view of uncertainty.[11] They assume that it is close to nonexistent in some situations (and hence that point forecasts can be made with ease) or, more commonly, that it exists and that its effect is like being confronted with a steel wall — impenetrable and opaque — against which the only response can be to abandon systematic, analytical rigour and rely instead on intuition. This all-or-nothing approach, however, is mistaken. It is possible to analyse what Courtney calls 'residual uncertainty' — that which is left after the best possible analysis of what separates the unknown from the unknowable. Four forms of residual uncertainty can be distinguished: level 1, a clear enough future; level 2, a limited set of possible future outcomes (alternate futures), one of which will occur; level 3, a range of possible future outcomes; and level 4, true ambiguity in which there is a limitless range of possible future outcomes. Level 4 is in fact rare and will not persist. Most strategy decisions face level 2 or level 3 uncertainty. In both cases a variety of tools can be used to analyse the uncertainty confronted. These include scenario analysis.[12] More is said about this in the discussion of step 5.

> ### » The rationale for steps 3 and 4: The future as two discrete periods

One way to make the task of trying to calculate future performance somewhat easier is to divide it into two parts. The first part is the value generated in what is referred to as the **explicit forecast period**, and the second is the present

explicit forecast period: the period during which a proposed strategy can be expected to provide for the organisation a competitive advantage and for which managers feel that they can sensibly make estimates of sales, costs and investments

value of cash flow after the explicit forecast period. The latter is variously called the terminal, residual or **continuing value**. Step 3 is the analysis of cash flow during the forecast period. Step 4 is the analysis of cash flow in the post-forecast period. By dividing the future in this way, the following definition can be offered:

continuing value:
the value of the cash flow generated during the post-forecast period

Value = Present value of cash flow *during* the forecast period
+ Present value of cash flow *after* the forecast period

There are two reasons for dividing it like this. One is that, in the majority of industries, a seven- or eight-year forecast period is the longest period managers feel that they can sensibly put estimates of sales, costs and investments. Beyond that, the implications of changes in economic conditions, competition and technology are too uncertain to forecast, at least with any hope of precision.

The second reason is that seven or eight years is the longest period that any marketing strategy can normally expect to deliver a **differential advantage**. For many strategies the period will be much less. A strategy creates value when it produces returns that exceed the cost of capital and thereby generates positive net present value. A firm's ability to generate these above normal profits depends upon it being able to offer customers something other companies are unable to match. This 'monopolistic advantage' enables it to earn profits above those normally expected by the capital market. The source of this competitive advantage may be innovation which has given the business superior products or processes; it may be brand names which customers trust and value; or it may be the possession of licences, sunk costs or natural monopolies which restrict competitors from entry to the market.[13] However, such advantages do not last. High profits attract competitors, substitutes appear, prices fall and above-normal profits fade away. The calculation of the continuing value captures this change. In the initial forecasting period the business may earn returns *above* the costs of capital, but after this they are assumed to fall to the market average.

differential advantage:
a competitive advantage that allows a firm to offer products that are perceived by customers as better value than those of competitors

» Cash flow and its determinants: The forecast period

In this third step, as noted, the focus is on estimating cash flow for each year of the forecast period. The task of estimating cash flow in the residual period constitutes the fourth step, and is considered in the next section.

Cash flow is the difference between operating cash inflows and outflows. It is often called **free cash flow**. Cash flow is the source of corporate value because it determines how much is available to pay debtholders and shareholders. Young and O'Byrne describe it this way:

free cash flow:
residual cash flow that is 'free' to be paid to investors

> Because investments tie up cash, their value is based on the amount of future cash flows that will accrue to investors. Free cash flow can be thought of as the amount of cash flow left over from the company's operating activities after expected investments have been made. It is from this residual cash flow that companies can then return cash to their capital providers. In brief, free cash flow makes it possible for companies to make interest payments, pay off the principal on loans, pay dividends, and buy back shares. These are the four ways that companies return cash to their capital providers, and therefore, the expectations of such cash flows will be the ultimate determinant of a company's value from a capital market perspective.[14]

Cash *inflows* are a function of two elements: sales and the operating profit margin. The operating profit margin is the ratio of pre-interest, pre-tax operating profit to sales. Operating profit is sales less the cost of goods, selling and administrative expenses and less depreciation costs. Cash *outflows* are a function of three elements: the cash taxes the company actually pays, and the additional working capital and fixed investment the business will incur in achieving its sales.

To illustrate how these cash flows are calculated, consider Alpha Company with current sales of $100 million, operating profit margin of 10 per cent and a cash tax rate of 30 per cent (see table 2.1). Management introduce a new marketing strategy to accelerate the company's growth. They believe that seven years is the longest period over which it makes sense to attempt detailed forecasts. Over this forecast period, sales are predicted to grow at 12 per cent a year in money terms. The operating profit margin and tax rate are forecast to remain the same. The net operating profit after tax, as noted earlier, is usually called NOPAT.

Table 2.1 Alpha Company: Cash flow forecasts ($ million)

YEAR	CURRENT	1	2	3	4	5	6	7
Sales ($ million)	100.00	112.00	125.44	140.49	157.35	176.23	197.38	221.07
Operating margin (10%)	10.00	11.20	12.54	14.05	15.74	17.62	19.74	22.11
Tax (30%)	3.00	3.36	3.76	4.21	4.72	5.29	5.92	6.63
NOPAT	7.00	7.84	8.78	9.83	11.01	12.34	13.82	15.47
Additional working capital		2.16	2.42	2.71	3.03	3.40	3.81	4.26
Additional fixed capital		2.64	2.96	3.31	3.71	4.15	4.65	5.21
Cash flow		3.04	3.40	3.81	4.27	4.78	5.36	6.00

working capital: net current assets — that is, current assets less current liabilities — comprised of inventories (stocks and work in progress), receivables (debtors owing money to the business) and payables (the business's creditors)

fixed capital: durable assets which are used repeatedly or continuously over a number of years to create products — such as buildings, motor vehicles and plant and machinery

Growth normally requires additional investment. Management estimates that *incremental net working capital* (debtors, cash and stock, less creditors) will grow at 18 per cent of sales. That is, every additional $100 in sales will require an additional $18 investment of cash in working capital. *Incremental net fixed capital* investment is defined as capital expenditures in excess of depreciation. It is net of depreciation because depreciation was deducted in calculating the operating profit. (An alternative approach that is often used is to add back depreciation to NOPAT and deduct gross investment to calculate free cash flow. This produces the identical result to deducting net investment from NOPAT.) In developing its strategy for the forecast period, management will put in its own estimates for capital spending. In the example, incremental capital investment is taken to be 22 per cent of sales. The cash flow that results is shown in the table.

The determinants of cash flow (or free cash flow) can be summarised, then, as:

CASH IN: determined by:
    1. Sales growth
    2. Operating profit margin

less

CASH OUT: determined by:
1. Cash tax
2. Incremental working capital
3. Incremental fixed investment.

All five components have to be estimated as part of the forecasting process. As noted, there are undeniable challenges in trying to do this accurately.

Step 4: Estimate continuing value

Recall from step 3 that continuing value is the value of the company's expected cash flow in the post-forecast period. Two of the key issues that arise at this point are, first, choosing the appropriate method or formula for determining continuing value and, second, interpreting the strategic significance of the proportion of total value represented by continuing value.

» Perpetuity and other methods

Unfortunately, there is no unique method of calculating continuing value, and different methods often produce sharply different results. The choice of method depends upon a careful judgment of the competitive strength of the business and the value of its brands at the end of the forecast or planning period. The most common method of estimating continuing value is the **perpetuity** method. This assumes that, after the forecast period, competition will drive the return the business earns down to the cost of capital. The effect of this is that further investments, even if they expand the business, do not change its *value*. As a result, future cash flows, after the forecast period, can be treated as what finance managers call a 'perpetuity' or an infinite stream of identical cash flows. As Rappaport points out, the perpetuity method:

> ... is *not* based on the assumption that all future cash flows will actually be identical. It simply reflects the fact that the cash flows resulting from future investments will not affect the value of the firm because the overall rate of return earned on those investments is equal to the cost of capital.[15]

perpetuity: an investment offering a level or even stream of cash flow for the indefinite future

Using the perpetuity method, the present value (at the end of the forecast period) is calculated by dividing the net operating profit after tax by the cost of capital:

$$\text{Perpetuity terminal value} = \frac{\text{NOPAT}}{\text{Cost of capital}}$$

To calculate the present value of the terminal value this figure has to be discounted back over the appropriate number of years. For example, if the net operating profit at the end of a seven-year forecasting period is $8 million and the cost of capital is 10 per cent, then the perpetuity continuing value is $80 million and the present value of this continuing value is $80 million divided by $(1 + 0.1)^7$ or $41 million.

There are a variety of other methods to calculate continuing values.[16] Some companies use the *perpetuity with inflation* method. This adapts the standard perpetuity model by assuming that operating profits after the forecast period grow at the rate of inflation. In periods of inflation this will give a higher estimate of the continuing value. The choice of which of the two to use depends upon whether managers believe the firm will have the ability to raise prices in the long term alongside inflation. This will depend upon industry conditions, the business's position in the market and the organisation's ability to maintain its competitiveness over the longer run.

Another common approach to estimating terminal values is the **price/earnings (P/E) ratio** method. Here one looks up the average P/E ratio for mature companies in similar types of industries and uses this to multiply net operating profit in the terminal year. For example, if the net profit was projected as $8 million in the seventh year and the average P/E was 11, the continuing value would be $88 million and its present value $45 million. An alternative is the **market-to-book (M/B) ratio** method. This calculates continuing value by multiplying the projected book value of assets by an average M/B ratio for similar companies. So, if the book value of assets in the terminal year is projected to be $60 million and the average M/B ratio is 1.5, the continuing value is estimated at $90 million.

price/earnings (P/E) ratio: the market price of the share divided by earnings per share

market-to-book (M/B) ratio: the market value of the business divided by the book equity value

Both these methods can be criticised. Book value nowadays is a poor measure of the real value of a company's assets. Inflation and intangible assets such as patents and brands mean market values are often substantially higher. Inflation and arbitrary accounting choices also often bias earnings. Finally, in choosing ratios, finding a sample of truly similar companies is no simple task. On the other hand, calculating continuing values always depends on judgment. Essentially the purpose of value analysis is to estimate market value — to estimate what investors would pay for a business. When you can observe what they actually pay for similar companies, that is valuable evidence. P/E and M/B ratios can act as common sense checks to test the validity of more scientific methods of valuation.

» Interpreting continuing value

The continuing value figure is of prime concern in shareholder value analysis because it is usually larger than the value created in the forecast period. This is illustrated in figure 2.1 where, for a variety of industries, the continuing value figure represents most of the value of the average firm. This is especially the case for growth companies that are likely to generate little or no profit and free cash flow in the early years. Care has to be taken, however, in interpreting these percentages. A large continuing value, as Copeland, Koller and Murrin point out:

> ... does not mean that most of a company's value will be realized in the continuing value period. It often just means that the cash inflow in the early years is offset by outflows for capital spending and working capital investment — investments that should generate higher cash flow in later years.[17]

The concept of continuing value is very important for marketing. For companies that have identified new market opportunities, it usually makes sense to spend heavily on new product development, developing the brand and opening up new markets. In this way, they pre-empt competition and build a leading strategic position in the industry. While such strategies create value, they absorb rather than generate cash in the formative period. Aggressive marketing strategies may well lead to minimal profits and free cash flow in the early years, but simultaneously be creating enormous value, which is reflected in the high figure for continuing value and in a rocketing share price. The continuing value reflects shareholders' recognition that in later years, perhaps five or more years ahead, the company will then start generating high free cash flow. Microsoft, Intel, AOL, Nokia and Dell are examples of companies that have followed exactly this pattern.

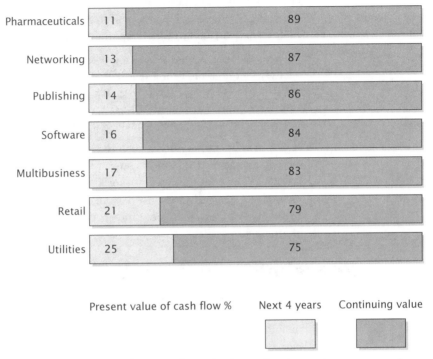

Figure 2.1 The significance of continuing value in total company values
Source: Value Line.

In contrast, companies that create high profits and free cash flow in the forecast period tend to be mature businesses or businesses where the management believes it does not have opportunities to invest, perhaps because competition is too strong. In these situations, management will be taking out costs, minimising fixed investment and reducing working capital. Here the continuing value will be small, recognising that the business's competitive position will not be worth much in the future.

Step 5: Calculate and interpret the results

The key tasks in this final stage are to discount both the forecasted free cash flow and the continuing value to the present. This is done using the WACC. The value of operations is then calculated by adding the present value of the explicit period to the present value of the continuing or residual period. A variety of adjustments are then required, most importantly that of subtracting the market value of all debt. This gives us a measure of enterprise value, one which reflects the effect of the proposed strategy. This can be compared with something usually referred to as the baseline shareholder value. This is a measure of the current (pre-strategy) value of the business assuming no additional value is created or destroyed. In the next section, where Rappaport's free cash flow approach to shareholder value is discussed, an illustration is presented of what the calculation entails.

A word of warning is necessary at this point. Valuation, as Copeland, Koller and Murrin observe, is as much art as science, is inherently imprecise and is highly sensitive to small changes in assumptions about the future.[18] For that reason it is important for companies to develop a variety of different scenarios, to derive valuations for each scenario, to examine critically the assumptions underlying each scenario and to attempt to determine the probability of each scenario. They make an important point:

> The purpose of valuing a company is always to help guide some management or investment decision, be it acquisition, divestiture, or adoption of internal strategic initiatives. The results must be analyzed from the perspective of the decision at hand. Since uncertainty and risk are involved in most business decisions, think of value in terms of scenarios and ranges of value that reflect this uncertainty.[19]

It is critically important to undertake sensitivity analyses of the forecasts. Decision makers have to ask: how much change in the cash flow forecasts, risk levels, or continuing value would be needed to change our decision? An example of how to use sensitivity analysis is provided in chapter 4 in the section on strategy valuation and in chapter 8 in the section on simulating alternative scenarios.

Shareholder value: A single metric?

There are, in fact, a variety of approaches to measuring shareholder value. Accordingly, the novice encounters a variety of competing terms — including free cash flow, shareholder value added, economic value added, market value added, cash flow return on investment (CFROI) and cash value added. The various approaches to measuring shareholder value are linked to different consulting companies, each of whom are staunch advocates of the virtues of their particular approach: free cash flow and shareholder value added are associated with LEK/Alcar, economic value added and market value added with Stern Stewart & Company;[20] and cash flow return on investment and cash value added with Boston Consulting Group and HOLT Value Associates.[21]

Pioneering work on the free cash flow approach was done by Alfred Rappaport.[22] His methodology informs much of the discussion in this chapter and the remainder of the text. It is an economical and efficient approach in that it requires less data and less manipulation of the data than the other approaches. Its focus is entirely on the future, and it does not depend on an opening capital or balance sheet value.

Economic value added (or EVA®), by contrast, is based on an assessment of the cost of capital resources used in the businesses. As such, it requires a starting balance sheet. To measure capital resources, a host of adjustments need to be made to remove distortions in the formal accounting figures (although, in practice, as few as 13 adjustments are usually recommended). The idea with economic value added is to measure shareholder value in terms of the difference (or spread) between the economic returns a company earns (measured as net operating profits after taxes) and what it has to pay for the capital resources needed to run the business (measured in terms of capital employed multiplied by the WACC). Furthermore, where the free cash flow approach is concerned with measuring shareholder value over a period of several years, economic valued added focuses on shareholder value on an annual basis. This is often claimed to be one of its major advantages, for whereas the accuracy of the free cash flow approach will not be revealed until the forecast period has run its course, the proponents of economic value added say that it provides an interim measure that can be used to track how well the business is meeting the tasks of value creation. They also argue that the year-by-year focus of the EVA approach to shareholder value can be complemented by measuring something referred to by Stern Stewart as **market value added (MVA)**. The latter involves a longer-term perspective and is built on the notion of summing the single period measures of shareholder value. More formally, MVA is the present value of the stream of future expected EVA.

market value added (MVA): the present value of the stream of future expected EVA

Note that both the free cash flow approach and the economic value approach are built on a common economic foundation and will lead, in theory, to identical valuations for the business. Conceptually, the present value of the sum of the annual spreads (using the EVA approach), when added to the measure of the capital invested in the business by its investors, can be shown to be equivalent to the present value of the firm's free cash flows. But while there is no conflict between the two methods they do provide different insights. The cash flow approach is very effective for valuing different strategic options. This makes it especially useful for exploring how investments in marketing can contribute to building long-term shareholder value. EVA, as noted, can be useful for judging ongoing performance and determining whether current policies are creating value. In this book the focus is on the cash flow method, but managers need to be aware of the parallel EVA approach.

Before analysing the two approaches in more detail, mention should also be made of yet another approach to measuring shareholder value, one that uses **cash flow return on investment (CFROI)** and the related concept of cash value added. This method changes the focus by using a rate of return rather than the use of dollar amounts characteristic of both the free cash flow and EVA approaches. One of the benefits of the CFROI approach, its proponents argue, is that it facilitates comparisons between investments and between businesses by measuring them in terms of an internal rate of return. They also argue that it eliminates the size bias inherent in the use of value measures that rely on dollar amounts. The downside is that it is highly complicated and heavily data intensive. It also depends on a particular conception of the economic life of assets, which some analysts find contentious.[23]

cash flow return on investment (CFROI): the sustainable cash flow generated by a business in a given year, expressed as a percentage of the cash invested in the firm's assets

Rappaport's cash flow approach

The steps described earlier for calculating shareholder value are based on the approach recommended by Rappaport. For him, the total value of a firm or business unit is called its corporate or **enterprise value**. It consists of the amount belonging to the holders of its debt and equity. The equity portion of the enterprise value is the **shareholder value**. That is:

enterprise value: the total value of a firm or business unit, expressed as the sum of its debt and shareholder value

Enterprise value = Debt + Shareholder value

Rearranging the equation, shareholder value can be expressed as:

shareholder value: the equity portion of enterprise value (enterprise value less debt)

Shareholder value = Enterprise value − Debt

So, to calculate the shareholder value of a business, its total or enterprise value must be calculated first, and then the value of its debt must be subtracted. What then is enterprise value and what is debt? Rappaport defines enterprise value using the two concepts discussed earlier: it is the present value of cash flow from operations during the forecast period plus continuing or residual value (the present value of cash flow during the post-forecast period). For greater precision, Rappaport adds a third component: the current value of marketable securities and other investments that can be converted to cash and that are not essential to operating the business. Debt he defines as the market value of debt, unfunded pension liabilities and the market value of other claims, such as preferred stock.[24] Deduct debt from the sum of the three components of enterprise value and we have a measure of shareholder value.

» An illustration of Rappaport's approach

Table 2.2 utilises the information about projected cash flows drawn from the sales growth, operating margin, tax and capital requirements summarised in table 2.1. The discount factor is $1/(1 + r)^t$ where r is the weighted cost of capital (10 per cent) and t is the year in question. Multiplying by this factor discounts future cash flows to their present value. The continuing value is calculated for each year using the perpetuity method. For example, the continuing value at the end of year 1 is computed as follows:

$$\frac{\text{NOPAT}}{\text{Cost of capital}} = \frac{7.84}{0.1} = \$78.4 \text{ million}$$

To bring the $78.4 million back to the present value it is multiplied by the appropriate discount factor, 0.909, to obtain $71.27 million.

Table 2.2 Alpha Company: Calculating shareholder value

YEAR	CASH FLOW	DISCOUNT FACTOR	PRESENT VALUE	CUMULATIVE PRESENT VALUE	PRESENT VALUE OF CONTINUING VALUE	CUMULATIVE PV + CONTINUING VALUE	SHAREHOLDER VALUE ADDED
Base					70.00	70.00	0.00
1	3.04	0.909	2.76	2.76	71.27	74.03	4.03
2	3.40	0.826	2.81	5.57	72.53	78.10	4.07
3	3.81	0.751	2.86	8.43	73.82	82.25	4.15
4	4.27	0.683	2.92	11.35	75.20	86.55	4.30
5	4.78	0.621	2.97	14.32	76.63	90.95	4.40
6	5.36	0.564	3.02	17.34	77.94	95.28	4.33
7	6.00	0.513	3.08	20.42	79.36	99.78	4.50

Other investments	7.00
Enterprise value	106.78
Value of debt	25.00
Shareholder value	81.78

The cumulative present value of cash flows for the entire seven-year forecast period is $20.42 million. When the continuing value at the end of the period of $79.36 million is added, the total value of $99.78 million is obtained. Typically, for a growth company, the terminal value is substantially higher than the value created in the forecast period.

To illustrate the distinction between enterprise and shareholder value, it is assumed that Alpha also has other investments of $7 million and debt of $25 million. The other investments are added to the total value to arrive at an enterprise value of $106.78 million. The debt is then deducted to arrive at the $81.78 million figure for shareholder value. Suppose the company has 20 million shares outstanding, and that other investments and debt were planned to remain the same over the forecast period, then the marketing strategy behind table 2.1 would lead to a predicted rise in the implied share price from $2.60 to $4.09 per share — a pretty satisfactory performance.

Shareholder value added in table 2.2 provides another insight into the success of the strategy in creating value during the forecast period. Where the shareholder value figure shows the absolute economic value predicted over the forecast period, economic value added shows the change in value. An increase in value means that management has succeeded in making investments that earn returns above the cost of capital required by the capital market. The value added by this seven-year marketing strategy is $29.8 million. The year-by-year increase in value is calculated by the annual change in 'cumulative PV plus continuing value' totals.

Table 2.3 summarises the expected results from the proposed marketing strategy. The first column summarises the beginning or baseline value of the business — the value of the business before the marketing strategy is introduced. In the base year the business has a NOPAT of $7 million, which would capitalise it, using the perpetuity method, as worth $70 million. Adding other investments and deducting the market value of debt leads to an equity value of $52 million. The new marketing strategy anticipates faster growth and investing at returns that exceed the cost of capital. Unless there are other strategic options that lead to even higher shareholder value added, the proposed marketing strategy looks attractive to shareholders.

Table 2.3 Alpha Company: Shareholder value summary

($ MILLION)	BEFORE STRATEGY	WITH STRATEGY
Cost of capital (%)	10	10
PV forecast cash flows	0.00	20.42
PV continuing value	70.00	79.36
Total present value	70.00	99.78
Other investments	7.00	7.00
Enterprise value	77.00	106.78
Debt	25.00	25.00
Shareholder value	52.00	81.78
Shareholder value added	0.00	29.78
Shares outstanding (M)	20	20
Implied value per share ($)	2.60	4.09

Economic value added

EVA® is the trademarked version of what has long been referred to as economic profit. The economic profit model is very intuitive. It starts, like the cash flow model, by recognising that value is created when the return on capital employed exceeds the cost of capital. This is the fundamental principle of valuation:

$$\frac{\text{Return on capital employed}}{\text{Cost of capital}} = \frac{\text{Market value}}{\text{Capital employed}}$$

In other words, investors will push up the market value of a company when it earns a return higher than they can obtain on other investments carrying similar risk — that is, value is added when

$$\text{ROCE} > r$$

where r is the company's weighted average cost of capital. Economic profit or EVA measures the value created in a company in a single period of time. Economic profit differs from accounting profit in that it does not deduct just the interest on debt, but instead deducts a charge for all the capital employed in the business. From an economic viewpoint, charging for all the capital resources tied up in the business makes sense. The capital charge is arrived at by applying the company's cost of capital to the amount of capital employed in the business. Specifically,

$$\text{Economic profit} = \text{NOPAT} - \text{Capital charge}$$
$$= \text{NOPAT} - \text{Capital employed} \times \text{Cost of capital}$$

An alternative way to define economic profits which brings out the central importance of return on capital employed is

$$\text{Economic profit} = (\text{ROCE} - r) \times \text{Capital employed}$$

The difference between return on capital employed and the cost of capital — that is, $(\text{ROCE} - r)$ — is called the **return spread**. Spread times the amount of capital determines economic profit. Only when the spread is positive is management creating economic value. For example, if Alpha had an initial capital of $47 million, a return on capital employed of 15 per cent and a cost of capital of 10 per cent, its economic profit or EVA for the year would be approximately $2.3 million.

return spread: the difference between return on capital employed and the cost of capital

EVA is generally used to analyse current or past performance. But it can also be used, like the cash flow method, for the crucial job of valuing marketing strategies. The value of a company equals the amount of capital employed, plus a premium or discount equal to the present value of its projected economic profit:

$$\text{Value} = \text{Capital employed} + \text{Present value of projected economic profit}$$

The logic behind this formula is straightforward. If a business earned exactly its cost of capital, r, each period so that the spread was zero, then the discounted value of its projected economic profits would be zero also, and the value would equal the original capital employed. A business is worth more than its initial capital only to the extent that it earns more than its cost of capital. So the premium to capital employed must equal the present value of the company's future economic profit.

It is easy to illustrate that both the cash flow and economic profit valuation approaches give the same results. Looking first at the cash flow method, Alpha has a baseline cash flow before net investment (i.e. NOPAT) of $7 million. Using the perpetuity method, the present value of the business is then $70 million. Using the EVA approach, the value of the business is its initial capital employed of $47 million plus the present value of its economic profit of $2.3 million:

$$\text{Present value economic profit} = \frac{\$2.3\,\text{m}}{0.1} = \$23\,\text{m}$$

Alpha's total value then is the identical $70 million.

Comparing cash flow and EVA

The major advantage claimed for EVA is that it can link current operating performance to value creation (see marketing management case in practice 'EVA's role in changing ANZ'). Calculating economic profit demonstrates whether value has been created for that period. If the return on capital employed has exceeded the cost of capital — that is, a positive return spread exists — economic value has been added.

Marketing management in practice: EVA's role in changing ANZ

ANZ banking group startled the market in July 2000 when it decided to 'reconceive the bank as 21 specialist business units,' each subject to its own strategic plan and each competing with the others for resources from the corporate centre. The bank based its new approach on the view that if the company were split into discrete parts, management could focus on the returns produced by each business unit, then direct capital to those with the best prospects.

Initially sceptical, the market has warmed to ANZ's specialisation strategy, particularly after the bank produced a record profit of A$1.87 billion and a return on equity of 20.2% for the 12 months to September 30 [2001].

ANZ's chief financial officer, Peter Marriott, says an important element in managing the change has been the use of performance-measured economic value added (EVA) ... Marriot uses EVA because it is a highly developed system that enables him to measure the performance of the bank overall, each business unit, individual products, customer groups and individual corporate customers.

'In a bank, you are always looking at risk-reward trade-offs,' Marriot says. 'We used to have a lot of high-risk corporate borrowers because we wanted the high margins that we could demand of them. But you have to allocate more capital for big, high-risk borrowers. Since we started using EVA in 1995, we have got out of a lot of those higher-risk credits; our analysis told us that the margins were not sufficient reward for the capital that was allocated. We can pull out the EVA for any corporate customer.'

Part of the aim of the specialisation strategy is to determine the parts of the business in which ANZ has a competitive advantage ... Marriot says EVA helps in this process because it allows the bank to calculate the economic profit for individual products and services.

Martin Concannon, the managing director of Stern Stewart Australia, says this process is extending beyond financial services. 'Any business that is considering outsourcing and partnering must be able to measure the value it is adding in its individual business units. There is a need for sophisticated measurement tools.'

Concannon says the other big application for EVA is in determining executive remuneration. Because discrete parts of the business can be analysed, the managers of those business units can be rewarded for their own performance ...

Source: Extracts from John Kavanagh, 'EVA's Role in Changing ANZ', *BRW*, November 22–28 2001, p. 73.

By contrast, it is not easy to get a simple measure of performance for a single year from looking at cash flow. Companies can be generating great long-term value and showing declining or even negative cash flow. Many successful entrepreneurial businesses start like this. While profit growth is spectacular, the high return on capital invested encourages a rate of investment that exceeds NOPAT. Issuing new debt or equity finances the deficit cash flow. As long as returns exceed the cost of capital, current shareholders will still be better off despite the dilution of their stake. Cash flow is greatly affected by discretionary investments in fixed assets and working capital. Management can easily delay investments simply to inflate cash flow. In a given year, the level of cash flow does not provide information about whether a strategy has created value; economic profit does.

The problem with economic profit is the arbitrariness of the calculation of capital employed and consequently of the estimation of the capital charge and the return on capital employed. The cash flow method does not require any estimates of balance sheet values, but the economic profit approach crucially depends upon them. Different companies and consultants use different assumptions in calculating capital. Some use the book value of assets; others seek to adjust to current or replacement values. Distortions arising from accounting conventions are sometimes corrected. These conventions include prudential procedures for bringing forward expected losses, deferred tax provision and other timing adjustments. Some capitalise rather than expense research and development, marketing investments and goodwill. The form of adjustments will vary between different types of business. Companies whose assets are mostly intangibles — brands, patents and contracts — will be particularly tricky. Comparisons of EVA across companies need to be treated with considerable caution.

A consequence is that EVA can give varying estimates of value added. However, if the focus is on year-to-year *changes* in economic profit rather than on the absolute value then the problem of measuring capital employed disappears. Change in EVA is then identical to shareholder value added.[25] Either can be used as a performance measure.

Finally, it needs to be re-emphasised that looking at a single year is dangerous. Value creation is a long-term phenomenon. High cash flow, high shareholder value added or high economic profit in a single year can easily mask declining long-run competitiveness. It is easy to boost all three in the short term by cutting back on long-term investment and marketing support. But such actions will result in a decline in the continuing value of the business and eventually in the share price. To determine whether a strategy makes sense, long-term cash flow or economic profits have to be estimated and discounted by the cost of capital to get a true valuation.

Managing expectations

A basic principle of shareholder value is that a company's share price is determined by the sum of all of its anticipated cash flows, adjusted by the cost of capital. If the company is expected to generate more cash, perhaps because it develops a new product or has a great advertising campaign, its share price will go up. Conversely, if expected cash flow falls, perhaps because a major new competitor is invading its market, the share price will go down. The crucial implication of this principle, as has already been indicated, is that the task of management is to maximise the sum of these cash flows.

Proponents of SVA argue that the value of a share is determined by forecasting dividends over an indefinite time period. Near-term earnings generally explain only a small proportion of the share price. For the major stocks, forecast dividends in the next five years account for only an average of 20 per cent of the market value of the share price. For high-growth stocks, the percentage is even smaller. Indeed, many companies in fast-growth industries such as the Internet, mobile phones, cable television and biotechnology have seen their shares soar long before they have generated a cent in current earnings for their shareholders. There is not much evidence of short-termism when it comes to valuing businesses with winning strategies in high-growth markets.

Still, many marketing managers are not convinced that the stock market takes a long-term view. They point, in particular, to the excessive attention given to quarterly earnings figures (the opening case, on the Foster's Group, might be cited as an example). However, the attention to current earnings announcements does not contradict the model. Short-term earnings do not themselves have much impact on the share price. However, they may lead investors to reconsider their longer-term forecasts of cash flows. Cash flow consists of earnings less the amount reinvested in the business. Changes in earnings, therefore, do have a big effect on cash flows. If managers fail to deliver earnings according to expectations in the short term, it may lead investors to question the long-term strategy. To optimise their investment portfolios, investors continually probe for information about the long-term prospects of the companies whose shares they hold. Earnings announcements are an important source of information for investors making and revising long-term forecasts. But shareholder value is not determined by short-term earnings; it is determined by discounting long-term expected cash flow. If marketing can convincingly present strategies that promise long-term growth in cash flow, there is plenty of evidence that this will be rewarded by a rapid rise in the company's market value.

The lesson is that expectations are critically important. As Copeland, Koller and Murrin explain, a major challenge awaits the managers of companies that become publicly listed. They have to deal not only with the 'real' market but also now with the financial (or capital) market. At that point, they have to learn to manage expectations:

> If you create lots of value in the real market (by earning more than your cost of capital and growing fast) but don't do as well as investors expect, they will be disappointed. Your task as manager is to maximize the intrinsic value of the company and to properly manage the expectations of the financial market.

> Managing the expectations of the market is tricky. You don't want their expectations to be too high or too low. We have seen companies convince the market that they will deliver great performance and then not deliver on those promises. Not only does the share price drop when the market realizes that the company will not be able to deliver, but it may take years for the company to regain credibility with the market. On the other hand, if the market's expectations are too low and you have a low share price relative to the opportunities the company faces, you may be subject to a hostile takeover.[26]

Limitations of shareholder value analysis

The essence of the shareholder value approach is that managers should be evaluated on their ability to develop strategies that earn returns greater than their cost of capital. The advantages of this approach are that it maximises the value of the firm for investors and creates the cash flow to enable it to meet the claims of other stakeholders — employees, suppliers and the community. It is superior to traditional accounting approaches in that it avoids the short-termism inherent in targeting earnings, ROI or payback criteria. In an age where **intangibles** — brands, skills, customer and supplier relationships — are the primary assets, accounting or book value has little use for valuing businesses.

intangible assets: non-material assets such as technical expertise, brands, or patents

But, like any technique, managers need to be aware of the assumptions and approximations needed to apply shareholder value analysis to real-world problems. Incorrect assumptions and inadequate estimates of the required data can, and will, lead to poor forecasts of shareholder value and incorrect decisions. The main areas of sensitivity are the following:

- **Forecasting cash flows.** The key inputs to the analysis are forecast of sales growth, operating margins and investment requirements for at least five years ahead. These critically depend upon good judgments about the evolution of the market in the future and, in particular, the firm's ability to sustain a differential advantage. Such estimates can be far out due to biases on the part of the managers making them, inadequate knowledge of customers and competitors, and unpredictable events. Nevertheless omnipotence is not a prerequisite for the use of scientific methods. In addition, most well-managed companies have made five-year forecasts of sales, profits and cash flow as part of their annual planning process — so shareholder value analysis does not require any new data.

- **Cost of capital.** Calculating shareholder value requires discounting the cash flow stream of each business unit by the weighted average costs of debt and equity. Each business unit within the company will have its own cost of capital depending on its risk exposure and the amount of debt needed to finance the assets of the business. Estimating the cost of capital is not easy and different estimates will give different present values. Of particular difficulty is estimating the unit's risk premium. It is generally difficult to find similar publicly quoted companies to estimate share price volatility so indirect weighting systems are often used. These subjective indices mean that the cost of capital figures used can easily be a percentage point or two out.

- **Estimates of continuing or terminal value.** Shareholder value calculations split the estimation into two components: the present value of cash flows during the planning period and a terminal value which is the present value of the cash flows that occur after the planning period. For growth businesses the overwhelming proportion of value arises in the terminal value. Unfortunately, it is difficult to be too confident about this value. As we have seen there are a variety of methods for coming up with an answer, including the perpetuity approach, perpetuity with inflation, and the market value multiple approach. However, each can give very different estimates of terminal value. In the end, the choice is a matter of judgment.

- **The baseline.** As noted earlier, the value created by a strategy is calculated by estimating the shareholder value if the strategy is employed, and then deducting from it a baseline shareholder value. The baseline or pre-strategy shareholder value is normally taken to be the current value of the business assuming no additional value is created or destroyed. This conveniently allows the present value of the business to be estimated by the perpetuity method of dividing net operating profit by the cost of capital. But this assumption that profitability will be maintained and any new investment will earn its cost of capital can be unrealistic. As the industry matures, excess capacity and competition will often put pressures on profits, leading to an erosion rather than a maintenance of value. In this case the value created by the strategy will be underestimated unless a more realistic baseline value is used. In some cases, where the baseline strategy amounts to harvesting the business, the pre-strategy value might be the business's liquidation value.

- **Options for growth.** If a business is to be sustainable it needs to develop options which will allow it to explore new growth opportunities. Option theory plays a major role in capital markets, but until recently it was not used in business decision making. An option is the purchase of an opportunity, but not a requirement, to go ahead with an investment at a later date. Innovative companies make many decisions like this. A European retailer makes a small acquisition in Australia to learn about the market before deciding whether to make a major commitment. Faced with technical and market uncertainties about its new product, a company can decide whether or not to build a $50 million new plant, or alternatively, it could build a $5 million pilot plant and then build the factory in a year's time if it looks successful. The $5 million investment represents the purchase of an option and may be a sound investment if uncertainty is high. Shareholder value analysis cannot directly handle options. If managers did not use this type of experimentation, then innovation and growth would certainly be deterred. Fortunately, most companies seem to make option decisions on a judgmental basis outside the normal capital appraisal frameworks. More recently, decision theory and financial options theory have been extended to begin to give insights on how to evaluate these types of problems.[27] Options are unquestionably important and the high valuations the financial markets give to many growth companies clearly reflects the value being attached to the firm's options.

- **Stock market expectations.** Shareholder value analysis assumes that if a strategy increases the implied value per share, this will be reflected in an increase in the actual or market share price. In other words, shareholder returns are a function of discounting future cash flows to their net present value. There is ample evidence that this is true in general. Earnings per share have virtually zero correlation with share price movements over time, while discounted cash flows explain around 80 per cent of price changes.

  Nevertheless, as noted earlier in the discussion of managing expectations, in the short term there can be significant discrepancies. Actual share prices are determined by investors' expectations; implied values are determined by the expectations of managers. These may differ on account of differences in the information available to investors and to differences in judgments about the implications of the information. To reduce these differences, it is important for the board to test the strategic and marketing assumptions behind their managers' forecasts. It is also important that they effectively communicate to the market the long-term rationale behind their strategies. The opening case suggests that the Foster's Group had not done this very well.

SVA and non-publicly listed companies

The discussion in this book focuses on publicly listed companies. It would be incorrect, however, to assume that SVA cannot be used by private companies. The situation becomes more complex but techniques are available for estimating the cost of capital when market prices for the company's stock are not observable.[28] These techniques, which essentially involve the use of a proxy capital structure based on an analysis of what the company would look like if it were publicly listed, are also relevant for divisions within a publicly listed company. With the latter, one technique that can be used is the so-called 'pure-play approach'. This involves an examination of a group of publicly traded companies that compete in a single line of business similar to that of the division under analysis. Variations of this approach will also need to be used by publicly listed companies contemplating entering a new line of business, different to what they presently do. In such a situation, the company's existing cost of capital is irrelevant. Modifications can also be made to SVA techniques — again through the use of proxies — enabling them to be employed by regulated companies and government businesses.

It also needs to be said that, even when there are severe technical challenges to the use of shareholder value metrics, organisations will always benefit from an adherence to the philosophical underpinnings of SVA: the imperative of focusing on value creation; the importance of generating cash flow; the use of an opportunity cost approach in which the return on invested capital is compared with what could be earned if the capital were invested elsewhere; the need to understand the drivers of value; the need to have a forward-looking and long-term approach to value creation and performance, rather than a backward-looking and short-term perspective; the adoption of an outsider's perspective of what happens within the organisation; and the realisation that marketing initiatives should be analysed, not in terms of expenses, but as investments that contribute to long-term value creation.

Why shareholder value is superior to accounting-based performance measures

In spite of the acceptance, in principle, that the task of management is to maximise returns for shareholders, most companies and fund managers still have not adopted value-based management. Accounting earnings rather than cash flows still form the basis for evaluating performance and valuing businesses. The financial press and analysts' reports consistently focus on short-term earnings, earnings per share and price/earnings ratios. Despite the clear contrary evidence, the belief still persists that good earnings growth will lead to a parallel growth in the market value of the company's shares. Similarly, managers erroneously believe that if they concentrate on improving return on investment (earnings divided by assets) and return on equity (earnings divided by the book value of shareholder funds), the share price will automatically follow.

Problems with earnings

There are four reasons why earnings are a poor measure of performance compared to changes in shareholder value:

1. First, unlike cash flow, which underpins SVA, accounting earnings are arbitrary and easily manipulated by management. The demise of the giant US corporation, Enron, is the most notorious example in recent times of how misleading earnings figures can be. Different, equally acceptable, accounting methods lead to quite different earnings figures. Prominent examples include alternative ways to compute the cost of goods sold (LIFO versus FIFO), different methods of depreciating assets, and the various choices in accounting for mergers and acquisitions. Complaints have arisen in the United States that companies are using whatever definition of earnings that will put their performance in the best possible light: choices include net income (sometimes called reported earnings), operating earnings, core earnings, pro forma earnings, adjusted earnings and EBITDA (earnings before interest, taxes, depreciation and amortisation).[29] Different countries have different accounting regulations too, so international companies are frequently quoting different earnings on different stock markets. For example, SmithKline Beecham recently reported its profits as £130 million in the UK but only £90 million in the USA. Not surprisingly, the flexibility of reporting procedures gives management ample opportunity to manipulate reported earnings for their own purposes — opportunities which are commonly taken.[30] But however managers choose to report profits, none of their manipulations or adjustments have any effect on the company's cash flow or economic value. While profits are an opinion, cash is a fact.

2. Second, unlike cash flow, accounting profits exclude investments. A growing business will invariably have to invest more in working and fixed capital, so that it could easily have positive earnings, but cash could be draining away. On the other hand, depreciation is deducted in the calculation of earnings even though it does not involve any cash outlay. So for a mature business with assets still being depreciated, earnings could well understate cash flows.

3. Third, earnings ignore the time value of money. This means that even consistent earnings growth can reduce shareholder returns. The economic value of any investment is the discounted value of the anticipated cash flows. The discounting procedure recognises that money has a time value: money today is worth more to investors than a money return tomorrow. Consequently, shareholder value will increase only if the company earns a return on the new investment that exceeds the cost of capital used in the discounting process. Taking a simple example, suppose a company has current earnings (and cash flow) of $20 million and a cost of capital of 10 per cent. It decides to invest $25 million to increase the future levels of earnings by 10 per cent. Unfortunately, while profits and cash flow rise by an agreeable $2 million, the shareholder value of the company falls. This is because when the increased annual cash flow is discounted, it is valued at only $20 million, or $5 million less than the original investment. Shareholders could have done better investing the money themselves elsewhere.

4. Fourth, and perhaps most crucial from a strategic viewpoint, is that profits produce a short-term managerial focus. Rising earnings can easily disguise a decline in shareholder value because earnings ignore the future implications of current activities. For example, earnings can quickly be boosted by cutting advertising or customer service levels. In the short run this is beneficial, but in the long run it will erode the company's market share, future earnings and shareholder value. Similarly, many activities that lower short-term earnings such as investing in brands and building customer relationships can increase long-term cash flows and shareholder value. The focus on short-term earnings discourages growth-oriented strategies that increase long-term competitiveness and shareholder value. Taking all these problems into account, it is not surprising that there is little or no statistical correlation between earnings per share growth and total shareholder return as measured by dividends and share price appreciation.

Problems with return on investment

Seeking to link earnings to levels of investment, managers routinely measure performance by looking at return on assets (ROA) and return on equity (ROE). The former tends to be used at the business unit level, the latter at the corporate level. Unfortunately, since both use earnings in the numerator, they are subject to all the previous weaknesses, plus some additional ones.

The main new problem is that assets are valued in an equally arbitrary way to earnings. Different, but equally valid, depreciation procedures or capitalisation policies will lead to different valuations of both assets and equity. With today's information-age companies the implications of the capitalisation problem are striking. The growing importance of knowledge-based companies makes intangible assets far larger than physical assets. However, these intangible assets such as brand names, patents, R&D, training and customer loyalty, do not normally appear on the balance sheet. One implication is that it is impossible to use ROA or ROE to evaluate different types of company. For example, pharmaceutical companies and businesses with strong brands would have higher ROAs than traditional manufacturing businesses even if their economic returns were identical, because the assets of the former do not appear in the denominator. As companies gradually invest more in knowledge and less in physical assets, it also makes comparing a company's ROA over time a dubious indication of performance.

Studies show that ROA generally overstates the true return on investment.[31] The bias is greater for mature companies. Mature companies will often have higher ROAs than growth companies because depreciation policies and inflation will have tended to lower the net book value of their assets. Such figures then often deter management from moving away from declining businesses because they wrongly believe that ROA is correlated with value. Only when SVA is conducted using estimates of future cash flows can it be seen that the growth businesses are often immensely more valuable, and that there is often an inverse correlation between ROA and shareholder value added.

Turning to return on equity, this has all the above problems plus another one. ROE is calculated as ROA factored by gearing — the proportion of assets financed by debt rather than equity. Provided that it earns more than the cost of borrowing, more debt increases the ROE. Even if the amount of debt exceeds the optimal level, further borrowings increase ROE even while the value of the company declines due to increased financial risk.

Managers and analysts use accounting earnings presumably because they are easy to calculate. But earnings, and all the various valuation measures (P/E ratios, earnings per share) and performance standards (ROI, ROA, ROE) which utilise them, are subject to fundamental practical, conceptual and empirical weaknesses. Practically, their measurement is arbitrary and subjective. Conceptually, they are inappropriate because they do not measure changes in value. Earnings are the result of past decisions; value changes are based on future cash flows. Empirically, earnings-based measures do not predict changes in the returns accruing to shareholders. Shareholder value analysis works because it overcomes all three weaknesses. It is fact based, conceptually robust and highly predictive of actual changes in the market value of businesses. And, unlike accounting numbers, shareholder value calculations are unaffected by the shift from industrial companies to knowledge-based companies built around intangible assets.

Summary

1. Shareholder value is an evaluative tool, and its use by management indicates a commitment to measuring performance in a transparent and consistent manner.

2. The task of marketing strategy is to increase the value of the business for its shareholders. This is achieved by increasing the sum of all its anticipated future free cash flows, adjusted by a discount rate known as the cost of capital.

3. There are two common approaches to valuing marketing strategies: the cash flow method and the economic value-added method. Both will produce the same result given similar assumptions. Using either method, it is crucial to remember that looking at one year's figures can be highly misleading. Value creation is a long-term phenomenon. Marketing strategies, in particular, can only be valued properly after the long-term cash flow is properly projected.

4. Whether the cash flow or economic value-added methods are used, shareholder value analysis comprises five main steps: analyse historical performance; estimate the cost of capital; develop estimates of performance during the explicit forecast period; estimate continuing value (the cash flow generated during the post-forecast period); and calculate enterprise value, compare it to the estimate of baseline (pre-strategy) shareholder value, and interpret the results.

5. One of the major challenges of publicly listed organisations is to manage the expectations of investors. Effective communication of the nature of, and rationale for, the company's long-term strategies is critical.

6. Shareholder value analysis, and its philosophical underpinnings, are just as relevant for private companies and government businesses as they are for publicly listed companies, but do require the use of proxy capital structures.

7. Like any analytical method, the results depend upon the accuracy of the information used. In particular, it requires good judgments about future sales, operating margins and investment requirements. However, such judgments are inevitably required from managers responsible for strategic

decisions. The other particular inputs required from the analysis are estimates of the cost of capital and the continuing value of the business. Managers should always attempt to analyse uncertainty, rather than rely solely on gut feeling or instinct.

8. While the limitations of shareholder value analysis (SVA) should be acknowledged, SVA is superior to accounting-based measures of performance. Yet, organisations persist with measures such as earnings and return on investment as the principal basis for evaluating performance and valuing businesses.

key terms

beta coefficient, p. 48	intangible assets, p. 64
capital structure, p. 47	market-to-book (M/B) ratio, p. 54
cash flow return on investment (CFROI), p. 57	market value added (MVA), p. 57
	net present value (NPV), p. 46
continuing value, p. 51	NOPAT, p. 44
cost of capital, p. 45	perpetuity, p. 53
differential advantage, p. 51	price/earnings (P/E) ratio, p. 54
discounted cash flow (DCF), p. 46	return spread, p. 60
enterprise value, p. 57	shareholder value, p. 57
explicit forecast period, p. 50	weighted average cost of capital (WACC), p. 47
fixed capital, p. 52	
free cash flow, p. 51	working capital, p. 52

review questions

1. Describe the principles of shareholder value analysis.
2. How can shareholder value be used to evaluate alternative marketing strategies?
3. How could a business unit marketing manager use shareholder analysis to demonstrate to the board the effectiveness of his or her marketing strategy?
4. What are the main assumptions required that could lead to poor estimates of the shareholder value added by a marketing strategy?
5. What are the similarities and differences between the free cash flow and economic value-added methods of determining shareholder value added?
6. What are the major limitations of shareholder value analysis?
7. Why is shareholder value superior to accounting-based measures of performance and valuation?

discussion questions

1. Relying on single-year measures of performance is seriously misleading. Discuss.
2. Should the pay of chief executives be linked to long-run performance?
3. Why is it necessary, in shareholder value analysis, to divide the future into two discrete periods?
4. What are the philsophical underpinnings of shareholder value analysis?
5. Why do so many businesses persist with accounting-based measures of performance?

debate | questions

1. Should non-profit organisations adopt a shareholder value approach?
2. Is it impossible to manage the expectations of investors?
3. In determining which strategies to implement, is there always an important role for reliance on gut feelings?
4. Does the fact that the future is uncertain make nonsense of forecasts?
5. Does shareholder value analysis offer anything relevant or useful to those working in the public sector?

case study | The wealth makers

See how the mighty have fallen. Thanks to their sheer size, Telstra and News Corporation remain in first and second place on the annual list of market value added (MVA) compiled by Stern Stewart. But both groups lost ground sharply during 2000–2001.

MVA is a company's stockmarket capitalisation, minus its capital (including retained profit and other surpluses) and borrowings. In other words, it is a measure of how much the market valued a company over and above the funds employed — at 30 June 2001, in the case of the Stern Stewart list.

Investors downgraded Telstra because of the global slump in the telecommunications industry. News Corporation fell as investors reconsidered its prospects for earning growth ...

Stern Stewart's second measure of a company's performance, EVA®, is a company's latest after-tax annual earnings, minus the cost of capital appropriate to its industry. Profit is adjusted in various ways, such as excluding capital write-offs and goodwill amortisation. Stern Stewart says that companies should not get away with writing off their mistakes. Negative EVA is not necessarily bad; some companies with a strong MVA result have negative EVA because the market expects strong future growth.

Another Stern Stewart measure, future growth value (FGV®), suggests how much a company's market value reflects investors' expectations of growth. The calculation first determines what the company would be worth if its present net profit continued indefinitely, discounted at the company's cost of capital. The difference between that and MVA is what investors are paying for growth.

Telstra improved its EVA slightly during 2000–01, but the market's expectations of growth nosedived, as shown by the lower FGV. News Corporation performed even worse. Its EVA was already in negative territory in 1999–2000, but it went much lower during 2000–2001. FGV fell as investors turned away from media stocks ...

The mining group Rio Tinto had a strong year in terms of MVA ... Stern Stewart says: 'Rio Tinto was the greatest MVA wealth creator in 2000–2001, thanks to long-term capital discipline and strong growth in EVA, up by almost $1 billion in 2001.' ...

As a group, the banks were outstanding. Stern Stewart says: 'The big four created $22 billion in shareholder wealth (MVA) in the 2001 financial year and banks in total added $26 billion. The total 150 companies on the list increased MVA by only $11 billion. In other words, excluding the four banks, total MVA would have fallen by $11 billion.' ...

In aggregate, telecommunications companies recorded the biggest fall in MVA, at $31 billion ... Not far behind telecommunications, media companies dropped $30 billion in aggregate MVA ... Retail stocks added $7.4 billion MVA in aggregate during 2000–2001 ... Health and biotechnology companies on the list had an aggregate increase in MVA of $4.8 billion ... Alcohol was another strong sector adding $3.7 billion in aggregate MVA ...

In the lower reaches of Stern Stewart's rankings — in the territory of minus MVA — unfashionable industries predominate. The two listed cinema stocks, Amalgamated Holdings and Village Roadshow, sank deeper. Other struggling companies in out-of-favour industries included Smorgon Steel, Orica and Caltex.

(continued)

Australia's biggest and brightest

MVA RANK 2001	COMPANY	MARKET VALUE ADDED ($M) 2001	MARKET VALUE ADDED ($M) 2000	ECONOMIC VALUE ADDED ($M) 2001	ECONOMIC VALUE ADDED ($M) 2000	FUTURE GROWTH VALUE ($M) 2001
1	Telstra	50 880	71 802	2 603	2 331	27 401
2	News Corporation	37 018	62 203	−4 432	−1 900	74 137
3	Rio Tinto	29 369	19 521	−465	−1 372	32 172
4	National Australia Bank	29 129	21 253	664	336	24 174
5	Commonwealth Bank	21 562	15 456	−227	1 099	23 809
6	BHP Billiton	16 480	15 307	271	−1 007	14 322
7	ANZ Banking Group	14 544	8 980	49	144	14 230
8	Westpac	13 764	11 439	425	111	10 393
9	Woolworths	10 441	5 481	373	291	4 480
10	Wesfarmers	9 652	2 278	29	22	9 382
11	Optus	8 313	13 719	−691	−236	13 254
12	Woodside Petroleum	8 199	6 443	937	140	−459
13	Brambles	8 185	9 081	−85	85	8 996
14	CSL	6 181	4 099	38	−1	5 773
15	Macquarie Bank	5 875	3 851	−18	60	5 988
16	WMC	5 468	3 622	83	−692	4 945
17	Coles Myer	4 626	4 558	−23	137	4 997
18	Foster's Group	3 971	2 901	197	79	1 400
19	Harvey Norman	3 929	3 401	41	63	3 483

Source: Stern Stewart & Co. EVA & FGV (Future Growth Value) are registered trademarks of Stern Stewart & Co.

Source: Extracts from Philip Rennie, 'The Wealth Makers', *BRW*, 22–28 November 2001, pp. 68–73.

Questions

1. How has shareholder value been measured? What further measures could be used to more accurately determine value?
2. Which of the top performing companies are likely to continue adding value for shareholders? Assume that each company is pursuing new market opportunities. How does this affect EVA®, MVA and FGV®?
3. Compare EVA between 2000 and 2001. Which companies created more value and what factors possibly contributed to this increase?

end notes

1. The five steps are based on those outlined in Tom Copeland, Tim Koller and Jack Murrin, *Valuation: Measuring and Managing the Value of Companies*, 3rd edn, New York: John Wiley & Sons, 2000. See chapters 9–13.
2. Copeland, Koller and Murrin, *op. cit.*, p. 157.
3. Copeland, Koller and Murrin, *op. cit.*, p. 164.
4. Copeland, Koller and Murrin, *op. cit.*, pp. 165–6.
5. See Andrew Black, Philip Wright with John Davies, *In Search of Shareholder Value*, 2nd edn, London: Prentice Hall, 2001, pp. 36–40, for a comparison and assessment of the two techniques.
6. 'Is Beta a useful risk meter?', *Shares*, January 2002.
7. For an introduction to the debate, see Black and Wright with Bachman, *op. cit.*, pp. 32–4, and S. David Young and Stephen F. O'Byrne, *EVA and Value-based Management: A Practical Guide to Implementation*, New York: McGraw-Hill, 2001, pp. 169–76.
8. Black and Wright, *op. cit.*, p. 44; italics in original.
9. Copeland, Koller and Murrin, *op. cit.*, p. 235.
10. George Day and Liam Fahey, Valuing marketing strategies, *Journal of Marketing*, **52** (July), 1988, p. 47.
11. Hugh Courtney, *20/20 Foresight: Crafting Strategy in an Uncertain World*, Boston: Harvard Business School Press, 2001.
12. For a review of these tools, see Courtney, *op. cit.*, especially chapter 6 and the appendix.
13. For a comprehensive account of the sources of competitive advantage see John Kay, *Foundations of Corporate Success*, Oxford: Oxford University Press, 1993.
14. Young and O'Byrne, *op.cit.*, p. 24.
15. Alfred Rappaport, *Creating Shareholder Value*, 2nd edn, New York: Free Press, 1998, p. 43.
16. For a detailed discussion see Copeland, Koller and Murrin, *op. cit.*, pp. 267–88.
17. Copeland, Koller and Murrin, *op. cit.*, p. 267.
18. Copeland, Koller and Murrin, *op. cit.*, p. 293.
19. Copeland, Koller and Murrin, *op. cit.*, p. 291.
20. G. Bennett Stewart III, *The Quest for Value*, New York: HarperCollins, 1991. See also Joel M. Stern and John S. Shiely with Irwin Ross, *The EVA Challenge: Implementing Value-added Change in an Organization*, New York: John Wiley & Sons, 2001, and Young and O'Byrne, *op.cit.*
21. Bartley J. Madden, *CFROI Valuation: A Total System Approach to Valuing the Firm*, Oxford: Butterworth-Heinemann, 1999.
22. Rappaport, *op. cit.*
23. Young and O'Byrne, *EVA and Value-based Management*, pp. 382–3.
24. Rappaport, *op. cit.*, p. 33.
25. On this equivalence see Rappaport, *op. cit.*, pp. 121–8; G. Bennett Stewart III, 'EVA: Fact and fantasy', *Journal of Applied Corporate Finance*, Summer 1994, p. 78.
26. Copeland, Koller and Murrin, *op. cit.*, pp. 52–3.
27. For an introduction to option theory in business see Thomas E. Copeland and Philip T. Keenan, 'How much is flexibility worth?', *McKinsey Quarterly*, no. 2, 1998, pp. 38–49.
28. For an overview of these techniques, see Michael C. Erhardt, *The Search for Value: Measuring the Company's Cost of Capital*, Boston: Harvard Business School Press, 1994.
29. 'Confused about earnings?', *Business Week*, 26 November 2001.
30. Terry Smith, *Accounting for Growth: Stripping the Camouflage from Company Accounts*, 2nd edn, London: Century, 1996.
31. Rappaport, *op. cit.*

Value drivers

By the time you have completed this chapter, you will be able to:

- identify the financial, marketing and organisational value drivers of the business
- understand how the three sets of value drivers relate to each other
- define marketing in terms of shareholder value
- understand how delivering value to customers is the basis for creating shareholder value
- explain the significance of the firm's differential advantage
- understand the increasing importance of measures of customer satisfaction, loyalty and trust in modern businesses
- describe the essential requirements for delivering customer value.

scene setter

The customer relationship management challenge for Standard Chartered Bank

Standard Chartered Bank (SCB) of Hong Kong took a conscious decision in 1994 to move away from its traditional product focus and to become committed instead to enhancing the customer's experience. 'We wanted to differentiate ourselves much more around understanding our customers and in the way we service them,' says Steven Parker, head of Customer Sales and Services. Having decided to get close to its customers, SCB came to an embarrassing realisation. It did not even know whether some of its customers were men or women — such was the quality of the information that the bank possessed.

Standard Chartered defines its approach to customer relationship management (CRM) as 'actively managing the customer relationship over time, in a coordinated way across products and channels, in order to increase benefits to the customer, and to increase profits for the bank.' A central component of becoming customer-focused for Standard Chartered has been discovering what customers hope to achieve, and analysing their banking patterns and preferences. Only by finding this basic information has it been able to take a needs-based approach to servicing its customers.

For example, a customer may have a preference for self-service and thus be informed of Internet banking services as opposed to traditional banking services. The focus is on the need and how a differentiated product may be offered to fulfil this need. The aim, according to Parker, is about changing the whole process to make it more customer oriented and also modifying the marketing process so as to better understand customer segments and customer needs.

One of the major challenges that the bank confronted with the implementation of CRM was changing the mindset of staff. As CRM is mainly a mindset, the emphasis proposed by the bank was to 'think customer, think customer experience, not just a product approach.' In order to engrain CRM into the culture of the organisation, various approaches were adopted. Incentive programs were introduced for staff, incorporating commission rewards. In addition to this, regular training sessions were held to ensure that the importance of the customer was maintained.

The bank says that the benefits from implementing CRM include improved sales and marketing effectiveness (including improved share of wallet, product utilisation and customer retention). There has been an improvement also in operational efficiency (including better coordination of resources across the businesses and better resource allocation through value/profit-based targets and metrics). Furthermore, the bank now offers differentiated customer packages that better serve the needs of their clients and build a stronger relationship. For example, the company was able to assign personal relationship managers to banking clients who maintain daily deposits greater than HK$8000. This advanced the notion of the bank's attentiveness, which in turn reinforced loyalty. Different banking plan options were offered to clients according to their various needs.

Source: Adapted from Grace Onntai Tan, 'CRM are you a boy or a girl?', BusinessOnline, January 2002, www.bolweb.com.

Introduction

The challenge for managers is less that of knowing about the technicalities of how to calculate shareholder value and more that of understanding what drives its creation. Accordingly, this chapter presents a framework that outlines and analyses the main drivers of shareholder value. The concepts discussed here will be referred to throughout the remainder of this book. Having introduced in chapter 1 the notion of value-based marketing and examined there the synergistic relationship between marketing and shareholder value, and having explained in chapter 2 just what shareholder value analysis involves, the final building block for fully appreciating the discussion in parts 2 and 3 of this book is to make clear how the various drivers of shareholder value can be categorised and to show how they relate to each other.

For those wary of the material covered in chapter 2, it needs to be stressed that value-based marketing is not primarily about numbers and making complex calculations. It consists of three main elements. First, it is a set of beliefs about the objectives of marketing. The basic belief is that the primary task of marketing is to develop strategies that will maximise returns for shareholders. Second, it is a set of principles for choosing marketing strategies and making marketing decisions that are consistent with these beliefs. These principles are based on estimating the future cash flow associated with a strategy to calculate the shareholder value added. Finally, it is a set of processes that ensure that marketing develops, selects and implements a strategy that is consistent with these beliefs and principles. To draw on the definition of value-based marketing offered in chapter 1, the ultimate aim is to build relationships of trust with high-valued customers and to create a sustainable differential advantage.

The processes that underpin the achievement of this aim concern the management of the financial, marketing and organisational value drivers of the business. The *financial value drivers* are those key ratios that have the most significant impact on shareholder value: the overall level of cash flow, as well as the timing, duration and riskiness of cash flow. The *marketing value drivers* are the customer-oriented strategies necessary to drive improvement in the financial ratios. They are the marketing assets the firm has developed: its marketing knowledge, its brands, the loyalty of its customers and its strategic relationships with channel partners. The *organisational value drivers* are the core capabilities, systems, skills, motivation and leadership styles needed to create and implement the shareholder value orientation in the business.

This is a long chapter composed of three discrete sections devoted to each of the three sets of value drivers, and you can pursue each of the sections separately. They are presented here in one chapter because collectively they constitute a single framework. This is illustrated in figure 3.1, which shows each of the value drivers as being linked in a hierarchical fashion. The logic of figure 3.1 is that the financial value drivers are heavily influenced by a set of marketing value drivers, which in turn are embedded within a collection of organisational value drivers.

Section 1 | Financial value drivers

Marketing is central to creating shareholder value. The shareholder value approach used to evaluate marketing strategies employs exactly the same model as investors use to value shares. A marketing strategy makes sense if it is likely to enhance the value of the business. The approach starts with the recognition that the economic value of a business, like any other asset, is determined by discounting forecast cash flow by the cost of capital. A marketing strategy, then, needs to demonstrate that it can increase this discounted cash flow.

Figure 3.1 The drivers of value in a business

The first step in applying the model is to identify the financial value drivers that determine cash flow. As we shall see, it is not just the level of cash flow that is important but also its timing, duration and riskiness. Cash flow that occurs early is worth more than that occurring later, because money is discounted. Marketing strategies that create enduring cash flows — perhaps by building strong brands — are worth more than strategies that promote only short-term gains. Finally, marketing strategies that are very risky are worth less, because the cash flows they are expected to create are discounted with a higher cost of capital. In other words, to invest in a high-risk marketing strategy, investors will want the expectation of higher cash flow.

To achieve their financial objectives, managers need strategies. Many executives, in embracing shareholder value, have not understood that marketing is essential to achieve financial performance. One of the aims of this section is to make clear that marketing crucially influences each of the financial value drivers that determine shareholder value. As noted above, there are four such drivers:

1. **Anticipated level of operating cash flow.** The greater the future free cash flow anticipated, the more will be available for distribution to shareholders and the greater the market value of the business.

2. **Anticipated timing of cash flow.** Because cash received today is worth more than cash received tomorrow, the speed with which markets are penetrated and cash flow generated positively influences value. This is taken into account through the use of a discount rate.

3. **Anticipated sustainability of cash flow.** The more lasting the cash flow, the greater the value created. This depends upon the durability of the firm's differential advantage and the perceived growth options it has available. The long-term ability to sustain positive free cash flow should be reflected in the firm's continuing value figure.

4. **Anticipated riskiness of future cash flow.** The greater the perceived volatility and vulnerability of the firm's cash flow, the higher the cost of capital used to discount the return. More predictable cash flows have a higher value.

Level of operating cash flow

The most fundamental determinant of shareholder value is the anticipated level of free cash flow. This, in turn, is influenced by three things: sales growth, the net operating profit margin after tax (NOPAT), and the level of investment (see figure 3.2).

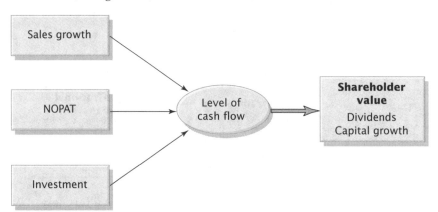

Figure 3.2 Determinants of the level of operating cash flow

Sales growth

The most important way of increasing the level of cash flow and shareholder value is via sales growth. After all, additional cash flow is simply growth less the additional cost and investment to achieve it — that is,

Additional cash flow = Sales growth − (Added costs + Investment)

As long as the added sales are profitable, and do not require disproportionate investment, cash flow rises. Of course, it is possible in the short run to increase cash flow without growth, by cutting costs and investment. However, such policies are one-off and will often lead to a decline in cash flow in the years ahead. Investors usually see through such policies in their valuations of companies.

Growth brings other benefits. Often it enables the business to gain economies of scale. This means it will be able to lower unit costs and increase the utilisation of its investment, further increasing cash flow. In a new market it may well pay to invest in growth even though the business is not yet profitable and additional sales do not increase cash flow. In many of today's growth markets, it is important to obtain a critical mass of customers to achieve profitability. Unless it has critical mass, the business may not have the level of sales to secure adequate distribution or to spread its overheads over a sufficient volume to have a viable unit cost structure. Again, whether this type of market penetration strategy makes sense depends upon carefully forecasting cash flows over a long period ahead.

Growing companies also make it easier to attract and retain staff. Able people know that growing companies offer more security and opportunities for advancement. In later chapters we examine the task of developing successful growth strategies. Successful growth strategies depend upon building marketing assets. These intangible assets include marketing expertise inside the business that provides the knowledge base to recognise growth opportunities. They also include brands that customers have confidence in. Loyal customers are additional marketing assets that facilitate higher growth. Finally, strategic partnerships with other businesses enhance growth opportunities by providing additional resources and growth ideas.

Net operating profit margin after tax

The amount generated for net investment and dividends is not determined by sales growth alone but rather by the balance after costs have been deducted. The net operating profit margin after tax (NOPAT) measures this relationship. Improving NOPAT has a crucial impact on shareholder value. There are three ways in which marketing can improve the operating margin:

1. **Higher prices.** If the Beta Company has a NOPAT of 7 per cent, then if it could increase its average prices by as little as 5 per cent without losing volume, after-tax profits would rise by 50 per cent.[1] Even if it lost 5 per cent of its volume to competition as a result of this price increase, NOPAT would still increase by 20 per cent.[2] In chapter 8 we explore a variety of marketing strategies for raising prices without losing significant volume. These include developing strong brands, demonstrating value to customers, segmenting customers by price sensitivity, multibranding and creating exit barriers. But by far the most effective marketing strategy in the long run is innovation — developing new products which meet customer needs better than the alternatives currently on the market.

2. **Cost decreases.** With global competition and increasing information available to customers, all companies are aware of the importance of becoming low-cost suppliers. With most businesses having pre-tax operating margins of 10 per cent or less, small cost cuts have disproportionate effects on the bottom line. Today's efforts to cut costs include new approaches to more effective supply-chain management, business process reengineering, outsourcing and the more effective use of marketing resources.[3]

3. **Volume growth.** Volume growth tends to improve the operating margin because overhead costs do not increase proportionately. In the short run the effect can be very big. For example, suppose a company with spare capacity increases sales by 30 per cent. If half its costs were variable —

bought in materials, components and variable labour — then a current NOPAT of 7 per cent would be doubled to 14 per cent.[4] Over the long run, however, most costs are variable to a greater or lesser extent: capacity has to be increased, marketing and administrative overheads rise and the business needs to spend more on R&D to support its broader line of business. Nevertheless, the effect of market-led growth on the operating margin is generally positive. While bigger companies do have higher overheads in absolute terms, as a percentage of sales overheads are usually lower. Economies of scale normally occur across a broad area of costs.

Investment

tangible assets:
material assets such as factories, equipment, machinery and stocks

intangible assets:
non-material assets such as technical expertise, brands or patents

Managers invest in **tangible assets** like equipment and stocks, and also in **intangible assets** such as brands, customer relationships, market research and training. Reducing investment produces an immediate jump in cash flow, but in the long run such actions can be extremely counterproductive. The purpose of investment is to increase long-run growth and cash flow. The golden rule is that investment creates value if the net present value of the cash flow is positive. Or, expressing it in equivalent economic profit terms, investment creates value if the return on the investment exceeds the cost of capital.

As long as the return on new investment exceeds the cost of capital, investment increases shareholder value. This is illustrated in table 3.1. Here, a company earns a return on new investment of 20 per cent. Under the first scenario it invests 25 per cent of its profits; under the second it invests 35 per cent. With the conservative investment strategy, it has a higher cash flow over the first 8 years and, indeed, over the whole of the 10-year planning period, the present value of the forecast cash flow is greater. Under the high-investment strategy, however, annual cash flow overtakes in year 9, and then the lead continually widens. For the reader who cares to work out the result on a spreadsheet, assuming an 11 per cent cost of capital, the high investment strategy generates a significantly greater shareholder value. This is reflected in the greater continuing value figure in year 10.[5]

Table 3.1 Cash flow projections with high and low investment levels

	25% INVESTMENT RATE			35% INVESTMENT RATE		
YEAR	NOPAT	INVESTMENT	CASH FLOW	NOPAT	INVESTMENT	CASH FLOW
1	100.0	25.0	75.0	100.0	35.0	65.0
2	105.0	26.3	78.8	107.0	37.5	69.6
3	110.3	27.6	82.7	114.5	40.1	74.4
4	115.8	28.9	86.8	122.5	42.9	79.6
5	121.6	30.4	91.2	131.1	45.9	85.2
6	127.6	31.9	95.7	140.3	49.1	91.2
7	134.0	33.5	100.5	150.1	52.5	97.5
8	140.7	35.2	105.5	160.6	56.2	104.4
9	147.7	36.9	110.8	171.8	60.1	111.7
10	155.1	38.8	116.3	183.8	64.3	119.5

Managers need to avoid wasteful investment in both tangible and intangible assets. However, as the example illustrates, not investing sufficiently in profitable marketing opportunities is equally value destroying.

The **threshold margin** is a useful tool for marketing managers. It shows the relationship between the three influences on the level of cash flow: growth, margin and investment requirements. The threshold margin is the pre-tax operating profit margin necessary to finance value-creating growth. It is the minimum pre-tax operating profit margin on additional sales necessary to maintain shareholder value. It is calculated as:[6]

threshold margin:
the pre-tax operating profit margin necessary to finance value-creating growth

$$\text{Threshold margin} = \frac{(\text{Incremental investment rate}) \times (\text{Cost of capital})}{(1 + \text{Cost of capital})(1 - \text{tax rate})}$$

incremental investment rate:
management's assessment of the proportional increase in fixed and working capital required for each unit of additional sales

Using the example of Alpha Company mentioned in chapter 2 (see table 2.1), the **incremental investment rate** totals 40 per cent, the cost of capital is 10 per cent and the tax rate is 30 per cent. Substituting into the formula gives:

$$\text{Threshold margin} = \frac{40\% \times 10\%}{1.1 \times 0.7} = 5.2\%$$

If the additional growth that marketing is planning to generate gives an operating profit margin of over 5.2 per cent, then value is created. The threshold margin depends on the additional working and fixed capital necessary to finance growth, the cost of capital and the tax rate. The higher these are, the higher the threshold margin that is required on additional sales. This is illustrated below:

Threshold margins for varying rates of investment and costs of capital

COST OF CAPITAL (%)	INCREMENTAL INVESTMENT PER $ OF SALES (%)			
	30	40	50	60
8	3.2	4.2	5.3	6.3
10	3.9	5.2	6.5	7.8
12	4.6	6.1	7.7	9.2

In Alpha's case, since managers believe they can get an operating margin of 10 per cent, then value is clearly going to be created. The difference between the actual (or expected) operating profit margin and the threshold margin is called the **threshold spread**. In Alpha's case the spread is 4.8 per cent (10 − 5.2). The size of the threshold spread is a key determinant of value creation. More specifically, the value created by a strategy in a given period, t, is given by the following equation:

threshold spread:
the difference between the actual (or expected) operating profit margin and threshold margin

$$\text{Shareholder value added} = \frac{(\text{Incremental sales in period } t)(\text{Threshold spread in } t)(1 - \text{tax rate})}{(\text{Cost of capital})(1 + \text{Cost of capital})^{t-1}}$$

For example, using the above equation on Alpha, and using the data in year 2 in table 2.1, we have:

$$\text{Shareholder value added} = \frac{\$13.44 \times 4.8\% \times (1 - 0.30)}{0.1 \times (1 + 0.1)^1} = \$4.11 \text{ million}$$

Timing of operating cash flow

Besides the amount of cash flow a marketing strategy generates, its timing also affects the value that is created. For example, if the cost of capital is 10 per cent, $10 million free cash flow received at the end of the first year of a product's launch has a value of $9.09 million; if it is not received until year 3, the value is only $7.51 million.

More and more companies are giving emphasis to rapid implementation and time to market, for these help to accelerate cash flows. The importance of timing is summarised by Young and O'Byrne, who point out that the ability of management to deliver positive cash flows on time is critical to value creation:

> Delays in project implementation caused by logistical, technical, or personnel problems can lead to delays in the receipt of future cashflows by several months or more. Even if all the cashflows materialize as anticipated, if they arrive later than originally expected, the present value of the cashflows declines. Sometimes, such delays are all that it takes to transform what would otherwise be a positive NPV [net present value] project into a value destroyer.[7]

Marketing strategies contribute in a variety of ways to accelerate cash flow, and in the process create shareholder value:

- **Faster new product development.** Many companies are redesigning their new product development processes to reduce the time from initial idea to final launch. Methods include using cross-functional teams, conducting development processes in parallel rather than in series and cutting out unnecessary steps.[8]
- **Accelerate market penetration.** Once a product is launched, it needs to gain quick market acceptance. Marketing can speed up this process through the skilful use of pre-marketing campaigns, promotions to gain early trial and leveraging the early adopters to obtain word-of-mouth advertising.
- **Creating network effects.** Many new products can gain from network externalities. The bigger the installed base (achieved or expected), the more desirable the product often becomes. Customers want products that will be standard in the market. For example, people bought VHS video recorders rather than Betamax or Philips 2000 because VHS had become the standard. Marketing can leverage network effects by such strategies as licensing and aggressively building the installed base.
- **Using strategic alliances.** Alliances can speed up market penetration by giving access to additional distribution. For example, in the United States McDonald's has an agreement to put its restaurants in new Wal-Mart stores. Alliances are particularly important in allowing companies to penetrate international markets more rapidly.
- **Leveraging brand assets.** There is evidence that consumers respond faster to marketing activities when they trust the brand. They are more willing to try new products under the umbrella of a familiar brand and they respond more to the advertising and promotions of familiar brands.

Sustainability of cash flow

The third determinant of value is the anticipated sustainability of the cash flow. This determines the assumptions used to calculate the continuing value of a marketing strategy. Some products are fads, achieving rapid prominence but then disappearing after a few seasons. They fail to create continuing value because of changes in fashion, new competitors or substitute products. On the other hand, some brands, like Holden, Victoria Bitter, Vegemite, Mortein or Golden Circle, last for generations. The share prices of the companies that own these brands reflect their high continuing values. Two factors affect the duration of the business's cash flow: the sustainability of its differential advantage and the options it creates.

Many companies come up with products that have a differential advantage, but do not succeed in creating enduring cash flow because the advantage is not sustainable. It is quickly copied by competitors, substitutes appear, or strong buyers use their power to squeeze the supplier's margins. A key task of marketing is to build barriers that enhance the sustainability of the differential advantage. Superior marketing expertise allows managers to track customers' needs and customer satisfaction, and then to build new sources of value for them. High customer satisfaction increases customer retention and loyalty, which are the most effective means of creating enduring cash flow. Chapters 7 and 9 will discuss how brand-building investments add layers of emotional values and confidence to the product, which make it more difficult for competitors to erode the customer franchise.

Investors' perception of the sustainability of cash flow is also affected by the options they believe the company possesses. Options are opportunities to enter new markets in the future. Investors may perceive options being created by technical research and development that the company is undertaking. This explains the high valuations attached to some biotechnology stocks. Options may also be seen in marketing ventures that the company is exploring in high growth markets. A loyal customer base also offers valuable options because such customers are also likely to be willing to try new products that the company may launch in the future. Of particular importance are strong brand names. Trusted brand names such as Virgin and Disney have been shown to offer options because they can be extended to cover different product areas to offer new growth opportunities. Nokia's share price reflects not just its continued leadership in mobile phone handsets but also investors' beliefs that it is well positioned to enter the emerging market for mobile Internet services. Companies that lack these marketing assets have future cash flows that are perceived to be less sustainable.

The risk attached to cash flow

The fourth factor determining value is the risk attached to forecasting future cash flows. Cash flows that are seen as particularly difficult to predict because of the volatility and vulnerability of the market in which the business is operating are penalised by a higher discount rate. Investors expect bigger rewards for investing in risky ventures than safe ones.

By reducing the volatility of the firm's cash flow, marketing can cut the firm's cost of capital and add value. The most effective way to reduce the volatility and vulnerability of a firm's cash flow is to increase customer satisfaction, loyalty and retention. High customer satisfaction and loyalty reduce the vulnerability of the business to attack from competitors. As we see in the next section on marketing value drivers, this also makes costs and investments more predictable. Loyal customers have lower and more foreseeable servicing costs. A high retention rate also means that less needs to be spent in chasing new customers.

Marketing has a portfolio of policies to increase customer satisfaction and loyalty. These include market research, initiatives to improve customer service, and loyalty programs. Programs to build channel partnerships also reduce the volatility of cash flow. Sharing information with distributors and suppliers can reduce unpredictable fluctuations in requirements, reduce stocks and lead to more predictable costs and investments.

Section 2 | Marketing value drivers

Shareholder value and its financial value drivers are the objectives of business but they are not the strategy. It is a big mistake to target these measures directly; instead managers need a strategy on how to influence them.

For example, in principle, raising prices increases the threshold margin spread. But if a company simply announces a 10 per cent price increase, it is likely to lose customers fast. Losing market share will erode profits, allow in new competitors and could fatally erode the long-term competitiveness of the business. Improving average prices and margins has to be achieved through a marketing strategy that might well include targeting different types of customers, introducing new products and changing the mode of distribution. Similarly, raising the return on capital employed is an objective, not a strategy. Achieving it requires a fundamental rethink about the effectiveness of how the company approaches the market. Simply targeting to cut capital employed will be counterproductive. It would be likely to lead to declining efficiency, eroding service levels and missed opportunities.

Marketing strategy lies at the heart of value creation. It is the platform on which are based growth, profitability and return on investment. Marketing strategy defines the choices about which customers the business will serve and how it will create customer preference. By targeting appropriate markets and creating a differential advantage, the firm gains the opportunity to grow and create the margin spread that is the basis for value creation. If the firm is locked into markets where there are no opportunities to grow and if it lacks a differential advantage, no amount of financial engineering will create value for investors.

Marketing, as was argued in chapter 1, is about managing markets; and value-based marketing is about delivering the benefits customers need and developing their trust and loyalty. Only by creating such relationships can the firm achieve profitable growth and shareholder value. The starting point for this marketing process is to understand the benefits that customers need and develop a proposition that they will regard as offering superior value. The next step is to develop a product that customers will trust and want to continue to do business with.

Marketing, then, can be defined as follows:

> Marketing is the process that seeks to maximise returns to shareholders by developing and implementing strategies to build relationships of trust with high-value customers and to create a sustainable differential advantage.

This defines the objective of marketing in the business enterprise and the strategies that contribute to it. The objective is to maximise returns to the owners of the business, as measured by its long-term dividend stream and capital growth. The specific contribution of marketing lies in the formulation of strategies to choose the right customers, build relationships of trust with them and create a differential advantage.

Choosing the right customers is important because some customers do not offer the potential to create value, either because the costs of serving them exceed the benefits they generate, or because the company does not have the appropriate bundle of skills to serve them effectively. It wants long-term relationships with its chosen customers because loyal customers make possible faster and more profitable growth. A firm's ability to earn a return above the cost of capital depends upon it maintaining a **differential advantage** — a reason why target customers perceive the firm as offering superior value to competitors. A strategy to create a differential advantage is based on understanding the needs of customers and the strategies of competitors.

The discussion in this section is organised principally around three key steps that are required for value-based marketing to be implemented. First, the organisation must develop a deep understanding of customer needs; without this it cannot create enduring customer value. Second, it must create a differential advantage and determine the value proposition that it will offer to customers. Third, it must seek to build a long-term relationship with customers. Each of these is considered in turn.

differential advantage:
a competitive advantage that allows a firm to offer products that are perceived by customers as better value than those of competitors

Creating customer value: Understanding needs

Figure 3.3 shows that there are two key elements in building a differential advantage. One is to understand customer needs; the other is to satisfy those needs in ways that are superior to competitors. Indeed, the essential idea of marketing is offering customers superior value. By delivering superior value to customers, management in turn can deliver superior value to shareholders. This formula — customer value creates shareholder value — is the fundamental principle of capitalism. In a free-enterprise system individual consumers choose how to spend their money. In turn, firms compete with one another to attract the patronage of customers. Firms making offers that do not appeal to customers go out of business because they do not generate the cash flow to pay their suppliers of materials, labour and capital.

Meeting customer needs

The marketing approach to creating customer value is based on three principles. First, it recognises that in choosing between competing companies, the customer will select the offer that he or she perceives to be of best *value*. Second, customers do not want products for their own sake, but rather for meeting their *needs*. These needs may be emotional (e.g. to look good), economic (e.g. to cut costs) or, more likely, some combination of both. Value is the customer's estimate of the product's ability to satisfy these needs. Third, rather than having just a one-off transaction with a customer, the firm will find it more profitable in the long run to create *relationships* whereby trust is established between them and customers remain loyal and continue to buy from the business.

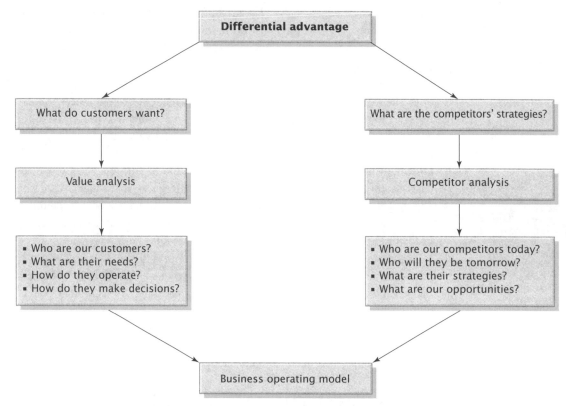

Figure 3.3 Developing the differential advantage

To get into a position to offer superior value to customers, the company must first understand their needs. The basic idea of marketing is that whatever product the company produces, the customer does not want it! What the customer wants is to satisfy his or her needs. The teenager insists on a particular brand of sports shoes, not because they intend to use them for jogging, but because they are seeking the approval of their peers. The advertising agency buys a new graphics software package, not because they want the product, but because they are convinced that it will enable staff to work more efficiently and thereby improve profitability.

Customers naturally want to deal with companies that they believe will address their needs. Understanding customers better than competitors can is a challenging task. It requires research on the whole customer experience, not just the ordering decision. Figure 3.4 illustrates how marketing must understand the problems leading up to the purchase, the choice criteria the buyer has in mind, how the buyer will proceed through ordering, installing, learning about and using the product, and what after-sales support he or she should expect. It is this whole experience that determines the buyer's perception of value. Within each of these stages, depending upon the needs of the individual buyer, there will be one or two critical interfaces between buyer and seller that will drive the customer's perception of value and the decision of whether or not to buy again. These may be the supplier's willingness to pull out all the stops when the customer needs fast repairs to the equipment, or their ability to put together effective training for the customer's operatives. These are often called 'moments of truth'. Detailed knowledge of this process and management of these moments of truth are the foundations for a strategy to deliver customer value and create competitive advantage.

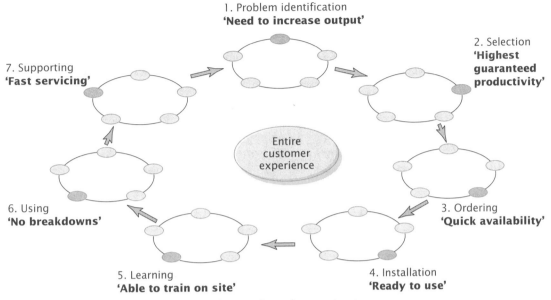

Figure 3.4 Understanding the purchasing process

Differences between consumer and business-to-business markets

Some companies produce for final consumers but most produce for other businesses. Needs, purchasing behaviour and product use differ in these two markets. Actually, managers need to understand both markets and develop two separate strategies. Consumer goods companies generally must first sell to other businesses. The Procter & Gamble brand manager has to make toothpaste appealing not only to consumers but also to the big supermarket chains that will decide whether or not to stock the brand, and how much support they will give it. Similarly, the demand for all business goods is ultimately derived from the demand for consumer goods. The amount of steel bought depends on consumer purchases of cars and the type of cars they buy. A shift in consumer tastes, for example, could see aluminium or plastic substituting for steel in cars.

The sources of the differences between the two markets lie in the number of customers and the professionalism of the buying processes. Whereas firms in consumer markets count their customers in millions, in business-to-business markets four or five customers can account for 80 per cent of a supplier's profits. This results in larger customers with greater bargaining power. The supplier normally deals directly, one-to-one, with these major customers and has a detailed knowledge of their wants and buying processes. Purchasing is increasingly professional as buyers seek to construct efficient supply chains that will allow their businesses to compete effectively. Today, buyers look for partnerships with a few chosen suppliers who can share responsibility for optimising key areas of the value chain. While individual buyers will always be influenced by personal and social factors, motives tend to be much more rational in business purchasing than in consumer buying.

Suppliers are chosen more for their perceived value in improving the buying firm's economic performance.

In some ways consumer marketing is less sophisticated than business-to-business. Consumer marketers do not know their individual customers and they employ mass marketing techniques such as advertising that treat all customers, or at least large segments of them, as alike. The huge numbers of buyers typical of consumer markets has meant that the marketer usually deals with them through intermediaries such as shops or dealers. They have not had one-to-one communication with, or acquired knowledge about, the needs and buying patterns of individual consumers. Modern information technology, however, is beginning to change this picture. The Internet and related developments promise to transform consumer marketing from mass marketing to something closer to the type of one-to-one marketing that exists in many business markets.

Understanding the decision-making unit

Meeting customer needs is complicated because, except for the most routine decisions, buying is rarely the choice of a single individual. In consumer buying, parents may do the supermarket shopping, but other members of the family, and perhaps friends, will have influenced their choices. In business buying, technical people, finance, marketing, shop floor and top management may influence the key purchasing decisions. In contrast, the influence of the manager formally responsible for purchasing may be slight. Studies suggest up to seven roles in the purchasing process: initiators, users, influencers, deciders, approvers, buyers and gatekeepers.

Understanding these roles in the buying process is important because the participants are likely to want different things from the supplier. For example, in buying breakfast cereals, the parent may want to choose a healthy brand for the family, but the kids want one that tastes sugary. In industrial buying, purchasing managers tend to be heavily influenced by price, technical people by product specifications and top management by overall impact on the bottom line. Marketing needs to understand the power relationships in these buying units and to communicate the appropriate messages to each of the important influencers.

Existing, latent and incipient needs

The most obvious way to discover the needs of customers is to ask them. But sometimes simply asking customers what they want is not enough.

Wants or needs can be classified into three groups. **Existing needs** are those for which consumers consider satisfactory solutions already exist. Here, opportunities for new products are limited since they will be competing head-to-head with similar products. **Latent needs** are needs that people have, which are not yet satisfied. Customers can easily articulate these needs in market research. People would like a cure for flu or cancer. Portable PC users would like a battery with a longer life, and so on. Profit opportunities are much greater for companies that can meet latent needs since solutions represent innovations for which, temporarily at least, no competition exists. **Incipient needs** are needs that people have, but which they do not know about until they see the solution. Customers were unlikely to articulate the

existing needs: needs for which consumers consider satisfactory solutions already exist

latent needs: needs that people have and can express but which are not yet satisfied

incipient needs: needs that people have, but which they do not know about until they see the solution, and hence are presently unable to articulate desire for Post-It notes, compact disc players, Sony Walkmans, Internet banking or automated teller machines. In areas of rapid technological and social change, buyers are likely to lack the foresight to predict the new products they would buy. Companies often have to follow up on novel technologies and the insights of their researchers without the benefit of direct consumer research. Rather than the classic marketing approach of first researching needs, in many situations the product breakthroughs occur first, and then the pioneering company has to find customers afterwards.

But it is a mistake to think that companies like Sony or 3M, which often proceed like this, create needs. Unless the invention meets an underlying customer need, and customers perceive it offering an advantage to current products on the market, it will not succeed. Such products as mobile phones, compact disc players and on-board navigation systems for cars were not suggested by consumers. But they succeeded because they offered them demonstrable benefits. Technology-led innovation is very risky.

Sony and 3M have managed to escape what Hamel and Prahalad refer to as the 'myopia of the served market'.[9] The risk for companies that focus exclusively on the existing needs of existing customers is that they may concentrate on making incremental, rather than bold, improvements in product design. They may also tend to make 'me-too' products that merely provide missing features or services already being offered by competitors.

In overcoming the problem of detecting latent and incipient needs, a variety of techniques are now available. Ulwick, for example, argues that the nature of customer interviews can be greatly improved if they are designed to ask customers only for the outcomes they desire, not for the solutions. The aim is to discover what the customer is really trying to achieve in using a product, leaving the company with the responsibility for devising the appropriate solution. He provides a methodology for achieving this.[10] Leonard and Rayport argue that it is important to concentrate on what people do, rather than what people say. They outline a process by which firms can engage in 'empathic design', a form of contextual inquiry in which participants are observed *in situ* (be it at home, in the office, in the factory, or in wherever work is done and products are used). Close observation of customers actually using the product can reveal a number of things, including unarticulated needs: witnessing the problems that customers encounter with a product that they do not realise can be addressed.[11] Sometimes useability laboratories are used for this method of understanding customer needs (see marketing management in practice 'Testing the pain threshold'). Another way of uncovering unarticulated needs is by using Zaltman's Metaphor Elicitation technique. The aim with this technique is to probe the attitudes and feelings of individuals relative to specific subjects (product/situations) deeply and systematically through the use of metaphors and visual images. The method involves clipping magazine pictures, taking photographs and generating collages, which in turn are the basis of in-depth interviews in which the individual is asked to explain the nature and meaning of individual images, as well as images combined to form a collage, to represent their views on the subject under investigation. The technique is based on the view that the best way to understand customers is through the use of research tools that engage their nonverbal, especially visual, modes of thought and communication.[12]

Marketing management in practice: **Testing the pain threshold**

There's more than just money riding on the next generation of mobile phones. After falling flat on its collective face with the overhyped and underwhelming launch of WAP (wireless application protocol) services, the telecommunications industry has enlisted the help of psychologists to ensure it does not repeat the same mistakes while it prepares for the next revolution in wireless networks.

Third-generation, or 3G, networks will become possible this September in Australia when the spectrum is released. Services and products will be launched gradually — Telstra is not expected to show its hand for another two years ...

In the outer Melbourne suburb of Clayton, behavioural science specialists at Telstra Research Labs are conducting an experiment with 150 carefully selected subjects to determine what people want, like or are prepared to tolerate from 3G services.

'Human expectations and reactions may seem an obvious thing to measure, but it's somewhat revolutionary from an engineering perspective,' says Garth Price, general manager, research, at Telstra's Research Labs.

Academics from the University of Melbourne have been following teenagers into nightclubs, universities, schools and homes to build up a complete picture of mobile habits, which the researchers hope will help bridge the gap between product designers and those they design for ...

The Telstra experiment is the work of a small wireless research team drawn from a group of about 20 human factors specialists employed by the telco. They work with product engineers to help ensure the human element is not neglected in the dazzle of new technology ...

The wireless experiment under way is noteworthy both for its scope and its timing. It will take six months for all 150 subjects to be put through an intensive, two-hour process, testing out a 3G network that will not be launched commercially until 2004 ...

As well as giving the subjects a taste of the mobile future with interactive video and internet-based applications, the Telstra experimenters also treat their subjects to what the leader of the research team calls 'excruciating delays'. The aim is to discover at what point in which applications and at what speed frustration levels rise.

The University of Melbourne study, titled Customers of the Future, has been conducted by the university's Interaction Design Group, which includes sociologists, anthropologists, psychologists and IT specialists. It is focused on improving technology design and development ...

The group is using traditional research methods as well as 'shadowing' its subjects to establish the future needs of mobile customers. It is not simply a matter of recording which features or services are preferred and why.

Even the most ardent technophile would not describe SMS text messaging as userfriendly, but this has not stopped fast and furious use of the service, especially by 16- to 22-year-olds who are the focus of the mobile study.

'Young people are obviously prepared to tolerate poor useability in some instances. Good end-user design is about understanding those trade-offs,' [the leader of the University of Melbourne's research team, Steve] Howard, says ...

Telstra Research Labs is, at least, clear on the potential benefits, particularly in regard to its wireless future.

3G products can run at speeds of 380 kilobytes per second and beyond. But it appears technology developers now understand the concept of overkill. If the wireless research group can demonstrate that desirable products need only run at 140 kb/sec, Telstra could alter capital expenditure.

Telstra's general manager of research, Garth Price, refers to the 3G experiment and other user-focused research as customer engineering, on the basis that it is just one more input to be defined and measured.

'What we are particularly interested in now is not so much technology but whether customers will use it,' Price says.

Source: Extracts from Emma Connors, 'Testing the pain threshold', *Australian Financial Review*, 22 March 2002.

Building differential advantage

As figure 3.3 shows, value-based marketing not only requires a focus on satisfying customer needs: it also has a competitive dimension. Management must be aware of both what customers need and what competitors are offering them. The firm must seek to satisfy the needs of target customers more effectively than competitors. A differential advantage is necessary for two reasons, one marketing, the other financial. First, a differential advantage is necessary to maintain preference. Only by having a differential advantage can the business profitably attract new customers or prevent existing customers defecting to competition. Second, a differential advantage is necessary if a business is to maintain earnings above the cost of capital — that is, to generate shareholder value. Without the barrier of a differential advantage, competitors can easily enter the market, copy the company's offer and compete away its premium profit margins.

A differential advantage is a perceived difference in value that leads target customers to prefer one company's offer to those of others. It is created by offering customers superior value. **Value** is the customer's perception of the effectiveness of a good or service in meeting his or her needs. It is a trade-off between performance and cost. Value can be increased by offering customers more performance or benefits for the same cost, or the same benefits for a lower cost.

Since customers have different preferences and constraints, the optimum value will differ among them. Some customers will put a greater emphasis on benefits, such as innovative product features or services; others will place a greater weight on price or convenience. Hence, in any market there will be different viable **value propositions**, depending on the customers targeted. The choice management makes is called the company's market positioning strategy. This refers to the choice of target customers, which defines *where* the firm competes, and the choice of value proposition, which determines *how* it competes. Both of these are discussed in detail in part 2 of this book. Here we provide an introduction to the two key ways in which a firm can build a differential advantage.

value: the customer's perception of the effectiveness of a good or service in meeting his or her needs

value proposition: the organisation's view on how and by what means its product offering provides unique and superior value to the customer

Strategies that offer more: Competing on benefits

Some companies compete primarily on the basis of offering more benefits. Such a strategy reflects the fact that some customers are primarily interested in selecting suppliers that offer the best solutions and are willing to incur more costs to get them. At least two types of positioning strategy can be distinguished for companies choosing to compete on this dimension.[13]

1. **Product leadership.** Some companies target customers who want the latest technology and products with the most innovative features. Examples include 3M, Sony, Glaxo, NTT DoCoMo, Apple, LG and Intel. These companies invest heavily in research and development, prioritise hiring the brightest talent and build organisational cultures focused on creativity and innovation. The financial advantages of successful product leadership are the opportunities to achieve rapid growth and to obtain premium prices. Some customers place a high value on outstanding service. Companies with a value proposition based on service include Singapore Airlines, Hyatt, American Express and the US department store Nordstrom. Businesses competing this way need first to identify the types of customers who will pay more to be pampered.

2. **Customer intimacy.** This strategy involves communicating with customers on an individual basis to learn about their needs and develop tailored

solutions which directly improve the customer's performance or experience. It is now often called one-to-one marketing and promises to be one of the most successful strategies of the information age. Customer intimacy has been a common strategy for business-to-business suppliers with a small number of customers. Companies such as McKinsey, Saatchi & Saatchi and Boeing have long seen this as their positioning. But today, led by such organisations as Amazon.com, Federal Express and Lexus, we see it spreading into areas where previously advertising and mass marketing played central roles.

The characteristics of a customer intimacy strategy are:

- the construction of data banks to hold information on the preferences and buying behaviour of individual customers
- the use of information technology (Internet, telephone, fax) to allow direct, one-to-one communication between the firm and the customer
- the organisation of marketing around customers and brands (see marketing management in practice 'Billabong: Surfing high')
- the tailoring of individual product solutions.

A stimulus for the growing popularity of this strategy is the increasing difficulty of maintaining uniqueness in products. This has resulted in competition shifting from delivering quality products to the provision of solutions that enhance the customer's overall experience or performance (see marketing insight 'Category management — developing customer intimacy'). Another stimulus is information technology which is making it increasingly cheap and easy to store individual data and to communicate on a personalised basis.

Marketing management in practice: **Billabong: Surfing high**

The Billabong brand was established in 1973 by Gordon Merchant, who wanted to create a brand for 'functional products for surfers to help us better enjoy our sport'. During the 1970s and 1980s, Billabong established its brand credibility with the young surfing community as a designer and producer of quality surf apparel. Merchant started selling Billabong products in Japan, Europe and the United States in the early 1980s through licensees. In the late 1980s and early 1990s, the brand was extended into other youth-oriented activities such as snowboarding and skateboarding. In 1998, a group of investors provided capital to convert Billabong's licensed US operation into a directly controlled business. The Billabong brand now covers 2200 apparel and accessory lines in Australia, 800 in North America and 700 in Europe. The Billabong brand is sold in 63 countries.

Billabong International listed on the Australian Stock Exchange in August 2000. Its shares, issued at $2.30, are now trading at $8.25. In the 12 months to June 2000, Billabong reported a net profit of $380.2 million, 15% higher than forecast.

A study of the most valuable brands in Australia, conducted by the brand valuation consultancy, Interbrand, between August and November 2000, placed Billabong in eighth spot with an estimated value of $850 million. The high valuation of Billabong is the result of its steady and successful global expansion and its ability to compete in a buoyant surf and leisure market which has an increasing number of competitive brands (Rip Curl, Quiksilver and myriad newer brands). For 38 years, Billabong has stuck to its core brand proposition: contemporary, relevant, innovative products of consistent high quality.

Maintaining the integrity of the Billabong brand has meant appealing to a wide variety of customers. It operates in a market heavily influenced by image and association, and has sustained its success by strong non-mainstream marketing support, for example sponsorships such as the Billabong Challenge international surf competition, as well as heavy investment in on-line promotion and in-store merchandising. The surf and street brands are also keen to stress their humble beginnings and not appear too 'corporate'.

According to Interbrand's chief executive, John Allert, 'The story underpinning the success of the Billabong brand is that the company has created a brand that has salience and resonance with people in a psychographic rather than a demographic set. The company has been able to capture a massive pool of earnings simply because the brand has resonated with people of a particular mindset in countries as diverse as Spain, the US, the UK, Indonesia and Australia, and Billabong can be described as a global, Australian-owned brand.'

The most valuable brands in Australia are those that receive the greatest attention from management in order to maintain a dominant or near dominant position in their market. This requires a mix of marketing support and means ensuring that the product offered under the brand name is relevant to the consumer.

Chief Executive of Billabong, Matthew Perrin emphasises how Billabong is almost paranoid about its brand, ensuring it remains true to its surfing origins and is not placed on myriad products. The company did consider launching a range of sunglasses and footwear since its float, but decided that such products would hurt its surf/ski brand image. Expansion will be achieved by acquiring other brands, not extending its own brand, over the next 18 months. In July 2001, Billabong bought US-based clothing brand Element for an estimated $20 million. The acquisition will help Billabong consolidate its position in the surf, ski and skateboarding markets. The stock market approved of the move, which sent stock up 7 per cent to a record high of $5.79.

One factor driving the success of the surf, ski and skate brands is the expansion of brands aimed at women. In the past five years, floor space devoted to women's wear in shops that stock big-selling surf brands has increased from about 30 per cent to 60 per cent. Billabong has increased the number of stores in Australia that carry its product from 600 to 650 in the past ten years.

Source: Adapted from Simon Lloyd, 'Brand power', *BRW*, 29 November–5 December 2001, pp. 49–54.

| Marketing insight: | **Category management — developing customer intimacy** |

The most significant development in recent years in the consumer goods area is category management. Suppliers of fast-moving consumer goods, such as Unilever, Procter & Gamble and Sara Lee, sell to final consumers via supermarkets. To attract final consumers these companies seek to develop appealing brands. But supermarkets have different buying motivations to final consumers. The supermarket's objectives are to increase its own business turnover and profitability. Most of the sales activities suppliers undertake to increase their market shares — such as developing new brands, promotions and advertising — do not help supermarkets; they merely produce brand switching within the store.

This creates conflict between the increasingly powerful retail chains and suppliers. Retailers retaliate by demanding better margins and cash incentives, and by developing their own private label brands that switch sales from manufacturer brands. Leading suppliers have responded by introducing category management. Category management is a partnership between a supplier and a retail group designed to grow the retailer's sales and profits in a merchandise area. For example, a category management team from Sarah Lee could work with Woolworths to develop a plan to increase the supermarket's sales and profitability in the biscuits category by 10 per cent per annum over the next three years.

Rather than trying to sell the reluctant retailer its variety of competing brands, the supplier uses its knowledge of the category to design a portfolio of brands, space layout, price points and promotions to maximise the client's growth and profits. Electronic data interchange can then link retail sales to the supplier's production line to cut inventories and optimise the supply chain. Category management aims to replace an adversarial relationship with a one-to-one partnership designed to increase the customer's performance.

Lower total cost: Competing on operational excellence

Rather than delivering the customer more product benefits, a company can instead seek a differential advantage by offering lower total costs or greater convenience. Lower total cost for the customer can include several dimensions. The most obvious one is offering customers the guarantee of consistently lower prices. A second way of offering lower total cost is emphasising product reliability, durability and low running costs. Volvo ads, for instance, show its cars offering decades of trouble-free motoring. Another element of cost that operationally excellent companies stress is convenience: the absence of tangible and psychic costs stemming from irritation and delays. The strength of these companies lies in the delivery of swift, dependable service. For example, DHL promises to accept telephone instructions from anywhere and to ship packages anywhere. It could not be easier or involve less total cost.

Criteria for a differential advantage

Treacy and Wiersema, in reviewing the differential advantages of today's industry leaders, suggest four rules:[14]

1. Provide the best offering in the marketplace by excelling in a specific dimension of value.

    Different customers buy different kinds of value. No company can be the best in all dimensions, so it has to choose its customers and focus on offering them unmatched value on one dimension. Customers recognise they have to make choices — they accept that if they buy from a supplier offering 'unbeatable prices', they are not going to get personalised service.

2. Maintain threshold standards on other dimensions of value.

    While outstanding performance is not expected in all dimensions, threshold standards are required. The lowest cost car on the market will not succeed if its reliability and service back-up are unacceptable.

3. Dominate the market by improving value year after year.

    Competition is continually raising the expectations of customers. What represents a differential advantage today will not do so tomorrow. Companies have to continually get better and faster than their competitors.

4. Build a well-tuned operating model dedicated to delivering unmatched value.

    Developing a winning value proposition requires companies to structure their operations specifically to deliver on that dimension. A business focusing on a value proposition of innovation and product leadership will require a quite different operating model from a company focusing on price leadership.

Business portfolios

For many organisations, the challenge of building and sustaining differential advantage occurs across multiple markets, each of which is at different levels of development. Companies often operate a portfolio of businesses — different industry sectors, technologies, countries or distribution channels. At the corporate level, the board has to decide which of these businesses it wants to be in and what priority they should have. Some of its business units may be in markets that do not have the potential to provide opportunities for growth or earn operating margins that exceed the threshold level. Others may offer tremendous opportunities but are not receiving sufficient investment and priority.

The mistake of many financially driven companies is to make this review static rather than dynamic. A static review focuses on the current profitability of the business units rather than their ability to create long-term value and to provide sources of differential advantage for the organisation in the future. Management must understand the need for continual change and evolution in today's rapidly changing environment. If the company is to survive it must move into new products, technologies, markets and distribution channels. To create value it must structure its portfolio dynamically. This means building a portfolio of activities across three types of businesses (see figure 3.5):[15]

1. **Today's businesses.** These are the core business units that should be generating the bulk of today's profits and cash flow. Usually they have only modest growth potential left. The management goals will be high levels of current profitability and cash flow. The strategy is to extend and defend the core businesses through incremental extension, updating and cost reduction. Those businesses that are not generating economic profit should be quickly fixed or divested.

2. **Tomorrow's businesses.** These are the company's emerging stars: new businesses that are already demonstrating their ability to win profitable customers and grow. The success of these businesses is likely to be already having a major impact on the share price as investors recognise their long-term cash generating potential. The task here is to invest in the marketing infrastructure to capture and defend the market opportunities against competitors.

3. **Options for growth.** These are investments that seed tomorrow's businesses. These are market trials, prototypes, research projects, alliances or minority stakes that the firm undertakes to explore the market feasibility of new ideas. Many will fail, but without a bundle of options being continually explored, long-term growth will certainly stall. The task of management here is to decide which of the options to pursue, based upon their estimates of the profit potential of the opportunities and the probability of success.

Eventually, a company needs businesses in all three categories. If it only has strong core businesses, then its current profitability and cash flow will be excellent, but its share price will disappoint because investors recognise the lack of long-term potential. On the other hand, if it does not have a strong core and only new businesses and options, management will lack credibility in their ability to extract value from the opportunities. The function of the board is first to weed out those businesses that fail to fit into any of these categories. Second, it needs to clarify to the unit managers where they fit in the portfolio, what their strategic objectives should be and on what measures they will be judged. Third, it needs to identify the scope for synergies among the businesses. Can value be added by sharing technology, brand names, distribution systems or common services?

Cochlear, Australia's biggest medical device company, and one that has excelled at providing shareholder value, is a good example of a firm that manages all three categories. Today's business is dominated by the bionic ear implant. Cochlear has also established what may become tomorrow's business by moving into production of a device that helps paraplegics control bladder and bowel functions. Aware of the need for options for growth, it is involved in long-term research into the use of stem cells to regenerate damaged hair cells in the ear. If successful, this would cure deafness and thereby eliminate the need for bionic ears.

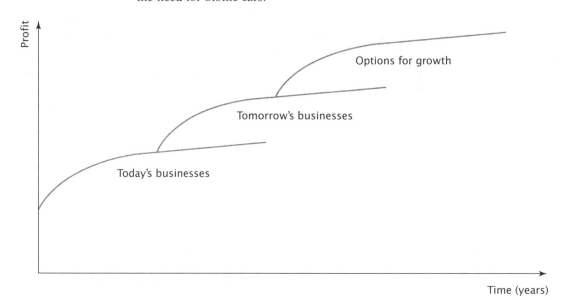

Figure 3.5 Building the sustainable business

The importance of building relationships with customers: The economics of customer loyalty

The first step in value-based marketing is to understand the needs of customers; the second aims at creating a differential advantage; the third seeks to convert this understanding and advantage into a continuing relationship with customers so that they buy again and again. Managers need to understand how such customer relationships are the fundamental key to creating value for shareholders. Accordingly, the discussion here focuses first on why relationships matter, and then goes on to explain how relationships can be developed.

By way of introduction, we can note the following findings on customer loyalty:

- **Loyal customers are assets.** A customer that generates a cash flow of $1000 for a supplier in its first year is likely to have a net present value (customer lifetime value) of around $50 000 if retained as a satisfied customer over 10 years.
- **Loyal customers are more profitable.** They buy more of the company's products, are less costly to serve, are less sensitive to price and bring in new customers.

- **Winning new customers is costly.** It costs up to six times as much to win a new customer as to retain an existing one. These are the costs of researching, advertising, selling and negotiating with new prospects.
- **Increasing customer retention.** The average company loses 10 per cent of its customers annually. Increasing customer retention by as little as 5 per cent can double the lifetime value of customers.
- **'Highly satisfied' customers repurchase.** They are six times more likely to remain loyal than customers who merely rate themselves 'satisfied'. Highly satisfied customers (sometimes called 'apostles') tell others about the company.
- **Dissatisfied customers (sometimes referred to as 'terrorists') tell others.** On average they tell 14 others. So, if losing a single customer represents the loss of an asset with a lifetime value of say, $10 000, this might just be the tip of the iceberg. The total value lost might be 14 times as great.
- **Most dissatisfied customers do not complain.** While they tell their colleagues, only around 4 per cent bother to complain. For every complaint received, another 26 customers will have had problems, and about 6 will have had serious ones.
- **Satisfactory resolution of complaints increases loyalty.** When complaints are resolved to the customer's satisfaction, these customers tend to be more loyal than those who never experienced a problem in the first place.
- **Few customers defect due to poor product performance.** Only 14 per cent defect for product reasons; two-thirds leave because they find service people indifferent or inaccessible.

Loyalty and growth

Shareholder value is determined by the company's growth rate and its ability to achieve an operating margin above its threshold level. For most companies, customer loyalty is the single most important determinant of long-term growth and profit margins. **Customer loyalty** refers to the customer's willingness to continue buying from the company. It is generally measured by the retention rate: the percentage of customers buying this year who also buy next year. A typical company — for example, a bank, car insurer or advertising agency — loses 10 per cent of its accounts annually. The average retention rate is therefore around 90 per cent.

customer loyalty: the customer's willingness to continue buying from the company

The effect of the retention rate on a company's growth is greatly underestimated by managers because new customer acquisition masks the effects of a high defection rate. However, a high defection rate makes profitable growth almost impossible to achieve. It is like a leaky bucket: the bigger the hole in the bucket of customers, the harder marketing has to work to fill it up and keep it full.

If management can increase the retention rate from the average of 90 per cent to 95 per cent, then it can massively increase the company's growth rate. Consider two companies, the first losing 10 per cent of its customers annually, the second losing only 5 per cent. If both companies are acquiring new customers at the rate of 10 per cent per year, the first will have no net growth; the second will have a 5 per cent net growth rate. Over 15 years, the first firm will be unchanged in size; the second firm will double. Table 3.2 shows the effects over a ten-year period of varying levels of customer retention in mature, moderate-growth and high-growth markets. In rapidly growing markets (that is, 20 per cent new customers acquired annually), a 5 per cent improvement in the retention rate increases the total number of customers by between 55 and over 100 per cent over a 10-year period. In mature (0 new customers) or low- to moderate-growth markets (10 per cent annual new customer growth), a high defection rate soon destroys the customer base.

Table 3.2 Growth in total number of customers over 10-year period

RETENTION (%)	GROWTH OF NEW ACCOUNTS (% PER ANNUM)		
	0	10	20
95	−34	55	252
90	−61	0	136
85	−77	−37	55
80	−87	−67	0

Loyalty and operating margins

If the effect of customer loyalty on growth is high, the effect on operating profits is extraordinary. In many industries there are vast differences between companies in profitability, even though their prices are pretty much the same. The major cause of this difference is variations in the customer retention rate. Customers who stay with the company are assets of increasing value — each year they tend to generate higher and higher net cash flow. A customer who has been with the company say seven years, typically generates six or seven times the amount of a new customer. Frederick Reichheld, a director of management consultants Bain & Company, identifies six sources making loyal customers more profitable:[16]

1. **Acquisition cost.** Obtaining new customers is very expensive in terms of such costs as advertising, direct mail, sales commissions and management time. It has been estimated that it typically takes six times as much to win a new customer as to keep an existing one.
2. **Base profit.** The base profit is the earnings on purchases before allowing for loyalty effects. Clearly, the longer a customer is retained, the greater the total sum of annual base profits.
3. **Revenue growth.** Loyal customers increase their spending over time. They learn more about the company's product line and, because they trust the company, are more inclined to put more of their business with it.
4. **Operating costs.** As customers become more familiar with the company, the costs of serving them decrease. Less time has to be spent answering questions and learning about each other's operations.
5. **Referrals.** Satisfied customers recommend the business to others. Referrals can be a very important source of new business in many markets. In general, personal recommendations are more powerful persuaders than advertising or paid-for communications.
6. **Price premium.** Old customers are normally less price conscious than new ones. New customers are usually attracted by bargains and discounted offers that earn the company low margins.

Figure 3.6 illustrates how these factors shape the cash flow over a customer's lifetime.

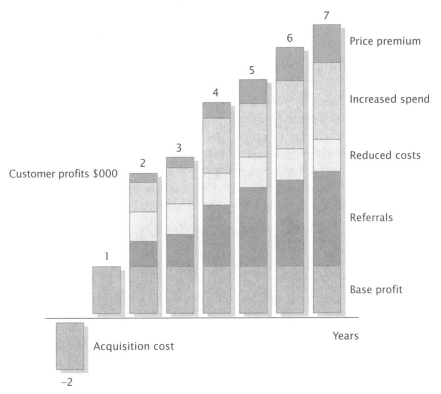

Figure 3.6 Cash flow over a customer's lifetime

customer lifetime value (CLV): the net present value of a customer, calculated in terms of the discounted value of the cash flow generated over the life of the customer's relationship with the company

The **customer lifetime value (CLV)** is the net present value of a customer — that is, the discounted value of the cash flow generated over the life of the relationship with the company. The cash flow is usually low or even negative at the beginning and then grows strongly over the years as a result of the factors described above. The major determinant of CLV is the retention rate. For example, for a credit card company, an average customer who stays only two years has a CLV of around $45, while one who stays 20 years has a CLV of over $1800. Reichheld shows the effect on the CLV of a 5 per cent increase in the retention rate for typical industries (see figure 3.7). For example, if a personal insurance company increased its retention rate from 90 to 95 per cent it would increase the customer net present value by 84 per cent — from, say, $840 to $1545. This occurs because with a 90 per cent retention rate the average customer stays with the company 10 years; with 95 per cent the average loyalty is 20 years.

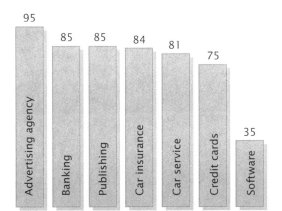

How much a 5% increase in loyalty lifts CLV

Figure 3.7 Effect of increased loyalty on customer lifetime value (CLV)

Growth plus margin effects on shareholder value

Putting the growth and margin effects together demonstrates the enormous impact on shareholder value of increasing customer loyalty. As shown above, increasing the retention rate from 90 to 95 per cent in a moderate-growth market would increase the number of customers by 55 per cent. So, for example, an insurance company with 100 000 customers would gain a net 55 000 over a ten-year period. This is the *growth effect*. But in addition, the average duration a customer stays with the business would double. As a result of lower average acquisition and operating costs, more referrals, revenue growth and higher prices, the average lifetime value of a customer grows by over 80 per cent. Using the above example, this is from $840 to $1545. This is the *margin effect*. The net result is to almost treble the value of the business from $84 million to $240 million:

Value with 90 per cent retention:	
Customers	100 000
Average CLV	$840
Business value	$84 million
Value with 95 per cent retention:	
Customers	155 000
Average CLV	$1545
Business value	$240 million

Given the importance of customer loyalty on shareholder value, it is striking how few companies measure retention rates. Without such information, managers do not know the lifetime value of their customers and miss crucial opportunities to increase their company's growth and profitability.

The foundations of customer loyalty

Except in situations of customer apathy, the influence of force of habit, or a lack of effective substitutes, loyalty cannot occur without customers being satisfied with the product on offer. Loyalty is dependent also on customer commitment, and this in turn depends on the existence of trust. Together, these constitute the foundations of customer loyalty.

Customer satisfaction

> **customer satisfaction:** a situation where the perceived performance of a product is at least equal to what the customer had expected

Fundamental to building loyalty is **customer satisfaction**. Customer satisfaction is defined as where the supplier's perceived performance is equal to the expected performance. More and more businesses now regularly measure, through surveys, customer satisfaction levels — though often the results may be misleading. The belief is that increasing customer satisfaction will increase loyalty and therefore future growth, profitability and shareholder value.

Unfortunately, research suggests that the link between customer satisfaction and loyalty is not so straightforward.[17] Typically, surveys measure customer satisfaction on a 1 to 5 scale where 5 is 'very satisfied' and 1 is 'very dissatisfied'. Loyalty is measured by repeat buying behaviour or intention to buy again. The relationship often appears to be non-linear (see figure 3.8).[18] People rating at either extreme end of the scale tend to have intense feelings about the company. Those in the middle, scoring 2, 3 or 4, fall into a 'zone of indifference' where there is little association between the satisfaction score and loyalty. Xerox, for example, found customers who rated the company 5 were six times more likely to repurchase than those who scored it 4.

Figure 3.8 Customer satisfaction and customer loyalty

The customers who score themselves at the very top end of the scale have been called 'apostles'. They are so enthusiastic about the company that they are like unpaid salespeople, spontaneously telling others about the company and recommending them to it. Those at the other extreme are called 'terrorists': they are so angry about the company's perceived performance that they actively 'bad-mouth' it and advise others not to buy.

Many marketing experts argue that in today's environment, faced with intense competition and buyers looking for the best deals, companies have to do more than satisfy customers, they have to 'delight' them. They have to try to convert as many as possible to apostles. A delighted customer is defined as one where the supplier's perceived performance exceeds expected performance. For two examples of companies wanting to delight customers, see marketing management in practice 'Making the customer a celebrity'.

The trust relationship

Customer satisfaction or delight measures how happy customers are with the company's product and with their recent transactions with the company. In the past few years, top marketing companies have moved away from focusing on products and transactions to building lasting relationships with customers. For suppliers, such partnerships are attractive because they replace the potential for destructive conflict with cooperation to achieve common goals. They shift the focus of negotiation from price to delivering total value to the customer. They also reduce the vulnerability to defection. Increasingly, customers want partnerships too. Japanese manufacturers have taught Western companies that long-term cooperation with a small number of suppliers is a better way to reduce costs, enhance quality and boost innovation than playing off one supplier against another. Both parties should gain from successful partnerships.

The creation of a long-term relationship depends upon a commitment from both sides to make cooperation work. Such commitment depends on trust — defined as a willingness to rely with confidence on the partner. Trust is the belief that neither party will ever act opportunistically to take advantage of the other party's vulnerabilities.[19] The new marketing emphasis is to move beyond satisfying customers with good products. The new aim is to develop trust relationships with customers that focus on working in cooperation to enhance the customer's performance or experience.

Marketing management in practice: **Making the customer a celebrity**

In February [2000], Just Jeans acquired the Peter Alexander mail-order sleepwear business, started by the Melbourne designer Peter Alexander in 1987. The business has a mailing list of 80 000 customers, and it turned over more than $7 million in 1999–2000.

Howard McDonald, the managing director of Just Jeans, says that thanks to Alexander, a culture of service permeates the organisation. 'He is the best one-on-one marketer I have ever met. Every customer is a celebrity.'

A recent problem demonstrates Alexander's approach. In March [2000], the company ran out of an item that was needed to complete 400 orders. There were two apparent choices: send the orders immediately and the missing item when it arrived, or delay dispatch for 10 weeks until the complete orders could be sent. Alexander suggested a third option. 'Peter said, "I will ring the 400 over the next four days and ask them",' McDonald says. 'He rang them. Ninety-eight per cent said, "You rang us? Absolutely, take your time, we're just delighted to hear from you".' Alexander says there are no tricks to providing good customer service. 'I knew if I broke trust with my customers that my business would fail.' ...

The chief executive of Woolworths, Roger Corbett, says that customers, when they deal with general merchandise stores, know that they trade a certain level of customer service for more competitive prices. However, Corbett does say that staff still need to be readily available to provide assistance.

Every complaint made to Woolworths is reviewed by a senior manager, and Corbett says the best way of dealing with a customer complaint is to turn what is a negative situation into a positive. He cites an example of a customer who complained that an advertised brand of men's underwear was not available in a Big W store. Management found that the product was there, but the customer had failed to find it. Rather than contacting the customer and explaining the misunderstanding, Corbett asked the manager to deliver six of the item to the customer's house. The customer was so pleased he said he would never shop anywhere else.

Source: Extracts from Michelle Hannen, 'The customer is not satisfied', *BRW*, 15 June 2001, pp. 65–9.

How to build relationships with customers

We have established so far that the notion of developing relationships with customers is fundamentally about an endeavour to build customer retention and loyalty. We have also established that there are powerful economic reasons — in terms of growth and operating margins — for trying to retain customers. Finally, we have shown that customer loyalty cannot be fully understood without considering the nature of customer satisfaction, customer commitment and trust.

We now turn to how managers can attempt to build a trust relationship with customers. The key steps in this planning process are shown in figure 3.9. The first step, determining the value proposition, provides a link to the earlier discussion of building differential advantage. If the firm is to build relationships, it must consider the value proposition that it will put to customers, and this in turn relates to the firm's differential advantage.

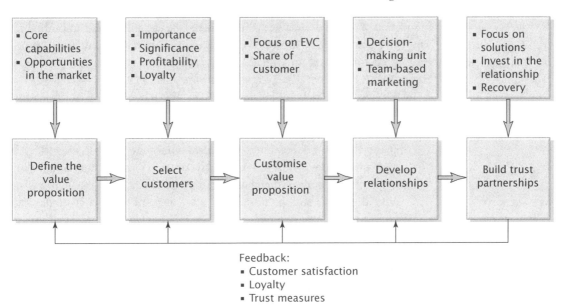

Figure 3.9 Customer value-based strategy

Defining the value proposition

Management has to decide how the firm is going to compete. Is it seeking a differential advantage based upon a value proposition of product innovation or low costs? The choice is determined by two key factors. The first is the firm's core capabilities — its unique combination of skills, assets and partnership relationships with customers and suppliers. These determine what the firm can do well. For example, a business is unlikely to be able to create a differential advantage based upon product innovation if it lacks a research and development base and experience in being first to market. Similarly, a firm today is not going to be competitive as a low-cost operator unless it has optimised the efficiency of each component of its supply chain.

The second determinant of the value proposition is the opportunities in the market. The value proposition has to match the wants of the customers. Of course, markets are segmented: some customers will want superior products, others will be more interested in services or low costs. But some market segments will offer more opportunities than others. The firm will need to research the size of the key customer segments, their growth, the amount of competition, average operating margins and investment requirements. It can then identify the profit potential of alternative value propositions.

Selecting customers

In today's increasingly competitive markets, successful marketing is about focusing on key customers. Many companies are willing to do business with any customer willing to spend. Such companies end up with large numbers of unprofitable small accounts. They fail to develop the sophisticated partnering skills big accounts expect and so end up with low margins, big overheads and high customer turnover. Numerous studies have shown that the 80:20 rule — 20 per cent of customers account for 80 per cent of the profits — is typical. Professors Cooper and Kaplan of the Harvard Business School suggested, in fact, that the situation is often much worse. Using activity-based costing they found that in most companies, 80 per cent of customers were unprofitable. They proposed the 225:20 rule, which stated that in many companies 20 per cent of customers account for 225 per cent of the profits. This of course means that 80 per cent lose 125 per cent of profits!

To select customers who will have a high lifetime value for the company, four criteria need to be used:[20]

1. **Strategic importance.** Strategic importance has three dimensions. First, the company should seek customers who desire its value proposition and so fit its core capabilities. Second, customers are strategically important if they are expected to grow, either because they are in fast growth markets or because they have strong competitive advantages. Finally, a customer can be important if they are an opinion leader. These lead customers can open the door to other customers who are influenced by them.

2. **Customer significance.** Significance refers to the percentage of total revenue and gross profit the customer accounts for. For example, is the customer in the top 10 per cent of accounts? Size is not always correlated with profitability. Some large accounts demand big discounts and onerous levels of servicing, which shrink the operating profit they generate. But size should be significant. Big customers should offer more opportunities, they are very difficult to replace and their loss can have a devastating impact on the business.

3. **Customer profitability.** The main reason why the majority of companies carry such a long tail of accounts is that they do not measure customer profitability. At best they measure contribution (revenue less variable costs). But contribution massively overestimates account profitability. Additional customers require more administrative support, warehousing, sales support, distribution and financing costs. Some firms are beginning to employ activity-based costing, which attempts to charge costs to products, channels and customers for the resources they consume. When such estimates are made, management is usually shaken by the losses that unfocused growth has brought. This inevitably leads to a strategy to refocus on the handful of profitable accounts and to make the others profitable or get rid of them.

4. **The loyalty coefficient.** If the company wants to create long-term partnerships, it needs to identify customers who would be interested in such a commitment. Some customers are inherently more loyal than others. In business-to-business markets, some purchasers are focused solely on price and they will switch from month to month according to which supplier is offering the best deal. For most companies, the lifetime value of these customers is very low. In consumer markets, too, some types of customer are inherently more loyal than others. In financial services, for example, there are striking variations in loyalty by demographic and social characteristics. In car insurance, loyalty is higher for married people, for home owners rather than renters and for those living in rural areas.

Customising the value proposition

Value-based marketing is about delivering benefits that improve the customer's performance. The focus is shifting from doing a small amount of business with a large number of customers, to a large amount of business with a smaller number of high-value customers. This allows the firm to add value by customising the solution.

Developing trust relationships with customers is based fundamentally on offering them value. Value is about improving the customer's performance or experience. Many companies do not offer value; they sell the products their company produces. Rather than understanding the customer's needs, the salespeople try to sell the features of their product — its quality or the services that accompany it. Such companies are production- or sales-oriented rather than market-led.

In most industries, competition leads to an evolution of value propositions (see figure 3.10). At the initial stage of the product life cycle, the innovator wins customers on the basis of its successful new product. It is unique and, if successful, offers customers benefits that are superior to the old solutions. But soon competitors copy the innovation, allowing customers to choose among a variety of suppliers. The effect of competition is to reduce prices and margins. Suppliers then seek to avoid margin erosion by emphasising value propositions typically based on the quality of their products and then the auxiliary features that are offered to support them (see marketing management in practice 'Aussie Home Loans'). But over time these distinctions erode. Usually there will be a number of suppliers, all offering products of acceptable quality, and with similar support. Buyers then increasingly focus on price, and the margins of suppliers sink towards the threshold level where, at best, they are earning just the opportunity cost of capital.

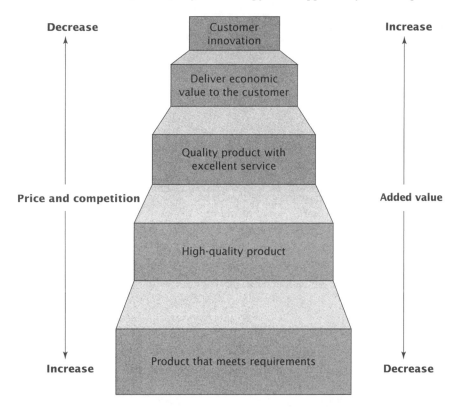

Figure 3.10
The value ladder

Ten years ago, in February 1992, John Symond started Aussie Home Loans. By using pricing power he transformed the Australian home lending market. 'When we kicked off, pricing was absolutely the value proposition,' Symond says. 'For the first five years, the value proposition for consumers was based on price.' Aussie Home Loans entered the market with a lower interest rate than the big four banks, and undercut their pricing further by charging lower (in most cases, zero) application fees. Symond's pricing power was also boosted by ill will among consumers about the banks: the big four were seen as expensive and exploitative.

The Aussie Home Loans experience highlights the most important element in pricing power: value. The American marketing consultant Thomas Winninger says value consists of seven components: service, response, variety, knowledge, quality, guarantee and price. In a paper on pricing written last year for the Professional Pricing Society, Winninger says: 'Note that price is only one component on this list. Always support value instead of defending or discounting price.' Winninger believes there are five questions a company needs to ask to determine where it provides most value to customers: 'How do I differ from my competitors? If I ceased to exist, why would my customers miss me? What do my customers want that I don't have? What need do I fill for my customers that no one else does? Who are my best customers and why?'

Symond addressed all five questions when he started Aussie Home Loans. But he says Aussie's pricing-power characteristics have changed markedly in 10 years. 'In 1997, when Commonwealth Bank cut its standard variable home loan rate out of the blue because of our competition, it was the start of the commoditisation of home loans,' he says. 'Since 1997, we have seen a proliferation of non-bank lenders enter the market and the banks are matching us on price. So today, pricing is nowhere near the value proposition that it was before.

'You cannot expect the average punter to remember that Aussie created competition in the home lending market by forcing down interest rates, fees and so on. Now we have to concentrate on the value proposition, knowing that while pricing is still an element, it will never play the same part it did when launching Aussie. Today, consumers value safety and security, convenience and service,' Symond says. Competitive pricing has become a given in the home loan market, and pricing power has come to mean value.

Source: Extract from Simon Lloyd, 'The Price Puzzle', *BRW*, 14 February 2002, pp. 42–9.

---

economic value to the customer:
an improvement in the customer's profitability

emotional value to the customer:
an improvement in the customer's experience

Leading companies today are recognising that, in the longer run, there is little profit to be made from selling product features alone (see marketing insight 'Companies shift from products to solutions'). The real returns are made from delivering customer benefits that are truly needed. We call this EVC, which in business markets normally means **economic value to the customer**. Economic value to the customer is created where the supplier finds ways of improving the customer's profitability by helping the customer increase sales, reduce costs, raise prices or lower its investment requirements. In consumer markets, EVC can mean emotional value to the customer. **Emotional value to the customer** is created where the supplier enhances the customer's experience by helping the individual obtain greater social, personal or psychological satisfaction. (EVC is discussed in detail in chapter 8.) The fifth and final step on the value ladder is where the supplier can transform the buyer's business by finding it innovative ways to compete and grow. Focusing on solutions that offer customers EVC and innovation is a much more secure way to create trust partnerships than focusing on product features alone.

Managers see a revolution sweeping through Western industry that has nothing to do with technology, the Internet or innovation. It is the switch that puts delivering solutions, rather than producing products, at the centre of the business.

Already such companies as IBM, General Electric, Boeing and ABB are seeing manufacturing accounting for a smaller and smaller part of their profits. Global competition and excess capacity have made products and basic services increasingly low-margin commodities. Rather than selling products and components, these companies see profits and growth coming from taking direct responsibility for increasing the performance of their customers. Durr, for example, the world leader in painting systems for car plants, has only one-tenth of its employees in production. The rest are working at the customers' premises operating the equipment and guaranteeing cost and quality targets. Castrol, a leader in industrial lubricants, is moving from supplying oils to running its customers' workshops to agreed performance targets.

Companies are positioning themselves as consultants, designing total solutions that will enable customers to increase their profits. They are also offering partnerships to deliver these results and give customers peace of mind. Boeing has set up a division to offer the airlines total fleet servicing. Ford is acquiring car service businesses so that they can offer total motoring solutions. General Electric now gets over half its profits from servicing customers rather than selling products. Such a transformation requires a complete mindset change — from focusing on internal efficiency to understanding what drives the effectiveness of the customer's business.

Developing and consolidating relationships

In discussing the final two components of building customer relationships identified in figure 3.9 — developing the relationship and building trust partnerships — we pay particular attention to what can be done when the business's customers are other businesses — by far the most common marketing situation. Partnerships are not built between companies but between individual managers. Trust and confidence in the capabilities and commitment of the supplier have to be developed on a person-to-person basis.

» The decision-making unit again

In business-to-business marketing, top management, middle management and the purchasing department all have a role in the development of customer partnerships. Normally companies do not sell directly to top management. But top management does control the purse strings, and their agreement is necessary before significant new investments can be made. The purchasing department is of course directly involved in buying arrangements. But the problem with purchasing executives is that they are generally transaction oriented. Their focus is on getting the best deal in terms of price, product features and payment terms. Because they do not have profit responsibility, they are less interested in initiating performance-based partnerships.

The most useful focus for initiating partnerships is middle management, defined here as the heads of business unit profit centres and functional departments. The former are evaluated by their profit performance; the latter by their ability to reduce costs. These managers have the primary incentive to respond positively to suppliers who have the capabilities and commitment to generate continuing proposals to increase the performance of their businesses. They have the most to gain. They are also in the best position to make proposals to top management to get funding for supply partnerships. When business unit heads are convinced that their suppliers can become partners to generate EVC for them, these managers become *allies* in winning the support of the top management.

» **Team-based marketing**

Developing partnerships generally requires a team-based approach from the company. Only a cross-functional team will have the expertise to put together a comprehensive plan to boost the customer's performance. Technical staff will be needed to understand the customer's operations, logistics people will be required to review the supply chain, development and marketing will be involved in putting together the offer, and financial staff in assessing the benefits to both parties. Teams also create an across-the-board commitment to the partnership. A successful ongoing relationship will depend on positive interactions between the businesses at many levels.

A team approach is also necessary in initiating the partnership. While the focus will be on the client's business unit manager, others in the decision-making unit cannot be neglected. Good communications need to be maintained with the purchasing management to align them to the objectives of the partnership. Top management also has to be brought alongside. Typically there will be multi-level communications: sales and purchasing people will be meeting, marketing will be leading the expert team negotiating with business unit management, and top management of the two companies will be in communication with one another developing trust and confidence.

Consolidating trust partnerships

Three points can be made about the task of developing and consolidating trust relationships. First, a partnership arrangement should be judged on its ability to deliver successful solutions for customers. Second, both parties need to invest time in understanding each other's businesses. Third, because problems and perceived breakdowns in trust are inevitably going to occur, it is important to have in place service recovery strategies that provide for investigating difficulties and resolving them to the satisfaction of both parties.

Section 3 Organisational value drivers

A company's success in managing markets depends upon it having a level of skills, capabilities and commitment that enables it to deliver superior value than that offered by competitors. Just as we need to examine the marketing drivers that underpin the financial drivers of shareholder value, we need to analyse the role of organisational drivers: the core capabilities, systems, culture and leadership styles needed to create and implement the shareholder value orientation and to operationalise strategy.

In most situations organisational capabilities and culture are more important than strategy. Looking at successful and unsuccessful competitors in an industry — for example, Singapore Airlines and Sabena; Sony and Philips; US General Electric and Britain's GEC; Coca-Cola and PepsiCola; David Jones and Harris Scarfe; Woolworths/Safeway and Franklins; Disney and Columbia — the real differences are not in their strategy but in how they implement it. We can compare, for example, Singapore Airlines and Sabena, the Belgian airline that ceased operations in November 2001. Both chose to target business travellers flying between major international hubs with a value proposition based on service. But Singapore was much more successful in delivering high levels of customer service and achieving extraordinary customer satisfaction and loyalty. Both possessed similar strategies but only one delivered it.

The 7-S framework

One of the most useful ways of auditing the effectiveness of the company's organisational value drivers is the 7-S framework developed by the McKinsey consulting firm (see figure 3.11).[21] The firm's analysis suggests that these drivers are essential for long-term performance. At the heart of the successful organisation is a set of *shared values* or vision that unites, challenges and gives direction to all the people working there. At British Airways it was to create 'the world's favourite airline'; at Saatchi & Saatchi it was 'nothing is impossible'. Shared values are not financial goals but the motivational drivers that make the former achievable.

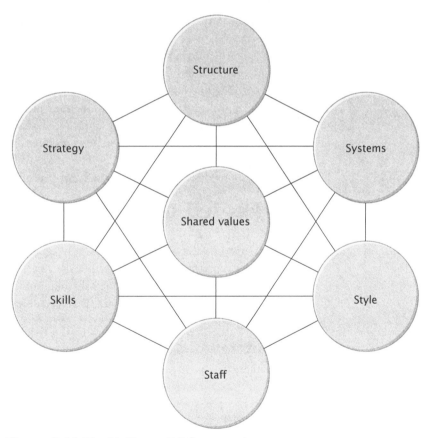

Figure 3.11 The McKinsey 7-S framework

Statements of shared values are meaningless unless they are supported by other drivers that make them operational. The first of these is a *strategy*. Strategy has to be customer led: a deep recognition, throughout the company, that achieving the vision depends on meeting the needs of customers more effectively than competitors. Primacy has to be given to listening to customers, understanding their operating processes and focusing on finding new ways to add value for them. *Structure* refers to how people are organised to work together. Today the emphasis is on empowerment, reducing functional barriers, delayering and encouraging knowledge workers to network widely. *Systems* refer to how information moves around the organisation and its network partners. Information technology which links customers, distributors and supply-chain partners has become a major source of advantage for companies like Dell, the American retailer Wal-Mart, or the British online bank First Direct, that use it to reduce costs and achieve outstanding customer responsiveness.

Staff concerns the background and culture of people who work for the organisation. Successful companies generally attract and socialise staff so that they are relatively similar in attitudes. They share a common outlook that also reflects the company's values. Goldman Sachs attracts hyper-ambitious MBAs from the top business schools; Hewlett Packard has an engineering culture; Saatchi & Saatchi attracts creative types. *Skills* are the distinctive capabilities that the people possess and which are the basis for the firm's ability to create a differential advantage. For example, Hewlett Packard possesses outstanding skills in measurement and computing; Sharp in flat-screen technologies; 3M in adhesives and substrates; Procter & Gamble in branding. *Style* refers to the behaviour of top management and, in particular, how effectively they communicate the values and priorities of the organisation.

The 7-S diagram emphasises the interdependence of the organisational value drivers. An inspiring vision is valueless unless the organisation has the strategy, skills, systems and motivated staff to back it up. Similarly, outstanding skills are not enough unless the structure empowers people to make decisions, the strategy is geared to applying the skills to what customers want, and the systems can deliver fast, cost-effective solutions.

The market-led organisation

Many managers still do not understand today's necessity of being customer oriented and confuse marketing with selling. A market-oriented business starts with understanding customer needs and then goes on to develop products to meet these needs. Production- and sales-oriented businesses work the opposite way: their shared values are very different to those of market-oriented ones.

Production- and sales-oriented organisations

Many organisations — not only in manufacturing, but also in services and government — are production oriented (see figure 3.12). They believe that if you have the necessary technical capabilities to produce good quality products at the right price, then, as in the case of the better mousetrap, 'the world will beat a path to your door'. If marketing is seen as having a role, it is about selling — using advertising, salespeople and PR to tell the public about your offer and to convince them to buy.

But in today's world these strategies cease to work. Because production- and sales-oriented companies design products with little or no input from customers, they are unlikely to be exactly what customers need. With overcapacity and intense competition in most industries, customers have plenty of choices and can usually do better. These businesses then can only find customers by slashing their prices. The results of ignoring customers are declining market shares and eroding margins.

Production orientation

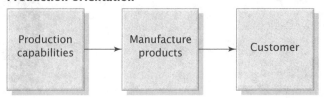

Selling orientation

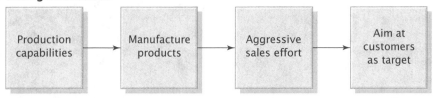

Market orientation

Feedback

Figure 3.12 Production, sales and market orientations

Market-oriented organisations

Today's top companies are customer led (see marketing insight 'Getting to grips with CRM'). This business orientation is often called the 'marketing concept'.

The marketing concept states that the key to creating shareholder value is building relationships with target customers based on satisfying their needs more effectively than competitors.

A market-oriented company starts by looking for market opportunities created by unmet customer needs. These needs are identified by carefully listening to customers, observing them and closely monitoring technological and environmental changes that impinge on markets. From this set of opportunities it aims to select those which seem to have the most potential and which best fit its competencies. The business then evaluates what production and marketing capabilities it will need, and how they should be resourced. Should it undertake these activities in-house or should it seek partnerships with other businesses already possessing these capabilities? Products are then tailored to the problems that customers have. Throughout the process, management continually obtains feedback by listening to customers. The aim is to create a good relationship between the company and its customers such that both parties see value in doing business with one another over an extended period of time.

Marketing insight: Getting to grips with CRM

Customer Relationship Management (CRM) allows companies to focus on getting greater value out of their customers through making business process more effective, but CRM still appears as somewhat of an enigma to a lot of companies. Intent on following the leader, systems are being installed eagerly, but what then?

A number of leading industry CRM specialists have offered their views on the implementation of CRM practices in Australia and offer their views on the benefits, challenges and issues that accompany development of CRM strategy.

The starting point for successful CRM is recognising the customer in the relationship. The Chief Executive of the Australian Direct Marketing Association, Rob Edwards, stresses the need to think about the customer in the relationship. How much do they want the relationship? Will it be mutually beneficial? A holistic view of the relationship is necessary. The basis of developing the relationship must come from input on what the customer desires. Differentiation comes through customer experience and how proactive companies are in getting products out to customers.

How is the CRM by-product integrated into a strategic view of a customer? Firstly it needs to be recognised that CRM itself is not new. What is new is that systems and processes that enable the practice are now technologically based. The technology has only recently begun to be adopted by Australian companies. Rod Bryan, CRM practice leader with Pricewater-houseCoopers, sees a number of projects failing because people try to implement a customer management tool, rather than true CRM. Raj Mendes, Asia Pacific CRM Leader with Cap Gemini Ernest & Young, says that 'The key issues appearing are that a number of CRM projects are failing and executives are not getting the return they expected. They are putting money into the technology but are not aware of the bigger picture.'

At the heart of CRM is the aim of managing your market and aligning this with your business strategy. The CRM leader with Deloitte Consulting, Tony Lucas, says many organisations do not view CRM as integral to their survival. 'CRM tends to be healthiest in markets where there are plenty of customers and a corporate culture that favours revenue-generation over cost cutting.' Another issue is that many companies view the Australian market as too small to necessitate or benefit from CRM. Mendes counters this by arguing that no company is too small to have a CRM strategy: 'What drives organisations are their customers, regardless of their size. The world is getting over-supplied by products and it is becoming more difficult to differentiate between them. Differentiation comes through customer experience and how proactive companies are in getting products out to customers.'

To be successful, CRM must be viewed as a central business philosophy. It has to be perceived as a key component in becoming a customer-centric company, one that helps build relationships that, in turn, maximise the lifetime value of the customer. CRM as a true one-to-one process takes us from the traditional objective of new customer acquisition to share of wallet and from developing short-tem transactions to developing customer lifetime value. CRM as a software solution enables businesses to develop, maintain and enhance the relationship. 'At the other extreme,' says Rob Edwards, 'I have had a bank call me at home to sell me a product I already had with them. If an organisation is going to offer CRM, it needs to take a holistic look at the customer and it better make sure it has the facts right. While CRM tools are powerful and can enhance a relationship, they can also do the opposite.'

Obviously implementation of CRM requires investment, not least the costs required in instigating organisational change, which is a key success factor. Mendes suggests that companies should take a strategic view of cost assessment and focus on return on investment instead. 'CRM is actually revenue generating and cost-cutting, especially as you bring in the Internet. This is evident in the banking industry where low value customers are being directed to the self-service Internet channel.'

Through understanding what customers really want, it is possible to fine-tune and tailor the offering to the benefit of both parties. 'We need to understand the cost and profit of each of them, then we can tailor offerings to make sure it is a profitable relationship,' suggests Bill Gibson, Chief Technology Officer at SAS Institute.

Source: Adapted from Gayle Bryant, 'Know your customers', *BRW*, 9 March 2001, pp. 82–4.

Organisational requirements for creating a market orientation

Managers cannot create a market orientation overnight. The organisation needs to have in place the assets and capabilities to provide unique value to customers. For example, Sony's ability to develop a successful value proposition based on product leadership rests on heavy investment and deep-rooted skills in microelectronics and precision mechanics. Wal-Mart's ability to dominate American retailing with its low-price value proposition is based on a huge investment in developing a unique low-cost sourcing and distribution system. The Australian company, Computershare, has achieved remarkable increases in offshore earnings, and dominant market share in many countries, because of its investment in technology and processes that enable it to offer registry services — lists of a client's shareholders, for a fee, based on the number of shareholders on the registry — on a global scale.

Developing and delivering a strategy to create customer value rests on the firm's resources and capabilities (see figure 3.13).

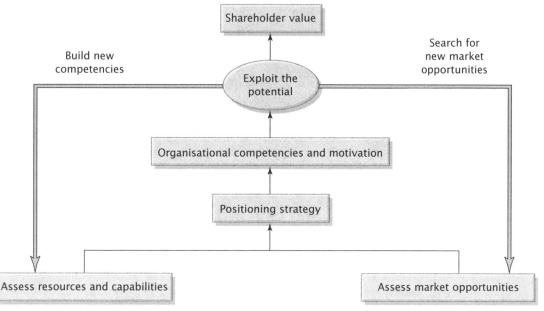

Figure 3.13 Developing and delivering customer value

Assessing resources

A firm's resources and capabilities have to be assessed at several levels. First, firms possess at any one time bundles of tangible, intangible and human resources. But some firms succeed in combining these resources more effectively than others to create superior capabilities. There is a further stage. Today a firm's success in creating a differential advantage depends not just upon its own resources and capabilities but how well it networks with other firms to leverage their capabilities alongside its own.

A firm's resources can be grouped under three headings:

1. **Tangible resources** are those assets that appear on the balance sheet: current assets, investments and fixed assets. Historically, the amount invested in such physical and financial assets, and the firm's ability to manage them efficiently, has determined its value.

2. **Intangible assets** normally do not appear in the firm's financial statement but today they have become far more important in determining the value of the firm. They are of three main types. *Reputational assets* are brand names and other trademarks that give customers confidence in the firm or its products. This confidence results in higher sales and often price premiums, both of which translate into higher shareholder value. *Proprietary technology* consists of patents, copyrights and trade secrets that allow the firm to profitably exploit unique knowledge. *Strategic assets* are inherited advantages that give the firm a monopolistic or unique market position. For example, Qantas's access to premier terminal space at the major Australian airports was a key constraint on its erstwhile challengers, Impulse and Compass. A problem for brewers outside of Victoria trying to compete against the Fosters' Brewing Group is the way that so many hotels are tied to Fosters through distribution agreements.

3. **Human resources** are the valuable knowledge and skills possessed by the organisation's staff and their ability and willingness to work cooperatively with others in the organisation. In today's knowledge-based society, it is the organisation's ability to attract and retain highly skilled people that is increasingly valued by investors.

Of particular importance are the firm's marketing resources. These consist of *marketing expertise* — the knowledge staff possess of customers' needs and the managers' skills in developing marketing strategies and making decisions about products, pricing, communications and distribution. Then there are the *brands* that have been created through marketing investment over time and which offer the promise of future profits. *Customer relationships* are other intangible marketing assets that are highly valued by investors. Then there are other *partnerships* with suppliers, distributors and agencies that augment the organisation's resources with additional knowledge and skills.

Organisational capabilities

Marketing resources are not effective in isolation. To build value-creating strategies, resources have to be brought together in collaboration.

Organisational capabilities are the firm's capacity to exploit a particular marketing opportunity. They are determined by the firm's resources and management's ability to integrate them in pursuit of a marketing strategy. Of most interest are those special capabilities that enable the firm to create a differential advantage. In their influential book, Hamel and Prahalad call these the organisation's **core competencies**.[22] They define core competencies as those special capabilities that make a disproportionate contribution to customer value, are relatively scarce and provide a basis for entering new markets. They comprise a set of skills and expertise that enable a business to deliver exceptional value to customers. Marketing is increasingly seen as the central core competency.

Sony's product leadership in consumer electronics is based on its early mastery in miniaturisation. Singapore Airlines' success in service is based on skills in selecting, training and motivating staff. Toyota's success with low-cost, high-quality cars is based on its operational excellence in supply chain management and manufacturing. It is more than just competencies, however, that determine whether a business generates value — it is also about

core competency: those organisational capabilities that make a disproportionate contribution to customer value, and which are relatively scarce and provide opportunities for the organisation to enter new markets

the culture and attitudes of people in the organisation. These determine whether competencies are applied appropriately. IBM in the 1980s, for example, had outstanding competencies. It was at the forefront of computer technology, it had brilliant staff across all areas of the business, and had exceptional access to major customers. However, it lacked the organisational drive to adapt to a changing environment and to deliver value to shareholders. The result was a collapse in its market share and in its share price. In recent years it has attempted to reposition itself, especially as a provider of e-business solutions.

Harvard Professor Michael Porter proposed the **value chain** as a powerful tool for appraising the firm's capabilities to create a differential advantage (see figure 3.14).[23] A firm is a collection of activities to design, produce, market, deliver and support its products. The value chain identifies nine strategically relevant activities that create value and incur costs. Five of these are termed primary activities and four are support.

The *primary activities* represent the sequence of bringing materials into the firm (inbound logistics), converting them into final products (operations), shipping out the products (outbound logistics), marketing them (marketing and sales) and servicing them (service). The *support activities* — procurement, technology development, human resource management and infrastructure — sustain the ability of the firm to conduct its primary activities.

> **value chain:** the collection of interconnected activities that are performed to design, produce, market, deliver and support goods and services, and that lead to the creation of value

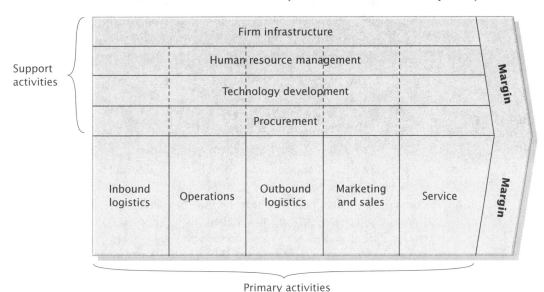

Figure 3.14 The value chain

The central task of management is to improve the firm's value chain by reducing the costs of these activities or improving their performance. The optimum structure of a firm's value chain will depend upon its market and its value proposition. For example, a company in the mainframe computer market will expect to operate on gross margins twice that of one in the PC industry, reflecting the higher investment it will have to make in sales, support and technology development. Similarly, a company with a value proposition based on price, such as Virgin Blue, will have quite a different value chain from one competing on superior service, such as Qantas.

Integrating capabilities: Processes and teams

The value chain describes sets of specialist activities — procurement, marketing, logistics, and so on — but the key to generating shareholder value is to integrate these activities into processes that add value for customers. Having brilliant specialisms will not be enough unless they are brought together and combined to generate fast, innovative and efficient solutions for customers.

Capability comes from combining a competence with a reliable process. While an organisation conducts a multitude of processes, the core processes that add value for customers can be grouped into three (see figure 3.15). The first is the *innovation process*, which analyses potential market opportunities, researches for solutions and develops marketable products. Without a steady stream of new products, the organisation will find its prices and sales being driven relentlessly down. Second, the business needs an efficient *operations process* — it has to be able to produce and deliver products that meet world-class standards of cost and performance. Finally, it must have an effective process for *customer creation and support*.

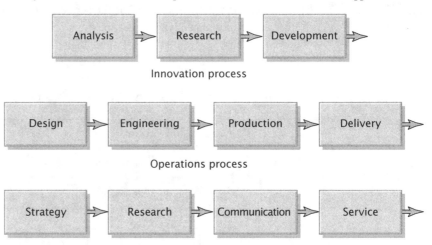

Figure 3.15
The core processes
of the business

There have been significant changes in the way successful firms organise their value-creating processes. In the past, firms were organised hierarchically and functionally. Individuals saw themselves as specialists rather than team players. Inputs to processes were organised hierarchically and each function performed its tasks sequentially. For example, in the innovation process, researchers would first produce ideas, designers would then develop a prototype, it would then be passed on to production for manufacturing, and finally marketing would be involved to develop plans to sell it. Each of the specialist managers would report to his or her functional head rather than to the general process manager.

Today, this type of functional organisation is increasingly giving way to *cross-functional teams*. The members of the team are chosen for their specialist skills but their duty is to accept joint responsibility for achieving process goals. Teams have responsibility not for functional inputs, but for the key processes that add value for customers. Typically these processes are about new product development, operations, and customer service and support. Employees no longer communicate through formal hierarchies but use multiple, informal networks to connect with others who have knowledge which may be valuable to the process. Properly used, these internal networks cut overheads, speed processes and motivate knowledge workers by giving them responsibility and trust.

Information technology has given added impetus to this new kind of direct, informal networking between knowledge workers. Computers and open access to information make redundant the role of bureaucrats in collecting, filtering and passing on information. Cross-functional teams then permit the number of organisational levels to be cut back, reducing overheads and facilitating faster processes. Perhaps the biggest gain from effective team working is its motivational impact on employees. By breaking work down into tasks that can be accomplished by self-managing teams, management releases the energies of their people. Employees can throw off the debilitating blanket of bureaucracy, can set themselves ambitious targets, and can see the results of their contributions in new products, faster processes or higher levels of customer satisfaction.

Networks: Augmenting competencies

The competitiveness of a firm's value chain depends not only upon the effectiveness of its internal, cross-functional networks but increasingly upon its external networks. The increasing need for knowledge about new products, new markets and new processes and for combining different technologies makes it difficult for organisations, however sophisticated, to operate autonomously. External networks — alliances, partnerships, joint ventures and outsourcing — have become the way to harness the disparate range of expertise and economic resources necessary to compete in today's changing markets. Many of today's fast-moving companies see the entrepreneurial task as being two-fold. First, they have to identify emerging opportunities in the market; second, they have to put together a network of companies with the collective set of capabilities to capitalise on the opportunity.

In the past, companies aimed at vertical integration — performing for themselves as many of the processes as possible from raw material supply to final delivery. For example, the Ford Motor Company had its own foundries casting iron and steel, its own factories making glass, tyres, engines and electrical components, and its own distribution business taking the assembled cars to its dealers. Today, however, most companies prefer to outsource non-core activities to a network of suppliers, distributors and partners. Networks allow companies to unbundle their business and focus only on those particular activities where they have unique capabilities to add value. Increasingly, competition is not between individual companies but between networks.

The decline of vertical integration and the growth of networks are due to the changing business environment outlined in chapter 1: notably, rapid technological change, the globalisation of markets and rising customer expectations. New technologies have meant that firms have had to rapidly obtain capabilities that were outside their traditional areas of competence. Sourcing such component products from outside is often the only practical route. Developing the capabilities internally would take too long, require too great an investment and be too risky. Similarly, globalisation has opened up new markets, but often firms lack the capabilities to exploit these opportunities. Finding business partners is an obvious solution.

Increasingly, the firm's value chain is part of a system for delivering solutions to customers (see figure 3.16). It is the effectiveness with which managers handle the whole supply chain and network of partnerships that determines the competitiveness of the firm. Again, information technology is boosting the facility with which such networks can be managed.

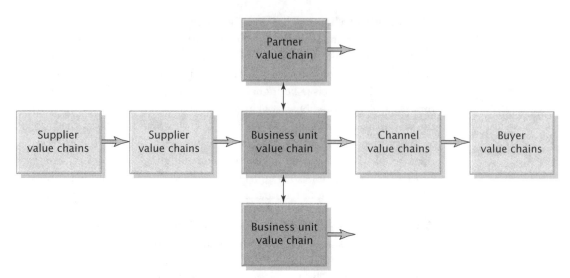

Figure 3.16 The firm's value chain system

The customer-focused organisation

The concept of the value chain allows management to explore how people can be organised internally to create greater value. But the external impacts of staff on customers also need to be optimised. In recent years, leading firms have been putting great efforts into making their organisations customer oriented.

In the past, customer focus was not the driving force behind the design of organisations. Instead, organisations were designed bureaucratically to optimise the efficiency of capital and to reduce risks. Top management formulated strategy and those at the bottom of the hierarchy undertook implementation. Job roles were clearly defined and employees were organised into functional departments (e.g. production, marketing, purchasing). To ensure that strategy was implemented correctly, controls in the form of supervisors, centralised information systems, budgets and formalised reporting played a major role. Communication was vertical: information went up and orders came down. Lateral communication across functions was limited and was the preserve of senior staff.

In recent years, three pressures undermined these bureaucratic organisations. One was the need to cut overhead costs as increasing global competition eroded the gross margins of many firms. Companies could no longer pay for the big head office staffs and the layers of middle management supervising and controlling the front-line staff. A second pressure was the need to accelerate the pace of innovation. While the formalised hierarchical structures worked well enough in steady-state industries, they were poor at stimulating innovation. Fast-paced innovation does not work well in organisations characterised by rules, rigid reporting procedures and tight job specifications. A third problem was that these organisations were not customer oriented. The front-line staff who dealt with customers were at the bottom of the organisational pyramid. People with talent did not want these jobs because they lacked prestige and autonomy. Real decisions and power lay at the top of the hierarchy — far away from direct contact with customers and the front line. Not surprisingly, customers frequently found such organisations unresponsive and their front-line staff unmotivated and unprofessional.

The right-side-up organisation

The new, more demanding market environment created the pressures to change organisations; information technology provided the means for change. Three features stand out in the way leading companies are reorganising to enhance customer orientation and shareholder value:

1. breaking into small, autonomous business units
2. turning the organisation upside-down
3. changing the role of top management.

» Breaking into small, autonomous business units

Large organisations cannot help but become bureaucratic, slow moving and unresponsive to customers. To counteract these problems, companies are breaking themselves down into small business units that have profit responsibility for a specific market, product or process. They are trading off the old priorities of scale economies and cost efficiency for the new agenda that prioritises innovation and customer responsiveness. For examples, see marketing management in practice 'Changing organisational structure to improve customer responsiveness'.

Marketing management in practice: **Changing organisational structure to improve customer responsiveness**

CEO Percy Bernevik transformed the global electrical giant Asea Brown Boveri. The business was radically decentralised with the creation of 1300 companies as separate and distinct entities — each with an average of 200 people and $25 million in annual revenues. Bernevik's idea was to create a federation of companies where employees would lose 'the false sense of security of belonging to a big organisation' and would develop the 'motivation and pride to contribute directly to the unit's success'. Each of the 1300 companies would have its own balance sheet and each retain one-third of distributable profits after paying a dividend to the group.

Management structure at the group level was also drastically changed. Eight layers of management were reduced to just one. The total number of employees at the head office of this $30 billion company was cut to under one hundred. The primary task of headquarters was to encourage and facilitate cross-company cooperation, with computer networks and knowledge sharing at the centre of this process. The focus for managers changed from vertical reporting procedures to an emphasis on horizontal integration, learning from others, sharing insights, and employing best practices wherever they exist.

Flight Centre's founder and chief executive, Graham Turner, organised his company into teams of seven people, which he believes is the most efficient size. The teams operate throughout the company, even in the global leadership team run by Turner. The teams are called families. Groups of four to ten shops are referred to as a village, and villages and their support businesses are grouped into tribes, each comprising about 120 people.

When John McFarlane became chief executive of the ANZ Banking Group he transformed it into a portfolio of 21 (now 16) different businesses. Each would have to establish a strong competitive position in its market, meet its cost of capital, and have a viable growth strategy. The theme of specialisation was based on the notion that entrepreneurial specialists create more value. The accounts are delivered with a picture and name of the chief executive of each of the 16 at the top of each file.

Sources: Sumantra Ghoshal and Christopher A. Bartlett, 'Changing the role of top management: Beyond structure to process', *Harvard Business Review*, January/February 1995, pp. 86–96; Philip Rennie, 'Flight Centre reaches for new heights', *BRW*, 14–20 February 2002, pp. 24, 35; John Kavanagh, 'John McFarlane', *BRW*, 18–23 April 2002, pp. 54–5; and Ian Huntley, 'Banking on a bonny future', *Shares*, January 2002, p. 24.

» Turning the organisation upside-down

Today, companies want to focus on customers and on those who are directly responsible for understanding and satisfying their needs — the front-line staff. Traditional organisations do not do this. The pyramid structure devalues the role of the front-line staff and promotes the importance of supervisory and staff positions. Power and rank go to those who can manipulate the politics of the organisation rather than those who satisfy customer needs.

Modern companies want to reverse this focus by turning the organisation upside-down and flattening it (see figure 3.17). The aim is to enhance front-line positions, improve knowledge about solving customer problems and enhance service. The new orientation recognises that the key to creating shareholder value is the loyalty of customers. This in turn depends on the skills and motivation of the front-line staff. To achieve this, companies have to recruit the best staff and invest heavily in their training and development. Finally, such staff have to be empowered to act on their own judgment about the right way of dealing with customers.

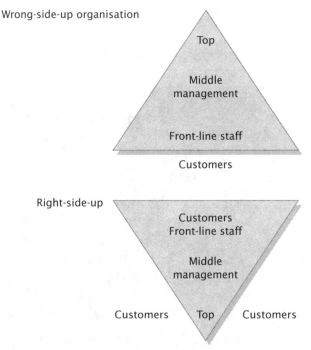

Figure 3.17 Wrong- and right-side-up organisations

The mission statement of Pepsico shows how the new upside-down organisation emphasises that the role of middle and senior management is to support the front-line staff in satisfying customers (see figure 3.18). If managers are not assisting the front-line staff by providing the products and tools that they need, then these managers are not adding value. The philosophy has led to new approaches to evaluating managerial performance. Evaluating the performance of front-line staff is often straightforward — customers can be asked to rate the way they perform. But deciding who should evaluate, and how the performance of middle and senior management should be judged, has been more problematical. In the new customer-focused organisation the answer is clear — ask the front-line the question: 'Are these middle managers helping you serve the customer?' Such an approach changes the outlook of middle managers. Instead of being controllers, they have to prove their value by becoming supporters and coaches, assisting the effectiveness of the front line.

PepsiCola — the right-side-up company

We will be an outstanding company by exceeding customer expectations through empowering people, guided by shared values

This requires
A consistent
Customer focus
For our company which all of our people understand and feel passionate about
An
Empowered organisation
Which is both motivated and supported to satisfy customers to the fullest extent of their capabilities
A set of
Shared values
Which guides all our decisions and actions

To make this a reality, we must turn the company 'right-side-up'.
A right-side-up company places the customer at the top, thereby acknowledging everything starts with the customer.

Those employees closest to the customers are at the top of the organisation. They must be empowered to satisfy customer needs. The rest of the organisation's role is to help those closest to the customers by providing resources and removing obstacles.

Figure 3.18 PepsiCola: The right-side-up company

» The role of top management

Today, the roles of the chief executive and top management are changing. In the past, the chief executive was seen as the company's top marketing strategist. He or she would define the company's markets and how it would create differential advantage. Once the strategy was formulated, top management would then design the organisational structure and systems required to implement the strategy. However, this view of strategy is looking increasingly anachronistic.

It is no longer realistic to assume top management has the superior knowledge to develop strategy. Relevant knowledge now lies in the front line, not in the corporate office. The real job of top management today is not to strive to achieve the impossible goal of being the marketing guru defining strategy, structure and systems. Instead, it is to release the knowledge and energy of the front line by developing and communicating a vision of the company's purpose, processes and people.

In large organisations it is all too easy for people to become disaffected by bureaucracy, cost cutting and the inevitable changes that threaten their security and careers. Shareholder value is not a goal that inspires staff. Work is more than an economic institution for people; it is also a social institution that involves a major proportion of their time, energy and relationships. To create involvement and motivation, top management needs to give the organisation a 'human purpose' with which employees can identify. Bob Allen did this at AT&T with his idea of being 'dedicated to becoming the world's best at bringing people together — giving them easy access to each other and to the information and services they want and need — anytime, anywhere'. So too has Jack O'Mahony, the chief executive of the Australian bionic ear manufacturer, Cochlear, which 'prides itself in being "A partner in Hearing for Life", supporting all its customers in working to improve the lifestyle of Nucleus cochlear implant recipients'.[24] Today, the real role of the chief executive is to shape the culture of the organisation and give it a meaning that encourages people to willingly contribute their energies and skills.

Summary

1. There are three sets of value drivers that influence shareholder value: financial, marketing and organisational.
2. The financial value drivers are the overall level of cash flow, and the timing, duration and riskiness of cash flow.
3. The level of cash flow is determined by a strategy's ability to achieve growth and adequate operating margins and by the level of investment required.
4. The financial drivers are the objectives of the business. However, achieving the growth and profitability targets depends upon strategy — especially marketing strategy.
5. Marketing is the basis for creating shareholder value. Only by meeting customer needs, developing customer preference and building customer relationships can an organisation achieve profitable growth.
6. Meeting customer needs, however, is not sufficient. The organisation also has to create a differential advantage: a reason why it should be preferred to competitor businesses. A differential advantage may be based upon offering consumers superior benefits, lower costs or some combination of the two.
7. The ultimate goal is to build partnerships with high-value customers founded on loyalty and trust. Customer loyalty is the real source of sound business growth and profitability. Customers are assets: the longer they are retained, the more value they should create.
8. Implementing a strategy depends upon the firm's organisational value drivers. Building successful customer partnerships depends upon the firm having the resources and capabilities to build outstanding processes, particularly in innovation, operations, and customer creation and support.

key | terms

core competency, p. 114
customer lifetime value, p. 99
customer loyalty, p. 97
customer satisfaction, p. 100
differential advantage, p. 85
economic value to the customer, p. 106
emotional value to the customer, p. 106
existing needs, p. 88

incipient needs, p. 88
incremental investment rate, p. 81
intangible assets, p. 80
latent needs, p. 88
tangible assets, p. 80
threshold margin, p. 81
threshold spread, p. 81
value, p. 91
value chain, p. 115
value proposition, p. 91

review | questions

1. What are the four financial drivers and how does marketing influence each of them?
2. What are the key challenges in building differential advantage?
3. Why is it difficult for a company to maintain and build its customer base?
4. What is the connection between developing customer relationships and building shareholder value?
5. What resources and capabilities does an organisation need to develop a successful marketing strategy?

discussion | questions

1. Marketing is central to creating shareholder value. Discuss.
2. What are the challenges for organisations in trying to understand customer needs?
3. Can you give examples of companies that have excelled at competing on benefits?
4. Why does customer loyalty have such a profound effect on shareholder value?
5. Can you give examples of companies that have 'selected' customers?
6. What are the organisational requirements to be a market-oriented company?

debate | questions

1. In essence, are consumer and business-to-business buyer behaviour fundamentally the same?
2. Is there such a thing as a loyal customer?
3. Does asking consumers whether they are satisfied tell a company anything very useful?
4. Are very few businesses customer-focused?

case study | **Understanding customers**

In the mid-1990s, executives of the Coca-Cola Company were talking about a new technique for identifying consumer needs that they called 'presearch'. According to the soft-drink maker, presearch involved using a variety of research models, tools and technologies to pre-empt consumer needs ... But, almost a decade later, the concept of presearch is still largely unknown.

Presearch is a method for picking new consumer needs and wants before they emerge or become obvious. It can involve new data-mining techniques, brainstorming and qualitative and quantitative research. It is an approach or technique that involves much more than customer research.

Suzan Burton, a senior lecturer in management at Macquarie Graduate School of Management, says the low profile of presearch is not surprising. Different companies, she says, have different ways to describe the technique of presearching: many simply call it research or strategic planning. Indeed, Coca-Cola's local marketing company has an insights and planning department, and a spokesperson had never heard of the term presearch.

Burton also believes that presearch is not very relevant to most Australian companies because the technique is most valuable to companies that are creating products that are

(continued)

'new to the world', such as companies involved in pharmaceuticals, food, beverages and information technology. Many of the big spenders on research in Australia are the local arms of multinationals, which adapt existing products and services for the local market.

Pinpointing customer needs involves more than researching customers, because they are not always able to say what they will need in the future. For example, based on market research, Internet banking and 3M's Post-it Note were widely underestimated by marketers. 3M's marketing department said at the time that it would be lucky to sell US$2 million of sticky labels; today, it is one of 3M's best selling products. Likewise, banks underestimated consumer demand for online banking. In both cases, the companies involved were focusing on established patterns of customer behaviour. 'Consumers are often very bad judges of their future needs,' Burton says.

The head of Commonwealth Bank's research and knowledge department, Elizabeth Moore, says it is a pity that the presearch concept is not more widely understood. 'It is about looking at your business through the headlights rather than the rear-view mirror,' she says. 'It is about investing the research dollar not in the past, but in the future. It is about looking outside the traditional market research perspective.'

Moore's department used presearch techniques when it worked on the integration of Colonial Group into Commonwealth Bank last year. Using customer databases, the department looked for issues that could be of concern to customers and key problems that needed to be dealt with before they occurred. Moore says that in the past, the normal strategy would have been to wait until customers had left and then conduct a survey of, say, 400 and ask them why. 'We wanted to deal with concerns before they became an attrition issue,' she says.

Commonwealth Bank is also using presearch techniques to develop new products. 'This is not an area that only the customers' points of view can solve,' Moore says. 'It's easy to have a fantastic idea that will appeal to a consumer. But it has to be implementable and profitable.' Moore assembles cross-disciplinary teams that include marketers, researchers and information technology staff. She also takes into account global trends, not just in the finance and banking sector but also in other service industries.

The managing director of Celsius Research, Martin James, says presearch enables research to be more focused, particularly with the help of computer software. 'Researchers are moving away from saying, for example, that the target market for Kit Kat is 4–24-year-olds. What presearch techniques do is ask "Should we be chasing the 14–25s or the 25 pluses?".'

Moore says: 'The real value in presearch is that it ensures every piece of research you do adds value to the business.'

Source: Adapted from Emily Ross, 'The customer is not always right', *BRW*, 31 October–6 November 2002, p. 43.

Questions

1. Just what is presearch? Why is it necessary?
2. How might presearch be done?
3. Do you agree that the technique is not very relevant to most Australian companies? Could the approach be used in situations other than the creation of new products?
4. Why is it difficult for consumers to say what they will want in the future?
5. What would be the organisational challenges in disseminating the results of presearch to the rest of the organisation and acting on the findings that it generates?

end notes

1. Assume initial sales are 100, costs are 90 and the cash tax rate is 30 per cent. With a 5 per cent sales increase and volume unchanged, sales rise to 105, costs stay the same, pre-tax profits rise from 10 to 15, and NOPAT from 7 to 10.5.

2. Working on the same example, assume that half its costs are variable. With a 5 per cent volume loss on the new price, sales slip to 99.75, variable costs drop from 45 to 42.75, then pre-tax profit increases from 10 to 12 and NOPAT from 7 to 8.4.

3. See, for example, Michael Hammer and James Champy, *Reengineering the Corporation*, London: Brealey, 1993.

4. Here sales rise from 100 to 130, variable costs increase from 45 to 58.5, fixed costs remain unchanged at 45, pre-tax profits go from 10 to 26.5 and NOPAT from 7 to 18.6 or to 14 per cent of sales.

5. Under the low-investment strategy, the present value of the continuing value is $754 million and the shareholder value is $1287 million. Under the high-investment strategy, the continuing value is $894 million and the shareholder value is $1393 million.

6. For detailed development of threshold margin see Rappaport, *Creating Shareholder Value*, 2nd edn, New York: Free Press, 1998, pp. 51–5. Rappaport calls the figure used here the incremental threshold margin.

7. S. David Young and Stephen F. O'Byrne, *EVA and Value-based Management: A Practical Guide to Implementation*, New York: McGraw-Hill, p. 76.

8. George Stalk and Thomas M. Hout, *Competing Against Time*, New York: The Free Press, 1990.

9. Gary Hamel and C. K. Prahalad, *Competing for the Future*, Boston, MA: Harvard Business School Press, 1994.

10. Anthony W. Ulwick, 'Turn customer input into innovation', *Harvard Business Review*, **80**, January 2002, pp. 91–7.

11. Dorothy Leonard and Jeffrey F. Rayport, 'Spark innovation through empathic design', *Harvard Business Review*, **75**, November/December 1997, pp. 102–13.

12. See, for example, Gerald Zaltman, 'Metaphorically speaking', *Marketing Research*, **8** (2), 1996, pp. 13–20.

13. The discussion here is influenced by Michael Treacy and Fred Wiersema, *The Discipline of Market Leaders*, London: HarperCollins, 1995. They identify three value disciplines: operational excellence, product leadership and customer intimacy.

14. Treacy and Wiersema, *op. cit.*, p. 205.

15. The discussion here builds on the three horizons framework presented in Mehrdad Baghai, Stephen Coley and David White, *The Alchemy of Growth: Kickstarting and Sustaining Growth in Your Company*, London: Orion, 1999.

16. Many of these findings are presented in an important book, Frederick F. Reichheld, *The Loyalty Effect*, Boston, MA: Harvard Business School Press, 1996.

17. Thomas O. Jones and W. Earl Sasser, Jr, 'Why satisfied customers defect', *Harvard Business Review*, November/December, 1995, pp. 88–99.

18. The term 'terrorist' has been used for some time. It was popularised in work by Heskett, Sasser and Schlesinger on the service–profit chain and is now part of the standard lexicon of 'customer types'.

19. For a complete review of this approach see Robert M. Morgan and Shelby D. Hunt, 'The commitment–trust theory of marketing', *Journal of Marketing*, **58** (3), 1994, pp. 20–38.

20. For an example of the use of rating systems to evaluate prospective customers see John O. Whitney, 'Strategic renewal for business units', *Harvard Business Review*, **74** (5), July/August 1996, pp. 84–99.

21. For a fuller description see Richard Tanner Pascale, *Managing on the Edge*, London: Viking, 1990, pp. 37–50.

22. Hamel and Prahalad, *op. cit.*, pp. 223–33.

23. Michael E. Porter, *Competitive Advantage: Creating and Sustaining Superior Performance*, New York: Simon & Schuster, 1985.

24. Cochlear, *2001 Annual Report*, p. 1, www.cochlear.com.

Part 2
Deciding where to compete

Value-based marketing strategy

chapter objectives

By the time you have completed this chapter, you will be able to:

- understand why systematic strategic marketing planning is necessary
- recognise the important differences between strategic planning at the corporate level and at the level of the business unit
- understand the role of a strategic position assessment and strategic focus assessment
- use the key components of a value-based marketing strategy
- develop performance measures for implementing and controlling the strategic plan
- show how the results of the strategic plan can be evaluated using shareholder value analysis
- outline the process for developing creative marketing strategies.

scene setter

The emerging importance of value-based marketing strategy

Marketers are under greater pressure than at any time they can remember... Why has their job become so difficult? Is high-profile American marketing consultant Regis McKenna correct when he claims marketing is dead?

The president of the Australian Marketing Institute, Tony Hart, says the pressure on marketers stems from a trend that has been strengthening for the past decade: shareholder demand for performance. 'To a very large extent, this new marketing landscape has evolved from the new business landscape,' Hart says. 'With the ever-growing need for increasing shareholder value, businesses have become obsessed with the bottom line. That means marketers have to deliver value to shareholders in the short term. There is an incredible amount of pressure, and I think many marketers have fallen by the wayside because of it. Marketing is an investment, but it is seen as expensive and a waste of money.'

Adding to shareholder demand for value are other issues that make the job of the marketer even more difficult. Products and services tend to be 'me too', making it harder for a company to find a clear point of difference for its brands, and the proliferation of media is diluting

> 'Because its purpose is to create a customer, the business enterprise has two — and only these two — basic functions: marketing and innovation. Marketing and innovation produce results; all the rest are "costs".'
>
> Peter F. Drucker

the effect of most marketing messages. Marketers find themselves being marginalised by their employers. Late last year, McKenna told a United States business magazine: 'Marketing is becoming an integrated part of the whole organisation. Who is responsible for setting the direction of a business? More and more, it's the CEO who is becoming chief marketer. The marketing function is being marginalised to advertising and PR.'

Hart agrees. He says the blurring of demarcation lines between the marketing director, financial controller, and chief executive over the past five years has left marketers feeling disenfranchised…'If you look at the major global companies, the marketing director has significant influence. In Australia, I don't think there is the same influence of the marketer in the boardroom. One reason is the emergence in the early-to-mid-1990s of the CEO with a purely financial background who did not understand marketing. But marketers have only themselves to blame for losing their influence. They sat back and let it happen.'

'What has not been well appreciated by company directors is that marketing controls the most valuable assets a company has — its brands, customer information, and product knowledge,' [Caroline] Trotman [a marketing director at the consulting firm Accenture] says. 'Assets are the key to whether shareholder value will be created or destroyed, and the way an organisation manages those assets determines how it gets a sustained competitive advantage. The attention boards give to those assets will have to change.'

Trotman is not as gloomy about the new marketing landscape as Hart. 'This is the age of marketing,' she says, 'but we have to face up to one issue: how does marketing market itself? As marketers, our biggest weakness is we do not talk the language of the boardroom.' …

Source: Extracts from Simon Lloyd, 'The board: The ultimate fight for share', *BRW*, 16 February 2001, p. 68.

Introduction

Part 1 of this book addressed the principles of value-based marketing. It examined the importance of shareholder returns as an objective, how to calculate the shareholder value added by marketing, and how marketing drives shareholder returns. This chapter presents an overview of the steps in developing such a marketing strategy. Chapters 5 and 6 consider in more detail the tasks of strategic objective assessment and strategic focus assessment.

Conceptualising marketing strategy

Creating long-term value is synonymous with achieving long-term competitiveness — the ability of the business to survive and prosper in a highly competitive global marketplace. So a strategy that creates value for shareholders should also enhance the security of employees, creditors, and the community at large. History has shown that firms cannot endure if they expand regardless of profitability, or if they do not adapt to changing markets.

marketing strategy:
a set of coherent decisions about a firm's approach to managing the market

A **marketing strategy** is defined as a set of coherent decisions about a firm's approach to managing the market. The decisions concern the choice of markets, and the customers within, that the business seeks to serve. The decisions also address how the business will meet customer needs, how it will create a sustainable competitive advantage, and how it will commit valuable resources to the served markets. A **value-based marketing strategy** is a marketing strategy that aims to maximise shareholder value.

value-based marketing strategy:
a marketing strategy that aims to maximise shareholder value

As emphasised in earlier chapters, marketing is at the heart of the strategy for creating long-term shareholder value. Without an outstanding competence in marketing, shareholder value becomes merely an accounting tool focusing on short-run profitability and cash flow.

Although marketing plays an important role at the corporate level, it is most potent at the business unit level — the level of the individual market and product. At this level, marketing's impact on shareholder value rests on the marketing plan. A marketing plan is a cornerstone of **strategic planning**. It is based first on the strategic position assessment, which evaluates the potential of the business unit's market situation and the broad direction by which shareholder value may be created. The strategic position assessment then leads to a definition of the business unit's strategic objective. Subsequently, the strategic focus and the marketing mix need to be addressed.

strategic planning:
a planning process focused on how long-term value for owners of the firm will be created

Once the marketing strategy is formulated, marketing management needs relevant performance indicators to ensure that the plan is kept on track over time. Finally, the financial implications of the proposed plan have to be tested through a shareholder value analysis to assess whether the marketing strategy is likely to maximise corporate value.

Why strategic marketing plans?

Developing a systematic marketing strategy is important. The functions of strategic market planning are to:

- facilitate the change process
- force managers to ask the right questions
- motivate and control
- balance the tyranny of accountants.

Facilitating the change process

The process of developing a marketing strategy forces management to objectively confront the current performance of the business today and its likely performance in the future. The remorseless pressures of day-to-day operational problems often hide the real fundamental issues facing the company. The plan starkly reveals whether the business has been successful in generating value for shareholders, in satisfying customers, and creating a competitive advantage in the market. Strategic marketing planning also provides a vehicle for piloting change. It sets the framework for thinking about the future, developing more ambitious goals, and identifying new options (see marketing management in practice 'destroyyourbusiness.com'). Knowing that the business has a clear direction can invigorate employees and instil confidence among investors.

Marketing management in practice: destroyyourbusiness.com

Few were surprised when *Fortune* magazine chose Jack Welch, chief executive of General Electric (GE), as its 'businessman of the century'. Since taking over in 1981, he had increased the value of the company from US$14 billion to more than US$400 billion, quadrupled sales to over US$100 billion and had grown profits six times to US$9.3 billion.

Despite the applause, at the end of 1999, only a year from retirement, Welch was still not satisfied and wanted more. The particular challenge he identified was e-business, both as an opportunity and a threat to GE's dominance. His response was to launch a major new initiative called 'destroyyourbusiness.com'. Welch believed that only by getting his managers to imagine the end of their current businesses could they really create something radical and new enough to survive into the next century.

The initiative was based on the three key elements that lay at the heart of Welch's transformation of GE in earlier decades. It was iconoclastic — nothing was sacred: products, channels, practices and systems were all up for challenge. It sought to learn and borrow from the best practices of other leading edge companies. GE envoys who went out to study the new e-business pioneers came back with alarming demonstrations of how GE was still too slow, too internally focused, and insufficiently customer-oriented for competing in 'Internet-time'. Last, the initiative sought to make determined use of GE's collective effort and intellect. A new set of 'workouts' was organised to stimulate all employees to challenge senior executives on current practices and to make recommendations for transforming the business and creating new ones.

Forcing managers to ask the right questions

Most products that fail do not do so because of events that could not have been anticipated. Rather, they fail because managers have not effectively analysed their customers and competitors. The marketing plan ensures that managers ask the key questions and do the vital analyses that determine success or failure. These centre on understanding the needs of customers, evaluating the competition and anticipating their likely strategies, and ensuring that the company can communicate a genuine competitive advantage. When managers have analysed the key questions, they are in a much stronger position to react effectively to the unexpected events that inevitably occur.

Motivation and control

Value-based marketing is based on two principles. First, the task of management is to create long-run value for shareholders. Second, its accomplishment depends on building relationships with customers founded on satisfying their desired benefits more effectively than competitors. The strategic marketing plan brings these two principles together. The objective and test of the strategy is its ability to create shareholder value. The process of strategy formulation focuses on choosing profitable customers and developing a value proposition that will make them want to do business with the company rather than competitors.

The structure of the plan aims at ensuring that managers do not pursue growth strategies that are not value-enhancing. At the same time, it encourages managers to invest heavily in growth if this will create long-run profits in the future. As the high values attached to shares in unprofitable Internet companies such as Amazon.com, Freeserve, and eBay demonstrated, there is no correlation between short-term profitability and value. Investors are quite happy to forgo cash and profits today if they believe the company is investing in a strategy that offers great long-run potential. In particular, value-based planning should discourage arbitrary cuts in marketing budgets to boost short-term profits and cash flow. Investors look through such cuts and often react to the moves by selling their shares, knowing that future profitability and competitiveness are being sacrificed.

Balancing the tyranny of accountants

The great majority of company boards spend too much time on the monthly, quarterly and annual budgets produced by their accountants. Such a focus leads to an overemphasis on short-term profit performance and an under-emphasis on the viability of the long-term strategy of the business. By delving into the details of the unit's costs and investments, the board demotivates management, discourages initiative, and blankets the entrepreneurship it should be encouraging under a stifling layer of bureaucracy.

The strategic marketing plan asks the board to consider what is important: Will the strategy create competitive advantage? Will it maximise shareholder value? While accountants look backwards, the strategic plan looks forwards; and it is the future not the past that determines the value of the business.

Corporate-level planning

In discussing strategic planning it is important to distinguish between the corporate or group plan and the business unit plans. Every company can be characterised in terms of **business units**. In big companies, there can be a very large number of business units: the engineering company ABB has over 1300; General Electric has around 200. In small to medium size companies, there might be only a few business units. Some small companies are, in effect, a single business unit. Indeed, they can be referred to as a business unit.

business unit:
an organisational unit with strategic and budgetary responsibility

A business unit may consist of a group of related products, a market, or a distribution channel. Because a business unit serves a specific group of customers and delivers a required benefit, a tailored marketing strategy is necessary. It is the responsibility of business unit managers to develop such a strategy with the aim of maximising long-run economic profits. It is this type of strategic planning which is the main focus of this chapter.

The corporate centre does not directly create value for customers; that is the task of the business unit. But headquarters can be very costly and absorb a substantial proportion of shareholder value. The largest companies spend an average of 1.3 per cent of annual sales on their headquarters. This amounts to an estimated 39 per cent of their equity value.[1] Some companies have costs three times this average figure, implying that cutting headquarters costs could sometimes have a big impact on the share price. How can the corporate centre justify loading the business with this overhead cost burden? Would it not be cheaper if all their functions and staff were allocated to the business units that have the profit responsibility and, hence, the incentive to manage costs more economically? Headquarters add value only if they enable the individual business units to generate additional profits that exceed the headquarters' costs. In principle, headquarters can add value in three ways, namely by:

1. driving organisational change
2. managing the shared value drivers
3. managing the business portfolio.

Driving organisational change

In successful companies, the corporate centre, and in particular the chief executive, is the catalyst for change. He or she communicates what the organisation's priorities should be. First of these is the belief that the central objective of all managers must be to develop strategies that will maximise shareholder value. Second is passionate understanding that in competitive markets, shareholder value is derived from delivering the benefits needed by customers more successfully than competitors. Only by delighting customers and building strong, continuing relationships with them can the company build the revenue stream that is the basis for long-term cash flow. Third is the recognition that in today's rapidly changing environment, the company must be continually sloughing off strategies that have worked in the past and finding new opportunities for growth.

An effective corporate centre puts in place a combination of formal and informal mechanisms for driving these priorities. The key mechanisms are:

1. **The strategic planning process.** In successful businesses, strategic plans, rather than accounting budgets, become the focus for managers. Business units are required to develop strategic plans that demonstrate how they will create long-term value for shareholders rather than short-term profits. Top management also looks to see that these strategic plans are firmly grounded on convincing assumptions about customers' needs and competitor reactions. The plans give management the information to question whether the business units are being sufficiently radical in responding to the problems and opportunities being created by today's rapidly changing markets and technologies, and whether they are creating sufficient growth options.

2. **The resource allocation process.** The centre is responsible for allocating resources among the business units and for creating new businesses and making acquisitions. Over time, these decisions will lead to a major reshaping of the company. Companies that manage for value allocate resources to businesses and new ventures when they promise a return that exceeds the cost of capital. There is no rationing problem. It makes sense for investors to forgo dividends and bring in new capital if management can earn returns that exceed the cost of capital. In this case, a business is

earning a better return than investors could earn if they invested the money themselves. An effective resource allocation process acts to continually reposition the company towards markets where market conditions allow the average company to make economic profits and where the business has a sustainable differential advantage — in other words, where the business is able to sustain economic profits that exceed the average of competitors by means of an economic cost advantage (which occurs when a firm's total costs, including capital costs, are lower than those of the average competitor) or by means of a differentiation advantage (which occurs when customers perceive its products as superior, and are willing to pay a higher price than is charged by competitors).

3. **Performance measurement and compensation.** Managers need feedback and incentives that motivate behaviour consistent with the objectives of creating shareholder value, customer orientation and growth. The first requirement is to give managers of the business units clear responsibility for strategy. As far as possible, each unit should be able to act as a separate profit centre and have total autonomy over how it buys, operates, and markets its products or services.

4. **Creating a sense of purpose.** In today's complex, knowledge-intensive organisations, strategy is not enough. Employees need a sense of purpose with which they can identify if they are going to be truly committed to the firm. Increasingly, the role of the chief executive is seen as providing this catalyst. Leaders such as Richard Branson of Virgin and Anita Roddick of The Body Shop, for example, articulated strong business philosophies which created an unusually strong alignment between company and employee beliefs.

Managing the shared value drivers

The ability of a multibusiness corporation to outperform a single business firm lies in whether the former can exploit economies from sharing resources or from transferring special capabilities which exist in one business to other businesses within the group.

» Shared services

All multibusiness companies have shared services. Typically, these will include accounting as well as tax, treasury, legal, human resources, and information systems. But shared services rarely create a differential advantage for the company in terms of either lower cost or superior quality. The key problem tends to be a lack of incentive within the centre to reduce costs or to meet the needs of their customers within the business units. The lack of customer focus often leads to the units duplicating corporate services. In dealing with corporate services, marketing management needs to answer two questions. Which services are best done centrally to minimise costs? Which should be decentralised to best match the requirements of their business unit customers? For those services that continue to be offered centrally, marketing management needs to find the least costly way to provide them, subject to quality standards. Sometimes, it will be possible to do this by creating an internal market in which central services have to 'sell' their capabilities to the business units in competition with independent suppliers.

» Leveraging resources

Much more important for creating shareholder value and, in particular, for creating new growth opportunities, are the resources. The centre has to catalyse the transfer of resources across businesses and, indeed, create new ones. As discussed in chapter 3, every successful business has resources that form the basis of core competencies, giving it unique opportunities for growth and profitability. These resources may be tangible assets such as first-class factories or equipment, intangible assets such as brands or patents, strategic assets such as licences and natural monopolies, or human resources in the form of highly skilled staff. For example, one of Qantas's core competencies in Australia might be its club lounge offer. One of Wal-Mart's core competencies in the United States might be its supply chain management.

The centre can add value in a crucial way by leveraging these resources across its business units. Hamel and Prahalad have shown how much of the growth of such companies as 3M, Sony, Canon and Honda has been due to the way they leveraged technical skills across their business units to create entirely new products.[2] For example, business units at Canon have developed core competencies in precision mechanics, fine optics and microelectronics. The centre continually encourages the discovery of new products and markets that can draw on the entire range of the company's skills. This has allowed Canon to move into a range of new opportunities from cameras, to calculators, printers, faxes, copiers and so on. For instance, when Canon identified an opportunity in digital laser printers, it created a new business unit and gave management the right to raid other units to pull together the required talent in engineering, optics, microelectronics and imaging.

Besides technical skills, marketing assets such as customer relationships are becoming increasingly important sources of leverage across business units. Virgin, for example, has built a brand name around the world symbolising underdog spirit, innovation, and genuine value, which has enabled it to move into businesses as diverse as record shops, airlines, soft drinks, railways, mobile phones and financial services.

To create these dynamic synergies across businesses, top marketing managers at the centre have to ask four key questions. First, what are the key strategic value drivers that can be leveraged across units? To preserve the autonomy and responsibility of business unit managers, the list of such shared drivers should be a short one. To meet the criteria, a resource must offer access to multiple markets. For example, 3M's special competency in coatings and adhesives has given it the opportunity to start new markets in Post-it notes, magnetic tape, photographic film and pressure sensitive tapes. It must also offer a customer benefit. The Virgin brand name, for instance, gives customers confidence in products bearing the name. Additionally, it must be hard for competitors to copy, otherwise any advantage is short lived.

The second question is: Are these shared resources receiving sufficient investment? Because the benefits of these value drivers are shared, there is a disincentive for any individual business to make sufficient investment. Unless the centre counteracts this, these capabilities will wither away. The third question is: Are any of the units exploiting the shared resource to the detriment of the company as a whole? For example, if a shared brand name is used on poor-value products or promoted using an inappropriate campaign, the residual damage to the company as a whole may be severe. The centre has to act as the guardian of the shared resource. The final question management at the centre should ask is whether these resources are leveraged to the fullest extent possible to generate growth. This means encouraging managers to look for growth opportunities in the form of new products and new markets where the company's special capabilities can form the basis of a competitive advantage.

Exploiting shared value drivers is an extremely critical function of the centre in the strategic planning process. Unless these drivers are proactively and aggressively managed, the company will lose major opportunities to create value and leave itself exposed to new competition.

Managing the business portfolio

The centre shapes the value-creating potential of the company through the way it allocates resources to the business units, funds new ones, and makes acquisitions and divestments. A review of the company's opportunities should start with the strategic position assessment. This involves examining each business unit and assessing the future attractiveness of its market and its competitive advantage. This then enables management to produce, for each business unit, a forecast of its future cash flow and the shareholder value it can create. When the value a unit can create is less than can be obtained from selling or liquidating it, then it is in the shareholders' interest to divest the business. The general rules for managing the business portfolio are:

1. **Invest in strategies that increase shareholder value.** This then puts the onus on managers to look for attractive markets, to focus on developing differential advantages, and to test that their plans create cash flow with a positive net present value.
2. **Encourage managers to look for new growth opportunities.** The centre should act as a catalyst challenging business unit managers to explore opportunities through increasing customer retention, growing share of customer wallet, winning new customers, and developing new products and distribution channels. They should also be triggering the creation of new business units to take advantage of emerging opportunities that build on key value drivers within the current business.
3. **Fund value-creating acquisitions and strategic alliances.** Not all new market opportunities can be exploited through internal development; sometimes it is faster or more economic to acquire or make alliances with other companies. The role of the centre is to help the search for candidates that may exploit the firm's strategic value drivers.
4. **Divest businesses that cannot create value for shareholders.** When, even after restructuring, a business unit looks incapable of generating value, management should divest it. Since the initiative is unlikely to come from the business unit managers themselves, this is a task for the centre.

The corporate centre: Recent trends

The role of the corporate centre varies considerably across companies. Michael Porter identified four types of roles.

1. **Portfolio management.** Portfolio management is where the parent company simply acquires a group of companies that it believes are attractive and allows them to continue operating autonomously, linked only through an internal capital market. This is often termed a holding company structure.

One current and successful example is Berkshire Hathaway, the holding company run by the world famous investor Warren Buffet. Holding companies will normally have a very small corporate centre focused on monitoring financial performance.

2. **Restructuring.** While holding companies like Berkshire Hathaway buy well-managed companies, others, like the British conglomerates Hanson and BTR, and US leveraged buy-out operators such as KKR, have created value by restructuring poorly run businesses. Here, the centre intervenes to change managers, dispose of underperforming assets, cut costs, and restructure liabilities.

3. **Transfer skills.** Some companies have corporate centres that seek to add value by transferring skills across business units. Philip Morris aims to create competitive advantage in newly acquired businesses by bringing in people with proven marketing and, especially, branding skills. To be successful, this policy requires similarities between businesses such that skills learned in one market will be valuable in the new one.

4. **Sharing activities.** The most important sources of value arise when the centre can exploit economies of scope from shared strategic value drivers such as brands, technical resources, R&D, distribution, and service networks. Porter suggests such sharing is facilitated by:
   - a strong sense of shared purpose
   - a mission statement that emphasises integrating business level strategies
   - incentives for cooperation across businesses
   - inter-business task forces and other vehicles for cooperation.

In recent years, the role of the centre in leading-edge companies has changed in a way that parallels changes in management more generally. This is a shift away from a controlling role to one more about encouraging and supporting. The key features of the transition can be summarised under four headings:

- a view of corporate headquarters less as the apex of the pyramid and more as a support service for the business
- less emphasis on formal systems and techniques, and more on relationships and informal interaction
- greater decentralisation and delegation of decision making to the business units
- emphasis on the role of the centre, and the chief executive in particular, as a catalyst and driver of organisational change.

Business unit planning

Strategic marketing planning takes place at the business unit level. Marketing strategy has to be bottom-up because the centre lacks the detailed knowledge of customers and competitors to develop practical options. The centre's role is to act as a catalyst and a facilitator.

The value-based strategic marketing plan of a business unit consists of at least four interrelated components:

1. strategic objective
2. strategic focus
3. marketing mix
4. strategy valuation.

Strategic objective

Every business unit needs a broad strategic objective (see marketing management in practice, 'Unilever's strategic objective'). The fundamental objective for every business unit should be to maximise shareholder value. However, such an objective is not actionable without more definitive guidelines. For innovative business units shareholder value creation can mean focusing on rapid sales growth and ignoring current losses and cash flow. In some cases, such as in the early days of the dot.com investment boom, start-up companies have been deemed extraordinarily valuable by investors even though they were not expected to show a profit for five years or more. Behind the valuations were investors' expectations of enormous growth potential and good profit margins once the start-up costs were out of the way. For other units — mature businesses in commodity-like markets, for example — shareholder value creation might be best achieved by allowing the business to decline and focus on maximising short-term cash flow.

Marketing management in practice: **Unilever's strategic objective**

To accelerate growth and shareholder value creation, Unilever, one of the world's largest consumer goods companies, reviewed its portfolio of businesses. Its objective was to identify those units that had the highest potential for generating return on investment. Many products were targeted for divestment. Of those categories it decided to keep, it set the following broad targets:

Rapid growth	Steady growth	Selective growth
Tea	Spreads	Frozen foods
Culinary products	Cooking products	Fragrances
Ice-cream	Oral products	Professional cleaning
Hair products	Laundry	
Skin products	Household care	
Deodorants		

Five strategic objectives can be assigned to a business unit:
1. divest
2. harvest
3. maintain
4. grow
5. enter.

Each of these is discussed in detail in chapter 5.

Assigning an objective depends upon whether investment in the unit is likely to generate a positive net present value. The strategic determinants of this are the attractiveness of its market and, most important of all, the possession of a differential advantage.

Consultants and academics have come up with various matrices to portray businesses along these two dimensions. The best known include the Boston Consulting Group, the GE–McKinsey matrix, and the Arthur D. Little model.[3] Our approach is the strategic characterisation matrix, illustrated in figure 4.1. The previous models were presented as capital rationing models: cash had to be funnelled from 'cash cow' business units to 'stars' and 'problem children'.

But today, companies geared to shareholder value recognise that there are no capital constraints if a business has strategies that will generate returns above the cost of capital. External finance is available to fund any and all businesses capable of delivering economic profits.

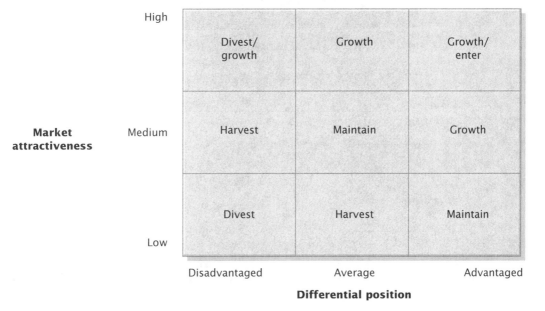

Figure 4.1 Strategic objectives and the strategic characterisation matrix

What most of these matrices agree on is that business units in attractive markets and with a strong differential position are much more likely to generate good returns than units without an attractive market or competitive strength. Figure 4.1 suggests possible strategic objectives, depending on the position of the business unit on the two dimensions. The objectives are clear at the two extremes; where they are more ambiguous is when one dimension is positive and the other is negative. Most problematical is a unit in a highly attractive market but with a weak differential position. These situations are often termed 'double or quit' — the business has to invest very heavily, often over a long period, to remedy its competitive weakness, or get out because of this weakness.

But these techniques should not be applied mechanically. Their real utility is to help managers analyse and organise information about the business, its market, and the competition it faces. The skill in applying these matrices is projecting what will happen to these markets over time and how the business position will be affected by the strategies of current and new competitors.

Strategic focus

Once managers have determined the strategic objective, the next step is to determine the marketing direction for achieving the objective. This direction, once set, is termed the strategic focus. A critical aspect of developing a strategic focus involves defining customer targets through a process called market segmentation and defining competitor targets by means of systematic competitor analysis. This is discussed in detail in chapter 6. Only by knowing exactly who the customers and competitors are and how they operate can a business deliver superior customer benefits.

Before the customer and competitor targets can be established, however, a primary strategic focus, or thrust, needs to be selected. Figure 4.2 shows that shareholder value can be thought of as being created in two ways: through increasing sales volume or through improving productivity. The latter means getting more value from the same, or even a lower, volume.

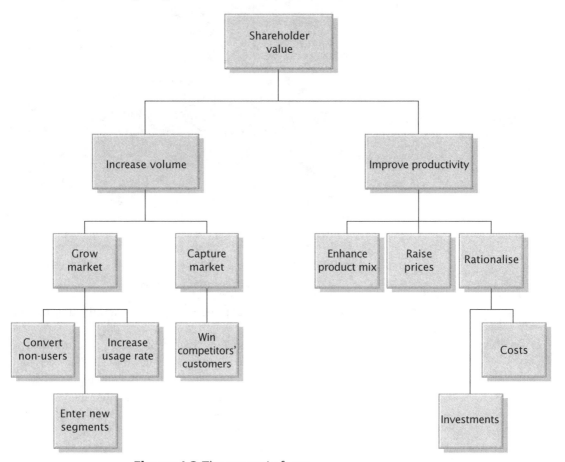

Figure 4.2 The strategic focus

The primary focus — volume or productivity — depends upon the strategic objective. If the objective is to enter the market or grow the business, the focus will be on increasing sales volume. If the strategic objective is to maintain market share, harvest, or divest, the focus will shift to improving productivity. As a market evolves, a business unit's focus is likely to change from volume to productivity.

It should be noted that a particular focus, for example a volume focus, does not mean that attention to productivity can be neglected; both a volume and a productivity goal are important, but depending on the strategic objective assessment a particular emphasis, or focus, is warranted to secure maximum shareholder value.

» **The volume focus**

At the beginning of a market's evolution, or when a business has developed a product with a strong differential advantage for a more mature market, the focus is on sales volume. The main tasks are to grow the market or, if the market is controlled by competitors, to capture the market.

A market can be grown by converting non-users, entering new segments and increasing the usage rate of products, typically in that order. Initially, a market has to be created for a new product. While an innovation, such as the mobile phone or the Internet, might eventually have a mass market, it is invariably a mistake to aim at the whole market at the beginning. The initial focus is to convert the innovators. These are the potential customers who will perceive the greatest value in the new product and have the resources to buy it. These are normally a small niche, perhaps only 2 or 3 per cent of the potential market. But these are important because they will be the first to adopt and will be the opinion leaders, whom the rest will follow.

As the market evolves, several key changes occur: the innovator segment becomes saturated; knowledge and interest in the innovation spreads to broader groups of potential buyers; more competitors enter the market; and the price falls, broadening the size of the market. The key move then is to enter new segments of the market to maintain growth. For instance, business-people initially purchased mobile phones. Then, the growth rate was maintained by household consumers entering the market, attracted by lower prices and the appeal of the product.

The next stage seeks to increase the usage rate among current or new customers. For example, Swatch made watches a fashion item and succeeded in getting many of its customers to buy several in different styles and colours. AstraZeneca in the United Kingdom grew its blockbuster drug Losec by finding new uses so that doctors prescribed it for a growing range of medical conditions.

The above-mentioned stages grow the market — the market expands. As the market matures, marketing strategy is increasingly a zero-sum game: sales volume has to be increased directly at the expense of competitors. Essentially, the market has to be captured from the competition, which entails one major task: winning competitors' customers. Rather than espousing the benefits of the product, the battle is about the superiority of the brand over competitive products that provide very similar benefits. At this stage, operating margins usually come under increasing pressure as buyers become more price sensitive — further sales growth is increasingly less profitable.

Just as target customers and competition change over time, so must the means of achieving volume. A company's differential is soon obsolete unless continually upgraded. Managers again have to consider the market dynamics by asking: How do we grow volume today? What should we be doing tomorrow?

In chapter 6, we introduce the concept of *growth innovation* (also referred to as the *growth ladder* concept). It describes how managers can manage profitable sales growth by growing markets efficiently. Initially, at the innovation stage, the product concept forms a generic advantage. For example, AOL initially had no real competition as an Internet service provider. It was able to grow by offering customers a gateway to the Net; but then competitors enter the market and to maintain leadership the innovator has to show it is a better alternative. AOL has to show it is a better gateway if its market position and profit margins are not to be eroded. Quality often becomes the next battleground. But soon quality ceases to differentiate and to prevent commoditisation, a new differential is required. The third level of competition is often the provision of added services to augment the basic product.

The ultimate stage of competition moves away from the product completely and focuses on solving the customer's problems directly. Products increasingly play a marginal role in the marketing strategies of leading-edge companies such as GE and IBM. They see themselves as winning and retaining high-margin customers by offering customised solutions that have direct and measurable effects on the customer's bottom line. Today, managers have to realise that competitive advantage is increasingly about information rather than hardware. More and more, value is created by providing information that enables customers to solve their problems better than before.

This requires careful market segmentation and competitor analysis — and combining the information with a self-analysis. In particular, it means that knowledge of the customers' and competitors' business and operations ranks in importance with knowledge of one's own operations and business. To sell computing systems or baked beans to customers, the supplier needs to know as much about what creates value for the customer — and how the competition creates value — as it does about its own computing technology or baked beans' recipes. Without such information, computers and baked beans are just commodities that can no longer generate value for shareholders.

» **The productivity focus**

As a market matures, two important changes usually take place. First, competition tends to consolidate with a small number of large players dominating the market. Second, customers become more sensitive to price as they perceive that a number of competitors are offering adequate products. In this situation, strategies to chase volume often cease to be value-generating. Aggressive moves trigger swift reaction as competitors seek to maintain capacity utilisation and the battle for market share leads to eroding profits and cash flow. For this reason, a better strategy is often to look to increase the cash flow from the volume the company has already achieved. Enhancing the product mix, increasing prices and rationalising are preferred ways to do this.

Enhancing the product mix is a particularly important way of boosting profits in mature markets. The first step is usually to segment the market according to particular benefits customers want or expect. Market segmentation based on price expectations of customers is a frequent approach. Greater focus is then given to higher-margin accounts. Often, line extensions and additional services aimed at less price sensitive customers can push average prices up. For example, Johnnie Walker pushed up the average price per bottle of its whisky by introducing a premium product, called Black Label, aimed at its more affluent customeers, to sell alongside its familiar Red Label brand.

A productivity focus should allow managers to be more confident in simply increasing the prices for existing products without having to augment the product mix. With volume growth no longer the main objective, it may pay to trade off the loss of some customers for higher average margins.

Finally, with the shift from a priority of volume to one focusing on profits, more effort can be put into rationalisation by reducing costs and investments. The supply chain can be reappraised to cut variable costs and overheads and to achieve savings in working capital and fixed investment.

Marketing mix

The marketing mix is the set of operating decisions that the firm makes to pursue its strategic focus in its target market. These decisions are often coordinated by the firm's branding concept and are centred on the four Ps: product, price, promotion and place. The four Ps are a simple — perhaps over-simple — reminder of the classes of decisions managers have to make to implement the marketing strategy. We shall turn to these decisions in detail in part 3 of this book.

Strategy valuation

Once the strategy has been developed, marketing management have to demonstrate that it is the best strategy for creating shareholder value. Usually, companies adopt planning processes that culminate in projected (often five-year) accounting statements. These show the sales, operating profits and the return on capital the business is projected to earn if the strategy is adopted. But such statements do not demonstrate that value will be created for investors. Value-based planning looks at marketing plans from the viewpoint of investors and asks if the strategy will generate a return that exceeds the investors' opportunity cost of capital. The strategy valuation process should enable business unit managers to answer such questions as: Does the proposed marketing strategy create value for the company's shareholders? Would alternative marketing strategies create more value? How sensitive is the strategy to the marketing assumptions and to unexpected changes in the industry environment?

Let us consider an example of the strategy valuation process. Fine Wines Ltd is an established family firm selling wine to customers through a direct mail catalogue, which is sent out quarterly. In recent years, sales and profits have stagnated due to increased competition from both retailers and other direct mail operators. With net operating profit after tax of $5.3 million (see table 4.1), and a cost of capital of 12 per cent, the business was valued at $44.17 million (that is, using the perpetuity method, continuing value equals NOPAT divided by the cost of capital). A new managing director proposes to relaunch the business as an Internet operation, GourmetFoods.com. An executive summary of her marketing strategy is as follows:

- **Strategic objective.** To create shareholder value by establishing market leadership in this new area of opportunity in e-commerce. The business would be launched initially in Australia and then rapidly developed throughout North America. In the first year, the product line would be limited to wine. But then a range of gourmet foods would be added and later a range of other luxury branded products.
- **Strategic focus.** The focus would be to increase volume and, specifically, to grow the market by attracting customers to switch from conventional retail channels to the Internet. Most consumers would be using the Internet for the first time in the purchase of wine and gourmet foods. The initial market to focus on would be high-income householders aged between 30 and 45. Later, the market would be broadened, as online buying becomes more common. The competition to watch would be conventional retailers, wine merchants and direct mail operators. Later, other online marketers would become direct competitors.

- **Marketing mix.** Establish a best-value brand. Key attributes associated with the brand will be:
  - *Product.* A broader assortment of wines and gourmet foods than are available in supermarkets and other competitive outlets. Expert online advice to help customers with their selection. Delivery within five working days.
  - *Price.* Prices to be at least 5 per cent below high-street prices. Creative use of promotions to encourage seasonal purchasing and create consumer interest.
  - *Promotion.* Heavy continuous advertising campaigns in national press. Promotion on major Internet portals, including Yahoo! and Amazon.
  - *Distribution (place).* State of the art warehouse located near Melbourne Airport. North American warehouse to be located outside Memphis. Distribution through the leading overnight delivery operator.

Table 4.1 Shareholder value from Fine Wines' new strategy

YEAR	SALES	NORMAL COSTS	START-UP COSTS	OPERATING PROFIT	NOPAT	NET INVEST-MENT	CASH FLOW	DISCOUNT FACTOR	$ MILLION DISCOUNTED CASH FLOW
Initial	50.0	42.5	0.0	7.5	5.3	0.0	5.3	1.00	5.3
1	65.0	55.3	10.0	-0.3	-0.2	6.0	-6.2	0.87	-5.4
2	84.5	71.8	10.0	2.7	1.9	7.8	-5.9	0.76	-4.5
3	109.9	93.4	10.0	6.5	4.5	10.1	-5.6	0.66	-3.7
4	142.8	121.4	10.0	11.4	8.0	13.2	-5.2	0.57	-3.0
5	185.6	157.8	10.0	17.8	12.5	17.1	-4.6	0.50	-2.3
6	241.3	205.1	0.0	36.2	25.3	22.3	3.1	0.43	1.3
7	313.7	266.7	0.0	47.1	32.9	29.0	4.0	0.38	1.5
8	407.9	346.7	0.0	61.2	42.8	37.6	5.2	0.33	1.7
9	530.2	450.7	0.0	79.5	55.7	48.9	6.7	0.28	1.9
10	689.3	585.9	0.0	103.4	72.4	63.6	8.7	0.25	2.2

Cumulative present value	-10.22
Present value of continuing value	119.27
Value of debt	10.00
Shareholder value	99.04
Implied share price (10 m shares)	$9.90
Initial implied share price	$4.42

forecast horizon: the time span for which a business unit plans into the future

Because this was a new market and one that would require heavy initial investment, management used a 10-year **forecast horizon** in assessing the value-creating potential of the strategy. As shown in table 4.1, management believed that their strategy could drive sales growth of 30 per cent a year. They anticipated a normal operating margin of 15 per cent, but saw very high start-up costs over the first five years, particularly in advertising. $10 million annually was set aside to create critical mass in brand awareness. Net investment and fixed and working capital was put at 40 per cent of incremental sales. Because of the higher volatility of Internet businesses, the financial director calculated a cost of capital of 15 per cent, as against 12 per cent currently. To finance the expansion, the board planned an initial public offering, selling up to 20 per cent of the shares on the stock market, and a borrowing facility of $10 million.

Table 4.1 shows a typical profile of an entrepreneurial business in a rapidly growing market. In the first year, operating profits fall due to the high start-up costs. Cash flow does not recover to the current pre-strategy level until the ninth year. But after year four, operating profits are projected to grow rapidly. Over the whole ten-year period, cumulative cash flow is negative, but this is greatly offset by the ongoing value of the business at the end of the planning period, when the present value of the continuing business is estimated at $120 million. After subtracting debt, this results in the strategy being predicted to more than double the value of the business to its shareholders.

» Simulating alternative scenarios

Before the board agrees to invest in this strategy they are likely to want to test management's assumptions. For example, how sensitive is the result to the 30 per cent growth forecast? The board might also want to explore alternative strategies to check whether they have found the optimal strategy. For example, what would happen if the high launch marketing spend was reduced? Or, how would a more aggressive pricing strategy affect shareholder value?

To explore the strategy's sensitivity to the growth assumption, management can rerun the spreadsheet with, say, 20 rather than 30 per cent sales growth. This, indeed, halves the value created (see table 4.2). While the result is still better than the 'do nothing' strategy by $5.38 million, the implied share price falls from $9.90 to $4.96.

Table 4.2 Fine Wines: Sensitivity of shareholder value ($ million)

STRATEGY	SHAREHOLDER VALUE	SV ADDED	SHARE PRICE ($)
Proposed strategy	99.04	54.87	9.90
20% growth	49.55	5.38	4.96
Cut start-up costs	70.94	26.77	7.09
10% price cut	57.11	12.94	5.71

Other strategies can be considered. Management believed that if the high marketing spend in the early years was cut from $10 million to $5 million, growth would be cut by 20 per cent (that is, from 30 to 24 per cent annually). The analysis shows that the effect of this would be to reduce shareholder value by nearly 30 per cent to $71 million. Finally, management explored an even more aggressive strategy of cutting prices by 10 per cent. They believed this would reduce the operating margin from 15 to 10 per cent, but boost revenue growth to 40 per cent annually. Unfortunately, the higher investment requirements and the lower operating margin make this an unattractive option. As table 4.2 shows, this is materially worse than the proposed strategy, reducing shareholder value by over 40 per cent.

The planning process

We now look at how marketing management can introduce this type of value-based marketing planning in their companies. In most companies, it will start with an educational process: a workshop to develop an understanding of the principles of value-based planning, the objectives of the process, and the importance of a market orientation.

A value focus

It is important to make sure that managers from non-marketing or non-financial backgrounds understand why creating shareholder value is their principal task. They need to be familiar with the principle of creating share-holder value — that the task of management is to develop a business unit strategy that maximises the net present value of long-term cash flow. Value-based planning is quite different from conventional planning built around budgets. Budgets focus on accounting profits; value-based planning focuses on value creation. In today's dynamic markets, there is no correlation between profits and the share price. Investors are looking at the potential of the business to create long-term cash, not short-term profits. Finding new growth opportunities from meeting new or unmet customer needs is the way to create long-term cash flow.

Understanding the objectives

Managers need to understand the objectives of the planning process. If the first objective is to drive business growth, the dead wood in the portfolio has to be cleared away and new opportunities to expand the business need to be found. The second objective might be to find a formula that will allow the business, and the people who work there, to win. Winning is about developing strategies that will give the organisation a lasting differential advantage in its target markets. Finally, implementing a strategy successfully depends upon building core capabilities that can result in delivering customer benefits efficiently and effectively. These core capabilities are assets, skills and systems that make possible customer benefits, and are difficult for competitors to emulate.

Being customer driven

Managers also need to appreciate that the foundation for both volume and profitability is solving customers' problems more effectively than competitors, as argued in chapter 3. Customers do not want products — they want solutions to their problems. The performance of a business depends on its knowledge of customers, their operations and problems, and its ability to innovate by bringing out new and superior solutions. The task of the planning process is to bring this knowledge and problem-solving outlook to the fore. Without this knowledge and outlook, the company becomes a commodity business, forced to compete largely on price. Commodity-based competition makes earning economic profits virtually impossible over a long period.

Developing the actual plan

The recommended process for developing the marketing strategy is outlined in figure 4.3.

» **Form cross-functional team**

The marketing department alone should not develop the marketing strategy. Genuine innovation relies on inputs from across the business — from technologists, market researchers, sales force, country managers etc. Involvement from across the organisation creates enthusiasm, accelerates the process and facilitates implementation.

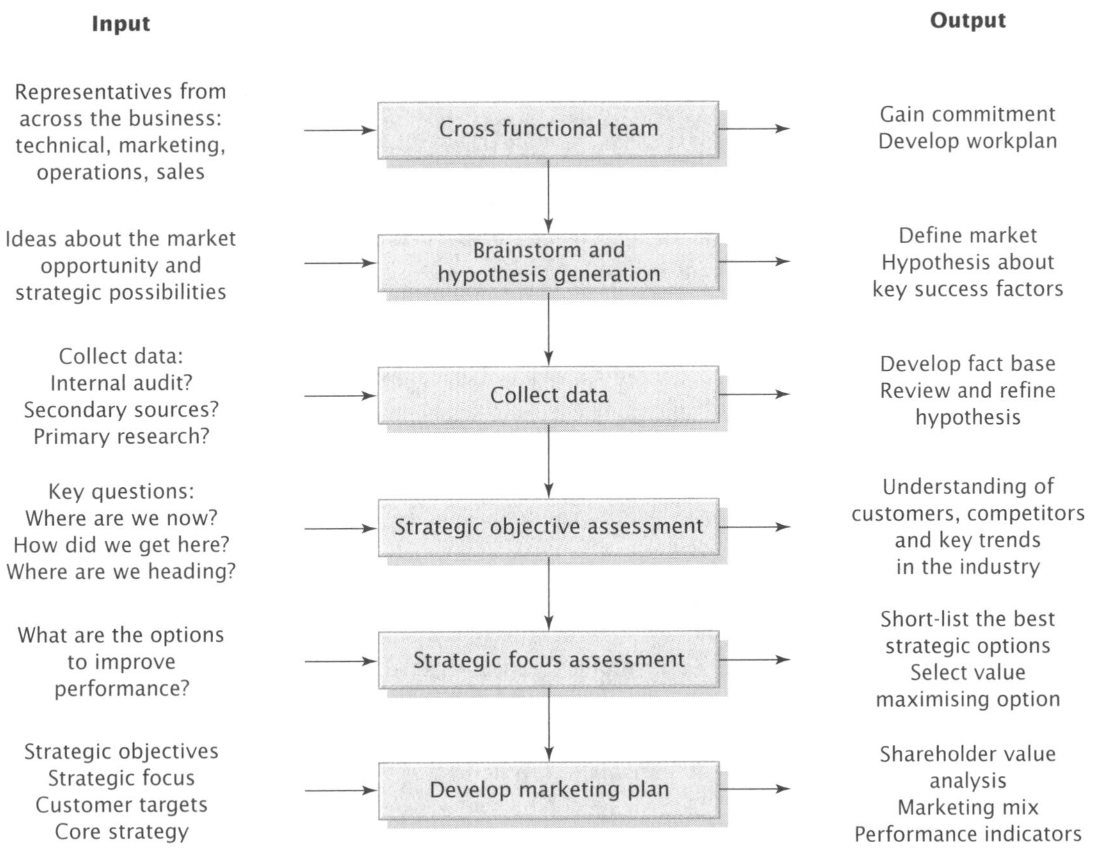

Input		Output

Input **Output**

Representatives from across the business: technical, marketing, operations, sales → Cross functional team → Gain commitment Develop workplan

Ideas about the market opportunity and strategic possibilities → Brainstorm and hypothesis generation → Define market Hypothesis about key success factors

Collect data: Internal audit? Secondary sources? Primary research? → Collect data → Develop fact base Review and refine hypothesis

Key questions: Where are we now? How did we get here? Where are we heading? → Strategic objective assessment → Understanding of customers, competitors and key trends in the industry

What are the options to improve performance? → Strategic focus assessment → Short-list the best strategic options Select value maximising option

Strategic objectives Strategic focus Customer targets Core strategy → Develop marketing plan → Shareholder value analysis Marketing mix Performance indicators

Figure 4.3 The process of value-based marketing planning

» Brainstorming and hypothesis development

Marketing is a creative process. Brainstorming is a good way of generating ideas from across the organisation and obtaining fresh insights about how to stimulate growth. The ideas that seem to be most relevant should then be formulated as hypotheses that, in principle, can be tested against data. For example, in a food company, a hypothesis might emerge that there is a big marketing opportunity for a fat-free range of desserts, or that prices could be raised across the current product line by 10 per cent without affecting volume. One of the tasks of the leader is to steer the team to develop hypotheses across the range of issues relevant to the plan.

Hypothesis-oriented planning is valuable because it leads to a focus on the critical issues affecting performance. It also helps in developing a consensus because hypotheses provide clarity about what is under debate. Finally, once the critical hypotheses are agreed upon, they provide guidelines on what is the key information to collect and how it should be analysed so that these hypotheses can be evaluated. Without hypotheses, it is all too easy to get drowned in excessive amounts of data and for the whole process to suffer 'paralysis by analysis'.

» Collect data to evaluate hypotheses

Once the critical issues have been identified, data will have to be brought together to analyse the issues and test the hypotheses. Some of the data will be internal, concerning the business unit's current and past performance.

Some will be secondary data available from published sources. Developing new ideas will almost always require primary data: original, purpose-specific information from surveys and focus groups to gauge customers' attitudes and problems. Good data are critical to make the plan rigorous and fact based.

» **Analyse data and conduct strategic objective assessment**
The data are then analysed to evaluate the hypotheses and to conduct a thorough strategic objective assessment. This will include looking at the current performance of the business and its main products. It will enable an analysis of the internal and external factors that have shaped performance in the past. It should provide the facility to project the growth and profitability implications of the unit's current strategy. Inputs to the assessments will be analyses of the probable strategies of competitors. Finally, the team will judge whether the present objectives are likely to fit the future environment and whether the results are likely to be satisfactory to the board and shareholders.

» **Conduct strategic focus assessment**
The team should then identify the best strategic focus for generating shareholder value. If a volume focus is selected, the team will have to short-list the best strategic options: convert non-users, enter new segments, increase usage rates and/or win competitors' customers. Naturally, productivity issues cannot be ignored and must be integrated.

Members of the team will have to debate and value the options and prioritise the alternatives.

» **Develop marketing strategy**
Here, the team develops its main conclusions and investment recommendations. The strategy will summarise the key issues, the overall strategic objective and focus, how the business unit's value proposition will be branded and the marketing mix. The shareholder value analysis will then be presented based on the sales, costs and investments forecast.

Accepting the strategy

Bartlett and Ghoshal reviewed how 20 large, successful European, US and Japanese companies sought strategy buy-in.[4] They found little similarity in their strategies, structures and systems, but a surprising consistency in how their leaders promoted strategies throughout the firm. They described it as a softer, more organic model built on the development of purpose, process and people. The overriding goal was to create a shared sense of commitment, belonging and common values throughout the organisation. The approaches to strategy buy-in can be summarised under three headings:

1. define the organisation's mission
2. build on the organisation's value
3. give meaning to employees' work.

Define the organisation's mission

Outside the ranks of top management, it is difficult to make strategies to increase shareholder returns an inspiring goal. Maximising the returns for outside investors is unlikely to enthuse inside staff who have their own goals and interests. What motivates employees is a sense of belonging and personal fulfilment. Successful leaders build on this by seeking to create a sense of organisational mission that employees can identify with. Generally, a **mission statement** should provide focus by defining what business the firm is in. It should state its core strategy, which describes how it is going to be successful. Finally, it should contain an inspiring goal to motivate staff and other stake-holders to commit themselves to the organisation's plans (see marketing management in practice 'Selections from company mission statements').

mission statement: a statement that provides a firm with strategic focus by defining what business it is in

| Marketing management in practice: | Selections from company mission statements |

Cochlear Limited
Cochlear strives to improve the quality of life for the hearing impaired by providing the highest quality products and life-long support for our implant recipients.

Accenture
To help clients change to be more successful. To align their people, processes and technology with their strategy to achieve best business performance.

Asics
(The company song of the leading Japanese sporting goods company)
Where the sacred torch is lit,
Builders of the corporation gather,
With sincere hearts, minds and actions,
Let us accomplish our mission.
Let us cultivate the frontier,
To the four corners of the world.
Young in spirit, ASICS.

AT&T
Dedicated to becoming the world's best at bringing people together — giving them easy access to each other and to information and services they want and need — anytime, anywhere.

British Airways
To create the world's favourite airline.

Ford Motor Company
To be a world-wide leader in automotive and automotive-related products and services as well as newer industries such as aerospace, communications, and financial services. Our mission is to improve continually our products and services to meet our customers' needs, allowing us to prosper as a business and to provide a reasonable return for our stockholders, the owners of our business.

Honda
We are dedicated to supplying products of the highest efficiency yet at a reasonable price for worldwide customer satisfaction.

Matsushita
Seven Principles
National service through industry
Fairness
Harmony and cooperation
Struggle for betterment
Courtesy and humility
Adjustment and assimilation
Gratitude

Build on the organisation's values

When management invent mission statements that are meant to inspire employees, but which are unrelated to the organisation's history or culture, all they inspire is scepticism and cynicism. Most companies should build their mission around the strengths and values the company already possesses. Ian MacLaurin turned around Tesco to make it Britain's largest, fastest growing and most profitable supermarket group in the 1990s by building on its historic reputation for competitive pricing. But he realised that this value focus had to be supplemented with a new emphasis on quality and innovation if Tesco were to meet the needs of increasingly affluent and demanding shoppers. 'Being the UK's number one for quality, innovation and value' was a mission to which staff could subscribe.

Creating a sense of purpose and commitment to the strategy involves more than inspiring speeches and mission statements. It requires getting the organisation involved in interpreting, refining and making it operational. This means tapping into the reservoir of knowledge and expertise that is widely distributed throughout the organisation. Tesco's MacLaurin had store managers, buying groups and operations people engaged in dozens of projects to operationalise the mission and get buy-in. He also sanctioned a major program of management education, training and organisational development to give the staff the knowledge and skills to move the organisation forward. Finally, implementing the mission also means developing indicators that measure progress. MacLaurin, for example, employed a market research company to provide regular feedback on how the Tesco brand was perceived by consumers and, especially, how its desired image for quality, innovation and value was progressing, benchmarked against key competitors.

Give meaning to employees' work

Successful leaders intent on gaining acceptance of their strategies consider how to gain the commitment of individual employees. Three initiatives stand out as encouraging such commitment. First, successful organisations recognise and celebrate individual accomplishments. People want to feel part of the team, not cogs in a huge machine. It is not just about recognising the organisation's stars, but also the efforts of all those who sustain the organisation. This has to be done in a meaningful way: front-line staff sees through PR gestures as meaningless attempts at manipulation. For example, London's leading advertising agency, Abbot Mead Vickers, has gained enormous loyalty and credibility by refusing to lay off staff even when it loses accounts or recession bites.

Second, organisations need to be committed to developing employees. This is more than just skill training; it is also about educating them and helping them to realise their full potential. In its recruiting, Accenture promises that their training prepares employees for working for anyone anywhere as well as for working for themselves. By developing its employees' potential, management shows that it recognises commitment has to be two-way.

Third, effective leaders foster individual initiative. Since the 1920s, when 3M was turned around, it has always shown that it recognises that innovation and growth depend on the initiative of individuals. Its processes recognise this, for example by the '15% rule' that allows employees to spend 15 per cent of their time on their own projects. Individuals' initiative can be stimulated by open information sharing in the organisation, by cooperation and by operating transparent and open decision making, allowing all with relevant knowledge to contribute.

To summarise, strategic marketing planning is a key process in creating value for the organisation. But plan buy-in depends on engendering the cooperation and commitment of employees throughout the business. This requires creating a sense of organisational purpose that people can identify with, and feel a sense of pride in its accomplishment.

Summary

1. The purpose of strategic marketing planning is not to forecast the future. Instead, it is to encourage managers to ask the critical questions about their changing markets so that they can identify the trends that are occurring and capitalise on the opportunities they offer.
2. Corporate level planning focuses on driving organisational change, managing the company's shared value drivers, and adapting the business portfolio to the changing marketing and technological environment.
3. Marketing strategy has to be formulated at the level of the business unit. Business unit managers have the detailed knowledge of changing customers' needs and competitive activities that are essential components for developing a value-based marketing strategy. They play a key role in the determination of strategic objectives and strategic focus, as well as the marketing mix.
4. Once a strategy is formulated, management have to test whether it looks likely to generate value for shareholders. It also has to consider whether there are other marketing strategies that would offer even greater returns.
5. The planning process and its successful implementation depend upon the involvement and commitment of the staff. They are the people with the detailed knowledge of the market and who have to make the strategy work.

key terms

business unit, p. 132
forecast horizon, p. 144
marketing strategy, p. 130
mission statement, p. 149

strategic planning, p. 130
value-based marketing strategy,
  p. 130

review questions

1. Why do companies develop marketing strategies?
2. What is the centre's role in the planning process?
3. What are the components of a value-based marketing strategy?
4. Illustrate how shareholder value analysis can be used to assess the potential of a strategic plan.
5. Describe the process of strategic marketing planning.
6. What additional considerations affect the successful implementation of marketing strategies?

discussion questions

1. How is value created at the corporate level and business unit level? What function does marketing strategy have at each level?
2. How can performance measures be implemented? What function do they have for controlling the strategic plan?
3. What is the role of marketing strategy relating to a market's life cycle? Critically analyse the potential for value creation over the market's life cycle at both the corporate and business unit level.
4. How can the value of a marketing strategy be assessed? Is this the same at the corporate and business unit level?
5. Can a value-based marketing strategy be developed for institutions in the public sector? Detail what the value-based marketing strategy would consist of and how you would assess it.

debate questions

1. Is strategic market planning more important in new, emerging or mature markets?
2. Should marketing planning replace financial planning as the cornerstone of value creation?
3. Will corporate centre decisions always dictate, or potentially override, business unit decisions? Is this an important consideration for value creation?
4. Do customers want relationships with organisations?

case study | Saha's value-based marketing strategy

The Saha Group 'brings happiness and smiles to the lives of . . . people around the world'.[5] Established in 1942, the Group has expanded and now owns more than 200 companies in a wide variety of industries employing more than 70 000 people. The Group produces more than 1000 products and services, which can be divided into 12 categories:

1. garments — the Saha Group subsidiary Thai Wacoal has nearly half of Thailand's lingerie market
2. textiles
3. leather goods
4. footwear — Pan Asia Footwear, Thailand's biggest shoemaker, supplies Nike, Reebok and Timberland
5. cosmetics and toiletries
6. household products
7. food and beverages — another Saha subsidiary, Thai President Foods, produces Mama instant noodles, which has a 60 per cent share in Thailand's instant noodle market and an 80 per cent share in Cambodia.
8. electronic and electrical products
9. sporting goods
10. services
11. distributors
12. logistics and sundries.

As the Group has grown, it has restructured the way that it manages its many subsidiaries. To encourage effective management, the Saha Group merged some subsidiaries and closed others that were underachieving. It has also targeted the mass market, as well as affluent urban dwellers with income to spend on new products such as snacks.

Product innovation and building their own brands, rather than licensed manufacture of foreign brands, has been part of the Group's survival strategy.

The retail scene in Thailand has changed radically with the arrival of multinationals on the retail scene. The Saha Group still sells more than 60 per cent of its product to small retailers, such as the traditional family-owned store, and has extended to them the same discounts that are normally offered only to larger retailers. The Group has also sought distribution channels outside of the large retailers to reduce their reliance on the big stores. However, the Group has been careful not to antagonise the large retailers and has produced house-brand products on request for some of their outlets. This balance means that the Saha Group will benefit no matter which group dominates the retail scene in Thailand.

Sources: Adapted from the Saha Group's web site, www.sahagroup.thailand.com; Bamrung Amnatcharoenrit, 'Saha Group seeks peaceful coexistence in retail trade', *The Bangkok Post*, 28 July 2002; and Supapohn Kanwerayotin, 'Homegrown market savvy', *Far Eastern Economic Review*, 27 September 2001, pp. 43–5.

end notes

1. Tom Copeland, Tim Koller and Jack Murrin, *Valuation: Measuring and Managing the Value of Companies*, New York: John Wiley & Sons, 1996, pp. 336–9.
2. Gary Hamel and C.K. Prahalad, *Competing for the Future*, Boston, MA: Harvard Business School Press, 1994.
3. For a summary see Peter Doyle, *Marketing Management and Strategy*, London: Prentice Hall, 1998.
4. Christopher A. Bartlett and Sumantra Ghoshal, 'Changing the role of top management: Beyond strategy to purpose', *Harvard Business Review*, November/December, **72** (6), 1994, pp. 79–98.
5. Quoted from www.sahagroup.thailand.com/product1.htm.

Strategic objective assessment

chapter objectives

By the time you have completed this chapter, you will be able to:

- evaluate the performance of a business
- assess the causes of its present performance, distinguishing between external or industry factors, and internal or competency factors
- take a view on where the business is heading, if it maintains its current trajectory
- identify the internal and external opportunities to increase the value of the business
- set strategic objectives for the products and markets that make up the firm's portfolio of businesses.

scene setter

Taking a long-term view

When Michael Chaney was preparing a speech for investors in 2000, he overcame one of his greatest challenges as a business leader focused on long-term shareholder value. The chief executive of the Perth-based conglomerate Wesfarmers decided to be boring. 'I know that I had addressed these guys the year before and the year before that,' he says of the conference in Perth ... 'The temptation is to think, "What will I tell them that's new, therefore interesting?" Because I can't tell them what I told them last year. They will say, "What's going on here? It's just the same old story".'

'But one of our great strengths is that the story is exactly the same as it was last year and the year before,' Chaney says. '[So] I said "You were all here last year and I'm going to tell you exactly the same story I told you last year about our philosophies, our objectives and how we run this company".'

Consistent strategy — in terms of how it is developed, executed and communicated — and consistent performance are hallmarks of an effective chief executive. Wesfarmers has been one of Australia's most consistently successful companies in recent years ...

Chaney says resisting the temptation to deliver something new is the biggest challenge for a chief executive who is attempting to focus on long-term shareholder value. 'The hardest thing is that people keep trying to deflect you,' he says. 'They say, "Where is the next big acquisition?" They are constantly trying to work out what we're looking at and what we will take over next.'

The chief executive of Leighton Holdings, Wal King, tells a similar story. He argues that chief executives need to distinguish between 'fragrance' and substance. 'It's easy to get mixed up in the fragrance cycle,' he says. 'It's extremely difficult for the chief executive not to be influenced.'

Chaney is a director of BHP Billiton, which has the vision statement: 'We seek to earn superior returns for our shareholders as the world's premier supplier of natural resources and related products and services.' In April [2002], the company's new chief executive, Brian Gilbertson, told a Securities Institute meeting: 'The first [word] is "superior", implying the primacy of our shareholders' interests.'

BHP Billiton's focus on shareholder value is supported by financial measures for the company's 'customer sector groups', which are based on products needed by particular customers, such as carbon steel manufacturers. The groups have to meet targets for earnings before interest and tax (EBIT) and cashflow, but they also have to meet a target for earnings before interest and tax and shareholder value added (ESVA), in which the EBIT is debited with a charge for the capital invested in the business.

'This measure provides customer sector group presidents with an additional tool, a self-discipline if you like, for judging new investments, acquisitions and disposals,' Gilbertson said. 'If a proposal before them detracts from ESVA, they will reject it.'

Gilbertson says: 'I think the past few years have seen the emergence of a new generation of resource executives, driven to achieve shareholder value rather than by emotional attachments to particular assets.'

Source: Extracts from Stuart Washington, 'Mr Consistency', *BRW*, 29 August—4 September 2002, pp. 58–61.

Introduction

During the past decade, most managers have come to accept that the objective of the firm is to maximise total returns to shareholders. If managers do not offer good returns to the owners of the business in the form of dividends and stock appreciation, then they are likely to be replaced. It is also accepted that the way to increase shareholder returns is to maximise the net present value of long-run cash flow.

Maximising shareholder value requires each business unit to have a process that encourages managers to develop strategic options, to evaluate these options in terms of their effects on shareholder value and to effectively implement the highest-value strategy. This process begins with the strategic position assessment — the point of departure in the strategic objective assessment process (see figure 5.1).

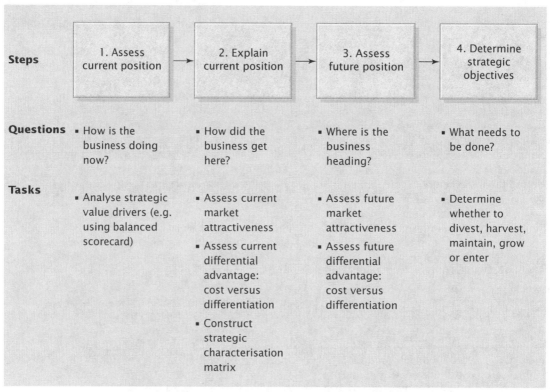

Figure 5.1 Strategic position assessment and the determination of strategic objectives

Overview of strategic position assessment

The strategic position assessment needs to be conducted at two levels: at the corporate level and the business unit level. At the corporate level, the focus will be on the value potential of the company's portfolio of businesses. At the unit level, the focus will be on the value and drivers of the individual products and markets. The methodology is the same; the difference is in the unit of analysis. In both, the outcomes will be conclusions about the future of the business.

The purpose of the strategic position assessment is to identify those parts of the business that are creating value and to leverage the drivers of value in the different markets by specifying strategic objectives. A simple way of thinking about the structure of the assessment is in terms of four questions. First, how is the business doing now? Is the business creating value? Which are its strong parts and are there any parts that are destroying value? The next two questions seek to understand the drivers of value. The second question is: How did the business get here? What explains its success or failure in creating value? The third question projects these drivers to the future by asking: Where is the business heading? What are the implications of its current trajectory? The final question addresses the strategic objectives and asks: What needs to be done? What actions are necessary to enhance the value of the business?

Assessing the current position

The first step in the strategic position assessment is identifying whether the business is performing successfully at the moment. In principle, this should be a straightforward question, but in practice, answering it is not simple at all.

Weaknesses of financial measures

Unfortunately, financial measures do not give reliable indications on whether current performance is creating the long-term value shareholders expect. The problem needs to be explored at two levels: the company as a whole and its constituent units.

» The company overall

For a publicly quoted company, the total return to shareholders in the form of dividends and share price appreciation is the natural way to judge the performance of its management. In the long run, this is certainly the case. But, as a short-run measure of performance, it is often not a good indicator. This is because a company's share price is determined by investors' expectations of the value of future cash flows. This leads to a number of paradoxes, especially over the short term. If investors appreciate a well-run company's strategy, the value of future cash flows will be fully incorporated in the current share price. The future share price of this well-managed company will therefore not appreciate more than the stock market average. Investors can do better investing in poorly managed companies, if they believe that market expectations have overestimated how bad these companies are doing. In the short run, good companies, therefore, may not deliver better shareholder returns than bad ones.

Because of this problem, managers tend to judge performance using accounting measures such as return on capital or earnings per share. But such measures are even more unsatisfactory. Far from being objective, earnings and capital employed are subjective and easily manipulated by different accounting methods. But even more seriously, these accounting metrics are short term and can be quite unrelated to the real job of creating long-term value for shareholders. Profitability can be easily boosted by cutting back on marketing, training and research to the long-run detriment of the business. New measures like economic value added may give a better measure of economic profit, but they in no way solve the problem of providing an indicator of long-term value creation.

» Operating units

Since the achievement of the company is the aggregate of the results of the operating performance of its individual businesses, it is even more important to judge their results. Unfortunately, this is equally difficult. Since the operating units normally do not have their own shares quoted on the stock market, looking at the total shareholder return is not possible.

The theoretically correct method of measuring the performance of an operating unit over a year is to look at the value management has created. This means comparing the value of the unit at the end of the year with that at the beginning. The obvious problem is that these values are based on highly uncertain forecasts of long-term cash flows. Since, generally, the managers who make these forecasts will be the same ones whose performance is being evaluated, there is considerable scope for biased results.

So again, as at the corporate level, performance is generally assessed using conventional accounting measures such as return on capital, profits or economic value added. None of these gives a reliable measure of the long-term value being created by managers; indeed, they will often be completely misleading. In some ways, these measures are worse at the operating unit level because they encourage deceptive comparisons across business units. For example, expecting a promising new business in a high-growth market to show the same levels of profitability as a mature business unit would seriously erode the potential of the newcomer. Units at different levels of development need quite different objectives and measures of performance.

Strategic value drivers

Because of the weaknesses of performance measures based on annual accounting measures and the subjectivity inherent in estimating directly changes in value, indirect measures have to be employed to decide whether current accomplishments are creating long-term value.

strategic value drivers: the organisational resources and capabilities that have the most significant impact on the firm's ability to create shareholder value

These lead indicators are termed the **strategic value drivers** of the business. Strategic value drivers are those organisational resources and capabilities that have the most significant impact on the firm's ability to create shareholder value. For example, key capabilities at 3M and Intel are their new product development abilities; at Billabong, brand management is a key driver; at Toyota operational efficiency is important; at Cochlear innovation is important. These drivers shape a company's ability to create and retain competitive advantage and continuing profitability. If managers' current actions are enhancing these value drivers, then long-term value is likely to be created. If these resources and capabilities are being neglected, then the firm's competitive position and long-term value is likely to erode. To measure whether value is being created in any one year management have to:

1. identify those organisational variables critically affecting competitive advantage and long-term cash flow
2. set target levels of performance on these variables
3. measure the performance achieved and compare this against target performance levels.

» Identifying value drivers

To identify strategic value drivers, the management team needs a fundamental understanding of their business. They need to be able to decide what are the most important factors determining the ability of the business to generate long-term cash flows. A strategic value driver should have three characteristics. First, it should be a current asset or capability that has a significant impact on the long-term value of the business. Second, it should be capable of being measured and communicated. Third, it should be capable of being influenced by management actions.

Most successful businesses will have a set of value drivers, including financial resources such as strong operating margins and cash flow; marketing resources including brands, customer loyalty and distribution partnerships; operating capabilities such as efficient manufacturing and supply chain processes; and learning capabilities in the form of training and development resources.

» Target levels of performance

Once the value drivers are identified, the levels of performance that are acceptable have to be determined. The best approach is to benchmark performance against a peer group or other companies that the business aspires to emulate.

It is important to recognise that the significance of a value driver and the appropriate level of performance depend on the nature of the business and its stage in the life cycle. For example, high returns on capital and positive cash flows are to be expected from mature businesses, whereas growth is a much more important measure of performance for a new business. Many new businesses will have high market valuations but little or no current profit. Here, investors are valuing the future cash flows that they believe will occur once critical mass has been established.

» Measuring performance

To measure progress, management has to set up the systems to collect regular, objective information on these drivers. These metrics are valuable if they form the basis for action. Targets have to be set, and individuals and groups have to be assigned responsibility for achieving results.

The balanced scorecard

Successful companies are accepting that performance and plans cannot be built around a single measure such as return on capital or earnings per share. Instead, they need a set of indicators to track performance and ensure that managers are achieving on the drivers of long-term performance. The most systematic and popular approach in recent years to developing such lead indicators has been the 'balanced scorecard' developed by Kaplan and Norton.[1]

The balanced scorecard was motivated by the recognition that companies cannot rely on short-run financial indicators to measure long-run performance. What is needed is a set of measures to link short-run achievement to long-run value creation. The way this is done is by getting managers to develop a model of their business (see Marketing insight 'Developing the balanced scorecard'). The model aims to identify what determines the business's long-run ability to generate cash. Each business will have its own key drivers and hence will have its own measures. But based on their research, Kaplan and

Norton suggest most businesses will have four common sets of perspectives (see figure 5.2):

1. financial perspective
2. customer perspective
3. internal perspective
4. innovation perspective.

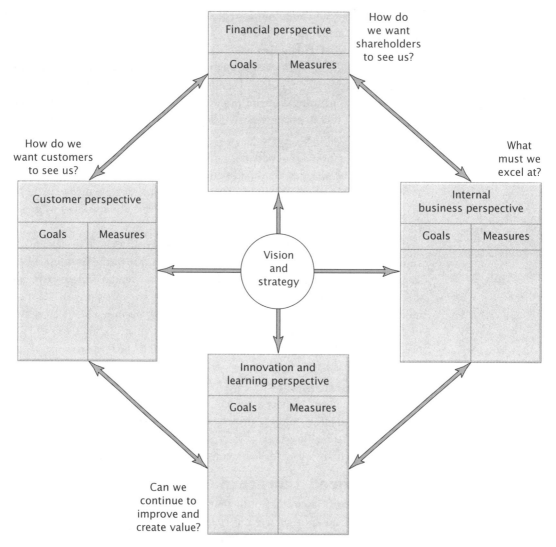

Figure 5.2 The balanced scorecard links performance measures.
Source: Reprinted by permission of *Harvard Business Review*. The balanced scorecard links performance measures from 'The balanced scorecard — measures that drive performance', R. Kaplan and D. Norton, Jan.–Feb. 1992, No. 1, p. 72. Copyright © 1992 by the Harvard Business School Publishing Corporation. All rights reserved.

» Financial perspective

The financial perspective incorporates the financial drivers of shareholder value. Normally, it will make sense for the business to set objectives for, and measure the performance of return on, capital employed, operating margins, economic value added, cash flow and sales growth.

The measures chosen and the target levels will depend upon the maturity of the products in the unit's portfolio. For businesses at the growth stage, the primary financial objective will be sales growth. When the business reaches maturity, profitability measures such as return on capital employed, economic value added and operating margins become more important. Finally, at the decline stage, cash flow will become the key financial measure.

Marketing insight: **Developing the balanced scorecard**

Developing the scorecard consists of eight steps:

1. **Preparation.** The firm must define the business unit for which the scorecard is appropriate. Normally, this will be a unit that has its own customers, distribution channels, production facilities and financial performance measures.

2. **Developing mission and strategy.** The management team receives briefing materials on the scorecard concept and internal documents describing the company's vision, mission and strategy. The scorecard facilitator interviews the executives to obtain their perspectives of the firm's objectives and ideas about scorecard measures. Often, a sample of customers and shareholders are interviewed to understand their expectations.

3. **Agreeing on the vision and what it means.** In a workshop, the top team debates the vision and strategy until a consensus is reached. They then identify the strategic objectives that are required for shareholders, customers, internal processes, and for the business' ability to improve, innovate and grow. Finally, they try to draft a preliminary scorecard containing operational measures for the strategic objectives.

4. **Drafting the balanced scorecard.** The facilitator documents the output of the workshop and interviews the executives about the tentative scorecard. He also seeks opinions about implementing it.

5. **Refining the scorecard.** In a second workshop, involving a larger number of senior managers, the organisation's strategic drivers and draft scorecard is debated. Subgroups are formed to review the proposed measures, link the various initiatives already underway to the measures, and start to develop an implementation plan. Finally, managers are asked to develop stretch objectives for each of the measures.

6. **Final approval.** The senior executive team meets to come to a final consensus on the strategy and scorecard and to agree stretch targets on the chosen measures. The team must also agree on an implementation plan including an action program, communicating the scorecard to employees, and developing the information to support it.

7. **Implementation.** A new team is created to implement the scorecard. This includes communicating it throughout the organisation, developing second-level metrics for decentralised units, and a new, comprehensive information system that links top-level measures down through shop-floor and site-specific operational indicators.

8. **Periodic reviews.** Each month, information on scorecard performance is reviewed. The balanced scorecard metrics are also evaluated annually as part of the strategic planning and budgetary processes.

Source: Adapted and reprinted by permission of Harvard Business Review. Building a balanced scorecard, from *Putting the Business Scorecard to Work*, by R. S. Kaplan and D. P. Norton. *Harvard Business Review*, Sept.–Oct. 1993, pp. 138–9. Copyright 1993 by the Harvard Business School Publishing Corporation. All rights reserved.

» **Customer perspective**

Growth and profitability depend crucially on the ability of the firm to satisfy its customers. Measures of marketing performance are normally leading indicators of financial results. Measurements will usually be required for market share, brand awareness and image, customer satisfaction, customer retention, customer acquisition and ranking of key accounts.

Some businesses have different types of customers whose perspectives require separate measures. For example, financial institutions will need to monitor both savers and investors; fast-moving consumer goods companies will need to look separately at both their trade customers and final consumers.

» Internal business perspective

The ability of companies to generate cash flow also depends upon the efficiency of their business processes: R&D, design, manufacturing, selling and distribution. The goals and measures should focus on those internal processes that have the greatest impact on customer satisfaction. They may include percentage of sales from new products, manufacturing cost, manufacturing cycle time, inventory management, quality indices and technological capabilities.

» Innovation and learning perspective

Long-run competitiveness depends on the firm's core capabilities and its ability to upgrade them over time. Many companies now have competency assessment centres to measure the skills and attributes of their employees. Others map out their key organisational competencies to identify strengths and weaknesses. Goals and measures can be set for competency developments in product development, purchasing, manufacturing, technology and marketing and sales.

The balanced scorecard emphasises that in a complex business there are no single measures that can summarise performance in the short run. High levels of current profitability can easily disguise a decline in the long-term competitiveness of the business. The appropriate metrics also vary with the maturity of the business. The balanced scorecard and lead indicator approach encourages managers to think about the strategic value drivers that generate long-term value. The goal of maximising shareholder value is not itself an actionable objective or basis for strategy. To make it actionable, managers have to think through what they need to accomplish and what competencies they will need to acquire.

Exploring the portfolio

It is not enough to look at performance at the aggregate level. To really understand the picture, aggregate performance needs to be broken down into smaller units to identify the real winners and losers. A company will disaggregate its results into operating units such as major product lines or countries; operating units will then in turn disaggregate performance by individual products, customers or markets. One of the most pervasive phenomena in organisations is the Pareto principle: 80 per cent of the results come from 20 per cent of the activities. In other words, usually only one in five of the organisation's products, customers or businesses is really profitable.

One of the most common presentations by management consultants is the profit waterfall showing the percentages of the company's total economic profit and capital employed by each of its business units, products or customer groups. The results are invariably eye-catching. The Pareto principle invariably holds. Usually, less than half of the company's invested capital is responsible for all the value created. Figure 5.3 illustrates a typical profit waterfall for a chemical company. Here, two major businesses accounted for 100 per cent of the company's economic profits. As much as 60 per cent of the capital was invested in business units that generated no profits.

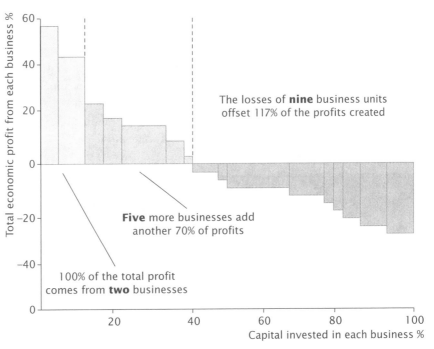

The losses of **nine** business units offset 117% of the profits created

Five more businesses add another 70% of profits

100% of the total profit comes from **two** businesses

Figure 5.3 Profit concentration in typical portfolio

The usual recommendation from the consultants is then to rationalise or sell the loss makers and focus future investment on those businesses earning the highest profits. The implication is that the smaller, more focused company will have much higher profits and a smaller capital base. But such a conclusion is very dangerous. It is certainly true that managers should be aware of which products are profitable and that many companies are making the mistake of persisting with businesses that have no future. But to confuse current profitability with value is misleading. The stock market often values very highly businesses that currently exhibit no economic profit. Value is based on long-term cash flows, not current profits. Current profits typically account for less than 5 per cent of the equity value of businesses in growth markets. Over-reliance on the profit waterfall can be highly damaging to a firm's efforts to encourage innovation. It will generally over-emphasise the value of mature businesses. Indeed, many of these mature businesses are profitable because they require little investment and brand building. Encouraging investment in them can be counterproductive because the incremental return on investment is low.

As for companies, the current performance of a product or customer group cannot be assessed from figures of current profitability alone. To judge their value, managers need to explore performance on the full range of measures that are lead indicators of long-term value creation.

Table 5.1 presents a simple illustration of the lead indicator approach for a company with four business units. Overall, the company looks to be doing well, with 18 per cent return on capital and a strong positive cash flow. But these averages disguise a more complex picture. Over 90 per cent of the profits come from the two business units, A and B. Unfortunately, these are declining businesses in mature markets. All the growth is coming from unit C and a recent acquisition, D. There is no straightforward answer to the question about which businesses are performing best. In accounting terms, A is best, generating over half the group's profits and most of its cash. But in terms of growth and from the perspectives of customers, operations, innovation and development, it is doing poorly. It is probable that the value of A is declining, while the long-term values of units B and C are increasing with their high levels of customer satisfaction, technical capabilities and innovation.

Table 5.1 Lead indicators to evaluate performance

		OPERATING UNITS			
	GROUP	A	B	C	D
Financial indicators					
Return on capital (%)	18	24	22	10	0
Operating margin (%)	9	12	12	3	0
Cash flow ($m)	12	10	7	−2	−3
Sales growth (%)	2	−2	−3	11	25
Customer indicators					
Market share		24	20	14	10
Customer satisfaction		3	3	4	5
Customer retention rate		3	3	4	5
Customer acquisition rate		2	1	4	5
Operations indicators					
Manufacturing costs		3	3	2	2
Quality		3	3	4	4
Technical performance		2	2	4	5
New product performance		2	1	4	5
Innovation and development					
Product development		2	2	4	5
Purchasing capabilities		2	2	3	3
Manufacturing capabilities		2	3	4	4
Technological capabilities		2	2	4	5

Indicators based on 5-point ratings: 5, excellent; 4, strong; 3, average; 2, weak; 1, very poor.

If C and D can capitalise on their opportunities and establish critical mass, they are likely to move into profits and become cash positive as the market matures. The task of the board is to ensure that the strategies are in place to achieve these goals. The board should be concerned about the threat to the value of units A and B from their mediocre performance in satisfying, retaining and acquiring customers and their weaknesses in development, innovation and operations.

Explaining the current position

The first question in the strategic position assessment asked: Where is the business now? It sought to analyse the current health of the company. The second question seeks to diagnose it. It asks: How did we get here? What have been the causes of the current successes and failures? It is an essential preliminary step to projecting the future of the business and determining the actions necessary to enhance its value.

Diagnosis starts with the basic economic proposition that there are only two ways in which a business can earn profits that exceed its cost of capital. One is to find attractive markets where competition is weak. Lack of competition then allows the firm to earn monopoly profits. The other is to possess unique resources and capabilities that enable the business to create a competitive advantage — in the form of lower costs or a superior offer (see marketing management in practice 'Centres of excellence'). In other words, success or failure can be explained by both:

1. external factors — the attractiveness of the market in which the firm is operating
2. internal factors — the specific resources and capabilities the business has inherited or developed, which allow it to develop a competitive advantage.

Marketing management in practice: **Centres of excellence**

... Graham Turner and his partners stumbled on a good idea in the 1970s but it was not until 1986 that they discovered the plot that would make it a huge global business. Since then, their collection of disparately branded general travel agencies which had numbered about 30 has been transformed into a world-leading air travel specialist. Last year, Flight Centre generated sales of $3 billion and made a profit after tax of $43 million. The company retains a stockmarket price-to-earnings ratio exceeding 40 in, arguably, the worst aviation market environment in history ...

The idea that Turner had seen in London in the 1970s was called a 'bucket shop' — primarily straight air fare shops which had been operating since the late 1950s specialising in discounted air fares. The plot he developed, starting in 1986, is probably simultaneously the simplest and most successful retail model in travel industry history. The principles that drive it are applicable to every business, regardless of industry.

According to Turner, Flight Centre has captured an Australian market share nearing 25 per cent, and his goal is to take that to 40 per cent. Simultaneously, he plans to make the company a global leader in the category. Already, one-third of the company's sales and profits are generated offshore. The model is now proven beyond reasonable doubt in countries like New Zealand, South Africa, the United Kingdom, Canada and the US.

Like many other entrepreneurs ... Turner has deliberately chosen to make his play in a mature market, with the usual characteristics of entrenched competition and narrowing margins.

There was, and is, no prospect that the market will expand overnight and the company will be carried on a wave of Nasdaq-like growth. Flight Centre's astronomical growth over the past 10 years has come from market penetration, cutting deep into competition by redefining the way things are done. What is the entrepreneurial creative thinking that has enabled some seemingly knock-about blokes, with little money to begin with until they floated the company in 1995, to reshape an industry and become the 'why didn't we think of that' envy of many established and well-heeled competitors?

There are a number of elements in Turner's approach:

1. **Unrelenting focus.** The London bucket-shop focus on discount air fares was a watershed discovery for Turner. Most travel agencies at the time were generalists undifferentiated, famous for nothing in particular, and struggling to deliver complex products to an ever-mobile workforce.
2. **Well-chosen timing.** Before 1986, it was illegal to advertise discounted air fares in Australia. Turner could see that the lifting of this barrier would create an opportunity for first-mover advantage, to make Flight Centre famous as leader of the category in which he had chosen to focus, with the very proposition that had previously been unmentionable.

   Long after deregulation, Turner says ... the decision to feature destination prices in Flight Centre's shop windows was an enormous help in establishing the company's difference and reputation.

(continued)

3. **Simplification as the key to a systems approach.** By narrowing the product focus, Turner saw that he could turn a hotch-potch travel outlet into a well-oiled machine, simultaneously providing value to customers and making a good profit.

   The company's net profit margin has progressively increased from 1.57 per cent in the 1992 financial year to 2.3 per cent in 2001 as it has learned how to create efficiencies.

   One of Turner's greatest strengths appears to be his ability to see the simplicity on the other side of complexity, the hallmark of people who have mastered their craft, and to convert that simplicity into a reality that can be replicated.

4. **An easily replicated system for everything.** Turner believes it merely common sense to have a business model that can be replicated and business processes that are systemised.

   'We bought a few small companies and it's interesting how unreplicable they are. You don't want to have a model where you have a neurosurgeon [key person] as part of your system, because they are hard to get hold of,' he says.

   Rolling out a new shop every couple of days, a hefty proportion of them offshore nowadays, has demanded a system that can be unfalteringly replicated.

5. **Rewarding people for the outcomes you want.** According to Turner, it is important to have each employee rewarded on the outcomes you want right from the start. It is also important that 'those outcomes are clearly measured, and that you've got the right people in the right places to produce those outcomes ... we've probably done that pretty well', he says.

6. **Pulling with human nature, not against it.** Turner's well-publicised human organisation model is down-to-earth, like the man himself. The company's 3000-plus staff work in small accountable teams of three to seven people (the 'Family') ...

   Shops and teams work in regions of four to 10 shops (the 'Village'). Villages are grouped with their support business of around 120 people (the 'Tribe'). 'Work is a part of people's social structure and if you work against it, it's a lot harder. There's nothing new about a lot of this stuff ... but it probably hasn't been applied directly to business before,' Turner says.

Source: Adapted extracts from John Lyons, 'Centres of excellence are Turner's prize', *The Australian Financial Review*, 13 November 2001, p. 43.

As with the assessment of performance, there are rarely simple explanations of the causes of success or failure. Managers tend to oversimplify and be biased in their analyses. A manager of a poorly performing business will invariably explain its failure in terms of external factors such as a declining market, excess industry capacity or aggressive competitors. A successful manager will usually explain performance in terms of internal factors such as superior products, excellent service or better marketing. Usually, both sets of factors play a role, and it is important to disentangle these causes since their implications for strategy are quite different.

Market attractiveness

attractive market: a market where the average competitor consistently earns a return above its cost of capital

An **attractive market** can be defined as one where the average competitor consistently earns a return above its cost of capital (that is, it is creating value for shareholders). Some markets do appear to be attractive for long periods of time, while in others it is much more difficult to earn economic profits. For example, US data reveal that companies in soft drinks and ethical pharmaceutical drugs earned an average economic return on equity of over 12 per cent above their cost of capital in the period 1976–1991. Companies in oilfield services, steel, textiles and mining were consistently unprofitable.[2]

The most important factors determining the attractiveness of the market are:

1. the size of the market
2. market growth
3. the competitive structure of the market
4. the cylicality of the market
5. risk factors.

» The size of the market

Big markets offer firms more opportunities to grow. For larger firms, only size-able markets will have the potential to generate meaningful increases in value. Larger markets may offer smaller firms the opportunities to find profitable niches where they can prosper without competing head-to-head with the major players. Big markets can also enable ambitious companies to build economies of scale.

» Market growth

It is easier to grow if the market in which the firm is operating is also growing. Non-growth markets are zero-sum: a business can only grow by taking customers away from competitors. Growth under these circumstances is usually associated with declining prices and profitability. Growth markets are non-zero-sum: all the competitors can grow, which acts to reduce destructive price competition and margin erosion. In high-growth markets, it is important to be ambitious. A firm's long-term competitive position can easily be undermined despite apparently satisfactory growth. For example, a business might be growing at 10 per cent annually, but if the market is growing at 20 per cent, its market share is rapidly eroding. Within a few years it might be overtaken by competitors that are able to achieve economies of scale and power over the distribution channels.

» The competitive structure of the market

The most important determinant of the average profitability of a market is its **competitive structure**.

There are five main elements of competitive structure:

1. **Intensity of direct competition.** In some markets, competitors are much more aggressive in seeking to win or maintain sales. Where this occurs, prices and profits are invariably reduced. Intense competition is most likely in markets characterised by:

   - **Excess production capacity.** The greater the excess capacity in an industry, the more likely competitors will cut prices and so erode profit margins in efforts to increase utilisation.
   - **Standardised products.** The more similar are the offers of competitors, the greater the chances of price-based competition and low margins.
   - **Many competitors.** The more players, the more likely is intense competition. With only a few competitors, tacit collusion will often maintain higher prices.
   - **Low growth.** In rapidly growing markets, the intensity of competition is reduced since they do not have to take customers from each other. As growth slows, excess capacity triggers price competition.

   In some industries, such as steel or textiles, all these characteristics are present, which act to eliminate profits for all but the most efficient producers.

2. **Buyer power.** The drive and ability of customers to reduce prices also has a major effect on the profitability of the industry. Buying pressure is a function of two forces: the price sensitivity of buyers and their negotiating power. The price sensitivity of customers is determined primarily by their profitability and the significance of the product's cost in their total expenditures. When times are tough for buyers and when they are spending significant sums with the supplier, there is a greater incentive to seek lower prices to restore their own margins.

competitive structure: the intensity of direct competition in a market, the power of suppliers and buyers, and the threat posed by new entry and by substitutes

The negotiating power of a customer is high where there are few customers, many suppliers, little differentiation between suppliers, low switching costs and opportunities for the customer to threaten to integrate backwards.

Generally, as markets mature, customer pressure puts margins under increasing threat. Over time, as buyers obtain more information about product features and suppliers' costs, their leverage increases. When this is combined with high price sensitivity, as it is for example in basic chemicals or auto tyres, buying power can cause profitability to disappear for all but the lowest-cost competitors.

3. **Threat of new entry.** If barriers to new entry are weak then it will be impossible for companies to maintain monopoly profits. The major barriers to entry are patents and legal regulations, economies of scale, high capital requirements to enter the market, strong brands, threat of retaliation and access to distribution channels. In some industries, such as soft drinks and pharmaceuticals, such barriers are crucial in explaining the high profit margins that have persisted. On the whole, however, globalisation, deregulation and the Internet are acting to reduce entry barriers in many markets.

4. **Threat from substitutes.** Substitute products are indirect competitors that can undermine demand and prices. There are different types of substitutes:
   - **Alternative products.** For example, if the price of steel rises, constructors can build bridges from concrete.
   - **New products.** Innovation can erode demand. For example, the fax replaced telegrams; e-mail, in turn, undermines the use of the fax.
   - **Elimination of need.** For example, new cars use less engine oil; eventually, sealed engines may make replacement lubricant unnecessary.
   - **Generic substitution.** All products, to some extent, compete with one another. For example, producers of TVs, computers, cars and holidays all compete for the limited incomes of households.
   - **Abstinence.** Consumers can often decide to do without the product if the price is unacceptable. Some industries are more prone to substitutes than others. For example, it is more difficult for customers to substitute away from ethical pharmaceuticals than it is for them to find substitutes for glass packaging.

5. **Power of suppliers.** Suppliers limit a market's profitability if they can drive up input costs faster than a market's customers will allow them to be passed on. Supplier power is likely to be high when:
   - few suppliers are available
   - suppliers have unique products or strongly differentiated brands
   - switching costs are high
   - suppliers can threaten to integrate forward
   - there are large numbers of small customers with weak negotiating power.

» The cyclicality of the market

Some markets, especially those for commodity products, are highly cyclical, with prices 30 per cent or more higher at the peaks than in the troughs. This results in companies swinging from high profitability to substantial losses over the years. The cause of the cycle is usually over-investment when profits are high, which then triggers excess capacity and a collapse of prices. Prices are only restored when mergers, or companies exiting the industry, reduce capacity. The performance of a firm in such a market is therefore highly coloured by the stage of the industry cycle.

» **Risk factors**

The attractiveness of a market is also affected by the risks involved, since such factors affect the rate used to discount future cash flows or economic profits. Risk factors include political stability and monetary considerations in the primary markets, infrastructure and the possibilities of regulatory interference, availability of skills and resources, and possible economic and tax considerations.

It is important to analyse all these external market factors when diagnosing a company's performance advantages. They emphasise that high profits and growth are not solely a function of strong capabilities and good management. Some industries, for long periods of time, are just easier in which to achieve performance. In some industries, however well-managed the firm, it is just extraordinarily difficult to create value for shareholders.

Differential advantage

Generally, however, the firm's differential advantage, or lack of it, has a more important impact on its value than the nature of its particular market. Even in the toughest markets, firms with a differential or competitive advantage are usually able to invest at returns that exceed their cost of capital. Similarly, even in industries where the average company earns high economic profits, firms without any differential advantage flounder. In other words, the variation of profitability within an industry exceeds the variation between industries. Ricardian profits are generally more important than monopoly profits.

To diagnose these internally generated sources of value creation, managers need to ask whether the business has held a value-creating differential advantage. If not, why not? The explanations of a firm's differential advantage, or lack of it, will be found in the firm's resources and the way they are integrated. If the firm has an effective set of lead indicators or balanced scorecard, which measures performance on the key value drivers, these should supply most of the answers.

When used in value-based marketing, a differential advantage has a precise meaning. A business has a differential advantage if it is able to sustain economic profits that exceed the average of competitors in its market. This differential advantage can be based on either of two strategies. The first is an economic cost strategy, which consists of a firm's total costs, including capital costs, being lower than those of the average competitor. The second is through a differentiation strategy, which consists of when customers perceiving its products as superior, are willing to pay a higher price than is charged by competitors.

» **Cost strategy**

In many commodity markets, developing a differentiation strategy is very difficult. Of course, every marketing manager can find ways of differentiating the product by augmenting it with additional services or advertising. But, without real innovation, it can often be very difficult, or impossible, to get buyers to pay price premiums sufficient to cover the costs of these additional features.

In such markets, superior profitability can only come through developing a cost benefit.

For value-based analysis, a cost benefit, or advantage, has a precise meaning. A business has a relative cost advantage if it has a lower total economic cost than the average of competitors in its market. **Total economic cost** means the sum of operating costs plus a charge for capital, where the capital charge is the cost of capital multiplied by the amount of capital employed in the business.

Note that this definition of an economic cost advantage is different from the conventional accounting method that looks only at operating costs. Unless the business recognises the cost of employing capital, investing heavily to reduce operating costs can actually increase total unit costs. This occurs if the increased capital charge is greater than the decline in operating cost. An example of this is the Saturn program at General Motors in the 1980s. GM spent billions on robotics and automation, only to find that companies like the Ford Motor Company, which focused on increasing the efficiency of its labour force, ended up with lower total economic costs per vehicle.

An economic cost advantage can create shareholder value in either of two ways. First, the business can charge the same price as competitors but earn a higher profit margin. Alternatively, it can charge lower prices and gain a higher market share.

Note that investing in a low-cost strategy may not always make sense. To create value, any investment to gain a cost benefit must be more than offset by the improvement in profitability over time, or the gain in market share, depending on how management chooses to exploit the benefit. Many companies have over-invested in efforts to gain a cost benefit only to find that innovation or competitive emulation quickly erodes the benefit.

» Differentiation strategy

Differentiation occurs when there is a perceived difference in delivered value that leads target customers to prefer one company's offer to those of others. Generally, differentiation strategies have been a more effective way of increasing returns to shareholders than cost-based strategies. This is illustrated in table 5.2, which lists companies among the Fortune largest 500 corporations with the highest sustained return to shareholders. The list is dominated by firms that have pursued strategies based on innovation, superior service and brand loyalty. Cost-based strategies are more vulnerable for two reasons. First, rapid change has meant that cost advantages based on scale and experience are often undermined by competitors innovating in terms of even lower-cost processes or distribution channels. Second, low-cost technology and systems have often been speedily copied by competitors.

However, developing a value-creating differentiation strategy is no easy task. Companies tend to overestimate the uniqueness of their offers. It is very common for managers to perceive their products as superior. Unfortunately, it is not their perceptions which count, but rather those of the customer. Differentiation occurs only if customers are willing to pay a price premium. If customers are unwilling to pay a price premium then the company does not have an advantage. The key requirement is customers being willing to pay more. If a business has such an advantage then management have three strategies to choose from. First, charge the full price premium by increasing the price to the

---

total economic cost: the sum of operating costs plus a charge for capital, where the capital charge is the cost of capital multiplied by the amount of capital employed in the business

point where it just offsets the improvement in customer benefits. Second, keep prices at the level of competitors and use its advantage to gain market share. Or, third, price above competitors but below the full premium to gain a combination of unit margin improvement and market share gain.

Table 5.2 Europe's best-performing companies: Total shareholder return 1994–1999

COMPANY	INDUSTRY	COUNTRY	TSR (%)
Nokia	IT hardware	Finland	1934
Aegon	Life assurance	Netherlands	978
Hennes & Mauritz	Retail	Sweden	872
Dixons Group	Retail	UK	738
Vodafone	Telecoms services	UK	726
UCB	Chemicals	Belgium	655
Synthelabo	Pharmaceuticals	France	612
Banco Bilbao	Banks	Spain	585
Bank of Ireland	Banks	Ireland	577
Smithkline Beecham	Pharmaceuticals	UK	522
Swiss Re	Insurance	Swiss	508
Pinault-Printemps	Retail	France	498
Allied Irish Banks	Banks	Ireland	493
Lloyds TSB	Banks	UK	479
Skandia Forsaking	Insurance	Sweden	478
Mannesmann	Telecoms services	Germany	476
Bank of Scotland	Banks	UK	451
Provident Financial	Speciality finance	UK	435
Ericsson	IT hardware	Sweden	434

If management's claim about possessing differentiated products is to be proved, they need to demonstrate that one of these three outcomes is occurring. The way in which this can be demonstrated is illustrated in figure 5.4. Here, managers believed that each of the five product lines had an advantage due to their superior quality and sales support. But the evidence from market research showed otherwise. Line A was perceived by customers as of lower quality than competitors; it sold at a lower price and still lost market share. Lines B and C charged premium prices, but customers obviously did not think these premiums were justified as market shares were also declining. Only D and E had an advantage. D charged higher prices and was holding market share; E charged parity prices but had gained over 5 per cent market share. Managers need to understand that being different is not the same as having a differential advantage. Unless the firm gains sufficient premium or additional share to cover the additional costs and investment, there is no added value.

Differentiation can be grouped into at least two sources. The first is product leadership where customers perceive the company offer as of higher quality, emotional appeal or more innovative (examples include Sony and American Express). The second is customer intimacy, or one-to-one marketing, where buyers see the company as being able to customise its offer to their personal requirements and deal with them on an individualised basis (examples are Federal Express and Roy Morgan Research in Melbourne). As with cost strategies, successful differentiation is based on the firm's resources and capabilities. Progress in building these resources and capabilities should be monitored through the choice of lead indicators.

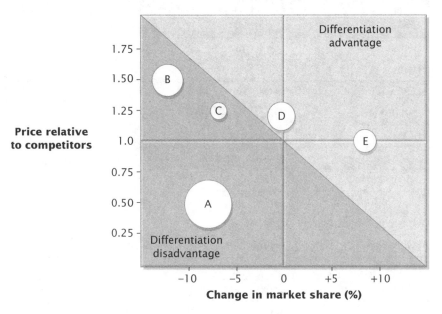

Figure 5.4 Measuring competitive differentiation

Market attractiveness and differential advantage

The analysis of the company's external and internal forces can be brought together in a strategic characterisation matrix.[3] This is illustrated in figure 5.5 for a company with four business units with different strategic characteristics.[4] The radius of the circles is proportionate to the turnover of the business unit. A business like A, in an attractive market and with a strong differential advantage, should always be creating value for shareholders. It may not currently be highly profitable if the market is new, but investment should earn long-run returns above the cost of capital. Ideally, a company would like to have most of its business in this part of the matrix. Companies like Microsoft and AMP are examples of companies with the majority of their businesses in attractive markets and possessing differential advantages.

Business B, on the other hand, has the opposite characteristics and will almost always be value destroying. It will produce economic losses and the return on investment will be less than the cost of capital. Outside the two extreme zones, for example for units C and D, the results are less clear cut. C will normally be in a better position than D because usually differential advantage has a bigger impact on profitability than market attractiveness. Normally, when a business has a significant differential advantage, it can generate economic profits even though it operates in an unattractive market. Businesses such as D are usually value destroying because the attractiveness of the market does not compensate for the lack of differential advantage.

Even when they are generating positive economic profits, they are highly vulnerable to deterioration in the economics of the market.

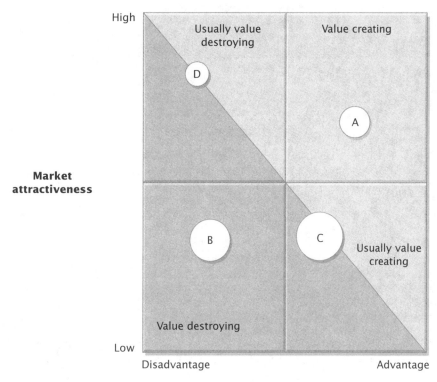

Figure 5.5 The strategic characterisation matrix

To summarise, the past performance of a company is explained by a combination of the attractiveness of the market and its differential advantage, with the latter generally the more important. To an extent, the two sets of factors overlap in that a competence of management should be in identifying attractive markets. Also, not all the features of the market are outside the control of managers. They can also develop strategies to improve the competitive structure of the market in their favour by, for example, creating entry barriers, or by mergers to reduce capacity. But it is important to disentangle the two different dimensions since they shape how the future of the business is likely to develop.

Assessing the future position

The first part of the strategic assessment was aimed at obtaining a factual picture of the performance of the company. The second part sought to explain this performance in terms of the attractiveness of the firm's markets and its differential advantages. The third part seeks to project where the business is heading under its present policies. It aims at predicting what the performance is likely to be, as a prelude to determining what new actions need to be taken.

Forecasting the future of the business on its present strategies requires projecting the characteristics of the market and anticipating the implications of the firm's differential position into the future (see marketing management in practice 'McDonald's looks to a McHappy future').

Marketing management in practice: McDonald's looks to a McHappy future

McDonald's has changed the way Australians eat in the 30 years it has been in Australia. Not only do we consume more fast food, we've started eating food faster. Ten years ago, 70 per cent of the people who ate at McDonald's sat down to finish their meal. Now that figure is 30 per cent. Today it's 'food on the move' as drive-throughs become more popular.

A typical McDonald's restaurant does 55 per cent of its sales to people who never get out of their cars — a figure rising all the time. The other takeaway customers come through the front door. Teams of McDonald's employees race each other to see how many cars they can process every 15 minutes — the record is 42 cars, or a meal served every 21 seconds.

But McDonald's won't stop there. It is looking at the City Link e-tag technology used in Melbourne so that people can have a stored-value tag on their car for easier sales, eliminating the need to stop twice; once to pay and once to pick up the goods.

On average, 450 000 people each year pass through each McDonald's store in Australia; the highest McDonald's customer-to-store ratio in the world. Today, McDonald's serves more than one million people a day through 710 restaurants in Australia. Last year, it had sales of $1.74 billion, up 0.6 per cent from a year earlier.

The company says it was hit hard by the introduction of the GST, which drove up prices and put off the price-conscious customers attracted to the golden arches. McDonald's will open about 25 new restaurants next year, which represents an easing in growth compared with five years ago.

But McDonald's Australia managing director Guy Russo says the slowdown in the company's expansion does not indicate that the Australian market has matured. 'I think it's a reflection that we went and put the accelerator down in the mid-1990s,' he said. 'We were neck-and-neck with KFC and Pizza Hut at that time. But, in the '90s, we decided to seize the moment when we saw how big demand was at that time. So we said, 'Let's get to where we want to be: faster, smarter, quicker.' We made a few errors in the middle of that period. We opened some restaurants we wished we hadn't opened. But basically now we have 700 restaurants and our nearest competitor has about 400 restaurants. We're growing by about 20 restaurants a year and our competitors are growing at about the same rate. So they're going to find it very hard to ever catch up.'

McDonald's has become aware of the need to go more upmarket, which means expanding the margins it earns from just selling burgers at low prices — but it has had to do so without hurting the McDonald's brand name. As a result, in March it will open its first Boston Market store in Australia, the fast-food chain the corporation took over in the United States. Boston Market has a sit-down food menu, with china plates and proper cutlery. To promote family eating, it won't have alcohol for sale.

'We might serve a million people a day, but in total more than 60 million meals get eaten a day in Australia,' said Russo. 'So that means we've got less than 1.5 per cent of all the food that gets eaten in a day. So what we want to do is tap into those other 60 million meals, but not be eating into the fast-casual food business.'

The company has always been conscious of being seen as a fast-food company rather than as a junk-food company; for instance, it has for years published information on the nutrition of its food. But now the company is moving in directions that would have been unthinkable 20 years ago. Salads, for instance, are being tried out in the Smith Street store in Melbourne, and sandwiches are being introduced as part of its new menu promotion.

'If you want to stay relevant in business, you've got to satisfy your existing customers by offering them more variety,' said Russo. 'But, at the end of the day, no matter what we put on our new menu, our biggest sellers will always be cheese burgers, Big Macs and Happy Meals. But the main reason for the change is that the Australian landscape has totally changed in regard to what's happened in the past 20 years. Chinese and Indians, and Italians, Greeks, and Europeans generally have made a big impact, and all those tastes have been brought into the new taste menu.'

McDonald's is also testing a new cooking system in Sydney called 'made for you', which will allow customers to design the burger or menu they want. McCafe is McDonald's Australia's export to the world. It is now in 19 countries, including the United States, Japan, France, Austria, Britain, Argentina and Brazil. One of Russo's goals is to increase the number of McCafes in Australia to 300 from 60.

The McDonald's story in Australia also throws up some quirky facts. For instance, the hamburger chain has become a symbol for protesters of what is bad about globalisation. Yet, during the S11 protests [in 2000] in Melbourne at the World Economic Forum, the McDonald's South Melbourne outlet, just around the corner from Crown Casino, had its biggest week ever as the protesters fuelled up on burgers to keep up the fight against globalisation that was going on down the road.

And the young McDonald's employees who work the drive-through counters get more than just an education in how a truly global organisation works. As one staff member said at the South Melbourne outlet, some customers in the middle of the night drive through in some form of undress, including total nudity, indicating how relaxed we have become with having dinner at the golden arches.

Source: Stephen Dabkowski, 'Many McHappy returns', *The Age* (Business), 27 December 2001, pp. 1–2.

Market attractiveness

We have looked at how the characteristics of the market affected performance in the past. Now the task is to assess how these characteristics are likely to change in the future and affect future performance.

Each of the dimensions of market attractiveness has to be evaluated. First, on the size and growth of the market, managers have to estimate how the growth rate will change over the next several years; we recommend a five-year time span. Of particular importance is taking into consideration how the market will be segmented and which customer segments are likely to be most attractive. The competitive structure of the market has to be evaluated, as does its impact on industry profitability. Will excess capacity be a problem? What are the strategies of the competitors and how will they affect the competitive intensity of the industry and the major segments? What implications will this have for prices and margins? Are customer pressures going to be a major issue? Are new competitors likely to enter the market? Are product substitution and new technology going to create pressures? Will suppliers be exerting significant cost pressures?

Similar projections need to be made about the industry cycle. Will cyclical pressures be favourable or not for prices and profits? Any new political, economic or societal risk factors also have to be considered. This research should lead to a profile of how market profitability and growth are likely to change over the next years. It should lead to a conclusion on whether the market is likely to become more or less attractive.

Differential advantage

Alongside the projection of developments in the industry, management has to assess how the differential advantage of the firm will shift over the coming years. If such an assessment is to be accurate and useful, it will require comprehensive quantitative information, not only on the firm's products, but also on those of competitors and on the changing needs of customers. For example, to estimate the relative economic cost advantage of the business, it will need to benchmark its costs against the major competitors for each stage of its value chain. Assessing the firm's differentiation strategy will require information on relative prices, market shares and consumer needs broken down by product and market segment. Since management is focusing on how these are likely to change in the future, it will also have to develop an understanding of the strategies of competitors and customers.

Figure 5.6 illustrates the results of such a differential position assessment for a speciality chemicals company. The larger circles show the projected improvement of the business from the current year (2001) to the forecast position in 2006, resulting from a major rebranding plan and a cost reduction program. The smaller points represent the changes in the competitive advantage projected for the business unit's individual products. Overall, the forecasts show a modest enhancement of the differentiation advantage of the business together with a significant move towards competitive parity in costs.

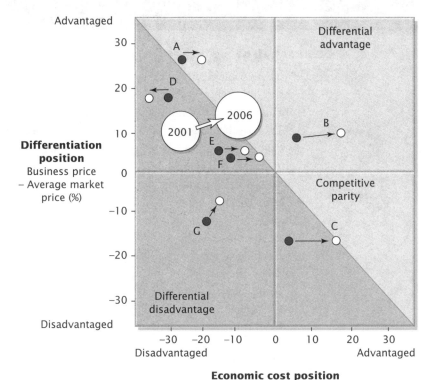

Figure 5.6 The competitive advantage matrix.
Source: Reprinted with permission of The Free Press, a Division of Simon & Schuster Adult Publishing Group, from *The Value Imperative: Managing for Superior Shareholder Return* by James M. McTaggart, Peter W. Kantes and Michael C. Mankins. Copyright © 1994 by The Free Press.

The next step is to integrate this analysis with the market attractiveness projections, using the strategic characterisation matrix, as illustrated in figure 5.7. This shows the strategic position of the business; most of its products are likely to improve from the projected enhancement of its differential advantage. Its major weakness is in the continued unattractiveness of its markets, characterised by little growth, tough competition and strong buyers.

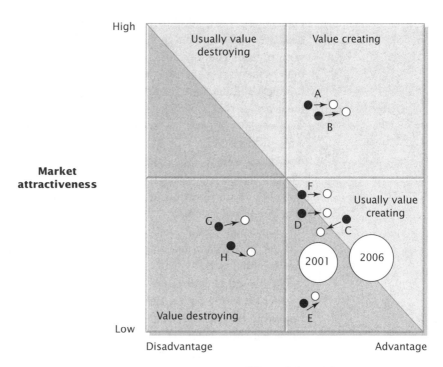

Figure 5.7 The strategic characterisation matrix

The final step is to input these projections into a forecast of the financial performance of the business and the shareholder value added over the planning period. In the previous example, management forecast an improvement in its already positive economic return on capital employed, but modest value creation on account of the lack of top-line growth.

Determining the strategic objectives

The strategic position assessment process cumulates in a set of broad strategic objectives, one for each of the business units. The strategic objective assigned to a business unit sets the broad path management have to follow in pursuit of the company's overall value-creating process. As explained in chapter 4, divest, harvest, maintain, growth and enter are the broad strategic objectives to be assigned. What the appropriate strategic objective is for a unit generally depends upon the assessment of the attractiveness of its market and the strength of its differential advantage (see figure 4.1 in chapter 4). The five strategic objectives can be distinguished as follows:

1. divest
2. harvest
3. maintain
4. grow
5. enter.

Divest

An essential element of value-based marketing is exiting from markets or market segments that do not offer profit potential and rationalising unprofitable products. Divesting from such losers cuts costs and shifts resources from uneconomical activities. By pruning the number of activities, it reduces complexity and allows managers to focus on those parts of the business that offer genuine opportunities for profitable growth. Many companies can double their value over a two- or three-year period simply by divesting from those products and customers that produce large, irreversible losses and increasing the growth of their most profitable units.

Divestment should be considered under combinations of high market attractiveness/disadvantaged differential position and low market attractiveness/disadvantaged differential position. The first, and more common, is when the product or activity is not making an economic profit and where there is little prospect of the situation being turned around. If the market is expected to remain unattractive — no growth, excess capacity, intense competition and powerful buyers — or if the company does not expect to achieve a genuine and significant differential advantage through a costs or differentiation strategy, then an exit strategy should be proposed.

The second circumstance when divestment should be considered is where another company values the business more highly than the current owner. Capturing this surplus creates value for the company's shareholders. The outsider's superior valuation might be due to the synergies it could achieve through lower costs, increased sales or reduced competition. Another reason for the higher valuation may be that the outsider has a greater management capability to turn the business around. This is often the case when the business is not a core activity of the current owner. Finally, an outsider may be willing to pay more than the current value of the business because they are simply excessively optimistic, or using the wrong criteria (for example, the effect on earnings per share) to judge the value of the acquisition. For example, Saatchi & Saatchi amazed the owners of the US advertising agency Ted Bates by offering twice their most optimistic valuation of their business. Subsequent events proved that Saatchi & Saatchi had grossly overpaid, the cost being born by its shareholders when the Saatchi share price subsequently collapsed. A similar example is HIH in Australia. The insurance company was perceived by many analysts as having paid too much for FAI. HIH is now bankrupt. Chief executives can be too accounting-oriented in their approach to divesting unprofitable products or businesses. Profitability and value are poorly correlated, especially in growth businesses. When new markets or technologies emerge, such as the Internet or mobile phones, entrepreneurial businesses are frequently unprofitable because of their high set-up costs and the importance of developing critical mass. At the same time, these unprofitable businesses are often highly valued by investors who are discounting their long-run ability to create profits. When executives divest such units, they destroy, rather than create, value.

Economic profits are more closely related to value in mature businesses. But even here, turning unprofitable businesses around may be a better option than divestment. The decision has to be based, in particular, upon management's ability to develop a differential advantage in terms of costs or a differentiated offering to customers. It also needs a hard-headed analysis of the future attractiveness of the market. Managers have to assess what market conditions — capacity, competition and customer buying pressures — imply for average profitability in the industry. In cyclical industries, taking a long-term view is particularly important. Depending upon where the business is on the cycle at any point of time, current prices and profitability can give very misleading signals of the trend. Managers need to look at the picture over a longer period to get an objective view of profitability and value potential.

Divestment and product rationalisation depend for their success on accurate data on economic profits. It is important that overhead costs and investment be allocated to products in a way that accurately reflects their usage. Without good economic information, the wrong products will often be sacrificed. Managers will often make rationalisation decisions based on volume, believing that low-volume products are less profitable than their high-volume counterparts. Once a proper allocation of costs and investments is made, it often becomes clear that many high-volume accounts are scarcely profitable because of the bargaining power of these customers. Many low-volume accounts are often discovered to be highly profitable because they are niche businesses, achieving higher prices, and selling to less demanding customers.

Another common problem in divestment lies in the links between the weak products and other parts of the business. It is common for the product under review to share costs, assets and customers with other more profitable products. Divesting the product will then mean reducing the profitability of the remaining businesses as they have to absorb the costs and assets. Often, too, there will be supply chain linkages. For example, shrinking the business unit's product line can reduce its level of influence over its dealers or retailers. Thus, the benefits of exiting one market or product must be weighed against the possibility of reducing the profitability of the whole product line.

Understanding of the linkages between products should not, however, be an excuse for inaction. Frequently, the savings from divestment will more than compensate for the side effects. When side effects are a major issue, there are often other options that can be considered. The business can source rather than manufacture products to maintain its product portfolio in a more economical manner. Alternatively, it may be able to find a strategic partner to share the costs of the business under review. In all circumstances, managers have to decisively attack the problems caused by businesses that are not adding value.

Two other issues are common barriers to sensible divestment strategies. One is the use of marginal analysis to explore investment and divestment options. This assumes a product is worth keeping if it makes any contribution to overheads and profits. Such an approach is particularly tempting to management faced with substantial excess capacity. Unfortunately, such a criterion allows the business to drift into carrying a large number of products that do not make an economic profit because they are not held responsible for either the overheads or capital they incur. In the longer run, managers have to accept that all costs and assets are variable. Marginal analysis makes it too easy to sanction entry decisions and too easy to postpone exit decisions.

The second obstacle is the desire of managers for size and growth. Growth is, of course, a crucial way to create value for shareholders, but only if it is, over time, profitable growth. In many companies, ill-considered incentives bias managers to non-value-adding growth. These include the pattern of paying managers according to the size of the business they manage, the prestige attached to running the biggest unit and incentives that reward volume rather than value. All these incentives encourage managers to add products and discourage them from sacrificing parts of their empires.

Management should review the business annually to identify candidates for divestment. Such a process involves four steps. First, identify divestment targets. These will be parts of the business that the strategic objective assessment forecasts cannot earn economic profits over the planning period on account of the inability of the business to build a profitable differential advantage or the unattractive nature of the markets in which they operate. Second, estimate the liquidation value of the business unit. This is the cash that could be obtained from selling off the fixed assets and releasing the working capital, less any exit costs (for example, for environmental clean-up). Typically, liquidating a business and taking the tax loss will produce a cash amount of 40 to 60 per cent of the book value of shareholders' funds. Third, estimate the highest operating value of the business unit under an optimal restructuring plan. As described earlier, this includes exploring all internal and external options to increase the long-term discounted value of cash flow that can be generated from the business. The final step is to determine the net divestment value. This is the present value of the after-tax proceeds from selling the business, liquidating it or spinning it off. If the net divestment value exceeds the highest operating value of the business, then the decision should be to divest the business.

In summary, divesting parts of the business that do not add value is a crucial way of increasing returns to shareholders. It is also an important precursor to a growth strategy by releasing management resources to focus on higher value activities.

Harvest

A harvesting objective is one that seeks to maximise the firm's cash flow from its existing assets. It is an appropriate objective when the firm has determined, first, that the business has sufficient potential for it to be retained rather than divested and, second, that increases in cash flow will come from the current volume of sales rather than growth. Indeed, harvesting is often accompanied by declining sales volume.

Harvesting — or milking the business — will apply to a combination of medium market attractiveness/disadvantaged differential position and low market attractiveness/average differential position (in other words, when the competitive advantage of the business is in unavoidable decline or where market conditions are deteriorating). This may be because new technology is replacing the company's core product or because the market demand is falling. Harvesting is a common objective in the pharmaceutical industry when a product's patent is about to expire. Tobacco companies around the world faced with a falling demand for cigarettes also employ it.

Companies pursuing harvesting strategies are willing to lose market share if this increases the cash flow. Cash flow can be increased in two ways. First, the company can increase operating margins by raising prices, cutting variable costs, cutting fixed costs and focusing on premium market niches. Second, it can reduce investment by reducing stocks and tightening up on payment terms, pushing suppliers for extended financing and reducing fixed assets. Such policies can dramatically increase cash flow quite quickly.

The problem with harvesting objectives today is that excessive efforts to increase margins and prune investment can lead to very rapid losses of market share. If that occurs, the market value of the business may fall precipitously. In such a situation, selling off the business may generate a greater value than harvesting.

Successful harvesting will often require tactical investments in marketing and promotion to discourage new entry. It will also mean ensuring that value levels do not fall below market expectations, especially in those niches where premium pricing is possible. To compare the value created by harvesting versus divestment, management needs to project the cash flow from harvesting under realistic competitive conditions.

Maintain

For some strategic business units, an appropriate objective is to maintain market share. This objective is different from harvesting, where management normally accepts that market share will erode. On the other hand, management does not aim at a more aggressive strategy of market share growth. A maintain objective applies to combinations of medium market attractiveness/average differential position and low market attractiveness/advantaged differential position. The conditions for a maintenance objective are that:

1. the business is earning healthy economic profits and marginal investments earn a return exceeding the unit's cost of capital
2. the market is not expected to decline over the foreseeable future and the business has a well-established competitive position
3. the market is dominated by only a small number of producers (usually no more than two or three)
4. there are significant barriers to new entry.

In this type of market, a competitive equilibrium or implicit collusion often occurs. Each major competitor knows that an effort to increase market share will lead to a rapid response from competitors and both prices and profits will tumble. Competitors earn higher profits by accepting the status quo. Such behaviour was apparent, for example, in the Australian domestic aviation market until 2000, where Qantas and Ansett shared the market roughly evenly — including all major airport terminals. Similar behaviour could also be observed in UK detergents, where Unilever and Procter & Gamble have shared the market approximately equally for decades.

The main objective in a maintenance strategy is to avoid price competition. Price competition is always the most damaging in its effects on value creation. For example, a price cut of 5 per cent for a company with a pre-tax operating margin of 8 per cent would see its profits drop by almost two-thirds. Price wars are what competitors fear most in these oligopolistic markets.

It is important for the established players to maintain barriers to entry since new competitors could quickly gain market share. Because lowering price is so unattractive for the incumbents, high levels of advertising support are often the best way to deter entry. Advertising expenditures are normally fixed costs and therefore offer the biggest competitors economies of scale that newcomers cannot match. In contrast, price cutting is like a variable cost: the bigger the company, the more it loses. A 5 per cent price cut costs a $40 million business $2 million off its bottom line; a $4 million business, on the other hand, loses only $0.2 million.

Besides high levels of advertising and communication expenditures, companies also need to maintain a focus on innovation. Unless they keep their products up to date, they will face market share erosion by either current competitors or new entrants. Maintaining market share does therefore require considerable proactivity from the incumbents to maintain the current position and keep out entrants.

Market signalling is another feature of a maintenance objective. Signalling is defined as the selective communication of information to competitors designed to influence competitors' perceptions and behaviour in order to provoke or avoid certain types of action.[5] Signalling can be used to deter competitive entry. Procter & Gamble has developed a formidable reputation for defending its markets. Clorox long dominated the bleach segment in Europe, a relatively small niche of the consumer soaps and detergents market. In 1990, it decided to extend into the mainstream US detergents market which was led by Procter & Gamble. Before Clorox's new product was even launched, Procter & Gamble rolled out its Tide With Bleach, employing a massive promotional campaign. Clorox soon had to withdraw, nursing losses estimated at US$50 million.

Signalling can also be used to discipline current players from aggressive moves. Alcoa, for example, deliberately over-invested in order to have available capacity to flood the market if the competitor did not toe the line on acceptable behaviour. Finally, it can be used to encourage mutual efforts to improve industry profitability. For example, the Australian and New Zealand petrol markets are characterised by price leadership, in the opinion of many industry commentators. Before raising prices, the leader firm usually tests the water and builds a consensus by press releases that announce 'unsatisfactory industry margins' and 'expected price increases'.

Grow

The first three objectives — divest, harvest and maintain — should ensure that investors' funds are not wasted on economically unattractive investments. But to create outstanding returns for shareholders, it is essential to possess growth businesses. Investing to achieve high growth makes sense as long as the business can earn a return on the invested capital that exceeds its cost of capital. As long as this return is achieved, the faster the business grows, the greater the value that is created for shareholders.

Such growth opportunities depend primarily on the firm possessing a differential advantage. Second, it depends on the attractiveness of the market. A growth objective applies to combinations of high market attractiveness/disadvantaged differential position, high market attractiveness/average differential position, high market attractiveness/advantaged differential position, and medium market attractiveness/advantaged differential position. The most obvious high-growth opportunities are to be found in the north-east quadrant of the strategic characterisation matrix (see figure 4.1 in chapter 4). With high-growth businesses, it is particularly important not to confuse profit or cash flow with value creation. Companies maximising value creation opportunities in high-growth markets will always have lower cash flows and generally lower profits in the early years than what could be achieved by reining back on growth. But holding back on opportunities for

market signalling:
the selective communication of information to competitors designed to influence competitors' perceptions and behaviour in order to provoke or avoid certain types of action

value creating investments to boost current cash flow and profits is a short-term strategy that erodes the value of the business and frequently means that the company fails to achieve the critical mass to be viable in the long run.

Marketing managers often appear to think that any strategy that achieves growth is successful. Of course, this is nonsense. Anyone can grow sales if the price is low enough or if enough is spent on advertising and communication. What the company needs is value-generating growth. These are additional sales that increase the net present value of the business. In other words, the additional sales must cover the investments, costs and the cost of capital incurred to generate the growth.

If marketers are often too optimistic about the value of growth, accounting-orientated management can be too conservative. One of the characteristics of many of today's markets is network effects, which suggest increasing rewards to companies that move fast and decisively in growth markets. A product has network effects or 'externalities' if the value to any one user rises with the total number of users of the product. A classic example is the telephone.[6] If you are the only owner of one in the country, it is not much use. The more people with phones, the more valuable it is to the user. Such network externalities are a marked characteristic of many of today's information-based industries.

Network effects mean that the first company to gain a big installed base sets the standard that makes it difficult to displace. New customers want to buy the product that everyone else has. For strategy, this has a number of implications. First, it stresses the importance of gaining a first-mover advantage. It also highlights the role of advertising and communication to make customers aware that your product is going to be the leader. Often, too, there are opportunities to form alliances to boost credibility in the future leadership of the product. Most controversially, it suggests the importance of penetration pricing at the early stages of these markets. It is worth subsidising early adopters through low prices. Microsoft, for example, gave its browser away free to get people to adopt it, counting on establishing it as the new standard.

Strategies like penetration pricing are risky. It will normally mean losing money in the early years with the hope of becoming the next Microsoft and recouping it many times after it becomes the dominant player. Companies that are insufficiently aggressive in their pricing are still likely to lose money in the early years and lose everything in the long run.

Enter

In a rapidly changing environment, creating value is not just about rationalising uneconomic businesses and improving current activities, it is increasingly about innovation. Innovation can take several forms:

- **New products.** Products are either new to the company, new to the market, or both, all of which can create value by adapting the company to a changing market. Examples are Diet Coke, which met the desire for low-calorie drinks, and Flora margarine, which met the desire for cholesterol-free spreads.
- **New processes.** These are operational innovations that allow the same products to be delivered at lower cost or with higher quality. For example,

Pilkington's invention of the float-glass process enabled it to capture much of the market for auto-glass. Dell Computer Corporation catapulted to leadership in PCs in the 1990s by cutting out the traditional dealer and interacting directly with consumers using the telephone or Internet. First Direct did the same in insurance, Amazon.com in book retailing, eBay in auctions, Direct Line in banking — the list is continually expanding.

- **New markets.** A company can achieve new sources of growth through exploiting new markets or market segments. Swatch, for example, developed the market for watches as fashion accessories, significantly increasing the size of the total watch market.

- **New marketing strategies.** These are innovative ways of marketing products. For example, Dixons became the number one Internet service provider in the United Kingdom by being the first to offer its service free to customers. It earned its revenue from taking a cut of the phone call costs rather than from subscriptions. Castrol became the leading machine lubricant by charging workshops a monthly fee for maintaining their machinery rather than charging per litre of oil.

An enter objective applies to a combination of high market attractiveness/ advantaged differential position. Here, determining high market attractiveness means forecasting the size of the targeted market, its growth rate, the competitive structure of the market, in particular the intensity of competition and the power of the buyers, cyclical factors, and the nature of the risks involved. If the industry is not going to be profitable on average — as industries like steel, airlines and textile manufacturing have been in the past — creating shareholder value is going to be very difficult, however good the company is. It is much better to swim with the tide than against it.

The second, and most important, criteria for entry is the firm's ability to create a sustainable differential advantage. This means achieving a low cost structure or differentiated offering that will lead to customer preference, and a preference that can be sustained when competitors inevitably seek to emulate it. This base upon which such a competitive advantage rests is, of course, the firm's resources and capabilities: the quality of the tangible and intangible assets it possesses, the skills and knowledge of its staff, and the drive and adaptability emanating from its organisational culture. Most successful innovations are, not surprisingly, based on leveraging the firm's current resources and capabilities to enter new markets or develop new positioning strategies.

An additional requirement for entry is overcoming the entry barriers to the industry. Attractive markets are usually characterised by high entry barriers in the form of patents, capital requirements or economies of scale. Their common feature is that they drive up the initial investment required to establish a viable position in the market. This means that the firm must have a really sizeable and sustainable competitive advantage to generate the margins that will achieve an economic return on this investment. Alongside barriers to entry, the prospective entrant must evaluate the likelihood of retaliation on the part of the incumbents, who will seek to deter entry. For example, Qantas and Ansett, the major airlines flying the Melbourne–Sydney route, successfully used price cuts to drive the new discounter, Impulse Airlines, out of the market in 2001.

In general, the most fierce retaliation occurs when the total market is not growing. The odds are better for entrants in growing markets because increased sales are gained without necessarily reducing those of competitors. In mature markets, acquisition can be a more effective means of gaining entry since it does not add to industry capacity.

Most managers do not understand the importance investors attach to a firm's ability to enter attractive markets. Much the greatest part of a company's equity value is based upon investors' expectations about the company's future products and markets rather than their current activities. As we have seen, on average cash flow over the next four years accounts for less than 20 per cent of a company's share price.[7] What investors are valuing are their expectations about long-term cash flow, which depends upon the options the firm has available and its ability to exploit these options.

Management accounting has not kept pace with our knowledge about how investors value companies. Accounting still overestimates short-term cash flows. It emphasises today's profit earners at the expense of tomorrow's. The standard discounted cash flow analysis accountants use to evaluate investment projects discourages many new opportunities by overemphasising the risk and cost of failure. More recently, financial options theory has presented a more effective way of judging new entry proposals. This approach reflects that entry decisions are not big, once-and-for-all choices, but rather a series of incremental investments, each one contingent upon the success of the previous one. If the feedback about the entry strategy is not promising, the company can usually pull out without further investment. Initial investments are options that allow the firm the opportunity to make subsequent investments if prospects look exciting at the end of the initial stage. Investors are valuing companies in terms of whether they have developed strategic positions to take up options in tomorrow's attractive markets.

The value-based plan

The strategic objective assessment provides the information for value-based planning. A value-based plan is a framework for restructuring the business to optimise its value for shareholders and can be used as a basis for the strategic focus and marketing mix decisions.

The focus of such a plan is on what determines equity value — long-term cash flows, not short-term earnings. The perspective marketing managers must take is that of the outside investor. This is a dispassionate approach that views businesses as investments in productive capacity that either earns returns above their opportunity cost of capital or does not. The units of analysis in the plan are the strategic business units, not the organisation as a whole. It is at the individual product-market level that competitive advantages are built and the strategic value drivers principally operate. The value and strategy of the company as a whole is primarily an aggregation of performance at the business unit level with a separate assessment of the value added, or otherwise, by the head office.

The task of management is to develop and implement a plan to increase the equity value of the business. A useful framework for describing the steps in this process is the McKinsey pentagon.[8] Figure 5.8 shows how the process of creating increased value can be divided into five stages.

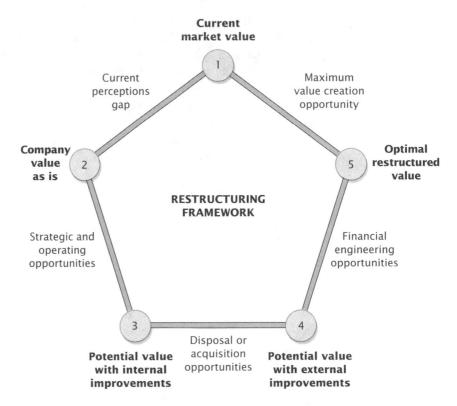

Figure 5.8 Value-based planning: The McKinsey pentagon

1. Establishing the current market value of the company

The first step in the analysis is straightforward if the company is publicly quoted. The current market value of the company can be calculated from the *Australian Financial Review*, *Wall Street Journal*, *Financial Times* or other widely available information sources. These sources provide the estimate made by outside investors of the discounted net present value of the company's long-term cash flow. The market-determined value should be fairly close to the managers' own discounted cash flow valuation. If it is not, the gap will be due to one of the following factors:

- **Unrealistic assumptions.** Management's perception of the future is based on unrealistic assumptions about the company's differential advantage or the attractiveness of the market in which it operates.
- **Insider information.** The management valuation may be higher if they have important information that has not yet been made available to investors (for example, about new product breakthroughs or strategic alliances).
- **Market expectations.** The market's valuation might be higher than that of management if investors anticipate a successful take-over of the company at a premium.

2. The value of the company as is

This stage examines how the company's market value is arrived at, and which are the company's most, and least, valuable businesses. It begins by breaking the company down into strategic business units. Cash flow projections have then to be developed for each of the units. These are based on projected sales growth, margins and investment needs — all of which should be available from the business plans. The finance staff will provide estimates of the cost of capital for each division. As described in chapter 2, discounted cash flow valuations are then calculated.

This process is illustrated for a speciality chemicals company, Ace Chemicals, in table 5.3.

Table 5.3 The value of the company 'as is', January 2002 ($ million)

ACE CHEMICALS	PLAN VALUES ($)	EXTRAPOLATION VALUES ($)	DIFFERENCE (%)
Foundry	485	410	+18
Steel	120	105	+14
Aluminium	30	35	−14
Headquarters	−95	−110	+14
Total	540	440	+23
Debt	−50	−50	
Equity value	490	390	+26
Stock market value	450	450	
Value gap	40	−60	
Gap (%)	9	−13	

The background is that Ace's recent performance had been disappointing, with little overall growth, stagnant profits and a sliding share price. A new chief executive had been brought in to improve the performance of the company. The company has three strategic business units selling chemical products to the foundry, steel and aluminium industries. It also has a corporate headquarters costing some $10 million annually. The first task was to use the profitability and growth forecasts from the business plan to calculate the net present values of the cash flows for each of the three units. The present value of headquarters costs were calculated by capitalising projected after-tax annual costs.

To provide a simple benchmark to assess the validity of the current business plan, the finance staff also ran a valuation based on extrapolating the trend for the previous five years. The analyses showed that, if the company continued on trend, its value would be 13 per cent below its current market value. The planned strategy, on the other hand, was envisaged to bring about a 26 per cent increase in its equity value. This would put the value of Ace above its current market value, but only by 9 per cent — not a particularly exciting figure for investors in the light of the poor performance in the past.

The new management team saw that the vast majority of Ace's value was represented by the value of the foundry business's cash flow. Aluminium is a particular problem, showing a decline in value against its past performance. The plan also projected a cut in headquarter's costs; even so, these would still represent a major drag on the company's equity value — almost 20 per cent.

The results of the strategic objective assessment that Ace had undertaken prior to developing the restructuring plan revealed the explanations of its position. The strategic characterisation matrix showed that the foundry's success was due to its strong differential advantage based on leading-edge products and an outstanding reputation for quality and service. With steel and aluminium, however, Ace's products were not seen as differentiated and the markets were characterised by intense price competition and strong buying pressures. Conditions in the aluminium market were expected to deteriorate further and Ace had no expectations of significant breakthroughs in products or costs.

Ace had also developed a balanced scorecard to monitor performance on its strategic value drivers. The financial indicators confirmed investors' disappointment with the company. When total shareholder returns were benchmarked against a peer group in the chemicals sector, Ace had significantly under-performed the average. The consumer indicators, while good for foundry, were weak for steel, and especially for aluminium. The indicators for internal operations and learning and development highlighted the weak technology and lack of new products in the latter areas.

What was clear from the valuation exercise and strategic objective assessment was that Ace was a vulnerable business. Even with the performance improvements envisaged in the plan, the equity value of the business was only 9 per cent above its current stock market value. Any deviations from the plan or unexpected developments in market conditions would risk a collapse of the share price.

3. The potential value with internal improvements

The new chief executive decided to develop a new plan that would more aggressively seek to increase long-term cash flows in the business. The three main determinants of higher cash flows are increased sales, higher operating profit margins and reductions in investment requirements. The core strategic value drivers that determine these dimensions of financial performance are increasing customer satisfaction, operational efficiency, quality management, the development of new products and the core capabilities that make possible further developments.

Action teams were set up for each business unit to undertake a fundamental reappraisal of the plan with the objective of significantly increasing the unit's value. In the steel products division, management first did a simulation to see the leverage of the different financial value drivers. They found that a 5 per cent increase in sales would generate a 20 per cent increase in the present value of the long-term cash flow; a 5 per cent increase in average prices could add 48 per cent to the unit's value, and a similar reduction in investment would add 8 per cent. Next, they benchmarked steel's value chain against the best competitors to judge the scope for improvements in product performance and productivity. These analyses, coupled with the strategic objective assessment, led management to believe that the business could perform at a significantly higher level. The major changes initiated were:

- **Sales performance.** The team were convinced that sales could be boosted without margin erosion by a modest increase in development spending on certain key projects, a new dealer partnership program to build greater loyalty and a refocusing of service staff around high potential customer accounts. Management also decided to invest in three strategic alliances with high-tech businesses overseas to develop potential new areas for growth. It was anticipated that at least one of these pilots would create a significant new income stream after five years.

- **Price increases.** There was scope to reduce the high level and range of discounts the business was giving. A segmentation analysis also suggested that certain specialised customers were not price sensitive if high levels of service and support were guaranteed.
- **Cost reductions.** Central buying and a vendor reduction program could reduce material costs. Also, new information technology permitted further savings in office costs.
- **Investment requirements.** Reducing the number of sites and a new logistics system would offer significant savings in working and fixed capital requirements.

Similar analyses in the other two business units also produced corresponding improvements in future cash flow. On top of this, it was also proposed to cut head office costs by half. Putting it all together, the Ace management team believed that the total value of the business could be increased by 40 per cent over the value in the original plan.

4. The potential value with external improvements

The next step is determining whether value can be created by external improvements. Such enhancements may be possible through either shrinking the business or expanding it. In the previous step, management calculated what the units were worth to the company. Perhaps significantly, more value could be created for shareholders if some, or all, were sold to other parties, spun-off and floated as independent businesses, or simply liquidated by selling their assets. Management can work with financial analysts to assess the price that might be obtained under each of these options. These sell-off options are often particularly attractive for unrelated businesses where other companies have more expertise, and could add more value than the current management. The cash received can then be returned to shareholders or reinvested to improve the core business if there are profitable opportunities available.

The alternative strategy is to consider strengthening the business through an acquisition. An acquisition might offer the potential to reduce costs or boost growth. While the overall success statistics for acquisitions are not high, the right combination can sometimes bring great rewards. Successful acquisitions depend upon being able to buy at a reasonable price and identifying genuine synergies in costs or marketing to justify the premium paid.

5. Optimal restructured value

The final stage of value-based planning is to determine what McKinsey refer to as 'the optimal restructured value' — what the business is worth with all the internal and external improvements. The final plan that was agreed by the board of Ace included selling off the aluminium business to a leading multinational for $60 million, halving the size of the head office, acquiring another foundry business in Taiwan, and a raft of new marketing initiatives that were projected to double Ace's growth rate over the next five years. The results of the value-oriented planning process are summarised in figure 5.9. The new team was confident that the new strategy would increase the equity value of the company by 80 per cent more than its current value, offering shareholders the prospects of significant real returns on their investments.

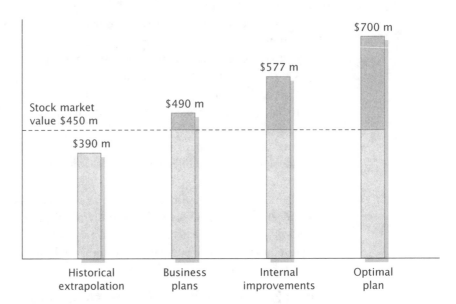

Figure 5.9 Ace Company: Creating shareholder value

Benefits of the strategic objective assessment

The strategic objective assessment is a crucial tool for management developing a strategy to create value for shareholders. First, it provides the information for a valuation of the complete business under its current strategy. If the company is public, it will also show whether its current market capitalisation over- or undervalues it. It also shows which products and customers are creating value, which are destroying it, and why. More generally, the assessment leads to the collection of a great deal of data about customers, competitors, the internal efficiency of the business and its progress in developing its resources and capabilities that are vitally important for developing strategies to create profitability and growth in the future.

Second, it forces management to consider the options open to it to create more value. If the market is not attractive, it encourages management to evaluate options to improve the average profitability of the industry. These might include efforts to improve industry capacity utilisation through mergers or joint ventures, and options to develop barriers to entry. Where the problems lie in a lack of differential advantage, managers can develop strategies aiming to reduce costs or achieve product differentiation. When neither of these is sufficient, it will energise managers to exit uneconomic businesses and search for new ways to grow.

The third benefit of a strategic objective assessment is that it identifies the business unit's strategic value drivers. Considering strategic value drivers pulls managers away from a sterile focus on accounting measures of performance to an assessment of the real resources and capabilities of the business, which determine its ability to achieve differentiation and a competitive economic cost structure. A differential advantage is based on offering products that are perceived by customers as better value than those of competitors. This has to be matched by an economic cost structure that is capable of delivering economic profits from the offer. These are the two determinants of the ability of the business to create long-term cash flow. The main strategic drivers are knowledge of customers, capabilities to innovate and manage brands, operational skills, and the ability of the organisation to learn and develop.

Unless managers focus on the strategic value drivers, they will not develop and adequately invest in them. Today, strategic assets that have in the past generated high returns soon become obsolete unless they receive attention and investment. Brands get dated, patents expire and skills become redundant. Tools such as the balanced scorecard ensure that this monitoring occurs and that the business continues to develop its assets and capabilities.

Understanding the strategic value drivers also encourages management to consider bold new strategies. IBM's turnaround in the 1990s, under Lou Gerstner, was based on the recognition that computer products were increasingly becoming low-margin, commodity items. Gerstner's team saw high-tech services and the Internet as the opportunities to find new sources of growth and profitability. To change the company, new options for acquiring Internet and servicing capabilities were developed — including closing manufacturing plants, a series of start-ups, investing in the service capabilities already existing in the different divisions and an all-out search for Internet and service companies that could be profitably acquired.[9]

Focusing on strategic value drivers rather than simply accounting numbers is also important because they can be leveraged to enter new markets and create new sources of profitable growth. Michael Eisner's success at Disney was based on his leveraging the strategic assets of the business — its famous cartoon characters. This was the basis for Disney's successful moves into retailing, publishing, movies and hotel development, which grew shareholder returns at an annual rate of over 20 per cent over the past decade. Similarly, Honda's skills in power train development allowed it to expand progressively into cars, lawn mowers, machine engines and generator markets worldwide. Strategic value drivers are invaluable, at both the business unit and corporate level, to the development of innovative marketing strategies.

Summary

1. To formulate a strategic plan, management must first understand the firm's current position and the forces shaping the future of the industry and its competitive position within it. This is the role of the strategic position assessment.

2. The first task is to assess whether management is currently adding value. This is often difficult to answer directly. Instead, it is necessary to determine the strategic value drivers that act as lead indicators to long-term value creation. The balanced scorecard is a useful framework for monitoring performance on these key capabilities.

3. The second task is to explain the current position. The success or failure of a business is caused by a combination of external and internal factors. The first is the attractiveness of the firm's market; the second is its differential advantage. Differential advantage is generally the more important determinant of value creation. It is a consequence of the strength of the firm's strategic value drivers.

4. Value is determined by future cash flow, so it is the future attractiveness of the market and the future differential advantage that must be projected. The purpose of a marketing strategy is to shift the business towards

attractive markets and build a sustainable differential advantage. This is the third task in strategic position assessment.

5. The end result of the strategic position assessment is that each business unit will be assigned a broad strategic objective that will form the basis for the strategic focus assessment. These objectives are divest, harvest, maintain, grow or enter.

6. The strategic objective assessment provides the information for value-based planning. A value-based plan is a framework for restructuring the business to optimise its value for shareholders and can be used as a basis for further marketing decisions.

key | terms

attractive market, p. 166
competitive structure, p. 167
market signalling, p. 182
strategic value drivers, p. 158
total economic cost, p. 170

review | questions

1. How do you assess whether a management team has created value during the past year?
2. Discuss the role of strategic value drivers in determining and assessing business performance.
3. How might a company use the balanced scorecard in its planning process?
4. What are the factors that shape a business's potential to generate value for shareholders?
5. Show how the McKinsey pentagon can be used to restructure a business with the goal of creating greater value for shareholders.
6. What determines the choice of strategic objective appropriate for a business unit?

discussion | questions

1. How do internal and external opportunities increase the value of a business?
2. Critically analyse the interaction of components required for explaining the current position of a business. Which component tends to dominate the analysis? Is this the same for:
   (a) slow growth commodity markets?
   (b) entrance into newly industrialised economies with moderate political and economic volatility (for example, Indonesia)?
   (c) Internet or electronic commerce companies?
3. Which is more likely to sustain and then maximise value creation: cost or differentiation strategy? How can a strategic objective assessment contribute to value creation of each?
4. How can a value-based restructuring plan maximise value creation?
5. How do the five strategic objectives create value? What function do they have for a strategic objective assessment?

debate | questions

1. Is it better to choose a cost strategy as opposed to differentiation strategy as a means of building differential advantage?
2. Do shareholders tend to have a preference for specific types of strategic objectives?
3. In your opinion, are some value drivers more important or valuable for sustaining differential advantage than others?

case study | **Biotech strategic position assessment**

You've walked past the shop a dozen times. You've admired it from every angle. It seems everyone has bought one. They swear by it. You know you should have it, but it seems so expensive. You keep waiting for the day when the shop owner drops the price. But it never comes. A steady stream of other shoppers walk in and buy that object of desire — and the next day, the sticker price increases. Again!

This is exactly the predicament many investors face with Cochlear, one of three manufacturers of hearing implant devices in the world, and one of Australia's most sought-after technology stocks ... [But] with the stock trading on an average price/earnings ratio of 78 ... [in 2001], many investors baulk at buying Cochlear.

They might have bought the stock in 1996, when it had a p/e of about 15, based on annualised half-year earnings, and a share price of $3. In March 1997 it traded on a p/e of 17, a year later a p/e of 25. In 1999, it started to look pricey when it hit a p/e of 40. Shareholders who have held the stock since December 1995 have increased their capital by a factor of 12, or 14 if they subscribed in the float ...

[Nonetheless, Michael Carmody, an analyst at Merrill Lynch] sees Cochlear as less risky than other industrials, arguing that in an environment in which the general trend is for earnings downgrades, the chances of disappointment from Cochlear are much lower. His insight is important because it helps us understand why the stock attracts such high multiples. He also thinks the stock is attractive because Cochlear enjoys high barriers to entry in its market, and is a leader in its field in technical innovation. Other factors that contribute to a lower risk profile include effectively no debt, and a strong leadership record under former chief executive Catherine Livingston, continued under Jack O'Mahoney, a seasoned medical products operator, who was formerly president of Howmedica, the orthopaedic division of Pfizer Inc., before its sale to Stryker Corp.

Cochlear is subject to several risks, albeit low-level ones. As a technology, it may be displaced by a biological invention. Cell therapy could be used to replace damaged cells in the ear. Professor Matthew Holley from the University of Bristol in England has differentiated mouse ear cell types, illustrating the concept at a basic level. However, cell therapy as a stand-alone intervention is most likely years away. According to Holley, it is more likely to be used in conjunction with cochlear implants, thus making them more effective, and perhaps enabling a wider application.

Cochlear's total sales reached $144 million last year. The recurring investment theme with Cochlear is that its value is a function of sales growth. In the past the company itself indicated sustainable growth rates of 18 to 20 per cent were reasonable. However, the market has viewed these rates as conservative. O'Mahoney agrees that the company can sustain 20 per cent plus sales growth during the next four years.

Merrill Lynch's Carmody forecasts average unit sales growth in the next five years of 23 per cent, followed by an average rate of 15 per cent in the subsequent five years. O'Mahoney backs his view: 'The market is very much bigger than people give us credit for. It is just difficult to get into in lots of ways.' He notes one estimate that 500 000 patients in the US could benefit from a Cochlear implant, plus another 200 000 in Germany, whereas fewer than 10 000 implants are being installed each year.

(continued)

O'Mahoney sees a challenge, and a big opportunity, in extending implant technology into the lives of people who go environmentally deaf. 'Basically, there is no need nowadays for someone who goes deaf to stay deaf. They can have an implant put in and resume normal activities.'

Background

The bionic ear or Cochlear implant was developed by Graeme Clark and his team at the University of Melbourne in the 1970s. In 1978, the system was successfully implanted into an Australian volunteer and in 1982 the first Nucleus 22 Cochlear implant was made available for commercial use.

The Cochlear implant systems involve a user wearing a microphone behind the ears that receives sounds and sends the sound waves via a thin wire to a speech processor, the size of a deck of cards, worn on the belt. The processor converts the sound waves to a coded signal. This coded signal is then sent along a wire to a transmitter located behind the ear, which sends a signal using radio waves to a receiver that has been surgically implanted beneath the skin. Electrical impulses are then sent along a wire through the ear canal to the Cochlear implant in the inner ear. The implant is surgically installed at the same time as the receiver.

The surgery involves connecting the Cochlear implant electrodes (24 of the Nucleus 24 system) to the existing hearing nerve fibres. The nerve fibres, when stimulated by sounds, send electrical signals to the auditory section of the brain. The bionic ear is not a hearing aid, which simply amplifies sound.

The Cochlear systems allow people with little or no hearing to hear again by using electrical signals to understand running speech. In its main North American market, the Nucleus 24 units sell for \$US23 000, although with other medical costs such as surgery and education and training, the overall cost to the individual is \$US35 000 to \$US45 000.

The surgical procedure required to install the Cochlear implant requires a day in hospital for an adult and a little longer for children. However, it takes several weeks before functionality is achieved, following a breaking-in program with an audiologist.

Source: Extracts from David Blake, 'Volume rising', *Shares*, May 2001, p. 22.

Questions

1. Using the balanced scorecard approach, critically evaluate Cochlear's strategic value drivers.
2. Having evaluated the strategic value drivers, explain and evaluate the company's current position.
3. Critically evaluate Cochlear's differential advantage.
4. What future challenges do you anticipate for Cochlear? What actions and strategies can you suggest to overcome these challenges?

end | notes

1. Robert S. Kaplan and David P. Norton, *The Balanced Scorecard*, Boston, MA: Harvard Business School Press, 1996.
2. James McTaggart, Peter W. Kontes and Michael C. Mankins, *The Value Imperative: Managing for Superior Shareholder Return*, New York: The Free Press, 1994, p. 89.
3. The literature on strategy is replete with matrices which similarly try to characterise the attractiveness and differential positions of business units. The best known are the Boston Consultancy Group's growth-share matrix, the General Electric matrix, the Shell directional policy matrix and the Marakon Associates strategic matrix. For a review see, for example, Gerry Johnson and Kevan Scholes, *Exploring Corporate Strategy*, London: Prentice Hall, 1999.
4. The following sections draw on the work of James McTaggart, Peter W. Kontes and Michael C. Mankins, *The Value Imperative: Managing for Superior Shareholder Return*, New York: The Free Press, 1994, pp. 85–154.

5. For a review of signalling see O. Heil and T. S. Robertson, 'Towards a theory of competitive market signalling', *Strategic Management Journal*, **12**, 1991, pp. 403–54.

6. For a good discussion of network effects and their strategic implications in information-based businesses see C. Shapiro and H. Varian, *Information Rules*, Boston, MA: Harvard Business School Press, 1999.

7. For recent statistics see Kris Butler, Stephan Leithner et al., 'What is the market telling you about your strategy?', *McKinsey Quarterly*, no. 3, 1999, pp. 98–109.

8. See Tom Copeland, Tim Koller and Jack Murrin, *Valuation: Measuring and Managing the Value of Companies*, 2nd edn, New York: John Wiley & Sons, 1996, pp. 327–58.

9. Doug Garr, *IBM Redux: Lou Gerstner and the Business Turnaround of the Decade*, New York: HarperBusiness, 1999.

Strategic focus assessment

By the time you have completed this chapter, you will be able to:

- explain the link between broad strategic objectives and specific strategic focuses
- explain the link between strategic focus and value creation
- evaluate the alternative ways a strategic focus can yield shareholder value
- understand how to balance a strategic focus in a business
- outline the process of growing a market
- analyse when diversification outside the company's traditional products and markets makes sense
- explain the market segmentation process
- evaluate competitor potential.

scene setter

The strategic focus of Wesfarmers

Patience comes easily to someone who once measured time in billions of years. So says Michael Chaney, one of Australia's most successful business leaders, and a former petroleum geologist ... Getting the time right has been a hallmark of Chaney's career and the growth of Wesfarmers, of which he has been managing director for the past nine years [prior to 2001]. In that time he has pushed the market capitalisation of Wesfarmers from $1.1 billion to $10 billion and done something that has eluded most Australian chief executives: made a success of a conglomerate structure.

Unlike many of his peers ... Chaney does not believe in the single-focus company. He acknowledges that being a conglomerate with a variety of operating divisions in different industries has caused problems for some companies, but he says the glue that holds Wesfarmers together is a total focus on creating shareholder value ...

Wesfarmers ... has a finger in many pies. It retains close links with its roots through its rural services division ... But the real strength comes from coal mining, hardware retailing, liquefied petroleum gas retailing, chemicals and fertiliser production. It also has operating interests in insurance, trucking and railways.

'When the rate of change inside the company is exceeded by the rate of change outside the company, the end is near.'

Jack Welch, former Chairman of General Electric

Chaney says: 'The key to Wesfarmers is shareholder focus and an unwillingness to be deflected from it. You can mouth the platitudes and say, 'We are here for shareholders' but, when it comes to looking for expansion possibilities, it is far better to have a choice of industries in which you can invest.'

'If you are a single-purpose company, it is too easy to make optimistic assumptions. The problem is that in Australia there are actually very few opportunities to grow. There are some but, generally, when they come along you have to take them, and you have, therefore, got to pay more than you might like because you know you are up against it. You start to justify that [the price] by saying things about the future being brighter than we first thought, and it might be that we can achieve higher revenues and lower costs. It becomes a mechanism to justify the price.'

Chaney says that at Wesfarmers, where financial discipline reigns supreme, it is a case of forming a value estimate of what an acquisition is worth and sticking to it ... A strict approach to financial discipline, based on measurement of return on capital employed and earnings per share, is a well-documented fact of the Wesfarmers philosophy ... 'We look for innovators', Chaney says. 'I want people who want to go the extra yard and do a bit more than their boss expects. I have come to the view that every dollar of profit is under threat, and unless you are innovating, unless you are thinking of new ways of doing business, such as new products, new services, new markets and new businesses, it means that you are going to go backwards.'

Source: Extracts from Tim Treadgold, 'Wesfarmers' winning ways', *BRW*, 13–19 September 2001, pp. 49–51.

Introduction

The strategic marketing plan links the strategic objective assessment with the strategic focus assessment, thereby organising information on which markets to serve and how to win a differential advantage in these markets. As discussed previously, the point of departure for strategy formulation is the strategic objective assessment. Once the strategic objective of the firm or business unit has been determined, the next step is to establish an appropriate strategic focus — the subject of this chapter.

Overview of strategic focus assessment

The main strategic focus of a firm depends on its strategic objective. As noted in chapter 4, if the strategic objective is to enter the market or grow the business, the main focus should be to increase sales volume. If the strategic objective is to maintain market share, harvest, or divest, the main focus should be to improve productivity.

To increase sales volume and to improve productivity are the two fundamental paths to value creation. They represent the two primary strategic focus options for a business unit.

There are two types of volume focus:
1. grow markets (sometimes also referred to as expand markets)
2. capture markets.

Markets are captured by winning competitors' customers. Markets are grown by increasing usage rates, converting non-users and entering new segments. Most scholars and practitioners would agree that a strategic focus on market growth is more effective in increasing sales volume and, thus, shareholder value than a strategic focus on chasing competitors' customers. But focusing on growing markets, if conducted properly, is an interrelated and difficult process. Ideally, the process centres first on existing customers, reinforcing loyalty, increasing purchases and selling new products to them (that is, increasing usage rates). Next, it looks to develop new customers with existing and new products (that is, converting non-users). Finally, it aims to develop new business through new distribution channels, international markets and entering new industries (that is, entering new segments). Later in this chapter, we will return to these steps in more detail.

There are three types of productivity focus:
1. rationalise
2. increase prices
3. enhance sales-mix.

Rationalisation involves trimming fixed and variable costs as well as reducing capital and asset investments. Price increases can be achieved directly by simply pushing prices up and indirectly by concentrating on high-value market niches or by price discrimination using regular and premium-priced products to serve different market segments.[1] Sales mixes can be enhanced by further dividing market segments according to the price sensitivity of customers and then aiming new line extensions and additional services at less price-sensitive customers. Among these three types of focus, a strategic focus on rationalisation is most popular, especially among executives with limited marketing background.

Evaluating the preferred types of strategic focus

Market growth or rationalisation are the preferred types of strategic focus. Growing markets has a direct effect on shareholder value by increasing the net present value of future cash flow. Many managers also believe that a rationalisation focus is an equally powerful alternative for creating long-term value. At first glance, this is not surprising. Cutting costs and investments can boost cash flow. But such actions rarely increase the value of the business substantially, because investors recognise that these actions do not create long-term profit growth. Such measures simply produce short-term gains, often at the expense of long-term growth.

One reason why rationalisation remains a popular alternative to growth is that many companies lack a market focus. They do not have long-term strategies in place to capitalise on emerging market opportunities. Managerial incentives also often conflict with a focus on long-term growth. In many companies, management bonuses are tied to annual profits. A failure to hit the year's budget is seen as penalising managers' pockets and, possibly, their careers.

Managers are also aware that rationalisation and growth focuses tend to work differently in their effects on profits and cash flows. Cutting costs and investments usually works quickly to increase profits and cash flows. While cutting back on such investments as in service staff, brand support and R&D will hit sales, this tends not to happen for a considerable time. Often, the negative effects do not show through until the managers responsible have moved on to other jobs. In contrast, creating profitable growth is costly immediately and it may take years before the positive results begin to show on the bottom line. In addition, rationalisation is relatively easy since it is about reconfiguring the firm's internal resources. Growth, however, is more difficult since its success is determined externally. It depends on convincing customers that your business offers them superior value to the other competitors in the market. Unfortunately, in career terms, rationalisation is often a more advantageous path than investing in market growth, especially when the firm's profits are under pressure and competition is fierce.

If a particular focus is implemented exclusively, it is clear that rationalisation is less useful as a long-term strategic focus than growth. It sacrifices long-term investment for short-term improvements in profitability and cash flow. In the longer run, these companies fail to meet the emerging benefits needed by their customers, miss new opportunities, and are left marooned in declining markets with yesterday's technology. And, even where there is waste, rationalisation can be executed only once; it does not offer continual opportunities unless new waste is 'created'. Accordingly, investors generally reward rationalisation pure-plays with a lower share price premium than they would otherwise reward a pure growth play.

In the best-case scenario, the company that chooses to pursue either a growth or rationalisation focus should not lose sight of the other focus. That is, if a growth focus is adopted, then rationalisation issues should not be completely forgotten; if a rationalisation focus must be adopted, then growth issues should not be ignored. Indeed, focusing on growing markets while controlling costs and scrutinising investments in the process is likely to be more effective than just striving for market growth at all costs. Likewise, concentrating on rationalisation while remaining open to growth opportunities is certainly more effective than looking the other way when a growth opportunity emerges.

To be sure, those companies that created the greatest shareholder value in the past decade, such as Dell, Flight Centre, Nokia and Microsoft, were all companies that grew profitable sales rapidly — they expanded their markets quickly and rarely lost sight of their profitability in the process. Logically, this is easy to understand: shareholder value is created by maximising long-term cash flows. And the primary determinant of cash flow is profitable sales.

Developing a strategic focus for superior shareholder value — a volume focus example

Financial markets clearly recognise, in large share premiums, the value of those companies that are able to integrate a volume focus with a concern for productivity, or vice versa, in such a way that cash flow is maximised. Naturally, there will be one principal strategic focus, depending on the strategic objective. Companies that neglect productivity or volume in pursuit of their main focus are less likely to fully maximise shareholder value. That is one reason why management should make a more integrated approach top priority. Interestingly, the evidence suggests that this does not happen very frequently. The boardroom agenda is all too often crowded out with day-to-day operating and administrative concerns that have little relevance to an integrated strategic approach to shareholder value creation. This section focuses on how such an integration might be achieved by examining how a volume focus can be achieved without ignoring productivity.

In a business geared to creating value for shareholders, top management should start by setting a shareholder value goal. For example, the new chief executive of Delta Company declares the goal of doubling the share price over a five-year period. As shown in table 6.1, the current equity value of the business, using the perpetuity method to calculate continuing value, is $46 million. This was close to the current stock market value of the company. Management understood that growing the equity value of the company depended upon a strategy to increase the net present value of future cash flow and communicating this strategy to investors.

Table 6.1 Growth and shareholder value at Delta

YEAR		1	2	3	4	5
Sales	100.0	114.0	130.0	148.2	168.9	192.5
Operating profit	8.0	10.3	13.0	16.3	20.3	23.1
NOPAT (tax = 30%)	5.6	7.2	9.1	11.4	14.2	16.2
Investment (40%)		5.6	6.4	7.3	8.3	9.5
Cash flow		1.6	2.7	4.1	5.9	6.7
Discount factor ($r = 10\%$)	1.000	0.909	0.826	0.751	0.683	0.621
Present value		1.4	2.2	3.1	4.0	4.2
Cumulative PV		1.4	3.7	6.8	10.8	15.0
PV of continuing value	56.0	65.3	75.2	85.7	96.9	100.4
Cum PV + CV	56.0	66.7	78.9	92.5	107.7	115.4
Debt	10.0					23.4
Equity value	46.0					92.0

After a strategic objective assessment, management believed it possible to set a two-part strategy centred on a volume focus to increase future cash flow, involving:

- **Rationalisation.** By rationalising the business processes, costs could be reduced sufficiently to drive up operating margins from 8 to 12 per cent over the next four years. The net increase in working and fixed capital to support sales growth was estimated at 40 per cent of sales (that is, each $100 of additional sales would involve new investment of $40). Most of the investment would have to be financed from profits. Management was willing to see the amount of debt increase from $10 million to around $23 million, but was not issuing more shares.

- **Market growth.** Management then looked at what market growth was necessary based on the above assumptions. As shown in table 6.1, by a process of iteration, an annual sales growth of 14 per cent would double the value of the business, increasing it from $46 million to $92 million.

Market growth was determined to be the main strategic emphasis. The next task was to consider whether and how such growth might be achieved without compromising rationalisation gains. What was clear was that the company was stagnating. Sales had been static for a number of years. No strategies to grow the market were being considered. It was obvious that the new management team needed to develop growth policies and to change the organisation and culture of the business. Essentially, there was a 'strategic gap' between what sales were desired and what were likely under current policies (see figure 6.1).

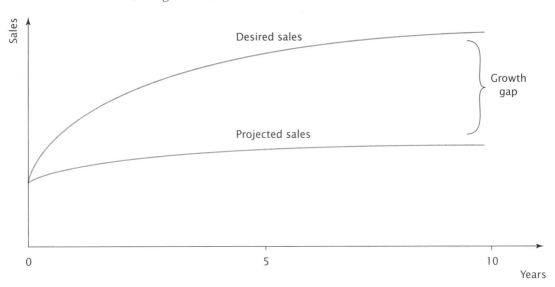

Figure 6.1 The growth gap

To fill this gap, the company must have new opportunities to grow markets. The concept of growth innovation (also referred to as the 'growth ladder' concept) is a useful framework that conceptualises a company's opportunities to grow markets as a nine-step progression. Growth innovation starts with consolidating the core customer base and then moving on to capitalise on less constrained opportunities for growth. Key to the concept is first establishing the fundamentals — ensuring that the business has the trust and loyalty of its existing target customers. The nine steps of growth innovation are:

1. increase customer retention rate
2. grow share of customer
3. gain new customers
4. develop new products
5. enter new markets
6. seek new distribution channels
7. pursue international growth
8. seek acquisitions and alliances
9. pursue growth outside current industry boundaries.

Step 1: Increase customer retention rate

The discussion here builds on the analysis of customer relationships in chapter 3. The starting point is to recognise that the first and most fundamental stage of growth innovation is ensuring that existing key customers have complete confidence and trust in the company. A typical company — a bank, insurance company or retailer — has a customer retention rate of 90 per cent. That means it loses 10 per cent of its customers every year. Or, to put it in another way, the average customer stays with the company for ten years. Increasing the retention rate has an enormous impact in raising profits and growth potential (see marketing management in practice 'The ascent of British Airways).

Marketing management in practice: **The ascent of British Airways**

Between 1982 and 1988, British Airways (BA) went from being a poorly perceived service provider with annual losses of over $300 million, to a premium airline that actively sought to excel in offering benefits needed by customers and to retain customer loyalty. The airline initiated a series of training programs designed to change the culture of the organisation so that all employees would be driven to meet customer requirements and to consequently increase customer retention. Staff were empowered to take initiatives in creating customer value and a reward system was put in place for addressing customer complaints. The airline also introduced new value structures designed for different customer segments. Premium value was provided to high-growth customer segments, particularly the trans-Atlantic business passenger. This entailed an active partnership with the customer, with BA providing loyalty discounts and luxury lounges in exchange for high service usage. As a result of this strategy, BA increased customer retention, significantly improved organisational growth and enhanced shareholder value with annual profits of over $1 billion.

Much of the research has focused on the effect of retention on increasing the profit or lifetime value of an average customer. But increased loyalty also has a powerful effect on the company's potential growth rate. Trying to grow markets without achieving customer loyalty is like trying to fill a bath using a bucket with a big hole in the bottom. Consider three companies, A, B and C. Each begins with 100 000 customers and each succeeds in attracting 10 000 new customers each year over a 10-year period. However, they differ in their ability to retain customers: A's retention rate is 80 per cent, B's is 90 per cent and C's is 95 per cent. In other words, an average customer stays with A 5 years, B 10 years and C 20 years.[2] The consequences for growth are that despite attracting the same number of new customers, company A's customer base ten years later has shrunk to 55 000, B's has remained unchanged, but C's customer base has grown to over 140 000.

Without loyal customers, it is almost impossible to grow a market. A high level of customer loyalty, on the other hand, makes growth much easier. If it wanted to double its customer base over the decade, company A would need to attract 42 000 new customers a year, while C would need only 17 000 a year.

To increase retention rate, management needs to put in place a number of initiatives, outlined in the following subsections.

» 1. Select and prioritise customers

customer selection: the practice of retaining valuable customers and allowing less valuable customers to go elsewhere

customer lifetime value: the net present value of a customer, calculated in terms of the discounted value of the cash flow generated over the life of the customer's relationship with the company

Managers need to understand that customers should not all be treated equally. **Customer selection** is necessary. The fact is that it is worth investing much more in retaining some customers than others. Among the retained customers, the most valuable need to be prioritised. Two criteria determine what priority they should receive: **customer lifetime value** and strategic fit. The potential lifetime value of a customer depends on its size, growth, profitability and loyalty potential. Strategic fit refers to the customer's need for benefits the firm can deliver via its value proposition.

Managers should segment accounts along these criteria and respond accordingly. For example, Swedish company Salo Polymers segments its customers into three categories based on the size of the account, its expected future development and the type of business relationship. The categories are partnership, base load and swing. A different product offering has been developed for each customer category. Salo offers a formal partnership proposal to priority customers. If the customer accepts, it agrees to buy a minimum of 80 per cent of its requirements from the company. The agreement covers product, credit terms, consignment stocks, technical and laboratory services, as well as advice on training on environmental, health and safety issues. For example, Salo will maintain consignment stock representing three weeks' average consumption by the partner. All partner orders are handled on the same day. Just-in-time deliveries mean that the customer does not need to maintain stock. All partners have an account manager who will take personal responsibility for the smooth operation of the customer's business. Base load customers do not have consignment stocks maintained for them. Laboratory and technical services have to be paid for. A more limited program of training on environmental, health and safety issues is offered. Orders are handled within three working days. Swing customers typically purchase most of their requirements from competitors. For these customers, the business relationship is limited to little more than delivery. If services are requested, they are invoiced at market rates. Swing customers are normally requested to open a bank guarantee before orders are accepted.

» 2. Customise the value proposition

Fundamentally, increasing the loyalty coefficient depends upon meeting the benefits needed by the individual customer. So, the first priority is listening to customers. Only by researching customers can management discover their desired benefits. Business-to-business marketing will focus on offering customers superior profitability through lower costs or enhanced output. For household consumers, it is often also about offering emotional value — confidence, prestige or trust.

Until recently, it was possible to customise solutions only when a company had a few customers. Most companies used variants of a mass marketing model. They designed products and services for a mass market, or at least a major segment of it. Consumers then had to choose the best approximation to their individual requirements. Loyalty was low because consumers would shift when a competitor came out with a better approximation to their requirements.

Information technology is changing this by providing new capabilities. First, computerised databases now allow companies to tell customers apart and remember their individual interests and purchasing history, even when the numbers of customers run into millions. Second, interactivity through the Internet, telephone or direct mail means that individual customers can communicate information about their wants directly to the company. Third, mass customisation technology means companies can now customise products to individual requirements. Companies like Dell and Amazon.com that pioneered this new mass customisation model found they could greatly increase the retention rate. What is the point of customers switching when their current supplier is giving them the exact product they want, when they want it, at a fair price? Especially when the company remembers what you bought last time, and your billing details, and can use this information to take the hassle out of ordering. It can even anticipate your requirements, suggesting new products that will interest you and keep you up-to-date. Peppers and Rogers call this new type of business the one-to-one enterprise.[3]

» 3. Enhance the value proposition

However successful a company is today, it cannot afford to rest on its laurels. New competition is always closing the gap on benefits differentiation. Changes in customer requirements and new technology continually make existing solutions obsolete. To maintain customer loyalty, the company has to maintain leadership by updating its products and the quality of its relationships with customers.

Keeping one step ahead involves close monitoring of customers, competition and technological trends. It also means taking a long-term view of what is required to maintain customer loyalty. It may mean pursuing new products even when they offer low margins and risk cannibalising current winners. For example, Hewlett Packard pioneered cheap ink-jet printing technology even though it competed with its own high-margin laser technology. Hewlett Packard recognised that while in the short run this cannibalisation reduced profits, in the long run it was the only way to retain customer loyalty.

» 4. Monitor customer satisfaction and loyalty

Since customer loyalty is the first step to achieving profitable growth, it is amazing that so few boards of directors insist on regularly measuring and monitoring it and its determinants. Improving customer satisfaction with the quality of the product's service component is the most direct way of increasing loyalty. Researchers have shown that there are normally five determinants of service quality that need to be monitored.[4] On average, customers weight them in importance as:

1. **Reliability.** The ability to perform the promised service dependably and accurately. (32 per cent of the total importance score)

2. **Responsiveness.** The willingness to help consumers and provide prompt service. (22 per cent)
3. **Assurance.** The knowledge and courtesy of employees and their ability to convey trust and confidence. (19 per cent)
4. **Empathy.** The provision of caring, individualised attention to customers. (16 per cent)
5. **Tangibles.** The appearance of the physical facilities, equipment, personnel and communications. (11 per cent)

Customers are satisfied if the service they perceive along these dimensions equals what they expected. Customers are delighted if the perceived service exceeds expectations. The model of figure 6.2 describes the main determinants of customer satisfaction.

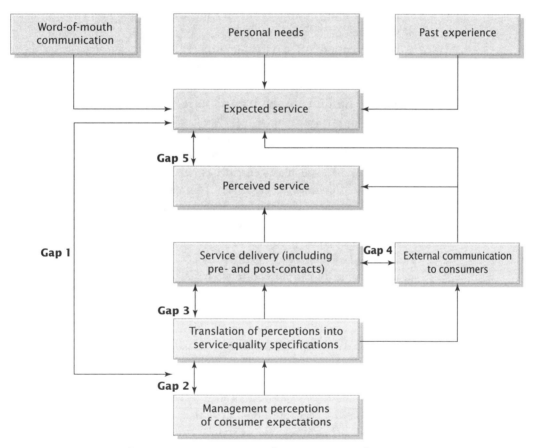

Figure 6.2 Determinant of customer satisfaction.
Source: Derived from Leonard L. Berry and A. Parasuraman, *Marketing Services: Competing Through Quality*, New York: The Free Press, 1991.

How should managers use customer satisfaction data? Movements in ratings are lead indicators of the ability to retain customers and, hence, achieve growth and profit goals. Only the highest scores — that is, delighted customers — really correlate positively with loyalty. Management should not be satisfied if large groups of key customers are not rating the service in the top box.

To motivate performance, especially among front-line employees, customer satisfaction should form a part of the reward and incentive system for staff.

The model also suggests where management should look to increase customer satisfaction. Figure 6.2 shows several 'gaps' which undermine service:

- **Misunderstanding of customer requirements.** This occurs where companies have not researched customers properly and are focusing on the wrong things. For example, managers think customers want higher-spec solutions when in fact their priority is greater reliability.
- **Poor specification of standards.** Management may not have set sufficiently clear specifications for staff to implement the desired standards. The managing director tells the switchboard to be customer-oriented but does not specify how.
- **Lack of capabilities.** Staff may lack the training or motivation to meet the standards specified.
- **Creating over-expectations.** Advertising and salespeople can promise too much, leading customers to have inflated expectations. The result is disappointed customers.
- **Misperception of service.** Consumers can misperceive the company's attentions. Highly attentive staff at a restaurant are sometimes perceived by customers as hassling.

» 5. Follow-up on complaints and defections

It is misleading for a company to rely on complaints as a measure of customer satisfaction. Most dissatisfied customers do not bother to complain. Even when they do, not surprisingly, front-line staff often do not pass the complaints upward to management. It has been estimated that on average only 4 per cent of dissatisfied customers complain. So, if a bank receives 1000 complaints a year, it probably has 25 000 dissatisfied customers.

But it is important to follow up on complaints for two reasons. First, angry customers can easily become what Xerox terms 'terrorists' — customers who actively bad-mouth the company to dozens of prospective purchasers. Such negative publicity can do enormous harm to a company's growth prospects. Second, complaints can generally be dealt with and customer confidence restored if the company responds quickly and generously. Some studies show that when complaints are resolved to the customer's satisfaction, such customers become more satisfied than those who never experienced a problem in the first place.

Companies should make it easy for dissatisfied customers to record their complaints. This way, problems can be identified early and dealt with decisively, before they become a tidal wave that washes away the company growth potential. Defections analysis is another growing tool. Here companies interview customers who have switched their business elsewhere. This gives direct, fresh insight into the causes of dissatisfaction, which is often more incisive than general measures of customer satisfaction.

» 6. Build customer partnerships

Increasingly, companies see the best way to create loyalty is to shift from a transactional to a partnership relationship with customers. By offering a formal partnership contract to customers, companies create a framework for mutual gain. Customers gain an organisational capability dedicated to improving their long-term performance. For the supplier partner, it means that it can trust in holding the account, gaining the majority of the business and the probability of increasing its sales with the client.

Normally, creating a partnership will mean assigning a dedicated account manager to the customer to coordinate the development of the relationship. Partnering today is increasingly about using information technology and, in particular, the Internet, to integrate the value chains of customer and supplier.

Full partnerships make sense only where the client's potential lifetime value to the company justifies the investment required. However, falling computing and communication costs are quickly lowering the costs of interfacing with customers. Many companies find it effective to tier partnerships. For example, Qantas Frequent Flyer club members are designated gold, silver or bronze tier members depending upon the value of the business they place with the company. The polymers company Salo offers customers partnership or base load relationships. Each tier offers a different level of benefits to the customer.

Step 2: Grow share of customer

share of customer: the proportion of total spending made by a single customer that goes to one firm

Once managers have in place an effective program to increase customer loyalty, the second step of growth innovation is to grow its share of the spending of these customers — to grow its **share of customer**. Over the past decade, there has been a major change of emphasis in marketing. Traditional marketing has focused on selling a single product to as many customers as possible; the new marketing focuses on selling as many products as possible to each individual customer. It is a shift from mass marketing to one-to-one marketing.

Several factors are breaking down the old business model. One is that products are becoming increasingly commodified. Virtually all industries have excess production capacity. Worse, in most of these industries it is proving impossible to retain significant technological or quality differences. Second, mass promotion, and particularly advertising, is increasingly costly. The average consumer is exposed to as many as 3000 ads a day. The fragmentation of television channels and print media make it more and more expensive to obtain the required impact. The result is that gaining market share is more and more expensive. Also, without real differences between offers, market share once achieved is difficult to retain against aggressive competitors.

But the greatest cause of the change is new technology and, in particular, the Internet. New information technology opens up markets to new competition by allowing the unbundling of the functions of providing information to consumers with that of the physical delivery of products. Consumers go to a retailer like Toys 'R' Us both to gain information about products and to physically obtain them. But now new Net-based companies can supply much more information to people over their home computers or TV screens. Then they, or their partner suppliers, can deliver the chosen product directly to their home. This is more convenient for the consumer, and for the supplier it means economies because there are no expensive shops and much less working capital to finance.

Equally important, information technology allows customisation. Companies can now communicate one-to-one with consumers, learning their individual requirements, storing this information and customising products and services. Until a decade ago, the technology was simply not available, or prohibitively expensive, for companies with large numbers of consumers to learn about them individually. This is strikingly illustrated, even now, by phoning the help-line number that appears on the packaging of most grocery products. Even though the consumer has been buying the Unilever or Procter & Gamble brand for decades, the company will have no information about his or her loyalty, importance or purchasing behaviour. Contrast this with a call to companies that have integrated the new technology into their business model like Telstra, Amazon.com or Vodafone, where the service representatives will immediately have the customer's whole purchase history before them.

The convenience, additional sources of differentiation and collaborative relationships information technology enable companies to increase their share of the customer's spend. Increasingly, successful companies will be selling benefits rather than product attributes. After all, it is benefits rather than products that ultimately meet consumer needs. For example, successful airlines will increasingly draw their revenues from the additional services they offer passengers. These include hotel bookings, car rentals, travel insurance and financial services. The airline has no need to own any of the other service providers: it simply brings them together under its brand umbrella to provide a convenient benefits package for the customer. As it collects more information about customer preferences, it can offer other things that might be of interest. It could suggest a theatre performance to somebody travelling to New York or Melbourne, make all the bookings and throw in a limo at a bargain rate. It could get flowers delivered before arrival and reserve a table at a favourite restaurant 15 minutes after curtain-down. If the customer's schedule changes, the airline will change not just its ticket, but all the other arrangements as well.[5]

Selling more to current customers means using information technology to communicate individually with customers, retain the information obtained and customise products and relationships to meet their needs. Then it requires being proactive in proposing additional benefits that will further improve the customer's total organisational performance or the individual's personal experience.

Step 3: Gain new customers

The first two steps get the basics right — they focus on delivering a value proposition that offers the quality of products and reliability that customers want. The result is a trust relationship with the individual customer that achieves a high loyalty coefficient and a growing share of the customer's expenditure. If this base is set properly, growing the number of customers is relatively easy (see marketing management in practice 'Vodka wins on cool'). High performance in the first two steps of growth innovation leads to high brand awareness levels and desirable brand images. New customers will want to do business with the company. Satisfied customers will also recommend the company to others. It is important to emphasise that value innovation aims to involve new customers — customers who have previously not been served. By not aiming to capture competitors' customers, value innovation avoids potentially zero-sum games.

Often it is more about selecting rather than gaining new customers. For example, First Direct is Europe's leading direct banking operation. It uses IT intensively to deal with customers as individuals and achieve high levels of service, 24 hours a day. Customer polls showed that 87 per cent of the customer base was extremely or very satisfied with First Direct, compared with an average of 51 per cent for its competitors. 85 per cent of its customers actively recommended the bank to friends, relatives and colleagues. In the past five years, First Direct achieved the largest net customer growth of all the UK banks and building societies. This was after rejecting about 50 per cent of applicants who it believed would offer low lifetime value to the bank.

Marketing management in practice: **Vodka wins on cool**

Wine and beer companies, as well as most spirit manufacturers, are grappling with how to attract younger drinkers, but vodka is still the rising star of the alcoholic beverages market, thanks to clever image marketing.

Although vodka has faced stiff competition from the booming ready-to-drink (RTD) market, some brands decided early on that if you can't beat 'em, join 'em. Guinness UDV Australia's launch of Stoli Lemon Ruski a few years ago helped fuel the growth in the RTD category and along the way boosted sales of mother brand Stolichnaya, which has since released Stoli Orange and Cranberry. Maxxium Australia's Absolut brand launched pre-mixed flavoured vodka, including Absolut Citron, Mandarin and Kurant. But the Australian vodka manufacturers are discovering a new consumer trend — the fickle and elusive but highly sought-after early adopter segment is reverting to pure vodka premium brands, and looking to hip vodka recipes in bars and clubs to satisfy its thirst for variety ...

Vodka's success hinges on its clever and hip marketing strategies and all brands have been active with advertising as well as on-premise and liquor store promotions and events.

Source: Extracts from Rochelle Burbury, *The Australian Financial Review*, 8–9 December 2001, S8.

Step 4: Develop new products

Strategists often use the Ansoff matrix (see figure 6.3) to discuss the growth options available to the firm.[6] The first three steps of growth innovation refer to the top left box, which Ansoff called market penetration. This is growth by selling more of the firm's current products in its existing market by increasing the customer retention rate, growing the share of customer and gaining new customers. Step 4 moves to a new element of the matrix — the top right, developing new products. In a rapidly changing environment, it is an essential step. Technological change, new competition and changing customer requirements are continually shortening product life cycles. In most markets, it is impossible to satisfy customers without an increasing stream of new products. Without an effective new product development process, a firm will face declining customer loyalty, loss of customer share and declining margins on its products. The topic of new product development is considered in more detail in chapter 8.

	Current products	New products
Current markets	1. Market-penetration strategy	3. Product-development strategy
New markets	2. Market-development strategy	4. Diversification strategy

Figure 6.3 The product–market expansion matrix

Step 5: Enter new markets

The fifth step of growth innovation is equivalent to the bottom left corner of the Ansoff matrix (see figure 6.3) — market development strategy, or entering new markets, using existing products. This is an obvious and common growth strategy, but managers often underestimate the difficulties of executing it successfully. There are three stimuli for this growth strategy. One is the opportunity to build on the synergies from current know-how or products. For example, Giorgio Armani decided to open a new chain called Armani Exchange. Another attraction may be the emergence of new growth markets. Caterpillar, which dominated the global market for large bulldozers, decided to enter the small equipment market when the heavy construction market matured. Glaxo took its anti-ulcer drug Zantac into the over-the-counter market after sales peaked in the prescription-only market.

But the most common stimulus to entering new markets is the **product life cycle**. Initially, a new product, because of its high price and limited communication, appeals to a specialist market. Then, over time, awareness grows and prices fall, offering opportunities to sell the product to a succession of new markets. For example, when mobile phones were first launched, very high prices limited the market to senior executives then, after a few years, the market expanded into the broader business community; later still, the household market offered growth opportunities and, finally, children became the fastest growing market.

Managers often think that moving into new markets is straightforward because it deploys current products or technologies. But this is a mistake: adapting to the needs of different markets is generally more difficult than developing new products. For example, Caterpillar and IBM all failed to make money when seeking to shift into the new markets. In the mobile phones market, Motorola lost its leadership as it failed to adapt to the different requirements of the new markets. The problems occur because these new markets have different needs, different operating processes and different buying patterns from the initial customers. This means that the products require different positioning strategies — and pricing, promotion and, especially, distribution channels have to be dramatically changed. Seeking to sell to new markets with strategies that worked for the original market is almost bound to fail.

Top management need to check that the new market strategy is soundly based by ensuring proper research has been done on the following questions:

- Who are the new customers and what are their wants and aspirations?
- How do these differ from those of our current market?
- Who makes the decisions and who influences the buying process?
- What is the positioning strategy and marketing mix that would ideally match the benefits needed by these customers?
- How different is our proposed strategy from this ideal?

Market leaders often come unstuck by not adapting sufficiently to emerging markets. When this happens, they are leapfrogged by new competitors, unencumbered by traditional strategies and channels, that can set up new market strategies that fit more effectively the needs of the new market.

product life cycle: the notion that products pass through distinct stages — introduction, growth, maturity and decline — each marked by different growth rates in sales volume and by increasing and decreasing unit profits

Step 6: Seek new distribution channels

The sixth step of growth innovation is innovation in distribution channels (a topic considered in detail in chapter 10). This will be one of the major sources of growth opportunities in the next decade. The main drivers of change are globalisation of markets, new information technology, computers and the Internet. In 1990, only 100 000 computers were connected to the Net; by 2005 the number of people using it will be over one billion. Already, this is producing huge changes in the way customers buy. Both in consumer markets, and even more in business-to-business markets, sweeping changes are occurring in the ways suppliers sell and distribute their products.

There are two fundamental questions managers should address when seeking to grow markets through distribution:

1. **Are there additional channels that can fuel growth?** The company can increase growth by adding new distributors to its current network to broaden or deepen its market coverage. Piggyback and co-marketing involve using the selling and distribution networks of other suppliers to create additional sales. Besides intensifying distribution, a company can add new channels. Web sites are becoming increasingly integrated into the growth strategies of firms. A company can also have parallel distribution by running two channels simultaneously. For example, Coles Myer sells its food products through its own shops and through its online operation Coles Online.

2. **Are there substitute channels that can fuel growth?** As the market changes and new technologies appear, a company may have to look to change its channels. In the early 1990s, Compaq became the market leader in PCs through its dominant position in leading retail channels. But, by the late 1990s, direct marketing had become the fastest growing channel. By cutting out the retailer, dealing directly with the individual customer over the telephone or Internet, and making to order, Dell was able to undercut Compaq's prices and build a closer relationship with consumers. By 1999, Compaq's channel leadership had become a liability rather than an asset. In 2002, it was merged with Hewlett Packard.

Step 7: Pursue international growth

Even the smallest companies have to exploit the growth opportunities presented by the global economy. Many companies are pulled into international marketing by the need to serve their customers. New stimulus is given by declining barriers to trade, deregulation of markets, global media and new trading and political entities like the European Union. Virtually all companies now face foreign competitors in their domestic markets. Indeed, the concept of a domestic market is losing much of its meaning; markets are increasingly regional or global.

In developing an international growth strategy, management has to make a number of strategic decisions.

» **Which markets?**

A company can choose to focus on a small number of markets or spread its efforts over a large number of countries. For all but the most experienced businesses, focus is the best strategy. Concentration allows a company to build knowledge in depth about its markets and it can focus resources to build strong distribution systems, critical mass and market share. In deciding on which markets to concentrate, the company needs to assess its market attractiveness, its competitive advantage and the country risks.

» **How to enter the market?**

Companies can choose between low-cost, limited-commitment methods of entering and developing overseas markets, and high-investment, high-goal approaches. They face the usual trade-off between risk and reward. Indirect exporting — paying independent agents or merchants to find customers — is a low-risk entry mode. Direct exporting gives more control. Licensing is another relatively low-risk method of developing a market. This allows a foreign company to use the brand name, patent or manufacturing process in return for a fee or royalty. Coca-Cola's enormously successful overseas growth has been based largely on having overseas bottlers licensing the company's brand name.

When a company is ambitious for greater control but still wishes to draw on outside skills and capital it can look to joint ventures. Joint ventures are increasingly being created when it is necessary to quickly put together large investments and complex technologies. Finally, the ultimate form of foreign commitment is direct investment and ownership of overseas-based assembly or manufacturing plants. This gives the firm the greatest control and upside potential; the downside is the greater risk and resource commitment required.

» **How to develop the market?**

A key problem in developing an international marketing strategy is deciding on how much tailoring there should be to local conditions. There are two extremes. One is a global strategy, where a company uses, as far as possible, a standardised marketing mix everywhere. The other is a multinational strategy, where the marketing mix is adapted to the local conditions in each country. As examples, Sony, National Panasonic and Coca-Cola have tended to follow the global standardised model; Unilever, General Electric and Nestle more the multinational strategy.

The ideal solution depends upon on how diverse local consumption patterns and distribution systems are. New electronics products are easier to standardise than traditional eating habits. However, the opportunities presented by globalisation and the desire to achieve scale economies have increased the pressure on companies to seek greater standardisation in their marketing. The ability to standardise varies with the different elements of the marketing mix. The basic product is often the most easily standardisable. With increasing transparency and fewer barriers to trade, there is also greater pressure towards convergence in pricing. Culture and language differences demand local adaptation in advertising, but again companies are tending towards sharing themes across countries and especially regions. Different historical developments make distribution patterns probably the most diverse element of the marketing mix today.

» **What type of organisation?**

Companies need to develop international organisations that reflect their commitment to international operations. An export department will be able to handle the limited commitments of a company involved in indirect or direct exporting. If the commitment grows to involve the firm in different types of overseas ventures and overseas sales become important, it will need to create an international division to control its operating units. In recent years, the largest and most experienced operators such as Procter & Gamble, Ford Motor Company, BHP Billiton and ABB, have switched to a global organisation.

Management plan brands, manufacturing and logistics on a global basis to maximise the company's operating efficiency and effectiveness. Country managers then are constrained to develop their own strategies within the parameters set by the global strategy. This new global thrust is being shaped by pressures on companies to achieve economies of scale and lever new products and expertise more rapidly across markets.

Step 8: Seek acquisitions and alliances

The next step is acquisitions and alliances. Managers in companies seeking high-growth markets assign these a major role.

The late 1990s saw record levels of mergers and acquisitions. One cause was the opportunities to boost efficiency created by the deregulation of such industries as telecommunications, transportation, financial services and the utilities. A second catalyst was overcapacity in many industries. Third was the race to become bigger. Companies saw markets and competition becoming increasingly global, and regarded becoming one of the top two or three players a necessity for long-run competitiveness.

Acquisitions have certain advantages over internal growth:

- Acquisitions are a faster way to win a market. Developing successful new products can take years; an acquisition can achieve the sales goal in weeks.
- Internal growth is costly. A competitive battle to win market share can be very expensive. Buying a business is less likely to cut industry margins.
- Some strategic assets such as well-known brands, patents and strong distribution channels are often difficult, if not impossible, to develop internally.
- An established business is typically less risky than developing a new one from scratch.

» High failure rate

Despite the popularity of acquisitions, studies over the years have shown that most fail to add value for shareholders in the acquiring company. The findings suggest the following:

- The bid premium paid by the acquiring company averages between 40 and 50 per cent over the acquired company's pre-acquisition value. The premium is lower for a friendly merger and higher for a hostile takeover.
- Shareholders in the acquired company are the big winners, receiving the benefits of the bid premiums. In two-thirds of take-overs, the value of the acquiring company declined after the acquisition. Taking a longer run view, only around a quarter of acquisitions were judged successful in delivering satisfactory returns to shareholders. The higher the bid premium, the more likely the acquisition was to fail.
- The chances of an acquisition being successful were improved when the acquirer had a strong core business before the take-over. The success rate was also higher where the company being bought was relatively small and in a related business.

What accounts for the failure of so many merger and acquisition programs to deliver profitable growth? The most important reason is that companies pay too much. With acquisitions costing up to 50 per cent more than the market valued the company, it is easy to see how this occurs. They overpay because they make overly optimistic forecasts of the market's growth potential or because they overestimate the synergies the acquisition will create. A second cause is poor post-acquisition implementation. Management fails to capture the potential synergies. Relationships with customers, staff and suppliers in the acquired company are eroded, damaging the value of the business. A third reason for poor acquisitions is the incentive systems in many companies. Often managers are compensated by the return they achieve on tangible assets. An acquisition adds to their top line, but the bid premium does not appear in the denominator. The result is that almost any acquisition increases the bonuses of managers even though shareholder value is being destroyed.

» Developing a successful acquisitions process

To increase the chances of acquisitions leading to profitable growth, a business needs a systematic acquisitions process. This should consist of the following stages:

- **Strategic analysis.** The process starts with an objective assessment of what the company needs to do to generate continuing value for shareholders. Are acquisitions necessary or would organic growth be superior? What types of acquisitions might enhance performance? This analysis should identify whether the company needs acquisitions to strengthen its present core business, or whether it should be looking for companies that will take it into new technologies or markets.

- **Search and screen.** The next task is to generate a good list of acquisition candidates. The screening process then eliminates candidates that do not fit the results of the strategic analysis. Additional screening criteria should include company size, cultural fit, current market share and quality of management.

- **Strategy development.** For the handful of companies that remain after the screening process, management has to assess in detail how they could leverage value from the company if it was acquired. How much cost could be taken out? How could sales be ratcheted up? How could best practices be transferred from one company to the other?

- **Valuation analysis.** The next issue is determining how much it is worth paying for the acquisition candidate. This is discussed further below.

- **Negotiation.** Effective negotiation is based on thorough preparation. In entering negotiations, the management team should be clear on what is the maximum price they are prepared to pay. They should also have assessed the value of the candidate to the existing owners and other potential buyers. They need to have assessed the financial position of the current owners, their objectives, strategy and likely negotiating tactics.

» Valuing an acquisition

How much should management be prepared to pay for an acquisition? The principles of valuation were described in chapter 2. As with any asset, the value of an acquisition is based on the net present value of the future stream of cash flow that is anticipated. For an acquisition, the fundamental equation is:

$$\text{Maximum acceptable purchase price} =$$
$$\text{Pre-acquisition value} + \text{Value of synergies}$$

If the prospect can be acquired for less than the maximum price, then the investment should generate a return above the cost of capital. The pre-acquisition value is the market value of the target before the prospect of the acquisition. This is the minimum the seller will expect. Invariably, the seller will hold out for a premium above this pre-acquisition value. This will be rationalised in terms of other potential bidders or the belief by the managers that the market underestimates the company's potential.

The amount the buyer should be willing to pay depends on the estimate of the synergies involved. Each of these synergies has to be identified and valued. The main synergies are:[7]

- **Cost savings.** Cost savings may increase the operating margin in the combined business. These are likely to be greater where the acquired company is in the same industry. Savings may be from economies of scale in purchasing, from eliminating duplicate jobs, facilities and other expenses, and from transferring best practices.
- **Investment savings.** Consolidation of the two companies may produce economies in fixed and working capital requirements.
- **Taxes and cost of capital.** Sometimes a merger will reduce the combined cash tax rate and the company's weighted cost of capital.
- **Sales growth.** This can occur when the acquirer introduces the target's products into a broader distribution channel. Sales enhancements are generally more difficult and uncertain to estimate than cost and investment savings.

The maximum acceptable price for a target is then calculated by valuing it using these synergies to upwardly adjust the original cash flow projection. The present value of these cash flows should normally determine the maximum price to be paid.

However, there are occasions when a higher price might be paid. This may be the case if the acquisition is a necessary investment as part of a much broader long-term strategy to gain differential advantage in the target market. Here, the whole strategy should be valued rather than any particular element forming a part of it. The specific acquisition can be thought of as purchasing an option allowing future opportunities to participate in the industry. Analogously, there are occasions when the company should pay considerably less than the maximum acceptable price. This is where there are other bid candidates that are cheaper, or where other initiatives such as joint ventures, strategic alliances or licensing could produce similar results more economically.

» Post-merger integration

Given the substantial premium an acquirer is likely to have paid, it is crucial that the post-acquisition implementation is handled effectively. In fact, studies show that most acquirers destroy rather than add value after the acquisition — acquired companies do worse after being acquired. To avoid this, a well-planned post-acquisition plan is required. Step one is to agree on strategy. Management in both companies should be in harmony about the objectives and focus of the new business. Step two is to communicate a plan to reassure customers, employees and suppliers. Step three is to implement the strategy for quickly progressing the synergies in costs, investments and sales. The last step is to develop a long-term strategic and organisational change program to leverage value from the merger.

» Alliances

Strategic alliances provide an alternative to acquisitions for accelerating profitable sales growth. Alliances differ in several ways from acquisitions. First, there is no bid premium involved so it should be easier to create value for shareholders. Second, alliances usually involve only parts of a company rather than the whole business as in the case of an acquisition. This should lower the overall level of risk. Third, alliances have to be carefully structured to allow for effective control. Finally, the motivation for alliances is often different from acquisitions. Acquisitions generally benefit from geographical overlap because of synergies from consolidating facilities, distribution networks and sales forces. Alliances, on the other hand, are usually intended to expand the geographical reach of the partners.

In an influential study of a large number of alliances in the 1990s, Bleeke and Ernst made the following findings:[8]

- Both acquisitions and alliances had roughly the same success rate in creating shareholder value.
- Acquisitions work better for core businesses and existing geographical areas. Alliances are more effective for edging into related businesses or new geographical areas.
- Alliances between strong and weak rarely work. When one partner has the major stake, it tends to dominate decision making and put its own interests above those of the alliance. A 50:50 split works best.
- Successful alliances must be able to evolve beyond their initial objectives. This means they must have autonomy and flexibility to respond as markets and technology change.
- Alliances and joint ventures have a limited life span. More than 75 per cent of the alliances that terminated ended with the acquisition by one of the parents.

Step 9: Pursue growth outside current industry boundaries

The final step of growth innovation involves opportunities for even more creative ways of achieving profitable sales growth. These involve growth outside the current boundaries of the company's industry. The most obvious alternatives are:

- **Vertical integration.** Forward integration, where the firm takes over ownership and control of its customers, can offer opportunities. For example, PepsiCo began acquiring its bottlers in the 1990s to gain greater control over sales effort. Such investment may enable the firm to achieve greater differentiation and avoid its margins being squeezed by an increasingly concentrating customer base.

   Backward integration involves moving into a supplier industry. In the past, car manufacturers produced around half of their components internally. Today, with the increasing importance of getting close to customers, forward integration has become more popular than backward integration.

- **Diversification.** Some companies have achieved enormous growth by transferring capabilities and intangible assets to quite disparate industries. The source of this creativity has often been based on taking a marketing view of the firm's business. Instead of defining it in product terms, management has defined the business in terms of meeting certain customer needs. For example, Gillette expanded from its core business of men's razors by redefining its mission first as men's grooming products. This took it into shaving creams, deodorants and aftershave. Later, the mission was expanded even further to personal care, which took it successfully into dental products, small appliances and stationery. Virgin defined its markets even more

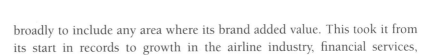

broadly to include any area where its brand added value. This took it from its start in records to growth in the airline industry, financial services, cosmetics, clothing, railways, telecommunications and the Internet.

- **Creating new businesses.** Creative companies that are alert to the opportunities created by changing technologies and changing consumer needs can create new businesses. Freeserve, a new Internet service provider, was started by Dixons, Britain's largest chain of electrical goods shops, in 1998. Ten months later Freeserve was launched on the stock market with a valuation of close to $6 billion. By then, it had leapfrogged established rivals such as AOL and CompuServe to dominate Internet access with a market share of 30 per cent. Prior to Freeserve, customers paid monthly subscriptions to the provider. Dixons' innovation was the insight that subscription fees could be waived and revenues earned from a slice of the telephone charges, advertising and e-commerce.

- **Leveraging relationships.** Some companies create whole new sources of growth by leveraging customer and supplier relationships to enter new markets. General Electric is a good example. Until the early 1980s, it was seen primarily as a supplier of industrial equipment and consumer appliances. But since then it has ratcheted up its growth rate by leveraging its relationships to move into a whole new set of growth businesses, especially in the service sector. Initially, it focused on financing the sale and distribution of GE products. Today, it is a leader in a broad array of financial and outsourcing services, ranging from railcar leasing and credit cards to reinsurance and equipment financing. Over the past decade, GE's total sales have been growing by 20 per cent and shareholder returns by 24 per cent a year.

- **Exploiting industry convergence.** Today, technological changes are leading to many industries converging. Examples are pharmaceuticals and genetic engineering, cable television and telecoms, and media, computers and the Internet. For industry leaders, such changes present opportunities as well as threats. Pioneers of new technologies tend to be small, making it financially feasible for current leaders to buy into them and dominate the newly converging sector. SingTel, Singapore's leading telecommunications company, has bought aggressively into the cable industry as they saw this becoming a key way of providing broadband digital services to households.

Implementing a strategic focus for superior shareholder value — a volume focus example

Many experienced managers can handle the task of rationalisation but stumble when it comes to growing markets. This is not surprising, since the perspective and skills are quite different. Building a successful growth business normally takes longer than fixing an unprofitable one. Rationalisation is essentially internally focused on the company's assets and costs; market growth, on the other hand, requires a focus on customers and the environment outside the firm. Market growth is more difficult because it is competitive; it is about getting customers to prefer buying from your business rather than the myriad of other companies. This requires having a differential advantage that is perceived as superior by customers. Finally, rationalisation can be directed from the top, but market growth requires a commitment throughout the business. In particular, it needs the enthusiastic support from the front-line staff who have the knowledge to generate ideas for growth and who have the task of implementing them.

The catalyst for integrating volume activities with productivity activities after designating the main focus based on the strategic objective is almost always a new chief executive. And even with a new chief executive, combining a particular volume focus with a concern for productivity, or vice versa, can take years since it requires a fundamental change in the company's culture. The task of preparing the introduction of a market growth orientation and making it the main strategic focus for a business unit traditionally concerned with productivity, for example, can be divided into three stages. The first is winning the commitment of the senior executive team. This requires an educational program to teach executives about marketing and developing market-led strategies. Frequently the chief executive will need to bring in new blood to provide experience and support for the strategy.

The second stage will be to set ambitious goals which signal change and stimulate progress. Jack Welch, legendary former CEO of General Electric, set the goal of doubling sales over a five-year planning period. Each GE division was asked to find two 'breakthrough' ideas that would significantly transform their growth performance. Sam Walton, founder of Wal-Mart, the world's biggest retailer, set the goal in 1990 of quadrupling sales, doubling the number of stores and increasing sales per square foot by 60 per cent by the year 2000. Such visible objectives signal what is expected from managers (see marketing management in practice 'Chief's lore of the jungle: Keep it simple').

Marketing management in practice: Chief's lore of the jungle: Keep it simple

... At the rostrum again last week, this time in Brisbane, [managing director of Wesfarmers, Michael] Chaney reiterated Wesfarmers' success was in no way rocket science. Rather, he says, it emanated from the company's simple objective: to provide a satisfactory return to shareholders. It is one which many other public companies will claim to share but which very few stick to with such rigid discipline as Wesfarmers has since it adopted it 17 years ago when it converted from a farmer co-op into a publicly listed company.

'The power of that statement was never very obvious at the time,' Chaney says. 'An important point is that the stated objective of the company was not something with an operational sort of flavour or vision, like to be Australia's major agribusiness or, subsequently, to be Australia's energy company or hardware company or, in fact, to be Australia's most successful conglomerate. It was simply ... a purely financial objective. That financial objective has allowed us to be absolutely dispassionate about the direction the group takes. Essentially, as long as the business concerned was an ethical one and fitted with our management philosophies, we would pursue it if the numbers added up.' ...

Chaney attributes Wesfarmers' success to several key factors: running its businesses efficiently and generating extra cash from them; hiring the best people it can find, even sometimes when it does not have a particular vacancy for them; developing a set of management systems which have a shareholder focus; developing a set of valuation principles and sticking to them; being positioned to evaluate opportunities as they arise and, finally, using its cash flow to make acquisitions and the management systems to run the acquired companies better.

Source: Extracts from Cathy Bolt, 'Chief's lore of the jungle: Keep it simple', *The Australian Financial Review*, 20 November 2001, S12.

The third stage is removing any organisational barriers that restrict managers from focusing on market growth. To generate growth options, the top team must sweep away a culture that penalises failure and mistakes, and thus less productivity. Fixed beliefs about what the company can and cannot do must also be challenged. Systems and budgets must be aligned to the new growth objective. For example, bonuses can be awarded for achieving top-line growth. Or, like at 3M, targets for new products can play a key role in the planning process.

Let us assume that volume is the principal strategic focus. How should such a strategic focus be implemented? We suggest developing a five-step process if the aim is market growth:

1. create the mindset
2. set the strategy
3. make it happen
4. build momentum
5. organise for growth.

Step 1: Create the mindset

Let us assume that market growth is the strategic focus. Building sustainable market growth on a productive business foundation requires management to understand that they need to operate in three market categories: today's businesses, tomorrow's businesses and **options for growth**.[9] They first need to appraise the current situation. If today's markets are generating good returns but they do not have any emerging markets or promising options, the task of management is to focus on proceeding through the growth innovation steps. On the other hand, if the core market is not performing, the initial task is to sort this out.

options for growth: Investments in research, experiments and trials that lay the foundation for the firm's most attractive new markets in the future

» Today's businesses

These are the company's current core markets and account for the bulk of the sales, profit and cash flow. The problem with today's markets is that they are inevitably maturing. For these established markets, management has three tasks. First, they want to get rid of any older businesses which are not generating adequate returns on capital and which cannot be turned around quickly. For those that remain, the focus is on rationalisation and operating efficiency, ensuring that these businesses are managed to optimise return on investment. The marketing task is to ensure that all profitable growth opportunities are explored in today's markets. It is fatal to treat these successful markets as cash cows: such attitudes will lead to a rapid erosion of market share. Instead the strategy must be to keep the brands up to date, focus on customer retention and retain the brands, for as long as possible, as thriving assets.

» Tomorrow's businesses

These are the company's star new markets. Businesses in these new markets are already demonstrating their ability to win profitable customers and grow rapidly. Management's job here is to roll out more business to capture critical mass and dominate the market in the same way they have done in 'today's markets'.

» Options for growth

These are investments in research, experiments and trials that seed 'tomorrow's businesses'. They are low-cost options for business growth that give the company the chance to learn about new opportunities. Many of these experiments will fail, in which case they can be dropped without major damage to the company; those that show promise can be developed and exploited. Given the high failure rate to be expected with options, companies should always be pursuing a bundle of them simultaneously.

Many managers over-focus on today's businesses because they generate the bulk of sales and profits. But this is a big mistake. Not only will their companies lose out on tomorrow's growth, but today's investors will penalise them in terms of the values they attach to their businesses. It is important to understand that the value investors attach to tomorrow's markets, and particularly an attractive bundle of options, can far exceed their current sales and profit contributions. Much of the shareholder value created by successful companies is based not on the success of their current markets but upon expectations about the management's capacity to generate future profitable market growth.

» **Sorting out the core**

If the company's core market is unprofitable, it is difficult to pursue market growth. A profitable core is necessary to generate the funds to finance growth. It is also necessary to give investors confidence in management's ability to achieve profitable growth.

Making an existing business perform depends upon achieving a strong strategic position in its market and efficiently executing a sound operational plan. For some markets, the chances of achieving a strong strategic position may look too formidable. In this case strategic divestment will be the appropriate action. Divesting those businesses that are seen as not offering adequate returns sends a decisive signal to investors about management's strategic intent.

For those mature markets that are kept, the task is to quickly create cash flow. Since for most of these markets the growth potential is limited, restoring profitability usually focuses on rationalisation to take out costs and reduce the amount of working capital and fixed assets employed. There is also often scope for improving margins by dropping unprofitable customers and targeting higher-margin accounts.

Step 2: Set the strategy

If the firm's market growth is to be profitable, it must be driven by a strategy to create a differential advantage. A differential advantage is developed by exploiting the firm's resources and capabilities. Management should look for growth opportunities that match its organisational resources and capabilities. To set strategy, the management team need to undertake three steps:

- assess the organisation's resources and capabilities
- search for growth opportunities that exploit resources and capabilities
- develop the resource and capability base.

The company cannot build a sustainable growth strategy from its current resource and capability base alone. In developing strategy, management will be made aware of resource gaps which need to be plugged. It will need to develop comprehensive training programs, recruit new talent with specialist knowledge and skills, develop additional technologies and form new relationships with customers, suppliers and distributors.

Step 3: Make it happen

Having ideas is not enough; ideas have value only when they are transformed into options through the planting of a new business. This may be achieved by initiating an R&D project, setting up a pilot plant or a test market, or making a small acquisition.

The early business books on corporate planning saw developing a growth strategy in highly rational terms. Strategic decision making was viewed as a logical process in which a plan is formulated through systematic analysis of the firm, its performance and the external environment. The strategy is then communicated to the organisation and implemented down through successive organisational layers.

However, the process in practice is much less structured and more diffused, and there is less of a dichotomisation between formulation and implementation. Mintzberg, one of the foremost researchers in this area, makes a useful distinction between intended, realised and emergent strategy.[10] **Intended strategy** is the strategy as conceived by top management. Even here, rationality is limited and the intended strategy is the result of a process of negotiation, bargaining and compromise, involving many individuals and groups within the organisation. **Emergent strategy** is the process by which managers adapt the intended strategy to changing external circumstances, their own strengths and weaknesses, and their own learning. **Realised strategy** is the strategy that emerges. Mintzberg suggests this tends to be only 10 to 30 per cent of the intended strategy.

Drucker calls this emergent process in successful growth companies a piloting approach.[11] A company takes small steps to learn more about the market opportunity and to gather the skills necessary to capitalise on it. Rather than a big, high-risk leap into a new venture, the piloting approach is a learning process. If they are going in the right direction, managers can accelerate their steps; if it looks a dead end, they can abandon the option without too much being lost.

For example, Lend Lease's move out of construction and property development and into various aspects of finance and banking can be described in terms of this piloting architecture: Lend Lease's wholly owned property trust helped it to acquire expertise in fund management. Early in the 1980s, it recognised two options for growth in the financial services sector, recently deregulated by the new ALP government. It purchased a 25 per cent stake in the newly created Australian Bank (the first retail bank to be created in Australia for many decades) and a 20 per cent stake in the large insurance company, MLC. In both cases a modest start was followed by a series of exploratory steps. However, things did not work out as Lend Lease had hoped in banking venture. Changes that were expected in Australian banking legislation did not happen. Despite the introduction of a variety of new products, the bank was never successful. Lend Lease was eventually to sell the Australian Bank in 1988, but shifted the cash management and mortgage loan portfolio to MLC. Things were different, however, in insurance and fund management. Lend Lease became convinced that MLC had great potential and increased its stake to 49 per cent in 1984, and eventually in 1988, with profits growing rapidly, decided to buy MLC outright. In the 1990s further steps were taken with the acquisition of two insurance firms, Capita and Australian Eagle.[12]

---

intended strategy: the firm's strategy as conceived by top management

emergent strategy: the firm's intended strategy after adaptation to changing external circumstances as well as top management's own strengths, weaknesses and learning

realised strategy: the emergent strategy that is implemented; typically only 10 to 30 per cent of the originally intended strategy

Step 4: Build momentum

A successful growth strategy depends upon putting together a difficult-to-imitate bundle of critical capabilities that make it possible to sustain a competitive advantage. A firm's capabilities depend upon its collection of resources: tangible assets, intangible assets and people. These resources, when integrated effectively, provide the firm with its special capabilities which, in turn, form the basis of its ability to grow the market.

Capabilities are not fixed; they can be acquired and developed. Indeed, it is the skill in acquiring and developing capabilities that determines an organisation's ability to develop a long-term growth strategy. Hence, companies should not take too narrow a view of their capabilities when considering growth opportunities. A company does not have to limit the search for opportunities to areas where it presently has the full range of capabilities; it should have the confidence that it can develop and learn new capabilities. Without this confidence, to quote Ghoshal and Bartlett, 'core competencies become core rigidities'.[13]

> **core rigidities:** abilities that define a firm's fundamental business core, but stifle its ability to adapt to competitive changes

The essence of the piloting approach is that capabilities need to be built and developed. It makes sense for the company to develop the most critical capabilities internally so that it controls the key sources of competitive advantage. But capabilities that are not so critical can be outsourced. Outsourcing, alliances, partnerships, joint ventures and the formation of economic webs have increasingly become the ways in which today's companies access manufacturing, development and IT capabilities. The need to quickly learn about new products, technologies and local markets makes it difficult for any organisation, no matter how large, to develop all the necessary knowledge in-house.

Step 5: Organise for growth

A business with a growing market has to be organised differently from a steady-state one. They need different structures, systems, processes and, generally, different types of managers. At the same time, they have to be linked to the centre if the company is to leverage the advantages of its size and its shared services, and exploit potential synergies across the group.

» Organisation

New businesses have to be organised differently from mature ones because their tasks differ. For mature businesses, the priority is running them efficiently. The business is well understood; the company has the capabilities to run it, and the market is familiar. The priority is to squeeze out more cash by controlling costs and investments and through marginal enhancements in the product and customer mix. For new markets and market options, the priorities are different. They are about achieving rapid growth, speed and decisiveness. Market uncertainty is much greater: customers, competition, channels and positioning are all new and changing. Many resources and capabilities have still to be acquired by the business.

If new businesses are reporting to the same line managers as the core business, there is a real danger that the new ventures will fail to flourish. First, managers will not give them sufficient priority; invariably, the new businesses will have tiny sales and often they will be making losses. Second, new ventures will have to conform to the same planning, budget procedures and performance measures as the mature businesses. If new ventures are held to the same profitability objectives as core businesses, the former will certainly wither away. Finally, speed is much more important in growing businesses. Tying managers in these ventures to the same approval processes found in mature business units would leave them floundering in the wake of more fleet-footed competitors.

Successful companies are responding in several ways to these problems. One approach is to assign responsibility to autonomous, cross-functional teams. Another approach often followed by companies like 3M, Johnson & Johnson, and IBM is to create a separate business unit. More recently, spinouts have become popular. Here, the company not only creates a separate unit, but establishes it as a separate company with some public shareholding. For example, Dixons spun out its Freeserve venture nine months after launch, offering 20 per cent to the public. The senior management team enjoy the excitement and, with luck, the financial rewards of running an independent public company. At the same time, the group company, as the majority shareholder, can enjoy the benefits of keeping the unit connected to the larger enterprise. All these approaches focus on the need to create fleet-footed small business units, with managers totally orientated to successfully growing the new ventures.

» Managing the talent

Because the task of managing mature and growing markets is different, so the management style has to be different. Most executives do not have the skills to create new markets. Established markets require managers who can optimise current operational processes and deliver consistent bottom-line results.

Tomorrow's businesses require managers to focus on top-line sales rather than bottom-line profitability. They need managers who are comfortable with ambiguity and changes in market requirements and operational processes. Managers who overemphasise consistency and discipline stifle risk taking and entrepreneurial flair. For managing options — explorations into new markets and technologies — the business needs visionaries. Commonly, they are younger, less experienced and naïve in the wiles of organisational politics. They will need the support and sponsorship of a senior executive at the centre who appreciates their special skills and can reassure the organisation about the venture's importance.

Any company needs a mixture of these disciplined operators, business builders and visionaries if it is going to manage effectively its present businesses and capitalise on tomorrow's growth markets. Too many managers focusing on disciplined processes and budgets detract from the future. Too few focusing on the basics threatens the present. Individual business units benefit from cultural homogeneity, but the company as a whole needs to have cultural heterogeneity.

» Systems and performance measurement

The type of planning used for mature markets does not make sense for new ones. For emerging markets there is much greater uncertainty and a greater focus on accumulating the necessary capabilities. Detailed annual operating plans and budgets are simply counterproductive.

Budgets, performance measures and rewards need to be different, reflecting the different objectives. In mature markets, the business budgets should focus on short-term profits and cash flow. Leading companies use cash bonuses to reward managers achieving short-term profitability goals. Managers who cannot achieve budgets are swiftly put aside. For growing markets, the focus is on long-term sales growth and value creation. Key measures are market share, customer acquisition and retention rates, the trend of profitability and expected net present value. Rewards need to reflect long-run value creation rather than achieving short-term budgets. To encourage an entrepreneurial culture, many companies offer executives equity participation. They are also more tolerant of failure than for mature markets.

With options, the focus is on estimating the potential rewards and the probability of success. In these businesses, learning takes place through experimental projects. Performance and rewards can be based on achieving results from project-based milestones. Increasingly, companies are exploring option theory to value these opportunities. The number of initiatives being pursued and the proportion of them that lead to a business launch can measure the overall performance of the business in creating options.

» Autonomy and integration

Growth and performance are best achieved by breaking big companies into small business units and giving their management teams as much autonomy as possible in running them. But if small businesses are best, what is the point of large companies? Surely investors would be better off if the company was broken up, the head office closed, and the businesses floated as independent companies.

Large holding companies only make sense if they can add value through either shared central services or exploiting synergies between the businesses. Small businesses can buy services outside but sometimes it can be cheaper or more effective to have them internally. The most useful services the centre can offer growing businesses include acquisition skills, financing capabilities, and legal and accounting support. The second possible source of added value are synergies. A business in emerging markets may possess lower costs and investment through sharing the company's existing facilities. Marketing synergies may enable it to use existing sales force, channels and networks. Businesses may also be able to cooperate in cross-selling opportunities. Finally, technological synergies may enable the emerging venture to utilise knowledge lying in other areas of the company.

Such synergies can be realised only if ideas are readily shared across the company. For the corporate centre, the challenge is to devise sufficient coordination and exchanges that offer the benefits of size, but without eroding the value of the entrepreneurial flair and sense of ownership that only devolved leadership can produce.

» Inspiring the organisation

Many of the most exciting new businesses in the past decade have been start-ups. But it is important that large businesses learn how to create new enterprises. How can corporate headquarters in large corporations motivate their managers to hunger for the challenges of growth and entrepreneurial activities? One way successful companies do it is through setting ambitious goals, such as achieving double-digit sales growth or doubling market share. Ambitious goals help create a change in culture in the organisation by raising the profile of market growth. They also stretch managers to be more imaginative by making them aware that the usual strategies will not be enough to reach the new goals.

The centre can also give managers the resources to achieve market growth. These are not solely financial resources but also include sweeping away the barriers to organisational growth such as bureaucratic planning and budgeting procedures. Top executives have to recognise that creating new markets requires autonomous organisations and systems that prioritise entrepreneurial efforts.

Neither ambitious goal setting nor adequate resourcing, however, is enough to inspire employees to great efforts year after year. It is hardly surprising that studies of the great growth companies like General Electric, Rubbermaid, 3M, Procter & Gamble, Sony and Microsoft all show that they have guiding ideals of leadership that transcend financial numbers. Ghoshal and Bartlett express this as follows:

> Strategies can engender strong, enduring emotional attachments only when embedded in a broader organisational purpose. Today, the corporate leader's great challenge is to create a sense of meaning within the company, which its members can identify, in which they share a feeling of pride, and to which they are willing to commit themselves.[14]

Segmenting the market and analysing competitors

An integral part of developing a strategic focus is establishing what to focus on. Volume cannot be increased and productivity cannot be improved without knowing exactly what benefits customers need and what kind of competition can be expected. Without this information, managers cannot ensure that all profitable growth opportunities are explored in today's businesses, that tomorrow's businesses are cultivated, and that the seeds for future options are sowed in the right places. Therefore, markets must be segmented and competitors must be analysed. These two processes are also key determinants of a business's marketing mix decisions. In the remainder of this chapter, we will focus on segmentation and competitor analysis in more detail. Both processes complement each other. We recommend focusing on customers first. After all, without customers, there is no competition.

Customer targets

Market segmentation is at the core of many marketing problems. The task of marketing is to identify and deliver the benefits customers need. But customers differ in their benefits needed; consequently, serving customers in a market effectively will require many different types of offer. Offering a single, undifferentiated product to the market leaves a supplier highly vulnerable to competitors making differentiated offers to particular market niches. This is why, for example, Nike offers over 300 varieties of sports shoes.

» Market segmentation

One-to-one marketing aims at tailoring individual offers for each customer. Modern computerised databases, direct marketing, and the Internet are all increasing the opportunities for such mass customisation. But in most cases, especially in consumer markets with millions of potential customers, to achieve scale economies and develop strategies, it pays to group customers in terms of similarity of benefits needed. This process is called market segmentation. The reasons for segmenting markets are fundamental:

- it permits prices, products, distribution and communication to be packaged to the benefits needed by customers
- by closer matching to benefits needed by customers, it leads to higher customer satisfaction
- by focusing on benefits needed by customers, it avoids commodifying the product and a consequent focus on price
- since customers differ in price sensitivity, it facilitates different pricing strategies and higher average margins
- it encourages growth and customer relationships through different offers over the customer life cycle
- it allows the company to pre-empt competitors by developing discrete offers customised to each segment of the market
- it stimulates innovation by focusing product development around the specific benefits needed by customers.

The tasks of marketing management with respect to market segmentation can be reduced to two principal phases: the actual segmentation of the market and the subsequent choice of target segments.

- **Segmenting the market.** Finding the most revealing way to segment a market is both an art and a science. There are always a number of alternatives and often several criteria will be used together. For example, car buyers can be segmented by age, sex, income, lifestyle, business or personal use etc. An advertising agency might segment prospective clients by size of budget, industry, local or global, profitability, attitudes to creativity or loyalty etc. The right choice will depend upon the specific market, its degree of maturity and the company's own resources and capabilities. Most modern segmentation schemes will be based on the benefits needed by customers. In terms of effectively revealing new business opportunities, a benefits-needed segmentation approach will be most useful.[15]
- **Choosing target segments.** Managers then have to decide which segments will be profitable to serve. This requires estimating the size of each segment, its growth rate, competition, profit potential and its fit with the resources and capabilities of the company. The aim will be to choose groups of customers who will have a high lifetime value for the company.

After choosing the target market segments, marketing management then needs to determine how to tailor the marketing mix to capitalise on the segments' value. A separate marketing plan needs to be developed for each market segment in which the business decides to compete. Normally, each segment will have a manager responsible for coordinating the resources and capabilities of the business and tailoring them to these customers. This will be explored in more detail in part 3 of this book.

» Dynamics of market segmentation

It is crucial for managers to appreciate that market segments are not fixed but highly dynamic: new segments are continually emerging and old ones disappearing. Capitalising on these dynamics is one of the most important avenues for companies to achieve growth and value creation. Two forces affect these market dynamics: changes in the environment and the evolution of the market.

- **Changes in the environment.** Over time, the demographics of markets change, new customer needs appear, novel technologies emerge, competition increases, markets deregulate and taxation policies change. All of these alter how markets are segmented. For example, in recent years, customers have become more concerned with diet and cholesterol. The result has been an explosive growth of health-orientated segments and the emergence of new low-fat and low-cholesterol brands in the food and beverages market. Increasing computer literacy has led to the rapid growth in the number of customers who want to bank and shop over the Internet. Managers who are alert to environmental changes and identify the opportunities they create can tap enormous value-creating opportunities. It is invariably easier and more profitable to capture market share by pioneering new segments than fighting head-to-head with competitors over established ones.

- **Market evolution.** One of the great confusions among managers is that between the product life cycle and the market life cycle. The product life cycle describes how total sales of a product evolve over time. The market life cycle describes how the customers buying the product change over time. The market life cycle is a much more important determinant of strategy. The key point is that markets do not grow in some uniform fashion; instead they grow by adding segments. The critical implication of this is that a business can continue to grow only by radical and often difficult changes in its positioning strategy. Failure to make these changes explains why once dominant players in a market, such as Hewlett Packard in calculators, Compaq in personal computers, Nissan in automobiles or Barclays in banking, lost out to new competitors with similar products but different marketing strategies. Figure 6.4 illustrates the relationship between the product and the market life cycles. Growth is spurred by new segments entering the market. Initially the product is bought only by a small group of innovators (segment S_1). For a new prescription pharmaceutical product these would be hospital consultants; for mobile phones they were higher managers. Innovators are those who first perceive the value of the product and have the resources to buy it. As awareness increases and prices fall, growth is taken on by a new segment of early adopters (segment S_2). Later, new segments emerge and repeat buyers take an increasing share of the market. For a company to maintain a leading position in the market, it has to change its focus, switching resources out of maturing segments into emerging ones.

Switching segments is normally quite difficult because the new segments have different needs and operating characteristics. The problems are not generally about adapting the technology, but rather about adapting the market positioning strategy. One of the most challenging problems is shifting distribution channels. For example the small, high-price innovator segment is often served by a direct sales force; for segment 2, distributors might be the most appropriate channel; for segment 3, mass retailers might be the answer; finally, for segment 4, with customers familiar with the product and price sensitivity high, the Internet might be the lowest cost and most effective channel. Channel conflict often handicaps such changes in an organisation. The difficulties of throwing off the past explains why many of today's market leaders are relatively new companies like Amazon.com, Cisco, Wal-Mart and eBay. They have not had to be concerned with cannibalising existing businesses or upsetting current channel partners.

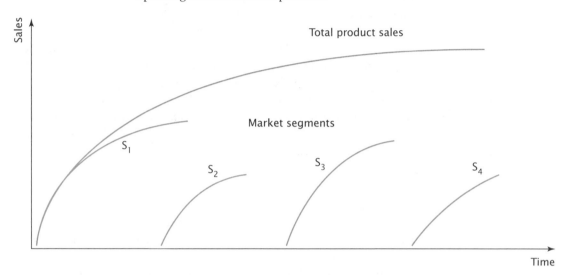

Figure 6.4 Market dynamics over the product life cycle

Who is the customer today? Who is it tomorrow? Developing a value-based marketing strategy therefore requires business unit managers to ask two questions. First, who are the target customers today? This is the easy question. A thorough analysis of the market should be capable of determining what target segments are the most profitable to serve today. But the second, and more difficult, question is more vital to the ability of the business to generate long-run value — that is, who should your customers be tomorrow? Unless the business can anticipate, or at least respond rapidly to, the newly emerging market segments, with their own specific needs and channel requirements, it will see its value erode.

Competitor targets

A strategic focus assessment is not just about seeking shareholder value by knowing exactly what benefits customers need, it is also about beating competitors who are playing the same game — that is, knowing what kind of competition can be expected. Managers need to analyse competitors around five questions.

» Who are the competitors?
The easiest competitors to identify are the firm's direct competitors, who are offering similar products to the same market. So, for example, Nokia competes directly against Ericsson and Motorola in the mobile phone market. But this can be too narrow and static a definition of the competition (see figure 6.5). The basic insight from marketing is that a competitor is someone

meeting the same benefit needed by customers, not necessarily with the same product. Indirect competitors are firms offering different products that meet the same benefit needed.

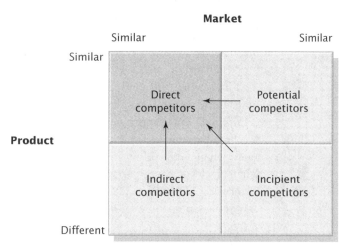

Figure 6.5 Different types of competitors

A striking example of indirect competition was the effect of the PC on the demand for encyclopaedias. Parents bought the Encyclopaedia Britannica in the belief that they were maximising the educational opportunities for their children. But, in the 1990s, the PC became the product for delivering this benefit aspiring parents needed. Britannica's traditional market was lost, not to competitive encyclopaedias, but to a completely different product and technology that delivered the same benefit.

There are also potential competitors that do not currently compete in the company's market segment, but may do so in the future. In the early stages of a market, different market segments often have different sets of competitors. But, as the market matures, the more successful of these niche players drive into adjacent segments until they cover the entire market with differentiated offerings. Smaller niche players, lacking economies of scale and scope, get pushed out of the market by larger and more aggressive competitors. Finally, there are incipient competitors who may become competitors as alternative technologies converge. For example, cable, satellite, wireless and traditional telecoms companies increasingly compete for the emerging communications markets. To summarise, in looking ahead at the strategy, managers again have to focus on the market dynamics and ask who are the competitors today and who might they be tomorrow.

» What are their likely strategies?

Second, management will need to anticipate the strategies of the key competitors and their likely reactions to the business's own plans. This includes assessing how aggressive they will be in seeking to gain market share, which market segments they will focus on, and whether their positioning will be around price or differentiation. Insights into these questions will be obtained from looking at their past behaviour, the strategic significance of the business to them, their financial position and the focus of their recent investments and R&D spending.

» **Where are they vulnerable?**

Developing a strategy to beat competitors requires identifying any weaknesses that can be exploited. The weaknesses may lie at the corporate level or at the level of the business unit. Impulse, an Australian low-cost airline, was crushed by Qantas who had identified the precarious nature of its corporate finances. Impulse's high level of debt and low operating margins meant that it was fatally vulnerable to relatively small erosions in price and market share.

More often it will be operating and marketing deficiencies at the business unit level that can be exploited. Glaxo was able to catapult Zantac into leadership in the huge anti-ulcer therapy market by exploiting the side effects said to affect patients using SmithKline's Tagamet. Qantas began to lose market share when Virgin Blue drew attention to its high prices. Tesco made gains when rival UK supermarket group Sainsbury introduced a poorly perceived advertising campaign. Dell Computer Corporation won leadership by exploiting Compaq's weakness in direct marketing channels.

» **Where are we vulnerable?**

The fourth question reverses the previous one. It asks: What are our weaknesses that could threaten our long-run position in the market? This involves projecting the implications of changes in the socio-economic, technological and market environments. Changing customer needs and the evolution of new segments have to be explored. The competitiveness of the company's differential advantage have to be objectively assessed. Questions that need to be asked are: How competitive are our products in range and quality? Do our prices offer genuine value? Are our promotional and distribution channels right for the consumers of today and tomorrow? Nowadays, any holes in the company's defensive wall are quickly exploited by aggressive competition.

» **What should we do?**

Finally, marketing management need to decide on an action plan that anticipates and responds to the competitive threat. The plan will seek to reduce the company's own vulnerability and attack the competitor's own area of weakness.

Summary

1. Rationalisation can produce short-run increases in cash flow but investors recognise that such policies cannot produce enduring gains.
2. The companies that have created the greatest returns for shareholders have mostly been businesses with an excellent productivity basis in high-growth markets. Combining a strategic volume focus with a concern for productivity is probably the most potent source of shareholder value.
3. Growth in sales volume creates shareholder value by increasing the future level of cash flow, accelerating the timing of cash flow, extending its duration or reducing the risks attached to future returns.
4. Growth innovation must start with consolidating the current customer base, increasing customer retention and winning a growing share of their spending. This forms the foundation for going on to gain new customers and developing new products and markets.

5. Any company that is to endure needs three types of markets: today's markets, tomorrow's markets and market options. The first provides the bulk of the revenue and cash but the last two account for most of a company's market value.

6. To grow markets, management has to create a growth mindset within the company, to build momentum and to sweep away the organisational barriers that constrain market growth.

7. Superior shareholder value cannot be achieved without knowing exactly what benefits customers need and what kind of competition can be expected. Market segmentation means knowing what benefits customers seek. Competitor analysis provides the means of knowing what kind of competition can be expected when meeting the benefits needed.

key terms

core rigidities, p. 222
customer lifetime value, p. 203
customer selection, p. 203
emergent strategy, p. 221
intended strategy, p. 221

options for growth, p. 219
product life cycle, p. 210
realised strategy, p. 221
share of customer, p. 207

review questions

1. Explain the links between growth and shareholder value creation.
2. Why has shareholder value become associated with rationalisation rather than growth?
3. Identify the different pathways to accelerate market growth.
4. Why is customer loyalty seen as the foundation for building a growth strategy?
5. Describe how to develop a growth strategy for a business.
6. Discuss the issues in implementing a growth strategy in a company.

discussion questions

1. When does diversification outside the company's traditional products and markets make sense?
2. What factors will influence the capacity to grow the share of existing customers? How can marketing facilitate this process?
3. Which component involved in developing a growth strategy is most significant for accomplishing growth innovation?
4. How can the product life cycle help determine effective market segmentation, and how does growth innovation impact on segmentation?
5. Is it possible to determine who an organisation's competitors are for growth markets? Is this the same for new markets?

debate questions

1. Can rationalisation provide sufficient value for shareholders?
2. Is prioritising the same as enhancing the value proposition for customers?
3. Is an alliance better than an acquisition?
4. Is competitor target analysis necessary if a firm continuously enhances its value proposition?

case study |ANZ delivers growth and value creation

For the financial year 2000–2001, ANZ Banking Corporation reported an increase in profit of 7 per cent from the previous period to $1.8 billion. The company's return on shareholder equity was 20.2 per cent. During the year ANZ moved to a strategy focused on 16 specialist businesses that were designed to be more customer-oriented.

Below are extracts from ANZ Chief Executive Officer John McFarlane's address to shareholders in the annual report for the financial year 2000–2001:

I am pleased to report another record result with the 2001 profit up 7 per cent on last year (18 per cent excluding discontinued businesses). Our good first half performance was repeated in the second half, despite the more subdued economy and weaker credit environment.

All but one of our specialist businesses grew their profits during the year, and all but four had double-digit earnings growth. This demonstrates the robustness of our strategy, our disciplined management and risk approach, and the strength and depth of our management team. It emphasises our focus on growing the top line, our caution on risk, our rigour on capital allocation and our decisiveness on costs.

The past four years has seen a major transformation of ANZ. We now have a more sustainable and balanced business mix, improved positions in a number of growth sectors, industry leading productivity, and considerably lower risk. The current uncertainties in the Middle East and South Asia provide further affirmation of our decision to sell Grindlays [a subsidiary].

All of this has resulted in a record share price, market capitalisation and shareholder dividend.

We have made good progress with our other stakeholders. The number of customers and market share across most measures has increased. Staff satisfaction has improved substantially. We have also taken a number of steps to earn the trust of the community, including a new ANZ Customer Service Charter, free transactional banking for those over 60, major concessions for Centrelink and Health cardholders and our moratorium on regional bank closures.

Of course, not everything has worked in our favour, and there are areas where we are not doing as well. Although we have made progress in areas of customer and community satisfaction, we have a great deal yet to do. It is well known that banks are not held in high regard by personal customers or by the community. Changing this perception of ANZ and contributing to changes in the wider industry is a major priority of ours over the next few years.

Again, while we have made substantial progress in Personal Financial Services, we remain underweight strategically in this area. In particular, we need to increase the number of customers in Metrobanking, Regionalbanking and Small to Medium Business. We also need a stronger position in Wealth Management.

We are also facing substantial competition for deposit funds, constraining our ability to grow assets — particularly from alternative investments. Plans are in place to increase deposits, but the real solution lies in diversifying our business by growing alternative revenue streams ...

We will continue to invest in selected growth segments and to improve the sustainability of our business mix. We are also paying particular attention to customer and staff satisfaction, in building our strategic position in our core businesses and in earning the trust of the community. We have plans for a major transformation of our branch network domestically over the next few years. Additionally, strategic opportunities at reasonable values are likely to present themselves, and we believe this will play to our advantage. As examples, we recently acquired a 75 per cent shareholding in Bank of Kiribati and signed contracts to acquire Bank of Hawaii's businesses in Fiji, Papua New Guinea and Vanuatu ...

Source: Extracts from ANZ Annual Report 2001, pp. 4–5, www.anz.com.au.

Questions

1. Critically assess the strategic focus at ANZ.
2. How has ANZ sought to create value for shareholders? How has growth been achieved to support this?
3. How is value being defined by ANZ? Is it accurate to suggest that ANZ is being too customer focused?
4. What factors contribute to the development of ANZ's growth strategy? Which consideration for developing a growth strategy is likely to be most significant for ANZ?
5. Is ANZ pursuing an acquisition or alliance strategy in its international operations?

end notes

1. See the examples in Peter Doyle, *Marketing Management and Strategy*, London: Prentice Hall, 1998, pp. 65–8.

2. Average customer tenure is calculated by taking the reciprocal of the defection rate. For example, if the retention rate is 90 per cent then the defection rate is 10 per cent annually. This gives a tenure of 1 divided by 10 per cent, or 10 years.

3. Don Peppers and Martha Rogers, *Enterprise One-to-One*, New York: Doubleday, 1997.

4. Leonard Berry and A. Parasuraman, *Marketing Services: Competing through Quality*, New York: The Free Press, 1991.

5. Drawn from *The Economist*, 26 June 1999, 'Survey: business and the Internet', p. 14.

6. Ansoff was the pioneer of the analytical approach to strategic planning. For his most recent work, see Igor Ansoff and Edward McDonnell, *Implanting Strategic Management*, 2nd edn, New York: Prentice Hall, 1990.

7. For a useful discussion and recent examples see Robert G. Eccles, Kersten L. Lanes and Thomas C. Wilson, 'Are you paying too much for that acquisition?', *Harvard Business Review*, 77(4), July/August, 1999, pp. 136–48.

8. Joel Bleeke and David Ernst, *Collaborating to Compete: Using Strategic Alliances and Acquisitions in the Global Marketplace*, New York: John Wiley & Sons, 1993.

9. This section borrows some of the ideas in Mehrdad Baghai, Stephen Coley and David White, *The Alchemy of Growth*, London: Orion Business, 1999.

10. Henry Mintzberg, *The Rise and Fall of Strategic Planning: Reconceiving Roles for Planning, Plans and Planners*, New York: The Free Press, 1994.

11. Peter F. Drucker, *Management Challenges for the 21st Century*, Oxford: Butterworth-Heinemann, 1999, pp. 86–7.

12. See Baghai, Coley and White, *op. cit.*, pp. 79–81.

13. Sumantra Ghoshal and Christopher A. Bartlett, *The Individualised Corporation: A Fundamentally New Approach to Management*, New York: HarperBusiness, 1997.

14. See Ghoshal and Bartlett, *op. cit.*, pp. 307–8.

15. For an excellent discussion about market segmentation, see Vithala R. Rao and Joel H. Steckel, *Analysis for Strategic Marketing*, Reading: Addison-Wesley, 1998.

Part 3

Deciding how to compete

7

Brands

chapter objectives

By the time you have completed this chapter, you will be able to:

- describe what a brand is
- understand how brands create value for shareholders
- explain how to build a successful brand
- assess the value potential in developing brand extensions
- explore the opportunities from updating brands and developing markets internationally
- show how a portfolio of brands can be structured systematically to control costs and maximise its effectiveness
- describe how brands are valued using discounting cash flow analysis.

scene setter

Brand positions

Most of us think of Nike as the world's most successful sports shoe and apparel company. But multibillionaire founder, chairman and CEO Phil Knight sees it a little differently; he calls Nike a marketing company. The shoes are just the company's most important marketing tool.

'For years we . . . put all our emphasis on designing and manufacturing the product, but now we understand the most important thing we do is market the product,' Knight told *Harvard Business Review*. 'The design elements and functional characteristics of the product itself are just part of the overall marketing process.'

This fundamental change in corporate thinking was critical in cementing the profile of the company's brand. Through clever advertising and high-profile product association, Nike has become one of the most powerful brand names on earth. The 'just do it' mantra has passed into the general lexicon, the 'swoosh' logo is one of the most immediately recognised in the world, and at the turn of the millennium all that work on developing the brand translated into total sales of US$9 billion, US$5.5 billion in sports shoes alone.

In the new millennium, brand is everything. Any company that launches a new product onto the market without sufficient brand development work is almost certainly destined to fail.

'These days, business people tend to think about brand at the forefront of any commercial proposition,' says John Allert, CEO of Interbrand Australia. 'Once it was technology, distribution, price or being first to market, but now people realise unless you achieve brand franchise with consumers, any commercial venture is an uphill battle.'

The franchise that brands build with customers is a make-or-break issue in the marketplace today. It goes beyond Coca-Cola's bonds with youth, or McDonald's relationship with young families. It means building an image and a relationship that extends far beyond its customer base and connects with governments, communities, analysts and investors.

The creation of UK telecommunications company Orange is an excellent illustration of how a well-considered brand can capture market share and create value for investors. In the two years following the company's launch in 1994/95, the company spent £45 million (then $91 million), more than 5 per cent of turnover, on building the brand. ABN Amro calculated that within two years the brand was worth £200 million and the £45 million investment had created £277 million in shareholder value. So, what had Orange done differently?

'It started with a name that had no baggage and didn't actually mean anything, giving the company total latitude to create the company brand and image it wanted,' says John Glynn, managing director of Brand Finance. 'And it didn't use telephones in any of its brand building because it didn't want to be painted into a corner as a pure telephony company, it strongly positioned itself as a communications leader so it could expand into data and the internet.'

When Knight changed his company's name from Blue Ribbon Sports to Nike in 1978, it is unlikely he realised how fundamental the name would become in the company's success. But Knight does claim the company was the first to recognise the true value of branding.

'It is hard to overestimate the importance of what the Nike brand means,' says Nike Pacific brand marketing director Carl Grebert. 'Externally it is a sign of quality, of inspiration and motivation for consumers. Internally, it drives everything we do throughout the entire company.'

Source: Extracts from Michael Cave, 'Australian Financial Review', *Boss Magazine*, May 2001, pp. 28–9.

Introduction

Part 2 of this book looked at the role of value-based marketing strategy in driving shareholder value. It examined the steps in developing a value-based marketing strategy and explained the process of strategic objective assessment and strategic focus assessment. Part 3 shows how to develop and manage a value-based marketing mix for maximum effectiveness. This chapter shows how the successful management of brands orchestrates this process.

The brand as an intangible asset

brand: an intangible asset that provides a differential market position; it is created by and, subsequently, affects the marketing mix elements

A **brand** can be described in many ways. We prefer a strategic perspective. A brand is about using the marketing mix elements to create a differential position in the market. A brand, in turn, can strengthen or weaken the impact of the marketing mix. Indeed, as we will explain, a good brand is the most effective way to orchestrate a firm's marketing process for superior shareholder value.

Intangible firm assets are usually much more important than the tangible assets that appear on corporate balance sheets. In the industrial era that ended somewhere in the early 1960s, possession of valuable property or efficient plant and equipment accounted for the stock market dominance of such companies as General Motors, Westinghouse and Unilever. They could turn out the cars, goods and chemicals the world clamoured for. But few of the world's most valuable companies in the 21st century — Microsoft, GE, Wal-Mart — rely for their profits on making things. They rely on market-based assets, for example customer, supplier and partner relationships centred on a brand's promise. When they do sell goods, their manufacture is often outsourced. In most of these top companies, the value of their tangible assets represents only a small percentage of their market value.

brand equity: the net present value of the future cash flow attributable to the brand. It is the incremental value above what an unbranded product would possess

Brands are classified as intangible assets. In many industries the equity in the company's brands is the most important intangible asset. **Brand equity** is defined as the net present value of the future cash flow attributable to the brand. It is the incremental value above what an unbranded product would possess. Brand equity arises from the strategic market position of the brand and the resulting trust that customers place in the brand. This trust creates a relationship between the brand and the customer that reduces risk and encourages preference, brand loyalty and a willingness to consider the new products that the company may offer under its brand name in the future.

There is clear evidence that strong brands create value for shareholders as well as for consumers. One study by Citibank and published by the *Financial Times* found that companies with well-known brands outperformed the stock market average by between 15 and 20 per cent over a 15-year period.[1] Other evidence lies in the high market value to book value ratios that usually occur for companies with strong brands. Finally, there is evidence in the high prices paid — typically five or six times book value — when branded goods companies are acquired.

A key question is who controls the brand and the relationship to the consumer. Most producers do not sell direct to the end consumer. So, for example, someone shopping for toys could think first of the supplier's brand (e.g. Mattel), a retailer that stocks toys (e.g. Toys 'R' Us), a new e-business (e.g. eToys) or a search engine such as Yahoo! that finds and may even recommend the best choice. In recent years, the power of the retailer's brand has grown at the expense of the suppliers. In the coming years, there is the threat that the greater efficiency of an e-commerce brand or search engine could dominate both. If a business loses control of its brand, the business risks being stripped of a means to a differential market position, and risks value migrating to whomever has the customer's preference. Creating and sustaining the brand is therefore the key to shareholder value in most industries.

A brand is something completely different from a **label**. A label is a name, symbol or design that is used to distinguish the firm's product. The firm's brand (or portfolio of brands) represents a strategic position in the market; the brand's equity is the result of a carefully managed marketing mix. As a strategic concept, a brand is the promise of added values to the customer.

A strong brand is one that is highly desired by its target customers. This affects each of the core business processes. It facilitates the product development process by giving customers more confidence in the quality and attributes of the products. Strong brands aid the supply chain management process by attracting suppliers and channel interest. They also enhance customer relationship management by creating emotional links over and above the functions of the product.

Table 7.1 lists the world's strongest brands as valued by Interbrand, a leading international brand consultancy.[2] While this particular list was compiled in the mid-1990s, little has changed. Year after year, the same brands dominate Interbrand's top-20 list. If one looks at the performance of these brands in their respective industries, one theme stands out — with few exceptions, companies that possess strong brands and, therefore, make the Interbrand list also appear to be top industry performers. And this is easy to explain — a strong brand indicates a strong strategic market position and trusting customers.

label: a name, symbol or design that is used to distinguish a firm's product

Table 7.1 The world's top brands

BRAND	BRAND VALUE ($ BILLION)	PERCENTAGE OF COMPANY MARKET CAPITALISATION
1. Coca-Cola	84	59
2. Microsoft	57	21
3. IBM	44	28
4. GE	34	10
5. Ford	33	58
6. Disney	32	61
7. Intel	30	21
8. McDonald's	26	64
9. AT&T	24	24
10. Marlboro	21	19
11. Nokia	21	44
12. Mercedes	18	37
13. Nescafé	18	23
14. Hewlett Packard	17	31
15. Gillette	16	37
16. Kodak	15	60
17. Ericsson	15	32
18. Sony	14	49
19. Amex	13	35
20. Toyota	12	14

Source: *The World's Greatest Brands.* Reprinted with permission from Interbrand.

The role of intangible assets

The modern resource-based theory of the firm is illustrated in figure 7.1.[3] A firm starts with certain resources — for example assets, human resources and an organisational culture. The quality of these resources and the effectiveness with which they are combined determine the firm's core business processes — the things it can do particularly well. So, for example, Optus has core business processes in telecomunications and Microsoft in writing software — those fundamental activities that generate value for customers.

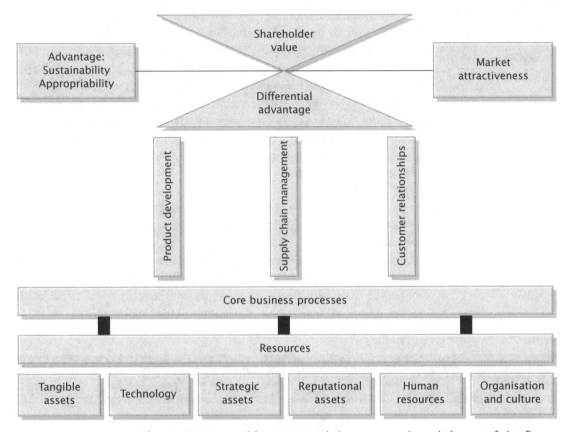

Figure 7.1 Intangible assets and the resource-based theory of the firm

These core business processes can be divided into three groups: (1) the product development management processes, which aim to meet benefits that customers need, (2) the supply chain management processes, which acquire inputs and efficiently transform them into customer benefits and (3) the customer relationship management processes, which identify customers, understand their needs, build customer relationships and shape the perceptions of the organisation and its brands.[4] The effectiveness with which the firm undertakes these processes determines its ability to create a differential advantage.

Whether this differential advantage translates into profitable, long-term growth is affected by two other factors. One is the sustainability of the firm's differential advantage. In some markets even strongly advantaged firms do not earn high returns because low entry barriers mean that the differential advantage is quickly copied. A second factor is the appropriability of the value of the advantage. Sometimes, parties other than the shareholders appropriate this value. These may be powerful customers, who are able to use their buying power to drive down the company's prices and so appropriate the value themselves. Sometimes, suppliers may appropriate the value. Star employees can occasionally use their specialised skills or fame to leverage the full value of their added value to the firm. Movie stars and rugby players are examples. Unions are also able to leverage their positions. Wage demands may make organisations that lead the market only marginally profitable, or even unprofitable, as value migrates from shareholders to the suppliers of skills.

Conventional balance sheets show only the firm's tangible assets. Tangible assets consist of its financial assets and physical production factors such as plant and equipment, land and locations. But tangible assets represent only a small fraction of the value of major companies. For example, the ratio of market value to book value for the world's top 20 companies averaged 15, and for the *Fortune 500* it averaged 8, implying that tangible assets represented between only 5 and 12 per cent of a company's total assets.

Most of the resources a modern company uses to build strong core business processes and value for customers and shareholders do not appear on the balance sheet. These intangible assets can be classified into five types:

1. **Technological assets.** These are proprietary technology in the form of patents, copyrights and trade secrets, or special know-how in the application of technology.
2. **Strategic assets.** These are licences, natural monopolies or other privileges that restrict competition from other firms.
3. **Reputational assets.** These are the name of the company and its brands, which convey the reputation of its products and fair dealings with customers, suppliers, the government and the community.
4. **Human resources.** These are the skills and adaptability of the firm's employees.
5. **Organisation and culture.** These are the values and social norms inside the firm that shape the commitment and loyalty of employees.

Brands as risk-reduction mechanisms

Brands create value for customers by helping them reduce risk. Today, customers are faced with an increasing array of competitive suppliers and products promising to meet the benefits they need. Making the right choice often involves risk because the products are new and complex, or because the customer has not had to make this type of decision before. Even if the buyer is willing to spend time evaluating the alternatives, judging products can still be tough. Goods and services that are hard to evaluate before purchase are said to be low in 'search qualities'. Services, like those offered by consultants, hairdressers or repair shops, are examples — it is difficult to know what the end result will be like until the service has been performed. Many of them have high 'experience qualities' — their quality can be evaluated after purchase. Some goods and services are, however, difficult to evaluate even after purchase, for example a medical check-up or a survey on a new property. These are said to be high in 'credence qualities'. Buying them can mean taking a risk. As the economy becomes more hi-tech and services become more dominant, consumer decision making gets more difficult as these tend to be high in experience and credence characteristics and low in search qualities.

Decisions are particularly challenging when complex criteria come into play. Particularly in consumer markets, decisions are often not based solely or even largely on economic or functional criteria of value. Products fulfil more than functional needs — they are also purchased to meet social needs, to seek status or for self-actualisation. In choosing clothes or a car, customers are looking for far more than functional values. They are looking not only for what the product will do for them but what it will mean for how others see them.

The consumer's anxiety and perceived risk is increased where the decisions are important ones. This is where the wrong decision entails significant financial or social costs. Of course, many decisions are not important in this sense. Buying the 'wrong' chocolate bar or magazine is generally not an important mistake. But most decisions absorb time. As people get more affluent, the value they assign to their time increases and they look for mechanisms to save time. Brands are one of the mechanisms to take time out of the purchasing process and to reduce risk.

Brand image

Successful brands create a relationship of trust with the customer. This relationship is based on the image customers have of the brand (see marketing insight 'Spin doctors and the quest for a perfect match'). A **brand image** is a set of beliefs about a brand's attributes and associations. A customer's image of a brand is built up from four types of source:

brand image: a set of beliefs about a brand's attributes and associations — an impression of the brand in the consumer's mind

1. **Experience.** Often, customers will have used the brand before. They will frequently have well-formed beliefs about its reliability and character.
2. **Personal observation.** Friends, acquaintances and others seen using it communicate beliefs about the brand's attributes and associations.
3. **Public opinion.** The brand may have appeared in the mass media or been analysed in consumer reports.
4. **Commercial presentation.** Advertising, display, packaging and salespeople are important in communicating messages about the brand's features and values.

Marketing insight:	Spin doctors and the quest for a perfect match

The prestige car manufacturers have determined what their customers like to drive and like to do, with brand experiences ranging from theatre to sport, driving clinics and motor racing. Advertising agency Young & Rubicam conducts a global survey on consumer perceptions of brands called the Brand Asset Valuator and, in Australia, has determined the likely characteristics of prestige car drivers by brand. Young & Rubicam found that each prestige car brand fulfils a unique role for its owner and different associations form a subtle, yet powerful, image.

Mercedes-Benz
The flagship prestige car — the one the others define themselves against. Mercedes drivers see themselves as having more self control and self assurance. Not a flashy car, but a sense of enduring achievement, though derived from corporate success, rather than individual or intellectual achievement. Brand analogies — Pierre Cardin, Omega, Bang & Olufsen.

Jaguar
Has a clear sense of almost arrogant leadership and heritage. Its typical driver is likely to be a self-made, high achiever, who is comfortable with being recognised as being a leader, with a sense of elitism carried from the boardroom to the golf course. Its English heritage purveys a sense of intellectualism — they would not notice the dog hair on the back seat. Brand analogies — Cartier, Chanel, Polo Ralph Lauren.

BMW
Also defines the benchmark for prestige cars, but appeals to the far more outer-directed. It expresses the enjoyment of driving — carefree but somewhat unapproachable. A BMW driver is eager to impress upon others their sense of dynamic achievement and success. They whole-heartedly embody their new found sense of hard earned success and feel this marks them out as being a 'cut above the rest'. Brand analogies — Blaupunkt, Giorgio Armani, Rolex.

Ferrari
The ultimate driving car with leading-edge performance. The most dynamic and stylish, derived from its Italian origin and Grand Prix pedigree. Like BMW, a Ferrari driver is similarly flashy. Beneath an often older body stirs a still fiery and impulsive person to whom money is of little concern. They love to feel they are living life on the edge. Brand analogies — Reebok, Calvin Klein, Gucci.

Porsche
Of similar pedigree to Ferrari, although more charming and carefree. A Porsche driver is looking to rediscover their youth, enjoy the things that make them feel good and has less to prove to themselves or anyone else about who they are. Brand analogies — Oakley, Harley-Davidson, Nike.

Volvo
More restrained, obliging, calm, down-to-earth and honest. It reflects a sense of levelhead-edness and conformity, being the complete antithesis of cars like Ferrari and Porsche. Brand analogies — Braun, Michelin, Samsonite.

Rolls-Royce
Clearly recognised as the original and traditional prestige car. In a class of its own, beyond prestige. A Rolls-Royce driver puts up with the sheer impracticality of a Roller as a symbol of their slightly quirky conservatism, even eccentricity. They have an 'unrockable' sense of self, which is typically borne out of having made it big, against all the odds. Brand analogies — YSL, Moet & Chandon, Chivas Regal, Harrods.

Lexus
More youthful, progressive, intelligent, approachable and friendly. Its driver shuns the whole prestige car symbolism, though the very idea of being anti-image is a statement in itself. Brand analogies — Tag Heuer, Nikon, Bolle.

Audi
The new Lexus, being similarly more intelligent and friendly, and is also felt to be better value. Its driver is typically small-scale affluent and possibly a more conservative yuppie. Brand analogies — Canon, Nokia, Sharp.

SAAB
The most trendy and daring. It is more fun, progressive and energetic. The open top and turbo Saabs really define the brand. A Saab driver is more alternative, liberal and a different person on the weekend. Brand analogies — Ray-Ban, Miele, Vogue.

Source: Rochelle Burbury, 'Spin doctors and the quest for a perfect match', *Australian Financial Review*, 22–23 July 2000, pp. 2–4.

There are three main types of brands. Each has distinctive brand images:

1. **Attribute brands.** These possess an image that conveys confidence in the product's functional attributes. Because it is often difficult for customers to assess quality and features objectively from the vast array of offers, they will often choose brands that appear to confirm their qualities. For example, Holden's brand proposition is about an Australian car manufactured to high quality standards. Aldi's brand image is of the lowest prices for staple food products. Persil communicates it 'washes whiter'. The McKinsey brand promises the highest quality strategic consulting. These are all 'beliefs about attributes' brands.

2. **Aspirational brands.** These convey an image about the types of people who buy the brand. The image says less about the product and more about a desired lifestyle. The belief is that acquisition of these brands associates the buyer with the rich and famous. Martini suggests it is the drink of sophisticated jet-setters. Rolex watches are shown on the wrists of leading professionals. The desire to create such images reflects the recognition that many products are bought not just to meet people's functional requirements but to buy status, recognition and identity.

3. **Experience brands.** These convey an image of shared associations and emotions. They go beyond aspirations and are more about a shared philosophy between the brand and the individual consumer. Successful experience brands express individuality, personal growth and a set of ideas to live by. Examples are Nike with its 'just do it' attitude, or Qantas with its 'the spirit of Australia' slogan. Coca-Cola's brand proposition is about sharing the experiences and values of the young generation. The Marlboro brand expresses the experience of rugged masculine values. For these brands, no claims are made about the superiority or special features of the product — the promise is about experience and shared associations.

The most effective brand image varies with the nature of the market. In business-to-business markets, where purchasing tends to be more functional, attribute brands are more important (see table 7.2). In luxury markets, aspirational brands play a big role. In consumer markets, many companies have been trying to create experience brands. Experience brands have a number of advantages over attribute and aspirational brands. The problem with attribute brands is that with today's sophisticated technologies it is virtually impossible to retain unique product features or qualities for any length of time. The availability of more objective information sources heightens the problem of attribute claims. For example, customers might read on the Internet that Holden cars are not more Australian than Ford cars, or that other retailers are as cheap as Wal-Mart.

attribute brand: a brand that conveys confidence in the product's functional attributes

aspirational brand: a brand that conveys an image about the types of people who buy the brand

Table 7.2 Famous international business-to-business brands

Andersen Consulting	GE	John Deere
Boeing	Glaxo	McKinsey & Co
Boston Consulting Group	Goldman Sachs	Merek
Du Pont	Harvard Business School	Microsoft
The Economist	Hewlett Packard	Motorola
FedEx	IBM	Reuters
Financial Times	Intel	Fuji Xerox

Aspirational brands are threatened by increasing affluence, the declining influence of social class and the growth of more individualistic lifestyles. In modern societies, people no longer feel the same need to imitate their betters or 'keep up with the Joneses'. Consumers are becoming more individualistic, preferring to spend money on what makes them happy than on trying to impress the neighbours. Experience brands are more robust because they do not depend on a product or a 'look'. Another advantage of experience brands is that, because they are about personal values, they are often capable of greater extendibility than attribute or aspirational brands. The latter tend to be restricted to their category or closely related markets. By contrast, experience brands can stretch to wherever a buyer's personal philosophy can be made relevant.

The archetype of an experience brand is Richard Branson's Virgin brand, which stands for an unstuffy, irreverent, us-against-them attitude. This has been stretched from music and entertainment to transport (airlines and trains), drink (vodka and cola), financial services, cosmetics, clothing, mobile phones and the Internet.

The most important thing about successful brands is that they differentiate. Today even the newest and most complex products can be copied. It is not difficult to produce a drink that tastes like Coca-Cola, a cigarette like Marlboro, a suit like Armani or a microprocessor that functions like Intel's latest Pentium. But people will not buy these products in the same numbers and certainly not at the same prices. People buy the well-known brands to reduce risk — people have confidence in their quality or trust their status.

The added value provided by strong brands in the different forms of risk reduction are often demonstrated. Bartle describes how a parity performance on taste, when two food products are tested 'blind', becomes a clear preference for one brand (brand B), when the two products are labelled (see figure 7.2).[5] In another example, for a household product, a clear performance deficiency is removed when brand identities are revealed (see figure 7.3). Blind product tests normally show a clear preference for Pepsi over Coke, but when the brands are labelled the preference changes overwhelmingly to Coke (see table 7.3).[6]

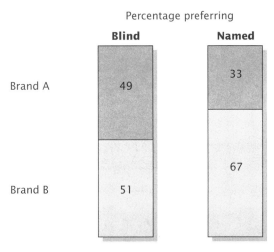

Figure 7.2 Blind versus named product test: food product

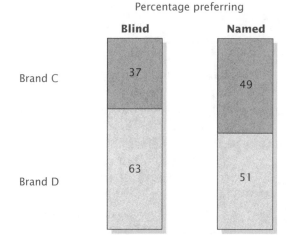

Figure 7.3 Blind versus named product test: household product

Table 7.3 Blind versus named product test: Coke versus Pepsi

	BLIND (%)	BRANDED (%)
Prefer Pepsi	51	23
Prefer Coke	44	65
Equal/Don't know	5	12

Source: Leslie de Chernatony and and Malcolm H. B. McDonald, *Creating Powerful Brands*, Oxford: Butterworth-Heinemann, 1992, p. 9.

The result of this added value is customer preference. Economically this means that strong brands obtain higher market shares, higher prices or, usually, a combination of the two.

Brands and shareholder value

This section explores how strong brands directly contribute to creating shareholder value. Brands contribute to the firm's capabilities in running its core business processes of managing its product development, supply chain, pricing and customer relationships. The effectiveness with which it runs these processes determines its ability to create value for customers and shareholders (see marketing insight 'At $9 billion, the Telstra brand is in a class of its own').

As we have seen, there are a variety of ways that the value of the business can be increased:

1. Increasing cash flows (e.g. by raising revenues, cutting costs or reducing investments).
2. Accelerating cash flows (earlier cash flows are an advantage because risk and time discount the value of later cash flows).
3. Increasing the residual value of the business (e.g. by increasing the size of the customer base).
4. Reducing the risk associated with cash flows (e.g. through reduction in both volatility and vulnerability of future cash flows, thereby effectively lowering the firm's cost of capital).

As we explain below, each of these four ways of increasing the value of a business is strongly influenced by brands.

At $9 billion, the Telstra brand is in a class of its own

Australia's 20 most valuable brands have a combined value of $28.1 billion, and the No. 1 brand, Telstra, represents almost 30 per cent of the total, according to an inaugural study by global consultancy Interbrand. The study found that Telstra had a brand value of $9.4 billion, dwarfing runner-up the Commonwealth Bank ($3.6 billion), followed by Westpac ($3 billion), ANZ ($2.5 billion) and National ($2.3 billion).

The Interbrand report said Telstra was a 'powerhouse of earnings, so that even though a relatively small proportion of earnings may be consigned as "branded earnings", the magnitude of the profit base drives the significant brand value amount'.

Service brands dominated the top 20, and newer brands made a strong showing ... Interbrand has produced an annual international 'billion dollar brands' league table since 1989, but this is the first time Australian brands have been valued.

Brands included in the study had to be Australian owned. They also had to have a brand value that could be isolated in terms of earnings from publicly available information, which led to some notable omissions, including Qantas, Coles Myer, AMP, NRMA, Foster's Lager, QBE, Goodman Fielder and Southcorp.

'Qantas ranked in the top three [in brand strength] but when we looked at the capital employed to take the Qantas brand and services to market, it impeded the brand to such a significant level there wasn't enough value to make the top 20,' Interbrand Australia's chief executive, Mr John Allert, said.

Interbrand uses a complicated methodology to value brands that consists of four elements: financial forecasting, which estimates economic earnings by intangible assets; the role of branding in determining earnings as a percentage of economic earnings; brand risk, where the risk rate of the forecast brand earnings is discounted to their net present value; and brand value calculation at the net present value of projected brand earnings.

Mr Allert said brand valuation had a critical role to play in investor relations, mergers and acquisitions, securitisation and licensing. 'Brands are no longer the marketing tools of marketers,' he said. 'They are strategic business tools and an identifiable asset that needs to be strategically managed to build shareholder wealth.'

Source: Rochelle Burbury, 'At $9bn, the Telstra brand is in a class of its own', *Australian Financial Review*, 30 November 2001, p. 18.

Increasing cash flow

Strong brands can increase cash flow in four ways.

1. **Obtaining higher prices.** Because customers have confidence in the attributes and quality of brands, or because brands offer desirable associations and experiences, customers usually pay a brand premium to purchase them. Brands like Mercedes, Microsoft and Qantas sell at substantial premiums to their rivals. A survey by Broadbent found leading grocery brands sold at a price premium averaging 40 per cent above retailer own-labels.[7] Other studies have shown that the price elasticity of strong brands is lower — implying that price increases result in smaller volume losses than for unbranded products. Of course, developing brands implies higher marketing costs so that incremental revenue is necessary to make brands economic. But price premiums are perhaps the most important way that brands create value for shareholders.

2. **Higher volume growth.** Instead of taking the full price premium that the brand may justify, a company can instead sell at, or close to, the average market price and use the brand's reputation to build higher volume. McDonald's, Dell and the Ford Motor Company are examples of companies

using their brand power this way. Most really strong brands such as Marlboro, Qantas and Intel are both leaders in share and sell at a price premium. Leading brands can gain scale economies in marketing and outspend smaller competitors to build growth. Another way in which strong brands increase growth is via **brand extensions**, which enable them to cover the market more fully or move into additional markets. Qantas's introduction of Qantas New Zealand is a classical example; so too is The Coca-Cola Company's Diet Coke (new line using an existing brand) and Virgin's launch of Virgin Mobile (new product using an existing brand) is another.

brand extensions: practice of using the same brand name to cover new lines in the current product category and to cover new products in different categories altogether

3. **Lower costs.** Brand leaders gain economies of scale that often result in lower costs. Buying power can mean lower variable costs. But it is in fixed costs, especially marketing and distribution costs, where brand leaders have their biggest advantage. Most marketing costs are fixed. For example, the minimum cost to run a national advertising campaign or national sales force is the same whether the brand share is 5 per cent or 50 per cent. This means that while brand leaders generally spend more in absolute terms than their smaller competitors, their unit marketing cost is lower.

4. **Higher asset utilisation.** Strong brands often have more opportunities to economise in fixed and working capital. They can obtain scale economies in plant and distribution. Suppliers and distributors also have a greater incentive to integrate their supply chains with companies possessing strong brands. This can lead to significant reductions in inventories, manufacturing and distribution assets.

Table 7.4 illustrates how these four factors operating together can augment the cash flow of a strong brand. Here the brand leader sells three times the volume of the follower and also has a brand premium of 10 per cent. Its buying power gives it a 5 per cent advantage in unit variable costs. The brand leader's fixed costs are $18 million more, yet in terms of fixed cost per unit, the follower is 20 per cent more costly. Both brands are assumed to have been growing sales by 5 per cent annually; the leader's investment rate is 40 per cent of NOPAT and the follower's is 45 per cent. The result is that the brand leader's market share advantage of 3:1 turns into a free cash flow advantage of 19:1. In addition, with its much higher marketing spend, the brand leader is in a strong position to increase even further its market dominance (see marketing insight 'The importance of market share').

Table 7.4 Brand strength and cash flow

	BRAND LEADER	BRAND FOLLOWER
Volume (m units)	100	33
Price ($)	1.00	0.9
Revenue ($m)	100	29.7
Variable costs ($m)	40 (0.4/unit)	13.86 (0.42/unit)
Fixed costs ($m)	30 (0.3/unit)	12 (0.36/unit)
Operating earnings ($m)	30	3.84
Tax ($m)	9	1.15
NOPAT ($m)	21	2.69
Net investment ($m)	8.4	1.21
Free cash flow ($m)	12.6	1.48

Accelerating cash flow

Brands can increase shareholder value by generating cash flows sooner than otherwise. The faster the company receives cash flow, the higher is its net present value. There is considerable evidence that consumers respond quicker to marketing campaigns when they are already familiar with the brand and have positive attitudes towards it.

This is likely to be particularly important for new products. One study found that brands with the strongest images in the personal computer industry, such as IBM, Compaq and Hewlett Packard, could expect customers to adopt their next-generation products three to six months sooner than brands with weaker images.[8] Strong brands can also get access to the major distribution channels faster. To the extent that brands lead to faster responses and stimulate earlier purchases, cash flow is accelerated and shareholder value is increased.

Marketing insight: The importance of market share

In both consumer and industrial markets companies attach great importance to market share. For example, both General Electric and Heinz have set their strategies around exiting from all markets where they cannot be number one or two. There is considerable evidence that in many markets only the top two brands in a category make an economic profit. As markets become increasingly global, these brand leaders become truly mega-brands.

The profitability of the brand leaders arises from three sources. First, brand leaders usually have lower unit costs as a result of economies of scale and purchasing power. Second, they can afford to spend more on marketing, enabling them to have a greater share of voice in the market and so boost sales even further. Third, they can obtain higher prices. Distributor economics pressure retailers and dealers to reduce the number of competing brands that they carry in a category. The brands most at risk are small-share brands, which have to resort to giving higher margins to distributors to maintain support.

The PIMS study of 2600 businesses found that, on average, brands with a market share of 40 per cent generated three times the return on investment of those with a market share of only 10 per cent. For grocery products the relationship appeared even stronger. Studies in both the United Kingdom and the United States indicate that, on average, the leading brand in a category earns around 18 per cent return on sales, the number two brand only 3 per cent, and the others are unprofitable.[9]

In recent years, 'network effects' have become important in adding to the critical significance of obtaining a high market share. For many products and services, especially those that are IT related, customers want to buy the brand leader. Buying the market leader gives them the assurance that the product is not going to be made obsolete by the emergence of new standards and that applications and networking with others will be facilitated.[10]

Increasing the residual value of the business

The residual value of the business is the result of increasing the continuing value of cash flow. Continuing value is the present value of a business attributable to the period beyond the planning period and it generally accounts for the majority of the value of the business. The continuing value reflects investors' views of the long-term ability of the business to keep generating cash. A strong case can be made for the importance of brands in enhancing continuing value. Striking evidence lies in the longevity of leading brands. Most of the world's leading brands, aside from those in completely new sectors of the economy like Microsoft and Intel, have been around for over 25 years. Brands like Coca-Cola, Nescafé, Persil, Heinz, Kit-Kat, Cadbury and Kellogg's have been around for up to a century.

Brands have longevity because consumers believe in them. Consumers are confident about their attributes and values and so continue to buy them, as long as they go on being managed properly. Users of early versions of the product not only buy later versions but also often buy new line and brand extensions. Equally importantly, they contribute to continuing value by referring the brand to other potential uses and new generations. Creating strong brands is one of the most important ways of increasing the long-term value of the business.

Reducing the risk associated with cash flow

The company's cost of capital is influenced by the risk attached to its cash flow. Cash flows that are more stable and predictable will have a higher net present value and consequently create more shareholder value. Strong brands reduce a company's vulnerability to competitive attack. While products are easy to copy, the evidence suggests that strong brands are not. Brand image is a significant barrier to entry and so acts to reduce the vulnerability of cash flow.

The volatility of cash flow is also often reduced for strong brands because brand loyalty promotes stability in operations. With a loyal customer base, the company does not have to risk major investments in winning large numbers of new customers. This is important because the cost of winning new customers is much greater than the cost of retaining existing ones.

How to build brands

A strong brand image B_S can be thought of as the combination of three elements: a good product (P), a distinctive identity (D) and added values (AV):

$$B_S = P \times D \times AV$$

The relationship is multiplicative, indicating that all three elements are necessary to create a successful brand. Developing a brand starts with having an effective product. Product effectiveness can normally be measured in blind product tests. Next, the product has to be given a distinctive identity through careful pricing, placement and promotion so that customers can recognise it and ask for it by name. This is usually measured by prompted and unprompted awareness. Finally, and most crucially, a strong brand has to have added values that elicit confidence in consumers that it is more desirable than similar products from competitors (see marketing insight 'Hot tips on creating a brand that's, like . . . cool'). Added values can be measured through market research into attitudes and preferences.

From products to brands

Having an effective product alone is not sufficient to earn economic profits. Competition only at the product level eventually makes it a commodity-type business and price becomes the major factor in customer choice. Most companies attach their names to their products so that they become recognisable, but again this is insufficient to create preference. These are not brands but labels (L), i.e. $L = P \times D$. A label distinguishes the product of a particular company but does not convey any added values. Preference depends upon the last ingredient — added value that gives customers confidence that this product reduces risk to levels not possible by others at this price level.

Hot tips on creating a brand that's, like ... cool

If brands think they are cool, they are in dangerous territory. Cool is not something that can be defined by a marketer — brands are rated cool by the market itself, according to research that seeks to unlock the code to cool. The George Patterson Bates Youth Gallery study found that 'cool' was a dangerous word, particularly because of a desire by marketers at some time in their career to create a cool brand.

A surprising array of products were mentioned in the focus groups of young people aged 15 to 24 in Sydney and Melbourne, including Melbourne Bitter, chess, Vietnam, Moonlight Cinema, sushi and vinyl records.

'To attempt to construct a cool brand ends up with a lot of misses,' Patterson's national director of strategy planning, Mr. Mike Morrison, said. 'People who use the brand are cool, not the brand itself. They bless the brand and give it its "coolness". Cool is dangerous because it's a "fat" word. Cool means everything and nothing and lacks precision. With this in mind, companies should not try to create cool brands but should try to join the dots on why things actually become cool.'

For a brand to be deemed cool by the youth market, it has to reject the traditional dictums of brand launches — mass distribution and mass advertising — to build its appeal, and instead use a 'discovery' marketing strategy.

'Marketers need to resist the temptation to launch new brands with great distribution in tons of markets. It flies in the face of cool brands. You need to dampen demand and limit distribution, which gives the brand its cachet,' Mr. Morrison said. 'If you want to gain respect, and that's the key word, it's "give me your props", or proper respect. Brands gain 'props' and are discovered and slightly known and almost obscure. They are far more interesting than brands that are famous.'

Patterson has developed a roadmap to 'cool' using results from the research. It is made up of nine stages and ends when the bubble bursts and the youth market moves on.

The road begins with experimentation, which leads to discovery and then to individualising the brand, creating a bubble of appeal when a brand is blessed as cool. Once the brand loses its individuality, the market rejects it and moves on to the next big thing.

'This market sees advertising coming a mile away and deconstructs it before it reaches their eyelids. If an ad says to the audience "this is what I think about you" then your brand is going nowhere,' Mr. Morrison said. 'When Red Bull launched, it used students as its "brand managers" and asked them to hold parties and supply Red Bull. It was a perfect way to give the brand a fabulous context."

Source: Rochelle Burbury, 'Hot tips on creating a brand that's, like ... cool', *Australian Financial Review*, 13 November 2001, p. 57.

The process of brand building is often described as a series of layers (see figure 7.4). The starting point is a product that meets a customer's needs. But however innovative or effective the product, it rarely forms the basis of a sustainable advantage. First, competitors can usually rapidly copy new products. For example, Gillette spent three years and over $2 billion developing its Mach3 razor. But one month after it was launched a retailer own-label copy of it had been introduced. In most markets today, there are not major quality differences among the leading competitors. Because manufacturing is often such a low-value activity, even the most innovative companies increasingly outsource making the product to third parties. A second problem is emphasised in the basic marketing concept — people do not want products, they want solutions to their problems. Products are not bought for their own sake, but for the benefits they provide.

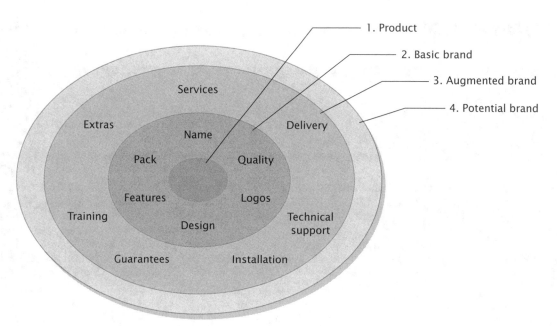

1. Product
2. Basic brand
3. Augmented brand
4. Potential brand

Services

Extras

Delivery

Name

Pack

Quality

Features

Logos

Training

Design

Technical support

Guarantees

Installation

Figure 7.4 The process of brand building

The second layer builds a basic brand around the product. The primary function of this stage is to differentiate the company's product from competitors and to make customers aware of it. At the same time, management will want to ensure that the differentiators are consistent with the added value they want to associate with the brand. The most obvious ways in which the basic brand is built, differentiated and customers made aware of it are through the choices of brand name, packaging, design and promotion.

The third layer of branding is the augmented brand. The objective here is to make the brand more desirable and differentiated by adding benefits. These typically include additional services such as free delivery, technical support, training, guarantees, credit and other financial terms. The final layer of branding is the creation of the potential brand whereby it succeeds in possessing the added values of emotional associations of confidence, status or identification that secure brand preference and loyalty. The potential brand status achieved by such brands as Sony, McDonald's and Qantas is usually the result of a long period of sustained investment in marketing communication allied to a strong concern for the product, its price and its placement.

Developing brand identity

Brand management centres on creating perceived added value for the company's offer among customers. The manager does this by shaping the brand's identity. The brand image is what the customer perceives of the identity. It depends on the strength, uniqueness and favourability of the brand's associations. The **brand identity** is the message about the brand that the marketer wants customers to receive. It represents what top management wants the brand to mean in the marketplace, and what it stands for. The customer's brand image is the result of how he or she decodes (interprets) all the signals emitted about the brand. The company's task is to get its message about the brand identity across to produce favourable feedback and responses in the form of purchase and brand loyalty.

brand identity: the intended impression of the brand that top management wishes to create in consumers' minds

» The brand communication process

On the basis that an appropriate brand identity has been developed, the three major problems in creating the desired brand image and feedback are:

1. **Wrong media.** Messages are communicated through personal media such as a sales force and impersonal media such as TV, newspapers and the Internet. The choice of media has a significant effect on the reach of the message and the confidence customers have in it.

2. **Competitive messages.** Customers are exposed to thousands of messages a day, of which only around 5 per cent are noticed and less than 1 per cent provoke some form of reaction. Without enormous expenditures, or luck, it is very difficult to get a message about your brand across. It is estimated to cost at least $100 million to create a new global brand. Today's new dot.com start-ups are routinely devoting 90 per cent of the capital they raise from investors on advertising in an effort to get their brand identities across.

3. **Other brand signals.** The company cannot control all the information being received about the brand. Customers also obtain information from past experience with it, from seeing others who use it, from other actions of the company and elsewhere. For example, there are more than 20 sites on the Internet devoted to attacking McDonald's for the damage the company is alleged to be doing to the global environment.

» The facets of identity

To build and subsequently manage a brand effectively one needs a model. A model identifies the variables constituting a brand, defines the relationships between the variables and predicts the effects of changes on consumer response. Developing a model of a brand is more difficult than modelling a product. The dimensions of a product are real and functional, e.g. speed, weight, size. However, those of a brand go beyond the product and are often emotional and perceptual, making it harder for managers to agree on what the attributes are and how they can be measured. But brands are so important to the business that managers and investors need models.

A model provides a language for executives to discuss brands in a meaningful and precise way. Without a common framework, it is difficult, for non-marketing managers in particular, to contribute to discussing the value and potential of a brand. When people do not contribute to the debate they tend to undervalue the importance of the brand, which can lead to weak management and inadequate investment. A model assists people to evaluate whether a brand is being managed effectively. Managers need to be able to judge, for example, whether an advertising campaign or a new design is consistent with the image of the brand and leverages its strengths. Finally, a model contributes to developing branding strategy. It illuminates the important issue of how to extend the brand to capture new growth opportunities.

Kapferer has presented an insightful model of a brand.[11] He suggests that the identity of most brands can be captured in six dimensions. Each dimension has to be managed to influence the customer's image of the brand. The six dimensions are:

1. **Physical.** This is the appearance of the brand in terms of its chosen name, colours, logo and packaging.

2. **Reflection.** This is the image of the target audience as reflected in the brand's communication, e.g. Coca-Cola reflects young people in its ads, even though the actual market is much wider.

3. **Relationship.** This refers to how the brand seeks to relate to the customer. Experience brands like the airlines Virgin Blue in Australia and Southwest Airlines in the United States position themselves as the customer's friend. An aspirational brand like Louis Vuiton invites you to join an exclusive club.
4. **Personality.** This is the character of the brand, e.g. IBM's personality is seriously professional, while Apple's is young and creative.
5. **Culture.** This refers to the background and values of the brand, e.g. Mercedes personifies German values, Nike celebrates the virtues of individualism.
6. **Self-image.** This is how the customer sees herself or himself in relation to the brand. For example, someone buying from The Body Shop may see herself as expressing her concern for the environment in choosing this brand.

In addition to the variables making up the brand identity, there is also the concept of the brand core. The core is the very essence of the brand — its DNA or guiding principle. The core of all the Virgin brands is the irreverent championing of 'us against them'. For Intel, it is advanced technology made effective. Figure 7.5 illustrates the application of the brand identity model to IBM and Apple.

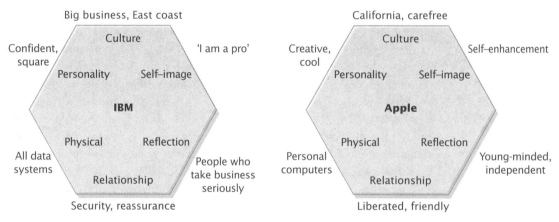

Figure 7.5: Brand identities for IBM and Apple

Issues in branding

Until relatively recently, the admired branding companies such as Procter & Gamble and Unilever employed a product branding philosophy. Each product was given an individual brand name and a unique market positioning was sought for it. This allowed each brand to be strongly differentiated and permitted the company to cover the market with individual brands targeted to each segment. It also reduced risk — a failure of one brand would not damage the rest of the business.

Brand extensions

Today, companies are shifting to extending brands — using the *same* brand name to cover new lines in the current product category, such as Diet Coke, and to cover new products in different categories altogether, such as Virgin Blue. One major reason is to reduce marketing costs. With costs of $100 million or more to develop a new brand with global reach, it is simply too expensive to launch different brand names. Companies increasingly want to focus their brand support around a smaller number of 'power brands'. A well-known brand name also facilitates new product acceptance among consumers and distribution channels who have been satisfied with the performance of the brand in the past, and will be willing to try its new offerings.

The changing concept of a brand also encourages brand extensions. Successful marketers are seeing that brands based around a shared experience are more resilient than attribute or aspirational brands. Experience brands break the tie between the product and the brand. In buying an experience brand such as The Body Shop, Virgin or Coca-Cola, consumers are not buying into a specific taste or design but rather into a particular personal philosophy. As long as the brand maintains its core values, consumers can accept its extension into different markets.

This is illustrated in figure 7.6. Product brands are limited in the perimeter of their brand extension possibilities to line extensions around an inner core. It is difficult to imagine the Persil brand stretching much beyond the washing area or the Whiskas brand being stretched beyond cats. Consumers would find such brand names attached to chocolate bars or financial services laughable. But aspirational brands and, in particular, experience brands have fewer constraints. Often, the experience brand can extend out from line extensions, to an outer core where consumers can make spontaneous associations with it, and then on to vast areas of latent potential that are consistent with the brand's core, yet are still outside the no-go area.

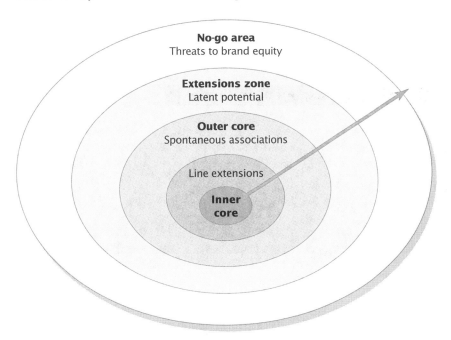

Figure 7.6 The perimeters of brand extension

Companies such as Virgin have become highly diversified businesses. The synergies arise not from financial controls, as in the old conglomerates such as ITT or BHP Billiton, nor from core technological competencies as at Mitsubishi or 3M, but rather from the synergies of sharing the same core brand. Until recently, strategists would frown on such diversification and advocate that companies should 'stick to their knitting'. This usually meant keeping to markets that utilised the same competencies. But in today's world, companies increasingly rely on networks and outsourcing arrangements to supply these competencies. For example, Singapore Airlines maintains Virgin's planes, Australia's AMP supplies its financial products, the Canadian company Cott produces its colas, and Deutsche Telekom its mobile phone facility. Production and technology skills are ceasing to be a constraint on the growth direction for companies with innovative ideas, strong brands and the new skill of managing networks.

The potential for brand extension is a key to the continuing value of companies. Strong brands give the company an option into new growth opportunities. Managers need to ask two questions. First, how strong are our principal brands? Second, are they principally attribute, aspirational or experience brands? Then, if the company has a strong brand, it can consider what new products could be built or acquired to leverage this brand strength.

Updating brands

Unilever's philosophy is that brands should have an infinite life. This may be correct, but what is certainly true is that products, brand themes and even markets can erode quickly. What makes brands fail? The foundation of any brand is its product. If the firm allows the quality of the product to erode, the brand will fail (see marketing management in practice 'Revitalising the Jaguar brand'). Even if the quality remains acceptable, technological advances, new competition, changing needs and new fashions invariably date products over time. No brand name can save a product that has become obsolete or irrelevant to consumers.

Marketing management in practice:	Revitalising the Jaguar brand

Founded in the 1920s, Jaguar was one of the greatest car brands, admired for its sporting successes and distinctive classic styling. But Jaguar failed to match the rising product quality standards that occurred in the car industry during the 1960s and 1970s. Disenchanted by their unreliability and poor finish, consumers switched to other brands, such as Mercedes and BMW. Eventually, the loss-making company was acquired by the Ford Motor Company. The first task was to improve Jaguar's quality and technology. But the new management recognised that these were entry requirements and were not enough to restore Jaguar to health. Chairman Walter Reitzle recognised that by the late 1990s 'there were no bad cars on the market; quality is now given, not a matter of differentiation'. Technology faced the same problem. Technology in the car industry was converging as the systems-supply industry consolidated. Today, if a car maker gets a lead on a new component, that advantage is fleeting. You might enjoy exclusivity on a breakthrough in technology for 12 months, maximum, says Reitzle. But because of the ramp-up curve involved in using technology, all your competitors will have it almost before the customer even realises that there is something new out there. In the late 1990s Jaguar was turned around. Between 1998 and 2002 sales volume nearly quadrupled. Once the quality and technology was brought back up to the market standard, what gave Jaguar the cutting edge was its unique brand. Through its marketing efforts, the business connected to a new community of customers who had little experience with the car, but who wanted to share the 'Jaguar experience'. This was a particularly British set of core values combining traditional style with a heritage of flair and sporting prowess.

Brand themes are also likely to get dated. The physical presentation of the product, including its packaging, colours and logos, will need to be updated if they are going to mirror current lifestyles. Similarly the brand's spokesperson and reflection need modernising as time progresses. Sometimes, the brand's market may erode, requiring radical repositioning. For example, more astute competition from Holden, a reduction in protectionist tariffs and the entry of new competitors sapped sales of Ford Australia. Consumers were less willing to sacrifice aesthetics for old-fashioned reliability. The brand had to be revitalised with new products, new themes and new relationships to fit today's car markets.

If a brand, or set of brands, ceases to generate value for shareholders, then management has four alternatives: repositioning, revitalisation, improving brand productivity or brand elimination.

» Brand repositioning

Repositioning the brand is a viable alternative if the brand has a weak position in an attractive market. There are several ways to do this:

- **Real repositioning.** Managers may need to update the product by improving its quality or updating its technology, functions or design. This is how Jaguar was turned around at the end of the 1990s.
- **Augmenting the brand.** Offering additional products and services alongside the core product can increase the brand's value. Hotels have added leisure facilities, bars and entertainment on top of their core product, accommodation.
- **Psychological repositioning.** The company can seek to change buyers' beliefs about the quality of the product's attributes, the status of the brand or the philosophy behind it. Unfortunately, people's beliefs, once formed, are difficult to alter.
- **Reweighting values.** Sometimes, buyers can be persuaded to attach greater importance to certain values in which the brand excels. Lexus, for example, emphasised quietness as a factor in choosing a luxury car.
- **Neglected values.** Occasionally, new attributes are introduced. In the United Kingdom, Unilever's new Radion detergent was positioned on the claim that it removes odours as well as dirt, an attribute not previously considered relevant in the market.
- **Changing preferences.** Sometimes, buyers can be persuaded to change their preferences. Scare stories in the media created a preference for non-genetically modified foods and ingredients.
- **Competitive depositioning.** In some countries, it is possible to use comparative advertising to undermine the value of competitors' brands.

» Brand revitalisation

Brand revitalisation is a strategy for when the brand is potentially strong but its current market is not sufficiently attractive to offer adequate profit opportunities. There are four ways forward:

1. **Find new markets.** Developing new international markets has been a key means of maintaining the growth of strong brands such as Billabong, Rip Curl, Coca-Cola, McDonald's and Qantas after they reached maturity in their home market.

brand revitalisation: strategy for when the brand is potentially strong but its current market is not sufficiently attractive to offer adequate profit opportunities

2. **Enter new segments.** Developing new segments is one of the most important ways to expand the market for a brand. Growing awareness in the market and falling prices are important stimuli, particularly in hi-tech markets. Line extensions are a flexible way to push into new market segments.

3. **Find new applications.** Companies can find new applications for the brand. The classic example is Arm & Hammer Baking Soda in the United States, which increased its sales by the factor 30 over the past 20 years by finding new applications for baking soda as a deodoriser and cleaner for refrigerators, sinks and animals, and even as a cleaning component in toothpaste.

4. **Increase the usage rate.** The average consumption rate can be increased, for example, by making the product easier to use (instant tea), reducing the disincentives to use (decaffeinated coffee), providing incentives for use (frequent flyer discounts) and finding new ways to increase the quantity consumed (large bottles).

» Improving brand productivity

brand profitability: the return on the total investment in a brand

When the market matures, it makes sense to take a harder look at **brand profitability**. First, costs — fixed and variable — can often be cut. However, management must recognise that reducing marketing spend may well lead to a long-term erosion of the brand's market share. Second, cash flow can be boosted by reducing working and fixed capital requirements. For mature products, it can pay to outsource production to contract manufacturers with lower cost structures. Third, raising prices will often boost short-term profits, even if volume declines. For example, if a brand has a contribution margin of 50 per cent and an operating margin of 8 per cent, then pushing up prices by 10 per cent will boost operating profits by a half, even if volume declines by 10 per cent.

Finally, in mature markets, it will often be possible to reduce the number of brands and product lines in the portfolio. Cutting off the tail of low-volume items will have a disproportionate benefit on working capital, with little volume loss. Nevertheless, all these measures produce benefits that are essentially short term and one-off. Management needs to simulate their long-term effects and value implications to check that long-term results are not being sacrificed.

» Brand elimination

Today, many companies have too many brands. Sometimes, it is because there is no longer a viable market for the brand and investing in repositioning or revitalising it does not look to be economical. Another common cause is where the company has grown by acquisitions and mergers. This frequently results in the company having a portfolio of overlapping and competing brands with no strategic rationale. With too many brands it then becomes impossible to support them adequately and marketing spend is spread too thinly to enable any of them to become genuine power brands. The result is that market share is undermined by smaller rivals which can focus their marketing investment behind a single brand to obtain critical mass. A 1999 report by KPMG found that two-thirds of mergers and acquisitions resulted in a net loss of market share and more than 80 per cent led to erosion of shareholder value.[12]

Companies such as Procter & Gamble and Colgate-Palmolive have shown that consolidating overlapping brands can cut costs, increase market share and boost shareholder value. This is illustrated in table 7.5 where a company consolidates two of its competing brands into one new brand. Market share by volume increases from 40 to 42 per cent because marketing spend is focused, effectively doubling the absolute level of brand support. Greater distribution power allows it to cut the level of trade discounts, which adds 1 per cent to the net price. Cost of goods is reduced because of greater buying power, and duplicated overheads are stripped out, resulting in a doubling of profits.

Table 7.5 Realising value through brand elimination

	BRAND A	BRAND B	NEW BRAND
Market share %	20	20	42
Cost of goods sold %	50	52	45
Gross margin %	50	48	55
Marketing %	25	25	25
Overheads %	15	15	12
Operating margin %	10	8	18

What prevents companies consolidating brands is fear over the loss of sales. How serious this problem will be depends on the degree of brand overlap and how the company implements the consolidation. Consolidating two brands into one is easier where the brands serve similar market segments, have overlapping brand images and when one is relatively weak. The problem is more complex where both are strong brands and they are serving different segments or distribution channels.

In implementing consolidation, a company has three routes to choose from:

1. **Phasing out the brand** is the appropriate approach if the brand to be eliminated has substantial brand equity and a significant base of customers. This policy keeps the old brand as long as necessary, but focuses promotion and development on the new brand. Effectively, it seeks to reduce the cost of carrying duplicate brands, with the objective of eliminating the overlap over time. Black and Decker followed this strategy after it bought the GE small appliances business. The GE brand was carefully phased out over a three-year period, allowing ample time for GE customers to understand the rebranding.

2. **Quick kill** means the immediate dropping of a brand name. This is a high-risk strategy but may become necessary if competition is ratcheting up the cost of supporting brands. It requires a very heavy investment in marketing and trade support if a loss of market share is to be avoided.

3. **Co-branding** is the most common transition strategy. Both brand names are kept on the new brand, giving consumers time to adjust. When Whirlpool bought Philips' household appliances business, the brand was marketed as Philips Whirlpool for the first six years. Another example is the way Westpac retained the name Bank of Melbourne after it acquired the

Victorian bank. To facilitate customer acceptance of the change of owner-ship, it was content simply to display the Westpac symbol next to the Bank of Melbourne logo.

Taking the brand international

Taking a brand into overseas markets is an obvious strategy for enhancing growth and shareholder value (see marketing management in practice 'Star-bucks' plans to profit from creating a home away from home for Australia's café habitués'). Indeed, in globally competitive environments it is an essential strategy to achieve scale economies and to justify the investment in the new products that will ensure the continuity of the company.

Marketing management in practice: **Starbucks' plans to profit from creating a home away from home for Australia's café habitués**

Starbucks [did] not [come] to Australia to teach the locals how to drink coffee, according to Peter Maslen, the man in charge of international operations for the world's biggest coffee-shop chain. However, the company may pass on a few lessons in how to build a brand ... 'Coffee consumption, and the coffee-house culture, is alive and well in Australia,' he says. 'I think it is a very sophisticated market, relative to many of the markets that we are in. We think we offer an alternative. But, in the end, the customer in Australia will be the judge. We will stand or fall on how well we can deliver' ...

The Starbucks chain has spread across North America, but it is still relatively small in over-seas markets. In 2000, it had 2500 shops worldwide, 350 of them outside the United States. Its biggest non-American markets are Britain and Japan, which each have 100 Starbucks out-lets. The company's [final] target is 10 000 shops in North America and 10 000 elsewhere. The move to Australia [in 2001 has] been on the drawing board for four years. The stumbling block was finding a local partner with the same 'cultural values' as Starbucks. The choice turned out to be Austrian-born restaurateur Markus Hofer.

For most Australians familiar with European-style coffee shops, Starbucks is different, and very American. 'Starbucks is a very people-oriented, community-minded organisation, almost in the extreme,' Maslen says. 'We never advertise. It is a brand built by really becoming involved in the community. We think we sell as good a coffee as anyone else in the world, but we also provide a very particular type of experience for our customers. We talk about it as the "third place" — home, work and then Starbucks.'

Maslen compares Starbucks to the pub in English society, without the 'downside' of alcohol. The target market is the entire family, from businesspeople using Starbucks as a meeting place during the day to children doing their homework after school. Starbucks shops in the US have leather armchairs, log fires, live music, the occasional poetry reading and a high proportion of cold drinks, including a Starbucks cold-coffee creation called Frappuccino. 'Think local' is the theme of each shop. 'We aim to be the biggest small company in the world,' Maslen says ...

Details of the deal with Hofer are private, but industry sources say Starbucks owns 95% of the venture and $40 million has been earmarked for developing Australian outlets. Maslen says Starbucks will not take market share from other coffee shops: it will build the total category. [In 2000,] the Australian coffee consumption [was] growing at 8.8% a year, but [it remained] far behind the market-leading Scandinavian countries and the US.

Maslen says a lot of Australia's coffee culture is tied to post-war immigration from southern Europe. Consumption in Melbourne, he says, is particularly well established. Although Starbucks and existing Australian cafes have coffee as a common theme, the real sales pitch for the newcomer is the 'home from home' atmosphere. Although Maslen says it works brilliantly with millions of people around the world, it might not be every Australian's cup of tea.

Source: Extracts from Tim Treadgold, 'Coffee chain blends home style with awareness', *BRW*, 5 May 2000, p. 36.

In developing overseas markets, a company can pursue one of three strategies. The first is multinational branding. This means developing different brands for each country and tailoring the marketing mix to local markets. This approach is broadly followed by Unilever, for example. The second approach is global branding where the brand name is standardised and the strategy is as far as possible similar in each country. The Ford Motor Company is an obvious example. The intermediate approach is regional branding, whereby companies such as GM try to build common brands and strategies in certain regions, such as Australia (Holden), continental Europe (Opel), or the United Kingdom and Ireland (Vauxhall).

» Local brands

The primary case for local brands rests on the great differences in language, culture and market conditions that still exist between most countries. A brand of breakfast cereal like Sanitarium that has meaning and broad appeal in Australia will rarely have the same resonance in Belgium or Finland. It seems obvious that an approach that designs the brand identity to the local language, preferences, traditions, climate and competition will do better. Another advantage of local branding is that it facilitates higher prices to be charged in less competitive markets. With common branding, parallel imports make differential pricing more difficult and this can lead to a significant loss of operating profit. A final important reason for local autonomy is that it encourages initiative, pride and responsibility for performance. Nothing destroys commitment like a faceless headquarters second-guessing local decisions and imposing strategies that the local management has not participated in developing.

» Global and regional brands

However, in most leading companies, there has been a significant shift towards regional and global branding. The drive to eliminate duplicate costs has been one reason. The cost of producing a TV commercial can easily amount to $3 million. The advertising agency McCann-Erickson claims to have saved Coca-Cola almost US$100 million in the past 20 years by producing commercials with international appeal. A global strategy facilitates a faster international launch, which reduces the danger of the brand being pre-empted by competitors. It also enhances shareholder value by accelerating cash flow.

On top of this, a number of forces in today's information society encourage a move towards global or regional branding. These include the growth of international business, the emergence of global media such as CNN and SkyTV, the explosion of tourism and international business travel, and the development of common standards like the Internet and GSM. All of these encourage the emergence of international lifestyles, or more accurately, the emergence of market segments that transcend geographical boundaries. Scientists in different countries want the same brands of equipment, teenagers the same clothing and yuppies the same symbols as their peers abroad. Finally, the pace of technological progress and innovation has meant that people are increasingly spending on new products that have fewer cultural heritages to hinder global branding.

Global brands can make more efficient use of the new international media and the Internet. They can also uniquely exploit the growing popularity of international events such as the World Cup, the Olympics and Formula One, and the sponsorship of international stars such as Tiger Woods, Michael Jackson or the All Blacks. International brands often also obtain a premium status from the glamour they possess. Finally, an international reputation facilitates brand extensions and entry into new markets. Global brands often have a stature that gives customers confidence in trying their offerings.

» Constraints on global branding

The constraints on global branding are external and internal. Some markets are still so idiosyncratic that global brands have limited potential. Often, a brand name does not make sense in another market. Snuggles fabric softener has to be translated as Cajoline in France and Cocolino in Italy, for example. Culture and tradition also prevent common approaches. For instance, a basic product like cheese plays different roles in different countries: in The Netherlands, it is mostly consumed at breakfast; in France it is served after the main course at dinner; in the United Kingdom it is mostly consumed at lunch in sandwiches. Different laws, climates and traditions can all create constraints on a common brand identity.

Factors internal to the organisation also have an important influence on the development of global brands. A key factor is history. The first international companies were European and were well established by the beginning of the 20th century. Then the slowness of international travel and rudimentary international communication forced these companies to delegate decision making to the local markets. Distance made central control from European headquarters simply impractical. Many companies like Unilever and Nestlé have maintained much of this pattern of multinational marketing until the present day. Global branding is much more associated with US and German companies and, later, the Japanese. German companies, which became prominent internationally after the Second World War, pursued an ethnocentric approach — they sold to a willing overseas market the products that had been successful in the home market, usually with only the minimum necessary adaptation. In the 1960s, Japanese companies such as Toyota and Sony introduced the first real global branding strategies. These were uniform products with a global brand name, designed to match the needs of international markets.

In recent years, the tendency has been to shift towards what is called **transnational marketing**. This might be loosely defined as seeking to standardise those elements of the brand where this is possible, but recognising that often it makes sense to adapt to local conditions. Generally, this approach leads to asymmetrical, pragmatic strategies; companies will invest in adapting to local conditions in the biggest markets such as the United States, Japan and Germany, but not in smaller countries. Traditional brands that are part of the culture and heritage of a market will be left as they are. New products, particularly those in new categories or using new technology, will be much more geared to a global approach.

The elements of the brand's marketing mix also vary in the degree to which they can be standardised. Generally, the core product is standardised across countries. Product functionality and use (e.g. how people listen to music or drive a bulldozer) tend to be fairly similar, internationally. Also, economies of scale are important here, as product development and manufacture are

transnational marketing: the standardisation of those elements of the brand where it is possible, and the adaptation of those elements to local conditions where it makes sense or is necessary

high-investment areas. The features of the basic brand — design, packaging, logo and name — can also often be standardised across countries, if planned systematically.

At the next level of branding — the positioning and communication — the difficulties begin to mount as culture, attitudes, language and economics impinge on the interpretation of the brand's meaning. The degree of standardisation possible varies with the market and the product. National values and traditions are still very important in food, but less so in electronics. Culture is less important in youth and more affluent markets than it is in mature, low-income ones. Moving further down the marketing chain to selling, promotion and distribution, these decisions are invariably specified locally because of sharp differences that normally occur in market and institutional characteristics across countries.

The shift from national to transnational branding and marketing is reshaping how companies are managed. Many of the biggest multinationals, such as Unilever and Procter & Gamble, have restructured to create international product divisions to replace the old country business units. Strategic decisions about brands are increasingly taken with a view to leveraging their full international potential and looking for global efficiencies in production and marketing. Most companies have sought to avoid building large central bureaucracies and rather aimed to use teams of local managers cooperating to develop international branding strategy.

Controlling the brand franchise

Today competition is not between single companies, but between networks. A network consists of all those companies in the supply chain that contribute components, services or knowledge to the ultimate product bought by the final customer. So IBM and its network of suppliers, partners and retailers compete with those of Dell to design and deliver desirable brands of personal computer to consumers. Coles Myer's network competes with that of David Jones to develop and execute the best retail concept.

» Who controls the brand?

All companies participate in networks. A key issue to participants in a network is who controls the brand. In general, the participant that controls the brand that consumers value makes the greatest economic profit. Traditionally the manufacturer, such as the Ford Motor Company, IBM or General Electric, has usually controlled the brand. The manufacturer normally tries to commoditise suppliers' inputs to push down costs and stimulate competition among them. But manufacturers do not always succeed and sometimes the supplier succeeds in wresting brand power from, or at least sharing it with, the manufacturer. Intel and Microsoft are striking examples of this phenomenon. The images of Intel and Microsoft are so powerful among final consumers that computer manufacturers are forced to purchase their components. The result is that much of the profit in the industry has migrated to these two component suppliers.

The distribution channels — wholesalers, retailers or the new e-businesses — can also control the brand power. One of the major trends in the past few decades has been the growth of retailer own-label brands. The large supermarket groups have succeeded in substituting their own brands for manufacturers' brands over an increasing percentage of their shelf space. Again, this has led to a transfer of value from manufacturer to retailer as the former's output has become increasingly commoditised, in other words, increasingly non-differential. Today, the growth of e-business is bringing in new participants to the struggle for who controls the consumer brand franchise. On the one hand, electronic commerce can restore the power of the manufacturer by allowing it to 'disintermediate' — cut out the retailer and go direct to the end consumer, as Dell did so successfully in the 1990s. On the other hand, e-commerce brings in a new breed of retailer like Amazon.com and eToys that can offer customers product ranges far superior to any that have been offered by retailers in the past. Other threats to traditional brand hegemony are the Internet navigators, including search engines such as Yahoo!, evaluators such as Consumer Reports, databases such as Auto Trader and software programs such as Quicken. All of these can become, and indeed are becoming, the brands in which more consumers are placing their trust. When this happens, power in the network changes in favour of the organisation that controls the most trusted brand.

The implications of a loss of brand control are severe. If a company's product is seen as a commodity or a mere label, it loses its ability to drive profitable growth. Customers will buy on price and there will be no barriers to switching to alternative suppliers. This is what happened to the personal computer manufacturers when they effectively ceded brand power upstream to the suppliers of their operating system and microprocessors. Computers became little more than low margin commodities while their suppliers, Microsoft and Intel, became immensely profitable. The same problem occurred with many textile and grocery goods manufacturers that became own-label suppliers to powerful branded retail groups. The enhanced bargaining power of the retailer often enabled them to appropriate all the economic profit of the manufacturers.

» Manufacturing or branding

Companies increasingly have to choose between investing heavily in brands or becoming contract manufacturers for other branded businesses. The problem facing many firms is that they have got 'stuck in the middle' as the tide of global competition has washed away established relationships.

Contract manufacturing is a rapidly growing area of business as companies increasingly outsource production. But global competition and global sourcing have made contract manufacturing much more demanding than it was in the past. To be a profitable contract manufacturer, a company has to minimise its cost structure on a global scale. Generally, this will mean locating production facilities in countries with the cheapest facilities and lowest labour costs, or where valuable resources are most abundant. It means minimising overheads and tight operational control.

Developing a strategy based on building strong brands leads to a different philosophy and organisation. A contract manufacturer focuses on production and costs; a branded business focuses on marketing and innovation. A contract manufacturer produces to a customer's specifications; a branded company has to discover what specifications consumers will want. The former has very low marketing costs; the latter needs to invest heavily in marketing to understand consumers and to build and communicate the brand. The personnel of a branded goods company have to be close to the market; those of the contract manufacturer have to be located where costs are minimised.

Given these completely different orientations, it is not surprising that trying to be both a low-cost manufacturer and a sophisticated marketer is increasingly a strategy that is difficult to make work. The danger is that in striving to be both, the company's philosophy and organisation becomes fatally compromised. It lacks, on the one hand, the cost structure to compete with global contract manufacturers and, on the other, the creativity and investment in branding to compete with those companies like Virgin and Amazon.com that focus entirely on innovation, marketing and branding.

Organising the brand portfolio

When a company goes beyond marketing one product, it has to decide how its products and brands should be related. It can market all its additional products under the same umbrella brand, as for example Canon does with its cameras, copiers, faxes and office equipment, or it can do the opposite, developing a separate brand name for each new product, as Procter & Gamble has traditionally done. In between, there are various other alternatives, including line brands, range brands and source branding strategies.[13]

A dilemma arises because management has to balance three partly conflicting goals. One goal is to differentiate the product from others it already markets. Generally, it only makes sense to introduce another product if it will do something differently, or appeal to a different group of customers. From this point of view, separate brand names are attractive. The second goal is to leverage the strengths and associations of the current brand name. This implies an advantage in using the existing brand name. Thirdly, cost factors have to be considered — the objective is not to maximise sales but to increase long-run economic profits. This again leads to an orientation to sharing brand names.

brand architecture:
a system that shows how brands in a firm's brand portfolio should be related to each other

brand portfolio:
a set of brands managed by the firm

The right **brand architecture** should result in a system that makes sense to consumers. The branding system should indicate to them how products are differentiated from each other. Managers inside the company should also understand the logic of the system and when a new product should have a separate name, or when it should share an existing name. Finally, the architecture should facilitate the growth in value of the **brand portfolio** as a whole by enabling it to be effectively communicated and promoted.

Brand architecture

The main difference between branding strategies is in the way they make the trade-off between differentiation and shared identity. There are six main brand strategies:

1. **Product brands** exist where the company assigns a unique name and positioning to each of its products. So, in the detergents market Procter & Gamble has Tide, Ariel, Vizir and Dash brands, each with its own target market segment and differential advantage. The Accor Group has developed multiple brands of hotels, each with its own positioning strategy — Novotel, Ibis, Formula 1, Sofitel, etc. The corporate name plays no role in the marketing of the brands to consumers — the focus is entirely on differentiation rather than shared identity.

2. **Line brands** are when a company has several complementary products sharing the same brand concept. For example, rather than individual product brands, L'Oréal sells a shampoo, hair spray, gel and lacquer under the Studio Line of hair products. Selling a brand line rather than individual brands can reinforce the brand's selling power and reduce marketing costs.

3. **Range brands** include a broader array of products than with line brands, but still limit the extension of the brand name to the same area of competence. For example, Nestlé uses the name Findus for its range of frozen food products and Heinz uses the Weight Watchers brand for its diet range.

4. **Source brands** are double-branded with a corporate or range name plus a product brand name. Examples are Kellogg's Corn Flakes, Castrol GTX and Johnnie Walker Black Label. The corporate name conveys identity and associations and the product brand focuses it to a particular segment.

5. **Endorsing brands** are a weaker association of the corporate name with the product brand name. Here the product brand is the dominant name and the umbrella endorsement merely aims to guarantee the brand's quality. Nestlé, General Motors and Johnson & Johnson follow this approach in endorsing, for example, their brands Kit-Kat, Holden and Pledge, respectively. An endorsing brand strategy is often an intermediate step as companies seek to shift away from product branding to range or umbrella branding strategies.

6. **Umbrella brands** are when one brand supports several products in very different markets. For example, Philips sells computers, phones, hi-fi, televisions, electric shavers and office equipment using the same name. This is the opposite strategy to product branding. Here the focus is on shared identity at the expense of differentiation. The main advantages are sharing brand-building costs. The main threat is what is called the 'rubber band effect' — the more the brand is stretched across different categories, the more likely the brand's identity is going to be weakened until its credibility and meaning are broken.

Choosing a branding strategy

Competing companies often adopt quite different branding strategies. In the hotel market, Accor uses product branding, while Sheraton uses source branding. In the Australian budget airline market, Virgin Blue launched under its umbrella brand Virgin. In the luxury car market, Toyota created a new product brand, Lexus. What are the criteria for deciding the right approach?

History again plays a big role. Many firms would not have the current number of product brands if they were starting afresh. Companies such as Procter & Gamble adopted a product branding approach in an era when competition was less fierce and margins were high enough to cover the heavy marketing costs involved in this strategy. Change today is difficult. For example, the Procter & Gamble name has no equity with consumers and so the type of umbrella branding favoured by Sony or Virgin is just not practicable.

A second factor is the power and type of brand. An umbrella or source branding strategy is not possible if the brand does not have strong added values, if it is little more than a label. Here, if a new product is thought to have potential, it is best launched under an individual brand name. Experience brands usually have more potential for umbrella or source branding than do attribute or aspirational brands. For example, BA aims to be an aspirational brand, so launching a budget brand would risk weakening its core values. In contrast, Virgin is an experience brand — 'us against them' — with core values that shift easily into a budget offer. However, if the brand is exceptionally strong, it is possible for aspirational brands to stretch downwards as long as the new product's status is indicated. For example, DaimlerChrysler indicates the positioning of the different Mercedes-Benz models by affixing the letters S, E, C and A to the appropriate ranges.

If a product is truly innovative in its attributes or concept, then product branding is attractive to highlight its originality. The Ford Motor Company wisely decided not to risk diluting the equity in the Jaguar brand by source branding. Product branding is also a way of reducing risks when there are hazards with a product's technology or side effects, which could be the subject of damaging publicity. Pharmaceutical companies selling novel medicines invariably use product branding.

A third factor is the attractiveness of the market. Developing separate brands is hugely expensive and most of the costs are fixed. Such an investment can only generate an economic return if the revenue and profits available are large. Umbrella branding is often the most effective way to enter smaller markets or where the opportunities to gain a high market share are limited.

Valuing the brand

The issue of whether brands should appear as assets on the balance sheet has become controversial. A spate of hostile take-overs and asset stripping of brand-rich companies led to the accusation that, because brands were excluded from the balance sheet, these companies were undervalued and easy prey to corporate raiders. Conventional accounting treats investments in internal brand-building as costs to be set against current profits. When brands were acquired externally, their 'goodwill' value was not carried permanently on the balance sheet, but had to be either amortised against profits over a number of years, or written off against shareholder funds. Thus, traditional accounting made developing or acquiring brands an unattractive proposition, especially in the short term before the additional profits they would generate could offset their costs.

The enormous and increasing divergence between the balance sheet and market valuations of companies has led to a prolonged debate in the accountancy profession about including brands and other intangibles. Currently, an unsatisfactory compromise has emerged at the international level. The International Accounting Standards Board has recommended that acquired brands, but not internally generated ones, be permitted to be capitalised and treated separately to goodwill on the balance sheet. If acquired brands are included they must be amortised over 20 years on a straight-line basis. For non-accountants this compromise is difficult to rationalise. It is hard to see why an acquired brand should be seen as a more valuable or secure asset than an internally built one. For example, Cadbury-Schweppes Plc can include Dr Pepper on its balance sheet, but not its Cadbury's or Schweppes brands. Similarly, it is not obvious why a powerful historic brand that does appear on the balance sheet should have to be amortised against profits even though it may be increasing in value.

The pros and cons of valuation

Behind the debate about brands on the balance sheet is a more fundamental controversy among accountants about what accounts are for.[14] The conservative wing believes that financial accounts should record only historical transactions, and assets should be valued at their cost, as only these have a solid factual base. Once accounts start trying to portray current 'values', it is argued, then they become subjective and inherently imprudent. This view argues that such revaluations are also unnecessary since the purpose of financial accounts is to provide facts not judgments. They are a means to an end, not an end in themselves. The interpretation of the value of a company and its assets is the responsibility of the user, not the accountant. This interpretation may use the financial accounts, but it will almost certainly require information from other sources about the industry, competition, stock market valuations and other factors relevant to future cash flow.

The liberal wing of the profession takes the view that financial accounts should be constructed to provide information that helps a wide range of audiences to make economic decisions. So investors should be able to see from the accounts what their shares are worth, banks and suppliers should be able to judge whether a company is safe to do business with and employees should be able to see how the value of the company is changing over time. This means that assets should be revalued to reflect current rather than historic costs. As far as possible, intangible assets should be included in the balance sheets and brands should be shown separately if their values can be identified. Also, an asset should only be depreciated if it is declining in value over time. If the value of the asset is increasing, not only should there be no depletion charge, but the asset should be written up in value every year.

brand valuation: the value of a brand as it would appear explicitly on the balance sheet (i.e. as it would appear as a separate item on the balance sheet)

The pros and cons of **brand valuation** largely reflect the views of the liberals and conservatives respectively. The conservatives argue against brands appearing on the balance sheet. First, any valuation of brands is highly subjective. Different methods and different valuers will give completely different valuations. Second, it is impossible to separate the earnings that are created from the brand name from those generated by the company's other tangible and intangible assets. Can one really separate the value created by the Cadbury's brand name from the values created by the quality of its product and its other intangible assets, including specialist skills and long-standing supply chain relationships? Third, all the arbitrary assumptions needed to come up with brand valuations would make financial accounts open to the criticism of being mere 'window dressing', devoid of a factual basis. Finally, it is argued that brand valuations are unnecessary since market values demonstrate that investors make their own forecasts of the future cash generating value of the business that clearly take into account all its tangible and intangible assets. It is better that investors take responsibility for their own judgments than for the company's accountants to publish their subjective estimates of the future.

The liberal case for valuing brands can be summarised under three headings. First, there is a clear conceptual case for treating brands as assets. Strong brands do offer their owners an enhanced and more secure cash flow than they would have without the brand. This is because they create a greater degree of customer preference and loyalty than weak — or non-branded products. Second, new methodologies permit brand earnings to be separated and valued in ways that are conceptually sound and practical to use. Finally, there are many situations where brand valuations are not a matter of choice — their use is a business requirement.

Uses of brand valuation

In recent years, brand valuations have become essential for a wide variety of purposes. These include:

- **Balance sheet reporting.** Many countries have now begun to require companies to show acquired brands on the balance sheet. To apply the new requirements, companies need defensible methods for valuing brands.
- **Mergers and acquisitions.** Up to 90 per cent of the price an acquirer pays for a branded goods company is represented by intangible assets, most of these being brands. Brand valuations play an important role in assessing whether such acquisitions can be justified.
- **Investor relations.** Companies such as Unilever and L'Oreal state as their central objective the creation of a portfolio of powerful brands. Brand valuations are an important way in which these companies can signal their strengths to the stock market.
- **Internal management.** Brand valuations are being used internally to judge the performance of different business units. They also encourage managers involved in budgeting decisions to assess the long-term impact on brand performance and not just the short-run effects of decisions on profits.
- **Licensing and franchising.** Companies often allow subsidiaries or third parties to use their brand name. An accurate valuation of the brand is necessary to arrive at a fair royalty rate.
- **Securitised borrowing.** As brands have become increasingly recognised as valuable assets, companies have been able to use their valuations as specific backing for loans.
- **Legal arguments.** Brand valuations are often used in legal cases involving such issues as damage to the brand caused by piracy, or in asset valuations for insolvency proceedings.
- **Tax planning.** Tax authorities are increasingly demanding companies charge royalties to their foreign affiliates for the use of their brand names.

Key issues in brand valuation

Any brand valuation methodology has to deal with the following issues.

- **Forecasting free cash flow.** The value of an asset is given by the net present value of its future free cash flow. This means forecasts have to be made of sales, operating profits, actual taxes to be paid and net investments in working capital and fixed assets. It is important that the forecast only refers to the sales of the brand being valued. If unbranded goods or other brands are also being produced, their figures must be excluded.
- **Calculating the brand value added.** This is a two-step process of identifying first the incremental cash flow generated by the intangible assets of the business, then separating the proportion of this additional cash flow that can be attributed to value provided by the brand name.
- **Determining the discount factor.** Future cash flows have to be discounted to their present day value. The discount rate that should be used depends on the vulnerability and volatility of the brand's cash flow.

Alternative valuation approaches

Assets can be valued using different assumptions and methods. If assets are being valued for tax purposes, the taxpayer will want to use assumptions that will produce a low value. Someone selling an asset will take an opposite approach. The method may also vary with the purpose of the valuation — the method that may be acceptable in a legal case may not be useful in an acquisition analysis. There are several 'traditional' brand valuation methods, as described next, and the modern approach, based on estimating the discounted value of future brand cash flow, which is described in detail in the following section.

- **Cost-based valuation.** This values a brand on what it costs to create. Here past advertising and other brand-building expenditures are converted into today's prices and added together. Such a method is sometimes used in legal cases to calculate compensation. But the fundamental problem with this method is that historical costs bear no relation to current values. In theory a brand could also be valued on a replacement cost basis, i.e. what it would cost to recreate now. But the problem is that a strong brand is by definition unique, so finding its replacement value is not normally a practical exercise.

- **Market-based valuation.** This values the brand on the basis of recent sales of comparable brands or businesses. For example, if a comparable company was sold at a multiple of four times book value, then this multiple can be used to value the current business. Tangible assets are then deducted from the implied stock market value to arrive at the value of intangible assets, and the proportion of these intangibles represented by the brand is estimated. The problems with this approach are that in practice it is complicated by companies often having several brands as well as some unbranded production, and that finding comparable companies and brands is very difficult.

- **Royalty relief valuation.** This values the brand by estimating what the company would have had to pay in royalties to a third party if did not own the brand name. The theoretical royalties that would be paid in the future are then discounted to arrive at the net present value of the brand. A number of the top accountancy firms regard this as the most effective valuation method. One problem with the approach is determining the royalty percentage to be applied to forecast sales. In practice, detailed information about rates is difficult to obtain, and they vary considerably according to arrangements about using patents, copyrights and shared marketing costs, as well as with the expected profits and market circumstances. Rates also tend to vary according to the industry and country being licensed.

- **Economic use valuation.** This values the brand's net contribution to the business by using a representative multiple of historic earnings attributable to the brand. So, for example, if a weighted average of the past three years post-tax brand earnings was estimated at $15 million and the earnings multiple is 10, then the brand is valued at $150 million. Until recently, this was the most popular method and it is still currently used by the magazine *Financial World* in its well-known annual estimates of the values of the leading US brands. The basic problem with this method is that historical earnings are a poor guide to future performance. Also, the method produces brand valuations that are highly volatile because they are so dependent on profits earned in the year the valuation is made.

Discounted cash flow valuation

Like the economic use method, the discounted cash flow (DCF) method estimates the return shareholders receive from owning the brand name. The difference from the earnings multiple approach is that the DCF approach is based on explicit forecasts of future earnings attributable to the brand. The advantage of this method is that it mirrors the approach investors use to value a company's assets and, therefore, it links brand values to share values. The approach deals explicitly with each of the three issues in brand valuation: forecasting cash flow, separating the value created by the brand from that attributable to tangible and other intangible assets, and identifying the appropriate discount rate. This approach to brand valuation has been recently developed and popularised by the Interbrand consultancy.[15]

» **Forecasting cash flow**

As with standard shareholder value analysis, the approach starts with managers forecasting sales and operating margins over a reasonable planning period, usually 5–10 years. Care has to be taken to eliminate any sales and earnings due to other brands or unbranded products. Cash flows after the planning period are estimated by a continuing value approach, usually the perpetuity method, which assumes that the brand continues to earn its cost of capital in perpetuity. The first two rows of table 7.6 show forecast sales and operating earnings for an illustrative brand.

Table 7.6 Valuing the brand ($ million)

YEAR	BASE	1	2	3	4	5
Sales	250.0	262.5	275.6	289.4	303.9	319.1
Operating profits (15%)	37.5	39.4	41.3	43.4	45.6	47.9
Tangible capital employed	125.0	131.3	137.8	144.7	151.9	159.5
Charge for capital @ 5%	6.3	6.6	6.9	7.2	7.6	8.0
Economic value added	31.2	32.8	34.4	36.2	38.0	39.9
Brand value added @ 70%	21.8	23.0	24.1	25.3	26.6	27.9
Tax (30%)	6.6	6.9	7.2	7.6	8.0	8.4
Post-tax brand earnings	15.2	16.1	16.9	17.7	18.6	19.5
Discount factor ($r = 15\%$)	1.0	0.87	0.76	0.66	0.57	0.5
Discounted cash flow	15.2	14.0	12.8	11.7	10.6	9.7

Cumulative present value	58.8
Present value of residual	64.8
Brand value	123.5

» **Estimating brand earnings**

This is a two-step approach: (1) separate earnings due to tangible assets from those due to intangible assets, and (2) separate intangible earnings into those attributable to the brand name and those attributable to other intangibles such as patents, special skills or monopolistic advantages.

• **Earnings on intangibles.** These are the residual earnings after the return on tangible assets has been deducted from total operating profits. First, the tangible assets employed in the business — for example, plant, ware-housing, creditors and stock — are calculated. These assets are valued at their realisable market value. Because they are included at realisable values, ownership risk is minimised, so a reasonable return is the risk free bor-rowing rate, usually taken as the yield on ten-year government bonds. Operating earnings less the capital charge gives economic value added. This residual profit is the return on intangible assets.

- **Earnings from the brand.** The next step is to judge the percentage of these intangible earnings that can be attributed to the brand. For some consumer goods, such as perfume or fashions, the brand is the major intangible item. For others, such as speciality chemicals or prescription pharmaceuticals, patents, technical know-how and personal relationships with key cus-tomers are more important than the brand name. In other words, they would sell almost as well under another name. Interbrand's approach involves two distinct steps. First, analyse the brand and its market to identify and rate the importance of the key strategic business drivers. Second, assess the extent to which each business driver is dependent on the brand. If the driver would be just as effective without the brand, then the brand makes no contribution.

» **Determining the discount factor**

Future brand earnings have to be discounted to arrive at their present value. The discount factor depends upon the volatility and vulnerability of these future earnings. Interbrand has developed a technique called the 'brand strength index' to determine the discount rate. A brand is rated on seven attri-butes that are taken to indicate the strength of the brand. Each attribute has the maximum score shown in parentheses.

1. **Market** (10). Brands in stable growing markets with strong barriers to entry are the most attractive. So food brands will score higher than high-tech brands on this attribute
2. **Stability** (15). Long-established brands that command consumer loyalty score better than new ones, or brands that have been erratically managed in the past.
3. **Leadership** (25). Strong brand leaders score better than brands with small market shares.
4. **Internationality** (25). Brands that have proven international acceptance and appeal are inherently stronger than national brands.
5. **Trend** (10). Brands demonstrating consistent volume growth score higher.
6. **Support** (10). Brands that have a record of receiving systematic and focused investment have a stronger franchise.
7. **Protection** (5). Brands with registered trademarks and strong legal protection score higher.

Brands can score up to a maximum of 100 points. The higher the strength score, the less risk is attached to the brand and the lower should be the dis-count rate. Interbrand has developed an 'S' curve chart with the brand strength score on the y-axis and the discount rate on the x-axis. So a perfect brand (scoring 100) has a discount rate of 5 per cent, somewhat higher than the average long-term real rate of return on a risk-free investment. An average brand with a score of 50 has a discount rate of 15 per cent.

A variation of the Interbrand approach, called 'Brand Beta Analysis', has been proposed by Haigh.[16] This calculates the appropriate discount rate from four factors:

1. **Risk-free rate of return**, taken as the 10-year government bond yield.
2. **Equity risk premium**, the extra return investors expect for investing in companies rather than 'risk-free' government bonds.
3. **Specific market sector risk** adjusts the equity premium. For example, the equity risk premium is generally lower in a stable food market than in a high-tech sector.
4. **Brand risk profile** is then used to adjust the average discount rate to the vulnerability of the specific brand.

For the brand risk profile, Haigh presents a scoring method, based on a list of factors analogous to the brand strength index, to produce a brand beta score, which is again marked out of 100. For example, Coca-Cola can expect a much lower risk rating than, say, Virgin Cola. The beta score varies from 0 for a perfect brand to 2 for an unbranded product. In the example of table 7.5, the risk-free rate at the time is 5 per cent, the average equity risk premium is 7 per cent, the specific market sector risk is averaged at 1.0, and it is a relatively new brand with an above-average beta calculated at 1.43, so the discount rate is then $5 + (7 \times 1.0) \times 1.43 = 15$ per cent.

The brand is valued in table 7.5 at $123.5 million. Of its forecast total earnings, approximately 17 per cent is attributed to earnings on tangible assets, 83 per cent to intangible assets and 58 per cent to the associations created by the brand name. Of the $123.5 million brand value, $58.8 million was due to cash flow added in the planning period; the remainder was its continuing value at the end of the period. This continuing value is estimated by the familiar perpetuity method. The continuing value reflects the fact that well-managed brands can last indefinitely.[17]

Summary

1. A firm's intangible assets are more important than its balance sheet assets in creating value for customers and shareholders. In many companies, brands represent one of the most valuable of these intangible assets.
2. Brands create value for customers by assisting them to reduce risks and by simplifying the choice process. Brand names may offer customers confirmation of their quality, status or the promise of shared experiences.
3. Brands create value for shareholders by increasing the level of cash flow, accelerating its timing, increasing the business's residual value and reducing the risk associated with cash flow.
4. Brand identities, once communicated, have to be periodically updated by brand repositioning and revitalisation. Improving brand productivity and eliminating redundant brands can also sometimes increase shareholder value. Brand identity may not correlate with brand image.
5. Today companies compete within a network of suppliers, distributors and partners. A critical issue is who controls the brand. Value in a network tends to migrate towards the organisation that holds the brand name.
6. Brands can be valued using discounted cash flow analysis. This links brand values directly to the company's own market value.

key terms

aspirational brand, p. 244
attribute brand, p. 244
brand, p. 238
brand architecture, p. 265
brand equity, p. 238
brand extensions, p. 248
brand identity, p. 252
brand image, p. 242

brand portfolio, p. 265
brand profitability, p. 258
brand revitalisation, p. 257
brand valuation, p. 268
experience brand, p. 244
label, p. 239
transnational marketing, p. 262

review questions

1. Describe how brands create value for customers.
2. How do brands create value for shareholders?
3. How are successful brands built?
4. Show how brand extensions can be a means of creating value.
5. Describe how a multiproduct organisation can structure its portfolio to control the costs and maximise the effectiveness of its brands.
6. Describe how brands can be valued. What uses can brand valuations have? How confident can you be in a brand valuation?

discussion questions

1. How and why do brands establish relationships with customers? How does the organisation of the brand portfolio contribute to the establishment and maintenance of this relationship? What is the link between the organisation of the brand portfolio and customer value?
2. Critically analyse the association between developing brand identity and brand extensions. How and why are the two components linked? Which of the two would be more important for the expansion of a brand internationally?
3. How can a company control a brand franchise? Is it more important to manufacture or brand? Is this the same for all markets?
4. Which brand valuation approach is more accurate and why? Can you suggest a new method of brand valuation? Use each method to estimate the value of your university's brand name.

debate questions

1. Are brands merely product names?
2. Are attribute brands more prevalent in the market than experience brands?
3. Is it more important to extend a brand or to create new brands? Is this the same for (a) growth markets? (b) mature markets? (c) volatile markets?
4. Is brand repositioning more beneficial for customer value creation or shareholder value creation?

case study | Branded Virgin — Sir Richard's empire expansion

Question: What do the following have in common?

- Cars
- Mobile telephones
- Wedding dresses
- Cars
- Music
- Hot air balloons
- Soft drinks
- Insurance

Answer: They've all been branded Virgins, along with more than 200 other disparate goods and services.

An eclectic range of products fall under the Virgin umbrella, and new goods are regularly added to the stable. You can now drink Virgin cola after touching up your Virgin makeup while flying on a Virgin plane. When you arrive at your destination, chances are that you'll be able to call your friends on your Virgin mobile phone to join you shopping with your Virgin credit card.

Has this enormous diversity hurt the brand? No, according to Virgin founder, Sir Richard Branson. Recent market research had Virgin in the top two most respected brands in the United Kingdom.[18] The Business Superbrands Council sees the Virgin Atlantic brand as 'distinctive, fun loving and innovative'.[19] While other famous brands, such as Microsoft and Coke, are associated with and specialise in one area, how has Virgin been able to diversify so successfully?

According to market observers, the Virgin brand has a strong reputation for innovation and taking on large competitors who may have become complacent or lazy. MT Rainey, managing partner of Virgin's ad agency Rainey Kelly Campbell Roalfe, stated 'If your products match that reputation, you can swap between diverse businesses'.[20]

Virgin is also inextricably linked with its flamboyant founder. Branson started in the 1970s with a student newspaper and mail order record service that soon turned into a discount music business. The Virgin umbrella now incorporates more than 200 companies and has made Branson a lot of money — not bad for a dyslexic whose headmaster wrote 'I predict you will either go to prison or become a millionaire'. He is well known for such stunts as wearing a wedding gown to launch Virgin Brides, making a Mad Hatter entrance on a float with transvestites and cheerleaders for high tea in Boston, and driving a tank into Times Square.

Despite his high-profile at the helm of Virgin, Branson feels that his staff are his key assets. He reasons that happy staff provide high standards of service, which contributes to high levels of customer satisfaction. This in turn services the interests of shareholders.

Not every Branson endeavour has been a success. One failure was a fire inhibitor; the partnership has since gone up in smoke. Branson failed in his bid to run the National Lottery and Virgin trains were plagued with service problems at the outset. Like other airlines, Virgin Airlines has suffered since September 11.

There are also some goods that Branson won't brand with the Virgin logo. Cigarettes are a notable example; he doesn't want to encourage young people to smoke.

Some observers have warned that there is danger in being too diverse and straying too far from what you know best. Alan Brew, principal at Addison Branding & Communications in New York, warns 'Virgin makes no sense; it's completely unfocused'. The Virgin brand may be diluted as it continues to extend into seemingly unrelated goods and services. Developing sub-brands of the parent brand may be a way of overcoming this problem.

What of the future? Expect Virgin cars fitted with Virgin mobile phones driving into the garages of homes equipped with Virgin products, all insured with Virgin insurance.

(continued)

Sources: Donna L. Goodison, 'Virgin's Sir Richard keeps reinventing, expanding brand', *Boston Business Journal*, 1 March 2002; www.bizjournals.com/, accessed 19 November 2002; *The Guardian*, 8 July 2002; media.guardian.co.uk/Print/0,3858,4448647,00.html, accessed 19 November 2002; Alison Smith, 'A good reputation is the key to Virgin's diversity', *Sunday Times*, 20 September 1997; www.btimes.co.za/97/0921/world/world.htm, accessed 19 November 2002; Chris Macrae, 'Branson on managing Virgin' www.allaboutbranding.com/; Virgin Online, www.virgin.com/aboutus/story.shtml; Melanie Wells, 'Red baron', *Forbes*, 3 July 2000; 'Sir Richard Branson', *The Guardian*, 8 July 2002.

Questions

1. How has brand equity been created at Virgin? What is the brand image of Virgin? Does the Virgin brand create value for shareholders and customers?
2. Does the diversification of the Virgin brand undermine value creation?
3. Is the Virgin brand managed correctly? What advice would you give for managing the Virgin brand in relation to:
    (a) future growth potential?
    (b) shareholder value creation?
    (c) a significant decline in the aviation sector that can potentially bankrupt Virgin Atlantic?
    (d) domestic (from the perspective of the United Kingdom) and/or international expansion into:
      (i) a new, emerging market?
      (ii) a new, mature market?
4. How would you measure the value of the Virgin brand?

end notes

1. Quoted from Leslie Butterfield (ed.), *Excellence in Advertising*, Oxford: Butterworth-Heinemann, 1999, p. 266.
2. Raymond Perrier, ed., *Brand Valuation*, London: Interbrand and Premier Books, 1997, p. 44.
3. The resource-based theory of the firm is described in M. A. Peteraf, 'The cornerstones of competitive advantage: A resource-based view', *Strategic Management Journal*, **14**, 1993, pp. 179–92; David Collis and Cynthia Montgomery, 'Competing on resources: Strategy in the 1990s', *Harvard Business Review*, July/August 1995, pp. 119–28.
4. Rajendra K. Srivastava, Tasadduk A. Shervani and Liam Fahey, 'Marketing, business processes and shareholder value: an organizationally embedded view of marketing activities and the discipline of marketing', *Journal of Marketing*, **63**, Special issue 1999, pp. 168–79.
5. John Bartle, 'The advertising contribution,' in Leslie Butterfield (ed.), *Excellence in Advertising*, Oxford: Butterworth-Heinemann, 1999.
6. Quoted from Leslie de Chernatony and Malcolm H. B. McDonald, *Creating Powerful Brands*, Oxford: Butterworth-Heinemann, 1992, p. 9.
7. Simon Broadbent, 'Diversity in categories, brands and strategies', *Journal of Brand Management*, **2**, August, 1994, pp. 9–18.
8. Kevin L. Keller, 'Conceptualising, measuring, and managing customer-based brand equity', *Journal of Marketing*, **57**, January, 1993, pp. 35–50.
9. Robert A. Buzzell and Barney T. Gale, *The PIMS Principles: Linking Strategy to Performance*, New York: Free Press, 1987; 'The year of the brand', *The Economist*, 25 December, 1988, p. 93.
10. See, for example, Larry Downes and Chunka Mui, *Unleasing the Killer App: Digital Strategies for Market Dominance*, Boston, MA: Harvard Business School Press, 1998.

11. Jean-Noel Kapferer, *Strategic Brand Management*, 2nd edn, London: Kogan Page, 1997.

12. KPMG, *A Report Card on Cross-Border Mergers and Acquisitions*, London: KPMG, 1999.

13. This section draws heavily on Kapferer, *op cit.*

14. This section is based on David Haigh, *Brand Valuation: A Review of Current Practice*, London: Institute of Practitioners in Advertising, 1996.

15. Raymond Perrier (ed.), *Brand Valuation*, London: Interbrand and Premier Books, 1997.

16. David Haigh, 'Brand valuation methodology' in Leslie Butterfield and David Haigh, *Understanding the Financial Value of Brands*, London: Institute of Practitioners in Advertising, 1998, pp. 20–7.

17. For one of the first major empirical studies in the marketing literature concerning the relationship between brand value and shareholder value see Roger A. Kerin and Raj Sethuraman, 'Exploring the brand value-shareholder value nexus for consumer goods companies', *Journal of the Academy of Marketing Science*, **26**, Fall, 1998, pp. 260–73.

18. Sir Richard Branson, quoted in Donna L. Goodison, 'Virgin's Sir Richard keeps reinventing, expanding brand', *Boston Business* Journal, 1 March 2002; www.bizjournals.com/, accessed 19 November 2002.

19. *The Guardian*, 8 July 2002; media.guadian.co.uk/Print/0,3858,4448647,00.html, accessed 19 November 2002.

20. Quoted in Alison Smith, 'A good reputation is the key to Virgin's diversity', *Sunday Times*, 20 September 1997; www.btimes.co.za/97/0921/world/world.htm, accessed 19 November 2002.

Prices

By the time you have completed this chapter, you will be able to:

- show how pricing decisions affect shareholder value
- explain the weaknesses of the pricing approaches commonly used in business
- describe the principles of developing value-based pricing
- propose a more effective approach to making pricing decisions
- outline the key issues in designing product-line pricing strategies, customised pricing, international pricing and promotional pricing policies
- plan price changes
- manage prices to ensure effective price realisation.

scene setter

Priceline's pricing strategy

Since its launch in April 1998, [Priceline] has moved beyond its initial business of selling cheap airline tickets, hotel rooms and rental cars to include groceries, gasoline, new cars, mortgages and phone service...

Priceline describes its business as a 'demand collection system' in which the web site serves as an auctioneer bringing airlines or other product together with consumers. For buyers, Priceline offers the prospect of low prices. For sellers, it provides an inexpensive outlet for goods and services, which otherwise might not sell at all. Like any retailer, Priceline seeks to profit primarily on the difference between what it charges customers and what it pays suppliers, although it charges a variety of fees as well ...

[Peter S. Fader, Wharton Marketing Professor] believes Priceline's enormously expensive marketing campaign is wasted because the company's services do not have long-term appeal to the mass market. Instead, he believes Priceline can attract and keep only a niche group of customers, those willing to go to considerable trouble for small savings ...

Its biggest revenue source is airline ticket sales, which serve as a model for most of its other operations. The goal is to offer customers large discounts, and to provide airlines some revenue on seats that would become worthless if empty.

To bid for a seat, the customer first submits a credit card number and irrevocable authorisation to charge the card if the bid is accepted. The customer must be flexible on airlines, flight schedules and intermediate stops. If the customer's bid is accepted, the transaction is final. If it is rejected, the customer must wait seven days to place a new bid for the same itinerary ...

'The beauty of this variable pricing model lay in the fact that it created "damaged goods" in the form of uncertainty,' according to [Professor Eric Clemons of Wharton]. 'If you were a student on a tight budget but with time to spare, it might not bother you to drive two extra hours to a distant airport, leave a day earlier than planned and fly back a day later, with layovers each way. On the other hand, a business traveller on a tight schedule would never pass up a regularly scheduled flight for a Priceline bid. So instead of losing a full-pay customer to a discount seat, the airlines could fill an otherwise-empty seat with a passenger who otherwise may not have even flown.'

Priceline had a hit on its hands and saw its stock price hit a record US$162 per share in April 1999 shortly after its IPO [Initial Public Offering]. Then, near the end of that year, the company decided to tap into a wider consumer market by launching the Priceline WebHouse Club, a service that let online customers name their own price for groceries.

Perhaps the company should have spoken to Clemons or some of his colleagues before launching the expansion. 'Variable pricing doesn't work for every situation,' he says. 'While it may attract incremental grocery sales in specific situations, this was the wrong application.'

One reason is because unlike financial instruments such as commodities futures, where supply and demand can fluctuate on a second-by-second basis, consumer demand for goods like groceries tends to be stable, enabling retail outlets to predict demand with relative accuracy and place their orders accordingly. So, the volume of 'damaged goods' like day-old bread may not be great enough to support variable pricing in the grocery segment — at least not on a widespread basis ...

Priceline found this out the hard way, and in October 2000 announced that WebHouse would shut its doors. Priceline's market value, along with that of many other Internet-based companies, has since plunged ...

Sources: Extracts from 'The problem with Priceline', 16 October 2000, www.knowledge.wharton; 'New Internet pricing models bring pain and fortune to retailers', 22 February 2001, www.knowledge.wharton.

Introduction

Pricing has a crucial impact on both the cash flow and growth potential of the business. Indeed, in many ways, pricing is the most important determinant of shareholder value. For the typical company, a 5 per cent price increase can boost operating profits by more than a half. In many industries, such as pharmaceuticals, management consulting or drinks, the purpose of marketing is considered as primarily about obtaining higher prices. This is because the results of successful innovation, brand building or adding value should be a willingness on the part of customers to pay more. Pricing affects shareholder value through its impact on the company's margin and the volume it sells. Ideally, a company wants to charge higher prices without this being offset by weak volume performance. Companies such as Glaxo, McKinsey and Microsoft have shown how this can be done.

Price is the only element of the marketing mix that directly produces revenue; all the others produce costs. The short-term impact of price changes on both profits and sales is usually much greater than other marketing mix changes. Price is also a highly flexible tool — while new products or changes in channels or communication policies can take years, prices can usually be adjusted very rapidly. In spite of its importance, few companies are good at pricing strategy. Most do not collect adequate information and rely on rules-of-thumb that lead to decisions that are very costly in shareholder value terms.

Trends affecting pricing decisions

Dynamic markets increase the need for better methods of pricing. In the previous century, consumers became used to sellers and retailers offering one price to everyone. But the information revolution and the Internet are destroying the simplicity of uniform pricing and bringing back individually negotiated prices and haggling. New web sites like PriceScan.com specialise in comparing the prices of sellers across the market; intelligent shopping agents like Jungle find the best deals for customers; online auction sites like eBay enable buyers and sellers to negotiate prices individually; and new business models like Priceline reverse the normal process by having buyers name the price they will pay and inviting sellers to respond. The information revolution makes markets more price-sensitive, placing greater pressure on suppliers' operating margins.

Pricing decisions are also becoming more critical due to the increasing complexity of markets. All markets are becoming more segmented, which has resulted in firms having to broaden their product lines with different products aimed at different types of customers. Gone are the days when Coca-Cola could offer a single brand to everyone — today it has Coke, Diet Coke, Cherry Coke, Caffeine Free Coke, etc. Successful business-to-business marketing is similarly shifting from commodity selling to speciality products. The result is that firms do not price products in isolation but have to develop product-line pricing strategies that take into account interdependencies within the range.

Another area of complexity is international pricing. Globalisation has meant that prices charged in one market affect the prices that can be charged in others. Last but not least, competition has also become more complex and diverse. In Australia, finally, the days have passed when Qantas simply had to compete against another me-too competitor, and Telstra against itself. Nowadays, competition comes from new lifestyle brands, like Virgin, that capture the imagination of consumers, and from a range of no-nonsense international companies, such as SingTel.

Overview of effective pricing decisions

Price has different effects on sales, profits and shareholder value. A price that optimises shareholder value is likely to be very different from that which maximises sales or profits. Different perspectives on pricing objectives is one reason why pricing has done so badly in practice. There are four principles underlying effective pricing. These are the need to base prices on what value is being offered to the customer, the need to customise prices to individual consumers, the importance of anticipating competitor reaction and, of course, the role of business strategy in shaping pricing decisions.

Broadly, effective pricing decisions flow from the strategic objective and strategic focus analyses. The first determinant of a price is the strategic objective. If rapid growth is the goal then penetration pricing — pricing below current full-cost — may well be a viable option. Its justification could be that it is necessary to pre-empt competition and gain critical mass, without which long-run viability is not possible. Also, volume growth is likely to reduce average costs through economies of scale, so that while the price is unprofitable at the beginning it may be profitable in the longer run. Pricing to achieve short-run profit targets can destroy a business's future in young, dynamic markets.

When critical mass is achieved, the strategic focus may shift the pricing intent to margin improvement. For example, when the zip maker YKK entered the European zip market, low prices were an essential part of its strategy. But after it had won a dominant market position, it was able to use its leverage to lead prices up to highly profitable levels. The target customer segment also plays an obvious role in the pricing decision. The price points in the luxury car segment will be much higher than those in the economy segment. Different market segments have quite different price elasticities because of their spending ability and specific choice criteria. Competitive strategies are also important. The prices charged by competitors will constrain the pricing options available for the business.

Naturally, the company's differential strategy has a crucial bearing on the price that it can charge (see marketing management in practice 'Price wars'). Fundamentally, the price a customer will pay for a product is determined by its perceived value, relative to competition. If a company is pursuing a 'basic product' or 'expected product' strategy then its price will have to be similar to the competition. If the differential strategy is based on offering superior economic value to the customer, then the upper limit on the price will be the additional value this represents. For example, if a steel company offers a fabricating solution that saves the Ford Motor Company $1 million a year, then this, in principle, is what the Ford Motor Company should be willing to pay at the limit. How close to this limit the steel company is actually able to price depends on its negotiating skill and the sustainability of its differential advantage.

Marketing management in practice: **Price wars**

Price wars are dangerous and costly battles and have widespread and detrimental impact on many industries. We look at two industries that have been affected and what strategies they have adopted to defend their positions.

1. Margarine wars

In 1999, three companies dominated 90 per cent of the Australian margarine industry: Goodman Fielder, Unilever and Peerless Holdings. A range of smaller companies held the rest of the market. And the margarine industry, one of the most unstable food markets in Australia, was in the middle of another price war. By late May 2001, 'the retail price of a 500-gram tub of margarine had fallen from $1.59 to below $1, sometimes as low as 70 cents.' Goodman Fielder felt the pinch. 'On June 8, Goodman Fielder announced that its operating profit for the 12 months to June 30, 2001, would be 5% below last year's result of $123.4 million'...

Rob Gordon, the Managing Director of Goodman Fielder's new consumer foods division... says the price war was restricted to low priced 'secondary' brands, including Goodman's ETA and Mrs McGregor and Peerless's Tablelands. Gordon says the price war was started by Peerless, which cut its prices heavily to persuade Woolworths to regularly stock its Tablelands brand in its supermarkets. 'This led to a brief but intense discounting campaign, which got (Peerless its) objective' says Gordon. With Tablelands now on the shelves at Woolworths, the discounting has abated...

Gordon says discounting wars are 'part and parcel' of a highly competitive industry. Historically, price wars in the margarine sector have been started by smaller companies trying to win market share ... [M]argarine's rise in popularity meant that consumers began to consider margarine a commodity, where the only difference between brands was price. Research shows that customers have no loyalty to a particular brand of margarine, switching brands up to 10 times a year ...

Gordon says Goodman has developed a three-part plan to reduce it's exposure to margarine price wars. The plan includes:

1. The creation of Goodman's consumer foods division, with an annual turnover of $1 billion. The enlarged business will be able to absorb the effects of any price wars.
2. Focus on its power brands, such as Meadow Lea, and slowly abandon secondary brands.
3. Attempt to increase earnings from its higher-margin brands, such as Paul Newman's Own pasta sauces.

Source: Extracts from James Thomson, 'Prices spread thin', *BRW*, Friday, 29 June 2001, p. 36.

2. Pizza wars

Home-delivered pizza is a fractious, difficult market, in which companies chase big-volume sales and learn to live with thin margins. Up-selling is the key to survival. Pizza delivery companies do not make money from pizza sold for $5 or $6 — they make money by persuading people to buy a bottle of soft drink or garlic bread with their pizza. Price competition in the home delivery pizza market is ferocious and relentless. The average price of a large pizza had crashed from about $16 in 1993 to about $6 in 1998. Fierce competition and the impulse buying habits of consumers force companies to constantly run TV advertising and employ a range of local-area marketing activities.

Pizza marketing is dominated by price, but not all home delivery pizza companies are obsessed with promoting low prices. Domino's has not yet mentioned price in its television advertising. However, it pushes price in the thousands of leaflets and product offers it puts in letterboxes each week, and it does not avoid price wars with its rivals. Pizza Hut, Pizza Haven and Eagle Boys Dial-A-Pizza aggressively push price, yet Domino's TV ads are 'clean', as Managing Director Fel Bevacqua puts it. 'We want our brand to be built on taste and quality, not price ...'

Some fast food companies claim that low prices and constant discounting have turned pizza into a commodity: people do not care who they buy pizza from, as long as they get the cheapest deal … Given the constant price-cutting, how can Domino's build brand loyalty? 'By being competitive on price, offering great service — which includes fast delivery and the attitude of our telephone operators and store staff — and promoting consistent brand image in advertising', says [Chris] Dibley [then group account director at Domino's ad agency].

Source: Extracts from Neil Shoebridge, 'Brand name bravery brings Domino's through the pizza wars', *BRW*, 18 January 1999, pp. 59–62.

The relationship between price and shareholder value

The basic objective in pricing is to choose a price that maximises the discounted value of the product's free cash flow. Free cash flow (CF) in any year is:

$$CF_t = P_tQ_t - C_t - I_t$$

where P is the product's price, Q is the volume of units sold, C is total cost, and I is the investment in fixed and working capital. Changes in prices can have a big effect on short-term profits, as most accountants are aware. For example, consider a company selling 100 million units at a price of $1, with a contribution margin of 50 per cent and an operating margin of 5 per cent. A 5 per cent price increase would double profits if volume remained unchanged. Even if the volume sold dropped by 5 per cent, profits would still rise by 45 per cent because of the reduction in variable costs.

Effect of 5 per cent price increase ($ million)

	NOW	VOLUME UNCHANGED	5% VOLUME LOSS
Sales	100.00	105.00	99.75
Variable costs	50.00	50.00	47.50
Contribution	50.00	50.00	52.25
Fixed costs	45.00	45.00	45.00
Operating profits	5.00	10.00	7.25

Other ways of increasing profits tend to be less powerful. For example, while a 5 per cent increase in prices can double profits, a 5 per cent volume increase, or a 5 per cent cut in fixed costs has only half that effect on the bottom line. To put it another way, a 5 per cent price cut could eliminate profits altogether, while a 5 per cent volume loss would only halve profits. **Price competition** can have a devastating effect on profitability. The implication is that it often makes more sense to defend prices than to defend volume.

price competition: practice of obtaining a differential advantage by offering comparable products at a lower price than the competition

Pricing has not had the attention its importance merits. In seeking to improve profits and cash flow, a great deal of attention has been given to reducing costs and capital employed. These have been the primary goals of re-engineering and supply chain management in recent years. Salespeople, and marketing people in general, have focused their efforts on increasing sales and market share. But the fourth variable in the cash flow equation, price, has been relatively neglected. Managers often appear to be under the mistaken belief that this is determined by the market and outside their control.

Basic price relationships

To discuss pricing, it is important to understand four general relationships:

1. **The demand relationship** relates price to the number of units sold. Almost always this is negative — the higher the price, the fewer units are bought. The degree of negativity is called the elasticity of demand. One of the key objectives of branding is to reduce the elasticity of demand, so that consumers will not so readily desert when prices rise.

2. **The revenue relationship** shows how sales revenue varies with price. This tends to be a bell-shaped curve — raising prices initially increases revenue but, eventually, the decline in units sold outweighs the price increases and revenue declines.

3. **The cost relationship** describes how total costs vary with price. This will tend to be linear — the lower the price, the greater the volume sold and the higher the total cost. The exact shape will depend upon the mix of fixed and variable costs.

4. **The investment relationship** describes how working and fixed capital vary with price. Lower prices mean higher volumes and greater investment. This tends to rise step-wise, as fixed investment tends to be added in large, discrete amounts.

These four patterns lead to the key relationships of price to profits and shareholder value. Both profits and value have a U-shaped relationship to price — in other words, there are optimal prices that maximise profits and value. The various relationships are illustrated in table 8.1. The first two columns show the demand relationship: as prices increase, volume declines. Often, salespeople believe that the firm should maximise sales, but, as can be seen, that means selling at the lowest price and incurring big losses and negative cash flow. Whereas the volume maximising price is $1, if the objective is to maximise revenue then the price should be $3. However, maximising revenue or volume ignores the costs and investments needed to support these sales. If the objective is to maximise profits — as assumed in most textbooks on pricing — then the price should be $5.

Table 8.1 Illustrating price relationships

PRICE ($)	VOLUME UNITS (M)	REVENUE ($M)	COST ($M)	PROFIT ($M)	INVESTMENT ($M)	CASH FLOW ($M)	VALUE ($M)
1	**17.0**	17.0	27.0	−10.0	21.3	−31.3	50.0
2	16.0	32.0	26.0	6.0	24.0	−18.0	150.0
3	14.0	**42.0**	24.0	18.0	24.5	−6.5	220.0
4	9.0	36.0	19.0	17.0	18.0	−1.0	**250.0**
5	7.5	37.5	17.5	**20.0**	16.9	3.1	200.0
6	5.0	30.0	15.0	15.0	12.5	**2.5**	100.0
7	3.0	21.0	13.0	8.0	8.3	−0.3	50.0
8	2.0	16.0	12.0	4.0	6.0	−2.0	10.0
9	1.0	9.0	11.0	−2.0	3.3	−5.3	−50.0
10	0.0	0.0	10.0	−10.0	0.0	−10.0	−70.0

The problem with maximising profits this way, however, is that it is a short-term solution. By selling only to customers who will pay $5, much of the market is left unsatisfied and this presents an open invitation to competition. The long-run result of short-run profit-maximisation is likely to be declining market share, loss of scale economies, and competitors obtaining critical mass and building the dominant brands. For example, such were the fates of Xerox in the copier market and the British motorcycle industry after they set short-run profit maximising prices. The right pricing decision is one that maximises the net present value of long-run cash flow, not short-run profits. This is the price that maximises value for shareholders. In the illustration, this value-maximising price is $4.

It is important to note that maximising volume, revenue, profits and share-holder value lead to quite different prices. In particular, in growing markets the value-maximising price will, often, be lower than the price that maximises short-run profits or cash flow. One reason is that market share effects are often important, either because the distribution channels will only support the brand leaders, or because network effects mean that customers attach value to buying the leading brands. A second reason is that scale economies or experience-curve effects mean that brands that do not grow fast suffer increasing cost disadvantages. Pricing, like strategy generally, requires taking a longer-term view.

Pricing in practice

The right price is the one that maximises value. In practice, such an approach is more challenging to implement since it requires collecting information to estimate long-run demand relationships, competitive strategies and the behaviour of costs over time. Instead, managers usually look to simpler mark-up formulas that add a standard margin to an estimate of the cost of the product or service. **Mark-up pricing** is a method widely practised on a day-to-day basis by, for example, accountants, solicitors and contractors.

mark-up pricing: a price set to add a standard margin to the cost of the product or service

Suppose a firm sells printers. It has a variable cost of $80 per unit, fixed costs of $2 million, and plans to sell 100 000 units annually. Then its unit cost is $100. If its standard cost mark-up is 33 per cent, then its price will be set at $133. Generally, the mark-up is expressed as a percentage of sales rather than costs. So, if a firm had a target sales mark-up of 25 per cent, then its price is given by:

$$\text{Price} = \frac{\text{Unit cost}}{(1 - \text{target return on sales})} = \frac{100}{1 - 0.25} = \$133$$

target-return pricing: a price set to achieve a target return on investment

A variation of this mark-up approach is **target-return pricing**. This method is popular among capital-intensive businesses such as public utilities and auto companies. Here, the firm aims to price to achieve a target return on investment. For example, if the printer company had $13 million of invested capital and it aimed for a 25 per cent return, then the target price is given by:

$$\text{Price} = \text{Unit cost} + \frac{\text{target return} \times \text{invested capital}}{\text{Unit sales}}$$

$$= \$100 + \frac{0.25 \times \$13 \text{ million}}{100\,000} = \$133$$

Managers like mark-up pricing because they find it easier to estimate costs than demand. It can also lead to more stability in prices if competitors are using the same methods. But mark-up pricing is not an effective way to price. It ignores demand and the perceived value of the product to the customer. For example, strong brands with added values should normally be much less price sensitive than weak brands. Mark-up pricing throws away the value created by effective marketing. It also ignores competition — standard mark-ups would be a disastrous policy if aggressive competitors were competing on price.

Mark-up pricing is also circular in its reasoning. For example, expected sales are a necessary input to determine the unit cost figure used in the formula to calculate the price. But unit sales themselves depend upon the price. Similarly, how is the percentage mark-up calculated? This must be dependent on demand and competition. In highly price-competitive markets, the percentage must be lower than in those industries where competition is less fierce. Managers need to make pricing decisions on stronger foundations.

Pricing principles

There are four key principles that underlie effective pricing:
1. Pricing should be based on the value the product offers to customers, not on its cost of production.
2. Since customers attach different values to a product or service, prices should be customised so that these value differences can be capitalised upon.
3. Pricing decisions should anticipate the reactions of competitors and their long-run objectives in the market.
4. Pricing should be integrated with the firm's broad strategic positioning and goals.

Pricing for value

The customer is not interested in what it costs the supplier to produce a product. The price a customer will pay for a product is determined by its value to him or her. If the customer believes competitors are offering similar products, then he or she will compare prices and choose the cheapest. But good marketing differentiates the product and creates a differential advantage by enhancing the satisfaction consumers receive. In addition, when customers choose a supplier, there are often associated costs that can dwarf the price paid for the product. Putting these two points together means that a company can differentiate its offer by offering more satisfaction, or lowering the costs associated with purchase and use of the product.

The additional customer satisfaction can be in the form of functional benefits arising from differences in the features offered, or psychological benefits arising from confidence in the attributes, status or experience associated with the brand. In business-to-business markets, the primary differences are functional. Economic value to the customer (EVC) is a key concept for pricing in such markets. EVC measures the value of the functional benefits offered by the supplier.

Consider this example from the construction equipment market. The established market leader in second-hand earthmoving equipment sells a bulldozer at a price of $50 000. Over the product's remaining economic life averaging 12 000 operating hours, the customer spends $20 000 on diesel oil and lubricants, $40 000 on servicing and parts and $20 per hour on labour, making a total remaining lifetime cost of $350 000. A new competitor with more advanced second-hand machinery enters the market and estimates the value of his product features as a precursor to setting prices. He offers two models. The first model has modern digital technology that has the effect of increasing bulldozer productivity by 10 per cent. The other, even more advanced model also has finishing technology that yields greater operating flexibility, which on average should enable the constructor to charge around $50 000 extra over 12 000 hours of work.

Figure 8.1 shows the economic value of the machines. The basic machine in the middle column 'saves' $30 000, implying that its EVC is $80 000. The advanced machine has an EVC of $130 000. At any price below the EVC, the customer makes more profit with the new machine, 'other things being equal'. How far the new competitor can charge the price premium reflected in its EVC depends on the ability of its salespeople to convince customers of its economic benefits. It also depends on persuading them that the support and service the company offers minimises the costs and risks in switching from the market leader.

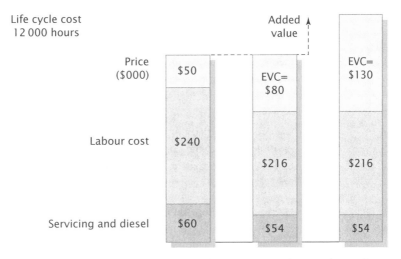

Figure 8.1 Pricing and economic value to the customer

In consumer markets, emotional value can be as important as economic value so that value-based pricing needs to estimate the worth of the emotional attributes. In the following section, we look at some direct and indirect methods for obtaining information from consumers about how much a brand is worth to them.

Note that **value-based pricing** is based on quite different assumptions than mark-up pricing and that it will produce quite different recommendations. Value-based pricing makes much more sense because it is based on value to the customer when the product is benchmarked against competitors' offers. It measures how much the consumer is likely to be willing to pay for the product, not how much it costs to produce it.

Pricing for customisation

Because of different attitudes and circumstances, customers differ in the value they attach to a product. Some people attach a very high value to owning a Porsche or having the latest mobile phone; others do not. If a company treats the market as homogeneous, it will throw away opportunities to create value for both customers and shareholders.

Consider first an industrial example. An agrochemical firm invented a new breakthrough herbicide that raised agricultural productivity by 20 per cent. The variable cost of the product was $2 (1 unit was sufficient to spray 1 hectare) and

value-based pricing: a price based on the total value that the product represents to the customer when it is benchmarked against competitors' offers. Essentially, value-based pricing measures how much the consumer is likely to be willing to pay for the product after taking all other product alternatives into consideration; not how much it costs to produce it.

fixed costs were estimated at $10 million. Statistics showed that there were 30 million cultivated hectares in the target market, yielding an average return to farmers of around $27 per hectare. The herbicide then had an average EVC of $5.40 per hectare. To incentivise use, the company decided to set the price so that half the EVC went to the farmer as increased profit. It believed it could then capture half the market, selling 15 million units. Unfortunately, despite a brilliant product, the budget suggested that the company would make virtually no profit. Its revenue would be $40.5 million (15 million × $2.70) but its costs would amount to almost the same sum (variable costs 15 million × $2 plus $10 million fixed cost).

Before abandoning the product, the company commissioned some market research. Like most markets, this one proved to be highly segmented (figure 8.2). The market could be divided into three segments of approximately equal size — around 10 million hectares each. The first was a low-value segment of rough grazing land in the north of the country, which yielded only $10 per hectare. A second segment of arable farming had a yield of $20, and the third was high-value fruit farming with a yield of $50 per hectare. The EVCs were then $2, $4 and $10, respectively. The research showed that at the original price of $2.70, the low-value segment would never buy because the price exceeded the EVC. In the middle segment, the incentive to switch was also quite low. But if the company focused on the high-value segment, it could sell at $5, offering an attractive incentive to the farmers and making a profit of up to $20 million (i.e. 10 million × ($5 − $2) − $10 million).

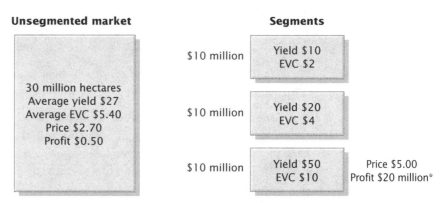

Unsegmented market

30 million hectares
Average yield $27
Average EVC $5.40
Price $2.70
Profit $0.50

Segments

$10 million — Yield $10 EVC $2

$10 million — Yield $20 EVC $4

$10 million — Yield $50 EVC $10 — Price $5.00 Profit $20 million*

*i.e. 10 million units × ($5 price − $2 variable cost) − $10 million fixed cost

Figure 8.2 Customised pricing, EVC and profitability

An important concept in pricing is the consumer surplus. The consumer surplus is the difference between the price the consumer would be willing to pay for a product and the price he or she actually pays. The existence of a consumer surplus means that the company is 'leaving money on the table' — missing out on profit that it could be making (see marketing insight 'What happened to Impulse?'). Consider an obvious example — pricing seats on an aeroplane. Suppose the demand curve for a discounted Melbourne–Perth flight is like figure 8.3. The price that just fills the 300-seater 747-300 brought into temporary service after Ansett's demise is $300, generating revenue of $90 000. The problem with this price is that the airline is passing up the consumer surplus represented by the triangle ABC — worth some $165 000 of revenue.[1] This is because many affluent customers who get the ticket for $300 would have been willing to pay substantially more. A more profitable ticket price for the airline would be $750, which generates revenue of $120 000. Here, the consumer surplus shrinks to the triangle ADE, but because only 160 seats are sold, the airline misses out on the revenue from the 140 unfilled seats.

Marketing insight: What happened to Impulse?

Many commentators suggest the decline in the Australian dollar, increased fuel costs and uncommitted investors are responsible for the Impulse Airlines' demise, but overseas experience suggests that it is more likely that Impulse simply had the wrong business model. A recent study shows that in the United States, an average of 4.8 carriers serve city pairs with a route density of more than 30 000 seats a week — a similar density to the Brisbane–Sydney and Sydney–Melbourne routes.

This suggests that there is more than enough demand for a third — and potentially a fourth — airline to operate on these key Australian routes. So where did Impulse go wrong?

The airline failed to compete effectively by dynamically pricing its fares to match demand at particular times of the day and week — that is, to price in a way that would have enabled it to capture maximum value from flights at premium times occupied predominately by business travellers. These travellers were, and still are, prepared to pay more than Impulse's fully flexible fares (but less than Qantas and Ansett fares).

In contrast, easyJet, a UK-based ... no frills carriers, constantly increases [or] decreases its price according to demand and the time of departure, so it captures much of the consumer surplus that Impulse overlooked. In fact, on some high demand flights, easyJet's prices exceed those of British Airways, despite its lower-value offering.

A significant part of Impulse's reported losses of $1 million a week could have been recovered had it priced to demand ...

Source: Alan Kallir, 'Impulse overlooked the fundamentals', *Australian Financial Review*, Friday 4 May 2001.

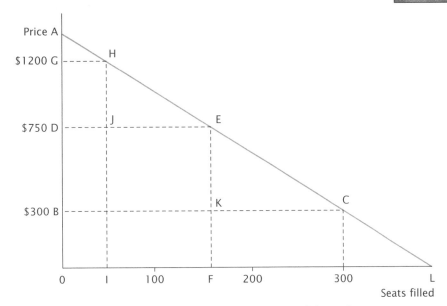

Figure 8.3 Pricing, consumer surplus and demand for airline seats

The obvious solution to this problem of minimising consumer surplus and maximising capacity is charging different prices to different customers. The airlines introduced First, Business and Economy Class to do this. In the example, the airline sells 50 first-class seats at $1200, 110 business-class seats at \$750 and 140 economy-class seats at \$300, generating total revenue of \$184 500. Table 8.2, which estimates the variable and fixed costs associated with the flight, shows that the three-class solution more than doubles profits compared to the single-price solution.

Table 8.2 Illustrating the profit impact of customised pricing

CLASS	PASSENGERS	PRICE ($)	REVENUE ($)	VARIABLE COST ($)	FIXED COST ($)	PROFIT ($)
Single-price strategies						
Maximising seats	300	300	90 000	30	70 000	11 000
Maximising profit	160	750	120 000	30	70 000	45 200
Customised pricing						
First	50	1200	60 000	100		
Business	110	750	82 500	50		
Economy	140	300	42 000	25		
Total	300		184 500	14 000	70 000	100 500

Even with three prices, profits are not maximised since there are still consumer surpluses represented by the triangles AGH, HJE and EKC. The best way of capturing these consumer surpluses is to negotiate a price with each customer. Individual customised prices would raise revenue by a further 38 per cent to \$255 000 and profits by a further 70 per cent to over \$171 000, if there were no additional costs involved. One of the important aspects of the Internet is that it opens up the possibility of low-cost, customised pricing on a much wider scale.

Customised pricing allied with product differentiation is, of course, very widely practised. Indeed, such tactics to capture consumer surplus are central to business-to-business strategy in virtually every industry.

customised pricing: a price developed uniquely for each customer

Pricing for competition

The company has to anticipate competitors responding strongly to a pricing strategy that aims at winning market share. Not only may competitors match a pricing move, but also a damaging downward spiral in prices can be triggered, leaving all the competitors worse off. In considering pricing decisions, managers therefore have to ask first: how will competitors react and what effect will these reactions have on profits? Second, is there a way of influencing competitors towards less damaging responses? As we shall see, competitor reactions and the ability to shape these responses depend on the nature of the industry.

» Competitor reaction

The importance of considering competitive reactions can be illustrated through game theory and, in particular, the famous Prisoner's Dilemma game.[2] The game is as follows. Suppose company A and B are the only producers of a certain product. There is only one client, who is willing to pay up to \$50 per unit for a one-off contract of 10 thousand units. The cost of producing the product, including an economic return on the capital employed, is \$10 per unit. The company that offers the lower price wins the contract; if both charge the same prices, the contract is shared equally between the two.

Figure 8.4 summarises the pay-offs of alternative pricing strategies. If both companies set their prices at \$50 and divided the contract, each would make a profit of $200 000. However, this strategy, though attractive, is not individually optimal. If A undercut B and charged $49, then A would win the whole contract, making $390 000 profit, and B would be out of the market. Unfortunately, this strategy is also going to occur to B, which will also seek to maximise its individual profits by cutting price. When price wars like this break out, the price is likely to drop substantially below $49. In fact, at any price higher than $10, the two competitors can improve their individual situation by undercutting the other and obtaining the entire contract.

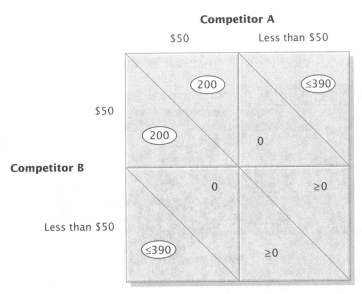

Figure 8.4 Pricing and the prisoner's dilemma

Only when both competitors are charging $10, and just making the minimum return necessary to stay in the market, is there no incentive for either to undercut the other. In the language of game theory, $10 is the only so called **Nash Equilibrium** of this game — the only price at which neither competitor can individually improve its own situation by reducing prices. But if the two competitors are charging $10, they are both much worse off than they could have been if they had shared the contract at $50.

The Prisoner's Dilemma game is a simplified model of price competition but it does highlight a conclusion that holds generally. That is, the individual incentive to cut prices can lead to consequences that leave every competitor worse off. This result, however, does not always occur. The most important oversimplification of the model is that it is a one-off, static decision. In practice, competitors can usually react to each other's price decisions. If a competitor anticipates that a rival will respond, then it may not engage in price competition. Take a simple example of a town with two petrol stations next to each other and customers purely interested in getting the cheapest petrol. To begin with, assume that both are charging the monopoly price — that price which maximises the joint profits of the two stations. What happens if competitor A lowers its price by 10 cents a litre? Competitor B, knowing that a price disadvantage will drive its market share to zero, is bound to immediately follow A's price down. Anticipating that this will happen, station A should not lower its price in the first place. The outcome of anticipating a competitive

Nash Equilibrium: a situation in which each player is making the best response given what the other player has chosen to do

reaction is the exact opposite of the Prisoner's Dilemma — monopoly pricing, rather than competitive pricing.

Note that it is easy to predict a cooperative rather than a competitive price outcome in the petrol station example because of the assumptions that were made. These include: price starts at the monopoly level; both competitors implicitly agree what this level is; information about prices is available immediately and without cost to both competitors and consumers; there are only two competitors and no substitutes for the commodity. However, most markets have more complex features than the petrol station example, making predictions about prices more difficult (see marketing insight 'Price competition and the Internet'). The key to anticipating competitive pricing behaviour is to look at the characteristics of the industry.

Marketing insight: **Price competition and the Internet**

On first glance, economic theory might suggest the Internet would reduce price competition. Prices become more transparent, consumers and competitors have much fuller information at very low cost, all factors conducive to industry cooperation.

However, what makes price competition more likely rather than less likely is the lowering of barriers to entry. New entrants do not need to invest in expensive stores or spend on costly customer lists. This should increase the number of firms and the differences among them, making high prices much more difficult to sustain. New entrants with no brand name and unable to fund large advertising campaigns will find it necessary to compete on price to get a toehold in the market.

Further, the reduction in search costs and the ease with which customers can compare prices on the Internet will encourage consumers to switch to lower price suppliers. Search and switching costs may be so low that negotiated prices become the norm. It may be much easier for customers to play suppliers off against each other, obtaining price quotes through e-mail and making offers and counter offers among a large number of sellers. For example, the Internet is already making it easy to play one car dealer off against another. Online auctions like eBay have become major growth businesses and online 'name your own price' businesses such as Priceline.com further reduce the ability of suppliers to coordinate prices.

» Conditions affecting price competition

Cooperation usually leads to more profitable outcomes than competition. Cooperation can be explicit, as when companies get together to fix prices. However, explicit cooperation on prices, or collusion, is normally illegal. The other way of restricting price competition is by implicit cooperation. This occurs when competitors learn to trust each other not to cut prices. This is more difficult, but a combination of price signalling and tit-for-tat often produces this outcome. **Price signalling** involves tactics to make more transparent what the firm's objective is. A company might signal its intention of not reducing prices by public commitment to its published price list or advanced announcements of price increases. Tit-for-tat is a specific strategy that begins by cooperating with the competitor then matching the last price move by the competitor. This simple strategy has been found to give the most profitable outcomes for both competitors in repeated Prisoner's Dilemma games. What industry conditions favour price cooperation rather than competition? There are several:

price signalling:
the use of tactics to make more transparent what a firm's pricing objective is

- **The number of competitors.** Such forms of implicit cooperation are more difficult to achieve where there are a large number of competitors.

- **Differences among competitors.** Where companies have very different cost structures, market shares and product ranges it is more difficult to reach agreement on a cooperative pricing strategy.
- **The short-run gain from price cutting.** Price competition is more likely to break out when there are potentially big short-run gains. These are greatest when firms have substantial excess capacity and when the products are relatively similar so that consumers can easily switch.
- **Price transparency.** Transparent pricing encourages cooperation. If rivals immediately observe price cuts, aggressive pricing is deterred. On the other hand, if prices are the result of complex, private negotiations it is harder for implicit cooperation to develop because rivals cannot assess their opponent's actions.

» Changing the rules of the game

Companies often seek to reduce price competition by changing the rules of the game. This involves shifting the above conditions to make them more favourable to cooperation. One way is to reduce the number of competitors through mergers and acquisitions. This may also reduce some of the differences between the surviving players, making cooperative behaviour more likely.

Another strategy is to reduce the gains to be had from price cutting. Building stronger brands through such actions as advertising, market segmentation and product differentiation reduces price sensitivity and the advantage rivals can expect from price cuts. Relationship marketing programs are particularly effective. For example, if a customer is a member of the Qantas frequent flyer program, the person is less likely to respond to a low price offered by Virgin Blue on the same route. This reduces the incentive for competitors to cut prices. Higher ticket prices are the result.

Finally, there are a variety of methods that companies can use to make their pricing more transparent in order to encourage competitors' trust. One way of avoiding price competition is for firms to follow a pattern of price leadership. Often, this is preceded by prior announcements to build a consensus. The firm will test the water by press releases announcing 'unsatisfactory industry margins', 'the need to recoup increased costs' and 'a price increase being expected soon'.

Pricing for strategy alignment

Prices are not determined in isolation but are influenced by the firm's strategy, the market positioning of the product, the other products it sells, and the various markets where it operates.[3]

» Value not profits

The firm's pricing should be geared to deliver value, not short-term profits. Value is measured by the net present value of the long-term cash flow that a pricing policy delivers. The value-maximising price can be higher or lower than the profit-maximising price. If prices fall over time, the price that maximises short-run profits may be below the value-maximising price. For example, some pharmaceutical markets are characterised by price elasticity and low variable costs, so that a lower price will increase profits. But in the Japanese market, the health authorities demand 50 per cent price cuts every two years. In this situation, a higher initial price may mean lower short-term sales and profits but higher long-term returns.

More usually, however, the value-maximising price is lower than the short-run profit-maximising price. One reason is that price elasticity is higher in the long run than in the short run. Lack of information about alternatives and switching costs means that it takes time for customers dissatisfied with the firm's relatively high price to find new suppliers. Second, high short-term profits stimulate new competitors eager to capitalise on the opportunities offered by high prices. Finally, in growing markets high prices can prevent the firm gaining the critical mass in market share necessary to be attractive to customers and distributors and so to be viable in the longer term.

» Price and positioning

Pricing is influenced by how the firm wants to position the brand. All markets are segmented. Historically, a three-tier segmentation of economy, mid-market and premium positioned brands has characterised many markets (figure 8.5). Customers normally choose brands from within a specific segment. For example, in the Australian car market the premium segment includes the BMW, Jaguar, Lexus and Mercedes-Benz brands; the mid-market includes the larger Ford, Holden, Mitsubishi and Toyota ranges, and the economy has the Daewoo, Hyundai and Kia ranges. Brands within a segment are termed a strategic group.

strategic group: brands competing with each other for the same customers within a segment

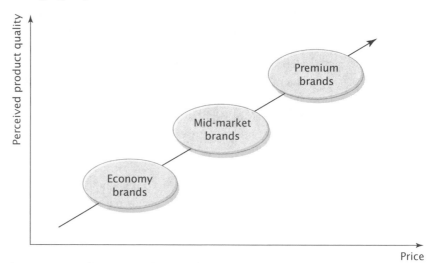

Figure 8.5 Three-tier value positioning map

Brands within a strategic group compete with each other to attract the same customers. The price elasticity within a strategic group is normally significantly higher than that between brands in different strategic groups. That is, a price cut by a mid-market brand will draw more sales from other mid-market brands than from other segments. Studies also suggest that where switching occurs between segments it is not symmetrical. Price cuts by a higher-quality tier are more powerful in pulling customers up from lower tiers, than lower-tier price cuts are in pulling customers down from upper tiers. In other words, customers trade up more readily than they trade down.

A company that competes in only one group is called a niche business. As markets mature, successful companies increasingly seek to compete in all the groups to achieve economies of scale and scope. One way to compete is to develop these groups from scratch. For example, Kodak supplemented its mid-market Gold brand with a cheap, new brand aimed at the growing economy segment and launched a new premium brand for the top end of the market. American Express pioneered Gold and Platinum cards. Sometimes, businesses are simply acquired. For example, Jaguar was bought by the Ford Motor Company to penetrate the premium segment; Daimler-Benz bought Chrysler to strengthen its position in the mid-market; VW bought Skoda to boost its share in the economy segment.

Pricing then has to be designed to fit into a market positioning strategy. Prices that position a brand below the diagonal in figure 8.5 will be perceived as poor value by consumers because their price is too high for the quality they are seen as offering. Pricing above the diagonal offers outstanding value with customers perceiving high quality brands at relatively low prices. A traditional approach to pricing follows the sequence:

$$\text{Design product} \rightarrow \text{Cost} \rightarrow \text{Price} \rightarrow \text{Market position}$$

But a strategic approach to pricing reverses the sequence. Management first defines its desired market position relative to its target customers and competing brands; this positioning defines the acceptable price, which in turn determines the acceptable level of costs. The product has then to be designed to meet the cost constraint. In summary, price determines cost — not the other way around.

One final point: while markets have traditionally been divided into three or four segments, the evidence is that the number is increasing. At the limit, every customer can be an individual segment for which a separate product is designed and a price is set. This is referred to as one-to-one marketing. Several factors shape this trend. One is rising customer expectations for individually tailored solutions. These expectations are fed by greater affluence and more competition among suppliers. The second factor is information technology, which facilitates one-to-one communication between buyers and sellers.

Finally, new production methods, from flexible manufacturing to new networking relationships among supply chain participants, increasingly facilitate customised solutions.

Setting the price

The firm has to set initial prices when it launches a new product or when it takes an existing product into a new market.

Defining pricing strategy

The firm's pricing strategy is given by the answers to two questions: how does it want to position the brand in the market? What marketing objective will maximise shareholder value? Market positioning is defined by the brand and its differential advantage. It involves choosing the type of customers to serve, and choosing the type of customer benefits to deliver. The choice of target customers will also imply a choice of target competitors. This market positioning choice will then determine the feasible range of prices that can be chosen. A price strategy also has to be dynamic — the right target customers and positioning today are likely to be wrong tomorrow. As a consequence, pricing strategy will change over time.

The brand's differential advantage — the value target customers perceive it to offer — will determine the price that can be charged. If a customer believes a new product will enhance profits by $1000, then this is the maximum price he or she should be willing to pay to acquire it. A company can charge anywhere between 0 and $1000. For example, Netscape decided to give its Internet browser away free, while Intel has been charging companies wanting to acquire its latest Pentium microchip. Charging a very low price — or even giving it away free — is usually termed market **penetration pricing**. Charging a high price, close to its value to the customer, is termed **skimming pricing**. In today's information-based economy, the choice between skimming and penetration pricing strategies has received renewed importance.

penetration pricing: a price set to maximise sales volume

skimming pricing: a price set to maximise unit margins

» Skimming pricing

With skimming pricing, the firm sets the price high to achieve high unit margins. It recognises that this will limit its penetration of the market and is likely to encourage competitors to enter the market. Companies such as Hewlett Packard, Glaxo and Du Pont have pursued this strategy in the past.

Skimming may be the best strategy for creating shareholder value under the following conditions:

- **High barriers to entry**, e.g. patents in the pharmaceutical industry, make it hard for competitors to enter the market with lower prices.
- **Demand is price inelastic**, e.g. in strategic consulting, customers perceive high value from obtaining the best advice. In some markets where product performance is difficult to judge, price may be taken as an indicator of quality.
- **High-value market segments**, e.g. in luxury goods, Rolex and Gucci can maintain premium prices because their customers are unwilling to trade down.
- **Few economies of scale or limited experience**, e.g. in some industries smaller companies do not suffer unit cost disadvantages.

Where these conditions do not apply, skimming pricing generally fails to optimise value.

» Penetration pricing

With penetration pricing, the firm sets the price very low to maximise sales volume. It recognises that this will mean losses or low profits in the early years but believes this will create shareholder value through achieving higher long-run cash flow and a greater continuing value for the business. This strategy has been pursued to a striking extent in the new information-based markets, notably in Internet businesses, where investors have attached enormous value to businesses with little or no profits.

Penetration pricing may be the best strategy for creating shareholder value under the following conditions:

- **Low barriers to entry**, e.g. Internet businesses are cheap to start up, making it very easy for competitors to enter the market with low prices. High prices in this type of market lead to rapid erosion of market share.
- **Demand is price elastic**, e.g. in commodity markets, both quality and performance are similar and price becomes the dominant factor in obtaining market share.
- **Network effects and critical mass**, e.g. in some markets customers see greater value and lower risk in buying the same brand as others — many people want Microsoft Office software because they perceive it is easier to swap files with colleagues, learn transferable skills and get the latest products. Small share brands are unattractive because they are not standard.
- **Economies of scale and experience**, e.g. in today's globalising market place, more and more industries offer cost economies to bigger companies.

Many of the problems of smaller companies lie in the advertising invest-ments required to build and sustain brands.

Table 8.3 shows how penetration pricing is the superior alternative under the latter conditions. Under a skimming pricing strategy, the company intro-duces a new product with a high price that captures a substantial proportion of the value it offers the customer. This leads to big cash flow in the early years but then this declines as new competitors enter the market with substantially lower prices. By contrast, under a penetration pricing policy cash flow is zero in the early years because of the low prices and high capital requirements to support the faster volume growth. But then once a critical market share is achieved, margins and cash flow improve rapidly. Note in the example that the cumulative cash flows over the 7-year planning period are identical. When the cash flows are discounted, the skimming pricing strategy value is $10.2 million greater. Nevertheless, the penetration pricing strategy delivers more than twice the shareholder value of the skimming strategy. The real difference lies in the continuing value of the two strategies: at the end of year 7, the skimmer has lost its market position and is economically worthless; the penetration strategy has a strong market position, resulting in a business with a continuing value of $63 million.

Table 8.3 An illustration of skimming versus penetration pricing and shareholder value

	CASH FLOW ($ M)								PV OF CONTINUING
YEAR	1	2	3	4	5	6	7	CUMULATIVE	VALUE
Skimming pricing	10	11	12	8	6	3	0	50	
DCF (r = 10%)	9.1	9.1	9.0	5.5	3.7	1.7	0.0	38.1	0
							Shareholder value		38.1
Penetration pricing	0	0	0	4	8	14	24	50	
DCF (r = 10%)	0	0	0	2.7	5.0	7.9	12.3	27.9	63.2
							Shareholder value		91.1

Estimating the demand function

Essential to a sensible price decision is an objective estimate of how demand will vary with price. Few companies make such estimates and instead rely on subjective judgments. Given the enormous impact price has on profitability and shareholder value, poor estimates are likely to be very costly. One problem is that different managers typically have sharply different views about the sensitivity of demand to price. Sales management invariably argue that customers are extremely price sensitive and push for low prices to maxi-mise sales. Accountants, on the other hand, are more concerned with margins and push for higher prices. Another handicap to rational decision making is that managers argue about what 'the customer' is like. In fact, there is never an 'identical' customer; individual customers differ greatly in their sensitivity to price — some are highly price sensitive, others are much less so.

» Price elasticity

price elasticity: the sensitivity of demand in response to price variation in a market segment

The sensitivity of demand in a market segment is called the **price elasticity** and is defined as:

$$\eta_p = \frac{\text{Percentage change in quantity}}{\text{Percentage change in price}}$$

For example, if the price is increased by 5 per cent and as a result the units bought fall by 10 per cent, the price elasticity is −2. Usually the minus sign is omitted, as the negative relationship is understood. If a change in price results in a more than proportionate change in quantity demanded, then demand is said to be price elastic; if a change in price produces a less than proportionate change in the quantity demanded, then demand is price inelastic (figure 8.6).

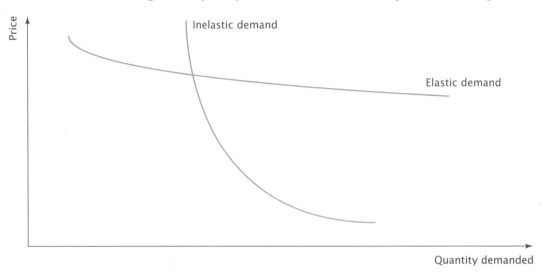

Figure 8.6 Elastic and inelastic demand curves

Managers would like their products to be price inelastic so that they can obtain higher prices without substantial volume losses. Much of the expenditure on advertising, branding and loyalty programs is aimed at reducing price elasticity and there is strong evidence that successful brands do have lower price elasticities. In general, price elasticity is reduced where:

• there are no goods substitutes available
• customers in the target segment perceive the brand as having added values that strongly differentiate it from alternatives
• customers have poor information about the products and prices that are available
• the product is only a small proportion of the customer's total expenditures
• the risks consequent to buying the wrong product are perceived to be high
• the decision maker does not pay for the product (i.e. it is charged on to someone else).

A fear facing many managers is that instant information and price comparisons over the Internet are increasing price elasticity, turning more and more products into commodities.

One has to distinguish between the industry demand curve and the firm demand curve. The firm or brand demand curve will normally be much more elastic than the industry curve. For example, a rise in the price of petrol will have little effect on total demand, but a rise in the price of one company's petrol price — if others do not follow — will have a huge effect on its sales. This is because it is easier to find substitutes for one firm's brand than for the commodity as a whole.

Studies show that the average price elasticity for products or brands is around 2. This means that a 1 per cent price increase reduces sales volume by

2 per cent. There are, however, huge differences across industries. It is interesting to note that price elasticities tend to be much greater than advertising elasticities. The average advertising elasticity is around 0.2, meaning a 1 per cent increase in the advertising budget increases sales by 0.2 per cent.[4] This implies that price is about 10 times as powerful as advertising in affecting sales.

Again, one has to remember that these advertising elasticities are averages and can disguise significant differences among segments. For example, Dolan and Simon found that overall demand for rail journeys was relatively price inelastic (less than 1.0), implying a price increase would increase revenue and profits.[5] But the overall demand is made up of two segments: commuters who are almost completely price inelastic — they have no alternative — and suburban off-peak users who are relatively price elastic. The obvious solution is to segment the market and introduce dual pricing to reflect the two different demand curves. Using the overall elasticity would be sub-optimal because it would lead to under-pricing of commuters and over-pricing and loss of revenue from off-peak users.

» Estimation methods

There are four main ways of estimating demand curves — expert judgments, customer surveys, price experiments and statistical analysis of past data.

1. **Expert judgments.** Typically, a number of industry experts are asked to predict volume at 'medium', 'low' and 'high' prices, and a consensus demand curve is developed. The advantages of this method are that it is simple and cheap and it is certainly preferable to traditional cost-plus pricing. Its major limitation is that experts' opinions can differ substantially from those of customers. This is particularly likely to happen where there are large numbers of customers with different price elasticities. The only way to get this important disaggregated information is through a consumer survey.

2. **Consumer surveys.** There are two approaches in common use. A direct price response survey asks consumers their probability of purchasing the product over a range of price levels. The demand curve is then plotted from those who say they would probably buy at each price. Again, this is simple and relatively cheap. The problems lie in its artificiality. In reality, consumers compare products across a range of attributes, not just price.

   In recent years, a new method, conjoint analysis, has become popular as a more realistic method of collecting information from consumers. First, the key attributes in the purchase decision have to be identified. For example, for a car they may include the brand name, price, engine power, fuel consumption and size. Second, consumers are presented with descriptions of models with different combinations of these attributes and asked to rank the alternatives in order of preference. Then a computer program calculates the value to the consumer of different levels of these features. From the result, one can construct a demand curve that predicts sales of any product at different price levels.[6]

3. **Price experiments.** In price experiments, prices are varied and the effect on demand is observed. These experiments can take place in a laboratory with a simulated shopping environment or actually in the market using different shops or different geographical areas. The Internet and direct mail catalogues, in particular, facilitate price experiments. The advantage of experiments over surveys is that actual consumer behaviour is observed,

although, unlike conjoint analysis, one does not get insights into which attributes could be altered to increase sales at a given price level.

4. **Analysis of past data.** In many markets, prices have fluctuated over time and the effects of these changes on demand can be analysed by statistical methods, most usually by regression analysis. Statistical methods can provide direct estimates of price elasticity as well as the effects of other variables such as advertising and different economic conditions. A problem with historical analysis often lies in obtaining reliable data. It can also be used only on established products. In practice, while models can be constructed to impressively fit past data, it is rare that these estimators are nearly as effective in predicting future demand.

Whatever method is used, it will need to be supplemented by managerial judgment. The previous estimation methods give an insight into the demand curve at a point in time. But to determine the strategy that creates the greatest value, management needs to augment this with long-term projections of the relationship between volume and price.

Estimating the cost function and investment requirements

Estimating the demand curve enables management to predict volume and revenue at different prices. But to estimate profits, management also need to predict costs, and to estimate cash flow they also need to predict investment requirements. Since the objective is long-term value creation, they need to know not just how costs and investment vary with sales levels but also how they will change over time.

» Predicting costs

Economies of scale mean that long-run unit costs usually decline with a higher volume. Companies have both variable and fixed costs; economies of scale apply to both. Greater purchasing power usually gives bigger firms an advantage in variable costs. Fixed costs include, of course, not just manufacturing but also management, R&D and, particularly, sales and expenses. Unit costs for most of these tend to be lower with bigger volumes. The implication is that lowering prices to boost volume may not cut margins proportionately because unit costs will fall.

Experience-curve effects describe how costs vary with learning. After studying large numbers of products, the Boston Consulting Group famously observed a remarkable regularity in how unit costs declined. They concluded that unit costs decline by a constant percentage (typically between 20 and 30 per cent) each time cumulative output doubles (see figure 8.7).[7] These findings had a major influence on business strategy in the 1970s and 80s. In particular, they emphasised the importance of market share. If a company grows more quickly than its rivals, it will move down the experience curve faster than them and open up a widening cost advantage. For instance, if Boeing achieves 60 per cent of the world market for large jets and Airbus holds only 30 per cent, then Boeing's unit costs should be around 25 per cent lower than Airbus (other factors being equal). Market share is viewed as the primary determinant of relative costs.

The experience curve has an important implication for pricing policy. It suggests that the firm should price its products not on the basis of its current costs, but on anticipated costs. For example, figure 8.7 shows a company with a price of $70 and a unit cost of $60 producing 100 000 units. Based on an experience curve analysis, however, it realises that if it could double its output, its costs would drop to $45 per unit. To drive for this volume, it decides to drop its price from $70 to $55. The price is initially unprofitable but once the volume goal is achieved the firm restores the unit profit target, but now with a dominant market share.

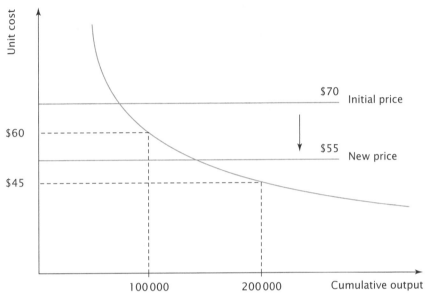

Figure 8.7 The experience curve

These dynamic cost relationships offer important insights into value-based pricing. In particular, they emphasise the dangers of cost-plus formulas and pricing aimed at maximising short-term profits. In growing markets especially, companies that do not maintain their market shares will often end up with non-viable cost structures, having missed opportunities to build scale and experience-curve economies. However, these relationships must be used with caution. If all the competitors are seeking to achieve scale and experience curve economies through ambitious strategies to build market share, then overcapacity will be the result and the anticipated superior profitability from market share will not emerge. A further problem is that focusing on opti-mising costs for existing products can open the firm to being leapfrogged by innovative products. Texas Instruments, for example, used experience-curve pricing to capture market share in calculators, but missed out on profitable new markets such as PCs, hand-held computers and mobile phones.

» Predicting investments

To calculate cash flow, incremental investment has to be deducted from after-tax operating profits. Incremental fixed investment is capital expenditures less the depreciation expense. A forecast of incremental fixed investment is usually obtainable from the long-term business plan. But this will have to be adapted to any revisions of the pricing strategy. The higher are predicted volume sales, the greater the fixed capital requirement. Incremental working capital investment represents net debtors, stocks and creditors that are required to support sales growth. Again, baseline forecasts are usually built from expressing the investment as a percentage of incremental sales.[8]

Projections need to be adjusted for pricing policy. For example, lower prices will tend to raise the historic relationship between investment and incremental sales. On the other hand, advances in technology may lower it. There is also evidence that economies of scale mean that companies with a high market share have lower percentage investment requirements than smaller companies.[9] Finally, any plans aimed at reducing investment (e.g. just-in-time stocking or manufacturing-to-order) have to be factored in.

Analysing competitors' strategy

Estimates of demand and pricing need to incorporate specific assumptions about competitors' current price-value combinations and their likely reactions to new product and pricing initiatives.

» Assessing competitors' values

Customers will choose products that offer the best perceived value. Value can be increased by improving perceived product quality or lowering the price. Competitive values can be compared using conjoint analysis or direct customer research. Here is an example of the direct research approach.[10] The method requires four steps:

1. **Identify the dimensions of quality.** Use focus groups to find out what product attributes customers are looking for when they choose suppliers.
2. **Weight quality dimensions.** Determine which attributes customers perceive as most important.
3. **Measure competitors along attributes.** Conduct a survey to determine how customers rate competitors' offers along the attributes.
4. **Discover value preferences.** Ask customers to rate which combinations of price and quality they prefer. Segment customers according to their preferences.

For example, a manufacturer of industrial cutting equipment was concerned about its poor market share and wondered if price was the problem. It undertook a research study in which customers rated the competitors and its own product X, as shown in table 8.4. The results were then mapped in figure 8.8. The investigation showed that there were three segments in the market: a premium segment led by competitor A; an economy segment led by C; and the largest segment in the middle, dominated by B. Product X's problem was clear: it was competing directly against B, but customers saw X's reliability and service as significantly inferior. It was positioned below the value line, offering an uncompetitive combination of quality and price. The obvious requirement for the company was to reposition X by either enhancing its quality or lowering its price, to improve its relative value.

In using these techniques, two caveats are needed. First, it is important to remember that all markets are segmented — not all customers desire the same value combinations. Pricing has to be geared to a specific segment. Second, the buying criteria generally vary among members of the decision-making unit. For example, in business-to-business markets, purchasing executives tend to be the most price sensitive; technical staff are more quality oriented; and senior executives emphasise lifetime costs and whether the seller can offer a potential competitive advantage to the company. Consequently, by strategically tailoring selling and communication to specific members of the buying unit, the supplier can partly shape the importance attached to the different attributes.

Table 8.4 Assessing price and value competitiveness

IMPORTANCE WEIGHTS (%)	QUALITY ATTRIBUTES	COMPETITORS			
		A	B	C	X
35	Precision	6	5	4	6
25	Reliability	6	6	3	4
15	Durability	5	3	2	5
20	Service	5	3	5	1
5	Delivery	2	5	5	5
	Weighted score	5.5	4.6	3.7	4.3
	Actual prices ($000)	29	21	15	22
	Market share (%)	27	45	20	8

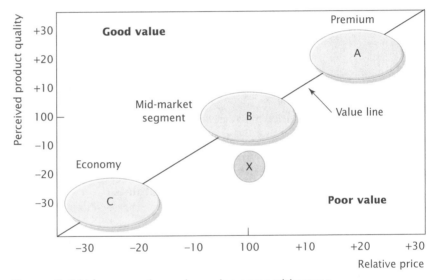

Figure 8.8 Value map: Assessing price competitiveness

» Anticipating competitor reactions

If a competitor sets a price to offer customers an outstanding value combination, it should anticipate competitors reacting to defend their market share. The company will not want to trigger a mutually damaging price war — which, as the Prisoner's Dilemma game illustrates, can easily occur. Anticipating competitors' reactions requires first understanding their strategic objectives for the product. How important is it for the company's future? This will suggest how hard they might fight to retain market share. Second, management need to estimate the company cost structure and financial strength. How much can they afford to cut prices and invest in defending the product?

Adapting prices to customers and products

Even though managers set initial prices, the price of a product is rarely set in isolation. Its price has to be set in relation to the other products the firm is selling and to the various markets and types of customer who might buy it.

Customised pricing

In the early days of the industrial era, such companies as the Ford Motor Company with its Model T and Coca-Cola with its ubiquitous curved bottle practised non-differential marketing. The same product was offered to the whole market at the same price. But in the second half of the 20th century, non-differential marketing gave way to segmentation and positioning. Companies varied their offers, tailoring products and prices to specific segments of the market. The information era has seen marketing strategies being customised even more precisely to customer needs with the emergence of one-to-one marketing. Airlines no longer just have three classes of tickets; any regular flight will contain people who have paid over a dozen different prices depending on when they booked, where they booked, who they booked with, how long they are away, their age, affiliation, past flights and so on. E-companies like Price-line.com even allow customers to name their own prices for a flight and invite airlines to compete. Internet auctions have become a rapidly growing pricing mechanism for many products in both industrial and consumer markets.

The importance of price on profits, cash flow and shareholder value has been constantly reiterated. A 5 per cent price increase can easily increase profits by 50 per cent or more. But in aiming to increase prices, it rarely makes sense to increase prices by 5 per cent to everyone. Consumers differ in price sensitivity. Some would switch to a competitor if faced with such an increase; others would not even notice. The same economic result is more likely to be achieved by raising the price by 10 per cent to half the customers, or by 20 per cent to a quarter of them. This principle of pricing is, as we have seen, based around capturing the **consumer surplus** — getting customers to pay the full amount that they are willing to pay.

consumer surplus: the excess between the price a consumer would be willing to pay for a product (rather than go without it) over the amount that the consumer actually pays for it

» **Constraints on price customisation**

For price customisation, or what economists call price discrimination, to work certain conditions are required:

- The market must be segmentable and the segments must show different price elasticities.
- Customers in the lower price segment must not be able to resell the product to the higher price segment.
- Competitors must not be able to undercut the firm in the higher price segments.
- The cost of segmenting the market must not exceed the extra revenue derived from price discrimination.
- The practice should not breed resentment against the firm and its products.
- The form of price discrimination should be legal.

Customised pricing techniques seek to meet these constraints. Greater competition and deregulation have encouraged price discrimination in more and more markets. New information technology facilitates price customisation. Scanners in stores and e-commerce companies can use software to monitor customer purchases and customise prices and promotions to each one. On the other hand, there is an increasing countervailing power with customers able to use the Web to compare prices instantly and discriminate between suppliers.

» **Customised pricing approaches**

Customised pricing is very important to creating shareholder value. A single price policy, on the one hand, loses the consumer surplus because the price is too low for some customers, and at the same time it loses revenue because it is too high for others. The aim of segmentation is to group customers by price sensitivity so that different prices can be charged. Most schemes do this only approximately. For example, airlines offer cheaper tickets to customers who stay over a Saturday; cinemas give discounts for children, but many of these customers who obtain lower prices are not very price sensitive and the company loses the consumer surplus. New information technology offers scope for better segmentation schemes. There are at least five basic approaches to customised pricing:

1. **Self selection.** By being offered different versions of a product at different prices, consumers can self-select and segment themselves according to their price sensitivity. This is done extremely widely in both consumer and business-to-business markets. In consumer goods, car companies offer a range of versions of the same model. For example, a customer for a new Mercedes C class can pay anywhere between $60 000 for the basic version to over $150 000 for the top of the range. Kodak offers Fun, Gold and Royal versions of its film for cameras. Microsoft offers its Office suite of programs in Professional, Standard and Small Business versions. The examples are endless today. Prices can easily vary by a factor of 10 from the cheapest to the most expensive variant, with the cost differences between them being minor. The advantage of this form of pricing is that since all variants are available, no one can object to it being 'unfair'.

2. **Controlled availability.** Controlled availability pricing differs from self-selection in that the customer does not have a choice about the price. As one-to-one marketing becomes more prevalent, it becomes possible to target different customers with different prices. E-businesses now offer individual customers special prices online, based on the information they have in their computer data banks of their past shopping patterns, and the price sensitivity these patterns imply. Supermarkets can do the same using the scanner data collected at the checkout. Sales promotions, coupons and direct mail catalogues can be similarly targeted. In the United States, for example, General Motors sent a US$1500 coupon incentive on a new car only to those who had expressed unhappiness with the previous model in a consumer survey. Victoria's Secret, the glamour underwear company, sent its catalogues with a US$25-off coupon to male addressees but not to females.

3. **Geographic pricing** is another type of controlled availability. Companies like The Gap, Nike and Ralph Lauren routinely charge 30 per cent or more in the United Kingdom than they do in the more price competitive US market. Controlled purchase locations also facilitate taking advantage of different price elasticities. For example, the low-price Eurail pass can be purchased only outside Europe; the operators naturally do not want it to be available to regular European travellers. Negotiated prices, long a feature of business markets, look likely to become more significant in consumer markets with the development of e-commerce.

4. **Buyer characteristics.** Different types of buyers are given different prices. Ideally, the criteria should be easy to apply and be effective in segmenting customers by price sensitivity. Common criteria are socio-economic variables such as sex, age, income, type of user and user status. In industrial markets, industry classification is often used. For example, some nightclubs allow women in free; children are allowed into many events at a lower price than adults; universities give scholarships to applicants from poor families; companies charge resellers less than they do end users; software companies sell new versions of their software to current users cheaper than to new users.

Today, however, such simple socio-economic categories generally do not sort customers out very effectively according to price sensitivity.[11] A better method is researching price sensitivity directly. This involves interviews to determine what factors are most important in the purchasing process to individual customers and then grouping customers by responses. Generally, the groupings do not correlate well with simple socio-economic or industry groupings. For example, studies by McKinsey and others have looked at industrial purchasing.[12] They found most markets, even mature commodity markets, could be segmented into three types of buying companies:

(a) **Price-sensitive buyers** who are primarily concerned with cost and less so with the quality provided. They exhibit little loyalty to suppliers.

(b) **Service-sensitive buyers** who require the highest levels of quality and often have special service and delivery requirements.

(c) **Relationship-oriented buyers** who want a close long-term commitment from their suppliers geared to developing superior customised products and processes. Research needed to be done on a one-to-one basis because price sensitivity did not match obvious industry characteristics such as end-user industry, company size or value added. Armed with the right segmentation information, the supplier is in a much more effective position to apply customised pricing. The same is increasingly true in consumer markets where price-oriented shoppers, for a particular product, rarely fall neatly into a clear socioeconomic group such as income or age.

5. **Transaction characteristics.** Transaction characteristics often facilitate price discrimination. Timing is one criterion. In the airline industry, a ticket booked well in advance and including a Saturday night stay is a signal of a price-sensitive customer. Prices are varied by season, day and hour. Coca-Cola has been considering new vending machines that will charge higher prices on days when the weather is hot. For hotels and airlines 'yield pricing' — finely tuned pricing to mop-up anticipated vacancies — is a key to profitability. Quantity is another transaction characteristic widely used in pricing, the assumption being that customers who buy large quantities are more price sensitive and therefore receive discounts. Banks offer higher interest rates on larger deposits. Supermarkets offer 'buy six bottles and get one free'.

Care needs to be taken with price customisation plans. First, customisation usually entails extra costs and investment for modifying the product and communication channels to individual customers or segments. The company needs to assess that the plans are profitable. Second, discriminatory pricing can lead to customer disaffection; it can also be illegal. Airline or hotel customers can get upset to discover that the adjacent customer is paying half the price for an identical service. It also changes the relationship between the customer and the company's service staff. Customers sometimes feel they cannot trust the representative to give them a fair deal and the transaction focuses on price negotiation rather than solving the customer's problem.

Product mix pricing

Companies have increasingly broadened their product lines to meet the different needs of customers and to capitalise on their different price sensitivities. This means that managers do not price a product in isolation but rather have to consider, in addition, its impacts on the sales and prices of other products in the range. Products in a range can be complements or substitutes. Complements are where sales of one product stimulate sales of another. For example, if Polaroid sells more cameras, it will also sell more of its film. For complementary products, the optimal product line price is lower than the stand-alone price. Substitutes are where sales of one product reduce the sales of another. For example, sales of a faster model of a Dell PC may reduce the sales of its slower model. Four common situations can be identified:

1. **Product line pricing**. There are several reasons why suppliers introduce multiple products. The most obvious is to meet the needs of different segments. For instance, Nike offers separate shoes for runners, tennis players and so on. A second reason is that separate products permit the firm to charge different prices and capitalise on different price elasticities. For example, Castrol sells a range of car lubricants from a low price GTX, to the more expensive GTX2 and GTX3, and up to a GTX7 in Japan. A broad product line also allows the firm to encourage customers to trade up over their life cycle. So Mercedes aims to capture younger buyers with its C class car and trade them up as they become older and more affluent with its E and S models. Finally, different products are sometimes tailored to adapt for differences among distribution channels. Discount channels operate on low gross margins; other distributors want exclusive products. A common solution to these conflicts is offering separate products. Sometimes these are under different brand names; sometimes the differences are in product quality or special features.

   Without a line of targeted products, firms would lose market share. The problem is that these products are at least partly substitutes for one another and low-margin products can easily cannibalise high-margin ones. Another danger is that downward extensions can threaten the exclusive image of the firm. It is important, therefore, to try to preserve the identities of the high-margin products and to set price points that take into account substitution effects.

2. **Product follow-on pricing**. Some products require the use of ancillary products. These follow-on products are complements. For example, it will generally be more profitable for producers of razors or cameras to price them lower than their optimal stand-alone prices to increase sales. The loss of margin is compensated by charging higher prices for the subsequent blades or film. The danger with the strategy is that the high prices of the follow-up products attract 'pirates', who capture much of the profits. Companies with follow-up products have to try to build unique designs, patents, or guarantees that lock customers into the supply of 'original parts'.

3. **Product options pricing**. To reduce the perceived price, a product may be advertised at a low, stripped-down price. At the point of purchase, the salesperson then seeks to persuade the buyer to add high-margin options. A typical buyer of a $120 000 Mercedes-Benz will be persuaded to add another $10 000 on options and features that will contribute disproportionately to the company's margin. In contrast, Japanese auto companies have historically bundled a comprehensive range of options in the sticker price to offer customers a superior value proposition.

   Options are complementary products and features. When they are bundled together, the customer will normally obtain a significant discount to emphasise the value of the offer. For example, Microsoft Office, which bundles Word,

Excel and PowerPoint, costs around 50 per cent less than buying the three programs separately. Without detailed information about elasticities across the market, it cannot be predicted whether bundling or separate pricing is optimal. Bundling can be profitable when it allows the company to tap unexploited consumer surplus. Unbundling is better when there are opportunities to exploit new markets through selling the products individually.[13]

4. **Product blocking.** Often, it makes sense for a firm to introduce a special product to block new low-price competitors from making inroads into the market. Cutting the price on the main product would be very expensive. Instead, the company launches a blocking or 'fighter brand' aimed at those price-sensitive segments most at risk from the new competition. The company will make little or no profit from the blocker product but this is compensated for by its ability to preserve margins on its less price-sensitive customers and to limit penetration by competitors.

International pricing

The globalisation of business has made international pricing a major issue. Currently, big differences can exist in the prices the firm charges for its product in different countries. The barriers to trade that permit such divergences to persist allow the firm to significantly increase profits by capitalising on differences in price elasticities. Unfortunately, declining trade barriers, notably in the new trade areas such as the European Union and the North Atlantic Free Trade Area (NAFTA), are markedly reducing the scope of such divergences, with potentially damaging implications for profitability.

» Pressures for price harmonisation

Several factors are making it difficult to sustain major price differences between countries. These include:

• **Elimination of trade barriers between countries.** This makes it easier to ship the product from a cheap country to an expensive one.

• **Decreasing transportation costs.** This makes it more profitable to undertake arbitrage transactions.

• **Growth of arbitragers.** Information agents and grey importers have been established to capitalise on opportunities from country price differences.

• **Superior information availability.** The information revolution has greatly enhanced the ability of companies to obtain up-to-the-minute data on international prices.

• **Increased globalisation of brands.** With brand names and packaging increasingly standardised, it becomes much easier for customers to accept grey imports.

• **Growth of international sourcing.** Corporate purchasing departments are increasingly focusing on identifying the lowest regional and global prices and demanding them from suppliers.

» International price alignment

Greater price harmonisation could be very damaging for many companies. Without careful planning, pressures for harmonisation can push prices to the lowest international price level with calamitous effects on margins (figure 8.9). To prevent this, companies are recommended to plan for a 'price corridor' with a mean price in between the highest and lowest price countries. This entails sacrificing some market share in the low-price markets and some margin in the high-price ones. But some price differences will be retained, implying an acceptance of some level of grey imports. The exact structure of this 'least worst scenario' depends upon details of the market sizes and price elasticities in the individual countries, the expected growth of grey imports resulting from the price differentials in the corridor and information on competition and distribution.[14]

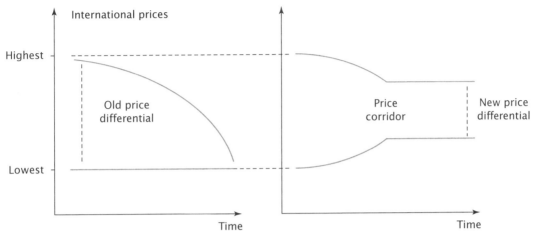

Figure 8.9 Planning for price harmonisation

Another important issue on international pricing concerns adjustments for exchange rate changes. A depreciation of the US dollar against the Australian dollar could wipe out the profits of an Australian exporter if it leaves its US dollar price unchanged. On the other hand, if it raises prices to maintain its equivalent Australian price, then its market share is going to collapse. As with the price corridor, the best solution is usually a compromise; in this case a 'moderate' price increase shares the burden of the change. As usual, strategic considerations have also to be taken into account. In particular, the longer-term repercussions on market position have to be considered. Adapting export prices to movements in exchange rates may be optimal in the short run but it may undermine the firm's long-run ambitions in the market.

Promotional pricing

Price cuts to stimulate purchase are widely and increasingly used by suppliers. In the United States, 75 per cent of major appliances are now bought 'on deal'. Sears sells 55 per cent of its goods 'on sale'. Promotions are used with the objectives of accelerating purchases, getting new customers to try the product, encouraging customers to buy more or gaining new sales from price-sensitive customers. The growth of promotional pricing reflects the increasing competitive pressures in many markets. It is a tempting competitive weapon because studies show that promotional price elasticities are often very high, up to four times normal price elasticities. A promotional price elasticity of around 8 means a 5 per cent temporary price cut typically yields a 40 per cent unit sales increase.

Promotional prices come in many forms. Some are trade promotions aimed at persuading retailers or distributors to carry the brand, or more of the brand. They include various forms of discounts, allowances and contests. Others are consumer promotions aimed at getting consumers to buy more. They include coupons, price-off, cash rebates, low-interest financing and sales events.

Promotions have grown at the expense of advertising in their share of marketing budgets. However, they are a controversial tool among marketing professionals. One problem is that the powerful effects of price promotions almost guarantee that competitors will have to respond. The result then becomes a zero-sum game in which all the suppliers lose margin. If money is diverted from advertising and long-run brand-building investments to promotions, this also threatens a manufacturer's long-run profitability. High short-run sales boosts are then outweighed by a decline in the brand's long-run competitiveness. Promotions also impose additional costs in the form of higher stocks and expenses in communicating and implementing the program.

But the biggest concern with promotions is whether they cannibalise regular high-margin business. Studies clearly show that most of those who buy on promotion are the company's regular customers, who would have bought anyway.[15] If the promotions encourage customers to load up, then normal sales decline in proportion to the incremental business in the promotional period. The high promotional price elasticities may, as a result, be somewhat illusory. Profit then suffers a major hit because the disproportionate level of sales in the promotional period carry a very low margin. The long-run effects may be amplified in promotion-prone markets. Consumers come to see the sale price as the 'normal' price and become unwilling to buy at the regular price.

In attempts to break the vicious circle of promotions, some companies, including such notable marketing heavyweights as Procter & Gamble and Aldi, have sought to substantially reduce price promotions in favour of 'everyday low prices'. They believe this will reduce supply chain costs, enable them to develop consistent brand images and offer customers a better deal over the longer run.

Sales promotions are likely to be more effective for smaller brands. Price promotions can give customers an incentive to trial their new product. It is also more difficult to make advertising cost-effective for small brands. Companies are also becoming more conscious about ensuring promotions do not damage the brand's image. One of the growing techniques is 'cause-related marketing' whereby the seller associates the promotion with a good cause, usually a charity.[16] In the United Kingdom, for instance, Pizza Express ran a levy on sales of its Veneziana pizzas, with the Venice in Peril campaign as the beneficiary. Tesco ran a highly successful promotion whereby customers earned points that could be used by neighbourhood schools to buy computers. In the United States, American Express ran a similar campaign to help renovate the Statue of Liberty in New York City. In Australia, examples of cause-related marketing include the efforts of Woolworths in organising an annual children's hospital appeal, while McDonald's has Ronald McDonald houses, which provide assistance to the parents of seriously ill children.

Changing the price

From time to time, management has to change prices. Naturally, price increases are more difficult to implement than price decreases. However, achieving price increases is often essential.

Price reductions

There are always pressures on management to reduce prices. When the industry is in recession and there is excess capacity, these pressures are amplified.

Sometimes, price cuts are used proactively to increase the firm's dominance in the industry. This may be particularly appealing if the firm believes that there are major economies of scale or experience-curve advantages to be had from greater market share.

Price cuts offer more value to customers and a higher market share may be expected. But there are dangers. First, price cuts are easy for competitors to copy. If they do follow, then all the players are worse off. Second, even if the company attracts new customers as a result of its price cut, these switchers are unlikely to be loyal and can switch again when a competitor takes an initiative. Third, price cuts can sometimes lead customers to question the quality or success of the brand, threatening its brand image. Finally, cuts can upset dealers or recent customers who see the value of their stocks depreciated.

Given the threat to profits that price cuts present, it is worth managers considering alternative ways to maintain or increase market share. These can include improving the perceived quality offered. After all, a 10 per cent cost increase is a lot less costly than a 10 per cent price cut. Another strategy may be to launch a **fighter brand** to serve those segments that have become most price sensitive.

Price increases

As we have emphasised, price is one of the most vital determinants of shareholder value. In periods of high inflation, obtaining price increases is easier. With an inflation rate of 20 per cent a year, buyers do not see a 23 per cent price increase as remarkable, but with low inflation such real price increases are much harder to obtain.

Strategies to obtain high prices can be seen in terms of a trade-off between timing and feasibility (figure 8.10). On the one hand, there are some techniques to improve prices that management can try immediately, but their feasibility is uncertain. On the other hand, there are some very straightforward ways of obtaining higher prices, but their deployment can take years. The only sure way of achieving higher prices is by finding ways to deliver greater value to customers. This may be via operational excellence, customisation, new marketing concepts or innovative products. For example, if a company can develop a new battery that will enable electric cars to operate with the flexibility of petrol-engine ones, or if a pharmaceutical company can develop a cure for cancer, then there will be no problem about attaining a price premium. Superior performance and innovation are the only sustainable means of obtaining better prices. The techniques for increasing prices are listed in order of their immediacy.

» Influencing sales psychology

Sales training and motivation can often produce higher **realised prices** relatively quickly. Generally, salespeople are more oriented to volume rather than profits. They are often so concerned about not losing a customer that they cave in too easily on price. Management needs to encourage salespeople to be more courageous — to be willing to take more risks in pushing for price increases. After all, the objective is to maximise long-term profitability, not sales volume. Sales force incentives can also be changed to encourage a focus on price or gross margins. Some sales teams are still bonused on volume, which invariably undermines efforts to improve profitability. Third, training in professional negotiating skills is crucial for managers involved in

fighter brand: a brand designed to defend the flagship brand against low-price competitors

realised price: actual price paid by customers after all discounts have been deducted from the invoiced price

price negotiations. Today, purchasing managers have become increasingly aggressive in their negotiating tactics.

Quick (but tough)

Sales psychology
- Courage
- Incentives
- Negotiating skills

Contracts and terms
- Escalation clauses
- Cost-plus formulas
- Discount reductions

Demonstrate value
- Sell packages
- Show EVC
- Build brands

Achieving higher prices

Segmentation and positioning
- Segment by price sensitivity
- Multibrand
- Trade-up
- Fighter brands

Create exit barriers
- Finance and equipment
- Brands and partnerships
- Training and development

Slow (but easier)

Deliver greater value
- Operational excellence
- Customer intimacy
- New products
- New marketing concepts

Figure 8.10 How to obtain higher prices

» **Contracts and terms**

With long-term contracts, there can be a significant gestation period between order and delivery. Skilled managers can often negotiate escalation clauses that allow them to protect margins by having prices rise automatically with inflation. Over time, such clauses can have a marked impact on profitability and avoid the necessity of annual price negotiations. Cost-plus formulas are another contractual approach to margin protection. Suppliers can agree to meet new customer needs on the basis of protected margins. Finally, discount reductions act in the same way as price increases. Many companies allow satisfactory list prices to be eroded into unprofitable realised prices by giving away unnecessary discounts for on-time payment, buying minimum quantities, seasonal discounts and other allowances.

» **Demonstrating value**

Most companies fail to optimise prices because they sell product features rather than demonstrating the value of their product to the customer. Focusing on product features invariably emphasises price as buyers compare competing products. There are several ways of focusing more productively on value to the customer. One is to sell packages rather than products. Packages include emphasising the services, technical support, terms and guarantees offered alongside the physical good, for example. Even more effective is demonstrating directly the economic value to the customer (EVC) of the product. This means showing the customer the lifetime savings accruing from purchasing the product. Another value creator is brand values that give customers confidence in the product's qualities or the experience associated with using it. When a blue chip company signs up with McKinsey or a woman buys Armani they are willing to pay a price premium because they perceive the brand as unique, conveying an image, reputation and confidence not possessed by competitors.

» Segmentation and positioning

Basic to any marketing strategy, and critical to pricing, is the recognition that customers differ greatly in price sensitivity. For some customers, price is the most important criterion, but for others quality, service or image are much more significant. If a 5 per cent price increase can increase operating profits by 50 per cent, then this 5 per cent increase is invariably best achieved by segmentation. That means recognising that some customers will not accept any increase at all, while others will accept a 10 or even 20 per cent price increase. Implementation requires researching what factors are most important in shaping the buying decisions of individual customers, grouping customers according to similarity of need, and then positioning different offers at different prices to each group, or indeed customising them to each individual buyer.

A further step permitting even wider scope for price discrimination is the development of a multibranding or line extension strategy. Here, differentially priced brands or lines are targeted to different segments of the market. So Distillers in the United Kingdom sell Johnnie Walker Red Label Scotch whisky at around $20, Black Label at around $55, Blue Label at around $180, and so on. Such a policy also often facilitates a policy of trading up, where customers start with an entry-level brand, for example the American Express green card, and are subsequently encouraged to move up to a more expensive option, such as the American Express gold or platinum card. A fighter brand is another tool for price segmentation. It allows a company to defend its market share without having to cut prices across its entire market. For example, Armani Exchange is a fighter brand for Giorgio Armani.

» Creating exit barriers

Skilful companies focus on creating exit barriers that make it difficult for customers to switch to cheaper suppliers. These include:

- **Provision of finance or special equipment.** Tetrapak, for example, leases sophisticated assembly line equipment to customers using its packaging. Switching suppliers would require customers to make major new capital investments.
- **Customer partnerships.** Suppliers can integrate into the customer's research and development work, making divorce a major problem. Outstanding levels of service can also increase the customer's dependency.
- **Brand images.** Customers who have developed associations and loyalty with a particular brand are reluctant to switch. Research shows that strong brands have relatively low price elasticities.
- **Training and development costs.** For example, it is costly and difficult to switch from Microsoft products once staff are trained and expert on their use.

- **Electronic links.** Where IT is integrating the two supply chains, changing suppliers entails increased risk and disruption.
- **Loyalty programs.** Where customers have built up privileges from loyalty programs, such as frequent flyer schemes, they are reluctant to write off these assets.

» Delivering greater value

In the long run, offering customers added value is the only way to obtain consistently high prices. All the other routes are one-off or limited opportunities that eventually erode market share. Without bringing new value to customers, competitors and new formats inevitably commoditise a company's products. Added-value strategies that permit premium pricing can be grouped into four:

1. **Operational excellence.** Customer value can be created by increasing the perceived efficiency of the current services offered to the customer. This effectively lowers the cost to the customer by cutting out hassle, inconvenience and the need to carry safety stocks. Service quality can be increased in five main ways:

   (a) **Reliability.** Performing services more dependably and accurately.

   (b) **Tangibles.** Customers respond to the professional appearance of physical facilities, equipment, personnel and communication materials.

   (c) **Responsiveness.** Greater willingness to help customers and to provide prompt service.

   (d) **Assurance.** Improving knowledge and courtesy of employees and their ability to convey trust and confidence.

   (e) **Empathy.** Providing more care and attention to customers.

2. **Customer intimacy.** Customising solutions on a one-to-one basis can enhance pricing power. When a customer receives a tailored solution, made and delivered to meet individual needs, the impression is created of getting exactly what is wanted rather than a compromised solution aimed at meeting the needs of a broader group with different needs. Today's information revolution is facilitating greater customer intimacy through (1) permitting flexible data banks of individual customer information to be constructed at very low cost; (2) allowing cheap one-to-one communication between the firm and individual customers; and (3) the development of fast, flexible supply chains that permit customised manufacturing.[17]

3. **New products.** The most obvious means of gaining a premium are to develop new products that offer customers superior economic, functional or psychological values. Customers value products that meet unmet needs or meet current needs in a superior way. Customers will pay more for pharmaceutical products that they perceive as more efficacious, batteries that last longer, computers that are faster, or equipment that is more productive.

4. **New marketing concepts.** New products require technological innovation; new marketing concepts add value by changing the way existing products are presented or distributed. They are more common than product innovations. New marketing concepts include:

   - **Identifying new markets.** For example, Lastminute.com identified a new market for customers wanting to go on holiday, go to a restaurant, go to a show or send a gift, immediately.
   - **New market segments.** Coke identified a huge market for diet cola. David Jones identified a major segment for pre-prepared gourmet foods.

- **New delivery systems.** The Internet, in particular, has stimulated new delivery systems of existing products that offer superior convenience or service to customers. Amazon.com's revolution of the book market is just one example.
- **New business systems.** Customer value can be created from offering customers services rather than simply the physical goods. Castrol launched Castrol Plus, which instead of selling lubricants to workshops offered a service that maintained the efficient running of customers' equipment.
- **New information.** New information can create value for customers. Suppliers such as Procter & Gamble and Cadbury offer supermarkets a category management service that enables retailers to increase the productivity of their space.

Price implementation

Effective pricing requires good strategy and good implementation. So far, we have focused on the strategic issues. Now, we turn to implementation issues.

Implementation concerns achieving the profitability that the pricing strategy is designed to obtain. There are two important issues: obtaining reliable cost data to measure customer and product profitability; and optimising realised prices as distinct from invoiced prices.

Differentiated costing

To target the right customers and prioritise the right products, it is important to have accurate measures of customer and product profitability. Typically, there are big differences in the costs of serving different customers and across different products in the line. For example, some retail chains want daily delivery to individual stores; others will accept twice a week delivery to a central warehouse. Others want special packaging and customisation. Products differ in the amount of R&D and technical service they require.

Most companies have standard cost systems that do not identify and allocate such differences in overheads. Tracking true customer and product profitability requires activity-based costing (ABC) that allocates both variable costs and overheads to the products and customers that incur them. When this is done, profit margins on high-value-added products can be lowered by up to 10 per cent. In general, standard costing systems overstate the profitability of high-end products and customer segments, allowing simple products to subsidise complex ones and low-end customers to subsidise high-end ones.

Achieving realised prices

There is often a significant difference between invoiced prices and realised prices, which can seriously impact on profits. Figure 8.11 illustrates this for a textile manufacturer selling to retailers.[18] The starting point in implementing a pricing policy is the list price. From this are normally deducted discounts for such things as larger orders and competitively negotiated terms to arrive at the invoice price. But in most firms the invoice price is not the actual realised price. From the invoiced price are deducted a whole new range of discounts for such things as prompt payment, volume bonuses and promotions. It is this realised price, not the invoice price, that determines the profitability of a customer or a product. Here the difference is big, amounting to almost 23 per cent off the invoice price per unit.

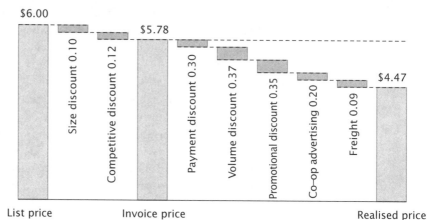

Figure 8.11 Realised prices versus invoiced prices

The problem is that management attention focuses on the invoiced price rather than the money the company actually realises. In fact, most accounting systems do not even measure realised prices. Many of these discounts get lumped into overheads and not allocated to individual products and customers. Again, with discounts varying enormously across transactions, the profitability of individual products and customers can be seriously misunderstood.

Summary

1. Effective pricing is of fundamental importance to strategies aimed at maximising shareholder value. On average, a 5 per cent price increase can raise economic profits by over 50 per cent. However, in the long run, premium prices can be sustained only by offering customers superior value. Charging premium prices without offering higher value will undermine the company's market position.

2. The pricing strategy that maximises shareholder value is different from one that maximises market share or profits. Pricing to maximise market share or revenue leads to prices that are too low. But the price that maximises short-term profits is generally too high because it ignores the implications of economies of scale, competition and market share on long-term cash flows. The value-maximising price is the one that maximises the present value of future cash flow.

3. Customisation is central to an effective pricing strategy. Many managers make dangerous generalisations about what price customers in their market will be willing to pay. The error is assuming that there is a typical customer. In fact, customers, even in what are considered commodity markets, differ greatly in their price sensitivity. For the company to achieve its twin objectives of growth and healthy margins, it must employ price discrimination — generally meaning providing different products at different prices to different customers. This way, it can both cover more of the market and capture the consumer surplus available from less price-sensitive clients.

4. Price elasticity is normally relatively high. Certainly, it is usually much higher than advertising elasticity. This means competitors are likely to react to price cuts, especially in mature markets. When a price war is triggered, all competitors can end up worse off. Consequently, pricing strategy needs to carefully assess competitive strategies.

5. Information technology and the Internet increase the price elasticity of most markets. The Web lowers the barriers to entry for companies competing on price. It also makes up-to-date information about products and prices more readily available to customers. Finally, it enables customers to be more proactive in negotiating prices and encouraging suppliers to compete for their customers.

6. Pricing strategy needs careful implementation. Most companies do not have accurate data on the costs of serving different customers and selling individual products. They also lack data on realised prices, which can be quite different from the recorded invoice prices. As a result of inadequate pricing and cost information, companies can be prioritising the wrong customers and wrong products.

key | terms

consumer surplus, p. 306
customised pricing, p. 292
fighter brand, p. 313
mark-up pricing, p. 287
Nash Equilibrium, p. 293
penetration pricing, p. 298
price competition, p. 285

price elasticity, p. 299
price signalling, p. 294
realised price, p. 313
skimming pricing, p. 298
strategic group, p. 296
target-return pricing, p. 287
value-based pricing, p. 289

review | questions

1. Illustrate how pricing decisions normally have a major impact on shareholder value.
2. Why is the price that maximises the firm's profits likely to be very different from the one that maximises shareholder value?
3. What should determine the choice between a penetration and a skimming pricing policy?
4. Show how customised pricing usually creates shareholder value.
5. Suggest some techniques that can be used by firms in highly competitive markets to increase achieved prices.

discussion | questions

1. How and why can understanding of competitive strategy and consideration of the competitive environment lead to the development and management of effective pricing policy?
2. What implications arise from the demand and cost functions involved in setting an optimum pricing strategy for creating long-term shareholder value?
3. How is pricing influenced by current marketing strategy? How does it influence future marketing strategy decisions?
4. How and why is an in-depth understanding of segmentation critical for developing a pricing strategy that maximises shareholder value?
5. Discuss the concept of economic value to the customer (EVC) and show how it can be used in pricing decisions.

debate questions

1. Should a company pursue promotional pricing?
2. Do you consider the Internet to present more challenges than opportunity for pricing strategy?
3. What strategies do you consider most effective in the implementation of a price increase?
4. Is it better when introducing a new product to adopt a skimming or penetration strategy? How and why does this vary between markets?

case study | **The Australian airline industry at the turn of the 20th Century**

When Impulse and Virgin Blue entered the market, Qantas and Ansett responded with discounted fares, but did not offer many seats at the new price. So this had relatively little effect on the newcomers who soon claimed operating profits, but just a few weeks later Qantas announced it would add extra capacity to its flight schedules presumably in order to offer more discounted seats.

On routes that were not served by Impulse and Virgin, no doubt the lowest fares of Qantas and Ansett were around 50 per cent of their full fares. But on routes served by the newcomers, the major airlines were charging about 20 per cent of those traditional fares. These discounts of 80 per cent meant that Qantas and Ansett might have sold at prices that were below their costs. And on some of the Impulse routes, Qantas announced flexible fares at half the previous level. The lower air fares led to reduced profits for Qantas and increased losses for Ansett.

It is not surprising that competitive entry erodes profit margins. It can make sense to lower air fares even though that loses money in the short term. But part of the pain at Qantas and even Ansett was voluntary. After all, an established company that drives out a newcomer by promotional pricing can hope to return to high profits that outweigh short-term losses. Because airline cost/revenue structures are complex, it is difficult to prove that deeply discounted fares have been too low to cover costs, which could warrant legal action.[19]

It is salutary to consider why the policies of Impulse and Virgin were in the national interest. The companies offered an attractive basic service and substantially increased air travel by those who couldn't afford the customary fares of the major airlines.

In the absence of competition from others and given their cost structures, Qantas and Ansett found it more profitable to ignore much of the low fare market.

Could an incumbent like Qantas have changed its style, reduced its costs and catered for lower-income private travellers? 'Management experts believe that long-established companies find it difficult, if not impossible, to make such a change. Generally, a new way of providing a service requires a new start–up company. In any case, there is no argument for imposing a basic service on all passengers. Instead, a happy market outcome would be for Qantas — and would have been for Ansett — to focus on those who want to travel in some style, while others are served by low-cost airlines.

Source: Adapted by the authors of this book from Gordon Mills, 'Air fares don't have to take flight', *Australian Financial Review*, 3 May 2002.

Questions
1. Why is the airline industry particularly characterised by intensive price competition?
2. Why do think that Impulse and Virgin entered the Australian airline market and what went wrong?
3. A principle underlying effective pricing is that it should add value to the customer offering. Has this been the case in the airline industry and what implications does this have for companies in the industry?
4. Discuss the implications that the price war poses for the industry.

end notes

1. The revenue in the triangle is given by $\frac{1}{2}$ base × height, i.e. ABC = 150 × \$1100 = \$165 000.

2. For a review of game theory applications to business see Howard Raiffa, *Decision Analysis*, New York: McGraw-Hill, 1997.

3. For more on pricing and marketing strategy see Harper W. Boyd, Orville C. Walker and Jean-Claude Larréché, *Marketing Management: A Strategic Approach with a Global Orientation*, Chicago, IL: Irwin, 1995.

4. Raj Sethuraman and Gerald E. Tellis, 'Analysis of the tradeoff between advertising and price discounting', *Journal of Marketing Research*, 28 May 1991, pp. 168–76.

5. Robert J. Dolan and Hermann Simon, *Power Pricing*, New York: Free Press, 1996.

6. On conjoint analysis see Jonathan Weiner, 'Forecasting demand: Consumer electronics marketer uses conjoint approach to configure its new product and set the right price', *Market Research*, Summer 1994, pp. 6–11; Dick R. Wittnick, Marco Vriens and Wim Burhenne, 'Commercial uses of conjoint analysis in Europe: Results and critical reflections', *International Journal of Research in Marketing*, January, 1994, pp. 41–52.

7. Carl W. Stern and George Stalk (eds), *Perspectives on Strategy from the Boston Consultancy Group*, New York: John Wiley & Sons, 1998, pp. 12–24.

8. For details on the methodology of forecasting investment requirements see Tom Copeland, Tim Koller and Jack Murrin, *Valuation: Measuring and Managing the Value of Companies*, New York: John Wiley & Sons, 1996, pp. 224–46.

9. Robert D. Buzzell and Bradley T. Gale, *The PIMS Principles: Linking Strategy to Performance*, New York: Free Press, 1987, pp. 74–6.

10. Adapted from Peter Doyle, *Marketing Management and Strategy*, 3rd edn, London: Prentice Hall, 2001, chapter 8.

11. John Forsyth, Sunil Gupta, Sudeep Halder, Anil Kaul and Keith Kettle, 'A segmentation you can act on', *McKinsey Quarterly*, no. 3, 1999, pp. 6–15.

12. Louis L. Schorch, 'You can market steel', *McKinsey Quarterly*, no. 1, 1994, pp. 111–20; V. Kasturi Rangan, Rowland T. Moriarty and Gordon S. Schwartz, 'Segmenting customers in mature industrial markets', *Journal of Marketing*, October, 1992, pp. 72–82.

13. A good discussion of price bundling is in Robert J. Dolan and Hermann Simon, *Power Pricing*, New York: Free Press, 1996, pp. 222–47.

14. Hermann Simon and Eckhard Kucher, 'The European pricing time bomb: and how to cope with it', *European Management Journal*, 10(2), June 1992, pp. 136–45.

15. A. S. C. Ehrenberg, K. Hammond and G. J. Goodhardt, 'The after-effects of price-related consumer promotions', *Journal of Advertising Research*, July/August 1994, pp. 1–10.

16. Hamish Pringle and Marjorie Thompson, *Brand Spirit: How Cause Related Marketing Builds Brands*, Chichester: John Wiley & Sons, 1999.

17. See Adrian J. Slywotzky, 'The age of the choiceboard', *Harvard Business Review*, January/February 2000, pp. 40–1.

18. Adapted from Michael Marn and Robert L. Rosiello, 'Managing price, gaining profit', *Harvard Business Review*, September/October 1992, pp. 84–93.

19. For further discussion of airline pricing in Australia, see chapters 11 and 14 of Gordon Mills, *Retail Pricing Strategies and Market Power*, Melbourne: Melbourne University Press, 2002.

9

Products

chapter objectives

By the time you have completed this chapter, you will be able to:

- describe the anatomy of a product
- analyse the value of a product mix
- explain the difference and link between invention and innovation
- critically evaluate the effectiveness of a new product development process
- apply the principles of shareholder value to new product development.

scene setter

Leveraging cholesterol for margarine products

Demographic changes and developments in nutrition have brought about significant adjustments to Unilever's value proposition in the food market. Customers are increasingly demanding food products that are nutritional, functional and beneficial for their health. Paradoxically, consumers continue to enjoy and demand products that are detrimental to these dietary ideals. This is especially true for margarine — a product customers remain apprehensive about when it comes to its high levels of cholesterol, but a product they continue to relish in large quantities.

Aware of this paradox in the margarine market, Unilever addressed the issue. The company conducted extensive research to define the nutritional needs of consumers using, or potentially interested in using, margarine. After segmenting the market based on dietary needs, Unilever decided to target 'baby boomers' — a segment characterised by pronounced dietary concerns and high consumption, and by high disposable income. The company believed that targeting this segment would generate significant economic returns on a new margarine product.

Unilever resolved to offer a modified margarine product, Flora Proactiv, while maintaining their existing margarine products. Flora Proactiv differed from existing offerings by being positioned as a dietary food product that contained cholesterol-lowering phytosterols.

Considerable investment was made in communicating the nutritional benefits of the new margarine to target customers. One of the messages in a television commercial went something like this: 'My father died young, and when I found out I had a cholesterol problem I just thought, "Well, I'm not waiting around for it to happen to me." So I started using Flora Proactiv, which actually reduced my cholesterol absorption. With Flora Proactiv I'm down from 6.5 to 4.5 in just three weeks. Now I can do anything I've been wanting to do for years.'

Flora Proactiv has been an enormous success in the United Kingdom and the United States. Competitors quickly followed with imitation products in the Australian market, such as Logicol by Goodman Fielder. By re-evaluating the nutritional benefits their customers need, Unilever has successfully created a valuable product.

Introduction

Without a value proposition, a firm cannot exist. A cornerstone of any value-based marketing proposition is the product. In today's marketing environment, firms increasingly customise their offers so that there is no standard product. The customer defines the product as much as the supplier. Also, firms increasingly augment their product with a range of attributes to increase their market competitiveness.

Defining products

Taking these issues into account, a value-based perspective yields a powerful definition: a **product** is anything that delivers a benefit needed by a customer. This means a product can be a physical good (e.g. balloon, chain), service (e.g. holiday, meal), technology (e.g. radar, wireless communication), person (e.g. Michael Jordan, Elvis Presley), organisation (e.g. World Trade Organisation, National Heart Foundation) or idea (e.g. socialism, safe sex). Importantly, a product can be a combination of these factors.

> **product:** something that delivers a benefit needed by a customer

To understand the implication of this, we start with the fundamental point that customers attach value to a company's offer in proportion to its perceived ability to help solve their problem and meet their needs. Customer needs can be separated into core needs and potential needs. A **core need** is the basic functional attribute a customer requires. A **potential need** is the ultimate goal of the customer. For example, a core need of a car buyer is to buy a car that runs reliably. The potential need of the car buyer might be to maximise the investment in the car by being able to sell the car after five years with minimal losses. The closer a car manufacturer gets to meeting the customer's potential need, the more value it can provide to the customer and the greater its ability to differentiate the offer.

> **core need:** the basic functional attribute a customer requires from a product
>
> **potential need:** the ultimate goal a customer hopes to achieve with a product
>
> **basic product:** those attributes of a product that meet the core needs of a customer
>
> **expected product:** those attributes of a product that a customer normally expects, for example friendly service
>
> **augmented product:** those attributes of a product that exceed what the customer expects
>
> **potential product:** those attributes of a product that fulfil all possible expectations and goals a customer might have when purchasing the product

The product hierarchy describes how a company can build the level of a product to enhance the value it offers its customers (figure 9.1). The **basic product** is the level of product offer that meets the core need of the customer. For a steel supplier this might be a specific grade and quality of steel. But buyers expect more than a basic product; they also expect hassle-free delivery, specific prices and payment terms, and technical support if necessary. The **expected product** is the set of product attributes that buyers normally expect when they purchase this product. But a supplier can go even further than this by augmenting the product to exceed what the customer was expecting. This is called the **augmented product**. For example, the steel supplier might offer steel coatings and finishing, or services such as machine maintenance on site and just-in-time delivery. Finally, there is the **potential product**, where the supplier offers a total solution to the customer's ultimate or potential need. For example, the steel supplier could offer a partnership that guarantees to take 5 per cent a year out of the car company's body manufacturing costs, thus improving the customer's bottom line by a defined and significant amount.

Today, it is increasingly difficult to earn economic returns from offering basic or expected products. Gradually, competition in established industries has shifted to the augmented level, whereby suppliers offer more services and features to differentiate themselves and seek to gain preference. But ultimately the best way of forging enduring relationships with customers is to focus on *their* ultimate or potential needs and offer them solutions which have direct value, rather than offering them more of your products.

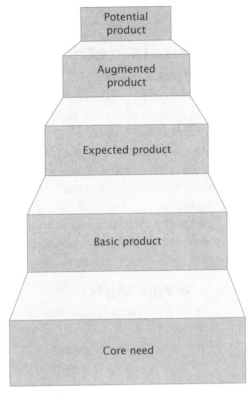

Figure 9.1 The product hierarchy

Product mix decisions

In developing product policy, business unit managers have two broad decisions to make:

1. How much should the business be investing in new product development or in modifying the existing products? The manager has to ask whether customers will pay enough to generate an economic return on the investment.

2. How many products should the business be offering to the target market? Here the manager has to ask whether the market segment is valuable enough to justify more products.

product mix: a firm's assortment of products

Basically, both questions are centred on determining the **product mix**, which can be defined in terms of product line breadth, length and depth. Breadth refers to how many different product lines a business unit carries. For example, Procter & Gamble has an extraordinarily broad range of products, including baby care, deodorants, dish care, hair care, skin care, oral care, laundry products and pet food. Length refers to the number of items within a product line. For example, Procter & Gamble's oral care category includes Crest toothpaste, Scope mouthwash, Fixodent denture adhesive and Gleem toothpaste. Depth refers to the number of variants of each item. For example, Crest toothpaste comes in many different varieties including liquid gel, baking soda, whitening control, tartar control, dual action, multicare whitening, cavity protection and sensitivity protection.

The answers to both questions are influenced by the following product mix determinants: the core strategy, the strategic objective of the business, its strategic focus, targeted market segments and competitive potential of competitors.

Product mix determinants
Core strategy

The first determinant of the product mix is the business core strategy. The core strategy will set the tone for how many resources are put into developing a new product or modifying an existing product. If the value positioning is around low price, then the necessity of minimising costs will lead to a 'basic product' positioning. While the breadth of the product mix might be large, the length and depth is likely to be moderate. If the value proposition is centred on service, the business will invest in an 'augmented product' strategy. If the proposition is customisation, then the company will be creating a 'potential product' positioning. In these two instances, any breadth, length and depth of mix is imaginable.

Strategic objective

The second determinant of these decisions is the business unit's strategic objective. In general, the more ambitious the growth objectives of the business unit, the greater the breadth, length and depth of its product mix. For example, a business like Amazon.com, whose share price is dependent upon achieving truly enormous sales growth, predictably increased the breadth of its product line. It started with books, but then added CDs to double its potential revenue sources, then auctions, and later a whole range of retailing lines. Without broadening its product line beyond books it could never have achieved the 10-year sales target of over $60 billion, since the entire book market was worth only $12 billion. Similarly, in its push to dominate its categories, the length of its product lines was expanded. For example, the number of different books it offered was increased to over three million. It also increased its depth, offering hardback, paperback and gift variants of most books. If such a company had become 'accounting oriented' and sought to increase profits by pruning the product mix and focusing only on areas that were currently profitable, its potential growth would have been curtailed, triggering a fatal collapse in the share price.

Strategic focus

The third determinant of the product mix is the strategic focus. Where a business shifts from a volume to a productivity focus, the product criteria change. Here the product mix is designed for more immediate profits than long-term sales growth. The length of the product line is likely to be reduced to cut costs, save on working capital and focus on the more profitable items. Management should explore the possibility of introducing premium-priced versions of the more successful products to trade up customers and to capitalise on the higher margins that can be made from less price-sensitive customers.

Targeted market segments

The targeted market segments also have an important influence on the product mix. As the market develops, it becomes increasingly segmented. It is vital to introduce products to match the needs of each segment if the company is to retain customer loyalty. For example, once consumers simply bought trainers. Nike built a dominant presence by identifying that the market was segmented: players of tennis, basketball and squash, joggers, serious runners and those who 'hang out' could all have targeted products. It was no contest between Nike's customised offerings and the mass-marketed products of their old-fashioned rivals. If a company has different customers with different needs — and that is virtually always — then it will need different products. Of course, the ultimate level of segmentation — increasingly possible in today's information age — is one-to-one marketing: a different 'product' for each customer.

Competitive potential of competitors

The competitive potential of competitors can also influence the optimal product mix. Some products are introduced to thwart the strategic ambitions of competitors. Xerox had its position undermined in the copier market after it declined to produce cheap, low-volume copiers for smaller offices. This allowed Canon to first exploit the small market and then use this opening to move up into the larger product heartland of Xerox. Rover's increasingly weakening position in the middle range sector of the car market was exploited in the United Kingdom when the luxury car makers, BMW, DaimlerChrysler (with Mercedes-Benz) and the Ford Motor Company (with Jaguar) moved downmarket with mid-level cars.

To prevent competitors threatening the core businesses, companies need to consider line stretching. Downward stretching occurs when a company located at the upper end of the market stretches its line downward to block a segment that would otherwise attract a new competitor. A good example is Armani. Giorgio Armani products (the original product line) are positioned at the top end of the fashion segment. Emporio Armani products are positioned at a lower price point. Armani Express products (the latest product line to be launched) round off the lowest price point targeted by Armani. Upward stretching is where a company at the lower end shifts into the higher end. Toyota soon recognised that its core competence in quality engineering could be leveraged in price segments above the low and mid-range. Thus, it decided to enter the luxury market with the Lexus product range.

When a company is attacked by low-priced competition, it often resorts to launching fighter products. These are products added to the line and targeted at price-sensitive accounts most at risk from the new competition. The aim is to segment the market and limit as far as possible the overall decline in margins caused by price competition. Fighter products will often be withdrawn if they succeed in eliminating the competitor. In 2001 Qantas introduced its City Flyer product between Melbourne and Sydney (a major Australian trunk route) in response to new price competitor, Virgin Blue. It is the classic fighter product: offer the market high-frequency flights between the two cities (much like a shuttle service) and competitive prices, thereby leveraging Qantas's excellent airport terminal presence.

New product development

New product development is a central aspect of value-based marketing. Unless augmented or replaced, efficient products are soon made obsolete by environmental changes that stimulate new customer needs, attract new competition and offer new technologies that provide better solutions (see marketing management in practice 'Slow death in the grocery aisles'. Unless rapidly occupied, viable new markets are soon lost to those competitors who are able to quickly obtain market share, establish industry standards and lock up distribution channels. If left with obsolete products and confronted with occupied market segments, marketing managers will face declining customer loyalty, loss of customer share and declining sales margins, to name just a few likely and immediate consequences — not to mention the implications for shareholder value.

Marketing management in practice:
Slow death in the grocery aisles

Late January 2002 was not a happy time for Revlon Australia. Its hair-care brand Flex was removed from Woolworths' supermarket shelves to make way for a shampoo and conditioner range based on Dove, a Unilever Australia toiletries brand. There is a chance Woolworths might take Flex back — if Revlon changes its product formula, packaging and marketing strategy. Flex is yet another example of a once-successful product biting the dust. At its peak, Revlon Flex had about 10% of the shampoo and conditioner market. It has since dropped to below 3%.

Woolworths' chief general manager, buying and marketing, Bernie Brookes, says: 'A brand has got to be getting at least 3–5% of the market to be safe on our shelves. The opportunity now is to re-invent the brand.' Brookes says the problem for Flex was that nothing had been done to the brand for a long time. It was tired and had little marketing support.

Unilever's marketing maestros have been working on pushing one of their star brands, Dove, into new product categories, such as deodorant (a Dove deodorant was introduced in 1999) and now hair care. Brookes is upbeat about Dove's long-term potential, but even by his figures it will have to fight to stay alive.

Woolworths' buying team sifts through more than 20 000 new products, line extensions and packaging rejigs each year, accepting just 2200, or 11%. That is the good news. Every year, Woolworths deletes 2000 lines. 'Eventually nine out of 10 new listings fail,' says Brookes. 'They may take 10 years but they will fail.'

It is a sobering statistic, and it is substantially higher than the accepted industry rule that 70% of new products die within two years. But few people are surprised. There are plenty of new-product success stories circling the Australian market, but few consumer marketers say they have a guaranteed way to reduce the new-product failure rate ...

[The marketing director at Cadbury Schweppes, Tim Stanford,] has used market research techniques such as choice modelling with some success at Cadbury. The Lion chocolate bar, which was successfully launched last year, was subjected to such pre-launch analysis — a process in which numerous sales scenarios are run through software algorithms based on consumer product trials, purchasing frequency and variations in distribution, packaging, promotion and price. 'The product almost lived up exactly to what the market research said we would achieve,' says Stanford, who has also had his share of failures using such techniques. He says research methods such as choice modelling are expensive, costing between $50 000 and $200 000, and are used sparingly at Cadbury. 'Some of our products we know intuitively will work.'

The marketing director at Arnotts, Peter West, takes a different line. 'We have doubled our market research investment in the past two years,' he says. 'The real focus has been on innovation.' In the past 12 months, Arnotts has put about 25 new product concepts through 350 consumer research trials. Another 30 ideas will be put to consumers in the next two years, and West says those that clear the hurdles will go into development. The three key development areas for Arnotts are product portability, including packaging and product refits such as Tim Tam Fingers; the premium biscuit segment, highlighted by the success of its Emporio biscuit range; and healthy eating — the Rix range of low-fat chips is now outselling Pringles (a brand owned by Procter & Gamble) with about $20 million in annual sales.

George Weston Foods' Noble Rise bread has also capitalised on consumers' preferences for more healthy, natural staple foods. In two years, it has become a $50-million brand, thanks to regular new line extensions and heavy promotion. Chris Langley, the marketing manager for Noble Rise and Tip Top, another Weston brand, says: 'People these days want to hang on to the traditional values in life but they want it in a contemporary offer. Fresh bread for them is getting Noble Rise in product forms they used to get from the local baker down the street. Every loaf is a little bit different, not perfectly formed.'

The latest Noble Rise variants, Tasty Crust White and Crunchy Toast White, are designed to highlight texture rather than flavor. Langley says: 'The big lesson is to have a unique point of difference but follow it up. Don't launch and leave it. We differentiated this brand but we've supported it with $7 million in media (advertising).'

One recent hit new product is Cadbury Dream, a white chocolate bar that has now entered European markets after doubling the size of white chocolate sales in New Zealand and Australia. Launched in New Zealand in 2000, Dream appealed to young women and extended the white chocolate category, which had been essentially a children's product in the form of Milky Bar. Stanford says Cadbury had been underperforming in the white chocolate market, but Dream solved that problem.

When sales of Dream were booming in New Zealand, Cadbury's rivals in the Australian confectionery market, including Nestlé and Mars, introduced new white chocolate products here. Nestlé's move to counter Cadbury Dream is more typical of what has been happening in new-product development in the past decade. Instead of launching a new brand, it used the Kit Kat brand to release a white chocolate variant. Earlier, Nestlé achieved big sales with Kit Kat Chunky. The core Kit Kat product mainly appeals to young women, but Kit Kat Chunky has been a hit with young men. Nestlé's share of confectionery bars sold through supermarkets increased from 10% to 12% during 2001 ...

Source: Extracts from Paul McIntyre, 'Slow death in the grocery aisles', *BRW*, 1–13 February 2002, pp. 60–62.

Accordingly, new product development is a central topic on the agenda of value-based businesses (see marketing insight 'Accelerating pressures to develop new products'). Top management has to champion new product development by continually asking three questions:

1. Are there new products that could be developed, purchased, licensed or imitated to meet customer needs?
2. Can variations of existing products extend the product range to meet a greater variety of customer needs?
3. Can existing products be improved to better meet targeted customer needs?

Of the thousands of new products being introduced annually, very few (some industry observers suggest less than one per cent) are **new-to-the-world products** — products that are new to both the firm and the market. A more frequent new product type is **line extensions** — products that are not new to the firm, but new to the market. Typical examples are new applications of a

new-to-the-world products: products that are new to both a firm and the market

line extensions: products that are not new to a firm, but new to the market

firm's core product to better fit special customer needs. These relatively low-tech marketing initiatives can be very valuable. For example, Coca-Cola's line extension Diet Coke is valued at around US$20 billion. Unilever's recent introduction of a tablet extension of its Persil detergent allowed it to overtake Procter & Gamble's Ariel as the number-one brand in the United Kingdom. Another major category of new product types is **me-too products** — products that are new to the firm, but not new to the market. Basically, these are a company's version of products already introduced by competitors. For example, Dell Computer Corporation followed the lead of Toshiba and Compaq in launching a line of notebook computers. But most products introduced today are not new products. They are **product improvements** — upgraded or redesigned versions of previous models launched by the firm. However, without these continual facelifts, new products would soon become obsolete or unfashionable.[1]

me-too products: products that are new to a firm, but not new to the market

product improvements: upgraded or redesigned versions of previous product models launched by a firm

---

Marketing insight:

Accelerating pressures to develop new products

Pharmaceuticals is one of many industries being forced to radically ratchet up new product development. In the past, patents meant successful new products earned huge profits for an average of ten years. When the patent expired, sales and profits usually collapsed under the onslaught of generic competitors. To maintain performance, successful companies reckoned that they had to bring out one new product every two years. But now investors want companies to bring out six new drugs a year, a 12-fold increase!

Expectations have been changed by three recent scientific revolutions — molecular genetics, informatics and automation, which are expected to lead to an explosion of new products. To survive, companies are looking at three strategies to ramp up their innovation activities. The first is outsourcing more of their R&D to new, niche companies with expertise in the new technologies. Second, they are boosting their own internal R&D budgets. The need to find bigger budgets has produced an explosion of mergers and alliances in the industry. Third, they are reengineering their new product development processes to accelerate the speed of development and launch and to ensure that they are closely linked to customer requirements.

Invention versus innovation

From a resource-oriented view, new product development is concerned with product attributes (remember that products can be physical goods, services, technology, people, organisations, ideas, or a combination of these factors). From a market-oriented view, new product development is concerned with customer benefits.[2]

Most of the marketing literature does not take into account that invention and innovation are two different aspects of the new product development process; the two concepts are used interchangeably and, sometimes, as alternative terms for 'new product development'. Adopting a value perspective sheds new light on the concepts. The difference is subtle, but critical: an **invention** is something that provides a new benefit; an **innovation** is something that has been commercialised and thereby tested by the market to determine whether customers need the new benefit.[3]

invention: a new product benefit

innovation: something that has been commercialised and thereby tested to determine whether customers need the new benefit it provides

Many inventions fail to find profitable markets because customers do not see them as offering benefits that are *needed*. For benefits to be needed rests on at least two factors. First, the benefits must be valued by customers. For example, a new watch, accurate to one second in a hundred years, would be a great technical feat, but would probably not be regarded as a substantial benefit by consumers. Second, the benefits must be considered unique (or rare) by customers. If customers perceive that products already on the market are similar or identical, the new product is not likely to be seen as necessary (all other marketing variables considered equal).

To be deemed a driver of shareholder value, an innovation must be tested against the following three criteria:

1. **Timeliness.** Speed in developing and launching new products is increasingly critical. Innovations that are delayed usually cost more to develop, earn lower margins and obtain smaller market shares than those that are fast to market.

2. **Marketability.** The company must have the capability to market the innovation. This includes designing a reliable and effective version of the product, producing it at a price customers can afford, establishing an effective distribution system to deliver and support it, and engaging in a dialogue with the market.

3. **Sustainability.** An innovation may offer meaningful and unique benefits, but unless it is inimitable and non-substitutable, it will not create much shareholder value. The product developer must try to erect barriers to imitation and substitutability, preferably also to market entry. In some industries, patents may provide a barrier, but more often it is achieved through an optimal marketing mix that yields a superior brand.

It is estimated that over 80 per cent of new products fail to generate a return to shareholders. Many are subsequently withdrawn. They fail because they are not an innovation in the first place, or do not meet the three criteria above.

The new product development process

To guard against these causes of failure, the business needs to develop processes and an organisational culture that increase the chances of successfully developing a stream of new products. An effective new product development process typically consists of the following steps (figure 9.2):[4]

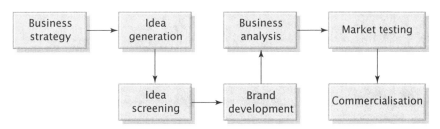

Figure 9.2 The new product development process

1. **Business strategy.** Management needs to articulate a business strategy that sets out its ambition to innovate. For example, 3M makes innovation the core of the company's strategy by demanding business unit managers achieve a minimum of 25 per cent of their profits from new products. Most companies will have a mission statement that identifies the markets, needs and technologies that form the scope of its activities. New product ideas will normally be expected to fall within this ambit defined by the firm's core capabilities.

2. **Idea generation.** New ideas come from many sources. Customers and technical research are two basic sources. But competitors, overseas markets, distributors and licensees can also be extremely fruitful. Virtually all sources depend on employees, and in particular front-line staff, identifying and championing the opportunities.

3. **Idea screening.** Once it has a stream of ideas, management needs to filter out those that are not worth pursuing. Companies often use screening techniques that rate ideas on their potential uniqueness, market potential and fit to their capabilities and business strategies. There are two types of errors in a screening process. Type I errors result from not screening out ideas that subsequently fail. They lead to financial losses from developing and promoting products that do not meet benefits needed by customers. Type II errors are harder to recognise, but can often be much more costly. These are mistakes in dropping ideas which could have been successful. (For some examples, see marketing management in practice 'Type II errors in new product development'.)

Marketing management in practice:	**Type II errors in new product development**

'The telephone has too many shortcomings to be seriously considered as a means of communication. This device is inherently of no value to us.'
Western Union internal memo, 1876

'The wireless music box has no imaginable commercial value.'
David Sarnoff, 1923

'Who the hell wants to hear actors talk?'
H. M. Warner, Warner Bros, 1927

'I think there is a world market for maybe five computers.'
Thomas Watson, chairman of IBM, 1943

'We don't like their sound, and guitar music is on its way out.'
Decca Recording Co. rejecting the Beatles, 1962

'There is no reason why anyone would want to have a computer in their home.'
Ken Olsen, President of Digital Corporation, 1977

'The Web — it's not going to be that profound.'
Steve Jobs, President of Apple, 1996

4. **Brand development.** Ideas that get through the initial screening have then to be developed into brands. Branding involves defining the product idea in terms of the target market segment (who might buy it) and the value proposition (why they would buy it). The brand is a crucial determinant of the product's future marketing plan. Developing a brand is generally a difficult step because, initially, most new products could potentially be aimed at quite different segments and have different value propositions. For example, something as simple as a new cold remedy could be aimed at children or adults, severe or normal sufferers, those with headache or cough symptoms, etc. Similarly, the value propositions could be built

around efficiency, speed of action, length of action, fewer side effects or a low price.

Brands should be tested for their appeal by researching the following broad issues (the questions raised are by no means exhaustive):

- **Benefit.** Is there a customer benefit?
- **Market.** What types of customers are most interested in the benefit?
- **Need.** Do customers view the benefit as valuable and unique?
- **Usage.** When would the benefit be needed?
- **Distribution.** Can the benefit be offered to customers when needed?
- **Price.** Can the benefit be offered at an affordable price?
- **Communication.** Would customers understand and believe the benefit being offered?

5. **Business analysis.** Normally, the amount invested in the new product up to this stage is relatively low, but if it proceeds further costs and investment will now begin to accelerate. To make this go/no go decision management should require a detailed business analysis that will enable them to judge the potential rewards, risks and investments needed. In principle, this is the standard net present value calculation to determine whether the proposed project will create value for shareholders.

The first task will be to calculate the level and timing of cash flow over the planning period. This requires marketers to estimate the prices that can be obtained and the growth of sales over the period. Next, the different functional areas will need to estimate the costs and investment requirements for developing, making and distributing the product. Since these estimates will be very uncertain, it is useful to produce optimistic and pessimistic estimates, as well as a median forecast of cash flow. Finally, management will need to choose the discount rate to be applied to the project. The more risky the product looks, the higher the discount rate that will be applied. The expected net present value of the project is then:

$$\text{ENPV} = \sum_t \frac{p_t C_t}{(1 + r)^t}$$

where ENPV is the expected net present value of the new product, C_t is net cash flow in year t, p_t is the probability estimate attached to cash flow in year t and r is the cost of capital.

The go/no go decision should not be based solely on the results of this financial calculation. Broader strategic considerations need to be examined. A failure to invest in a new product area could give a competitor a strategic opportunity to enter the market and build a beachhead for subsequent expansion. Similarly, a decision to invest may offer profitable growth opportunities that are not reflected in the basic discounting formula. The theory of options is increasingly being used to value such strategic new product opportunities. Option theory calculates the net present value of a project by explicitly incorporating estimates of the value of the future options a new product may offer (see marketing insight 'Using options to value new product proposals').

The next stage involves developing a product concept capable of commercialisation. The product development work demands the close cooperation of a cross-functional team, with each member bringing in his or her specialist knowledge. A product has to be designed and developed to match the chosen brand concept and be capable of efficient production and delivery. There are a wide variety of market research techniques for developing and testing alternatives.

Marketing insight:

Using options to value new product proposals

The net present value rule can sometimes be misleading when applied to new products. When managers factor in the high levels of uncertainty about a new product's potential cash flows, the NPV will often be negative, indicating that the product proposal should be rejected. But such a decision may be wrong because management does not need to make a go/no go decision at the start of the new product development process. Instead, they can purchase an option by investing in research and deferring a decision until the results are known. This is an extremely common situation in developing new products and, indeed, in developing growth strategies generally.

Option theory was developed in finance in the 1970s. More recently it has started being applied in marketing decisions. Essentially, options are a combination of decision tree analysis and NPV. A simplified example can illustrate the approach. Management is considering a new product concept. The product will require a $100 million investment and if it succeeds it will be very profitable, generating an income stream with a present value of $150 million. The chances of success are put at 50:50. If it fails, then the present value of the income stream is put at $10 million. A traditional NPV analysis would put the expected value of the project at $80 million. Since this is less than the upfront investment of $100 million, it has a NPV of minus $20 million, which leads to a rejection of the product proposal.

But in practice, management will not put the whole investment upfront; instead, they will research the project. Suppose management takes an option to invest $10 million in research and consumer testing and delays a decision about proceeding further until the results are known after 12 months. If the development and testing are successful, management will launch the product and reap the profits of $150 million. However, since both the investment ($10 m + $100 m) and the returns are delayed by a year, they are discounted by the opportunity cost of capital, say 10 per cent, to $100 million and $135 million, respectively, or a net gain of $35 million.

The overall value of the new product, then, is $7.5 million (the average of $35 million and zero, less the upfront $10 million). Management should therefore proceed with further development and testing.

The technicalities in options analysis lie in calculating the discount rates to be used. Usually, these are considerably higher than the normal weighted cost of capital. In summary, option valuation is most important in situations of high uncertainty where management can respond flexibly to new information, and where the project value without flexibility is near breakeven. If the NPV is very high, the project will go full steam ahead, and flexibility is unlikely to be exercised. Optionality is of greatest value for the tough decisions — the close call where the traditional NPV is close to zero.

Source: Derived from Thomas E. Copeland and Philip T. Keenan, 'How much is flexibility worth?', *McKinsey Quarterly* no. 2, 1998, pp. 38–49.

---

6. **Market testing**. After a product has been developed and pre-tested, a company can test it further in a more authentic market setting, to get more reliable information about the size of the market and reactions to the elements of the product brand, and to anticipate any problems that may occur in the full launch. The product can be tested in a sample of shops or distributors. Consumer goods are often tested in a representative geographical area.

7. **Commercialisation.** Once it is decided to commercialise the brand, then the really major costs and investments in manufacturing and marketing are incurred. By then management hope that all the problems have been anticipated. Speed to market is increasingly important. Being first — provided it is done right — often offers major advantages in terms of higher profits and long-run market share.

Fast product implementation

Successful new products are quickly copied. If the company is to profit from its innovation, it needs to move fast and to establish critical mass. Speed may allow the company to establish a **first-mover advantage**.[5] A first-mover advantage is based on access to resources and capabilities that later entrants cannot easily acquire. The advantages include:

> **first-mover advantage:** an advantage based on access to resources and capabilities that later entrants cannot easily acquire

- **Patent and copyrights.** By establishing a patent or copyright, the first mover may possess technology, products or designs from which followers are legally excluded.
- **Scarce resources.** When key resources are scarce, e.g. locations for new supermarkets or specialised employees, first movers can pre-empt these resources.
- **Higher prices.** Prices are usually higher at the beginning of the market life cycle. The first mover can recoup higher margins before competition erodes prices.
- **Reputation.** The first mover establishes a reputation with customers, suppliers and distributors that cannot initially be matched by followers.
- **Standards.** When proprietary standards in relation to product design and technology are important, the first mover may have an advantage in setting the standard.
- **Experience.** Economies of learning suggest that the first mover can obtain a cost advantage by virtue of its longer experience.

Achieving first-mover advantage is not simply about being first but also about achieving sufficient scale to defend against ambitious followers. It requires heavy investment in marketing and product development. Strategic alliances and partnering are ways of sharing the costs of developing the market. Priorities in exploiting the growth opportunity will include:

- **Market development.** Initially, a new product is bought by a specialist niche but if it is successful it will spread to broader markets. It is important for the innovator to lead in the development of these new market segments; otherwise it offers a beachhead for new competitors. For example, Xerox, inventor of the copier, did not develop the market for small machines, which allowed Canon to enter the market and become a major rival.
- **Brand nurturing.** Creating and fortifying a well-known and trusted brand name can give additional sources of defence. Even when competitors copy the product, customers may feel more confident buying a familiar brand. Much of the success of companies like Gillette, Coca-Cola and Marlboro is due to their continuous investment in brand building.
- **Brand extensions.** Line extensions allow the product to be more finely tuned to the needs of specific customer segments. Such customisation makes it more difficult for competitors to find gaps.

• **Overseas markets.** The erosion of barriers to trade has made it danger-
ously myopic for a company to neglect the opportunities presented by
overseas markets. Exploiting such opportunities will often require the firm
to find partners with experience and resources already in place.

Consumer adoption process

When launching a new product it is important to consider how the market
will develop. It is generally a mistake to aim at all customers. People and
firms differ in their propensity to take up new ideas quickly. An important
idea in marketing is the consumer adoption process. Figure 9.3 shows the
typical development of a market from launch to maturity. Researchers term
the first $2\frac{1}{2}$ per cent of consumers buying the product innovators; these are
followed by the early adopters, early majority, late majority and, finally, the
laggards.

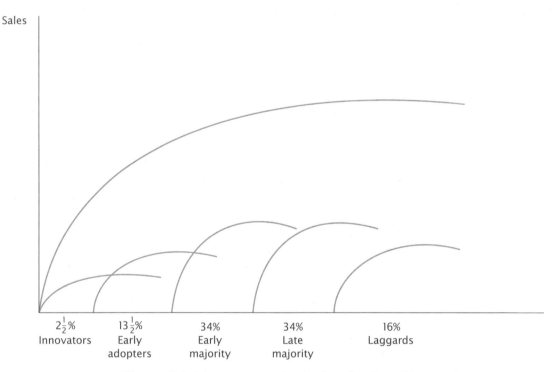

Figure 9.3 Adopter categories in the adoption of innovation

For a new product, it is important to focus on the innovators. The mass
market will not buy until the opinion leaders have taken up the product
first. The characteristics of innovators vary with the specific product, but in
consumer markets they tend to be younger, more highly educated, more
affluent and more cosmopolitan. In business-to-business markets, innovators
tend to be those customers who are more technically aware, who can gain
most economic value from the new product, and who can manage the risks
of trialling it.

The following characteristics of the new product also influence its speed of
adoption:

• **Relative advantage.** The greater the perceived added value offered by the
new product, the quicker it will be adopted.

- **Compatibility.** If the new product does not disrupt the customer's current practices and processes, it will be taken up more quickly.
- **Complexity.** Adoption will be facilitated if it is easy to understand and use.
- **Divisibility.** It helps if the customer can sample or trial the product before purchase.
- **Risk.** The greater the economic or social risk attached to failure, the more reluctant buyers will be in buying it.
- **Communicability.** Adoption is facilitated when the product's advantages are easy to show.

Summary

1. A product is anything that meets a benefit needed by the customer. This means products can be physical goods, services, technology, people, organisations or ideas.
2. The product hierarchy describes how a firm can build a product to enhance the value it offers its customers. The hierarchy is composed of basic, expected, augmented and potential products.
3. In their development product policy, organisations need to consider the product mix, which can be defined in terms of breadth, length and depth. The product mix is influenced by the product mix determinants: core strategy, strategic objectives and strategic focus of the business, as well as targeted market segments and competitive potential of competitors.
4. New product development is a central aspect of value-based marketing. Unless augmented or replaced, efficient products are soon made obsolete. There are two aspects of new product development from a value-based perspective: invention and innovation. An invention is a new benefit; an innovation is a new benefit that is actually needed by the customer.
5. Organisations need to develop processes and an organisational culture that increase the chances of successfully developing a stream of new products. This involves seven steps: business strategy, idea generation, idea screening, brand development, business analysis, market testing and commercialisation.
6. Successful new products are copied quickly. Speed may allow an organisation to establish first-mover advantage. Achieving first-mover advantage is not simply about being first but also about achieving sufficient scale to defend against ambitious followers. Organisations need to exploit growth opportunities for a new product. This involves market development, brand nurturing, brand extensions and overseas markets.

key terms

augmented product, p. 324
basic product, p. 324
core need, p. 324
expected product, p. 324
first-mover advantage, p. 335
innovation, p. 330
invention, p. 330
line extensions, p. 329

me-too products, p. 330
new-to-the-world products, p. 329
potential need, p. 324
potential product, p. 324
product, p. 324
product improvements, p. 330
product mix, p. 325

review | questions

1. How do we define a product and what considerations determine a product mix?
2. Why is new product development important and what processes are involved?
3. What advantages can a first mover derive in a product market?
4. What is the customer adoption process and why is it important for new or modified products?

discussion | questions

1. Is it possible to provide augmented or potential products in all markets?
2. Which step of the new product development process is the most important? Is this the same for product modifications?
3. Which is more likely to enhance shareholder value: product innovation or invention?
4. How could competitors undermine a first mover advantage in a product market?

debate | questions

1. Is new product development more important than product modification?
2. Can pursuing product breadth over product length more effectively increase shareholder value?
3. Is product invention more likely to circumscribe the competitive potential of competitors?
4. Is the product development process more important than product implementation?

case study | ING Direct: Straightforward, value-based products

The Australian banking sector has traditionally relied on high customer switching costs to maintain existing business and product offerings. Quality of service and product innovation have been peripheral concerns to proficient risk management and imperative of improved shareholder return. Much like their counterparts in the United States, Australian banks have placed minimal emphasis on enhancing product value or establishing new product markets. Furthermore, high overhead costs associated with extensive branch networks have mitigated low-cost product offerings. While the Australian banks have used their branch networks to leverage cross-product promotion, they have not attempted to reposition their products as low-cost offerings.

The International Netherlands Group (ING) recognised that a niche existed in the Australian market for low-cost financial products. ING Direct was launched in Australia in November 1999 offering a unique selling proposition — fee-free banking. The advertising message for the product was equally simple: 'Who says all banks are the same?' ING Direct offered a low-cost product alternative through branchless banking. This proposition was antithetical to the strategies of the existing banks. However, ING Direct was relatively unknown in Australia and this produced challenges in creating brand awareness, product differentiation and the need to convince customers of its security, because it was a branchless bank (customers can transact with ING Direct only over the Internet, its call centre or by mail). The head of marketing and communication at ING Direct, Amanda Houlihan, says that although ING Direct does not like to call itself a virtual bank, this was the way customers perceived it. That perception could have been a problem because Internet banking late in 1999 was relatively undeveloped and was viewed with suspicion by many consumers.

For at least six months after ING Direct was introduced, the main market segment it sought to reach was people aged 18–30, who are usually early adopters of new technology and are less suspicious of the Internet than older consumers. However, Houlihan says the bank's customers are now spread across all age groups.

When ING Direct started, the bank spent $3.5 million in three months ... on television and print ads, which were created to convince potential customers that ING Direct was not the same as other banks. This year it is spending $9 million on a campaign that started in January with a new theme — that banking with ING is 'straightforward'. Houlihan says research conducted earlier this year found that about 60% of consumers were aware of the ING Direct name, and that the 'straightforward' proposition was an advertising message that no other bank had used. Consumers responded enthusiastically. After the first eight months, ING Direct had 40 000 customers and $850 million on deposit.

In entering the market, ING Direct exploited two inter-dependent trends. First, deregulation of the banking sector has led to increased competition amongst suppliers of financial service products. Second, advances in information and communication technology have enabled finance companies, insurance dealers and other non-banking firms to enter the retail banking market without branch office networks (for example, firms like Coles Myer and Ford Motor Company now provide consumer credit). To be successful in the market, ING had to convince potential Australian customers that ING Direct was genuinely different from other banks. Its strategy was to use research to find a gap in the product range in the market and to create a product to fill the gap.

Amanda Houlihan says there were no guarantees that the ING Direct concept would work, which is why research was so crucial. 'We conducted two years of research to find whether there was an opportunity in this market.' The research found a lack of incentive to save among bank customers because of low interest rates in the latter half of the 1990s. The savings accounts that were available had superficially attractive interest rates, but they also had fees and conditions. 'What we wanted when we launched was to establish credibility very quickly,' Houlihan says. 'Obviously ING is huge internationally, but Australians had not heard of us. I think the main formula for our success was the fact we did enter the market with a single product offering. Our competitors probably would have viewed that as a potentially dangerous move because you are limited by just having one product, but we had a product that filled a void in the market, a product that people really wanted.'

ING's secrets of success can be summarised as follows:
- carefully researching the Australian market
- finding a niche in the crowded banking sector
- creating the right product with a unique selling proposition
- quickly establishing brand credibility
- investing in mainstream advertising to demystify its brand and product
- focusing on getting a single product right before looking at new products.

Source: Adapted with extracts from Simon Lloyd, 'Direct approach', *BRW*, 27 September–3 October 2001, p. 41.

Questions

1. What level of the product hierarchy has ING Direct leveraged and how does this create value for both customers and the shareholders of ING Direct?
2. How would the product mix determinants have influenced ING Direct's decision to enter the Australian market? Outline how each of the product mix determinants would have been employed by ING Direct.
3. Which of the three main questions for new product development would have been most important for ING Direct? Are there new products that could be developed, purchased, licensed or imitated to meet customer needs? Can variations of existing products extend the product range to meet a greater variety of customer needs? Can existing products be improved to better meet targeted customer needs?
4. How could ING Direct capitalise on its product implementation?

1. For a classification of new product types see Bryan A. Lukas and O. C. Ferrell, 'The effect of market orientation on product innovation', *Journal of the Academy of Marketing Science*, **28** (2), 2000, pp. 239–47.

2. For reviews, evaluations and applications of the resource-based view of the firm and associated concepts, such as dynamic capabilities and core competencies, see Jay Barney, 'Firm resources and sustained competitive advantage', *Journal of Management*, **17** (March), 1991, pp. 99–119; George S. Day, 'The capabilities of market-driven organisations, *Journal of Marketing*, **58** (October), 1994, pp. 37–52; Kathleen M. Eisenhardt and Jeffrey A. Martin, 'Dynamic capabilities: What are they?', *Strategic Management Journal*, **21** (October/November), 2000, pp. 1105–21; Richard Makadok, 'Toward a synthesis of the resource-based and dynamic-capability views of rent creation', *Strategic Management Journal*, **22** (May), 2001, pp. 387–401; C. K. Prahalad and Gary Hamel, 'The core competence of the corporation', *Harvard Business Review*, **68** (May–June), 1990, pp. 79–91; Birger Wernerfelt, 'A resource-based view of the firm', *Strategic Management Journal*, **5** (April/June), 1984, pp. 171–80.

3. For an excellent discussion of the need to merge resource-based theories with market-based theories see Richard L. Priem and John E. Butler, 'Is the resource-based "view" a useful perspective for strategic management research?' *Academy of Management Review*, **26** (January), 2001, pp. 22–40; Jay B. Barney, 'Is the resource-based "view" a useful perspective for strategic management research? Yes', *Academy of Management Review*, **26** (January), 2001, pp. 41–56; Richard L. Priem and John E. Butler, 'Tautology in the resource-based view and the implications of externally determined resource value: Further comments', *Academy of Management Review*, **26** (January), 2001, pp. 57–66; Yiannis E. Spanos and Spyros Lioukas 'An examination into the causal logic of rent generation: Contrasting Porter's competitive strategy framework and the resource-based perspective', *Strategic Management Journal*, **22**, 2001, pp. 907–34; Additional perspectives are offered by George S. Day and Robin Wensley, 'Assessing advantage: A framework for diagnosing competitive superiority', *Journal of Marketing*, **52** (April), 1988, pp. 1–20; Shelby D. Hunt, *A General Theory of Competition: Resources, Competences, Productivity, Economic Growth*, California: Sage Publications, Inc., 2000; Shelby D. Hunt and Robert M. Morgan, 'The comparative advantage theory of competition', *Journal of Marketing*, **59** (April), 1995, pp. 1–15.

4. For interesting discussions of new product development excellence see Melissa A. Schilling, 'Technological lockout: An integrative model of the economic and strategic factors driving technology success and failure', *Academy of Management Review*, **23** (April), 1998, pp. 267–84; Candida G. Brush, Patricia G. Greene and Myra M. Hart, 'From initial idea to unique advantage: The entrepreneurial challenge of constructing a resource base', *Academy of Management Executive*, **15** (February), 2001, pp. 64–78; Constance E. Helfat and Ruth S. Raubitschek, 'Product sequencing: Co-evolution of knowledge, capabilities and products', *Strategic Management Journal*, **21** (October–November), 2000, pp. 961–79.

5. For a review of the literature on first-mover advantage, see Marvin B. Lieberman and David B. Montgomery, 'First-mover advantages', *Strategic Management Journal*, Summer Special Issue, **9**, 1988, pp. 41–58; Marvin B. Lieberman and David B. Montgomery, 'First-mover (dis)advantages: Retrospective and link with the resource-based view', *Strategic Management Journal*, **19**, 1998, pp. 1111–25.

Distribution

Distribution

chapter objectives

By the time you have completed this chapter, you will be able to:

- understand the functions of distribution channels and the ways they affect shareholder value and brand equity
- assess the advantages and disadvantages of direct, indirect and mixed distribution systems
- understand the factors influencing the choice of channel structure
- analyse the means by which distribution channels can be reviewed and the forces influencing inertia in distribution channels
- understand the reasons why channel conflict can occur and the means by which it can be resolved
- analyse the role of the Internet as a distribution channel.

scene setter

Distributing movies: The digital future

In the next few years we will see the beginnings of a revolution in the way movies are distributed to the home and to the cinema. Technologically, the future of the cinema is digital. Hollywood studios are planning to distribute films digitally for downloading over broadband Internet. If they can get past the regulatory authorities, it could be big business for the studios. Already Movies.com is eyeing the market beyond broadband Internet distribution, looking to release movies through cable television on a pay per view basis and increase its return from 50 per cent to 60 per cent. This would compete directly with video/DVD stores; a business opportunity the studios missed in the '80s.

The other potential digital distribution method is via satellite direct to the cinemas. The financial benefits are manifold. Distributors could eliminate the US$2000 to US$3000 they pay for each film print, an expense that can represent 10 per cent or more of a movie's production budget. A typical US release opens on more than 3000 screens ... Print costs are about US$2500 per screen, which means that the distributor pays more than US$7.5 million for film prints that could be almost eliminated by digital distribution. The cost of shipping the film to the cinemas in heavy steel canisters is also considerable, but disks or satellites would make this redundant. When a film's run is over, the disk or the data could be erased rather than returning the print to the exchange.

There is a large element of risk for a distributor in estimating how many prints to strike. Will audience demand be great or small? It's anyone's guess ... Using the Internet or satellite, distributors would no longer have to guess the turnout for a new movie. If a movie was a hit, the distributor could strike a new disk or send data via satellite to the cinema.

Another potential cost saving of digital distribution is that exhibitors won't have to operate duel systems in their theatres ... Digital images tend also to be more stable than photographic emulsions. A 35mm print ages rapidly, but a digital 'print' would be just as good on the 100th screening as on the first. And the sound would be CD quality rather than the compressed optical track that is used on a photographic print. Finally, the digital distribution era will offer exhibitors increased revenue by downloading from satellite exclusive sporting or cultural events that work best when seen in a crowd ...

Ideally, the studios would prefer to ditch the middlemen and have complete control over their products. They would prefer that consumers never owned a copy of a movie but paid each time they saw a film, whether in a cinema or at home.

They could send their digital package by satellite or disk directly to the cinemas for first release and then offer the home market a DVD or a download from the Internet. None of this augurs well for the corner video stores, which have already been hit by the release of DVDs.

Source: Extracts from Peter Crayford, 'Focus on Digital', *Australian Financial Review Weekend*, 28 March–1 April 2002, p. 51.

Introduction

The element in the marketing mix called 'place' is concerned with the channels of distribution that the business employs to reach the target market. The term **distribution channel** captures the idea of an interlinked and interdependent group of partners that connect the producer to the end-user, be it consumers or business users. The distribution channel is the downstream part of the overall **supply chain**. The upstream part is the supply of components and raw materials to producers.

Today, innovation in distribution is becoming one of the most significant ways firms can create competitive advantage. The triggers have been the desire of consumers for greater convenience, global competition, forcing companies to search for new ways to cut costs and capital employed, and facilitating technologies, notably information technology and the Internet. New distribution strategies are offering consumers greater benefits in terms of convenience, speed, accessibility and lower costs that are offering pioneering companies opportunities to leapfrog competitors. Besides market advantages, these companies can often significantly reduce their operating costs and investment.

The macroenvironmental changes mentioned above, and discussed in detail in chapter 1, have forced companies to review their assumptions about the best means of reaching their markets. The appropriate response must be strategic, with channel decisions being viewed as choices from a wide and varying assortment of alternatives. Managers must move beyond a preoccupation with the purely tactical, such as maintaining power balances, managing conflicts and minimising transaction costs. Too often, as Anderson, Day and Rangan complain, the distribution method used by a company is merely an appendage to its strategy, something that is 'the result of opportunistic, reactive, one-by-one decisions accumulated over time and frozen by perceived barriers'.[1]

This chapter presents the strategic choices as well as the tactical responses. It begins with a consideration of the functions of distribution channels. It then discusses the task of choosing channel structures, and considers the additional strategic choices that arise from the decision to use indirect channels. It also discusses the task of reviewing distribution systems once they have been put into place and avoiding the inertia that so commonly afflicts them. The chapter concludes with an analysis of the Internet as a distribution system, a topic considered further in chapter 12.

distribution channel: the means by which a producer makes available its products to the final customer (or end user)

supply chain: the set of upstream linkages between suppliers and producers and downstream linkages between producers, distributors and customers, through which products are created and sold

The functions of distribution channels

Most companies employ a multi-function, multi-channel approach. Different organisations are chosen for different functions, and some functions are handled by several intermediaries simultaneously. A computer company might use a market research company to gather information, a transportation company to handle delivery, banks to finance receivables and inventories, and then sell through its own sales force to large accounts and use independent retailers and a web site to sell to smaller customers.

The functions that channels perform can be grouped into four categories:

1. **Informing**. The marketer needs information about what customers want, or might want. Customers need information about what the company can offer.

2. **Selling.** The company has to promote its products and negotiate on prices and terms.
3. **Delivering.** Goods have to be stored, broken into bulk and transferred from the company to its customers.
4. **Financing.** Inventories, accounts receivable and associated risks have to be managed and financed.

The question is not whether these four functions have to be performed, but who can perform them most efficiently and effectively. The key channel decisions that management must make are who should perform these activities. Organisational success will depend increasingly on the ability to combine these functions creatively among different players in the pursuit of cost minimisation and greater responsiveness to customer needs. More important still will be the ability to reconfigure — through a process of channel decomposition and recomposition — the players responsible for different functions.[2]

It is partly because of the variety of functions performed in a distribution system that the participants in the system will have different views on the nature of the product that is sold and the benefits that it provides. Consider an agribusiness firm selling tea tree oil. The wholesaler will be interested in whether the brand ensures rapid stock turnover and in whether the way it is packed enables the breaking of bulk; that is, dividing the product into quantities or volume that suit the needs of the next tier of the distribution channel. The wholesaler has no interest in the intrinsic benefits provided by the product — the ones that are relevant to the final consumer. The chemist store that purchases the tea tree oil from the wholesaler is more interested in whether the product will achieve regular sales and whether it is attractively packed so that efficient use is made of shelf space. Other retailers who purchase the oil may include a powerful group of supermarkets. For both types of retailers, as well as for the wholesaler, the product is less a consumer good and more like a component in an industrial process. It is only the final consumer, who chooses to buy the tea tree oil as a natural antiseptic to heal a wound, who truly sees it for what it was intended — a product that satisfies a consumer need.[3]

The consumer in this example does not have direct personal contact with the manufacturer. The link is indirect, and an important question is how the constituent parts of the distribution channel fit together. It is much better that there be close relationships between the members of the channel than having a situation in which the product moves only as part of a series of discrete and remote transactions between independent entities. But this only underlines the challenges involved in trying to manage channel arrangements, a point explored in more detail below. Ideally, the distribution system should be structured in such a way that delivery costs are minimised while simultaneously reducing the sense of psychological and geographical distance between supplier and customer.

Three basic influences on customer satisfaction are the support service provided to customers (such as customer assistance), the recovery process for counteracting negative experiences and the provision of what is sometimes called extraordinary service; that is, service which is aimed directly at the customer's personal preferences to such an extent that the product is perceived as being customised.[4] In each case, these tasks are best performed by the part of the distribution system that is closest to the final consumer. One of the potential advantages of service organisations is that there is usually some direct personal interaction with customers. With many manufacturing firms, however, as in the tea tree oil example, the part of the distribution system that is closest to the final consumer is the one furthest from the producer. This impairs responsiveness, and this in turn affects sales volume and, hence, shareholder value.

The effect of distribution arrangements on shareholder value

The nature and efficiency of the distribution system have a major impact on shareholder value.[5] One of the major influences on the level of cash flow is the volume of sales. This is directly affected by the performance of the distribution system. Cash flow will be affected by the nature and quality of the customer service provided, the order cycle time, the order completion rate and invoice accuracy. Some of these same elements influence the timing of cash flow. Superior distribution arrangements — those that are more reliable and responsive than those of competitors — can have a positive influence on customer loyalty, thereby increasing the level of operating cash flow and reducing the risk attached to it.

Recall from chapter 2 that cash flow is equal to cash in (which, in turn, is determined by sales growth and operating profit margin) less cash out (taxes, incremental working capital and incremental fixed investment). The distribution system, together with the upstream part of the supply chain, can make a powerful contribution to reducing operating costs. Net operating profits can be increased through efforts to minimise transportation, storage and warehousing, handling and order processing costs.

A supply chain that reduces the time from order placement to order fulfilment and delivery will improve customer service and accelerate cash flow. It will also help to reduce costs by eliminating non-value-adding activities. The nature of a company's order processing systems and inventory control mechanisms influences costs. Improvements in them contribute directly to the achievement of time compression, a concept explored in more detail below. Inventory carrying costs, likewise, are expenses that influence operating profits.

Some of the major components of a manufacturing company's distribution system, such as trucks, distribution centres and depots, warehouses and automated handling systems, can represent major components of its fixed investments. Improving the efficiency of these investments will improve shareholder value. In some cases, the use of third-party suppliers of logistics services can lower these sorts of fixed investments. Another option is to lease instead of purchasing some of the fixed capital components of the distribution system. As always, what is needed is a careful analysis of the costs of financing the capital investment used in the company's distribution networks to determine what sort of return it generates.

Christopher and Ryals point to the need for identifying opportunities for time compression along the pipeline that links suppliers, producers and consumers. This is an important means by which the receipt of cash can be accelerated:

> Enhanced and accelerated cash flow can be achieved if the total end-to-end pipeline time can be compressed. This is because, firstly, the shorter the pipeline the less

working capital is locked up in it. The analogy with an oil pipeline works well — the longer the pipeline the more oil it contains. Secondly, the shorter the pipeline the more responsive to demand the company can be. Hence the opportunity for improved sales volume through having the right product in the right place at the right time.[6]

Time compression is the key to reducing, possibly even eliminating, the lead-time gap. This term refers to the all too common situation in which it takes longer to procure, make and deliver a product to the consumer than he or she is prepared to wait. This was a problem that faced Apple when it introduced its new iMac computers into Australia in 2002. Production problems were responsible for delivery delays of up to two months after the customer had ordered the computer.

The conventional solution is to carry inventory, but as inventory increases, and the time it remains idle is extended, cash flow is reduced (see marketing insight 'Stock up and save'). Carrying inventory is associated with a variety of other problems. Marketplace dynamism puts the holder of inventory at risk, especially when customers' buying habits are subject to rapid change and competitors are offering new products. And as inventory costs go up, profits are reduced.

There are opportunities, however, right along the pipeline, to deal with this problem. Direct access to sales and usage data has been improved by the use of electronic data interchange and, more commonly now, the Internet. This is markedly superior to a situation of relying on the step-by-step transmission of data from one channel member to another. The various partners in the channel can enjoy instantaneous access to the same data, thereby improving responsiveness and scheduling. Information is a key ingredient in demand management, be it information about anticipated demand and actual customer sales and usage. Without this it will be difficult, if not impossible, for goods and services to be produced quickly and flexibly and for supplies to be replenished at the time they are needed and in the quantity required.

Direct, indirect and mixed systems

Many businesses would prefer to distribute their products to their target customers through a **direct distribution system**; that is, a company-owned means of distribution, such as a sales force. The system is directly controlled by the company and is dedicated solely to company products — two powerful advantages. Another advantage is that a direct system provides greater opportunities to offer value-added services.

direct distribution system: a company-owned means of distribution

In practice, however, the barriers imposed by physical and psychological distance have meant that most companies do not sell their goods directly to final users; instead, they use intermediaries such as agents, distributors, wholesalers, transport companies and retailers. This sort of reliance on intermediaries is referred to as an **indirect distribution system**. While direct systems offer superior control, a key drawback is that they also mean taking on all the distribution risks, including the high costs. The use of intermediaries is often the most cost-efficient way of distributing products. Selecting, training and maintaining a sales force is too expensive and too much of a drain on resources for many companies. Intermediaries also offer superior customer reach. They are usually the most effective means of obtaining

indirect distribution system: distribution that relies on intermediaries external to the company

desired levels of market coverage. The advantage of intermediaries lies also in their experience and the economies of scale and scope that they possess. Value can be generated by the use of specialists who have the relevant capabilities. It follows that a higher return may be achieved from investing in expanding the firm's core business than in establishing its own channels.

Marketing insight: **Stock up and save**

It is a big, expensive problem that has plagued grocery retailers and their suppliers for years — how to avoid stock shortages in their stores. The grocery retailing sector loses sales of between $500 million and $1 billion a year from running out of stock, and the cost to their suppliers is $450–$750 million a year. These are big figures in any industry, but they are particularly worrying in the grocery business, in which profit margins are thin and sales growth modest.

Increasing inventory is not the answer. Suppliers and retailers have to work together to solve the core problem, not just the symptoms, says Andrew Reeves, the managing director of Coca-Cola Amatil (CCA), one of the biggest suppliers to the grocery retailing industry. Reeves says CCA is achieving substantial benefits from working with large retailers on pilot programs to deal with the problem of running out of stock. He says co-operation between retailers and suppliers is essential because of the number of variables along the supply chain that result in empty spaces on the shelves.

A report published [in 2001] ... by Efficient Consumer Response Australasia (ECRA), a group that draws together suppliers, retailers and others in the industry, says that 5–10% of products are out of stock in grocery stores at any given time. The report says the instinctive response of increasing inventory often exacerbates the out-of-stock problem because the excess stock clogs the supply chain. The leader of the consumer packaged goods industry practice at PricewaterhouseCoopers, Michael LaRoche, says the additional inventory also ties up working capital and does not deal with the cause of the problem. LaRoche, who worked on the ECRA report, says the solution requires manufacturers and retailers to work together; however, research has found a 'collaboration gap'. He says trading partners do not understand the effect they have on each other at each stage in the supply chain.

LaRoche says there are several areas in which retailers and their suppliers might not realise they can work together, such as product labelling, sales forecasting and changing the amounts in which goods are ordered. He describes the collaboration that is happening as rudimentary. Effective collaboration, he says, requires compatibility, commitment, capability and control. The senior executives of retailers and suppliers need to be committed to working together, sharing information and jointly tackling technology issues.

Suppliers are often the biggest losers from goods being out of stock, because shoppers will switch to a rival product. The deputy director of the Australian Food and Grocery Council, Harris Boulton, says that being able to find a desired product on the shelf clearly produces consumer satisfaction. Grocery retailers can lose 20–40% of sales because of stock shortages, and suppliers can lose 30–50% of potential sales.

The ECRA report says that 80% of the problems that cause stock shortages occur in the store, such as shelves not being filled routinely or low stock levels not being recognised and acted upon. The head office or distribution centre of the manufacturer accounts for 10% of shortages, and the remaining 10% is the result of problems at the retailer's head office or distribution centre. Although most of the problems are at the retailer's end, Boulton and Reeves say that suppliers have a key role to play in reducing the out-of-stock problem.

Boulton says some retailers are inviting suppliers to send staff to their stores to track stock movements and work with employees on making improvements. 'They say it is money well spent, and the savings from making that investment far outweigh the costs of having the person there.'

Source: Extracts from Jan McCallum, 'Stock up and save', *BRW*, 23 August 2001, p. 43.

There are nevertheless drawbacks in the use of intermediaries. One is a loss of control over a critical marketing function. This may, in turn, give rise to opportunistic behaviour. The channel might, for example, put greater energy and time into representing competitors' products. Another potential drawback is the possibility of conflict between channel members. In part, this depends on whether the indirect system is 'short' or 'long', and this, in turn, depends on the number of layers that separate the producer from the final consumer. It is increasingly common to find distribution systems that are combinations of both direct and indirect channels. These are referred to as **multiple-channel** or **hybrid-channel systems**.[7] These may involve a situation in which different channels are used for different customer segments, such as a PC manufacturer that uses a sales force for business customers and retail stores for household consumers. An alternative configuration is for the channel members, rather than serving different segments, to perform complementary functions — different channels are used for the same customers. An individual customer of David Jones, for example, may choose to buy online at the David Jones web site or visit the David Jones department store. Those wanting to buy Nike sportswear can buy them from dedicated Nike stores as well as from a variety of sports stores, clothing stores and department stores. A flight with Qantas can be purchased from the company direct either by visiting a Qantas sales centre, or by using the Internet or by working through an offline or online travel agency.

The challenges associated with multiple-channel systems are principally to do with handling potentially complex coordination and management issues, including maintaining the loyalty of different channels. There is also the potential for consistency in product positioning to be threatened when the same product is offered at different prices in each channel. This may not be a problem if different channels serve different customer segments, but as products proliferate and customer segments fragment, customers may shift between channels. The task of minimising direct comparisons is made difficult, too, when customers wear different hats for different purchasing occasions. They may act as price-sensitive customers who seek out the no-frills channel on some occasions, and service-sensitive customers patronising the full-cost channel on others.[8]

multiple-channel/ hybrid-channel system: a combination of direct and indirect distribution systems

Choosing the channel structure

The first major strategic choice, then, is a configuration decision. Management must determine whether to use a direct or indirect distribution system or some combination of the two. Channel decisions are influenced by the familiar marketing strategy parameters. Ideally, the channel configuration should create a differential advantage by matching the service needs of customers more effectively than competitors. So planning should start with research into the service needs of target customers and into the effectiveness of the competitors' channels.

Different customer segments have different needs. The choice of channel must be informed by an understanding of these needs and of the fact that they can and will vary from one segment to another. The more diverse are the needs of different segments, the more likely that multiple or hybrid channels will be used.

One approach to understanding the basic determinants of channel structure is that of Rangan, Menezes and Maier, whose interest principally is in channel selection for industrial products. They argue that structure will reflect the requirements of customers with respect to eight distribution functions:

product information, product customisation, product quality assurance, lot size, assortment, availability, after-sales service and logistics.[9]

1. **Product information.** For some products, notably those that are new and/or technically complex, and those that have a rapidly changing technological component, customers are likely to demand more information. When information requirements are high, customers usually prefer a direct channel system.

2. **Product customisation.** An inherent feature of some products is that they must be customised to meet the customer's production requirements (such as special steel for manufacturers of surgical instruments). As a rule, the greater the degree of customisation, the more that customers prefer a direct channel.

3. **Product quality assurance.** Where, say, a manufacturer's operations depend critically on the integrity and reliability of a product, the manufacturer is likely to prefer a direct channel as a means of obtaining the required quality.

4. **Lot size.** The issue here is how much the customer outlays for the product. If it has a high unit value or if it is to be used extensively, it will usually involve careful pre-purchase evaluation. Direct channels tend to be preferred when lot size requirements are large.

5. **Assortment.** Where the desire is to be able to purchase a broad range of products, including product line breadth and complementary products, from a single supplier (one-stop shopping), then indirect channels tend to be preferred.

6. **Availability.** Where customers have unpredictable usage rates for a given product, or where it is imperative that a product be available as and when needed (say because of volatile and unpredictable shifts in demand), customers usually rely on indirect channels and may readily switch from one supplier to another.

7. **After-sales service.** Where the demand for after-sales service, such as installation, repair, maintenance and warranty arrangements, is high, customers will generally seek indirect channels for the relevant product.

8. **Logistics.** If logistics requirements are complex, such as will be the case in transporting hazardous chemicals, and where those requirements involve product-specific investments, direct channels are usually preferred.

These, of course, are not the only influences on the choice of channel structure. Many others have been suggested. Lambin, for example, provides a list of factors affecting channel structure and groups them in terms of market factors, product characteristics and company variables. Under market factors he includes the number of buyers, geographical dispersion, the quantity purchased and the seasonality of purchases. Under product characteristics he lists perishability, complexity, newness, weight, variability and value. Under company variables he includes financial resources, assortment sought and desire for control.[10] His matrix suggests, for example, that direct channels are likely to be associated with situations in which, with respect to market or customer influences, the number of buyers is small, geographical dispersion is limited, and large quantities are purchased. In line with Rangan, Menezes and Maier, he suggests that the more complex the product, the higher its value, and the more customised it is, the more will direct channels be favoured. New products and perishable products will also tend to be distributed through direct channels. Furthermore, when the company has large financial resources and/or wishes to exercise a high level of control, it will tend to favour direct channels.

The key point is that channel design should be based on a careful consideration of the variety of influencing factors and an understanding of the relative importance of each one. Furthermore, as will be argued below, there needs to be a dynamic aspect to this assessment. Managers need to understand that the relative importance of the influencing factors will change over time as markets evolve and customer requirements become increasingly varied.

The distribution structure that is chosen needs to meet certain requirements. Four are especially important:[11]

1. **Effectiveness.** The extent to which the channel design addresses customer needs.
2. **Coverage.** The opportunities given to customers to find the product and appreciate the value it offers them.
3. **Cost efficiency.** The costs relative to the benefits of greater coverage.
4. **Long-run adaptability.** The ability of the design to handle new products and to incorporate new channel forms.

The last of these is considered in more detail below.

In designing channels, management need to ask some more specific questions. What is the 'best' configuration in fast changing, 'high velocity' markets? Do such environments favour channel specialists or channel generalists? What happens when and if the environment stabilises? Anderson, Day and Rangan argue that multiple channels are most commonly found in turbulent market environments, a reflection of the plurality within the market and the attendant need to have multiple channels for different buying patterns. Diversity is the key to coping with turbulence, especially if the channels employed represent a portfolio of options to be used or discarded as circumstances evolve, such as a return to market stability. Diversity may mean a combination of direct and indirect channels, as well as various forms of each of these. It may also mean a combination of specialist and generalist distributors (such as a specialist pen store and a generalist stationery/office supply store such as Officeworks). Again, in highly uncertain markets it is wise to use both types as part of a bundle of options. The greater the turbulence, the more difficult it is to determine in advance what type of channel is most appropriate. Options provide flexibility. The alternative is to commit to a channel that is subsequently recognised as inappropriate and which offers at best the prospect of incremental modifications.[12]

Strategic reviews of distribution channels: adopting a forward-looking approach

Channel decisions, as has been made clear, involve strategic choices. The amount a business should be willing to invest in channels will depend on the strategic objective. The strategic focus will also shape the appropriate channels. (The notions of strategic objective and strategic focus were introduced in chapter 4, and were discussed in detail in chapters 5 and 6.) If the focus is to convert new customers to the business, a more aggressive channel will be required than if the focus is on maintenance of cash flow. As the market evolves and becomes more segmented, the business will increasingly be pulled into developing multiple channels to cover the market and match the different needs. Similarly, the core strategy will be an important influence. If, in line with the reasoning presented earlier, the strategy is around customised solutions to the potential problems customers are facing, a more direct channel will be required to allow for closer contact between the customer and the production division. If, by contrast, a business is selling basic or expected or standardised products, and using low prices as the value proposition, an indirect sales channel will be more efficient.

The search for competitive advantage is a game played in a dynamic, and in some cases highly turbulent, environment. Accordingly, strategies are tried, discarded and amended. They evolve. There is a need for constant review and re-evaluation of all aspects of competitive strategy. Channel strategy is no exception. It is imperative to review channels continually. There are several reasons why market-oriented companies need to do this:

- **Opportunities to innovate.** New distribution channels offer the opportunity to create whole new markets. Lastminute.com created a unique concept using the Internet to sell exclusive last-minute deals for flights, entertainment, gifts and hotel rooms (see marketing management in practice 'New distribution channels offer opportunities to create new markets').
- **Accelerate growth.** A company can outgrow its distribution channel. For example, British confectionery company Thorntons relied on sales from its own shops for two decades. To increase its growth opportunities, it began to sell to supermarkets and chain stores as well.
- **Changing customers.** New customers or changing customer needs can make existing channels obsolete. As customers become more familiar with a product, distribution tends to migrate from high-price, full-service retailers to low-cost channels, such as mail order, telesales or the Internet.
- **New technology.** New technology can make current distribution channels obsolete. The impact of ATMs and telephone and Internet banking is predicted to halve the number of bank branches in the next decade. With new low-cost technologies, competitors do not need to make enormous investments in bricks and mortar to compete.
- **Poor performance.** Current distributors may be performing inadequately. Perhaps they have more profitable alternatives or lack the skills and knowledge to exploit the supplier's product range.

Marketing management in practice: **New distribution channels offer opportunities to create new markets**

Two young British entrepreneurs set up Lastminute.com in 1999 to exploit the growing availability of the Internet. They recognised that for the first time the Net offered the opportunity to publicise exclusive last-minute deals for a whole range of items including flights, entertainment and hotel rooms — even diamonds have been sold on the site. Their target market was 'yuppies' — the cash-rich, time-poor people who can take off at the last minute. This was just the audience that was already online. Within six months the company had 200 000 registered users. Following the success of the UK site, localised versions of the web site were launched in France, Germany and Sweden in 1999. A joint venture was formed with the Australian online company, Travel.com.au, in August 2000 to handle business in Australia and New Zealand. In the same year another joint venture agreement was signed for an operation in South Africa. Since then Lastminute.com has further expanded its European presence with the launch of web sites in Italy, Spain and The Netherlands. By March 2002 the company had over 5 million registered subscribers in Europe.

Reviews of channel arrangements involve an assessment of what presently exists, what has been used in the past and what might be tried in the future.

It may be that contextual, firm-specific resource constraints lead to a less than optimal initial channel selection. For example, a small-to-medium enterprise that manufactures high-tech products may not have the financial resources to employ its own salesforce, even though the product characteristics and customer requirements suggest that a direct channel is appropriate. The important issue is to avoid being locked into an inappropriate design. The aim should be to structure the existing or initial arrangements so that the option exists of creating something in the future that better meets customer requirements. The selection of channels may always be subject to constraints, but it is important to understand the loss imposed by such constraints. This is best done by analysing the loss in terms of the unconstrained solution.[13]

Even where the initial choice of distribution channel seems appropriate, it is unlikely to remain so for the reasons outlined above. And even in a relatively stable environment, reassessment will be necessary because of the influence of the product life cycle. The choice of channel should incorporate a dynamic element. The challenge for managers is to anticipate how customer requirements will evolve as the product moves through the introductory stage to maturity. Distributors usually play a critical role in meeting the information needs of innovators and early adopters. In later stages, with growing product acceptance and knowledge, the principal role of distributors is likely to shift to that of handling volume and service requirements. Personal computers, for example, were first sold by manufacturers' sales forces. Later, office equipment distributors became a lead channel, then retailers, and now mail-order firms and the Internet are the fastest growing channels. The added value of distributors tends to decline as products shift from high service to low-cost channels. Channel design must be forward-looking to ensure that such changes can be accommodated.

In a turbulent, high-velocity environment, the task of trying to predict an appropriate channel configuration is simultaneously more important and more difficult. The appropriate response, as explained earlier, is to hold strategic options. In practice this means trying out many different ways of reaching the market, and realising that each of them provides different openings and different sources of information about the best choice of future configurations. Anderson, Day and Rangan note:

> As the market clarifies, the manufacturer can judiciously sell some options (e.g. sell out a distribution joint venture or liquidate an equity position in a distributor), fail to exercise some options (cease distributing through the channel entity) and call some options (invest in them more heavily by purchasing equity, injecting resources or cultivating commitment).[14]

Options are useful, too, in making decisions about international marketing channels. A retailer, for example, may purchase an option in one or more international markets by buying a small local firm to get a better understanding of the nature of the market and its potential, and of the local regulations and practices governing distribution arrangements, before making a more serious commitment. From a shareholder value perspective, options are a portfolio of investments in long-term growth. They are a collection of small-scale pilot projects. As such, they are perfectly amenable to real options analysis as a means of evaluating them.[15]

Options make it easier to reconfigure distribution arrangements but they do not eradicate the challenges of introducing change. For many firms the task of changing distribution channels is fraught with difficulty. One reason for this is that it is likely to introduce conflict between the current distribution channel and the emerging one. For example, the early 1990s saw the growth of direct selling of personal insurance products. For the existing players this was a problem since they relied on independent brokers to sell their products. Fearing the loss of broker support, they were deterred from selling direct to the public. As a result, they lost a major share of the market to new entrants.

Similar problems face many businesses today — locked into large investments in site locations, historical distribution networks or sales forces, they find it hard to slip into the new wave of low-cost, information-based distribution systems. Often, the result is the emergence of a new generation of industry leaders. This issue is explored further in the next section.

Inertia in distribution channels: forces for and against

For all the importance of regularly reviewing channel structures, it is of course true that channels, once established, can become troublingly rigid. The challenges of initiating and implementing change may sometimes be deemed sufficient reason for a company sticking with the status quo. This may happen even in situations in which management acknowledge that inertia weakens the company's competitive situation. It is certainly true that long-term relationships, contracts, infrastructure and systems linking channel partners cannot be quickly altered.[16] It is also true that many firms have invested heavily in their existing distribution channels. Close relationships have been developed with distributors or, having chosen the direct route, branches have been opened, employees hired, training provided, product-specific knowledge developed, routines introduced and services supplied.[17] In many cases, such investments will be channel specific, in the sense that they will have little value if alternative channels are chosen. This is the case, for example, with traditional retail banks. The investments made in the establishment of bank branches, their promotion, their employees, and the day-to-day procedures to be followed in the branches, are all investments which would be of little, if any, value if the branches were to be replaced by Internet banking as the most important distribution channel.[18]

A feature of such investments is that, traditionally, they were seen as a source of competitive advantage by extending market coverage. They were also seen as a means, through the extension of the banking network, by which additional relationships could be nurtured and competition restricted. The Internet has now changed that perception. For some banks, the heavy investments made in their traditional branches have become a liability. At the very least, the branches are no longer perceived as a protective barrier to entry. ING, for example, has enjoyed considerable success in Australia in the provision of banking services, but it operates entirely online. Banking services can now be provided to anyone anywhere who has access to the Internet. Furthermore, the services offered to customers are likely to be superior, at least in terms of a wider and deeper variety of offerings, the elimination of queuing, instantaneous transactions and lower charges. Of course, not every consumer will accept such arguments — witness the continuing furore in Australia as more and more bank branches are closed in rural areas. The fact remains, however, that the banks themselves have been forced, through technological change, to reconsider the role, efficiency and effectiveness of their investment in branches.

As this example suggests, the pressures for change have forced even the faint-hearted to look anew at existing distribution arrangements. Inertia is gradually being overcome. Alternatives are being examined in the context of trying to determine a design that will provide competitive advantage. There are three forces that have led to the re-evaluation of customary channel arrangements: the proliferation of customers' needs, shifts in the balance of channel power and changing strategic priorities.[19]

1. **Proliferating customer needs and rising expectations.** More firms are now able to provide increased variety in product offerings. They can do so through the use of database technology and flexible manufacturing techniques. In some cases they have been able to exploit the ability of the Internet to allow a direct dialogue with consumers. Some businesses have moved closer, using the same means, to address the needs of individual consumers, not just broad segments. Distributors have also taken advantage of technological improvements to automate functions that enable them to respond more quickly to customer orders and to provide customised products. Customer expectations have changed in response to this situation. Customers have grown accustomed to a situation in which the products being offered more closely address their individual needs. Increasingly, they take for granted the provision of greater services, ready availability and rapid order fulfilment. As customer expectations have risen, so too have the pressures on distribution channels (see marketing insight 'Let's get personal').

2. **Shifts in the balance of channel power.** There has been increased concentration within distribution channels. Consolidation in retailing has seen the emergence of distributors with substantial purchasing and bargaining power. In many instances, power has shifted from the producer to the intermediary. The rise, for example, of high-volume chain retailers, such as Toys 'R' Us, and of regional and national joint purchasing units, has been associated with increased pressure on suppliers to provide discounts, price concessions and additional services. The shift in the balance of power has been hastened by the threat of backward integration, with distributors showing a willingness to act as direct competitors to some of their suppliers. Distributors have also emerged as more knowledgeable buyers, as a result of the insights gained into suppliers' costs through negotiations with the suppliers on private-label products. In addition, they have benefited from the insights that transaction-processing systems provide into their own operations and those of their customers.

3. **Changing strategic priorities.** Increasingly, firms are rationalising their activities, concentrating on the things at which they are best able to provide superior value. They are also forming new relationships and alliances — a confederation of sorts — with a variety of specialised partners. By this sharing of activities, the expertise and resources of the partners can be collectively harnessed. In the process, firms are increasingly looking anew at all activities. Channels are no exception. Questions are raised about who, within and outside the firm, should be responsible for order fulfilment, inventory management, logistics, distribution and after-sales service. Questions are asked also about how channel collaboration can be fostered and managed. Indicative of this rethinking, Narus and Anderson talk of 'adaptive channels' in which distribution networks are perceived as 'webs of

capabilities embedded in an extended enterprise', and in which the sharing of resources and capabilities creates profit-making opportunities that could not be exploited by any firm within the network alone.[20] Such arrangements are especially useful in providing the critical skills necessary to respond to unusual or infrequent, but nonetheless important, customer demands.

Marketing insight: **Let's get personal**

A corner shopkeeper in the 1950s who kept handwritten lists of his or her customers' preferred groceries, and delivered them when necessary, was just as much involved in relationship marketing as the retailing chain of the 21st century that builds vast databases about customers and communicates with them over the internet. The fundamentals are the same ...

The difference for the marketer of today is that loyalty to brands and retailers of those brands has become flimsy. The executive director of the Australian Centre for Retail Studies, Ian Clark, says: 'One of the biggest problems retailers face today is that customers are very well trained in what they want. Customers are fickle, very cynical, and they shop very broadly across brands. They are less loyal to retailers than they were even five years ago, and this makes the business of building relationships with them increasingly difficult.'

Clark says that retailers are responsible for this change in attitudes. 'Retailers are paying the price for training shoppers very well in recent years.'

He says consumers have been trained to look for bargains, and that has impeded the process of relationship marketing, because the assumption among many retailers is that consumers, as a group, shop only on the basis of price. He says this is a fallacy. 'Retailers have to increase customer intimacy and understand that people are looking for genuine value rather than engineered "specials". People are prepared to spend money if it is in a niche where they see the retailer having a critical mass of product that the consumer identifies with. At the bottom end, there are lots of people looking for value — the working poor, who are 'needs shoppers' — and they are being well catered for among retailers at the moment.

'At the other end, you have the early baby-boomers, empty-nesters with no mortgage who are looking for indulgences, home enhancement and lifestyle. They want service, respect and choice. For them it is a matter of: "Who is my retailer of choice who understands my needs?"'

The director of the Centre for Customer Strategy, Ross Honeywill, agrees with Clark that customer relationship marketing for retailers is complicated by differences in expectations among types of consumer. 'We need to drill down to the fact that it is very hard to draw conclusions about retailing in general,' he says. 'There are actually two markets, the high-margin and the low-margin markets.'

Honeywill says customers in the low-margin market are 'price and sale-event' oriented. 'Forget location, location, location. They are after price, price, price. This is the group of consumers who will drive across town to save 2 cents on a litre of petrol. They have a low sense of control over their life and, from a retail point of view, they come out of the woodwork only when they can have a win.'

He points to the success of the retailer Harvey Norman, achieved by accurately focusing on customers in this group, for which price is the biggest element in the relationship between seller and buyer. 'With low prices and no interest for two years, promotional events and high brand marketing, Harvey Norman has reached and motivated this group.'

The high-margin group is made up of customers who demand a more personal relationship with the retailer, Honeywill says. 'They are looking for quality, see themselves as individual consumers, and so look for individuality. They want a relationship with the retailer that involves some kind of personal connection. The experience is more important than the transaction.'

Source: Extracts from Simon Lloyd, 'Let's Get Personal', *BRW*, August 23–29 2001, p. 63.

Inertia is also being overcome by the globalisation of markets. Another factor is the willingness — indeed the requirement in many instances — of foreign competitors to experiment with alternative distribution arrangements (see marketing insight 'Patient Aldi is buying carefully'). One of the lessons from international marketing — not sufficiently appreciated in discussions of domestic channels — is that while distribution links can give the appearance of an effective means for locking out new entrants from a market, strategies can be devised to circumvent the status quo: The case of Canon breaking Xerox's control of the British photocopier market by using local independent distributors, or the case of Komatsu using new channels to enter the US farm machinery market, or Honda using non-traditional retail outlets for motorbikes indicate that there are often creative alternatives available.[21] Examples like these underline the importance also of not paying excessive deference to established procedures.

Strategic choices when using indirect distribution channels

The choice of an indirect channel necessitates other strategic decisions to be made. One is to decide on the number of intermediaries — a market coverage decision. Another relates to the choice between a conventional or a coordinated vertical structure.

The number of intermediaries: Market coverage strategy

The decision about the number of intermediaries to be used will be influenced by the strategic objective. Another consideration is the shopping/purchasing habits of the consumers of the distributed product.

There are three choices in determining the market coverage strategy: exclusive, intensive and selective.

1. **Exclusive distribution.** This strategy, as the name suggests, involves the use of only one retailer or dealer in a given geographic area. Within the particular product category for which the contract has been negotiated, the distributor does not sell competing brands. By definition, competition between channel members is low, probably non-existent, and market coverage will generally be very low. This form of distribution is used in particular for **specialty goods**. These are specific (usually up-market) brands, exotic and rare products, and sophisticated items. Products sold through exclusive arrangements can be more readily differentiated in terms of product quality, prestige and service excellence.

   speciality goods: specific brands, exotic and rare products, and sophisticated items

2. **Intensive distribution.** The aim with this strategy is to maximise sales by attempting to maximise the number of retailers selling the product, the number of storage points and brand exposure. Inevitably, competition between channel members is intense. The strategy is appropriate in particular for **convenience goods** (goods purchased often, in small quantities, and with little thought or effort, such as jars of instant coffee) and for other low-involvement products. Convenience goods include staple goods (such as most food items), impulse items (the unplanned purchases of things such as a detergent on temporary promotion at the local supermarkets) and emergency goods (such as light bulbs).

   convenience goods: goods purchased often, and with little thought or effort; they include staple goods, impulse items and emergency goods

3. **Selective distribution.** This strategy attempts to balance the desire for maximum market coverage with that of minimising competition between channel members. It is the middle ground between intensive and exclusive distribution. Selective distribution is generally used for **shopping goods**. These are goods that involve high perceived risk by the consumer. The higher risk means that consumers are more inclined to spend time and effort in comparing products in terms of their quality, price, design and features. Examples include furniture, major appliances and items of clothing (those that are relatively expensive and bought infrequently). Generally, the selection of shopping goods will involve visits to different stores to inspect and compare different brands.

shopping goods:
goods that involve high perceived risk by the consumer

Marketing insight: **Patient Aldi is buying carefully**

Aldi might not have a store on every corner yet, but retail industry consultants say the German discount grocery chain will become the third force in Australian supermarket retailing. Aldi, which opened its first store in January [2001], has since opened 16 more at an estimated cost of $34 million.

There are several reasons why Aldi is a threat to Coles Myer and Woolworths:
- By devoting most of its product range to private-label products, it can pitch itself as a low-price alternative to existing grocery retailers.
- It is prepared to pay a premium for good store sites.
- It is a global giant, with more than 4800 stores in 11 countries.
- It has demonstrated a long-term commitment to the Australian market.

A senior consultant at the retail consultancy Strategic Horizons, Ian Clark, says Aldi has been slower than expected in opening stores, not because it is scaling back its plans but because finding suitable sites is difficult. 'They've got very deep pockets and they are very patient,' Clark says. Most grocery retailers in Australia lease store sites; Aldi is willing to buy land and build stores where it cannot find stores to lease or buy.

The associate director of retail and property at KPMG, Justin Ganly, says that Aldi has been paying top dollar for sites, particularly in regional areas. As a result, Aldi is likely to get the pick of retail locations. Aldi's real estate strategy, he says, indicates it is making a long-term investment in Australia.

All of Aldi's stores are in New South Wales, mainly in working-class areas, and they are served by a distribution centre at Minchinbury in Sydney's outer west...

Established in Germany's Ruhr Valley in 1948, the privately owned Aldi operates 4800 stores in 11 countries, including Britain, the United States and France. It has annual sales of about €35 billion ($66 billion). It differs from local retailers by offering a limited range of about 700, mainly private-label, products developed for Aldi. By comparison, Coles Supermarkets and Woolworths offer up to 20 000 items, largely national brands. In Aldi stores, national brands represent less than 5% of stock.

Aldi customers are charged for carry bags, stock is displayed in the shipping cartons and staff costs are minimal. The few staff in each store perform various tasks, including checkout and stocking shelves, in return for above-award wages. Ganly says discount supermarkets in Australia turn over $8000–10 000 per square metre a year on average, so Aldi stores, which are about 1200 square metres, should turn over an estimated $9.6–12 million each.

So far, Aldi's share of Australian grocery retailing is below 1%. Clark believes that the figure will be 5% by 2011, representing annual sales of $2.5 billion, based on the industry's current turnover. Ganly says the effect on Coles Myer and Woolworths may be negligible because grocery retailing is growing about 5% a year. On the assumption that Aldi stores perform in line with other discount grocery retailers, Ganly says: 'Aldi could have the effect of taking out one year of growth.'

Source: Extracts from Michelle Hannan, 'Patient Aldi is buying carefully', *BRW*, September 27–October 3, 2001, p. 37.

Vertical structures

The term **conventional vertical structures** refers to the traditional distribution model in which channel members act independently of each other, each pursuing their own objectives, and doing so with little regard for the performance of the channel overall. The individual members of such structures are autonomous; system-wide goals do not exist. Each channel member is a customer of the other, with each link a separate buyer-seller exchange. The limit of the wholesaler's interest is with making sales to retailers, not the retailer's sales to their own customers. And the retailer is likely to see itself as a purchasing agent for its own customers, not as an agent for the supplier organisations. Motivation becomes a critical issue. The business must strive to convince the wholesaler or retailer to purchase and then to 'sell on' the offering to the next layer in the channel. The situation is akin to encouraging individual players to pass the baton to the next player.

More recently, coordinated vertical structures have arisen. They are usually referred to as **vertical marketing systems (VMS)**. In this case, each channel member is a partner to the other. They work collaboratively to achieve maximum marketing impact for the system as a whole. Each channel member takes the initiative to exercise the necessary coordination to effect this goal. In contrast to conventional vertical structures, team members replace autonomous players. Cooperation, commitment and trust become critical relationship variables, tying the team members together. These do not happen spontaneously. Considerable investment of time and money is required, as is the ongoing exercise of centralised coordination.[22]

Three types of vertical marketing systems (VMS) have emerged: corporate, contractual and administered.[23]

1. **Corporate VMS.** In this case, high levels of coordination and control are achieved by production and distribution activities being joined through common ownership. The firm that owns the other parts of the channel could be a manufacturer engaging in forward vertical integration, thereby controlling how the product is delivered, presented, installed and repaired. Another advantage is that the producer has direct contact with the final consumer. Alternatively, a retailer or wholesaler may engage in backward vertical integration. A retailer, for example, may decide to manufacture some or all of the products that it sells. Another example is BRL Hardy, one of the largest producers of fine wines in Australia. It exports to over 60 countries. It has more than a dozen wineries and has 3200 hectares of company-owned vineyards, though it also obtains supplies from over 1000 independent grape growers, who work closely with it to provide quality fruit.

2. **Contractual VMS.** Here the channel activities are performed by individually owned firms whose activities are coordinated as a result of legal agreements specifying the responsibilities and rights of each partner. There are three types of contractual VMS. One is retailer-owned cooperative systems — independent retailers joining together to purchase or lease wholesale facilities. Another is wholesaler-sponsored voluntary chains. These are independent retailers choosing to affiliate with an existing wholesaler and agreeing to use a common storefront design, business format and name and purchase system. The third is franchise systems — an agreement between the franchisor and a franchisee; examples include McDonald's, H&R Block, 7-Eleven, Harvey Norman and Muffin Break.

3. **Administered VMS.** Here coordination is achieved neither by ownership nor by long-term contracts but through the influence of a dominant member of the system. The system requires trust and voluntary sharing of information. What it needs in particular is one member of the channel, usually the manufacturer, to be recognised as the leader. The leader must motivate the other channel members to see the benefits of cooperation and coordination. Procter & Gamble is one company that has had some success with such a system.

In the last 20 years or so, vertical marketing systems have emerged as the dominant mode of distribution in the field of consumer marketing. They can be viewed as a new form of competition, *channel system competition*, in which complete channels compete against other complete channels. This differs from traditional vertical competition in which competition occurs between opposing channel members at different levels of the same channel; that is, retailers versus wholesalers and manufacturer versus wholesaler. Vertical marketing systems help to eliminate the sources of conflict that are common in conventional vertical structures.[24]

A major disadvantage of vertical marketing systems, however, is that they involve constrained decision making. The decisions of channel members on things such as store hours, involvement in a cooperative advertising program, merchandise depth and width, and vendor selection may be constrained or limited by the existence of contracts. They may also be constrained by the exercise of various forms of power by a channel member. The ability of a channel member to determine how best to pursue goals, such as the maximisation of shareholder value, may suffer in circumstances of constrained decision making.[25]

The cooperation achieved in an administered VMS may sometimes arise spontaneously but more commonly it is achieved through the exercise of power. Where a channel member is able to control or influence the marketing strategy of an independent channel member, we can say that it is exercising **channel power**. Two types of power can be distinguished: coercive and non-coercive.[26] The essence of *coercive power* is that one or more channel members are threatened with punishment if they do not act in a particular way. *Non-coercive power* is power that derives from the promise by one channel member to another of rewards, assistance or expertise, or of the benefits of being associated with the member's brand and overall image.

channel power: a situation where a channel member is able to control or influence the marketing strategy of an independent channel member

The use of both types of power may be either contingent or non-contingent. With coercive power that is contingent, the dominant channel member signals in advance that punishment will result only if there is non-compliance. The idea is to modify behaviour by the use of threats. When it is non-contingent, punishment is unilateral and occurs without prior warning. With non-coercive power that is contingent, the dominant channel member makes clear that rewards will be received only as a result of compliance, whereas non-coercive power that is non-contingent will involve the unconditional provision of rewards. The idea with unconditionally providing rewards is that the dominant channel member solicits the cooperation of other members by making them feel a sense of gratitude or benevolent respect.

These various forms of power will influence the level and type of satisfaction felt by channel members. They will also affect the sense of commitment of one member to another. These, in turn, will help to determine whether channel relationships endure.[27]

Channel conflict

Conflict is likely to occur in all distribution channels, even within the essentially cooperative approach of vertical marketing systems. The term **channel conflict** refers to the tension that emerges when a channel member believes that the actions of another channel member are interfering with its goal attainment. Conflict can be manifest — actual interference is happening. Alternatively, it can be perceived to exist or be imminent. It can also differ in terms of frequency, importance and intensity (from minor to major).

There are many reasons why conflict may occur. The goals of one channel member may be incompatible with another's. For example, the manufacturer that wants additional shelf space for its new insect spray may encounter a supermarket that is unconvinced that there will be demand for the product. Behaviour may be outside the range of what is deemed acceptable for that role. This happens, for instance, when orders are not processed within a reasonable amount of time. Opinions may differ on domain issues — such as who is responsible for transhipments, who is in control of functions such as the determination of the final selling price, and who is assigned to which sales territory. Perceptions may differ. A retailer and a manufacturer may have, for instance, very different interpretations of what an acceptable gross margin is for a particular item. One channel member may believe that it has already well exceeded its contractual obligations while another may feel that it has not done nearly enough. There may be conflicts also because of communication breakdowns. In addition, as explained earlier, the need to review channel structures and, should it be necessary, modify or replace existing arrangements will almost certainly produce conflict.

Channel power can be a way of dealing with channel conflict, but it may also be a cause of it. Conflict resolution can take a variety of forms. It must begin, obviously enough, by trying to isolate the cause of the problem. If the problem is essentially perceptual, for example, an attempted solution will be to use persuasion or negotiation to try to bring perceptions into alignment. A key issue is whether the parties can solve the conflict themselves or whether they require (or indeed will accept) third-party mediation. In either case, the goal must be to avoid a zero-sum situation in which 'resolution' of the conflict means the victory of one party at the expense of the other. Unless the losing party is forced out of the channel, problems will reappear soon enough in situations where conflict resolution is a zero-sum game.

It needs to be stressed that conflict is not always dysfunctional. Some degree of conflict may prevent complacency among channel members and may even encourage innovation. It may be also that disagreements are not always purely negative but may arise because of differences of opinion on how the channel as a whole can best achieve goals such as customer value. In this case, the disagreement is about the best way to realise common goals. Conflict that arises because assumptions have been questioned, or because alternatives have been suggested, may ultimately have a positive effect on the relationship between those who are presently in conflict. And this may ultimately lead to an improvement in the performance of both of them.

The distribution system and brand equity

In chapter 7, brand equity was defined as the net present value of the future cash flow attributable to the brand. Marketing channels can be important determinants of brand equity and, hence, of the cash flow generated by a brand. Of all the components of the channel design, retailers have the greatest effect on brand equity. What is at issue is not simply whether a retailer stocks the branded product. Brand equity can be subtly influenced by how the brand is presented by the retailer, the knowledge and persuasiveness of the retail staff with respect to the brand and its positioning, and the nature of the in-store promotional campaign. It is influenced also by the retail outlet's internal environment — its ambience, the cleanliness and presentation of products, and the sense it projects of suitability for the purpose. Another influence is the store's external image. This may damage brand equity if the product is being sold in a store that does not fit appropriately with the product's positioning.[28]

One of the reasons for direct distribution systems, in the form of company-owned stores, is a concern to maximise brand equity. The display and presentation of the branded product can be more effectively controlled. Such stores can also be the most effective means of customer education about the brand. In some ways, too, company-owned stores serve as means of hedging bets with retailers who continue to push their own labels.

Another influence on brand equity will be the choice of intensive, selective and exclusive distribution systems. Of these three, intensive distribution is the weakest mode when the aim is to build brand image. There will be difficulties, in particular, with product positioning because of the lack of control generally associated with intensive distribution channels. Prices may be discounted, customer service may be poor, and cooperation is difficult to achieve with so many dispersed retailers.

Since retailers can have a major influence on brand equity, producers need to determine how they can influence retailers. There are two major strategies. One is the use of a **push strategy**, in which the manufacturer attempts to persuade retailers — by offering them incentives — to carry, display and promote its products. Incentives may be, for example, training the retailer's sales staff, providing gifts and free merchandise to the retailer, and supplying it with product literature and catalogue materials. The other is a **pull strategy**, in which the producer circumvents retailers and targets consumers directly by mounting a promotional campaign. If the campaign is effective, consumers will request the product from the retailer. In this case, the influence is exercised indirectly. A pull strategy is a long-term investment in building brand equity. As Lambin puts it: 'A strong brand image is an asset for the firm and is the best argument for obtaining support and co-operation from intermediaries.'[29] Often, producers will use a combination of push and pull, such as cooperative advertising. This refers to the situation in which the retailer advertises a product locally and the manufacturer reimburses part of the expense of doing so.

push strategy: a strategy in which producers aim to get retailers to offer their products by directly influencing the retailers

pull strategy: a strategy in which producers aim to get retailers to offer their products by influencing consumers, who in turn demand the goods from the retailers

The Internet as a distribution channel

Information technology is having a major impact on channel design decisions. We have already examined how it has led to a re-evaluation of the economic worth and strategic significance of investments in bank branches. This example demonstrated the Internet may transform some traditional distribution systems into expensive liabilities that no longer provide the sorts of barriers to entry that they formerly did.

Perhaps the most profound impact of the Internet on distribution arrangements, however, is its encouragement of **disintermediation**. This refers to a process in which intermediaries are bypassed and, as a result, new forms of direct channels are created and/or indirect channels are shortened by reducing the number of layers. Disintermediation is not new but it has greatly accelerated in the Internet era. Part of the attraction is the promise of lower prices. A recent Australian advertising campaign for Merrill Lynch HSBC, promoting its online stockbroking service, has the by-line: '5 good reasons to get rid of your stockbroker'. The company's advertisements encourage the reader to visit www.mlhsbc.com.au and 'to start making money for yourself, not your stockbroker'. In other markets, as will be explained in chapter 12, new intermediaries called **infomediaries** are being created to help shoppers find the best deals from among the multitude of companies selling online.

For established businesses — bricks-and-mortar organisations — the Internet creates both distribution challenges and opportunities. It provides them with the chance to exploit more fully their brand, their experience in fulfilment and customer service operations, and their established relationship with suppliers. Each of these are advantages which pure dot.coms lack. Taking advantage of these capabilities and resources, they may be able to serve existing segments better by creating a web-based business that provides customers with an alternative, and possibly superior, channel. They may also be able to serve new segments, now accessible because of the web site. And with both existing and new segments, they can offer cross-channel delivery and returns, another advantage they enjoy over pure dot.coms. For example, when the US bookseller, Barnes & Noble, responded to the competitive threat posed by Amazon.com by creating its own online business, barnesandnoble-.com, it was able to use its established network of bookstores as convenient places to pick up merchandise ordered online or, if need be, to return items deemed unsatisfactory.[30]

Potentially, a major challenge for established businesses who use the Web as an alternative distribution channel is the risk of cannibalisation of their existing business. This happens when customers desert existing stores, branches or dealers in favour of the new online business unit. Merrill Lynch, for example, runs the risk of cannibalising its existing business, comprising thousands of brokers, by moving into low-cost online trading. The extent of cannibalisation, however, can be easily exaggerated. It may be that the online business creates more customers and/or more spending by existing customers. Certainly there is evidence that customers who shop in multiple channels spend more heavily than those who shop in a single channel.[31]

Digitisation and networks — two essential ingredients in the Internet revolution — have major implications for how companies organise their distribution. The two primary functions of retailers and distributors are providing information (about availability, prices, the suitability of alternative products, etc.) and supplying goods. The traditional logic of using intermediaries is that,

disintermediation: the elimination of intermediaries or agents between the supplier and the consumer

infomediary: an online site that provides specialised information on behalf of producers of goods and services and links them to their potential customers

since the supplier has only a limited number of products, while customers desire a vast number of different products, it would be hopelessly inefficient for each producer to go to each customer, and vice versa. This is illustrated in figure 10.1, which shows three producers, a farmer, a food processor and a beverage manufacturer. Each is marketing to ten consumers. If there are no intermediaries, as in scenario A, then the costs of thirty separate contacts have to be paid. But with an intermediary (scenario B), only thirteen contacts are required.

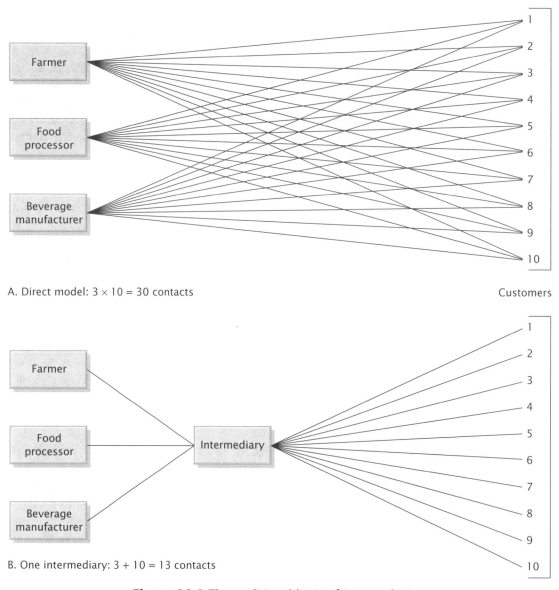

A. Direct model: 3 × 10 = 30 contacts

Customers

B. One intermediary: 3 + 10 = 13 contacts

Figure 10.1 The traditional logic of intermediaries

The Net changes this logic by permitting the separation of the economics of information from that of products. Over the Net, companies and customers can interact at almost zero cost, so the model of scenario A is viable.

What makes the direct model attractive to consumers is the potential of lower prices, greater assortment, more convenience and customised service.

What makes it attractive to suppliers is lower costs, competitive advantage and the value-enhancing opportunities that accrue from a direct relationship with the customer. Most online marketers still need to handle the physical distribution of their goods. But when this is separated from the information function, it can normally be handled from one or a small number of central distribution points, often by third parties like DHL or Mayne Logistics.

This change offers disintermediation opportunities and with it big cost savings. For example, if airlines do direct booking and ticketing on the Internet they save agency commissions of at least 10 per cent. For an airline issuing a million tickets a year this amounts to a saving of around $120 million. A computer company selling direct can save around $600 per machine by eliminating the retailer. The network world is also creating opportunities for new types of intermediaries to help buyers steer their way through the deluge of information.

The most exciting distribution breakthroughs are for digital products, such as software, that can be downloaded from the Internet. And, as the scene setter at the start of the chapter shows, more products are becoming digitised. Films and music look to be increasingly downloaded, and newspapers and books may follow. More troublesome are physical products that have to be delivered by conventional logistics and which incur significant shipping costs that can negate the advantages of e-commerce. Some of the earlier pioneers invested in sophisticated web sites, but failed to invest sufficiently in logistics and distribution. The result has been easy ordering, but late and erratic delivery (see marketing insight 'Promising online distribution'). Such hiccups can quickly erode customer loyalty.

Marketing insight: **Promising online distribution**

Losing customers is bad news in any industry. For e-commerce companies selling to consumers, it is doubly devastating because customer acquisition costs are so high.

According to a recent study by the Boston Consulting Group, the average pure Internet retailer spent $141 to acquire a single customer. The only way that kind of investment can be recovered is if the customer returns again and again.

This is why, in certain e-commerce circles, fulfilment is the 'f-word' that doesn't get aired in polite company. After winning customers with a heady mix of deep discounts and hyped promises of convenience, many online retailers throw their investment away because of poor fulfilment.

Estimates of the proportion of transactions that go bad vary. Companies in the online industry claim only 5 per cent of orders have problems. Some experts say the number could be 30 per cent or higher ...

In December [1999], at the height of the pre-Christmas selling period, *The Wall Street Journal* ran a number of prominent stories about US e-commerce fulfilment stuff-ups.

The newspaper chided online retailers for making extravagant promises that they were unable to keep. It said e-commerce companies had only themselves to blame because they spent a fortune on marketing to create a demand they could not meet.

In many cases, customers who ordered Christmas gifts didn't receive them in time, the newspaper reported. What's more, because e-commerce companies take credit-card payments at the time of ordering, some customers didn't have cash to buy last-minute replacement gifts.

(continued)

Poor fulfilment of goods ordered online is not just a US phenomenon. A recent study by APT Strategies, *Successful eFulfilment: The last Mile in eBusiness*, found that Australian online retailers were all failing on this front. It found that in some cases as many as 30 per cent of ordered goods were being returned.

Paul Koffler of APT Strategies says that a major problem is that Australian online retailers fail to put as much emphasis on fulfilment as they do on creating attractive looking web sites. He says: 'Our research indicates that fulfilment is an afterthought, driven into the forefront when crisis occurs.'

Koffler says fulfilment is part of the three equally important components of successful online retailing. The other two are the front — end usually an online catalogue — and the payment system.

He says that fulfilment systems for online retailers can be broken down into five parts: A front end, which gives customers delivery options and tells them of the progress of their orders; a distribution centre, which, depending on the business, can be centralised or decentralised, in-house or outsourced; the physical delivery system, which moves goods from the distribution centre to the customer; and customer service returns, where unwanted or wrongly delivered goods can be sent back for a refund.

He says: 'They have a pallet mentality. Few of them have systems in place for dealing with single items to individual customers.'

The direct-to-consumer model is not as deeply entrenched in Australia's distribution system as in, for example, the US and the UK. They have long traditions of catalogue shopping where customers order a number of single items that are picked, packed and dispatched in individual lots.

In the US and UK, online retailers are learning the lessons from catalogue companies. Big online retailers have been buying up catalogue operations to integrate their physical distribution systems with their technology systems.

This is less of an option for e-tailers in Australia, where there is not a tradition of catalogue shopping. Strong unions present a further problem. To some extent, Australia's courier industry is less developed.

In 1999, Greengrocer.com managing director Douglas Carlson told a seminar in Sydney that the biggest obstacle his business faced was that couriers wouldn't handle out-of-hours deliveries which was precisely what his customers wanted. Carlson has responded with his own fleet of refrigerated vans, enabling evening deliveries.

In the US and UK, certain companies, for example Kozmo.com and Ziproaund.com, offer customers delivery within two hours. Here most online retailers who don't operate their own fleets can't do much better than deliver on the next working day ... if you're lucky.

In theory, there's no reason an Australian online retailer could not offer a similar turnaround. Consider pizza deliveries. If small businesses around the country can take orders and deliver hot food to local customers within 30 minutes, delivering CDs and books shouldn't take weeks. Koffler says some online retailers are working on these issues and that a new breed of distribution and fulfilment specialists is appearing that will, over coming months, radically change the way goods ordered over the net are delivered.

In particular, expect to see after-hours delivery become the norm rather than the exception.

One last issue facing online retailers is that their lack of a physical presence is a barrier for some customers. For example, customers would prefer to return unwanted goods to a collection point rather than wait for a courier.

Koffler's answer to this one is surprisingly elegant. He suggests that online retailers hook up with service-station convenience stores.

He says that with their many locations and long hours, they could make a powerful distribution partner for online retailers.

Source: Bill Bennett, 'Online retailers need to speed up delivery', *Australian Financial Review*, 16 May 2000, p. 44.

Summary

1. Innovation in distribution is one of the most significant ways in which firms can create differential advantage. The nature and efficiency of the distribution system can have a major impact on shareholder value and on brand equity.

2. Most companies employ a multi-channel, multi-function approach. Channel design should be based on a careful consideration of the variety of influencing factors — such as market factors, product characteristics and company variables — and an understanding of the relative importance of each one. Furthermore, there needs to be a dynamic aspect to this assessment.

3. Distribution channels must be strategically reviewed. A forward-looking approach is necessary. There are powerful forces creating inertia in distribution channels but a proliferation of customers' needs, shifts in the balance of channel power and changing strategic priorities provide countervailing forces to this inertia.

4. Market coverage strategies involve choices between exclusive, intensive and selective distribution. There are choices also in vertical structures, between conventional structures and vertical marketing systems. Vertical marketing systems, in turn, comprise corporate, contractual and administered systems.

5. Channel conflict is likely to occur. Channel power is both a potential source of conflict and a means of overcoming it.

6. The Internet has the potential to revolutionise distribution arrangements, especially through the encouragement it provides to disintermediation. For established businesses, the Internet creates both distribution channels and opportunities.

key | terms

channel conflict, p. 361
channel power, p. 360
convenience goods, p. 357
conventional vertical structures, p. 359
direct distribution system, p. 347
disintermediation, p. 363
distribution channel, p. 344
indirect distribution system, p. 347
infomediary, p. 363

multiple-channel/hybrid-channel system, p. 349
pull strategy, p. 362
push strategy, p. 362
shopping goods, p. 358
speciality goods, p. 357
supply chain, p. 344
vertical marketing system (VMS), p. 359

review | questions

1. Why is distribution important and how does it impact on marketing decisions?

2. Why is channel structure important? What considerations need to be made for different customer groups and markets in choosing a distribution channel?

3. How does a forward-looking approach improve shareholder value?

4. What factors have led to a re-evaluation of customary channels arrangement? How does a firm's response to these improve shareholder value?

5. What choices need to be considered when using an indirect distribution channel?

discussion | questions

1. Which function that channels perform is the most important for shareholder value creation?
2. How can distribution create, increase and sustain shareholder value? How does this differ across markets and channel structures?
3. Why do distribution channels have the potential to create new markets?
4. How can a firm successfully manage intermediaries?

debate | questions

1. Is distribution less important for creating shareholder value than other aspects of marketing (say, for example, branding)?
2. Is a direct distribution system likely to be more beneficial for a firm than an indirect one?
3. Can channel conflict create value?
4. Is distribution a component of brand management? Is it subservient to brand management?
5. Consider, for a variety of different markets and customers, the contribution of the Internet as a distribution channel. Is its contribution more important for some markets and customers, and less for others?

case study | **Online support**

If one of Britain's wealthiest young entrepreneurs has her way, Australian women will soon be trying on new bras not in department stores and lingerie shops but at home, or even at the office. Glasgow-born Michelle Mone has built a personal fortune of £10 million ($30 million) since the August 1999 launch in Britain of her creation, the Ultimo Bra, a garment that helps women to greatly enhance their cleavage.

The bra, which has silicone gel sachets sewn into the fabric, has been one of the most successful new products released in Britain and the United States in the past two years, and in mid-September [2001] it arrived in Australia. But it is not being sold in shops. It will be distributed via the Internet and by consultants selling direct to customers at home and work.

Mone says the decision to use Australia as a testing ground for direct selling was based on pricing and convenience. The Ultimo Bra is not cheap; it costs $87.95. By comparison, the bras of one of the most expensive established brands, Calvin Klein, sell for $59.95 in Myer and Grace Bros stores. Mone says the Ultimo's price would have been higher if it had been sold in stores, because of the retail mark-up on wholesale prices, which can be as high as 300% ...

'We have decided to go with online and direct selling so we can give Australian women more value for money,' Mone says. 'The product is top-of-the-range, using expensive fabrics and a type of silicone liquid on which we have a worldwide patent, so what women are getting is exceptional quality at an affordable price.' She says women are often uncomfortable buying bras in shops, and want a personalised service. 'Our research shows women are sick of going into department stores, waiting around in fitting rooms, and would prefer this in the comfort of their own home.'

Mone's company, MJM International, which she established in 1996 with her husband Michael, has set up a local subsidiary and established the Ultimo Academy ... [T]he Ultimo Academy ... recruit[s] consultants to be trained in fitting the new bra, as well as receiving instruction in small-business skills. Consultants, who earn ... commission ... organise gatherings along the lines of Tupperware parties, and ... also visit offices by invitation.

Mone's only competitor in direct lingerie selling is a small company called Can Can Lingerie, which has no online selling presence. But her Internet sales will face competition. No Regrets, a lingerie e-tailer that was set up in November 1999 by the JeansWest founder, Alister Norwood, offers a range of about 200 products, most of them at discount prices.

Mone is not fazed. She says the Ultimo Bra concept has no direct rivals among 'push-up' bras. The only similar product, a cleavage-enhancing bra in Bendon's Elle Macpherson range, was taken off the market early this year [2001]. Instead of silicone, it used a combination of oil and water.

Since its release in Britain in 1999, the Ultimo has become one of the top three bra brands, alongside the long-established Warner and Triumph brands.

In the US, the Ultimo has been a spectacular hit, thanks, in part, to some unsolicited celebrity endorsement. The actor Julia Roberts said in March 2000 that her cleavage in the film *Erin Brokovich* was boosted by an Ultimo bra. (She had bought the bra on a shopping trip in London.) This created a six-week waiting list for the garment before its official US release in May last year. Saks Fifth Avenue has since put the Ultimo into its 62 US stores.

Mone's venture has not stopped with a bra. Ultimo is, she says, a new brand rather than a new product. A swimwear line has been released overseas, but the full range will not be available in Australia until February 2002, because MJM's factories in Scotland and Hong Kong are only just keeping up with demand from Britain and the US.

'We are not just a gel bra company, even though this is what we are famous for,' Mone says. 'Individual products come and go, but we are very conscious that we are creating a new brand, which I want to turn into a global lifestyle brand to compete with, for example, Calvin Klein.'

Mone says MJM is developing bras without gel implants, bras for larger women, maternity bras and 'glamor' bras to complement the original Ultimo product. It will extend its swimwear range into beachwear next year. 'We are also working with a scientist to develop a skin-care range to be launched next [northern] spring.'

Source: Extracts from Simon Lloyd, 'Online support', *BRW*, 11–17 October 2001, p. 45.

Questions

1. Why was the decision taken to distribute the Ultimo Bra in this way in Australia? Critically analyse the factors that would have been considered in choosing this distribution structure.
2. Based on your answer to question 1, is the present form of distribution system correct? Could another form of distribution have been developed that would have led to greater shareholder value creation?
3. How could indirect distribution improve the existing system and increase shareholder value?
4. Will the present distribution improve brand equity? Will this be the same across geographic markets?

end notes

1. Erin Anderson, George S. Day and V. Kasturi Rangan, 'Strategic channel design', *Sloan Management Review*, **38**(4), 1997, p. 59.
2. Anderson, Day and Rangan, *op. cit.* p. 68.
3. This is based on Dennis Adcock, *Marketing Strategies for Competitive Advantage*, Chichester: John Wiley & Sons, 2000, p. 219.
4. Thomas O. Jones and W. Earl Sasser, Jr, 'Why satisfied customers defect', *Harvard Business Review*, November/December, 1995, pp. 88–99.
5. This section draws on Martin Christopher and Lynette Ryals, 'Supply chain strategy: Its impact on shareholder value', *International Journal of Logistics Management*, **10**(1), 1999, pp. 1–10, as well as Malcolm McDonald, Martin Christopher, Simon Knox and Adrian Payne, *Creating a Company for Customers: How to Build and Lead a Market-Driven Organization*, London: Financial Times Prentice Hall, 2001, chapter 5.

6. Christopher and Ryals, *op. cit.* p. 6.

7. See R.T. Moriarty and U. Moran, 'Managing hybrid marketing systems', *Harvard Business Review*, **68**(6), 1990, pp. 146–55.

8. See Moriarty and Moran, *op. cit.* pp. 146–55.

9. The following section relies on V. Kasturi Rangan, Melvyn A. J. Menezes and E. P. Maier, 'Channel selection for new industrial products: A framework, method, and application', *Journal of Marketing*, **56**(3), 1992, pp. 69–82.

10. Jean-Jacques Lambin, *Market-Driven Management: Strategic and Operational Marketing*, London: Macmillan, 2000, pp. 521-22.

11. Anderson, Day and Rangan, *op. cit.* p. 67.

12. Anderson, Day and Rangan, *op. cit.* pp. 65–66.

13. V. Kasturi Rangan, Melvyn A. J. Menezes and E. P. Maier, 'Channel selection for new industrial products: A framework, method and application', *Journal of Marketing*, **56**(3), 1992, pp. 69–82.

14. Anderson, Day and Rangan, *op. cit.* p. 64.

15. The term 'real options' is used to distinguish them from financial options. For a guide to real options analysis, see F. Peter Boer, *The Real Options Solution: Finding Total Value in a High-Risk World*, New York: Wiley, 2002; Tom Copeland and Vladimir Antikarov, *Real Options: A Practitioner's Guide*, New York: Texere, 2001; and Lenos Trigeorgis, *Real Options*, Boston: MIT Press, 1996.

16. See A. M. Weiss and Erin Anderson, 'Converting from independent to employee salesforces: The role of perceived switching costs', *Journal of Marketing Research*, **29**(1), 1992, pp. 101–15.

17. Niels Peter Mols, 'Organizing for the effective introduction of new distribution channels in retail banking', *European Journal of Marketing*, **35**(5/6), 2001, p. 667.

18. Mols, *op. cit.*

19. Anderson, Day and Rangan, *op. cit.* pp. 59–61.

20. J. A. Narus and J. C. Anderson, 'Rethinking distribution', *Harvard Business Review*, July/August, 1996.

21. Adcock, *op. cit.* p. 220.

22. Barry Berman, *Marketing Channels*, New York: John Wiley & Sons, 1996, chapter 12.

23. See Berman, *op. cit.* pp. 529–44.

24. Lambin, *op. cit.* p. 524.

25. Berman, *op. cit.* p. 523.

26. See John F. Gaski and John R. Nevin, 'The differential effects of exercised and unexercised power sources in a marketing channel', *Journal of Marketing Research*, **22**, 1985, pp. 130–42.

27. Inge Geyskens and Jan-Benedict E. M. Steenkamp, 'Economic and social satisfaction: measurement and relevance to marketing channel relationships', *Journal of Retailing*, **76**(1), 2000, pp. 11–32.

28. Hugh Davidson, *Even More Offensive Marketing*, London: Penguin, 1997, p. 551.

29. Lambin, *op. cit.* p. 533.

30. Thomas R. Eisenmann (ed.), *Internet Business Models: Text and Cases*, Boston: McGraw-Hill/Irwin, 2002, pp. 320–21.

31. Eisenmann (ed.), *op. cit.* p. 322.

Promotion and communication

11

Promotion and communication

chapter objectives

By the time you have completed this chapter, you will be able to:

- evaluate the different promotion tools available for communication
- understand how effective communication creates shareholder value
- show the dangers of treating communication as an accounting cost rather than an investment
- describe how communication works to influence the choices customers make
- know how to define the objectives of a communication plan
- develop a comprehensive communication strategy
- understand how to conduct a shareholder value analysis of alternative communication strategies.

scene setter
Hotels: Hyatt's hat-trick

The Chicago-based hotel group Hyatt International Corporation has launched its biggest global marketing program to date in an effort to redefine its portfolio of Park Hyatt, Grand Hyatt and Hyatt Regency brands...

Hyatt is hoping that the campaign will consolidate its position as the world's biggest privately owned hotel owner and operator by building loyalty among its existing customer base of three distinct types of guest, and attracting business from rival groups such as Inter-Continental, Sheraton and Marriott.

Hyatt's senior vice-president, marketing, John Wallis, says: 'As the publicly owned hotel companies have grown through acquisition in recent years, primarily to satisfy the demands of the market, we ended up as the world's largest private hotel company, trying to see how we should position ourselves within that marketplace. We undertook a complete rethink of our whole product.'

Three advertising campaigns have been developed... to distinguish between the three types of Hyatt. Past campaigns have focused only on Hyatt as a 'masterbrand', making little distinction between the hotels in its portfolio.

Internationally, Hyatt operates 18 Park Hyatt hotels (including Sydney, Canberra and Melbourne), 18 Grand Hyatts (one is in Melbourne) and 137 Hyatt Regency properties (including Adelaide and Perth).

Wallis says: 'We have our three brands and have been singularly successful at positioning those hotels in a given market-place. For example, the Park Hyatt Sydney is recognised as the finest pub in Sydney. The Park Hyatt Tokyo is recognised as the best. What we were failing to do was to put what we had achieved so well in indi-vidual cities into a global context as a total brand.'

'We realised that our Parks and Grands of tomorrow would be developed in gateway and capital cities, while our Regencies would be in secondary cities. We then started looking at the demo-graphics of the three brands. We did a lot of research, asking existing customers why they were staying in each of the par-ticular brands and found that the Park Hyatt customer wants to be recognised by the staff but wants to be in a discreet environment. The Grand Hyatt customer wants to be seen, and knows that they are part of the glamor end of town. And the Regency customer is your road war-rior, the guy who has to do 60 nights on the road every year and really just wants a place where he can get in, get a fast check-in, get into his e-mails, spend a bit of time exercising, relax, rejuvenate and get the hell out.'

Price also plays a big part: the average price in any city for a Park Hyatt room is US$285, a Grand Hyatt room is US$180, and a Hyatt Regency US$130.

The new ads for Park Hyatt feature sumptuous photography... The Grand Hyatt ads depict what Wallis calls the 'I want to be seen to have made it' guest; the Regency ads focus on rejuvenation and are aimed at a younger market.

Wallis says the most succinct statement of the new campaign's goal is by analogy: 'What we are trying to do is become the BMW of hotel groups, in that, unlike any others, we have a 7-Series, a 5-Series and a 3-Series.'

Source: Extracts from Simon Lloyd, 'Hotels: Hyatt's hat-trick', *BRW*, 12 April 2001, p. 45.

Introduction

It is not enough for a firm to produce a good product; it also has to communicate its values effectively to potential customers. Today, the number of products competing for the customer's attention is so great that gaining share of mind is a major problem. The business has to invest in promotion tools and communicate to make people aware of the product, to show the value of its functional and emotional attributes, to persuade them of its advantages over competitive products, and to reassure customers once they have bought it. For a new company, unless it invests in communication, its offer will be slow to take off, it will be quickly copied by competitors, and it will fail to get the level of market share necessary to achieve critical mass.

Overview of promotion and communication decisions

promotion tools:
advertising, sales promotion, public relations, personal selling and direct marketing instruments, including direct mail, telemarketing, TV shopping and the Internet

Promotion tools cover advertising, sales promotion, public relations, personal selling and the increasing array of direct marketing instruments, including direct mail, telemarketing, TV shopping and the Internet. These promotion tools serve as channels for communication.

Advances in information technology mean that communication is increasingly being seen as a two-way, interactive process. It is not just about the company broadcasting information about itself and its products, but also about finding ways to encourage customers to talk to the company about their needs and their degree of satisfaction with the company's current products and services. Companies, new and old, big and small, spend a great deal of money on communication. Table 11.1 shows what the top advertisers in Australia spent at the turn of the millenium. Figure 11.1 shows that on advertising alone, companies like Procter & Gamble were investing up to 15 per cent of their sales and figure 11.2 reveals companies like Nissan were investing as much as 100 per cent of their operating profits.

Table 11.1 The Top 10 advertisers in Australia 2000

RANK			
2000	**1999**	**ADVERTISER**	**2000 ($M)**
1	9	Federal Government	140–145
2	1	Telstra	140–145
3	2	Coles Myer	137–142
4	4	Nestlé Australia	80–85
5	6	Toyota	70–75
6	3	Unilever	65–70
7	7	McDonald's	65–70
8	5	Woolworths	65–70
9	15	Harvey Norman	65–70
10	8	Village Warner Group	60–65

Source: 'Will your Business grow in 2002?' Adapted from *BRW*, 9 March 2001.

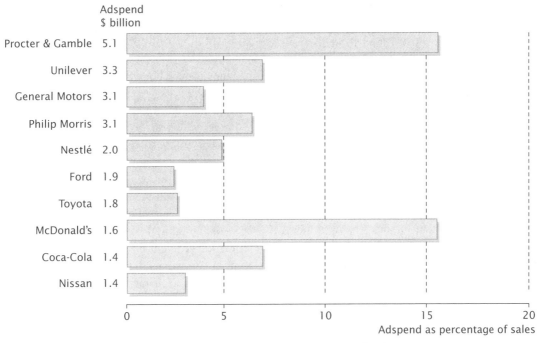

Figure 11.1 Adspend as a percentage of sales

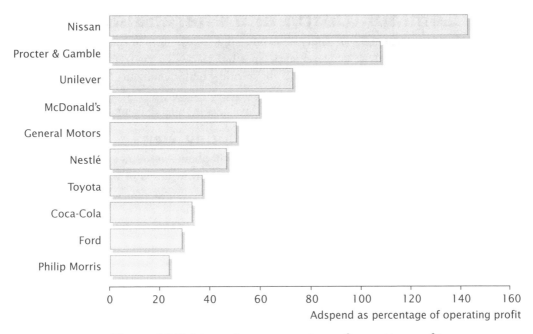

Figure 11.2 Adspend as a percentage of operating profit

The key promotion decisions are how much the total promotion budget should be, how to allocate it across the communication channels, and what message the firm should communicate to the audience. These decisions are all consequences of prior strategic decisions. The size of the promotional budget is mainly a function of the strategic objective management has determined for the business unit. If it is a new business with an objective of rapid growth, it is likely to require a large budget. While accountants treat this spending as a current expense, much of it is in fact an investment that builds up an intangible asset in the form of brand equity. The benefits of the current spending, in terms of positive awareness and attitudes to the business, carry over well into the future. In many of today's new markets, it is crucial to build a brand quickly to pre-empt competition. This means a high communication spend is an essential entry requirement.

The strategic focus will determine the objective of the communication. When the strategic focus is on volume, which involves increasing cash flow from selling more products to more customers, then the objective of communication is to win competitors' customers, increase the usage rate, convert non-users or enter new segments. When the strategic focus is one of productivity, which involves increasing cash flow from the product volume the company has already achieved, then the objective of communication changes from increasing product turnover to maintaining the existing base.

> **communication strategy:** the allocation of promotion tools (advertising, sales promotion, public relations, personal selling, direct marketing) to maximise the net present value of future cash flow

The characteristics of the target market segment play a central role in every aspect of the **communication strategy**. Consumer behaviour will determine the most effective communication channels. Consumer attitudes to the business, its products and its competitors will determine the most appropriate message. Thorough audience research is a prerequisite to effective promotion planning. The message will be designed to communicate the value proposition of the business.

Communication and shareholder value

Managers are generally confused about the role of communication. Normally they take a functional perspective, marketing managers being generally positive about communication spending and accountants being suspicious. These two functional perspectives are evaluated and then contrasted with the approach taken by rational investors in judging communication spending.

The traditional marketing view

Few marketing professionals think about their strategies in financial terms. They view the task of communication in terms of increasing market share, sales, awareness, or shaping the brand's image cost-effectively. This has been confirmed in numerous studies. For example, one study asked financial directors what criteria their marketing departments used to justify their marketing and communication budgets:[1]

Q. Which criteria are set by your marketing department?

	%
Sales volume	57
Market share	26
Awareness levels	35
Brand image	11

Source: IPA/KPMG.

But such criteria do not make sense for budgeting decisions. If the objective is to maximise sales, market share or awareness, too much will be spent on communication. Spending more can always increase these levels, but beyond a point, increases in sales or awareness will cost more to gain than they bring in incremental economic profit. Another problem is that awareness and brand image have a weak correlation with sales and almost none with profit or value. Rolls Royce cars had a great image and universal awareness but these did little to halt declining sales and share price.

The accounting view

In contrast, conventional accounting takes a very short-term view of expenditures on communication. Only spending on tangible assets is treated by accountants as investment. This means spending on communication is treated as costs to be deducted immediately from revenue on the annual profit and loss account. Consequently communication spending, and in most instances even marketing spending as a whole, is only justified if it increases sales sufficiently to maintain profits. The accounting model is:

Communication spending → Incremental sales → Incremental profits

For example, suppose a brand has the current profit structure shown in the first column of table 11.2. How does the financial director respond to a promotion proposal to increase communication spending next year by, say, $5 million? First she calculates the break-even point, based on the current situation (column 1). She does this by dividing the additional cost ($5 million) by the brand's profit contribution. The profit contribution is simply the value of sales less variable costs ($100 million – $50 million = $50 million). In percentage terms, the profit contribution is 50 per cent of sales. By dividing $5 million by 50 per cent, the financial director determines (as shown in column 2) that sales must increase by $10 million (to $110 million) if the additional communication spending is to maintain operating profits at their existing level. If she wants the spending to guarantee a target profit improvement, say to boost profits from $10 million to $15 million, then, as column 3 in the table shows, marketing needs to promise an additional $20 million sales — a growth of 20 per cent in one year.

Table 11.2 Communications budgeting and break-even ($million)

	1	2	3	4
Sales	100	110	120	105
Variable costs	50	55	60	52.5
Profit contribution	50	55	60	52.5
Communication spending	10	15	15	15
Overheads	30	30	30	30
Operating profit	10	10	15	7.5

This short-term view has several negative implications. First, it becomes very difficult to get marketing investments such as promotion through a board of directors. It is rare to expect communication spending to produce enough short-term sales growth to meet the break-even figure. In general, the elasticity of demand with respect to communication and the profit contribution margin are not high enough to achieve the short-term break-even sales level. For example, studies suggest that the short-term **advertising elasticity of demand** is rarely above 0.2.[2] This means that an increase of $5 million in

advertising elasticity of demand: the extent to which demand increases as a result of a given increase in advertising expenditure

the communication spending might expect to increase sales by only around 5 per cent.[3] As column 4 of table 11.2 illustrates, this result would be an expected drop in profits from $10 million to $7.5 million.

Not surprisingly, faced with pressure to increase profits, marketing expenditures, especially promotion expenditures, are the first things management look to cut.[4] They see — generally correctly — that cutting such spending leads to little short-term sales loss and consequently a significant increase in the bottom line.

But such a policy has three weaknesses. It ignores the long-term effects of communication spending. The investment to develop a brand, for example, increases not just this year's sales but sales on into the future. The accountants' view highlights their different treatment of tangible and intangible assets. If accountants applied the same reasoning to tangible assets, companies would never invest, since plant and equipment rarely pays off in its first year. The accountant's approach leads to a dangerous bias against intangibles — those knowledge-based assets that are the key to competing in today's information age. The second weakness is that it assumes that if the company does not spend the money, sales and margins will continue at their current level. But as we shall see, in competitive markets this is not likely to be the case. If a brand receives inadequate support, both its sales and operating margins are likely to erode as it loses saliency to consumers and the trade. Finally, since investors take a long-term view of the value of assets they are not likely to react positively to the company pursuing short-term policies. Cuts in promotion budgets generally have a negative effect on the share price, even though they may increase profits in the short term.

The value-based view

The approach of value-based marketing contrasts with both the traditional marketing and accounting viewpoints. It evaluates communication spending, not in terms of sales or immediate profits, but rather in terms of its projected impact on the net present value (NPV) of all future cash flow. It employs the same criterion as outside investors use.

The value-based theory of communication is represented in figure 11.3. Much of the organisation's communication spending is an investment to build intangible assets. These assets are the organisation's brands and its relationships with customers and other value chain partners such as retailers and suppliers. Developing a communication strategy also builds the organisation's knowledge and understanding of its markets. These assets enable the firm to enhance the effectiveness of its core business processes. For example, powerful brands, marketing expertise and strong relationships enable it to be more effective at launching new products, maintaining customer loyalty and running an efficient supply chain. In turn, these processes increase the firm's potential to increase shareholder value.

As we have seen in earlier chapters, the NPV of cash flow can be increased in four ways: (1) by increasing the level of cash flow, (2) by accelerating its timing, (3) by increasing its duration, and (4) by reducing the risks attached to it (figure 11.4). Communication expenditures, through the assets they create and the business processes they enhance, can influence all four levers.

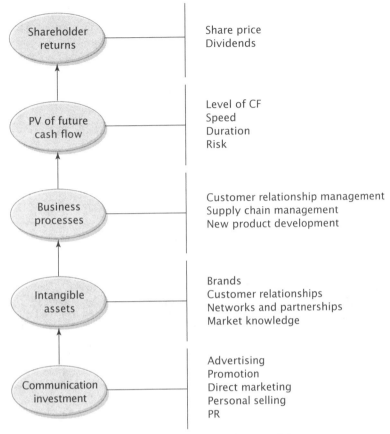

Figure 11.3 The value-based communication model

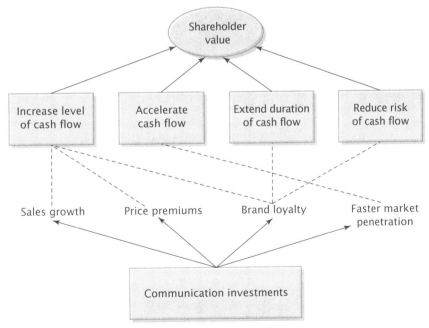

Figure 11.4 Communication and the NPV of future cash flow

Many studies confirm that effective communication can increase the level of cash flow mainly by stimulating short- and long-run sales growth and by building a price premium for a brand. It can accelerate the timing of cash flow through a faster penetration of the market. The longevity of positive cash flows can be increased through the brand loyalty that communication contributes to creating. Finally, the risks attached to future cash flows, and hence the company's cost of capital, can be reduced through the effect of communication investments in building barriers to entry and reinforcing customer loyalty.[5]

Factoring in plausible assumptions about these effects, the dilemma illustrated in table 11.2 can be reconsidered in value terms rather than short-term profit terms. Suppose if the additional communication spend of $5 million a year is not approved, marketing predicts that revenue will decline by 2 per cent a year. In contrast, with the additional spend, marketing predicts that they can maintain prices and grow volume by a conservative 1 per cent a year. The finance staff then estimate the cash flows and shareholder values resulting from the two strategies as follows:

YEAR	1	2	3	4	5	PRESENT VALUE OF: CUM.	CONT.	TOTAL
Cash flow (no increase)	6.5	5.4	4.4	3.5	2.5	17.6	12.6	30.2
Cash flow (with increase)	3.4	3.7	4.1	4.4	4.8	15.1	32.8	47.9

The results clearly demonstrate how short-term policies destroy shareholder value. If the additional spending is not made, cash flow is indeed higher for the first three years. But by year 4, investing in the brand begins to pay off as the cash flow benefits from increased sales and maintained gross margins. The table also shows the present value of the cumulative cash flows, the continuing value of the business at the end of year 5, and the total value of the business to shareholders. The investment strategy increases shareholder value by $17.7 million. This is because, without the new level of communication spend, profits erode sharply over the period, undermining the continuing value of the brand.

Balancing the evidence

The above argument is not to suggest that all communication spending is effective in increasing shareholder value. Money is certainly wasted if the communication strategy is poorly planned and executed, so that the sales targets are not achieved. It also destroys shareholder value if the growth is achieved but not at an adequate operating margin to cover the added investment required.

Management should not take marketing's sales forecasts on trust and they should hold them accountable for achieving the targets that are agreed and which form the basis for justifying the marketing spend. But the major point of the above analysis is to identify the dangers of a short-run accounting focus. This is not mere theory but is evident every day in the stock market. Growth stocks in new industries such as the Internet and biotechnology are routinely valued in billions of dollars even though they have no free cash flow and communication expenditures vastly exceed sales. Investors are recognising in their valuations that these expenditures are not costs but investments to attract customers, who will spend money on the web site over a long period of time. They are investments in innovation.

High communication costs are not merely a feature of new companies, as figures 11.1 and 11.2 illustrate. Companies like McDonald's, Unilever and Nestlé spend heavily to defend their valuable current market shares and protect their price premiums.

Communication and customers

The main objective of communication is to positively influence customers towards buying the company's products. How communication works and its potential to influence people depends upon the type of decision the customer is making.

Factors influencing buying behaviour

The firm's communication is only one of many factors influencing the buyer's decision process. The various factors shaping choice can be grouped into four.

1. **The buyer's role.** Organisational buyers make different decisions than people buying for themselves or their households. For example, a senior manager will expect to fly business class when he represents his company, but on holiday he will fly economy. Organisational buyers often have different constraints, attitudes and objectives than personal consumers.

2. **The buyer's background.** The cultural, social and personal background of the buyer influences decisions. For example, governments are concerned that the benefits of Internet access are currently being enjoyed most by more affluent, younger households and by males more than females. Political, technological and economic forces also affect decisions. For example, firms increase their advertising budgets when the economy is growing and cut back in recessions.

3. **The buyer's experience.** A person buying his or her first car approaches the decision quite differently from someone who changes their car every year. If the buyer has made the same decision many times before, the choice will generally be a routine, low-involvement one. If he or she is satisfied with the previous service, they are likely to buy from the same source. For someone who has never bought before, the decision is a much more complex problem, requiring more information, an evaluation of the alternatives and often involving more people.

4. **The buyer's information sources.** When buyers need to supplement their experience, they have several sources of information including:
   - **Personal sources.** Information can be obtained from family, friends and neighbours. Organisational buyers can draw on the knowledge of other functional experts within the business.
   - **Public sources.** Television, newspapers, consumer-rating organisations and the Internet all provide information, comment and criticism about businesses.
   - **Experiential sources.** Buyers can often learn about the product before purchase by handling, examining and trialling it.

- **Commercial sources.** The buyer receives information in two ways. First, from the company's presence in the market, the buyer perceives the quality of its products, level of its prices and placement in its distribution channels. Second, the buyer can be influenced by the firm's promotion tools — its advertising, sales promotion, public relations, personal selling and direct marketing activities (each of which is discussed later in the chapter).

This review suggests why most studies have found the direct effect of commercial communication spending on buying behaviour to be small. The firm's communication is only one of many factors shaping decisions. Most other forms of information are more credible than commercially sponsored communication. People recognise that advertising messages are biased. Finally, there are so many thousands of other commercial messages every day competing for the buyer's attention that it is difficult to have a strong impact.

Communication mechanisms

The way advertising communication or other forms of promotion work depends upon the type of decision the buyer is making. It works differently when the buyer is choosing coffee than it does when he or she is choosing an airline flight. It works differently for an organisational buyer than it does for an individual consumer.

» Types of buying decisions

Buying decisions can be categorised on two dimensions: involvement and rationality.

buying decision involvement: the amount of investment in time and effort, and the number of people contributing to the decision-making process

Buying decision involvement refers to the amount of investment in time and effort and the number of people contributing to the decision-making process. The investment is likely to be high when the decision is unique so that the buyer or buying team has little experience, when a large amount of money is involved, and when a mistake would pose major economic or social costs. In these circumstances, buyers need to search for information to decide their needs, to identify and evaluate the alternatives, and to make an efficient choice. Conversely, the degree of involvement is likely to be low for routine decisions, low-cost decisions and when there are minimal risks. The two extremes are called extensive problem solving and routine problem solving. Most grocery shopping is an example of routine problem solving, but the purchase of a house will be an example of extensive problem solving.

A buying decision is rational if choice is based primarily on the perceived functionality or economics of the product. Most business buying is rational, as are most purchases of household essentials such as washing powder, petrol and life insurance. Decisions that are low on rationality are those that are made on the basis of subjective feelings or image. Perfumes, beer, confectionery and sports cars normally fall into this category.

Figure 11.5 shows a simple categorisation of buying decisions on the basis of degree of rationality and degree of involvement. Note that extensive problem solving or high-involvement decisions can be rational or subjective. Examples of category 1 decisions would be an organisation's choice of a new information system or a young entrepreneur's choice of a delivery van. Category 2 decisions include choices of clothing, perfumes, whisky or sports cars. These are perceived as important, high-risk decisions by consumers, but image and associations play a more important role in the choice process than functionality and economics. Category 3 decisions are most consumables. Buyers are broadly rational, but because they are such frequent purchases, buyers do not need more information. Category 4 represents impulse items — choice is often random or a response to specific stimuli. Examples include purchases of soft drinks and confectionery.

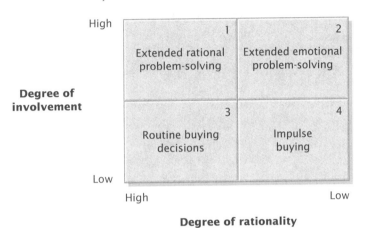

Degree of involvement

	High	
	1 Extended rational problem-solving	**2** Extended emotional problem-solving
	3 Routine buying decisions	**4** Impulse buying

High — Low (Degree of rationality)

Figure 11.5 A categorisation of buying decisions

» A typology of communication models

The way in which advertising communication and other forms of promotion work depends on the type of buying decision that a firm is seeking to influence. The task of communication in influencing routine decisions is quite different from that in high-involvement decision making. There are two sets of models describing how communication works; one describes its application to high-involvement decisions, the other to low-involvement decisions.

high-involvement communication models: models that describe the role of communication in high-involvement decisions

1. **High-involvement communication models.** These models best describe the role of communication in high-involvement decisions. They envisage the communication strategy assisting the buyer going through the learning process that precedes purchase. In the extended rational problem-solving situation (category 1 decisions), this is a cognitive (rational thinking) process. The model used to represent this category is often referred to as the rational model. First, the task of communication is to make buyers aware of the product, then it has to get them to understand its features, then they have to be persuaded to desire it, which then hopefully culminates in purchases. Emotional or image-oriented extended problem solving (category 2) follows a different hierarchy that is an affective (emotions and feeling) rather than a cognitive process. The model used to represent this category is often referred to as the image model. After creating awareness, the task of communication is to build positive feelings about the brand, rather than an understanding of its function. The rational model can be described as 'think, feel, do'; the image model is 'feel, think, do'.

Both types of high-involvement models see communication as an aggressive activity geared to increasing sales. They are a reasonable way to describe the tasks of communication in situations when buyers have limited experience and information, and where the decision is important or high risk. They would also apply when a company is launching a new product or relying on direct-response marketing. Here, the tasks are to create awareness, create preference and win new customers.

2. **Low-involvement communication models.** These models, which include the so called rational-reminder models and image-reminder models, best describe the role of advertising communication and other forms of promotion in low-involvement purchase situations. They mirror the two high-involvement models. The main reason why consumers buying groceries or colas, or businesses buying consumables like oil or packaging, spend little time on the decisions is because they have made them many times before. Here the task of advertising is not to aggressively build awareness, comprehension or preference. This is already achieved. For example, virtually every adult in Australia is aware of Telstra or Victoria Bitter (VB); they understand the products, have attitudes to them and many have used them before.

> **low-involvement communication models:** models that describe the role of communication in low-involvement purchase situations

In such low-involvement purchase situations the task of communication is defensive. Its first role is not to win new customers, but to retain current ones. Given that some of these mature markets are huge, this is an important role. Without continuing communication, the brand's market share would erode and with it the value of the brand to shareholders. The second role of communication in these situations is to defend the brand's price premium. Most successful brands have significant price premiums that contribute greatly to their value for investors: Telstra and Victoria Bitter are no exceptions.

Image-reminder models maintain the brand's value by reminding customers of a brand's continuing presence and relevance. Without being reminded, some customers would eventually forget and drift to other brands. Rational reminder models act to reinforce buying decisions by confirming that customers have made the right choice and that their brand is still good value. Over time, communication models will reposition the brand to keep it relevant as fashions, tastes and attitudes change.

Understanding the nature of the market and the appropriate communication model is critical for managers defining the objectives of communication and evaluating its results. For example, the low-involvement models show that in many situations, it is not realistic to expect communication to increase sales. The fact that an advertising communication, for instance, does not increase sales does not necessarily mean that it does not create value for shareholders. On the contrary, great value may be created by preserving the brand's market share and its operating margins, and sustaining its long-term cash flow.

Developing a communication strategy

Figure 11.6 on the opposite page illustrates the steps marketing management needs to consider when developing a systematic communication strategy for a brand.

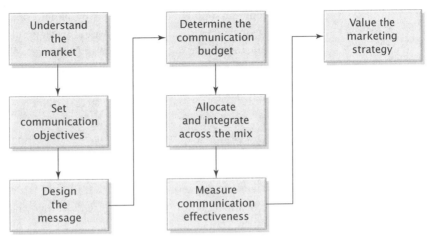

Figure 11.6 Developing the communication strategy

Understand the market

As always, the process starts with understanding the market. There are three main issues to research. First, marketing managers need to review the brand's performance and potential. This means looking at its marketing performance in terms of growth and market share, and its financial performance in terms of economic profits and cash flow. The aim is to understand how well it is doing and to assess its potential to generate future cash. Managers need to understand the attractiveness of the market and whether the brand possesses a differential advantage.

Next, its communication profile has to be audited. This requires researching customers and others who influence the buying process to discover the level of awareness of the brand and its communication efforts, their understanding of the brand's key features and message, and finally their attitudes to the brand and the way it is communicated. The aim is to uncover what strengths can be built on and what weaknesses need to be overcome.

Third, managers need a detailed understanding of customers and the buying process so that they know who to aim at and what messages and media are going to be most effective. This includes researching what types of customers are buying the brand and why they are buying it, looking at how they use the product and where they buy it from, and finding who influences the decision process and how they influence it. The conclusion should be a clear definition of the most valuable customers to aim at, and an in-depth understanding of how to effectively communicate to them the brand proposition.

Set the communication objectives

It is important to set objectives for the communication strategy. The technical and specialised nature of communication means that much of the work will be done by outside agencies: advertising agencies, PR companies, direct response businesses, etc. Objectives align the different activities to common goals; they also provide standards to judge the effectiveness of the work.

Objectives should be specific, measurable and operational. Ultimately, the primary objectives of a communication strategy are to increase, or at least maintain, long-term sales and operating margins. The problem is that it is difficult to make these operational as communication objectives. Generally, it is impossible to disentangle the effects of advertising or other forms of promotion from the myriad of other factors influencing sales and margins. In addition, the purchase is often the end result of a long process of customer decision making. Current communication investments, therefore, may not fully be reflected in sales until well into the future. Similarly, today's buyers of established brands like Qantas or IBM are influenced not just by current communication expenditure but by that which took place in the years before.

As a result, communication objectives are normally framed in terms of intermediate goals which better meet the criteria of being specific, measurable and operational. As noted in the discussion of communication models above, the buying process consists of three stages. The first is the cognitive stage — customers have to be aware of the product and understand its benefits. The next is the affective stage — positive attitudes, liking and preferences for it have to be induced. Finally comes the behavioural stage: purchase, repeat purchase, or intermediate measures such as intention to buy or repeat-buy. Since these variables are easy to measure through surveys or customer panels, a standard way of setting objectives is to target improvements in these variables.

Judgment is required to determine which are the most important measures and what are reasonable targets. For rational high-involvement decisions, cognitive measures are generally the most important. Buyers have to understand the special features and benefits the product offers. For image or emotive decisions, affective criteria are more important. Targets also have to be appropriate to the market situation. For mature, established brands in low-involvement markets, it is unreasonable to set ambitious targets for cognitive and affective measures or for big sales increases. Such targets are unlikely to be met, and setting them shows a misunderstanding of the role of communication in such situations. For established brands, the main communication task is to maintain current performance levels or to produce marginal repositioning.

Design the message

Once the cognitive, affective and behavioural targets have been set, then communication messages have to be developed to achieve the objectives. Given the volume of products competing for the attention of buyers, messages have to have impact; to capture attention, they also have to suggest benefits that are desirable, exclusive and believable.

» Message content

rational appeals: claims made in advertising, or through other forms of communication, about the brand's uniquely superior attributes or economic value to the customer

The message may be rational or emotional in appeal. **Rational appeals** make claims about the brand's uniquely superior attributes or economic value to the customer. In the past, brand managers at companies like Procter & Gamble were taught to write the message around a unique selling proposition (USP). Such messages make sense for attribute brands and where decision making is highly rational. They are still common in business-to-business markets. But increasingly the problem is that it is difficult to sustain real differences in functionality or cost.

Today, more messages are **emotional appeals**. They seek to present added values over and above functional or economic differences. Some offer aspirational messages, associating the brand with status and desired lifestyles. Others offer experiences or shared emotions. These can be based on negative or positive motivations. Negative appeals use fear, guilt or shame to influence people's behaviour (e.g. stop smoking, avoid drinking and driving). Evidence shows that overly negative campaigns are not usually effective. Positive appeals use humour, pride or affection to achieve their goals. The evidence suggests that communication that is liked tends to be more effective.

emotional appeals: claims made in advertising, or through other forms of communication, about the brand's added values over and above functional or economic product difference

» Message presentation

Effectiveness depends on the presentation as well as the content of the message. The style of the message can be one-way or two-way. Personal selling and potentially the Internet can be highly effective because they permit interaction between sender and recipient. Two-way communication permits the sender to tailor the message to the recipient's needs. Even for conventional advertising and direct response communication, getting consumer involvement increases the effectiveness of the message. This can be done by presenting the disadvantages as well as the advantages of the product, or leaving some ambiguity in the message to involve recipients and encourage them to draw their own conclusions.

Many messages are delivered by spokespersons such as celebrities or opinion leaders to increase the impact and credibility of the message. Expertise, trustworthiness and likeability are the characteristics of sources who are most credible to audiences. The message's effectiveness is also a function of the creativity of the phrasing of the wording, the tone and the visual appeal of the message. Most communication messages are pre-tested against consumer groups to monitor impact and credibility.

Determine the communication budget

With spending on communication routinely representing 15 per cent or more of sales, more effective budgeting potentially has a big impact on profits. But few managers in either marketing or finance know how to approach the decision of how much to spend. We explain how managers should decide on how much to spend on communication.

» Conventional approaches to budgeting

Deciding how much to spend on communication is difficult in practice because it is hard to judge the effectiveness of the expenditure. Many other factors such as the product's quality, its price, competition and economic conditions are affecting sales simultaneously. Effectiveness is also not just about how much is spent but how creatively it is spent. Some companies and their agencies get much more from a given budget than others. Many companies appear to give up any attempt to budget rationally.

The **incremental budgeting method** is employed by many companies, whereby they increase last year's budget by a given percentage. The **percentage of sales method** is also common, where the communication budget is set at some percentage of current or anticipated sales. Other methods that research shows are widely used include **competitive parity** — spending the same percentage as competitors — and the **affordability method**, where the company spends what it feels it can afford from the budget.

incremental budgeting method: a budgeting approach whereby a company increases last year's budget by a given percentage

percentage of sales method: a budgeting approach whereby a company sets the communication budget at some percentage of current or anticipated sales

competitive parity method: a budgeting approach whereby a company simply decides to spend as much as its competitors

affordability method: a budgeting approach whereby the company spends what it feels it can afford from the budget

None of these rules of thumb are rational because they do not consider the basic question of how different levels of communication spending might affect sales and cash flow. They lead to budgets that can easily be a hundred per cent too much or too little.

» **Objective and task method**

This method is regarded — incorrectly — as the superior method in many marketing circles. The idea is to define a specific objective. For example, a marketing manager decides that a 3 per cent trial rate is sufficient to establish a new product in the target market. Then the task that must be performed to achieve this objective is determined. In our example, this might include determining the number of advertising exposures needed per person in the target market to achieve the 3 per cent trial rate. Finally, the costs of performing the task are estimated.

The problem with the objective and task method is that much of the detail is spurious. There is no justification for a specific trial rate. In our brief example, how does the marketing manager know whether 2, 3 or 5 per cent trial rate is sufficient? After all, it is a new product. Past experiences with other products, and their trial rates, might not apply in this case. Different assumptions concerning trial rates and exposures necessary to stimulate a product trial would give very different budgets.

» **Value-based budgeting**

Since the objective of marketing is to maximise shareholder value, the right way to determine the communication budget is to spend that amount which maximises the NPV of the brand's future cash flow. This means considering the trade-off between communication spend and other investments to increase returns. It also means evaluating the implications of different levels of spending. The first step is to estimate how sales will vary with communication spend. This can be done directly or by separating out the components of revenue. For example, net revenue growth for a mobile phone operator is best estimated by predicting the number of subscribers it gains, the average spend per subscriber and the number of years an average subscriber is retained.[6]

There are three ways to estimate the sales response function. First, an econometric approach can be used, which correlates variations in spending with variations in sales. The data can be either historical or based on differences occurring cross-sectionally in different geographical areas. This method is most appropriate for mature products and where markets are relatively stable so that conditions in the future are not going to be too different from the past.[7] Experimental estimates can be used for new products. This involves varying the levels of spending in different regions and assessing the response function.[8] The third approach is consensus estimates. This requires members of the brand team to use their best judgments to make predictions about sales at 'low', 'medium' and 'high' levels of marketing spend; from these estimates a consensus response curve is developed.

The resulting levels of spend and sales forecasts are input into a shareholder value analysis to estimate the shareholder value added for the different budgets. Figure 11.7 illustrates this for the beer, Buzz, showing the shareholder value added with annual communication budgets of 5, 10 and 15 million euros. Note that market share is always maximised with the maximum communication budget, but the objective is to maximise value, not sales. Table 11.3 shows the calculation in detail for the optimum communication spend of 10 million euros. Here, managers forecast sales reaching 35 million euros and the brand having a shareholder value of 27.8 million euros.

Communication budget
(euros)

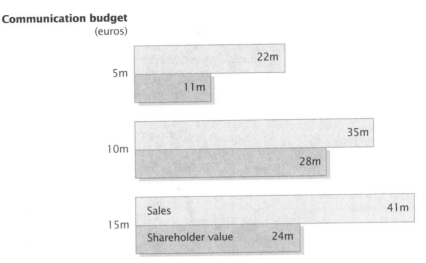

Figure 11.7 Value-based budgeting for communication investments

Table 11.3 Optimum communication budget for Buzz Beer

YEAR	1	2	3	4	5
Sales (euros m)	30.0	33.0	35.0	35.0	35.0
Communication budget	10.0	10.0	10.0	10.0	10.0
Operating profit	3.0	3.3	4.2	5.3	7.0
NOPAT	3.0	2.6	2.9	3.7	4.9
Net investment	15.0	1.2	0.8	0.0	0.0
Cash flow	–12.0	1.4	2.1	3.7	4.9
PV of CF	–10.9	1.2	1.6	2.5	3.0
		Cumulative present value			–2.6
		PV of continuing value			30.4
		Shareholder value			27.8

Allocate and integrate across the communication mix

The budget has to be allocated and integrated across the various communication channels — advertising, sales promotion, public relations, personal selling and direct marketing. Companies even within the same market can employ very different strategies. Developing an appropriate set of channels will have a marked effect on the success of a campaign. Each of the channels has certain characteristics, and advantages and disadvantages.

» Advertising

Companies can use advertising in a range of media including TV, radio, newspapers, magazines, billboards and web sites. The aims can be long-term brand development or quick sales response. The general features of advertising are:

- **Legitimise the brand.** Exposure in major advertising vehicles expresses the company's commitment to the brand and conveys a measure of confidence among buyers.

- **Creative expression.** Advertising, through the use of pictures, colour and language permits a more creative presentation of the brand's emotional and functional benefits.
- **Image building.** Advertising over a long period can be the most effective way of building a distinctive personality for the brand.
- **Economical.** Advertising can be a relatively low cost means of exposing the company's message to large populations. The downside is that it generally has smaller effects than personal selling or promotions.

» Sales promotion

Sales promotion tools include money-off vouchers, samples, contests, trade-in allowances, gifts, exhibits and tie-ins. Their general features are:

- **Impact.** By offering direct inducements to buyers, they can have strong and quick effects on sales. Normally, the elasticity of demand with respect to promotions is significantly higher than for advertising.
- **Trial.** Promotions can be an effective means of obtaining customer trial in low-involvement markets where other communication vehicles do not receive attention.
- **Expensive.** Promotions, particularly where they involve price reductions, can be expensive. They can also reduce margins by displacing sales from periods when promotions are not being offered.
- **Image erosion.** Excessive use of sales promotions can damage the quality image of a brand.

» Public relations

Public relations (PR) can include lobbying politicians and the media, publications, press handouts, speeches, charitable donations and sponsorships. Its main features are:

- **Credibility.** News stories and features are more credible sources of information to buyers than ads and promotions that are obviously biased and paid for.
- **Imprecise.** It is more difficult to control the message and target it to particular groups than with conventional commercial communication.
- **Low cost.** Effective PR can obtain substantial free media exposure.
- **Difficult.** PR cannot depend on gaining effective access to the most important media or community stakeholders. It depends on the perceived importance and interest of the message.

» Personal selling

Using the company's own sales representatives is a highly effective way of building up an understanding of the company's offer and creating preference. Its main features are:

- **Two-way.** Two-way communication is always more persuasive than one-way. The salesperson is able to modify and tailor the information to the reactions and wants of the customer.
- **Closure.** Personal selling allows the deal to be agreed. It also puts the buyer under psychological pressure to respond to the representative's visit.
- **Relationships.** Personal selling facilitates the development of friendships and lasting relationships that encourage continuing business.
- **Expensive.** Personal selling is normally a much more expensive form of communication. With keeping a salesperson on the road costing up to $300 000, an individual sales call can easily cost $600.

» Direct marketing

A significant trend in recent years has been the growth of direct marketing channels. The explosion of access to the Internet looks certain to give this an even greater impetus. Direct marketing includes mailings, catalogues, telemarketing, e-mail and electronic shopping. Its main features include:

- **Personalised.** The message can usually be addressed to a specific person and customised to their individual circumstances.
- **Responsive.** Direct marketing usually invites a behavioural response from the buyer. Where effective, direct marketing can lead to a rapid increase in sales.
- **Interactive.** Messages can be prepared quickly and can be changed depending on the customer's response. The new online medium even allows two-way communication, which is richer and more effective than one-way messages. For marketers, it offers often dramatically lower costs, continually updated information about customers, greater flexibility and the ability to build relationships with customers by storing and retrieving information about their preferences.
- **Targeted.** Direct marketing can be precisely targeted to specific market segments.
- **Convenient.** Direct marketing is more convenient for customers — they can often order 24 hours a day, 7 days a week, right from their homes or desk.
- **Diverse.** Direct marketing allows more choice by separating the physical goods from the information about them. Unlike, say, shops where the presentation and storage of the goods take place in the one location, direct marketing can present a huge catalogue of choices, which do not have to be stored at multiple locations. A central warehouse and direct marketing offers economies of scale with maximum variety.[9]

What determines the right mix of communication for a brand? The allocation the manager should make depends on the following factors:

- **The company's objectives and capabilities.** If the company's aim is to increase awareness in the mass market, then advertising is the obvious medium. On the other hand, if it wants to create trial, sales promotions are attractive. The resources available also influence the options. Television advertising is very expensive; PR can be cheap.
- **Characteristics of the target market.** If the target market consists of a relatively small number of customers, direct selling is likely to be effective. If the market consists of millions of customers, then mass media will be better.
- **Type of product.** In general, personal selling is the most effective vehicle for products that are expensive, complex and high risk, and for markets with few, large buyers. Advertising and sales promotion are more efficient for products that are cheaper and routine, or where emotions play an important role in the choice process.
- **Push versus pull strategy.** An important factor is whether the company is pursuing a push or a pull marketing strategy. A pull strategy uses advertising and consumer promotions targeted at end-customers with the aim of getting them to induce the retailer or other channels to stock the product. Pull strategies create a demand from consumers. A push strategy directs selling and promotions to the trade with the aim of persuading retailers and distributors to carry the product and in turn promote it to customers.

- **Stage of market evolution.** The mix of communication instruments tends to shift as the product and market evolve. For a new product, advertising and PR are usually the most appropriate vehicles to build awareness. In the mature phase, sales promotions and personal selling can become more important. In the decline stage, advertising, PR and direct selling are cut back as there is little new to say about the product and declining margins make it difficult to justify high investment. Sales promotions will often be necessary to stimulate the trade to continue to push the product.

Integrated marketing communication

The new information technology has spurred another trend towards greater efforts to produce **integrated marketing communication**. This means seeking to combine advertising, sales promotion, public relations, personal selling and the increasing array of direct marketing techniques in a synergistic manner to produce greater clarity, consistency and effectiveness in the way the business communicates to its target markets. The problem until now has been that each of these promotion tools has usually been controlled by different managers and different external agencies that have set their own communication objectives. Much can be gained by bringing these together and developing integrated, multi-stage, multi-vehicle communication campaigns.[10]

integrated marketing communication: the combination of advertising, sales promotions, public relations, personal selling and direct marketing techniques to produce effective and consistent communication with the target market

To make the communication investment effective, it is important for management to integrate the various elements of the communication mix around a common set of objectives. In recent years the major advertising agencies, such as Saatchi & Saatchi, J. Walter Thompson and Young & Rubicam, have bought agencies specialising in sales promotions, direct marketing and public relations with the aim of making an integrated communication offer to clients. But this move has not been noticeably successful — most clients still prefer to choose their own set of specialist agencies and to develop strategies for individual elements of their communication mix.

Often, these activities are poorly coordinated — each agency working in isolation, developing its own messages, themes and modes of presentation, and reporting to different specialist managers within the client company who are jealously guarding their own areas. The results are communication efforts that fail to exploit the synergies between the company's advertising, direct marketing and PR initiatives, and that do not maximise the effectiveness of the often large investments made.

Integrated communication can be stimulated by a number of measures. First, management should have a single budget for marketing communication. One manager should have responsibility for the company's entire communication investment. The company's communication specialists should plan the communication strategy as a team and work out how it should be coordinated and implemented. Finally, senior managers should evaluate the results of the communication strategy as a whole in terms of overall, rather than specialist, goals. The world's biggest advertiser, Procter & Gamble, has recently adopted this approach to encourage its managers and their specialist communication agencies to work as a team. It has moved away from the traditional approach of paying agencies a commission on the work they do, to paying them a performance fee based on the overall sales achieved by the business unit.

Communication effectiveness

In spite of the huge sums being spent on communication, companies spend relatively little on judging whether their investments have paid off. More is spent on pre-testing campaigns than on post-campaign results.

» Pre-tests

Before the national or international launch of a major communication campaign, companies will sometimes test it in one region to assess its effects on sales. If the campaign fails, it can be dropped before more is spent. But because such real market tests take time, most companies rely on more flexible copy testing services. These involve showing proposed ads to audiences of potential consumers and having the messages rated for their ability to attract attention, achieve cognitive effects and impact on customers' attitudes and intentions to buy. Most advertising agencies are sceptical about such pre-testing, arguing that the methods over-emphasise the rationality of consumers and ignore the ads' non-verbal effects on subsequent behaviour.

» Post-tests

More companies, like Procter & Gamble, want to judge the success of communication spending through its effect on increasing sales. But caution is necessary in using short-term sales increases as a measure of value generation. Many factors affect sales besides communication investments. A longer period than a year has to be used to judge the effectiveness of an image-building campaign. Another factor, which we explore in the next section, is the benchline for judging sales effects. For many brands, especially in mature markets, the communication spend is necessary to prevent sales and margins declining. Looking at increased sales, therefore, may seriously underestimate the economic effect of the investment.

Managers can benchmark the effectiveness of their spend against competitors by comparing their **share of voice** to market share ratios. For example, the table below shows the three competitors in a market. Company A has a communication effectiveness score of 1.1 — its market share is 10 per cent higher than its relative communication spend. B, spending the same amount as A, is much less effective. Company C is the most efficient with a score of 1.3, suggesting it could profitably increase its market share by spending more on marketing communication.

share of voice: a company's communication expenditure on a product expressed as a proportion of all communication expenditure by it and rival firms on that product

	COMMUNICATION EXPENDITURE	SHARE OF VOICE (%)	MARKET SHARE (%)	COMMUNICATION EFFECTIVENESS*
A	$10 000 000	40	44	1.10
B	$10 000 000	40	30	0.75
C	$5 000 000	20	26	1.30

* Market share divided by share of voice

Caution is required in such comparisons. For example, mature products benefiting from their past investments in the brand would expect to have higher scores than new ones. Differences can also be due to factors other than communication effectiveness. For example, C's high score could be the result of lower prices or superior quality.

Most evaluations of campaigns are still based on examining their communication effects. There are a variety of market research services that seek to answer such questions such as how effective the campaign has been in creating awareness, building comprehension and achieving positive attitudes to the brand. Unfortunately, while these measures give useful diagnostics they are generally, at best, only weakly associated with sales and profits. As always, the only really satisfactory measure of the communication investment is whether it creates shareholder value, a subject we return to in the final section.

» Generalisations about communication effects

There has been a vast amount of research on communication, especially on advertising. As always, when human behaviour is concerned, there are no laws that can predict responses. There are big variations in the effectiveness of different communication campaigns depending on their creativity of execution, the competitive response, the nature of the market and the differential advantage of the product. Nevertheless, it is useful to summarise the general conclusions of the research as this provides some broad benchmarks on what can be expected from communication spending.

- The direct effect of communication on sales is usually small. Most studies find advertising elasticities around 0.2 or less, compared to elasticities of up to 2 for price promotions. This implies that a 10 per cent increase in advertising would increase sales by 2 per cent, while a 10 per cent price cut would increase sales by 20 per cent.
- Communication is often critical for new brands. The advertising elasticity is higher for new brands. Communication creates awareness and comprehension, and signals the brand's quality.
- Once brands are established, the role of communication is to reinforce existing buying behaviour. Communication adds value by maintaining sales and prices rather than increasing them. While these may appear modest goals, they can have a major effect on the value of the brand.
- The effect of communication on maintaining price levels can be as important as its effects on volume. Brand advertising tends to reduce price sensitivity allowing the firm to obtain higher gross margins and be less sensitive to price competition.
- Advertising has diminishing effects in terms of short-term sales results. The first exposure to an ad has the biggest effect on consumers' purchasing behaviour. After the third exposure, effects are usually very small. This means that reach soon becomes more important than frequency.
- Communication is more effective when the brand has a differential advantage. Such an advantage can be based on functional or emotional attributes.
- Because communication elasticities are normally low, the payoff will vary with the brand's profit contribution. High communication budgets are unlikely to create value on low-margin products.

These conclusions suggest that the power of communication, and particularly advertising, has often been exaggerated. The satisfactory experience of customers and sheer habit tend to be more important than communication in maintaining sales. For new brands, companies have to employ additional and more powerful means to capture initial sales, including aggressive pricing, samples and word-of-mouth endorsements. At the same time, shareholder value is a long-term phenomenon. This means that small advantages in communication effectiveness will compound over time into surprisingly large value differences. This is illustrated next.

Value the communication strategy

Typically, both marketers and accountants have an incorrect understanding of how communication expenditures should be judged. Whether the money is spent on short-term promotions or image-building advertising, the campaign should be evaluated in terms of its effect on future cash flow and, thus, on shareholder value. Generally, such a value-based approach will lead to quite different, and much superior, decisions on communication spending. In short: a value-based approach is the principal approach that should be used in valuing and selecting communication strategies.

We have shown that there are two broad types of communication problems: high involvement and low involvement. In high-involvement purchasing situations the buyer is searching for information about the attributes or emotional benefits offered by competing products. The function of communication here is to help buyers solve this problem by providing information to take them through the process of learning about the product and building attitudes favourable to purchase. The ultimate test of this type of communication is whether it succeeds in increasing the number of buyers and the value of sales. Low-involvement buying is different. Here buyers are familiar with the product and have bought it before. The function of communication is not persuading customers to try it, but to reinforce current purchasing habits.

To determine whether a given investment in communication creates value in high-involvement situations is straightforward. Managers have to forecast the effects of the expenditure on the components of sales, estimate the resulting free cash flows, discount them and calculate the shareholder value added. This is similar to the case summarised in table 11.3. The problem becomes more controversial, however, in the low-involvement situation when communication expenditures do not increase sales. Is it in the shareholders' interest to spend money on communication when there is no increase in sales or profits? The answer to this very common problem is presented in marketing management in practice 'Biscuit value'.

Marketing management in practice: Biscuit value

Sigma, from Associated Biscuits, is a brand leader in the impulse biscuit market. It had succeeded in maintaining sales despite the growth of retailer own-label brands and competitive new product launches from Cadbury and Nestlé. Awareness is very high and consumer attitude and usage studies confirm the brand's strong profile and franchise. However, a newly appointed finance director is less impressed about the brand, pointing to its low operating margin, lack of growth in recent years and heavy spending on promotions tools. He observed that spending on communication amounted to 10 per cent of sales and exceeded profits by 150 per cent.

The marketing manager had proposed a communication budget of $3 million, the same as in the previous year. But the finance director had calculated that the break-even on this expenditure amounted to $7.5 million ($3 million divided by the contribution margin of 50 per cent) and was unwilling to endorse the budget unless marketing could promise such a sales increase. He stated that profits would be higher without the campaign, with a cost saving of up to $3 million. He demonstrated this on a spreadsheet to the marketing manager. Column A shows the budget, column B shows the profits with no communication support, and column C shows the budget, with the communication budget halved. Column D shows profits if advertising is eliminated and sales decline as a result by 5 per cent.

(continued)

The marketing manager was alarmed since this clearly showed — to his surprise — that profits were significantly higher without the communication support. He also knew that there was no way that sales next year would increase by the 25 per cent necessary to achieve the break-even on the communication budget.

	\$ million			
	A	**B**	**C**	**D**
Sales	30	30	30	28.5
Variable costs	18	18	18	17.1
Contribution	12	12	12	11.4
Communication	3	0	1.5	0
Overheads	7	7	7	7
Operating profits	2	5	3.5	4.4

The manager discussed the problem with a friend who was a city investment analyst. The analyst criticised the financial director's approach. She said the director was using an old-fashioned accountancy approach, which investors had jettisoned years ago. Investors, she said, were interested in long-run performance, not just next year's results. Also, she said, shareholders were interested in cash, which was a much more objective and relevant figure than accounting profit. Finally, she thought the financial director was taking a very naive and short-term view of marketing and consumer behaviour. Surely, she pointed out, cutting communication support would lead to long-term erosion of the brand. It would also hit margins because retailers would need to be offered more discounts to give shelf space to a declining brand.

Using a laptop, she suggested they explore three valuations: the value of the brand to shareholders with the past strategy being continued, the value using the financial director's plan and an alternative strategy to boost operating profits.

Value with the continuing strategy

Under the continuing strategy, the marketing manager believed that Sigma could hold market share and profits would remain around the present level for the foreseeable future. This meant shareholder value could be estimated by the perpetuity method. Assuming a tax rate of 30 per cent and a cost of capital of 10 per cent, then the value of the business was now worth \$14 million.[11]

Value under the financial director's plan

The marketing manager reconsidered the implications of the financial director's plan. He thought that the idea of losing 5 per cent of sales if advertising and brand support was abandoned was reasonable. But if there was no brand support in the future years, he thought it obvious that sales would continue to decline. He estimated this decline as around 2.5 per cent a year. Having negotiated with the major retail chains, he knew that a declining brand would become unattractive to them and he would have to pay higher discounts to retain shelf space. He figured this would have the effect of eroding prices by 2 per cent a year. Table 11.4 shows the new scenario.

Table 11.4 Implications of eliminating discretionary communication spending, \$million

Year	0	1	2	3	4	5
Cases (m. units)	20.00	19.00	18.53	18.06	17.61	17.17
Unit price (\$)	1.50	1.47	1.44	1.41	1.38	1.36
Sales	30.00	27.93	26.69	25.50	24.36	23.28
Variable costs	15.00	14.25	13.89	13.55	13.21	12.88
Contribution	15.00	13.68	12.79	11.95	11.16	10.40
Communication and marketing	3.00	0.00	0.00	0.00	0.00	0.00
Overheads	10.00	10.00	10.00	10.00	10.00	10.00
Operating profit	2.00	3.68	2.79	1.95	1.16	0.40
NOPAT	1.40	2.58	1.96	1.37	0.81	0.28
Net investment		-0.83	-0.50	-0.48	-0.45	-0.43
Cash flow	1.40	3.40	2.45	1.84	1.26	0.72
DCF	1.40	3.09	2.03	1.38	0.86	0.44

Cumulative present value	7.81
PV of continuing value	1.75
Shareholder value	9.56

In the first year, the financial director was correct — profits and cash flow would be higher if the advertising and marketing budget were cut. But from the second year, profits and cash flow would fall precipitously as market share and prices eroded. At $9.56 million, shareholder value is one-third less under this policy than under the current strategy.

Value under an alternative strategy
The analyst suggested that if the financial director was determined to improve short-term profits, then a strategy that might do less permanent damage to the brand would be to raise the price by 5 per cent. She suggested that a leading brand like Sigma would be expected to have a lower than average price elasticity, say around –1, suggesting this might erode the number of cases sold by around 5 per cent. They were pleased with the numbers that were generated from these assumptions — operating profits jumped by nearly 40 per cent to $2.77 million and shareholder value increased to $19.38 million. The market share loss over the planning period was only 5 per cent as against nearly 15 per cent under the financial director's plan.[12]
In summary, the three options gave the following figures:

	SHAREHOLDER VALUE ($)	MARKET SHARE, YEAR 5 (%)
Current policy	$14 000 000	34
Finance director	$9 560 000	29
Alternative policy	$19 380 000	32

Summary

1. It is not enough to have a good product; its values have to be communicated to create awareness, to build an understanding of its benefits and to develop positive attitudes towards it. Without a decisive communication strategy, competitors can catch up and usurp the brand's position in the customer's share of mind.

2. Usually, neither marketing nor accounting managers know how to evaluate spending on communication. Marketers usually look at awareness and sales, accountants focus on the impact on short-term profits. Neither set of measures correlates with shareholder value.

3. Investing in communication increases shareholder value by creating and developing intangible assets which enhance the effectiveness of the business' core processes.

4. The firm's commercial communication activities are only one of many factors affecting the buying process. In general, their effects are quite small. Nevertheless, small differences in communication effectiveness can compound over a long period to significant differences in the value of the business to investors.

5. There are two broad model categories of how communication works — the high-involvement models and the low-involvement models. The former see the role of communication primarily as persuading new customers to buy; the latter see the communication role as reinforcing current buying behaviour.

6. Much communication investment is primarily about reinforcement. Such spending can still create shareholder value even though its effect on increasing sales is minimal.

review questions

1. How does communication create shareholder value?
2. Contrast how accountants and marketing managers conventionally judge the effectiveness of spending on communication.
3. How does communication influence buyer behaviour?
4. Describe how communication objectives will differ for mature products and new ones.
5. Describe the steps in developing a communication strategy.
6. Show how to evaluate the potential effects on shareholder value of a communication plan.

discussion questions

1. Discuss the considerations that accompany the development of a communication strategy.
2. How do buying decisions affect the development of a communication strategy?
3. How does value-based budgeting differ from conventional budgeting approaches? Assess its usefulness in developing value-based communication strategies.
4. How would the communication strategy differ for two companies: (a) an *established* company, with high brand credibility, introducing a new product to the marketplace, and (b) a *new* company introducing a new product to the marketplace?

debate questions

1. Should companies allocate resources to activities that produce more tangible results, such as new product development, rather than promotion and communication?
2. Would company managers be more resourceful to focus their communication strategy on direct marketing initiatives rather than on less accountable communication strategies?
3. Is it reasonable to suggest that the concept of integrated marketing communication is a fad with a short-term focus?

case study | Light beer communication

At Lion Nathan, David McNeil has been instrumental in positioning Hahn Premium Light as the 'best tasting' beer and overcoming perceptions of light beer as 'wussy' and lacking in taste.

McNeil says that light beer has traditionally been seen as something that people drink when they are driving — it's rarely a choice of beer. He saw an opportunity for a light beer positioned on taste and quality. And so began an ambitious plan to position Hahn Premium Light as a beer of choice.

At the heart of the brand's marketing activity was a TV campaign featuring Michael Caton, the star of the Aussie battler movie, *The Castle*. McNeil says the TV campaign was an opportunity to break away from the predictable advertising of the past. Michael Caton was chosen to front the ads because his character is in keeping with Hahn Premium Light's brand value. While Caton's aesthetic taste leaves a lot to be desired in the ads, his taste for beer is right on target. The campaign's basic message is what you see is what you get — it is the idea of good taste/bad taste that really shines through in the ads.

What started off as an ambitious plan to reposition Hahn Premium Light has turned into a runaway success, surpassing initial expectations and propelling the brand to a position of market leadership in 2002. Hahn Premium Light knocked Foster's Light Ice off the top spot and became market leader in every state except Victoria. In NSW, it became the market leader two years ahead of schedule. McNeil says the results of the Hahn Premium Light marketing push are in keeping with the two original objectives — to transform Hahn Premium Light into the leading light beer and grow the light beer market. The campaign also saw the brand rewrite Lion Nathan's sales books with the new brand's sales jumping by 83%.

McNeil puts the success of the campaign down to a mix of forward planning and seizing an opportunity in the market. He believes the campaign was about uncovering an opportunity and assessing the risks one by one. Hahn Premium Light must now focus on maintaining its market leadership in the face of competition. 'The best indicators of the future are the behaviours of the past. I've got one eye on what's been tried and tested and two eyes on where we're headed', McNeil says.

Source: Adapted from 'Australia's Ten Most Effective Marketers', *B&T Marketing & Media*, 14 January 2002, www.bandt.com.au.

Questions

1. How would you evaluate the effectiveness of the Hahn Premium Light marketing campaign?
2. How do you think Lion Nathan shareholders evaluate the new brand's communication strategy?
3. Which factors associated with this campaign contributed to Hahn Premium Light's success?
4. Do you think Hahn Premium Light will sustain its competitive position in the market? How will the communication strategies change in the future?

end notes

1. *Finance Directors Survey 2000*, sponsored by the Institute of Practitioners in Advertising and KPMG, London: IPA, 2000.
2. Demetrios Vakratsas and Tim Ambler, 'How advertising works: What do we really know', *Journal of Marketing*, **63**, January 1999, pp. 26–43.
3. The increase in sales is given by the elasticity times the percentage increase in the spend: 0.2×25 per cent = 5 per cent. Sales would be expected to grow from $100 million to $105 million.
4. *Finance Directors Survey 2000*, sponsored by the Institute of Practitioners in Advertising and KPMG, London: IPA, 2000.

5. A good summary of supporting studies is in Rajendra K. Strivastava, Tasadduq A. Shervani and Liam Fahey, 'Market-based assets and shareholder value: a framework for analysis', *Journal of Marketing*, **62**, January 1998, pp. 2–18.

6. For a good example see, 'The FTSE's bright, the FTSE's Orange: How advertising enhanced Orange PLC shareholder value', *The IPA Advertising Effectiveness Awards 1998*, London: IPA, 1999.

7. For a full account see Dominique M. Hanssens, Leonard J. Parsons and Randall L. Schultz, *Market Response Models: Econometric and Time Series Analysis*, Boston, MA: Kluwer, 1990.

8. Leonard M. Lodish, Magid Abraham et al. 'A summary of 55 in-market experimental estimates of the long-term effects of advertising', *Marketing Science*, **14**(3), pp. 133–40.

9. For an excellent discussion of the implications of this separation of the economics of information from the economics of physical items, see Philip Evans and Thomas Wurster, *Blown to Bits: How the New Economics of Information Transforms Strategy*, Boston, MA: Harvard Business School Press, 2000.

10. For detailed examples of integrated communication, see Stan Rapp and Thomas L. Collins, *Beyond Maximarketing: The New Power of Caring and Daring*, New York: McGraw-Hill, 1994; Ernan Roman, Integrated Direct Marketing, Lincolnwood, IL: NTC Business Books, 1995.

11. After tax profit or NOPAT is $1.4 million. Dividing by the cost of capital at 10 per cent gives $14 million.

12. It should be straightforward to rework table 11.4 on a spreadsheet to check this alternative strategy.

chapter 12

Value-based Internet marketing

Value-based Internet marketing

chapter objectives

By the time you have completed this chapter, you will be able to:

- understand the development of the Internet and its key features
- describe the drivers of the new economy
- assess how the Internet is reshaping marketing and competition
- show how it can create value for customers and shareholders
- analyse how the Internet affects marketing strategy
- understand how Internet businesses and strategies are valued
- summarise how companies need to respond to the threats and opportunities from the Internet.

scene setter
Don Tapscott

Don Tapscott, who co-authored Digital Capital: Harnessing the power of business webs in 2000, [has an] undying faith in the net... [This] led to a robust debate with Harvard strategist Michael Porter at the World Trade Congress in Davos [in 2001]...

On one issue — dotcoms — they agree. Porter says the dotcoms measured performance in ways that were unreliable, and had 'only a loose relationship to economic value'. Tapscott says dotcoms were doomed from the start because they used 'indirect measures, like clicks and stickiness, which were not about creating value for customers'.

'But we have a fundamental disagreement on what conclusions you draw from all of this,' Tapscott says. 'Porter and many other people are throwing out the baby with the bathwater. They conclude that (the dotcom crash) shows that the net is not really important, that e-business was a mistake, that there's no such thing as the new economy, and that conventional business thinking is not only necessary, it's sufficient to compete today.

'That's very dangerous because the internet is not about creating dotcoms. It's a new, publicly available infrastructure that's lowering the costs of transactions, partnering and knowledge exchange.

'Every now and then, a technology comes along that is so profound, so powerful, so universal, that its impact will change everything. It will transform every institution in the world. It will create winners and losers, it will change the way we do business, the way we teach our children, communicate and interact as individuals.'

Lou Gerstner, Chairman of IBM

'Knowledge used to be something that was pretty much internal to an organisation. The main relationships we had in the past were internal to the organisation. It's amazing to think that, but it's true. You had your relationship with your boss, your secretary, your subordinates and your project team. Such relationships were often carefully defined — you were part of the human resource with roles, responsibilities, reward systems and the like.

'Great thinkers, like Alfred Sloan, who took GM to prominence years ago, developed entire theories of management based on this paradigm. But did GM really have relationships with its customers? Car makers did market research to understand customers. They did mass marketing to establish brands. They sold vehicles and repaired them. But few customers would describe this as a relationship in any significant sense of the term.'

Central to Tapscott's theories is relationship capital — a new term for the intangible value involved in exchanges with customers, suppliers and other partners. Relationship capital, he says, is now 'more important than the capital contained in land, factories, buildings and even big bank accounts'.

Organisations that make full strategic use of the net have higher relationship capital because they are faster and more interactive. The focus of online retail, for example, is the customer (his or her needs, tastes, demographic and so on), whereas in conventional shops, Tapscott says, the point of reference is merely the old-fashioned classification and movement of goods.

But is relationship capital, as a measure of an organisation's worth, another example of the flawed performance measures used by dotcoms? Not if you believe in the net's ability to create new and more effective ways of communicating, which Tapscott says is happening already.

... business relationships are becoming a new form of wealth and of competitive differentiation. Companies with good relationships can compete better than those without.

Source: Extracts from Fred Pawle, 'The internet Don', *AFR Boss*, February 2002, pp. 23–5.

Introduction

The growth and speed of the impact of the Internet on business and society has had few precedents. From the mid-1990s through to the bursting of the technology stock bubble in April 2000, the point was made on every business platform that 'The Internet changes everything'. Jack Welch, at the time chairman of GE, the world's largest and most admired company, said that for GE, 'the Internet ranks as priority No. 1, 2, 3 and 4!' The chief financial officer of Cisco, which before the downturn of early 2000 was the world's third most valuable company, claimed that the Internet fundamentally changes the rules of business. He suggested that firms that did not rapidly adopt Internet technologies were heading for extinction: 'It's no longer about the big beating the small, it's about the fast beating the slow'.

This sort of rhetoric is now much less common. The obsession with the Internet has temporarily waned, many technology companies have disappeared, and hype has been replaced by more sober assessments of the impact of the Internet. Where once stock markets valued Internet-related businesses at multiples that enormously exceeded traditional companies, a more cautious view now prevails. Indeed, there is a resurgent scepticism in some quarters about the role of the Internet; a growing number of companies have become more wary of making the commitment to having an online presence. A survey of Australian businesses by Dun & Bradstreet in January 2002 was able to compare the answers given by 400 executives a year earlier to the same set of questions. Almost half of all executives questioned in 2002 said they did not use the Internet for business transactions, and cited security and reliability as major concerns. This was a 20 per cent increase on a year earlier. Other executives, by contrast, were making more extensive use of the Internet, with more than 12 per cent of businesses conducting 20 per cent or more of their business online. This compared with 8 per cent a year before. In January 2002, 50 per cent of the Australian firms that had their own web site called it 'an integral part' of the way they do business. This was up from 43 per cent from the 2001 survey. But there was also a jump to 34 per cent of the number of executives who said a web site was 'not important' to their business and that they did not own one. In short, there is an apparent trend towards a more marked division between those companies who are making the Internet a critical part of their business activities and those who have decided to reject it outright. Some Australian firms have become more sceptical that the Internet will have a positive impact on their business. Such firms are in the minority but as of early 2002 are part of a growing minority.

Despite this caution, it would be wrong to suggest that the rise of the Internet was ephemeral, its impact exaggerated, and its potential overrated. Investors continue to believe, with reason, that the future is in information technology. Although both Microsoft and Cisco suffered during the US downturn in technology stocks, both continue to exhibit enviable profit margins and cash generating capabilities, far in excess of most old-economy businesses. There can be no doubt that a paradigm shift is occurring in the way companies need to do business in the future. While the business plans of many dot.coms proved to be fundamentally flawed, leading to their rapid demise in the aftermath of April 2000, it is also true that the Internet offers such enormous improvements in operating efficiency and market effectiveness that, in many markets, traditional ways of doing business have been seriously questioned.

In analysing the impact of the Internet on business, we need to recognise that there is a spectrum of companies from **pure dot.coms** (companies that were created from scratch to take advantage of the Internet) to **bricks and mortar** companies (traditional players who are conducting business 'the old way'). For many of the latter, the key issue is whether, and more especially to what degree and in what ways, they should embrace the Internet to transform existing practices and to enter new markets. They need to assess the revenue streams to be produced by offline and online activities and determine how they will allocate resources between these activities.

Where once the rhetoric was about the imminent extinction of bricks and mortar firms that did not quickly transform themselves into so-called 'clicks and bricks', there is presently, as noted, some scepticism in some countries about whether the transition is even necessary. This is perhaps not surprising when one remembers that e-commerce is still very small, accounting for under 1 per cent of consumer spending, even in the United States, by far the most advanced e-economy. While most of the hype prior to the technological stock price collapse in April 2000 focused on consumer web sites such as Amazon.com, Lastminute.com and Freeserve, it is in fact business-to-business marketing — which typically involves big companies buying from suppliers online — that has dominated e-commerce, accounting for about 80 per cent of Internet spending. But even business-to-business e-commerce, according to eMarketer, accounted for slightly less than 2 per cent of all business-to-business trade in the United States during 2001, and only 11 per cent of US corporations reported fully implemented e-business strategies.

Such percentages indicate that there is room for very considerable increases in the volume and value of e-commerce. eMarketer estimates that worldwide business-to-business e-commerce will rise from US$823 billion at the end of 2002 to US$2300 billion at the end of 2004. International Data Corp. (IDC) is even more optimistic. It expects the total worldwide value of goods and services purchased by businesses through e-commerce solutions will increase from US$282 billion in 2000 to US$4.3 trillion by 2005, with purchases increasing in the United States at a compound annual growth rate of 68 per cent from 2001–2005, 91 per cent in Western Europe and 109 per cent in the Asia–Pacific.

This chapter begins by describing the growth and development of the Internet and the key features for marketing. It argues that the Internet is fundamental for marketing and that its impact has to be assessed not merely in terms of projected sales increases online. The Internet, we show, radically affects how the firm communicates with its customers and builds relationships with them. We explain the three fundamental drivers of e-business: digitisation, the network economy and one-to-one communication with customers. The chapter then shows how these change the economics of firms and industries, destroying the effectiveness of traditional value chains and ushering in a new wave of information-based competitors, offering more to customers and operating with much lower levels of costs and assets. We then show how marketing needs to be adapted to capitalise on the value-creating opportunities offered by information technology. The chapter explores the

---

pure dot.coms: companies created from scratch to take advantage of the Internet

bricks-and-mortar: traditional companies, with a material presence for customers, who may or may not also operate online implications for market positioning strategies and the traditional tools of the marketing mix. Most markets will see an explosion in the number of Internet-based competitors and gaining the attention of customers will be a major concern. We look at some of the practical issues of Internet marketing in this hyper-competitive environment. Finally, the chapter explores the special problems of valuing Internet companies and strategies, when these are not expected to generate significant cash or profits for several years.

The growth and development of the Internet

The Internet refers to the web of computer networks that is making possible today's cheap, instantaneous global communication. Public interest in the Internet first exploded in 1994. But its origins go back 30 years earlier. Research into the Internet started in the United States and Europe in the early 1960s. In the United States the objective was to create an emergency military communication network that would be invulnerable to nuclear attack. In Europe the aim was to develop a communication system that would allow academics to share research ideas. The first practical implementation of the Net occurred in 1969, when the University of California at Los Angeles was connected to the Stanford Research Institute. In the following years, today's universal Internet standards were developed, including the @ symbol in addresses (1971), remote accessing of computers through telnet (1972), multiple-person chat sessions (1973), and the downloading of files through ftp (1973). After these developments the embryonic Internet spread quickly among academics. In particular, the research community soon adopted e-mail as an effective means of communicating with colleagues.

Growth of the Net

In the early to mid-1990s, three breakthroughs brought the Internet out of academia and into a much broader community. First, the US National Science Foundation, which effectively regulated the Internet, ended its ban on the commercial use of the Net. Second, low-cost computers and new software made it much easier and cheaper to access the Net. The Apple Macintosh, using a Graphical User Interface (GUI), was introduced in 1984. Microsoft did not launch its first Windows software until 1990. Third, the development of web browsers (which facilitated customer use, just as the GUI-based software had done) and web servers made it possible for people to navigate the Net more easily and for organisations to put richer content on to their web sites. In 1993 Mosaic software allowed images to be viewed over the Internet. The Netscape browser was launched in 1994 and Microsoft launched the Internet Explorer 1.0 the following year. For consumers this meant ease of use (no longer having to rely on obscure commands) and much richer content by the employment of multimedia (the combined use of pictures, sound, and even video, with text).

These breakthroughs created a communication and marketing revolution that is still ongoing. Now, anyone connected to the Net can communicate with anyone else through open, universal standards, instantaneously and at almost zero cost. Companies can communicate with other companies, individuals with other individuals and companies with individuals. Firms suddenly found themselves able to create marketing material that had global reach for very low cost. Small businesses could compete on a much more even footing with the largest firms in the world. Customers found that they could quickly find product and company information at the click of a mouse. Even more fundamental, companies and customers could engage in a dialogue and learn from each other.

Since 1994 the number of people connected to the Net has grown exponentially every year. Estimates of the global Internet population are notoriously imprecise, but according to NUA there were 407.1 million online as of November 2000, compared with 201.05 million in September 1999, 147 million in September 1998, and 74 million in September 1997. eMarketer's estimate of the number of Internet users worldwide for 2000 was 446 million. Despite the events of September 11, and the existence of a global economic downturn, eMarketer's projection in February 2002 was that the number of users would continue to rise rapidly, reaching 709 million by 2004. As the online population grows, new segments and new opportunities emerge (see marketing insight 'The rise of the cyber-senior').

Marketing insight: The rise of the cyber-senior

It is 9.15 am on Thursday, March 22, and at the Wesley Conference Centre in Sydney's Pitt Street, about 300 people — all aged over 55 and most of them well into their 60s and 70s — are jostling for a seat in the centre's Lyceum Theatre. Within a few minutes, the small auditorium is packed and latecomers have to make do with the limited standing room. The audience is mostly women, and some are clearly over 80 years old. At 9.30am sharp, a representative of the New South Wales Ageing and Disability Department stands on the small stage and welcomes the audience before introducing the first speaker.

Why are these people here and in such numbers? It is certainly not because they want to hear about nursing homes or the latest developments in walking frames. The numerous speakers lined up to address the gathering are not aged-care specialists or health fund representatives. They are product managers and customer relations executives from Telstra, Microsoft and Dick Smith Electronics.

Welcome to TechnoSeniors, a two-day event comprising seminars, workshops and tutorials to help older people with computer technology and, more specifically, to get them started as Internet users ...

The event is a reflection of a phenomenon occurring all around Australia: Older people are taking to technology in numbers that are growing exponentially, and the over-55 age group is the fastest-growing group of new Internet users in the country ...

Although absolute numbers of Internet users over 55 are still low compared with younger people, the growth rate is impressive. According to the Australian Bureau of Statistics (ABS), between May 1998 and May 2000 there was a 220% leap in the number of people over 55 starting to use the Internet, compared with 57% for those aged 18–24, 76% for those aged 25–39, and 67% for those aged 40–54. ABS figures also show that during the same period, ownership of PCs among the 55-plus age group surged by 91%. The bureau says that in May 2000, 21% of people over 55 owned a PC. The NSW Government, through its Seniors Card project, carried out research during 2000 which found that, of a sample of 200 000 seniors in the state (NSW has 1.1 million people over 60), 35% of those aged between 60 and 64 had a home computer, 26% of those aged between 65 and 69, and 19% of those between 70 and 74.

The growth in Internet usage among seniors presents an outstanding marketing opportunity for companies that have dismissed the seniors market as too hard to reach, particularly online. So far, companies have been slow to pick up on the market, but they are starting to realise the potential.

(continued)

If Internet use among older people continues to grow at the present rate, the implications for marketers will be enormous. The ABS estimates that between 2011 and 2031, the number of people in Australia aged over 65 will grow from three million to five million.

One of the problems for marketers chasing the 55-plus age group online has been the paucity of web sites devoted to the needs of this group of people. To date, only a few purely commercial sites have been established, the biggest of which is SeniorLink. The only other dedicated site, seniorcomputing, is a community site run by the Australian Seniors Computer Clubs Association.

The founder and managing director of SeniorLink, Andrew Campbell, says the site, which went live in mid-1998, was designed to fill the information technology void for seniors. 'There was clearly a lack of knowledge about IT and how it could benefit their lives,' he says. 'We felt if we could educate them we could fill a niche position, which is what we did. SeniorLink evolved out of a training company in which we had 17 individuals going round to people's homes showing them how to use their PCs.'

Six months after forming the training company, Campbell put up a web site to support the trainers' activities. The commercial potential of the site was soon apparent when the health and skin-care products company Blackmores began advertising with banner ads and sponsorship of the site's health index page. Blackmores also sponsored the site's e-mail newsletter, with weekly information on products and a link to its own web site. Its feature pages on SeniorLink have achieved click-through rates of 17.5%.

Campbell says other advertisers have started to use SeniorLink over the past two years. The site now has 7000 subscribers, a figure that is growing at an annualised rate of 25%.

'Around 80% of SeniorLink members use computers for personal reasons including e-mail, genealogy, game playing, shopping, general entertainment and research in areas such as travel, health and finance,' Campbell says. 'The remaining 20% use computers to also aid their small businesses, manage investments and do things like the bookkeeping for their children's companies.'

He says that although advertisers have been slow to see the potential of older consumers online, the situation has changed rapidly in the past six to nine months. But the most frequent access for men and women aged over 55 is still biased towards the big software companies, search engines and Internet service providers. For example, the Internet user measurement company Media Metrix found that in January 2001, the top five sites visited by men aged 55 and older were microsoft.com, msn.com, yahoo.com, ninemsn.com and passport.com. The most popular corporate site was westpac.com.au, but it ranked 19th.

'Our audience is intelligent, interested and hungry for information — you can see that in their response to permission marketing, promotions and the general marketing that runs on the site,' Campbell says ...

According to the *Seniors Internet Survey* 2000 by AMR Interactive, older people are attracted to the Internet because of e-mail, access to cheaper products and services, and because it offers an alternative information and sales channel for people with mobility problems. The study found that seniors were most likely to visit travel, government services and share-trading sites.

But there are hurdles for marketers. The costs associated with buying a computer and getting online are an obstacle to almost 30% of the 55-plus age group, according to AMR Interactive. Among those already on the Internet, online shopping, for example, has been hampered by a number of concerns: older people prefer to examine products in person, they are worried about the safety of payment systems, they prefer face-to-face transactions, and they are worried about privacy and the integrity of suppliers.

Source: Extracts from Simon Lloyd, 'Rise of the Cybersenior', *BRW*, 30 March 2001, p. 64.

The number of Internet users, however, varies considerably from one country to another and one region to another. As of early 2002, approximately 50 per cent of the population were Internet users in the United Kingdom, United States, Sweden, Canada and Hong Kong.[1] In Germany, New

Zealand and Singapore it was around 1 in 3, in Australia and Britain 1 in 4, in France 1 in 5, in Malaysia 1 in 11 and Thailand 1 in 13. The amount of material on the Web is increasing even faster than the number of users. The number of Internet domain hosts (those with addresses ending in edu, org, com, and so on) has also risen rapidly, from approximately 30 million in January 1998 to about 147 million in January 2002. Around one million new pages are being added to the Net per day. The majority of these pages are in English (68 per cent in 2000), with the next most important languages being German and Japanese, each constituting only 6 per cent. The speed with which the Internet has been embraced can be put in perspective by using data on the number of years it took for various forms of mass media to be adopted by 50 million users/households in the United States: 38 years for radio, 13 years for television, 10 years for cable, and only 5 years for the commercial Internet.

Three factors make the continued rapid growth of the Internet a certainty. One is the explosion of new Internet access devices in addition to the personal computer, such as mobile phones, personal digital assistants, digital TV and games machines. The second is the rapid development of broadband communications which enormously expands the speed and amount of information that can be accessed by customers. Third, and most important, is the sheer amount of customer-focused innovation being released by companies racing to capitalise on the opportunities presented by the new technology.

Evolution of the Net

» Web sites

The web sites that organisations are using to market themselves are increasing in sophistication. Three types of sites can be distinguished in terms of the degree of feedback and individual customisation they offer.[2]

1. **Type I: publishing sites**. These are the most basic sites. The company moves its promotional material online, which can be read by visitors like a newspaper or magazine. The sites can be interesting to look at if the company employs effective design and graphics; they can also have sound, video and pictures. But their main limitations are the lack of customisation and interaction. The same information is provided to everyone and the company gets no feedback from customers in the form of communication or purchases.

2. **Type II: database sites**. In addition to publishing capabilities, these sites can respond to individual customer requests and permit buying and selling. A typical Type II site is Travel.com.au. A customer can ask for flight details from one airport to another; the site responds with the options, prices and other information. Customers can then book tickets if the offers meet their requirements.

3. **Type III: personalised sites**. These are the most advanced sites that use information provided by customers to personalise and customise responses. These sites dynamically create individual web pages that may anticipate the needs of the customer and suggest products that will meet their needs. An early example was Amazon.com's site, which initially welcomes the returning customer by name, suggests books that match his or her reading interests, and remembers the address and billing details to take

the hassle out of ordering again. Type III sites are important because they form the basis for the beginning of online relationship marketing, whereby a company learns over time about the needs and purchasing behaviour of individual customers and uses this information to customise solutions to their specific requirements. In addition, visitors are given the opportunity to personalise the site, such as the way the *Australian Financial Review* site allows subscribers to be informed of stories on specific industries and companies that they have chosen.

» Types of e-commerce

Electronic commerce refers to the trade that actually takes place over the Internet, usually through a buyer visiting a seller's web site and making a transaction there. But the influence of the Web — for example, as a source of information — stretches much wider than this. For example, in 2000 only 3 per cent of new cars in America were bought over the Internet, but over 40 per cent of buyers involved the Net at some point, with customers using it to compare prices or look at the latest models.

E-commerce involves individuals and companies. It has grown exponentially, around 50–100 per cent annually since 1994. It can be classified into four types (figure 12.1). By far the biggest and most rapidly growing sector is business-to-business (B2B), accounting for about 80 per cent of revenues. Companies like GM, Ford, GE, Cisco and Oracle have transferred just about all their purchasing to the Web. Suppliers and buyers are putting their capacity or business requirements on to their web sites or B2B exchanges and asking for responses. Fourteen of Australia's top 100 companies, including Telstra, BHP Billiton, Qantas, Coles Myer and Foster's Group formed corProcure in 2000. The aim was for it to act as an electronic marketplace (a group of companies from non-competing industries joining together to purchase items such as office and cleaning supplies, fuel, energy, legal services and telecommunications). The electronic market still exists but corProcure now has a single owner, Australia Post. The next biggest sector is business-to-consumer (B2C), which includes the retail activities on the Web, such as bookselling by Amazon.com, travel arrangements by Travel.com.au, automobile purchases by Carline, and online stockbroking by CommSec. The third sector is consumer-to-business (C2B), which takes advantage of the new power the Internet provides to drive transactions the other way round. For example, Priceline.com allows would-be customers to state how much they will pay for airline tickets or for a car, leaving the suppliers to decide whether to accept the offers. Letsbuyit.com facilitates customers to aggregate their individual purchases to gain discounts from businesses. The fourth sector, consumer-to-consumer (C2C), includes the burgeoning growth of consumer auctions run by such companies as eBay and QXL.

	Business	Consumer
Business	**B2B** CorProcure GM Cisco	**B2C** Amazon Wishlist CommSec
Consumer	**C2B** Priceline Accompany Letsbuyit	**C2C** eBay QXL Onsale

Figure 12.1 The e-commerce matrix

As we shall see, the drivers of all this growth and innovation are the Internet's ability to offer consumers lower prices, greater convenience and products that better match their requirements. For companies, it offers often dramatically lower operating costs, access to burgeoning new markets and striking competitive advantages over the incumbent competitors.

» Intranets and extranets

The Internet provides a universal common standard for communicating between computers. Internet marketing is the use of Internet technology to reach out to customers. Most companies divide their Net activities into three categories: the public Internet, the extranet and the intranet. Each of these differ in their goals, the type of users and the organisational responsibility for managing them.

The public Internet is the most familiar use of Net technology. It includes the entire Web and the Net activities of the company that are available to everyone. The public Internet includes an enormous growing array of information provided by companies, individuals, governments, universities and the media. The marketing department manages the public Internet in most companies.

intranet: web sites internal to the company and available only to its employees

Intranets are web sites that are internal to the company and available only to its employees. Their goal is to share information throughout the company. This might include messages from senior management, information about employee activities, payroll and benefits information, and other managerial processes. The intranet is also used to coordinate dispersed teams working on common projects, and to support sales and marketing staff.[3]

extranet: web sites that connect the intranet of an organisation with its trading partners, suppliers and distributors

Extranets combine features of both the public Internet and intranets. They limit access by registration and passwords to exclude unwanted parties and to facilitate payment mechanisms. Extranets are at the core of most business-to-business commerce. They connect the intranet of an organisation with its trading partners, suppliers, distributors and customers. Protected by a firewall, an extranet allows trusted partners to share collaborative business applications such as developing new products, procurement and customer service and support.[4]

Drivers of change in the new economy

Three forces are driving the growth of the Internet and e-commerce: digitisation, networks and customisation. These in turn are reshaping the role and tools of marketing and the ways companies create value for shareholders.

Going digital: Moore's Law

The digital concept is very simple. Something is digital when all its properties and information are stored as a string of zeros and ones. The smallest piece of this digital information is called a bit. All the text, pictures, music and videos seen on a computer screen or sent over the Internet are simply strings of bits. Digital devices that process bits are now all around us in the car, in the home, in digital cameras, digital TVs and digital telephones. Everything on the Internet is digital. The essence of the information revolution is this transformation of information into digital form where it can be manipulated by computers and transmitted by networks. Computers and digital devices are all built on semiconductors (or chips). The remarkable phenomenon about semiconductor production is the striking productivity gains that occur. Chips are becoming cheaper, smaller and more powerful at an amazing rate. The significance of this is that computing power has apparently boundless possibilities because of its power, cheapness and applicability.

This feature was first codified by Gordon Moore, founder of Intel, into what is now accepted as an equation of enormous power.

> Moore's Law states that every 18 months, computer processing power doubles while cost stays constant.

Every 18 months, you get twice as much power for the same price, or the same power for half the cost. For example, computer power that cost $3000 ten years ago would cost $24 today, and only 18 cents ten years from now! Moore's Law has proved to be remarkably accurate for the past 30 years, and most scientists expect it to hold for the next 30 years too. It means computing power is becoming almost free. It also means that storing, processing and communicating information becomes incredibly cheap. This provides new ways for marketing to create value for customers and shareholders. Let us look at some of the implications of Moore's Law.

» Resource substitution — 'Atoms to bits'

In the new digital world bits replace atoms. To create shareholder value it means managers must seek to substitute cheap digital resources for those that are expensive — labour, raw materials and capital. So to stay cost competitive banks are replacing branches with the Internet; companies replace paper with online documents; letters and telephone calls are replaced by e-mail; service staff by online customer support. Digital substitution also allows firms to become more effective as well as to reduce costs. Firms can offer benefits to customers that were virtually impossible before, such as '24/7' (twenty-four hours a day, seven days a week availability and service). Web sites can offer information in multiple languages, or even instantaneous translation.

» The developing digital environment

Currently many customers find the digital interface a poor substitute for the richness of shopping in the real world. But broadband access, faster connection speeds and advances in software are making cyberspace increasingly realistic, stimulating and user friendly. Web sites can now create a virtual space to simulate or enhance the real world, whether it is a shop, classroom or office. Customers can get feedback and interaction, and shopping agents can give advice or compare different products. Two- or three-dimensional images allow customers to 'walk around' products and even try them out under simulated conditions. Finally, the product assortment and information available on a well-designed Web site can far exceed any 'bricks and mortar' site.

» Digitising marketing processes

Moore's Law and the developing digital environment create major opportunities to increase the efficiency and effectiveness of marketing. To exploit these, the first step is to map out in detail the firm's marketing processes.[5] At the aggregate level these processes consist of first understanding customer needs, then involving customers in the design of products. Next, the products have to be communicated, sold and delivered. Finally, customer service has to be provided and customer relationships built. The second stage looks for opportunities to substitute digital material. Market research materials can be converted to online formats; the firm's intranet can be a vehicle for cross-functional new product development; web sites can augment the selling efforts; online customer support can be used to build an interface with customers. The third stage is to fundamentally redesign marketing processes to capitalise on digital capabilities. For example, the airlines are redesigning their marketing processes to cut costs and deal directly with the customer, eliminating the travel agent. The whole process, from enquiring about schedules and availability, making reservations, to obtaining an 'e-ticket', has now been digitised.

Networks and Metcalfe's Law

Moore's Law puts cheap computing power into the hands of millions. The Internet permits all these users to be linked together into a universal communication network. Once people are networked, new sources of consumer and shareholder value are created that go beyond the acceleration of computing power predicted by Moore. Digitisation is a technological phenomenon; networks that allow millions of people to communicate with organisations and with one another are social phenomena.

What explained why the Internet was so valuable was a law, proposed by Robert Metcalfe, founder of 3Com Corporation.

Metcalfe's Law states that the value of any network is proportional to the square of the number of users

For example, a telephone service is not very valuable if only a handful of people is connected. Its value rises rapidly the more users are connected. When the Internet was used by only a handful of academics, it was not very valuable. Now that hundreds of millions of people and organisations are connected, it becomes essential. The explosion of connectivity that the Internet created has implications that promise to fundamentally change how businesses create value for their customers and shareholders.

» Unbundling products and information

Companies have traditionally provided customers jointly with both information and products. For example, shoppers go to a car showroom to collect information about features, credit terms, prices and availability. They visit a bookshop to see what is available and suitable for reading on holiday. This joint supply leads to compromises since the economics of information are very different from the economics of goods. Traditional bookshops and car showrooms are ideal neither for purchasing nor for obtaining information. For example, the information provided by a car dealer is biased and shoppers cannot see the range of competitors' cars that they might also want to consider. As a place to purchase cars, showrooms are too small to be efficient, nor can they carry a full inventory, even of their own brand. The Net is breaking these compromises across a range of industries, offering better solutions for customers. Book businesses like Amazon.com and car sites like Autobytel now separate the economics of information from that of products. Information is most effectively provided on the Internet, where it can be complete and unbiased. Products can be most effectively delivered from a single site, where economies of scale can be reaped and an encyclopaedic assortment held.

» Unbundling value chains and reshaping industries

The separation of the supply of products and information is only one form of unbundling. Businesses typically undertake multiple processes. They undertook these processes internally rather than purchasing them in the market because transaction costs made it more economical to do it that way.[6] Cheap information networks change all this, making it more efficient and effective to specialise and focus on core competencies. Bundled companies are ceasing to work as customers use information networks to find cheaper or better specialists. Figure 12.2 illustrates this for a large assurance company.[7] Ten years ago it was a fully integrated business undertaking its own administration, investment management and selling in-house products through its own large direct sales force of 15 000 representatives. During the 1990s it was attacked by new competitors with specialist innovative products and undermined by new channels of distribution like the Internet and independent financial advisers. Like many companies, it survived by unbundling. Today, virtually all its processes and most of its products are outsourced. The company is at the hub of a network of specialists, virtually rather than vertically integrated.

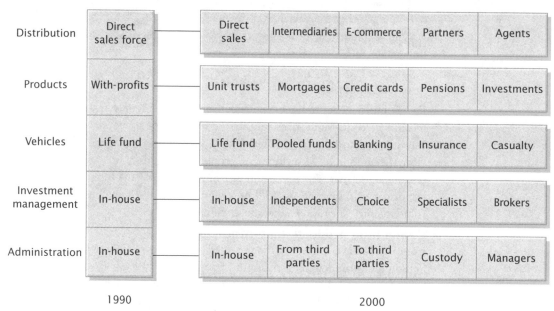

Figure 12.2 The unbundling of life assurance companies, 1990–2000

» The growth of specialists

A company is vulnerable if any of its processes or products can be undertaken more effectively by a specialist. The advantage of integrated generalists disappears when customers can do their own integration. The computer industry is a good example of the growth of specialists. Once dominated by vertically integrated companies like IBM and DEC, it has been taken over by a myriad of specialists competing with one another at each stage of the value chain. Customers can use cheap information networks to put together any combination of components. Newspapers are another example of an industry threatened by unbundling and specialists. Newspapers jointly supply news, features and advertising. But each of these products can be done more effectively now by specialists. Classified ads for jobs or homes can be accessed more easily through specialist searches on web sites. If such ads migrate to the Net, the whole economics of the newspaper industry, with ads subsidising the cover price, is deconstructed. Worse, Net specialists like Yahoo!, Freeserve and Alta Vista are providing free 'newspapers' over the Internet, actually configured to the special interests of individual readers. Networks break down industry entry barriers, ushering in new competitors and exposing the weakness of the traditional leaders.

» Disintermediation and reintermediation

Networks can undermine the business of many wholesalers, distributors and retailers. In some cases, producers can now achieve faster, cheaper communication and interaction themselves with customers, and then supply directly. This enables producers to take out distribution costs and recapture control over the customer relationship. Companies such as Dell in computing, the UK firms Direct Line in personal insurance and First Direct in banking, and the Australian firm CommSec in stockbroking have leapfrogged into industry leadership by such **disintermediation**.

At the same time new types of intermediaries are emerging, the so-called **infomediaries**.[8] With the exploding volume of information on the Net, customers are finding it increasingly difficult to identify and evaluate the myriad of alternatives offered by an expanding number of specialist web competitors. The new infomediaries help customers through the maze by comprehensively searching for what is available, tailoring their recommendations to the individual customer's requirements, and providing unbiased advice. These new infomediaries can be portals (e.g. Yahoo!), virtual communities (e.g. Motley Fool), Net companies (e.g. Amazon.com) or shopping agents (e.g. ValueStar).

Individual customisation

The third driver of the phenomenal growth of the Internet and e-commerce is the opportunity it offers for **one-to-one marketing**. The essence of successful marketing is meeting the needs of the customer. When the company precisely meets the needs of the customer, the customer is satisfied and a basis for long-term loyalty is established. Until recently, at least in markets with large numbers of customers, this was hardly possible. Companies lacked the ability to interact and learn about customers on an individual basis. In some cases, companies used broadcast media, advertising the same message to everyone. And even when markets were segmented and differentiated messages were sent, communication remained one-way (figure 12.3). Even if companies had learned individual requirements, it was generally too costly to customise products. Businesses were built around the economics of mass production of standardised products.

Moore's Law and networks break the need for these compromises between economies of scale and customisation. The increasing numbers of customers connected to the Internet permits the company to identify its important clients and to have a one-to-one dialogue. The shift to the networked organisation enables the firm to consider the possibility of **mass customisation**.

The benefits to the customer of individual customisation are a more precise matching to his or her specific requirements — greater value. In the past, customised goods and personalised service have been the privilege of the elite. Only the rich could afford to have their clothes, homes or cars customised

disintermediation: the elimination of intermediaries or agents between the supplier and the consumer

infomediary: an online site that provides specialised information on behalf of producers of goods and services and links them to their potential customers

one-to-one marketing: a form of marketing involving mass customisation and two-way, direct, communication between the producer and the consumer

mass customisation: offering products tailored to the individual customer and made to order

and made to order. Digitisation and networks democratise consumption, making customisation affordable to the many rather than the few. Personalisation becomes cheap because it is automated, made virtual, and leverages existing digital assets. So Internet pioneers such as Dell, Yahoo! and Amazon.com offer customers what they want, how they want it, when they want it.

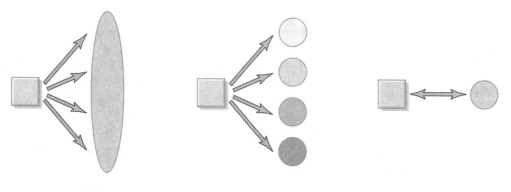

| One message broadcast to all customers | Different messages broadcast to each segment | One-to-one interactive messages to each individual |

Figure 12.3 From broad messages to interaction

These changes also help individuals make more rational decisions in purchasing situations where they lack experience. New online services like Value-Star rate difficult-to-evaluate, unstandardised services such as local garages, hospitals and house repairers. Amazon.com helps customers choose books by recommending titles bought by other customers who have similar tastes. New opportunities are appearing everywhere for marketers that can develop personalisation techniques that help customers match products to tastes and eliminate unpleasant purchasing experiences.

For companies that succeed at individually customising their communication and products, the benefits are stronger customer relationships. This in turn increases the lifetime value of their customers and feeds directly into the shareholder value equation.

Creating value through the Web

We need to look at how the Web offers enormous opportunities for managers to create shareholder value, and why failing to take advantages of these opportunities is destroying shareholder value at record rates in traditional businesses. Since shareholder value is based primarily on offering customer value, we start by summarising what benefits customers can obtain from web-based businesses.

How the Web creates value for customers

The Web offers customers seven benefits that together account for the growth of online buying.

» Customisation

As noted above, the Internet provides the potential for customers to have products personalised to their requirements, offering them higher delivered value. Customisation can be either in terms of how the offer is communicated

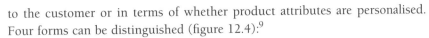

to the customer or in terms of whether product attributes are personalised. Four forms can be distinguished (figure 12.4):[9]

- **Cosmetic** customisers present a standard product differently to different customers. For example, many web sites give a personalised greeting to regular visitors, but the content of the site is unchanged.
- **Transparent** customisers provide individually customised products, but do not explicitly communicate this personalisation. For example, the latest sites make 'smart offers' — personalised presentations of goods, based on the visitor's history. The idea is to work out the visitor's needs and preferences without asking.
- **Adaptive** customisation uses the same product and message but the product has multiple settings, allowing the buyer to customise it. For example, Spinner.com offers over 100 channels on its Internet music service, with editable presets for adaptive customisation.
- **Collaborative** customisation is the ultimate one-to-one marketing. It involves the company conducting a dialogue with individual customers to help them define their needs, to identify the precise offering that fulfils those needs, and to make customised products for them. Business-to-business extranets are emerging examples of this form of customisation where purchasers provide the supplier with ongoing feedback through the new product development process.

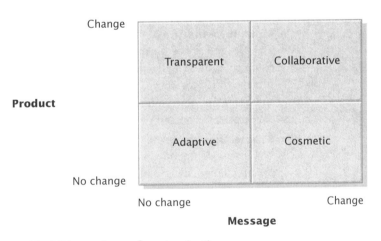

Figure 12.4 Dimensions of customisation

» Greater assortment

Web-based businesses can provide consumers with a much greater product assortment than bricks and mortar companies. Constraints on space and the need to achieve an economic asset turnover mean that conventional retailers and intermediaries can stock only popular items. The economics are completely different for online sellers — there are no space constraints in the virtual world, and centralised inventory holdings and networked contractors make it effective to stock a much larger numbers of items. So Amazon.com or CDNow carry one hundred times the number of titles of a normal shop. Chemdex, a speciality chemicals supplier to laboratories around the world, carries almost a quarter of a million products, far more than conventional geographically based suppliers.

» Lower prices

For some consumers a major attraction of the Web is the possibility of obtaining lower prices. The basic reason why online businesses may offer lower prices is that they have lower operating costs and a higher utilisation of assets than a conventional business. A second reason is that Net businesses often face greater price competition, as Internet buyers may visit several sites to make comparisons. An offsetting factor, however, is shipping costs that have to be added to the product. For digital information goods such as software, airline tickets and research reports that can be delivered over the Net, shipping costs are near zero. For bulky or perishable products shipping costs can eliminate any price savings. Those companies selling products that have a high value-to-weight ratio enjoy a considerable advantage.

» Greater convenience

Internet shopping offers great convenience. Customers can shop when it is convenient for them, from their offices or home. Most sites offer 24/7 access and service. There is no hassle about parking the car or being disappointed that the wanted item is unavailable. Customers can do extensive comparison shopping without rising from their chair. Shopping agents will even do the comparison shopping for the customer. For example, using MySimon.com to shop for a product, the customer is requested to supply his or her choice criteria (e.g. brand, type, price range, etc.); the service then quickly responds with a list of alternatives fitting the criteria and places where the products can be bought.

» More information

The Net offers customers almost unlimited information about products and companies, at virtually zero cost. Before ordering, customers can consult consumer guides for comparative ratings, visit specialist web sites for opinions and enter online communities to discover the views of other users. They can check prices, availability, specifications, service and features.

» Greater assurance

Web-based competitors can often give customers greater confidence that their requirements will be satisfied. They retain information about previous visits and requirements forming the basis of a continuing relationship. Automated processes can remove the inconsistencies that occur with people-based service providers. They can also introduce services that specifically reassure customers that their business is on track. Federal Express customers, for example, can check online the exact location of their parcels and get up-to-the-minute details on delivery times. That said, there are many consumers who use the Web for browsing but who remain reluctant to buy because of concerns with security and privacy related to the disclosure of credit card and personal information. There may be greater assurance for many customers about their requirements being satisfied, but this does not always coincide with an amelioration of concerns that the information obtained by online businesses will not be used in ways that the customer deems inappropriate.

» Entertainment

As companies shift to more sophisticated Type III web sites, shopping on the Internet becomes increasingly entertaining and challenging. With broadband communication, high-speed modems and full-motion video, this will increase. People today still enjoy the challenge and novelty of buying online.

Companies are amplifying the entertainment quotient through aligning chat rooms, instant messages and discussion groups alongside their direct ecommerce function. The rapid growth of auction sites like QXL and eBay owes much to the excitement customers get from being in active bidding competition with others.

How the Web creates value for companies

Why do businesses exploiting the Internet tend to enjoy share price multiples far in excess of traditional companies? To understand why investors anticipate high sales and profit growth from these firms, we need to explore their economic advantages. Hanson distinguishes between improvement-based business models and revenue-based models.[10] We can also add a third type — mixed business models, which incorporate both benefits. Two other important benefits of Internet-based business are the acquisition of valuable customer information and the opportunity to make more effective investment decisions as a result of better measurement tools.

» Improvement-based business models

Improvement-based benefits from the Web create shareholder value in three ways: cost savings, enhancing the brand image and greater marketing effectiveness. These benefits should be available to any firm, not just information or technology specialists.

- **Cost savings.** Cost savings have been a major reason for using the Web, especially in B2B. Some firms have made savings of hundreds of millions of dollars a year (see marketing management in practice 'Why Cisco uses the Web'). Posting manuals and customer support documents online can produce big savings. Online customer support also works out much cheaper than any other form of interaction. In banking, it has been calculated that the cost of a customer receiving personal service at a branch amounts to $3 per transaction, as against $1.20 by telephone, 60 cents using an ATM, 30 cents using a proprietary PC banking service and only 6 cents by Internet banking. At heart, customer self-service lies behind many of these savings. Customers do more of their own searching and problem solving rather than relying on the company's staff.
- **Enhancing the brand.** Traditional organisations such as the ABC, Fairfax and Cadbury are using the Web to enhance their brands. Creative, high quality web sites can give customers fresh insights into the capabilities and reach of the company and build stronger relationships with them. The Internet has also created powerful new brands such as portals like Yahoo! and Freeserve, and new Internet retailers such as Amazon.com and Travelocity.
- **Greater business effectiveness.** The Internet can also revolutionise the firm's value chain, allowing it to do new things and to do old things better. It can greatly enhance marketing effectiveness by allowing a closer dialogue with customers. It can spread information about customers throughout the organisation. It can be used to support outside sales people, dealers, retailers and suppliers. For example, Glaxo's sales representatives can obtain immediate details of stock conditions, order status and delivery times over palm computers. Ford's web site directs customers to the nearest appropriate dealer. Dell's extranet gives suppliers real-time details of its requirements.

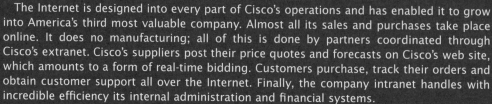

Cisco Systems, the maker of data-networking equipment, is one of the most aggressive companies in using the web site for its marketing. Cisco estimates its annual cost savings from using the Internet at over $500 million a year. This is more than 8 per cent of its revenue and 40 per cent of its profits. It saves $270 million a year from replacing printed product manuals with online documentation; $130 million is saved by online distribution of its software products; $125 million from customer support savings, especially reduced numbers of telephone calls; and $10 million from online recruitment.

The Internet is designed into every part of Cisco's operations and has enabled it to grow into America's third most valuable company. Almost all its sales and purchases take place online. It does no manufacturing; all of this is done by partners coordinated through Cisco's extranet. Cisco's suppliers post their price quotes and forecasts on Cisco's web site, which amounts to a form of real-time bidding. Customers purchase, track their orders and obtain customer support all over the Internet. Finally, the company intranet handles with incredible efficiency its internal administration and financial systems.

» Revenue-based business models

Improvement-based business models create indirect benefits because they do not immediately lead to a sale. Revenue-based business models, in contrast, generate direct benefits in the form of revenue from customers. In the coming years these direct benefits will be the biggest source of shareholder value creation. There are two types of revenue-based models: one obtains revenues from purchasers, the other from providers paying fees to reach web site users.

1. **Purchase-based revenue models.** These are likely to become the most important online revenue generators. Revenues are dominated by B2B sales. But B2C e-commerce will also accelerate as consumers gain better access to computers, faster connection speeds and greater familiarity. Companies create revenues in three main ways. Sales of the company's products are the biggest and most obvious way firms such as Dell, Cisco and Federal Express have grown. A second way is pay-per-use whereby customers pay for information. Many online job search businesses charge this way. A third way is charging annual subscription fees, as do the *Financial Times* and Reuters business services.

2. **Provider-based business models.** Here the company obtains revenues not from users, but from other companies wanting to gain access to the web site users. These include sales commissions from providing links to other companies' sites, banner advertising, sponsorship and sharing access charges with telecoms operators. Provider-based business models generate the revenues for some of the most famous web brands, such as AOL, Yahoo!, Freeserve, AltaVista and Lycos.

» Mixed models

Many companies create both improvement-based benefits and revenue-based benefits. Companies such as Dell and Cisco have streamlined their value chains to optimise their costs and asset utilisation, developed effective supply chain networks and built powerful brands. At the same time, they have achieved fabulous growth by moving sales online and using their web sites to attract income from customers, advertisers, sales commissions and sponsorship.

» Information for relationship management

Digitisation and networks allow companies to collect and hold detailed information about their customers. Previously, the interaction often took place between the customer and an intermediary. This enabled the retailer or intermediary to build the brand and own the customer relationship. When this happens the supplier can be commoditised and the value in the supply chain appropriated by the intermediary or the customer. Only by holding consumer information and achieving direct interaction can a real relationship management program to build loyalty and enhance the lifetime value of customers be created.

» Superior investment allocation

Unlike broadcast communication such as television or newspaper advertising, online marketing investments can often be directly evaluated in terms of their financial payoff. Marketing can then be held accountable for their spending because management can tell with considerable accuracy whether the spending created value. This greater ability to track online investments also allows managers to determine which types of investments — banner ads, prospect fees, sponsorship — work best to increase long-term profits. The effectiveness of online marketing is evaluated through the analysis of web chains stored in the servers. These are the sequence of steps a visitor clicks through to arrive at the company's web site. From web chains it can be determined whether, say, a banner ad bought on Yahoo! is generating visitors and creating profitable sales. Web chain analysis can show the effectiveness of alternative strategies in achieving impressions and impact, and the expected value of prospects and customers that are stimulated.

Implications for marketing strategy

The Internet is rapidly changing the nature of markets and marketing. We review how it affects the nature of markets, creates new marketing opportunities, reshapes positioning strategies and the marketing mix, and finally its implications for implementing strategy.

From caveat emptor to caveat venditor

From buyer beware to seller beware. In the past, high information costs protected the profit margins of many businesses. In the physical world, buyers face all kinds of obstacles to getting the best deal — far-flung suppliers, limited time to do research, intermediaries who hide the information. For consumers, it was generally just too tiresome to drive to three different places to save $2. The Web changes the nature of markets and marketing. Internet commerce is likely to shift the balance of commercial power to the buyer.[11] Several factors strengthen the hands of buyers and intensify competition between suppliers.

- **Instant choice.** On the Net, competition is just a click away. If people are not satisfied with the price at Amazon.com, they can go to barnesandnoble.com.
- **Comparison shopping.** There is a wealth of information on the Net to compare prices. CompareNet, for instance, offers detailed information on hundreds of thousands of consumer products.
- **Purchasing power.** The Net allows consumers and corporate buyers from all over the world to band together, pool their purchasing power, and get volume discounts. For example, GE divisions pool purchases to get price reductions of around 20 per cent on more than $1 billion worth of goods bought online.

- **Global reach.** The Net eliminates the geographical protections of local and national businesses. Car dealers selling online, for example, have even drawn buyers from different countries.

New market opportunities

Electronic commerce creates entirely new high-growth markets and new sources of differential advantage. The main sources of opportunities arise from the following:

- **Declining market entry barriers.** In the physical world new competitors were deterred from entry to many markets by the scale economies possessed by the incumbents, an inability to obtain distribution or good locations, established brand names and a lack of information among buyers. In the virtual world most of these barriers erode. In industry after industry — computers, travel, books, distribution, financial services — established leaders are being challenged by new online entrants.
- **Deconstructing value chains.** The increasing weaknesses of vertically integrated companies — high in costs and assets, inflexible and insufficiently specialist — are forcing companies to unbundle their value chains and outsource more and more of their products and processes. Such unbundling and the growth of virtual companies create an array of opportunities for specialist firms able to contribute products and processes to these networked organisations.
- **Convergence of industries.** Common digital technologies and the Internet are leading many industries to converge. This is most obvious in the huge computer, communication and content industries. Content companies like Time Warner need the new distribution technologies and networks possessed by computer and communication companies like AOL and Yahoo! The latter need content to make themselves more attractive choices to customers. The results are new market opportunities and a rush of mergers, acquisitions, alliances and partnerships as firms try to capitalise on the new synergies.
- **Superior customer value.** As argued earlier, online marketing can offer customers superior value through lower prices, greater choice, more convenience and one-to-one communication. These benefits enable companies that can quickly capitalise on them to possess differential advantages to outflank established competitors.
- **Greater shareholder value.** Investors see potentially successful online business as offering great shareholder value. This comes first from their high growth potential, which is in turn the result of the superior customer value they can offer. Second, it results from their lower operating costs and higher asset utilisation.

New marketing strategies

The core of marketing strategy is segmentation and positioning. Segmentation refers to the choice of customers the firm is targeting for its product or service. Positioning refers to the differential advantage or choice of value proposition that the firm hopes will attract customers in the chosen market segment to its offer. In the new information environment both these dimensions have to change subtly but significantly.

» From segmentation to personalisation

Only in the past decade has it been possible for companies in mass markets, such as Unilever, David Jones and Woolworths, to obtain and process information on individual consumers. Traditionally, information about consumers has been obtained through sampling. A few hundred or thousand consumers would be interviewed about their attitudes, wants and buying processes and the results would be partitioned and averaged by profilers such as age, sex, income or, sometimes, lifestyle characteristics. The aim of the market research would be to group customers into a handful of market segments with similar wants and characteristics. Then products and communication would be aimed at each of these segment averages. The result would be a compromise — products and messages that met the needs of some consumers better than others. It was often not clear how good or bad the fits were since companies did not obtain direct feedback from individual consumers.

Digitisation and networks are making such compromises less necessary. Companies can now enter a dialogue with individual customers.[12] Of course, for companies with thousands or even millions of customers, investing in detailed interaction with all of them is not cost effective, so segmentation is still necessary. But the objective of segmentation is different; the aim is to segment not by similarity of needs but rather by the potential lifetime value of the customer to the organisation.

A typical example of this type of segmentation by customer value is employed by Dell Computer Corporation (see figure 12.5). Dell segments its customers into five classes according to their potential value to the business. The greater the value, the more Dell invests in the relationship. Companies such as the Ford Motor Company have bought over 250 000 computers from Dell. Such exclusive corporate customers are electronically linked into Dell's intranet and Dell service employees permanently man the customer's premises, taking complete responsibility for customising the computers and software and for ensuring that performance meets world-class standards. Platinum customers too get extraordinarily high levels of personalisation. Next come 'contracted', and 'registered,' customers, and at the bottom the 'all customers category' made up of individual customers or businesses that are not interested in forming a relationship with Dell.

The Dell model illustrates the principles of modern segmentation: first, the use of information technology to understand customers and offer superior value to all of them; second, the need to establish priorities — it pays to invest more in customers that have the highest future lifetime value to the business — and third, the aim is to build relationships through individual customisation of communication and solutions.

» From selling propositions to customisation

Traditionally, marketing has focused on seeking to develop a unique selling proposition that would give the firm a differential advantage in a market or market segment. In the new networked world differential advantage is gained not from selling an unbeatable proposition to as many people as possible, but from matching the needs of the individual customer more precisely. It is about making *to* order rather than making *for* orders. The traditional marketing model has been based upon maximising the sales of a single product or brand by selling it to as many people as possible. The new model is based upon selling as many products as possible to each individual customer. In the language of economics, economies of scope become more important than economies of scale.[13]

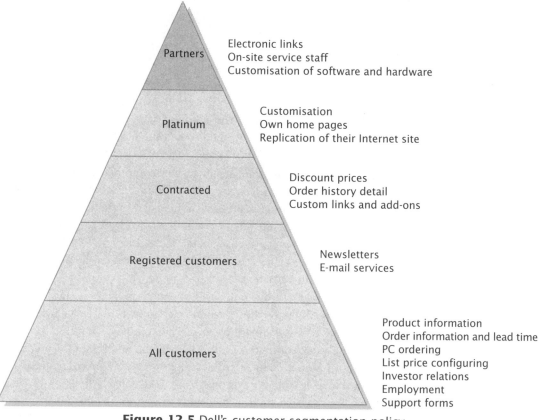

Figure 12.5 Dell's customer segmentation policy

What makes the transformation possible are the new capabilities that today's information technology provides. Digitally stored databases allow companies to tell customers apart and remember their individual requirements and purchasing behaviour. Interactive networks allow individual customers to talk to the company and update their learning. Mass customisation technology and networked organisations mean companies in a variety of industries can increasingly customise their products at low cost.

What is forcing companies to adapt is that the old business model cannot any longer meet the increasing expectations of consumers. In attempts to meet the growing variety of consumer needs, suppliers such as Procter & Gamble or Du Pont and retailers and intermediaries such as supermarkets and distributors are being forced to carry inventories of ever increasing product ranges. A typical supermarket will carry 30 000 stock keeping units, and a supplier might have 100 varieties of steel or shoes. No single customer will want more than a minute fraction of such variety. The modern competitor is unbundling information from supply. The information about the available variety is put on the web site, the individual's requirement is then customised after the order is received, and finally it is delivered to the home or business.

The changing marketing mix

Implementing marketing strategies in the information age requires companies to significantly adapt their marketing mix.

» Product policy

The second half of the twentieth century was marked by companies expanding the number of products in their ranges. Expanded variety, however, brought higher costs and investment requirements as inventories rose, and with it greater customer confusion. Online marketers recognise that customers want not more choice, but less. They want a single offer that is tailored to their exact requirements rather than having to choose among a plethora of imperfectly fitting options. Personalised communication and customised solutions made to order is a response that makes more sense for both customers and companies.

Customisation also allows companies to augment their products and differentiate them. Many products such as banking or insurance have become commodities. But what can differentiate them and create customer loyalty are personalised additions that enable them to meet requirements more effectively. These might be 24/7 access, helpful web sites, customised portfolio planning services or e-mails on special opportunities.

More generally, customisation shifts the company from competing in manufactured goods to competing in services. Services are increasingly a more attractive area in which to compete. In the modern economy the service sector is twice the size of the goods sector and growing more rapidly. Services too tend to be more profitable. This is because goods are standard and much easier for customers to compare. Also customers do not really believe there is much difference in quality between products such as computers, cars or detergents. Because services are hard to standardise they are more difficult to compare. Buying services is more risky. Customers often use price as an indicator of quality — high price means good service. The car industry is typical. Excess capacity and fierce price competition mean that few car companies make consistent economic profits. In contrast, margins on servicing cars, insuring and renting them are very attractive.

» Pricing policy

Online markets bring in many innovations in pricing. Interactive communication can reverse the locus of the pricing decision. Conventionally, businesses have set the price to customers, but now we have, in addition to B2C, C2B and C2C. In C2B, online intermediaries like Priceline are allowing consumers to state what they will pay for cars or airline tickets and companies have to respond. On C2C auction sites such as QXL, the company can be left out entirely as consumers sell unwanted goods to other consumers.

Online marketing facilitates much greater price discrimination. Using data banks that rank customers by anticipated value to the company or following web chains that indicate the customer's price sensitivity, suppliers are increasingly offering customised prices to online shoppers. Used effectively, such individualised pricing can capture the consumer surplus and maximise profitable sales.

One of the most striking phenomena of the new online companies has been the use of very aggressive pricing or even, as illustrated by companies like

Netscape and Freeserve, giving the product away free. Such strategies can sometimes be justified in terms of achieving critical mass, earning revenues on subsequent transactions, or new business models based on selling access to advertisers or other companies, rather than making money from users. For example, the most successful start-up in business history was Buy.com which achieved sales of $125 million in 1998, its first full year. This online super-store's business model relies on underselling rivals, sometimes at or below cost, and making profits off advertising.

Pricing is certainly even more critical in online markets. Customers have more information about prices than ever before, which is likely to increase price sensitivity in most markets. Companies seeking to dominate new markets are using low prices more often. But profits are so sensitive to price that ill-considered aggression can easily destroy the chances of new companies ever creating value for shareholders.

» Communication policy

The communication mix that companies have employed reflected the tra-ditional trade-off companies have been forced to make between what Evans and Wurster call 'richness and reach'.[14] **Reach** refers to the number of people receiving information. **Richness** refers to the detail of the information and whether it can be customised through a dialogue between buyer and seller. Some communication media, such as TV advertising, allow high reach but sacrifice richness. Others, such as a sales force, allow richness but are too expensive to achieve high reach. With a given communication budget, man-agers choose a communication mix to achieve the best combination on the budget line (figure 12.6). The significance of the Net is that it promises to enable much higher levels of reach without sacrificing richness. As such, it is leading to significant changes in the communication mix.

reach: the number of people receiving information

richness: the amount of information and degree of customisation of the information supplied

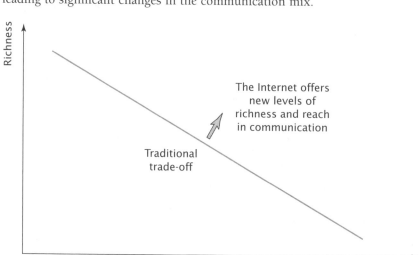

Figure 12.6 The change in the richness/reach trade-off

Traditional advertising is a high-reach, low-richness medium since it employs a one-to-many communication model that allows only limited forms of feedback from the customer. The Internet operationalises a model that facilitates interactive multimedia one-to-one communication — a rich form of communication. Online communication differs in another important way.

With conventional advertising the message is sent by the seller to customers, but with online communication the customer has to seek out the supplier's message. Online communication is self-selecting; the customer must be motivated to want to read the supplier's communication.

The most common form of online advertising is the banner ad, generally appearing at the top of the computer screen. The objective is to induce the user to click to the advertiser's web site. Online advertising possesses a number of potential advantages. One is that the advertiser can target the most valuable customers and not waste money on unproductive reach. This is achieved by having the banner appear only to customers with particular socio-demographic profiles, or who key in relevant words when using search engines. Increasingly, advertisers can target promotions and ads on a one-to-one basis and thus build rich interactive relationships with users, one at a time. This is achieved through the personal information the user supplies when registering with a site or through 'cookies' — small data files stored on the user's hard disk, which reveal to the supplier the user's search patterns. Another strength of web communication is its ability to provide extensive product information, unlike traditional media. Finally, online advertising creates the opportunity for immediate interaction with customers, either by providing more information or completing an online order.

Controversy surrounds the effectiveness of advertising online. The main problem surrounds the creative limitations of small banner ads to motivate interest. Certainly click-through rates are very low, typically about 2 per cent, meaning that 98 per cent of ad impressions do not produce action. However, this underestimates the effectiveness of the advertising since many of these impressions will be noticed by viewers and build brand awareness and interest.[15] Nevertheless, it is noticeable that new dot.com companies themselves have become massive users of traditional TV, radio and newspaper advertising. Traditional media still seem to be more effective in creating rapid awareness and impact. Indeed, the cost of conventional media campaigns to create consumer interest and trial has become the major barrier to entry for new online companies.

The personalised communication enabled by the Internet has encouraged the development of **permission marketing**. Traditional advertising often interrupts consumers when they are attempting to do something else, and this may well lead to negative feelings. Permission marketing seeks the permission of consumers for the delivery of advertising and e-mail It seeks to create mutually beneficial and trusting relationships by asking people what they are interested in, asking for permission to send them information, and to provide it in a way that the consumer finds entertaining, educational or interesting. Most commonly, it requires the consumer electing to receive information by clicking a 'yes' box. If it is to work properly, consumers must be given the opportunity not only to opt in but, should they so desire, opt out. And the latter should be something that the consumer recognises as easily done. The aim of permission marketing is to achieve ever greater levels of permission.

permission marketing: e-mail marketing that seeks the permission of consumers for the delivery of advertising and offers

» Distribution

As pointed out in chapter 10, digitisation and networks have led to a re-evaluation of how companies organise their distribution. The Net changes the traditional logic of using intermediaries. It permits, we argued, the separation of the economics of information from that of products. Over the Net, companies and customers can interact at almost zero cost, so direct sales from, say, the farmer to the consumer, the food processor to the consumer and the beverage manufacturer to the consumer are now viable. What makes the direct model attractive to consumers is the potential of lower prices, greater assortment, more convenience and customised service. What makes it attractive to suppliers is lower costs, competitive advantage and the value-enhancing opportunities that accrue from a direct relationship with the customer. Most online marketers still need to handle the physical distribution of their goods. But when this is separated from the information function it can normally be handled from one or a small number of central distribution points, often by third parties like DHL or Mayne Logistics. This change creates the opportunity for disintermediation to be introduced and, with it, potentially large cost savings.

Speed to market

Marketers have always recognised that speed to market can offer important strategic advantages. Being first, or at least early, to the market makes it easier to establish the brand's differential advantage. It can give it the opportunity to obtain the best locations and the best distribution deals. Pioneers also become magnets for companies wanting to form strategic alliances and partnerships. But the networked world adds another dimension to the importance of speed to market. This is the so-called 'network effect'. Metcalfe's Law explains this — the more users a company obtains on its network, the more value customers perceive in it. If one web site carries the most holiday-break bargains, why would anyone want to consult the number 2? The leading network can develop a virtuous circle, attracting more and more customers from the also-rans.

Marketing plays the key role in developing fast-to-market strategies. It requires very ambitious objectives to dominate the market sector. Clear strategies are required to identify customers who are likely to be opinion leaders, anticipate how the market is likely to develop, take a global perspective, since the Net has no geographical frontiers, and put together a creative communication campaign. Hype appears to play a particularly important role in network markets. Most of these publicity campaigns feature the entrepreneurs in a central role. Many Internet companies make celebrities of their founders, particularly if they are young and visionary leaders. Hype has two advantages: it is a lot cheaper means of grabbing attention than mainline advertising and it also shapes consumer expectations, giving the impression that the network is big and rapidly growing.

But the most obvious characteristic of most of the Internet businesses that do establish critical mass is the very high levels of marketing investment in the early years. This means years of low profits and negative cash flow. Managers schooled in traditional accounting find these business models impossible to understand. But investors using shareholder value models do understand that minimal profits and cash in the early years can be consistent with creating substantial value through creating long-term cash flows. They also have practical examples in such companies as Microsoft, Yahoo!, EMC and Cisco, which are now through their adolescence and generating high profits and cash flow.

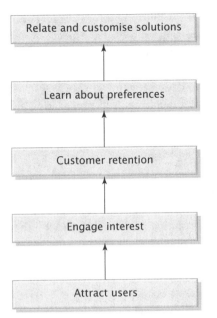

Building Net brand value

The interactive, one-to-one character of the Internet makes building Net brands different from classic brand building. Responsiveness as a brand attribute, the evolution of the brand in response to customer needs and the increased frequency of interaction with the brand become key issues. Opportunities expand for dialogue with customers about the brand, which in turn encourages a move towards the individualisation of the brand. Yet online branding retains the marketing fundamentals — the need to understand the customer, environmental analysis and building differential advantage. The process of Net brand building can be described in a five-stage process (see figure 12.7).[16]

Figure 12.7 Marketing to the digital consumer

Attracting users

Traffic building is critical for success and it is the major challenge facing web marketers. Unlike direct and traditional marketing where the message is essentially imposed on customers, Internet marketing requires them to voluntarily seek out a web site. With two million sites competing for users, generating traffic is expensive and difficult. Ways to attract users fall into five main categories:

1. **Domain names.** A good domain name can be an important traffic builder. The domain name is the address that customers use to find a web site. Like a brand name, a successful domain name should be easy to recall and be related to the positioning of the brand. Examples include David-Jones.com.au, Holden.com.au, Cocacola.com, and Hyatt.com. Well-chosen names make it easy for users to remember and find the site without having to rely on search engines.

2. **Portals.** If a potential customer does not know the domain name, a search engine or directory such as Yahoo! or Google is the usual next step. There are two major problems with these portals. One is that none is inclusive — only one in a hundred web sites are listed in all top four search engines. Second, and even more frustrating to the user, a search will often list thousands of entries. If the desired site does not appear in the first dozen entries many users will give up. Such factors mean that ambitious online marketers cannot rely on high traffic generation from search engines.

3. **Publicity and word-of-mouth.** Publicity and word-of-mouth are highly effective in generating users. The Net amplifies the speed of feedback from users to potential adopters: e-mails, online forums and discussion groups can quickly spread good or bad news about a site (see marketing insight 'Intel finds bad news travels fast'). Word-of-mouth follows the same dynamics as Metcalfe's Law, diffusing through the network of individuals who communicate with one another. Increasingly the heightened speed and power of word-of-mouth made possible by the Internet is referred to as **viral marketing.** A well-designed viral marketing strategy, targeting

viral marketing: online marketing relying on word of mouth

opinion leaders, can be highly productive for diffusing information about a new site. Viral marketing is about harnessing the positive aspects of network effects. It is based on the notion that the new offering is more likely to be trusted when the messenger is a trusted friend or acquaintance. It represents, therefore, a subtle form of endorsement. One of its major advantages is that it is cheap. It is also, by definition, self-propagating and once it has reached 'epidemic' levels there is little that the competition can do about it. Two notable examples of how viral marketing was used to spread the adoption of a new product were Hotmail and ICQ.

4. **Banners and buttons.** Banner ads that encourage users to click through to the advertiser's site are a growing business. Online advertising is sold like traditional advertising, with a rate charged per thousand impressions. In addition, alliances and barter, with sites running banner ads for each other, are common. Banner ads have the advantage that their effectiveness can be measured, which facilitates trial and experimentation. But click through rates are normally very low and, as noted, there is still scepticism about the effectiveness of this form of advertising.

5. **Traditional advertising media.** New online companies are heavy users of traditional advertising media. This can be more effective because target users are still not heavy users of the Internet. TV and radio are highly effective for creatively developing new brands, and newspaper ads allow the presentation of a high level of content. Particularly with B2C brands, it is difficult to create quick awareness without using traditional media. In addition, with web addresses increasingly integrated into them, traditional ads have direct traffic building effects.

Engaging interest

Once users have been attracted to a site it is essential to capture their interest and attention, otherwise they click out without looking at more than a couple of pages. The objective is to increase the visit duration. The longer the duration, the more time there is to communicate the messages of the site, the more chance to build commitment and loyalty, and the more opportunity to expose the user to advertising or alliance partners.

Interest is a function of the creativity of the site and the quality of its content. Creative site programming is increasingly essential to engage users. Simple Type I sites that transfer content from conventional brochures or advertising do not work because they fail to create interaction. Successful sites are interactive, easy to use and entertaining. Simple guidance through the site is important. Users have limited tolerance for inappropriate material before abandoning their visit.

Content, or the substance of the site, is even more important. A web site must have a perceived differential advantage to engage users' interest. This may be a reputation for offering more bargains than competitive sites, greater variety or superior customisation. Being fast to market, and creating the largest network, can be key ways to create and sustain such a differential advantage.

Another technique for creating user interest is the development of online communities.[17] These bring together users of the firm's products or services to share ideas and applications. For example, Palm has created an online community for owners of its personal digital assistants where owners can join Palm user groups, participate in discussion boards, and tell 'cool' user stories. The British pharmaceutical company Bristol Myers Squibb has a site, womenslink.com, that allows women to exchange opinions and advice about common problems. Firms see such community building as a way of generating loyalty, customer involvement and recurring traffic.

Customer retention

Because winning new customers is so difficult and expensive, retaining them becomes even more valuable. The enormous value of high retention to the cost of building a web site and the chance it has of becoming successful is easy to demonstrate.

Suppose a new web site has 50 000 active users and aims to grow to 100 000. It decides to run a banner advertising campaign costing $20 per thousand impressions and the click-through rate is estimated at 2 per cent. The cost for acquiring each new visitor is then $1. It decides to buy 1 million banner impressions each month until its objective is reached. Table 12.1 shows how the cost and time to build a successful site increase if retention rates are low. If retention were 100 per cent, so that all new visitors became loyal users, it would cost $70 000 and 2.5 months to reach the 100 000-user target. With a 90 per cent retention rate it costs $100 000 and takes 4 months. The lower the retention rate the higher the cost and the longer the time needed to reach the goal. With retention rates below 80 per cent the objective can never be reached with this strategy.

Table 12.1 Effect of customer retention on marketing costs and speed of growth

MONTHLY RETENTION RATE (%)	ADVERTISING COSTS ($)	TIME NEEDED TO REACH 100 000 REGULAR USERS (MONTHS)
100	70 000	2.5
95	80 000	3
90	100 000	4
85	140 000	6
80	380 000	19
75	—	Not possible

Source: From *Principles of Internet Marketing*, 1st edn, by W. Hanson © 2000. Reprinted with permission of South-Western College Publishing, a division of Thompson Learning.

Achieving high retention is about maintaining ongoing contact with users. Engaging a visitor's initial interest and maintaining loyalty are subtly different problems. Customers can visit a site initially out of curiosity but they will not return without a reason. To achieve high retention, the first requirement is for the content to be strong and kept continually up to date. Developing an effective online site is not a one-off project, but requires continued resource commitments over time. Many companies have seriously underestimated the costs of maintaining fresh ongoing content. One way companies seek to manage costs is by outsourcing web site maintenance to specialist third parties. Another approach is to involve users in maintaining interest levels. For example, a sports shoe company could allow its site to be used by athletic associations to publicise events and results. The site then begins to embody characteristics of an online community.

Another way of enhancing retention is to build switching costs that make it costly for users to shift to competitive sites. This occurs with shopping agents and financial sites such as Quicken. To exploit the advantages of these technologies customers have to invest time and energy providing personal information and details of their requirements. The more consumers have to invest in a site the less they wish to repeat the process elsewhere.

Learning about preferences

The unique feature of digitisation and the Net is the facility they offer the company to learn about customers, and exploit this learning to create value for them and for its shareholders. Online marketers need to design their web sites to make this learning possible. The more managers know about the importance, preferences, attitudes and behaviour of customers, the better it can meet their needs. Learning can be gained from registration processes, questionnaires, surveys, e-mail communication, cookies and web chain analyses. Rapid software advances are providing more and more power to mine and utilise these information banks for creative marketing.

Customised relationships

The end result of the model is a series of profitable transactions with customers. Knowledge about customers enables the firm to target high-value prospects. The particular advantage of the Net model is that it allows personalisation. It means that the company can add value by developing customised communication and products, cross-selling more products to individual customers, and developing individualised pricing and promotional strategies to optimise differences in response rates.

Valuing Web strategies

Many people, especially at the peak of the dot.com boom, were astonished at the prices investors attached to shares in new Internet companies. Journalists argued that markets had become irrational, sound investment principles had been thrown out of the window and the stock market was just a casino. But this was not the case. As will be shown, the valuations attached to Internet stocks can be explained by exactly the same shareholder value principles that have been used throughout the book. What investors are valuing are the long-term cash flows that may be generated by companies that have mould-breaking ideas that could generate explosive growth.

Three things make it hard to value the strategies of these entrepreneurial businesses. First, like many start-ups, they typically have losses in the early years because of the high marketing costs in acquiring new customers. Second, these companies may be growing at very high rates — in the early years of the Internet boom the successful ones were showing annual growth rates of 100 per cent or more. Finally, the fate of these companies is extremely uncertain.

Some analysts use rules-of-thumb to judge values such as multiplying the number of customers by industry values. For example, in buying mobile telecoms company Orange, Germany's Mannesman valued it at $3000 per subscriber. But such methods make little sense since they make no attempt to project the long-run profits and cash flow the business may generate.

Applying basic principles

The way to think about valuing Internet marketing strategies is to return to the fundamental discounted cash flow techniques on which shareholder value is based. The only practical difference is that a longer planning period forecast is required. For established businesses, a planning period of 5–7 years is normally satisfactory, since any differential advantage that enables them to return surplus profits is usually eroded by then, so that a continuing value formula can be used to estimate the businesses' values beyond the planning period. Some Internet businesses reshape their industries. When this happens, network effects may enable the most successful of them to sustain their competitive advantage and extend it into additional markets, just as Amazon.com and AOL are doing today.

To see how basic financial principles can explain very high valuations for start-up businesses, we can consider the example presented in marketing management in practice 'Valuing Krypton: An Internet start-up'.

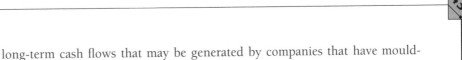

Marketing management in practice:	**Valuing Krypton: An Internet start-up**

Krypton, an Internet start-up from Belgium, was valued at over $300 million when it was launched on the stock exchange. What amazed journalists about the high valuation was that the company was making losses of $12 million a year, on sales of a mere $3 million. But what investors had learned from talking to Krypton's management were that the losses were partly due to high start-up marketing costs and that the company had global marketing opportunities with major companies. Analysts were predicting sales growth of 70 per cent annually for the next five years, 50 per cent for the following five years, and 25 per cent for the next ten years. Yet, investors recognised that these forecasts were very speculative. This explained Krypton's high cost of capital, estimated at 15 per cent — 50 per cent above that of the average company.

Table 12.2 illustrates the forecast results for a sample of years. It shows that these assumptions comfortably justified the $300 million valuation. It also illustrates the pattern of development of successful Internet businesses. It was not until year 7 that the company was expected to move into profit and it is year 8 before free cash flow turns positive. Indeed, it is year 14 before the present value of the cumulative cash flow becomes positive. The message is that, in spite of managers' views to the contrary, the valuations investors often give to high-tech businesses are striking illustrations of how financial markets do take a long-term perspective.

Table 12.2 Using the DCF method to value an Internet start-up, $million

YEAR	1	5	7	10	15	20
Sales	1.0	6.8	15.3	51.6	157.6	480.9
Costs	5.0	9.1	14.2	36.0	99.6	293.5
Operating profit	−4.0	−2.3	1.1	15.7	58.0	187.4
NOPAT	−2.8	−1.6	0.8	11.0	40.6	131.2
Investment	1.0	0.6	1.7	5.7	10.4	31.7
Cash flow	−3.8	−2.2	−0.9	5.3	30.2	99.4
DF ($r = 15\%$)	0.870	0.497	0.376	0.247	0.123	0.061
DCF	−3.3	−1.1	−0.3	1.3	3.7	6.1
PV of cum. CF	−3.3	−10.4	−11.5	−9.4	5.4	30.7
PV of cont. value	−16.2	−5.3	2.0	18.1	33.3	53.4
Cum PV + CV	−32.5	−10.6	3.9	36.1	66.6	106.8

NOPAT, net operating profit after tax; DF, discount factor; DCF, discounted cash flow; PV of cum. CF, present value of cumulative cash flow; PV of cont. value, present value of continuing value; Cum PV + CV, cumulative present value of cumulative cash flow plus continuing value.

Some extensions

Because of the difficulties of making forecasts 10 or 20 years ahead, analysts have looked for insights into dealing with such uncertainty. Two are of particular interest — the use of scenarios and the application of options theory.

» Using scenarios

A method favoured by consultants McKinsey is to run the type of discounted cash flow illustrated above under different scenarios about the company's prospects.[18] For example, in valuing Amazon.com, which was losing US$300 million in 2000, four scenarios were developed covering its future to 2025:

1. **Scenario A.** Amazon.com becomes the second largest retailer (after Wal-Mart) in the United States. It is able to operate with much less capital than traditional retailers and captures higher operating margins. This scenario led to an estimated shareholder value of $79 billion at the beginning of 2000.
2. **Scenario B.** This projected similar revenues to A, but had Amazon.com on margins and capital requirements around those of traditional retailers. This implied a value of US$37 billion.
3. **Scenario C.** This projected more modest growth forecasts, and margins and capital ratios similar to the market average. This led to a valuation of US$15 billion.
4. **Scenario D.** This sees competition catching up to Amazon.com and the company ending up with only average retail economics. Here the company is worth only US$3 billion.

The next step is to assign probabilities to each of these scenarios. These were estimated at 5 per cent, 35 per cent, 35 per cent and 25 per cent, respectively, which led to an expected value of $23 billion, reasonably close to its actual valuation at the time of $25 billion. This type of scenario forecasting has a long history in economic and business forecasting. It is a useful way for investors and managers to think through the uncertainties surrounding the future marketing and competitive environment.

» Insights from options theory

Another way of understanding the values attached to high-risk businesses is to consider them as **options**. As discussed in chapters 3 and 6, investors value established companies when they possess three types of products or business units: today's businesses, tomorrow's businesses and options for growth. Today's businesses are those that are successful and highly profitable but are in maturing markets. Tomorrow's businesses are well established, growing businesses that are profitable but still require considerable investment. Options are the company's pipeline of R&D projects, joint ventures, experiments and trials, some of which may emerge as big winners in the future. Options give a company the opportunity to enter markets in the future, if they then appear to have good prospects. If some years down the line, the prospects do not turn out as good as expected, the company does not need to proceed, and will not have lost too much money.

option: a right, but not the obligation, to take an action in the future; for an investment it is the right, at some point in the future, to sell the investment, maintain it or expand it

To a significant extent, in buying shares in an Internet business, investors are buying an option. The Internet offers tremendous option opportunities. If an Internet company is positioned like, say, AOL or Yahoo!, with substantial content and a large subscriber base, it stands to make big gains when bandwidth in the home increases. Advanced telecommunications, movies-on demand, video telephones, work-from-home capabilities and a whole host of other potential future developments — industries worth billions — become possible. When and if this happens, these companies will have to make huge investments in infrastructure to handle the throughput. But these are options since these investments will only be made if the technology makes them valuable.

Valuing options is an important area of research in modern finance. One of the key implications of the famous Black-Scholes Option Pricing Model is that the higher the volatility of the share price, the higher the option value. Essentially this means that the spread of risk is such that companies with highly uncertain futures have a small chance of doing spectacularly well. In contrast, the chance of low-risk shares doing spectacularly better than expected is virtually zero — they have a low option value. For example, Amazon.com's share price has been three times more volatile than GE's in recent years. It can be shown that the implication of this is that an option to buy Amazon.com at three times the current share price over the next 5 years would be worth nearly 11 times that of a similar option to buy GE.[19]

Option theory provides a different insight into why investors pay high prices for start-ups that they consider as having potential. Like the basic discounted cash flow (DCF) and scenario approaches, it illustrates how investors understand the need to accept uncertainty and long-term time horizons if they are going to build wealth. It also illustrates how companies are rewarded for innovation and long-term marketing strategies.

Future perspectives

Many businesses have now learnt, the hard way, that the Internet is certainly not a source of immediate wealth. The importance of the Internet, however, cannot and should not be trivialised. It is worth summarising how management, and particularly marketing, needs to respond to the environmental upheaval that it represents. Twelve recommendations are presented under four areas: the new context of business, the new strategic priorities, the implications for value-based marketing and the implications for business organisation.

Recognise the new context of business

» 1. The Internet is a powerful force for change

The Internet, by creating instantaneous, universal and almost free communications changes the nature of business. It destroys the traditional model of business that links information to products. It unbundles industries, triggers new, better adapted competition and creates new distribution structures. The first industries to be transformed have been the 'low touch' industries such as computers, books, CDs, travel and financial services. But even 'high touch' businesses such as clothing, shoes and groceries are now feeling the impact. Here the effects are most immediate on the way the Internet is reengineering supply chains, cutting costs and accelerating asset turnover. It needs to be remembered that while online business-to-consumer commerce causes the most excitement, it is in business-to-business trade where the effects of the Internet are greatest.

» 2. Re-engineer the business model

The Internet is not an innovation that can be adapted to simply by improving the efficiency of the traditional business model or by adding a web site. It is what is termed a 'disruptive technology' that destroys previously successful business models.[20] Many businesses need to change radically because what were once assets have become liabilities. Compaq's strong relationships with distributors or Barclays Bank's network of branches became millstones around the companies' necks as more successful competitors established direct, one-to-one links with customers. Today, survival often means having to compete with, and cannibalise, one's traditional business model.

» 3. Customise marketing

The Internet is most of all a marketing phenomenon, shifting power to customers, giving them much more access to competitors, to lower prices and better products. Indeed, it is spawning a whole new class of infomediaries and exchanges whose sole function is giving buyers more information and helping them get the best deals. The Web is a threat because it is the customer — not the marketer — who decides whether to interact and who to interact with. The Web is an opportunity, however, for companies that grasp the new possibilities to customise their products to the needs of individual consumers and so form enduring relationships.

Change the strategy

» 4. Think outside the box

Changing strategy is not just about selling through the Web; it is about thinking creatively about the industry's whole value chain and the company's entire business processes. It means reappraising customer service and support and looking at how the Internet might offer radically new ways of communicating with customers, enhancing service levels and ensuring a better experience. Operations processes will have to be reengineered to permit the introduction of customised made-to-order products, to lower inventories and cut costs. New product development needs to be reviewed to expedite processes and consider new, unrelated products that could be cross-marketed to the customer base.

» **5. Move fast**

Competitors move fast in the Internet world. When Amazon.com moved into selling CDs online it took just 45 days to become market leader; it took only 9 days to seize leadership in video sales. Slow movers can find their market positions destroyed before they have even put together a plan. To move fast, companies have to outsource much more radically. There are now hosts of Internet specialists and contract manufacturers that can develop and host the site, make-to-order and handle distribution. Many of tomorrow's businesses are network organisations.

» **6. Take an offensive posture**

It is not enough to be first into the market; strategies have to be developed and resources obtained to exploit the first-mover advantage and critical mass. In the networked world, customers often attach the greatest value to the sites that have most users. This is why investors value high growth performance rather than profits in start-up businesses. Since online firms are all potentially competing in a global market, the marketing investment requirements to achieve critical mass can be very high.

Think shareholder value

» **7. Ignore accounting statements**

Accounting statements are flawed measures at the best of times, but for Internet, and high-growth businesses generally, they are particularly damaging. Their fundamental weakness is in treating marketing and other essential development investments as expenses to be deducted from current profits. This positively discourages managers from making rational strategic decisions in these crucial markets. The DCF shareholder value approach, by focusing on cash rather than profits, does not require a distinction between expenses and investments. It is the only sensible way to evaluate growth strategies.

» **8. Invest in a portfolio of real options**

The discontinuities in today's markets make the traditional new product development process inadequate. Now, leading businesses see innovation as more like investing in a portfolio of options that give them the right, but not the obligation, to invest in future markets and technologies should these opportunities crystallise. Often these options are not internal projects but minority stakes in start-ups. Like an investment portfolio, they recognise that only a few of their bets will succeed — but that those that do, can succeed spectacularly.

» **9. Patience is an essential**

Managers remain fixated by short-term profits and yearly earnings objectives. Such time frames make it impossible for companies to capitalise on the opportunities offered by the information revolution. They are also unnecessary. Shareholder value analysis, and indeed the valuations attached to many entrepreneurial businesses, demonstrate that investors are willing to accept extraordinarily long time frames before expecting a company to break even.

Restructure the organisation

» **10. Build networks**

New economy firms are built around networks. The information revolution has made vertical integration unnecessary and the speed of change has made it uneconomic. Creating virtual businesses with suppliers and partners offers speed, pooled expertise, lower costs and lower asset requirements. Using digital technology to form networks with customers creates relationships that build lifetime value out of expensively obtained assets.

» **11. Invest in human capital**

The Internet revolutionises communication inside organisations, making bureaucratic structures obsolete and releasing human capital. It also makes employees with exceptional skills more marketable. If organisations are going to hold on to these people, they will need to rethink payment systems and tie rewards more closely to the value employees create, and also make their work environments more rewarding.

» **12. Make managers responsible**

Top management has to take responsibility for building a culture that recognises that creating value depends upon innovation, marketing and growth rather than cost-cutting and downsizing. They have to build planning processes that stimulate the development of such strategies. Finally, they need to introduce evaluation and reward systems that help implement such strategies and reinforce the behaviour of managers.

Summary

1. The Internet is a 'discontinuous change' that will lead to a fundamental restructuring in all industries. The three sources of this shift are the increasing power and declining costs of digital technology, the explosion of connectedness brought about by the Internet, and the new opportunities to customise communication and products.

2. The Web creates benefits for customers by facilitating companies to offer individualised solutions to their needs, lower prices, greater convenience, more information, assurance and entertainment. The most immediate impact has been on 'low touch' markets such as computers and business-to-business purchases, but in the longer run few markets will remain unaffected.

3. The Web creates direct benefits for companies by creating new opportunities to gain market share and earn revenues. It also produces major indirect benefits in lowering costs, reducing investment requirements and enhancing business effectiveness.

4. The information revolution has major implications for marketing strategy. It changes the context of markets by increasing the power of customers over suppliers. It creates new marketing opportunities and leads to ways of thinking about segmentation and positioning. By breaking the trade-off between richness and reach it also leads to a reformulation of the marketing mix, emphasising direct one-to-one communication.

5. There is no mystery in valuing Internet marketing strategies or new Net businesses. The DCF shareholder value model used throughout the book explains these valuations very satisfactorily. The only differences in application lie in the longer planning period that has to be used and the greater uncertainties that arise in looking longer into the future. Scenario planning and options theory provide useful insights into coping with these uncertainties.

6. Internet businesses provide striking illustrations of the principles of value-based marketing: the importance of growth, taking a long-term perspective, and the significance of creating business processes that enable the firm to build superior relationships with customers.

key terms

bricks-and-mortar, p. 405
disintermediation, p. 415
extranet, p. 411
infomediary, p. 415
intranet, p. 411
mass customisation, p. 415
one-to-one marketing, p. 415

option, p. 435
permission marketing, p. 427
pure dot.coms, p. 405
reach, p. 426
richness, p. 426
viral marketing, p. 429

review questions

1. What are the drivers of the Internet revolution and how might the Internet be characterised?
2. How does the Internet create value for consumers?
3. How can the Internet create value for companies?
4. How does the Internet affect marketing strategy?
5. Can a new Internet company that has never made a profit and has sales of less than $1 million be rationally valued by the stock market at $100 million?
6. Develop the outline of a presentation to the board of directors of a large consumer goods company suggesting how they need to respond to the Internet.

discussion questions

1. Which type of electronic commerce is most likely to maximise shareholder value creation?
2. Which shareholder value principle is most appropriate for assessing organisational performance and value creation on the Internet?
3. How can differential advantage be established and sustained on the Internet?
4. How can strategic position assessment be utilised with the Internet?
5. Develop a value-based Internet marketing strategy for a company of your choice. Your company must be multi-divisional and currently pursuing various strategies off-line. Your analysis should demonstrate and support a logical association between your strategy and shareholder value creation. You MUST critically analyse the following issues in your response:
   (a) Shareholder value, including financial, organisational and marketing value drivers.
   (b) Creation of customer value and differential advantage.
   (c) How organisational requirements will support your strategy.
   (d) Assessment and explanation of current organisational position, particularly drawing on your strategic objectives.
   (e) Facilitation of value-based marketing strategy including corporate and business unit planning.
   (f) Assessment of brand equity and the impact of an Internet marketing strategy on your existing product lines.
   (g) The development and allocation of a communication strategy.

1. Is it easier to create shareholder value on the Internet than off-line?
2. Are the benefits of customisation offset by the high costs of implementing and monitoring such systems?
3. The Internet changes everything. Put the case for and against.

case study | Shopping that clicks

Three years ago, the boosters of online retailing were happily predicting that the Internet would kill traditional retailers. They were wrong. Rather than destroying bricks-and-mortar retailers, online retailing — or e-tailing — has been embraced by them. Successful e-tailers understand that the fundamentals of retailing still apply online. The unsuccessful e-tailers are in the dot-com graveyard.

The founding director of the Internet trading analysis company Global Reviews, Adir Shiffman, says consumers are looking for the same things online as in conventional stores. 'All of the same factors are going to apply online,' he says. 'Competitive prices, reliable customer service and trusted brands.'

Australians spent $3.8 billion online in 2001, up 31% from $2.9 billion in 2000. Shiffrnan says Australia's biggest retailers, including Woolworths, Coles Myer and David Jones, are well placed to attract shoppers on the Internet. With their well-known and trusted brands, and their ability to use existing supply chains to reduce costs, it is not surprising that these companies are among the e-tail survivors.

One conventional retailer that is doing well in e-tailing is the fabric and craft retailer Spotlight. During 2001, Spotlight Online consistently ranked among the top 20 Australian e-tailing sites, as measured by the number of unique visitors (individual visits to each site), according to the Internet ratings company Red Sheriff.

The chief executive of Spotlight Online, Brandon Chizik, says the online business's biggest advantage is its brand name. 'If we were called fabrics.com I think we would really struggle.' Chizik says the offline operation can also keep its costs down by making good use of the Spotlight supply chain.

Spotlight Online was born from a shop-at-home service and customer club started by Spotlight eight years ago for its regional customers, who received catalogues and could place orders through a call centre. The club grew to about 1.8 million members in metropolitan and regional areas. Three years ago, Spotlight developed a Web site and started putting its catalogues online.

Chizik says the shift to selling products online, which occurred in November 2000, was prompted by customer demand, and the subsequent development of the site has been responsive to customer requests. For example, the site features sections where customers can trade recipes, gardening tips and child-care advice, none of which relates directly to the products that Spotlight sells. 'We are building an online community here,' Chizik says. He says the skills learnt running a shop-at-home service were valuable when Spotlight developed its online division because the logistics and delivery functions were already in place. About $1.5 million was spent on the technology behind the Web site...

Another long-established retailer enjoying online success is David Jones, which moved into e-tailing in October 1999, when it started selling hampers online. The department store bolstered its online business in June 2000 when it bought the infrastructure behind the failed e-tailer The Spot.

David Jones has taken a cautious approach to e-tailing, steadily adding product categories to its Web site. The operations manager, Julie Coates, says caution has contributed to its success. Red Sheriff says David Jones ranked consistently in the top 10 Australian e-tail sites by unique visitors in 2001 and was the most-visited Australian shopping site in December.

Coates says David Jones regards e-tailing as another distribution channel, not as a new business. She agrees that conventional retailers have the advantage of being able to use an existing brand that customers trust, but says they must not damage the brand by failing to meet their customers' expectations online. 'David Jones is a pretty useful brand to have for your online business,' Coates says. 'But around that, people have an expectation of quality and service.'...

The increasing dominance of long-established retailers in e-tailing is becoming evident in online grocery sales. A senior analyst at the research company ACNielsen/Net Ratings, Andrew Reid, says that although online grocery retailing is developing more slowly than other types of e-tailing, it has great potential.

Shiffman of Global Reviews agrees. He says that just over 3% of total grocery sales in Australia are being conducted online, and it is the big, bricks-and-mortar retailers that are winning the battle for market dominance. Woolworths launched its grocery Web site, HomeShop, in 1998. In December 2000, it bought 26% of the e-tailer GreenGrocer.com.au for $12 million, before buying the remaining 74% for $7 million in October 2001, giving its online grocery business a combined turnover of $50 million. Although the division is not yet profitable, Shiffman says Woolworths' strategic approach to e-tailing will eventually pay off. 'They very much see it as a future growth business,' he says.

Source: Extracts from Michelle Hannan, 'Shopping that clicks', *BRW*, 31 January–6 February 2002, pp. 66–7.

Questions

1. What are the advantages that bricks-and-mortar retailing organisations have, compared to pure dot.coms, in competing online? Do you expect long-established retailers to enjoy increasing dominance in e-tailing?
2. Is David Jones correct to consider e-tailing as another distribution channel, not as a new business?
3. What would be the major challenges, and opportunities, for established bricks-and-mortar organisations in moving online?

end notes

1. There is a need for caution with these figures, for they refer to the total online population, not to active users. In some countries, notably the United Kingdom, active users are significantly fewer than the total online population.
2. Ward Hanson, *Principles of Internet Marketing*, Cincinnati, OH: South Western, 2000, pp. 10–14.
3. Randy J. Hinrichs, *Intranets: What's the Bottom Line?*, Englewood Cliffs, NJ: Prentice Hall, 1997.
4. Deborah Bayles, *Extranets: Building the Business-to-Business Web*, Englewood Cliffs, NJ: Prentice Hall, 1998.
5. Robert Hiebeler, Thomas Kelly and Charles Ketteman, *Best Practices: Building your Business with Customer-Focussed Solutions*, New York: Simon & Schuster, 1998.
6. For more on how transactions costs shape businesses see Larry Downes and Chunka Mui, *Unleashing the Killer App: Digital Strategies for Market Dominance*, Boston, MA: Harvard Business School Press, 1998, pp. 35–56.
7. Figure 12.2 is adapted from a presentation by Keith Beddell-Pearce, executive director of Prudential plc at the Warwick Business School, March 2000.
8. John Hagel III and Marc Singer, *Net Worth*, New York: McKinsey & Co, 1999.
9. James H. Gilmore and B. Joseph Pine II, *Every Business a Stage: Why Customers Now Want Experiences*, Boston, MA: Harvard Business School Press, 1999, p. 95.
10. Hanson, *op. cit.* pp. 126–7.
11. Donna L. Hoffman and Thomas P. Novak, 'Marketing in computer-mediated environments: Conceptual foundations', *Journal of Marketing*, 60, July 1996, pp. 60–8.
12. For convenience, the words 'consumer' and 'customer' are being used virtually synonymously. It should be remembered, as emphasised in an earlier chapter, that purchasing is generally a networked activity involving several members of the household or organisation. Marketers need to understand the whole buying process and experience. See Robin Wensley, 'The MSI priorities: A critical view of researching firm performance, customer experience and marketing', *Journal of Marketing Management*, 16, April 2000, pp. 11–27.

13. The earliest and most complete exposition of this change is Don Peppers and Martha Rogers, *Enterprise One-to-One: Tools for Building Unbreakable Customer Relationships in the Interactive Age*, London: Piatkus, 1997; see also Fred Wiersema, *Customer Intimacy*, London: HarperCollins, 1998.

14. Philip Evans and Thomas S. Wurster, *Blown to Bits: How the New Economics of Information Transforms Strategy*, Boston, MA: Harvard Business School Press, 2000.

15. Robert Kesnbaum, Kate Kesnbaum and Pamela Ames, 'Building a longitudinal contact strategy', *Journal of Interactive Marketing*, **12**, Winter 1998, pp. 45–53.

16. This model is adapted from Alexa Kierzkowski, Shayne McQuade, Robert Waitman and Michael Zeisser, 'Marketing to the digital consumer', *McKinsey Quarterly*, no. 3, 1996, 5–21.

17. John Hagel III and Arthur Armstrong, *Net Gain: Expanding Markets through Virtual Communities*, Boston, MA: Harvard Business School Press, 1997.

18. Driek Desmet, Tracy Francis, Alice Hu, Timothy M. Koller and George A. Riedel, 'Valuing dot-coms', *McKinsey Quarterly*, no. 1, 2000, pp. 148–57.

19. Stern Stewart Europe Ltd, 'Internet valuation: Why are the values so high?', *Evaluation*, **2** (1), February 2000.

20. Clayton M. Christensen and Michael Overdorf, 'Meeting the challenge of disruptive change', *Harvard Business Review*, **78** (2), March/April 2000, pp. 66–77.

glossary

advertising elasticity of demand: the extent to which demand increases as a result of a given increase in advertising expenditure, p. 377

affordability method: a budgeting approach whereby the company spends what it feels it can afford from the budget, p. 387

aspirational brand: a brand that conveys an image about the types of people who buy the brand, p. 244

attractive market: a market where the average competitor consistently earns a return above its cost of capital, p. 166

attribute brand: a brand that conveys confidence in the product's functional attributes, p. 244

augmented product: those attributes of a product that exceed what the customer expects, p. 324

basic product: those attributes of a product that meet the core needs of a customer, p. 324

beta coefficient: a measure of the association between changes in the share price of an individual company and the change in the main market index in which the share is quoted, p. 48

book equity: the value of shareholders' funds as recorded in the published accounts of the business, p. 20

brand: an intangible asset that provides a differential market position; it is created by and, subsequently, affects the marketing mix elements, p. 238

brand architecture: a system that shows how brands in a firm's brand portfolio should be related to each other, p. 265

brand equity: the net present value of the future cash flow attributable to the brand. It is the incremental value above what an unbranded product would possess, p. 238

brand extensions: practice of using the same brand name to cover new lines in the current product category and to cover new products in different categories altogether, p. 248

brand identity: the intended impression of the brand that top management wishes to create in consumers' minds, p. 252

brand image: a set of beliefs about a brand's attributes and associations — an impression of the brand in the consumer's mind, p. 242

brand portfolio: a set of brands managed by the firm, p. 265

brand profitability: the return on the total investment in a brand, p. 258

brand revitalisation: strategy for when the brand is potentially strong but its current market is not sufficiently attractive to offer adequate profit opportunities, p. 257

brand valuation: the value of a brand as it would appear explicitly on the balance sheet (i.e. as it would appear as a separate item on the balance sheet), p. 268

bricks-and-mortar: traditional companies, with a material presence for customers, who may or may not also operate online, p. 405

business unit: an organisational unit with strategic and budgetary responsibility, p. 132

buying decision involvement: the amount of investment in time and effort, and the number of people contributing to the decision-making process, p. 382

capital structure: the relative dependence of a business on equity versus debt as sources of funding, p. 47

cash flow return on investment (CFROI): the sustainable cash flow generated by a business in a given year,

expressed as a percentage of the cash invested in the firm's assets, p. 57

channel conflict: the tension that emerges when a channel member believes that the actions of another channel member are interfering with its goal attainment, p. 361

channel power: a situation where a channel member is able to control or influence the marketing strategy of an independent channel member, p. 360

communication strategy: the allocation of promotion tools (advertising, sales promotion, public relations, personal selling, direct marketing) to maximise the net present value of future cash flow, p. 376

competitive parity method: a budgeting approach whereby a company simply decides to spend as much as its competitors, p. 387

competitive potential: an organisation's assessment of the extent to which it is able, now or in the future, to compete in a market, p. 13

competitive structure: the intensity of direct competition in a market, the power of suppliers and buyers, and the threat posed by new entry and by substitutes, p. 167

consumer surplus: the excess between the price a consumer would be willing to pay for a product (rather than go without it) over the amount that the customer actually pays for it, p. 306

continuing value: the value of the cash flow generated during the post-forecast period, pp. 20, 51

convenience goods: goods purchased often, and with little thought or effort; they include staple goods, impulse items and emergency goods, p. 357

conventional vertical structures: the traditional distribution model, characterised by each channel member acting independently rather than cooperatively, p. 359

core competency: those organisational capabilities that make a disproportionate contribution to customer value, and which are relatively scarce and provide opportunities for the organisation to enter new markets, p. 114

core need: the basic functional attribute a customer requires from a product, p. 324

core rigidities: abilities that define a firm's fundamental business core, but stifle its ability to adapt to competitive changes, p. 222

cost of capital: the opportunity cost, or expected return, that investors forgo by investing in a company rather than in other comparable companies, pp. 18, 45

customer lifetime value (CLV): the net present value of a customer, calculated in terms of the discounted value of the cash flow generated over the life of the customer's relationship with the company, pp. 99, 203

customer loyalty: the customer's willingness to continue buying from the company, p. 97

customer satisfaction: a situation where the perceived performance of a product is at least equal to what the customer had expected, p. 100

customer selection: the practice of retaining valuable customers and allowing less valuable customers to go elsewhere, p. 203

customised pricing: a price developed uniquely for each customer, p. 292

delayering: removing or reducing the number of managerial layers within an organisation, p. 16

differential advantage: a competitive advantage that allows a firm to offer products that are perceived by customers as better value than those of competitors, pp. 51, 85

direct business model: a business model involving direct sales to the end user and, usually, close cooperation with suppliers, p. 14

direct distribution system: a company-owned means of distribution, p. 347

discount factor: the present value of $1 received at a stated future date; calculated as $1/(1 + r)^t$ where r is the discount rate and t is the year, p. 17

discounted cash flow (DCF): future cash flows multiplied by the discount factor to obtain the present value of the cash flows, pp. 18, 46

disintermediation: the elimination of intermediaries or agents between the supplier and the consumer, pp. 10, 363, 415

distribution channel: the means by which a producer makes available its products to the final customer (or end user), p. 344

downstream: that part of the supply chain in which the product moves from the producer to the buyer, p. 14

economic value to the customer: an improvement in the customer's profitability, p. 106

emergent strategy: the firm's intended strategy after adaptation to changing external circumstances as well as top management's own strengths, weaknesses and learning, p. 221

emotional appeals: claims made in advertising, or through other forms of communication, about the brand's added values over and above functional or economic product difference, p. 387

emotional value to the customer: an improvement in the customer's experience, p. 106

enterprise value: the total value of a firm or business unit, expressed as the sum of its debt and shareholder value, p. 57

existing needs: needs for which consumers consider satisfactory solutions already exist, p. 88

expected product: those attributes of a product that a customer normally expects, for example friendly service, p. 324

experience brand: a brand that conveys an image of shared associations and emotions, p. 244

explicit forecast period: the period during which a proposed strategy can be expected to provide for the organisation a competitive advantage and for which managers feel that they can sensibly make estimates of sales, costs and investments, pp. 20, 50

extranet: web sites that connect the intranet of an organisation with its trading partners, suppliers and distributors, pp. 10, 411

fighter brand: a brand designed to defend the flagship brand against low-price competitors, p. 313

first-mover advantage: an advantage based on access to resources and capabilities that later entrants cannot easily acquire, p. 335

fixed capital: durable assets which are used repeatedly or continuously over a number of years to create products — such as buildings, motor vehicles and plant and machinery, p. 52

forecast horizon: the time span for which a business unit plans into the future, p. 144

free cash flow: residual cash flow that is 'free' to be paid to investors, p. 51

high-involvement communication models: models that describe the role of communication in high-involvement decisions, p. 383

hypercompetitive markets: markets subject to intense competition and high levels of environmental turbulence, p. 11

incipient needs: needs that people have, but which they do not know about until they see the solution, and hence are presently unable to articulate, p. 88

incremental budgeting method: a budgeting approach whereby a company increases last year's budget by a given percentage, p. 387

incremental investment rate: management's assessment of the proportional increase in fixed and working capital required for each unit of additional sales, p. 81

indirect distribution system: distribution that relies on intermediaries external to the company, p. 347

infomediary: an online site that provides specialised information on behalf of producers of goods and services and links them to their potential customers, pp. 363, 415

innovation: something that has been commercialised and thereby tested to determine whether customers need the new benefit it provides, p. 330

intangible assets: non-material assets such as technical expertise, brands or patents, pp. 25, 64, 80

integrated marketing communication: the combination of advertising, sales promotions, public relations, personal selling and direct marketing techniques to produce effective and consistent communication with the target market, p. 392

intended strategy: the firm's strategy as conceived by top management, p. 221

intranet: web sites internal to the company and available only to its employees, pp. 10, 411

invention: a new product benefit, p. 330

label: a name, symbol or design that is used to distinguish a firm's product, p. 239

latent needs: needs that people have and can express but which are not yet satisfied, p. 88

line extensions: products that are not new to a firm, but new to the market, p. 329

low-involvement communication models: models that describe the role of communication in low-involvement purchase situations, p. 384

macroenvironment: the broad outside forces affecting all markets, including the major economic, demographic, political, technological and cultural developments, p. 6

market segmentation: dividing a market into discrete categories of consumers who share particular characteristics and who have a similar need, p. 11

market signalling: the selective communication of information to competitors designed to influence competitors' perceptions and behaviour in order to provoke or avoid certain types of action, p. 182

market-to-book (M/B) ratio: the market value of the business divided by the book equity value, pp. 20, 54

market value: the actual value of equity as reflected in the market price of shares multiplied by the number of shares, p. 20

market value added (MVA): the present value of the stream of future expected EVA, p. 57

marketing mix: a set of operating decisions, sometimes referred to as the four Ps — product, price, promotion and place, p. 10

marketing strategy: a set of coherent decisions about a firm's approach to managing the market, p. 130

mark-up pricing: a price set to add a standard margin to the cost of the product or service, p. 287

mass customisation: offering products tailored to the individual customer and made to order, pp. 11, 415

me-too products: products that are new to a firm, but not new to the market, p. 330

microenvironment: the specific developments affecting the firm's individual industry or market: its customers, competitors and suppliers, p. 6

mission statement: a statement that provides a firm with strategic focus by defining what business it is in, p. 149

multiple-channel/hybrid channel system: a combination of direct and indirect distribution systems, p. 349

Nash Equilibrium: a situation in which each player is making the best response given what the other player has chosen to do, p. 293

net present value (NPV): the net contribution of a strategy to the wealth of shareholders: present value of cash flows minus initial investment, p. 46

new-to-the-world products: products that are new to both a firm and the market, p. 329

NOPAT: net operating profits after tax, p. 44

one-to-one marketing: a form of marketing involving mass customisation and two-way, direct, communication between the producer and the consumer, pp. 12, 415

opportunity cost: the loss of other alternatives when one alternative is chosen, p. 18

option: a right, but not the obligation, to take an action in the future; for an investment it is the right, at some point in the future, to sell the investment, maintain it or expand it, p. 435

options for growth: Investments in research, experiments and trials that lay the foundation for the firm's most attractive new markets in the future, p. 219

organisation: the capabilities the firm possesses and how its staff are led, coordinated and motivated to implement strategy, p. 12

penetration pricing: a price set to maximise sales volume, p. 298

percentage of sales method: a budgeting approach whereby a company sets the communication budget at some percentage of current or anticipated sales, p. 387

permission marketing: e-mail marketing that seeks the permission of consumers for the delivery of advertising and offers, p. 427

perpetuity: an investment offering a level or even stream of cash flow for the indefinite future, p. 53

potential need: the ultimate goal a customer hopes to achieve with a product, p. 324

potential product: those attributes of a product that fulfil all possible expectations and goals a customer might have when purchasing the product, p. 324

price competition: practice of obtaining a differential advantage by offering comparable products at a lower price than the competition, p. 285

price/earnings (P/E) ratio: the market price of the share divided by earnings per share, p. 54

price elasticity: the sensitivity of demand in response to price variation in a market segment, p. 299

price signalling: the use of tactics to make more transparent what a firm's pricing objective is, p. 294

product: something that delivers a benefit needed by a customer, p. 324

product improvements: upgraded or redesigned versions of previous product models launched by a firm, p. 330

product life cycle: the notion that products pass through distinct stages — introduction, growth, maturity and decline — each marked by different growth rates in sales volume and by increasing and decreasing unit profits, p. 210

product mix: a firm's assortment of products, p. 325

promotion tools: advertising, sales promotion, public relations, personal selling and direct marketing instruments, including direct mail, telemarketing, TV shopping and the Internet, p. 374

pull strategy: a strategy in which producers aim to get retailers to offer their products by influencing consumers, who in turn demand the goods from the retailers, p. 362

pure dot.coms: companies created from scratch to take advantage of the Internet, p. 405

push strategy: a strategy in which producers aim to get retailers to offer their products by directly influencing the retailers, p. 362

rational appeals: claims made in advertising, or through other forms of communication, about the brand's uniquely superior attributes or economic value to the customer, p. 386

reach: the number of people receiving information, p. 426

realised price: actual price paid by customers after all discounts have been deducted from the invoiced price, p. 313

realised strategy: the emergent strategy that is implemented; typically only 10 to 30 per cent of the originally intended strategy, p. 221

return spread: the difference between return on capital employed and the cost of capital, p. 60

richness: the amount of information and degree of customisation of the information supplied, p. 426

share of customer: the proportion of total spending made by a single customer that goes to one firm, p. 207

share of voice: a company's communication expenditure on a product expressed as a proportion of all communication expenditure by it and rival firms on that product, p. 393

shareholder value: the equity portion of enterprise value (enterprise value less debt), p. 57

shareholder value analysis (SVA): a formal process in which strategies are analysed to determine whether and to what extent their implementation would increase shareholder value, p. 17

shopping goods: goods that involve high perceived risk by the consumer, p. 358

skimming pricing: a price set to maximise unit margins, p. 298

speciality goods: specific brands, exotic and rare products, and sophisticated items, p. 357

strategic group: brands competing with each other for the same customers within a segment, p. 296

strategic planning: a planning process focused on how long-term value for owners of the firm will be created, p. 130

strategic value drivers: the organisational resources and capabilities that have the most significant impact on the firm's ability to create shareholder value, p. 158

strategy: the business's overall plan for deploying resources to create a differential advantage in its markets, p. 12

supply chain: the set of upstream linkages between suppliers and producers and downstream linkages between producers, distributors and customers, through which products are created and sold, p. 344

tangible assets: material assets such as factories, equipment, machinery and stocks, p. 80

target-return pricing: a price set to achieve a target return on investment, p. 287

threshold margin: the pre-tax operating profit margin necessary to finance value-creating growth, p. 81

threshold spread: the difference between the actual (or expected) operating profit margin and threshold margin, p. 81

total economic cost: the sum of operating costs plus a charge for capital, where the capital charge is the cost of capital multiplied by the amount of capital employed in the business, p. 170

total shareholder returns: the combined returns to shareholders in the form of dividend payments and share price appreciation, p. 19

transnational marketing: the standardisation of those elements of the brand where it is possible, and the adaptation of those elements to local conditions where it makes sense or is necessary, p. 262

upstream: that part of the supply chain in which the producer obtains the parts, components and/or raw materials with which to make the product, p. 15

value: the customer's perception of the effectiveness of a good or service in meeting his or her needs, p. 91

value-based marketing: the process that seeks to maximise returns to shareholders by developing relationships with valued customers and creating a competitive advantage, p. 4

value-based marketing strategy: a marketing strategy that aims to maximise shareholder value, p. 130

value-based pricing: a price based on the total value that the product represents to the customer when it is benchmarked against competitors' offers. Essentially, value-based pricing measures how much the consumer is likely to be willing to pay for the product after taking all other product alternatives into consideration; not how much it costs to produce it, p. 289

value chain: the collection of interconnected activities that are performed to design, produce, market, deliver and support goods and services, and that lead to the creation of value, p. 115

value gap: the difference between the value of a company if it were operated to maximise shareholder value and its current value, p. 21

value proposition: the organisation's view on how and by what means its product offering provides unique and superior value to the customer, p. 91

vertical integration: achieving control and coordination of the procurement of supplies and/or of distribution by owning those who provide the supplies or distribute the product, p. 15

vertical marketing system (VMS): coordinated and collaborative distribution structures, with each channel member a partner to the other, p. 359

viral marketing: online marketing relying on word of mouth, p. 429

virtual business: an online business; one conducted on the Internet, p. 10

virtual integration: achieving control and coordination through information rather than through ownership, p. 15

weighted average cost of capital (WACC): the cost of equity and the cost of debt combined and weighted according to their relative contribution to the organisation's financing or capital structure, pp. 19, 47

working capital: net current assets — that is, current assets less current liabilities — comprised of inventories (stocks and work in progress), receivables (debtors owing money to the business) and payables (the business's creditors), p. 52

index